# Convention Sal
### Ninth

**James R. Abbey, Ph.D.**
Professor Emeritus
College of Hotel Administration
University of Nevada, Las Vegas

**Waterbury Press**

## Disclaimer

This publication is designed to provide accurate and authoritative information in regard to the subject matter covered. It is sold with the understanding that the publisher is not engaged in rendering legal, accounting, or other professional service. If legal advice or other expert assistance is required, the services of a competent professional person should be sought.
— *From the Declaration of Principles jointly adopted by the American Bar Association and a Committee of Publishers and Associations.*

Cover Photo: Courtesy of Gaylord Palms Resort & Convention Center

Copyright © 2016
Waterbury Press
1605 Iron Ridge Dr.
Las Vegas, NV 89117
Tel: 702-254-1530
Fax: 702-254-3824
Internet: www.waterburypress.com
E-mail: sales@waterburypress.com

All rights reserved. No part of this publication may be reproduced, stored in a retrieval system, or transmitted, in any form or by any means, electronic, mechanical, photocopying, recording, or otherwise, without the prior written permission of the publisher.

Printed in the United States of America

ISBN 978-0-9620710-7-2

# Contents

**Introduction** .................................................................................. ix

## 1 Introduction to the Convention, Meetings and Trade Show Industry ............................................................................. 4

The Convention and Meetings Industry Today ................................. 7
The Scope of Today's Meetings Market ........................................... 10
    *Types of Meetings, Who Holds Meetings, Types of Group Customers, Types of Meeting Facilities*
Trends in the Meetings Industry ...................................................... 19
    *New Technology, Changing Demographics, Strategic Meetings Management, Complex Contracts, Third-Party Meeting Planners, The Wellness Movement, Green Meetings and Social Responsibility*
Summary ............................................................................................ 32

## 2 Developing Your Marketing Plan ........................................ 38

The Difference Between Sales and Marketing ................................. 38
The Importance of Marketing ........................................................... 39
The Marketing Plan ........................................................................... 41
The Four Steps of the Marketing Plan ............................................. 41
    *Step #1—Conducting Marketing Research,*
    *Step #2—Selecting Target Markets and Positioning the Property,*
    *Step #3—Establishing Objectives and Action Plans,*
    *Step #4—Reviewing and Monitoring the Marketing Plan*
Putting a Marketing Plan into Action ............................................. 65
Summary ............................................................................................ 66
Chapter Appendix: Sample Marketing Plan ................................... 69

## 3 Organizing for Convention Sales ....................................... 76

Sales Structures ................................................................................. 76
    *The Sales Office, How the Sales Office Interfaces with Other Departments*
The Sales and Marketing Staff ......................................................... 83
    *Positions within Sales, Supplemental Sales Staff*
Managing the Sales Effort ................................................................ 92
    *Standard Operating Procedures, Sales Meetings, Assigning Account Responsibility, Evaluating the Sales Effort*
Sales Records and Filing Systems ................................................... 98
    *Hotel Filing Systems, Control Books and Sales Forms*
Sales Office Automation ................................................................... 106
    *Advantages of Automation, New Advances in Hotel Computer Systems, The "Virtual" Office, Additional Uses of Automation*
Summary ............................................................................................ 115

# Contents

## 4 Selling the Association Market .................................................. 120

Revenue Producers .................................................................................. 120
Requirements for Association Meetings ................................................. 121
Kinds of Association Meetings ................................................................ 124
    *Annual Conventions, State and Regional Conventions, Conferences, Seminars and Workshops, Board and Committee Meetings, Hybrid Meetings*
Characteristics of Association Meetings ................................................. 130
    *Cycle and Pattern, Geographic Restrictions, Lead Time, Kind of Sites, Voluntary Attendance, Convention Duration, Price*
Association Meeting Decision-Makers .................................................... 138
    *Association Director, Association President and Officers, Committee Chairperson, Board of Directors, Other Influences*
Sources for Finding Association Business ............................................... 143
    *Directories and Databases, Specialized Periodicals, Hotel Records*
Summary .................................................................................................. 148

## 5 Selling the Corporate Meetings Market .......................... 152

Requirements for Corporate Meetings ..................................................... 153
Kinds of Company Meetings ................................................................... 159
    *National and Regional Sales Meetings, New Product/Dealer Meetings, Professional/Technical Meetings, Management Meetings, Training Meetings, Stockholder/Public Meetings, Incentive Meetings*
Characteristics of Company Meetings ..................................................... 165
    *Small Meetings, Time Cycle, Lead Time, Geographic Patterns, Kinds of Sites, Attendance, Duration, Exhibits, Meeting Room Requirements, One Meeting-One Check, Multiple-Booking Potential*
Corporate Meeting Decision-Makers ....................................................... 175
    *Full-time Meeting Planner, Company President, Marketing and Sales Executives, Advertising and Sales Managers, Other Corporate Executives, Passenger Traffic/Corporate Travel Managers, Procurement (Purchasing) Managers, Training Director, Meeting Specialists/Third-Party Planners*
Sources for Finding Corporate Business and Decision-Makers ............. 182
    *Special Meeting Publications, Trade Directories, Publications, and Databases, Trade Associations, Convention and Visitors Bureaus, Lateral Referral and Account Penetration*
Summary .................................................................................................. 187

## 6 Selling Other Markets ............................................................... 192

Nonprofit Organizations .......................................................................... 193
The SMERF Groups ................................................................................ 194
    *Social Groups, Military and Other Reunions, Educational Meetings, Religious Meetings, Fraternal Meetings*
Government Agencies ............................................................................. 209

|   |   |
|---|---|
| Labor Unions | 212 |
| Incentive Meetings | 213 |
| Insurance/Financial Service Meetings | 217 |
| Medical Meetings | 220 |
| Summary | 224 |

## 7 Selling to the Meetings Market ............................................. 232

|   |   |
|---|---|
| Personal Sales Calls – Mastering Consultive Sales | 233 |

*Pre-call Planning, Opening the Sales Call, Getting Prospect Involvement, Presenting Your Property, Handling Objections, Closing and Follow-up*

|   |   |
|---|---|
| Telephone Selling | 245 |

*Telephone Techniques, Screening Prospects, Setting Appointments by Phone, Telephone Sales Call Follow-up, Handling Inquiries, Telemarketing*

|   |   |
|---|---|
| Sales Blitz Selling | 252 |
| Trade Show Selling | 253 |
| Selling with Convention Bureaus | 257 |
| Site Inspection Selling and Familiarization Tours | 261 |
| Summary | 265 |

## 8 Advertising to the Meeting Planner ............................. 270

|   |   |
|---|---|
| Print Advertising | 271 |

*Trade Magazines, Hotel Directories*

|   |   |
|---|---|
| Using Technology for Advertising | 277 |

*The Internet, E-mail Advertising, Fax Transmissions*

|   |   |
|---|---|
| Collateral Materials | 288 |

*Brochures, Other Collateral Materials, Specialty Items*

|   |   |
|---|---|
| Direct Mail Advertising | 294 |
| Planning an Advertising Strategy | 296 |

*Reach, Frequency, Timing and Consistency, Exchange Trade Advertising, Cooperative Advertising and Strategic Partnerships, Advertising Agencies*

|   |   |
|---|---|
| Public Relations and Publicity | 303 |
| Summary | 305 |

## 9 Negotiations and Contracts ........................................... 312

|   |   |
|---|---|
| Negotiations | 313 |
| Letter of Agreement/Contract | 316 |

*Names of Organization and Hotel, Official Dates, Number and Kinds of Rooms, Rates/Commissions, Arrival/Departure Pattern, Meeting Space, Complimentary and Reduced-Rate Rooms, Prior Visits, Working Space, Registration Control, Exhibit Space, Food Functions, Refreshment Breaks, Liquor, Gratuities and Service Charges, Audiovisual Equipment, Union Regulations, Master Account and Credit Procedures, Method of Payment, Termination/*

## Contents

*Cancellation Clauses, Damage Clause: Liquidated or Mitigated Damages, Gratuities and Service Charges, Attrition Clause, Arbitration/Dispute Resolution, Warranty of Authority, Insurance/Indemnification, Other Contract Matters*

Contract Standardization ........................................................... 341
Multiple-Meeting Contracts ....................................................... 342
Summary ..................................................................................... 345

## 10 The Service Function ........................................................ 352

Service Is the Key ....................................................................... 353
Who Services? ............................................................................ 356
*The Convention Service Manager, Increased Recognition, Convention Service Staff, Convention Service Managers at Convention and Visitors Bureaus*
The Transition ............................................................................ 367
An Overview of the Service Function ....................................... 369
Summary ..................................................................................... 372
Chapter Appendix: Convention Service Checklist .................. 375

## 11 Guestrooms ........................................................................ 382

Reservation Systems .................................................................. 382
*Hotel-Managed Reservations, Rooming Lists, Convention Center Housing Bureaus, Third-party Housing Companies*
Room Assignment ...................................................................... 390
*Rate Structures, Complimentary Arrangements, Priorities, Room Types, The Group History, Arrival/Departure Pattern, Other Hotels*
Managing Room Blocks ............................................................. 396
*No-Shows/Overbooking, Attrition*
Check-in/Check-out ................................................................... 403
*Check-in Procedure, Check-out Procedure*
Summary ..................................................................................... 408

## 12 Preparing for the Event .................................................... 414

Pre-convention Meeting ............................................................ 414
*Key Personnel Roster*
Resume (Specification Sheet) ................................................... 419
Banquet Event Order (Function Sheet) .................................... 421
The Importance of Communication ......................................... 427
Communicating Details Electronically .................................... 429
The Importance of Follow-up .................................................... 432
Summary ..................................................................................... 433
Chapter Appendix: Resume (Specification Sheet) .................. 435

# Contents

## 13 Function Rooms and Meeting Setups ........................... 442

Function Rooms ......................................................................... 442
*Types of Function Rooms, Function Room Size and Layout, Meeting Room Plans, Timetable for Setup and Breakdown*

Managing Function Rooms ....................................................... 452
*Sales Restrictions on Function Space, Function Room Charges, Function and Meeting Room Revenue Management, Release Dates, Several Meetings Simultaneously, Use of Meeting Rooms by Others, Employee Procedure Manuals*

Meeting Setups .......................................................................... 461
*Function Room Furniture, Basic Meeting Setups, Setups with Tables*

Breakdown of Function Rooms ................................................ 475
Meeting Rooms of the Future .................................................. 476
Monitoring Function Room Usage .......................................... 479
Summary ..................................................................................... 480

## 14 Food and Beverage Service ............................................ 486

Food Service .............................................................................. 488
*Types of Food Functions, Themed and Special Events, Off-Premises Catering, Changing Tastes, Types of Service, Chefs Tastings Pricing Food Functions, Attendance, Attrition, Function Rooms, Control Procedures, Staffing, Uniserve or Duoserve*

Beverage Service ....................................................................... 511
*Types of Setups, Hospitality Suites, Brands, Pricing Methods, Beverage Control*

Post-Function Actions .............................................................. 519
In-House Coordination: Large vs. Small Properties ............. 519
*Role of the Catering Manager, Servicing and Selling, Communication and Cooperation*

Summary ..................................................................................... 521

## 15 Audiovisual Requirements ............................................. 530

Types of Audiovisual Equipment ............................................. 531
*Sound Systems, Lighting, Screens, Projectors, Projector Stands, Multimedia Presentations, Simultaneous Interpretations, Virtual Conferencing, Other Presentation Devices*

Bandwidth and High-Speed Internet Access ......................... 547
Outside or Inside? ..................................................................... 549
*Audiovisual Specialists, In-House Equipment*

Charging for Audiovisual Equipment ..................................... 553
Union Regulations ..................................................................... 555
Summary ..................................................................................... 555

**vii**

# Contents

## 16 Admission Systems and Other Services ... 562

Convention Registration ... 562
Convention Security ... 568
    *Controlled Admission, Ticket Arrangements, Uncontrolled Admission, Exhibit Security*
Other Services ... 573
    *Signs & Notices, Convention Headquarters Room, Convention Hospitality Suites, Guest Packages, Telephones, Printing and Duplication, Decorations, Entertainment, Preferred Suppliers/Exclusives*
Guest/Companion Programs ... 585
    *Building Guest/Companion Attendance, Activities for the Attendee's Guests, Activities for Children*
Summary ... 592

## 17 Exhibits and Trade Shows ... 598

The Scope of Exhibits and Trade Shows ... 598
    *Types of Exhibits*
Exhibit Planning ... 600
    *Key Trade Show and Exhibit Personnel, Scaled Drawings, Layouts, Photo File, Timetable, Show Hours and Room Assignments, Labor Regulations, Insurance*
Exhibit Billing Procedures ... 616
    *Hotel's Rental Charge, Exhibition Service Contractor's Fee*
Convention Shipping and Receiving ... 619
    *Exhibit Shipping, Recommended Address Terminology, Shipping Methods, Incoming Shipping Costs*
Summary ... 624

## 18 Convention Billing and Post-convention Review ... 630

Convention Billing ... 630
    *The Master Account, Time of Payment, Guest Credit, Gratuities and Service Charges, Surcharges and Resort Fees, HSMAI's Suggested Payment Schedule*
Post-convention Review ... 647
    *Comparison with Projections, Function Attendance, Special Services, Individual Comments, Post-convention Reporting, Final Appraisal*
Summary ... 655

## Index ... 658

# Introduction

*Convention Sales and Services* was written to serve as both a primer for those interested in meetings and conventions as a career path and as an updated resource for those who are already involved in this exciting segment of the hospitality field. Earlier editions of this book have been tested on the firing line in university classrooms and in hotel sales offices throughout the world, and seasoned industry professionals worldwide have given glowing reviews to this comprehensive text. Neil Ostergren, CHSE, past president of the Hospitality Sales and Marketing Association International (HSMAI), says:

> *Convention Sales and Services* is the most complete and up-to-date textbook that I have come across in my 35 years in the hotel industry. The 18 chapters are full of pertinent information, not just for students being introduced to the industry, but for seasoned professionals as well. Anyone seriously interested in advancing his or her career in today's hotel industry who does not read this book will, in my opinion, be less successful in reaching his or her full potential.

This text was designed to take an in-depth look at the techniques necessary to effectively sell to and service the meetings and conventions market. This market segment has become increasingly important for hotel profitability – and it offers the opportunity for an exciting and rewarding career with practically unlimited potential. To be successful, it is important to become knowledgeable in the nuances of the sales and servicing processes – and to develop strategies that take both the perspective of the hotel and the point-of-view of meeting planners into consideration.

Today's meeting planners are knowledgeable and professional – and they expect their contacts in the hospitality field to exhibit these qualities as well. Planners are tech-savvy, and they expect hotel sales and service people to understand how to best communicate with them and to anticipate and be able to meet their specific technical needs. Since a partnership between hotels and planners is necessary to ensure the execution of rewarding and memorable meetings and conventions, this edition has been updated to reflect the increasing influence of planners on a hotel's sales and servicing efforts.

The text is divided into two parts. Part I offers practical insight into the various types of meetings and conventions, the types of organizations that stage these events and how to reach and sell to this important group segment. This section includes in-depth discussions on developing a marketing plan (the cornerstone to successful sales and marketing), analyzing a hotel property to determine which segments of the group market can be sold to and serviced successfully, practical advice on reaching each of the group market segments, implementing successful sales strategies and finalizing a group's events through negotiations and letters of agreement.

Part II details the various aspects of convention service. To ensure that an event flows smoothly, effective service procedures must be implemented and followed by a staff that is skilled and knowledgeable in the various aspects of each function. This section details specific requirements for group events, including guestrooms, meeting and function rooms, audiovisual requirements, food and beverage service and other aspects, such as event registration, convention security, and other services.

# Introduction

Comprehensive appendices at the end of several chapters include a sample marketing action plan, a convention service questionnaire, and a resume questionnaire for servicing meeting groups.

## Features of the Ninth Edition

### Industry Profiles

Each chapter begins with a profile of a seasoned industry professional who shares his or her insights into areas relevant to each chapter. These opening profiles include a photograph, brief biography, and personal advice on how to succeed in each area of expertise. Profiles of both hospitality and meeting planning professionals have been included to provide a balanced view of the relationship between hotels and their meetings and conventions customers.

As we mentioned previously, it is important to understand a planner's perspective regarding different aspects of the sales and servicing process. Therefore, many chapters also include additional profiles and advice from meeting planning professionals as well as boxes that detail how hotels are helping planners to meet specific needs for their events.

### Industry Profile

*Kevin Buchanan,*
*General Manager*

Hilton Garden Inn Providence Airport/Warwick

A 1994 graduate of Johnson and Wales University, Kevin Buchanan has served as the general manager of the Hilton Garden Inn Providence Airport/Warwick since the property opened in 2005. Over his 20-year career in the hospitality industry, Buchanan has been recognized with such honors as General Manager of the Year for Hilton Garden Inn and as the Rhode Island Hospitality Association Hotelier of the Year. Also employed by the Williamsburg, Virginia-based Newport Hospitality Group (NHG) since 2002, he was honored as General Manager of the Year. An active member of the Providence Warwick Convention and Visitors Authority for seven years, Buchanan also serves on the board of directors for the State Tourism Department for the city of Warwick, Rhode Island.

### The Sales-Focused General Manager

As general managers, we are responsible for leading everything at the hotel and delivering the results to contribute to its overall success. We help to drive sales and profitability as well as guest and team member satisfaction and ensure brand standards are met. To achieve that mission, it is important that general managers are involved in sales and that they make sales a priority on a daily basis.

# Introduction

## "Worth Watching" boxes

These boxes, which are new to this edition, provide links to videos that have been carefully selected to complement topics discussed in the text. Most videos are short (averaging three minutes in length), but each features either invaluable advice from industry professionals or tutorials on various topics.

> **WORTH WATCHING**
>
> Steve Bartolin, the former president and CEO and now chairman of The Broadmoor, explains the property's unprecedented guarantee to meeting planners dealing with an economic downturn at meetingsnet.com/video/broadmoor-guarantee-meeting.

> **MORE ONLINE**
>
> An excellent example of a RFP from the National Association of School Psychologists can be viewed at www.meetings-conventions.com/News/Features/The-Comprehensive RFP/ (scroll down to the "here" link). You can also view guides for meeting planners on what should be included in a RFP at www.conventionindustry.org/StandardsPractices/APEX/RFPWorkbook.aspx (click on RFP Workbook and scroll down to link to download the workbook) and at meetings.zentila.com/8secrets-download (registration is required for this free download).

## "More Online" boxes

These boxes, which are also a new addition to this text, direct the reader to Internet sites that provide additional information on the subject explained in each chapter. These sites are excellent resources for the student or professional who wishes to access more in-depth information on topics of interest.

## Internet Exercises

These exercises go a step beyond the "More Online" boxes, offering readers the opportunity to navigate specific websites in order to increase their knowledge and answer questions regarding chapter topics. As with the "Worth Watching" and "More Online" boxes, Internet Exercises are not simply "fillers" – they are invaluable resources that have been strategically placed to enable the reader to further explore the content discussed in the chapter.

---

### 🖥 INTERNET EXERCISE
### IACC Conference Centers

Visit the website for the International Association of Conference Centers at www.iacconline.com. Navigate the site to answer the following questions:

1. What are the differences between conference centers and conventional hotels and resorts in each of the following areas:
   - Focus and market segments
   - Facility design
   - Furnishings and equipment
   - Food and beverage service
   - Personnel
2. What are some of the industry *standards* and *guidelines* for conference centers?
3. What environmental initiatives are recommended to member conference centers?
4. What scholarships and awards does this trade association offer to students?

# Introduction

## "Best Practices" boxes

These boxes, which are included throughout the text, provide actual examples of how the principles detailed in each chapter have been used by hospitality properties to sell to and service the convention and meetings market. "Best Practices" boxes provide an opportunity for the reader to see exactly how the principles discussed in each chapter are put into action by leading hospitality firms.

---

**Best Practices**

**Hilton**  **Sheraton**

**"Hilton Hotels & Sheraton Hotels Form a Strategic Partnership to Capture Meetings Business in New York City"**

Hilton New York, Sheraton New York, and the Sheraton Manhattan, which are about 150 feet from one another in mid-town Manhattan, have 100 meeting rooms, more than 225,000 square feet of meeting space, and a combined total of 5,000 guestrooms. They can also accommodate up to 425 exhibits. Although they are competitors, the three hotels took advantage of an opportunity to market their combined facilities to appeal to meeting planners.

The three hotels created NY 5000, a partnership geared to a joint sales and marketing effort.

---

## Learning Objectives and Key Terms

Each chapter starts with a list of learning objectives and a chapter outline. These learning objectives prepare you for the chapter's content and help you to focus and organize your thoughts as you read.

Key terms used for convention sales and services are highlighted within each chapter. Definitions of each of these key terms are found at the end of each chapter.

## Key Terms

**American plan**—Charge includes room, food and beverage, and gratuities. Includes three meals per day.
**authorized signature**—Signature of person(s) with the authority to charge to a group master account.
**auxiliary business**—Affiliates and subgroups, such as exhibitors, who contribute to the overall value of the meeting. Often, this type of business that is brought to a facility because of an event is called **in conjunction with** business.
**billing instructions**—Notice as to how charges for an event should be handled and to whom invoices should be addressed.
**blanket service charges**—Service charges added into the room charge so that attendees do not have to tip during their stay. Primarily used with the American Plan (AP) system.

# Introduction

## To the Reader

It wasn't many years ago that students or convention sales and services staff who wanted to further their knowledge on specific topics had to either travel to see a speaker in person or wait until a DVD of the presentation was released. Today, however, the Internet has made it possible to instantly access presentations by experts via numerous video portals and to gain additional knowledge by browsing the articles, white papers, and other educational resources available online.

Studies have shown that when students are presented with communications that combine voice and visual elements, retention tops 65 percent. Therefore, this book offers links to a number of instructional videos that can be found online. Some of our sources include YouTube (www.youtube.com) and Vimeo (vimeo.com). Informative videos that can supplement your knowledge and help to further you career may also be posted on the websites of hotel chains, meeting planning organizations, and industry suppliers. One such resource is Hilton Elevated Discussions (HED Talks at hedtalks.connectplusat hilton worldwide.com). This site offers a number of videos by industry professionals speaking on such areas as "Building Connections," "Driving Results," "Creating Experiences," and "Doing it All Responsibly." Websites of professional groups, such as the Hospitality Sales & Marketing Association International (HSMAI at www.hsmai.org), also offer a wealth of educational resources.

This ninth edition includes three excellent features that enable readers to supplement their knowledge by using the Internet. New "Worth Watching" and "More Online" boxes provide links to videos and other educational content, such as white papers and articles on the latest developments in the hospitality industry. Internet Exercises offer the opportunity to navigate through selected websites to enhance your grasp of the key concepts presented in the text.

These features contain relevant material that has been carefully researched and strategically positioned within the text. The author strongly suggests that you do not skip over these important resources (or the illustrations and additional boxes referenced in each chapter); these materials have been developed and placed to provide in-depth coverage of each topic and to help you to better understand each concept — and retain that information.

Disclaimer: At the time of this writing, the Internet addresses provided in the text were correct. However, Internet addresses may change or sites may be removed. If a website is no longer available at the address listed in the text, a search engine can be used to find the new address or additional, related sites.

## To the Instructor: Supplemental Support Package

A comprehensive Instructor's Manual is now available in a downloadable format. This new, updated Instructor's Manual provides the following resources for each chapter:

- Chapter Overview
- Suggested Lecture Outline
- Class Activities, including suggested guest speakers and individual/group work.
- Supplemental audiovisual materials are suggested for several chapters
- Test Questions and a separate Test Questions with Answer Key file

Also included in the Instructor's Manual are:

- Mid-Term and Final Examinations and a separate Test Questions with Answer Key file
- Case studies (with answers to discussion questions) are also provided for a number of chapters.

## PowerPoint Presentations

A complete set of PowerPoint presentations is also provided for each chapter. These presentations include a comprehensive overview of each chapter, including many of the text exhibits, and can be shown "as is" or customized to meet the needs of the individual instructor.

This new, expanded edition of *Convention Sales and Services* is an invaluable resource that will enable students and hospitality professionals alike to stay up-to-date in the ever-changing meetings and conventions industry. It is the author's hope that, using the tools provided in this text, YOU will find success and career satisfaction in this challenging and rewarding field.

James R. Abbey, Ph.D., CHA<br>
Las Vegas, Nevada

## Acknowledgments

Over the years, students and instructors have provided reviews and suggestions for improving the text and Instructor's Manual, and seasoned industry professionals have contributed their knowledge, expertise, and advice to ensure that *Convention Sales and Services* remains one of the most comprehensive, practical, and up-to-date textbooks available for the meetings and conventions field. It would be impossible to list everyone who has contributed, of course, but each is gratefully appreciated (several of these industry professionals have been profiled at the beginning of chapters and within numerous chapters in the text). The author would, however, like to extend a special "thank you" to Gilbert Medina, audio-visual manager at The Cosmopolitan™ of Las Vegas, who leads the team that services and maintains all audiovisual systems at the 2,995-room luxury resort. Gilbert played a pivotal role in the revision of Chapter 15 (and related content in the Instructor's Manual) by reviewing the chapter in the previous edition of this textbook and providing updated information on the latest AV technology available for today's meetings and conventions.

The author also wishes to express his gratitude to his Las Vegas-based assistants who contributed to the production of this book:

- Donna Merrill, a professional advertising writer and editor who has worked on a number of editions of this book as well as on the author's *Hospitality Sales and Marketing*, assisted in the editing of this text, typed additions and corrections, and proofread the book in its various stages.
- Robert Wais, a talented graphics artist who has worked for prestigious companies in the U.S. and abroad, scanned the new illustrations, designed graphics, and is

responsible for the layout of this text and for the cover designs for this book and the three previous editions of *Convention Sales and Services*.

Last, but certainly not least, the author wishes to express his appreciation to the hospitality firms (large and small), trade publications, and hospitality professionals who not only contributed their expertise, but also granted permission for the use of their forms, exhibits, and advertisements to enhance the text of this book.

**James Abbey**

# Convention Sales and Services
## 9th Edition

### Industry Profile

## *Deborah Sexton, President and CEO*

**Professional Convention Management Association (PCMA)**

*After Deborah was hired as president and CEO of PCMA in 2005, membership in the organization reached an all-time high and attendance records continue to be broken at PCMA annual meetings. This award-winning industry leader, who is also President of the PCMA Education Foundation, is the author of the "To The Point" column, which appears monthly in the organization's magazine,* PCMA Convene.

## The Changing Face of the Meetings Market

As we mark another year for *Convene's* Annual Meetings Industry Forecast, both current reports and future predictions are positive. Here are some predominate trends and themes:

**Disrupters to the Status Quo.** Disruption to standard business models for travel, lodging, and face-to-face events is incredibly strong right now. Challenges facing government meetings are still significant, and the sheer number of Millennials with their different priorities is an impressive force…Look at each disruption as an opportunity to improve, and focus your efforts on doing just that.

**Potential of International Markets.** The most significant potential comes from the international side. Inbound international traffic increased last year and is expected to grow in the years ahead…And as many international destinations begin to develop their meetings offerings, there are real possibilities for new shows to be launched or existing international events to expand.

**Big Data.** Everyone is talking about big data, but only a small percentage are using it effectively. The potential for big data in the areas of uncovering marketing opportunities, customer service, and ROI is huge. But gathering this data is still cost prohibitive for many, and even then, those who have it must learn how to use it appropriately and translate it into business and marketing plans.

**Role of Technology Overall.** The ability to collect big data is just one of the seemingly infinite ways technology can improve meetings and travel. It's now been proven that virtual meetings allow us to expand the reach of our face-to-face meetings and attract new attendees. Though it has the potential to distract, social media can help to engage stakeholders in our missions when they're on site and throughout the year. And new technology has practical implications as well…event professionals will be able to monitor food-and-beverage supply levels, rentals inventory, delivery status, venue temperatures, and more – with just a swipe on their touchscreen.

**Job Prospects for Graduates Are Better.** How do graduates land a job in the field of their choice? I firmly believe that networking, volunteering in your chosen industry, and getting out and expanding your skillset will more likely land you your dream job than simply scouring job postings online. I can honestly say that every job I've been offered throughout my career was the result of connections I'd made while volunteering in the hospitality and meetings industry…Whether you're searching for that all-important first post-college job, or simply looking for a new career direction, there's much to be said for getting out and networking, helping a good cause, and showing what you can do.

### WORTH WATCHING

Deborah Sexton's excellent video on topics discussed in this chapter, including industry trends, meeting design, hybrid events, and globalization, can be viewed at hedtalks.connectionplushiltonworldwide.com (click on the Building Connections tab and then the Industry Trends video).

**Learning Objectives:**

This portion of your text introduces you to the nature and scope of today's growing and changing meetings market. When you have studied this chapter, you will:

- Be able to identify organizations involved in the advancement of professionalism in the convention and meetings industry.

- Be able to identify the types of meetings held and tell when and why each is typically used.

- Know the types of organizations that hold meetings and describe the types of group customers.

- Be able to describe the various types of meeting facilities.

- Be aware of the current trends that are impacting the meetings industry, especially the role of third-party meeting planners and the increased use of technology.

**Outline**

The Convention and Meetings Industry Today

The Scope of Today's Meetings Market

- Types of Meetings
- Who Holds Meetings
- Types of Group Customers
- Types of Meeting Facilities

Trends in the Meetings Industry

- New Technology
- Changing Demographics
- Strategic Meetings Management
- Complex Contracts
- Third-Party Meeting Planners
- The Wellness Movement
- Green Meetings and Social Responsibility

Summary

# 1 Introduction to the Convention, Meetings and Trade Show Industry

It wasn't too many years ago that training meetings would typically include a simple schoolroom setup of heavy tables and rigid chairs; the tables were often set with pitchers of water, glasses, and ashtrays, as many attendees smoked. The presentation was given at the front of the room, where the speaker would use a flip chart to illustrate points; some speakers used an overhead projector to show transparencies with additional information. Attendees were a passive audience; there was little interaction, either between the speaker and the audience or among the attendees. All or most of the attendees were men. Sessions were long, with all-day meetings broken up only by lunch and two coffee breaks (at which coffee, tea, and sugar-laden pastries were offered).

Today's meetings, which are likely to be attended by as many (or more) females as males, are a far cry from the meetings of the past. First, attendees are generally younger and they enjoy combining socializing with work. Since they grew up with technology, they typically carry at least two mobile devices (usually a smartphone and a tablet or notebook) to enable them to remain connected with their workplace, family, and friends.

Meetings are now participant-driven and, since today's attendees prefer to receive information in short spurts, they include numerous breakout sessions that allow attendees to brainstorm and add their input to the meeting. Meeting room setups are more likely to include comfortable seating and tables and chairs that can easily be moved by the attendees themselves, and some meetings are not restricted to typical meeting rooms – attendees may come together on rooftops or in outdoor settings.

Today's presentations are likely to include some form of computer-generated content, such as feeds of speakers from remote locations or inter-active presentations on monitors or touchscreen tables. Notes — or even the entire session — can be downloaded into a mobile device for future reference.

Refreshment breaks now include healthy foods, such as granola, fresh fruit, nuts, and juices and vitamin water. Breakfast and lunch menus are being designed to provide the proper combination of nutrients to keep attendees alert and focused. There is an increasing emphasis on "brain food" menus for lunch and dinner, and more locally grown produce and locally sourced meats are being included in meetings fare.

**Conventions**, too, have changed. It is not unusual for the program to include speakers from remote locations or multi-media presentations; today's conventions are often streamed in real time or videotaped to be viewed on the organization's website. Attendees' badges are becoming interactive, allowing them to share information with other attendees or exhibitors. Lighter, healthier foods are being served at convention luncheons and banquets.

Groups – corporations, associations, and non-profits – need to come together for a variety of reasons, so this market is expected to show continued growth. Meetings and conventions business already accounts for as much as 70 percent of sales volume at major U.S. hotels, and 15 to 20 percent of the revenue of smaller properties. Meetings are also big business in Canada. One study showed that meetings were attended by 70.2 million participants, resulting in $32.2 billion in direct spending and the creation of 235,500 full-year jobs (see sidebar titled "Meetings Activity in Canada"). More than 75 percent of these meetings were held in hotels and resorts. Mexico, too, has stepped up its efforts to attract meetings and conventions, but it is not only our neighbors to the north and south who are reaching out to associations and other groups to attract meetings and convention business.

## Chapter 1: Introduction to the Convention, Meetings and Trade Show Industry

**Trade shows** and conventions, including ITB Berlin, the world's largest tourism trade fair, have been held in Europe for many years, with Germany, Italy, and the United Kingdom among the major players. Today, trade shows and fairs are held in 42 European countries. There are a number of European associations that serve both trade show planners and exhibitors. The European Major Exhibition Centres Association (EMECA at www.emeca.eu) unites 22 leading venues that stage some 1,500 trade fairs annually. The International Congress and Convention Association (ICCA at www.iccaworld.com) is a large international association that represents over 1,000 meetings suppliers in more than 90 countries. This association offers a number of services to members (see box titled "The ICCA: Global Leader in International Meetings") and holds an annual ICCA Congress and General Assembly in sites around the world, including Buenos Aires (2015), Malaysia (2016), Prague (2017), and Dubai (2018).

| MEETINGS ACTIVITY IN CANADA | |
|---|---|
| Total meetings | 671,000 |
| Total participants | 70.2 million |
| Full-year jobs (equivalent) | 235,500 |
| Direct Spending | $32.2 billion |

Source: Meetings impact research study conducted by Toronto-based Meeting Professionals International Foundation Canada. To download MPIFC's complete research results, visit www.mpiweb.org.

---

### The ICCA: Global Leader in International Meetings

The International Congress and Convention Association (ICCA) was formed in 1963 by a group of travel agents who were determined to evaluate ways to get the travel industry involved in the expanding international business market. Today, the organization includes five sectors: Meetings Management (open to organizations and firms that organize events); Transport (airlines, trains, buses, and car rental firms); Destination Marketing (national, regional, and local tourism organizations, including convention and visitors bureaus); Venues (hotels dedicated to meetings, convention centers, and exhibition centers that target the international market); and, Meetings Support (media, IT/software companies, AV and production companies, venue management companies, and financial services).

The organization, which has become the global expert in international association meetings, offers a directory of its members in each sector, educational events, and free resources to meeting planners. Many of these resources can be viewed on the organization's website, www.iccaworld.com (click on the Associations tab).

Among the publications offered by the ICCA are annual reports that rank the top cities and countries for meetings attendance. In the latest survey, for example, Paris was the top city and the United States was the top country in the rankings. To view the latest statistics on the international meetings market, go to www.iccaworld.com/associations.cfm and click on the Download Report link at the bottom of the ICAA Statistics Report box.

---

As China opens its doors to trade, more U.S. companies are setting up branches there – and Chinese businesspeople are attending meetings in the U.S. in record numbers. Today, many U.S. brands, including Hilton, Hyatt, Marriott, The Ritz-Carlton, Sheraton, and Wyndham, have a presence in the China, and other chains also found in the country include Shangri La and Jin Jiang Hotels, which range from economy to five-star upscale hotels (see Figure 1.1). Businesspeople from the United States generally opt for familiar chains or five-star properties to ensure that they will get expected amenities and services.

Chapter 1: Introduction to the Convention, Meetings and Trade Show Industry

**Figure 1.1. A HOTEL CHAIN IN CHINA PROMOTES ITS SERVICES TO MEETINGS ATTENDEES.**

This ad promotes the Jin Jiang International Hotels chain, which operates numerous hotels, ranging from economy to upscale, in China, one of the fastest growing markets for meetings and conventions.
**Source: Courtesy of Jin Jiang Hotels.**

    Other countries making an impact on the meetings, incentives, conventions, and exhibitions (MICE) industry include Brazil, Russia, India, and South Africa (these countries, along with China, have been given the acronym BRICS). As with China, U.S. companies are opening offices in these countries and attendees from the BRICS nations are attending more meetings and conventions in the U.S. Domestic hotels are meeting the needs of these delegates by hiring multi-lingual staffs, offering signage and promotional materials in several languages, and providing instantaneous language translation devices at meetings.

Meetings and conventions business doesn't just fall into the laps of hospitality properties, of course. In order to effectively sell to and service the group market, you have to know the types of meetings that are held, determine who holds these meetings, and recognize the types of facilities that each segment of this market requires. You also need to keep abreast of trends in the meetings industry to stay a step ahead of your competition. In this chapter, we will provide an overview of today's meetings market, and we will discuss the trends that are shaping the needs of this market segment and their impact on the hotel industry.

## The Convention and Meetings Industry Today

The most recent study commissioned by the Convention Industry Council (CIC) found that the average association attendee spends approximately $322 per day while attending an annual convention.[1] The majority of that money was spent for hotel rooms and food and beverage (see Figure 1.2). When this daily expenditure is distributed throughout the economy, the multiplier effect is huge and has a larger, more far-reaching impact on the nation's economy. Figure 1.3 reflects this economic impact — $907 billion and over six million jobs.

While leisure travelers may represent larger numbers for the hospitality industry, meeting attendees—who frequently travel on an expense account—bring in the lion's share

*Figure 1.2. WHERE ASSOCIATION DELEGATES SPEND MONEY.*

**Where Association Delegates Spend Money**

- Food and Beverage: 29.5% $95.00
- Hotel Rooms and Incidentals: 47.1% $152.00
- Transportation: 9.5% $30.00
- Retail Stores: 10.9% $35.00
- Entertainment: 3% $10.00

*The average association delegate spends approximately $322 per day at national and international conventions. It is important to note that this estimate includes only association delegates; corporate delegates can be expected to spend an additional twenty to thirty dollars per day, as many are on expense accounts and usually entertain potential clients while attending meetings and conventions.*
**Source: Adapted from the Destination Marketing Association International's Expenditure and Impact Survey (EXPACT).**

## Chapter 1: Introduction to the Convention, Meetings and Trade Show Industry

*Figure 1.3. THE ECONOMIC IMPACT OF THE MEETINGS INDUSTRY.*

**Summary of Economic Impacts**

- Corporate/Business Meetings $132.1 Million (50%)
- Conventions/Conferences/Congresses/Trade Shows $106.6 Million (41%)
- Incentive/Other Meetings $24.3 Million (9%)

$263 Billion in Direct Spending — 1.7 Million FTE Jobs

**Multiplier Effect**

$907 Billion in Total Economic Impact — 6.3 Million FTE Jobs

*While direct spending from meetings totaled approximately $263 billion, supporting 1.7 full-time equivalent (FTE) jobs, the total impact of the meetings market business has an even larger, more far-reaching effect on the nation's economy. As a result of meetings and conventions, the demand for auxiliary goods and services also rose, generating a total of $907 billion, supporting 6.3 million FTE jobs. The meetings industry ranks higher than air transportation and automotive manufacturing both in terms of contribution to the GNP and in number of workers employed. Every year, meetings generate 250 million overnight stays by 117 million Americans and five million international attendees.*
**Source:** "The Economic Significance of Meetings to the U.S. Economy," a study conducted by PricewaterhouseCoopers for the Convention Industry Council.

of revenue in addition to benefiting properties by filling "soft spots" and generating word-of-mouth business. Therefore, the lucrative convention and meetings market is becoming an increasingly important—and competitive—target market for hotels.

No longer are conventions attended primarily by males. According to recent figures, as many as 44 percent of association meeting attendees and 39 percent of corporate meeting attendees are women. Therefore today's accompanying spouses are often husbands instead of wives!

Meeting and convention attendees are just as likely to be single as married, and are typically younger (25 to 40 years of age) and more affluent than convention delegates of two decades ago. Meetings are no longer attended primarily for fun; in most cases, meeting attendance must be considered worthwhile enough to justify the expense and time away from the office.

The economy has also played an important part in changing the meetings and convention market. For example, the previous 80 percent deduction for business meals and entertainment has been reduced to 50 percent, forcing meeting planners and convention delegates to "cut corners" and look for the best deals. This trend, in addition to deregulated airlines and increased competition for meetings and convention business in the hospitality

## Chapter 1: Introduction to the Convention, Meetings and Trade Show Industry

industry, has resulted in increased negotiation for group transportation, discounted room rates, low- or no-cost meeting space, and inclusive packages. Contracts for hotel services are now the norm, and many corporations and associations are signing multiple-meeting contracts. This trend not only provides a savings to the organization (contracts usually guarantee a percentage off the rack rate in exchange for multiple business), but also gives the advantage of having only one contract for multiple events.

Many hotel contracts are negotiated by meeting planners who, unlike the meeting planning clients of the past (who typically had little knowledge of the requirements for a successful meeting), are highly trained professionals. Thirty years ago, the Convention Industry Council (CIC) administered its first certification exam to just a handful of meeting planners who had taken its educational courses. Today, over 20,000 meeting professionals hold the CIC's Certified Meeting Professional (CMP) designation, and additional courses and certifications are offered by a number of other organizations as well (see box titled "The ABCs of Certification"). Professional groups such as Meeting Professionals International (MPI), the Professional Convention Management Association (PCMA), and the Society for Incentive Travel Excellence have been formed—and joined in force by meeting planners—for additional training and networking.

---

### The ABCs of Certification

**CMP — Certified Meeting Professional**
Convention Industry Council
www.conventionindustry.org

**CHSP — Certified Hospitality Sales Professional**
American Hotel & Lodging Association
www.ahlei.org

**CHME — Certified Hospitality Marketing Executive**
Hospitality Sales & Marketing Association International
www.hsmai.org

**CEM — Certified in Exhibition Management**
International Association of Exhibitions and Events
www.iaee.com

**CITE — Certified Incentive Travel Executive**
Society for Incentive Travel Excellence
www.site-intl.org

**CDME — Certified Destination Management Executive**
Destination Marketing Association International
www.destinationmarketing.org

**CSEP — Certified Special Events Professional**
International Special Events Society
www.ises.com

**CMM — Certification in Meetings Management**
Meeting Professionals International
www.mpiweb.org/education/cmm

**CPCE — Certified Professional Catering Executive**
National Association of Catering Executives
www.nace.net/cs/education/cpce

**CGMP — Certified Government Meeting Professional**
Society of Government Meeting Professionals
www.sgmp.org

---

*Increasingly, people within an industry seek to become "certified" or "licensed" in the skills of their profession. While certification is not essential, many meeting planners and suppliers recognize the importance of education, and take advantage of opportunities to improve their skills and update their knowledge through programs offered by their professional associations. The meetings industry is filled with an "alphabet soup" of certifications, many of which are earned at the association's regional conventions, at regional seminars, or through courses offered over the Internet. Many of the industry leaders who have contributed to this text have completed one or more of the certification programs listed above.*

The Convention Industry Council (CIC), recognizing the need for hospitality professionals to have guidelines and examples of common industry practices, has developed a number of standardized forms and tools under its APEX (Accepted Practices Exchange) umbrella. One of the most useful, whether you are a student or a seasoned professional, is a comprehensive listing of the terms commonly used in the hotel industry (see box titled "APEX Industry Glossary"). We urge you to refer to this glossary — and to the additional

Chapter 1: Introduction to the Convention, Meetings and Trade Show Industry

> **APEX Industry Glossary**
>
> The Accepted Practices Exchange (APEX), an initiative of the Convention Industry Council (CIC), developed a comprehensive glossary of terms that are typically encountered when dealing with meetings business — from setting up programs and meeting the specific needs of meeting planners to negotiating the final contract.
>
> These standardized terms guarantee that everyone is "on the same page" when requests are made — there is no doubt as to what a planner needs when he or she requests a lavaliere microphone or a podium. Of equal or even greater importance are standardized definitions of common meetings contract terms, such as arbitration, audit, and slippage.
>
> With approximately 4,000 terms defined, a student or an inexperienced meeting planner can become well-versed in meetings terminology by simply typing in a search term. The glossary is also an invaluable tool for seasoned professionals, as it is updated periodically with new terminology. To view this useful tool, which can be used to supplement the terms you learn in your text, log on to www.conventionindustry.org/StandardPractices/APEX/glossary.aspx.

**Source: Courtesy of the Convention Industry Council (CIC).**

tools developed by the CIC, which are featured in several chapters in this text — to better learn how to sell to and service the meetings market.

## The Scope of Today's Meetings Market

Despite rising costs for transportation and hospitality services, more and more meetings are being held. They are held for a variety of purposes: to keep abreast of today's ever-changing technology; to keep sales goals on track; to meet for group motivation and rewards; and many more. No longer are meetings limited to a few annual conventions that simply require a large ballroom for a general session and a few food functions, or small business meetings where attendees are informed by a speaker armed only with a flip chart and a few marking pens. Today's attendees—and planners—expect a lot more. Hotel **business centers** that are complete with computers, fax machines, and sophisticated communications equipment have become commonplace (these are discussed in Chapter 5); state-of-the-art audiovisual equipment is expected (an overview is given in this chapter and AV equipment is discussed in detail in Chapter 15); and many conventions have taken on the appearance of lavish productions—complete with exotic foods and decor—to attract attendees.

As with other industries, however, the hospitality industry is greatly affected by economic conditions and other outside factors. The most recent slowdown took place when a global recession impacted both businesses and the traveling public. Many meeting planners had to justify the time and expense of meetings held off company premises, while other corporate planners were forced to scale back their formerly lavish affairs and forego the use of upscale properties in the face of public outcry over the appearance of excess in a down economy. Association meeting planners and planners for social groups were also forced to rethink meeting locations and programs in light of shrinking travel budgets for both the groups and attendees.

Today, however, demand is slowly increasing — although many of today's meetings are smaller and planners may scale back certain options, such as food and beverage, for meeting attendees. Beverly Kinkade, former vice president of association sales for Sheraton Hotels & Resorts Worldwide, says:

## Chapter 1: Introduction to the Convention, Meetings and Trade Show Industry

> Small meetings are up, and so is training activity...Convention attendance is up in all industries...There is greater demand across the board.[2]

Now planners are seeing how economic cycles play a vital role in how hotels respond to group business. The greater demand, which is due in part to there having been virtually no growth in the upscale and luxury property category, has resulted in:

- Tighter availability of rooms, especially at peak times
- Fewer concessions on food and beverage functions
- Less flexibility in "comp" allotments
- Tougher negotiations of other amenities

Although the meetings industry is facing an uncertain economic climate worldwide, meeting planners will still face higher rates and stiffer penalties if they fail to fill space as hotels struggle to keep pace with rising costs. But, since the hospitality industry is highly cyclical, a wise hotelier knows that business lost today may be business lost tomorrow, when it is needed. Hotels are looking to hold on to future group business by working with planners, often suggesting flexibility with dates; groups looking for value as well as availability, for example, are urged to consider off seasons rather than peak periods for their meetings.

You still face a great deal of competition in selling your site and facility for today's meeting. If you land a piece of business, you remain very much involved. You have a strong vested interest in the success of the convention. If it goes well and you gain the approval of the event sponsors and attendees, you stand a better chance of getting the repeat business and recommended business that is so very important in the career of anyone in the hospitality business. To successfully compete in the marketplace, it is important to know:

- The types of meetings held
- Who plans and holds meetings
- The types of group customers with whom you'll deal
- The types of meeting facilities that can successfully accommodate different meeting groups

## Types of Meetings

In the interest of simplicity, we will use the term *convention business*. But we are actually dealing with an entire spectrum of meetings of all types. It would be simpler if all events were just called *meetings*; after all, that's what they basically are. But that's not the way it is. There are a number of not-quite synonyms for the term, with nuances of difference. The "More Online" box and the Key Terms section at the end of this chapter provide definitions of the more commonly used types of meetings.

Keith Sexton-Patrick, CMP, who has been the director of convention services at several properties including the Mohegan Sun, Sheraton New York Hotel & Towers, and Disneyland Hotel, says:

**MORE ONLINE**

To see the definitions of the most commonly used terms for meeting types, go to www.evenues.com/event-planning-guide/types-of-meetings (you can also do an Internet search for additional information on common meetings terminology).

Meeting terminology is important. Those in the hotel business who aspire to be true professionals seek to understand the differences in order to help the meeting planner produce a successful event. As a convention sales or service professional, you'll be working with an ever-increasing professional group of people. Only by knowing the groups and the purpose of their meetings can you help them toward the accomplishment of their goals.

Sometimes, an event doesn't seem to fit into any category, and it can simply be called a *meeting*. This is particularly true when attendees of a single organization meet to discuss organizational affairs (stockholder meetings and board of directors meetings are two examples). These meetings can attract both a local and an out-of-town clientele, and range from a few attendees to large groups.

It is important to understand these various differences in terminology in order to grasp the kind of event the client is trying to produce and to help the meeting planner to effectively carry it out. Much of it has to do with the projection of a desired image. While meeting descriptions are not scientific terms, but loose, often interchangeable ones, proper terminology can help people work together to achieve a tone or image for an event, and in that sense terms are important. For example, a *seminar* connotes something more cerebral than a *convention*. A *conference* in Chicago may be termed a *congress* in Geneva. A *conference* conjures up a picture of a small group in shirt-sleeves, while a *lecture* promises a more formal presentation to a passive audience.

Accurate communication is needed in the convention business, and the ability to use proper terminology is important. Those in the field should understand the various terms used to describe meetings and use them correctly to achieve the professionalism expected by today's more sophisticated meeting planners.

## Who Holds Meetings

Once you have determined that convention business, whatever the terminology, is worth going after, the next question deals with determining who holds meetings. Corporations and associations represent the two major types of meeting sponsors. But nonprofit organizations, such as governmental agencies, labor unions, and fraternal and religious organizations, also hold conventions, meetings, and trade shows. For convenience, we have broken today's convention business into three major categories:

- Corporations
- Associations
- Nonprofit organizations

**Corporations.** The corporate meeting is of extreme importance. Such meetings can be likened to an iceberg: a small tip protrudes above the surface while a huge mass floats beneath it. Companies have no need or desire to publicize their meetings, but meet they do. And often. They hold small meetings, large meetings, and middle-sized meetings. Business executives stress communication, and one of the most fundamental methods of intra-company communication is the meeting. Company meetings are a prime part of the market and growing rapidly. We will discuss how to target this lucrative segment in detail in Chapter 5.

Attending conventions and conferences is very definitely a part of professional and business activity. Such expenses as transportation, lodging, food, entertainment of clients, and registration fees are tax-deductible as business or professional expenses. Companies that stage meetings for dealers or their own staffs may deduct the cost of such events as business expenses. This has been a strong stimulant to meetings and conventions. It is also a strong factor in site selection, as those who attend look to such business trips as quasi-vacations.

Pharmaceutical, financial, and insurance companies are important to the hotel sales manager because they are such prolific meeting sponsors (many of these meetings are continuing training programs for personnel). The prize, however, is the *incentive trip* for their top salespeople. These deluxe events are produced in various sizes and durations. Such trips are free to attendees, which are usually individuals (and a guest) or small groups. Little is needed in the way of meeting space, but incentive trips are promoted a year in advance and therefore require more advanced planning. However, so many insurance company meetings are produced in such a variety of sizes and types that the insurance company meeting planner is a prime contact for all hotels, from the large property to the small inn.

**Associations.** The most visible convention organizers are the many associations throughout the country—indeed throughout the world, because many of them are truly international. Associations vary in size and nature. Their scope ranges from small regional organizations through statewide associations to national and international ones. In Chapter 4, we will detail the characteristics of association meetings, and provide sources for reaching association decision-makers. Associations can be divided into several general categories:

- Trade associations
- Professional and scientific associations
- Technical societies

### A Successful Career Servicing the Meetings and Conventions Market

Anne Hamilton
Vice President Global Travel
The Walt Disney Company

I grew up in the hotel business. My father owned several small properties on Miami Beach, so I learned the ins and outs of hotel operations from an early age. After graduating from Florida State University's hospitality school, I joined Hyatt in their corporate training program. I had rooms experience at that point, so I worked in food and beverage to balance myself.

In 1996, I joined Disney, and, as vice president of resort sales and services, I was responsible for all sales and services related to meetings, conventions, and incentive programs at Walt Disney World Resort. We are fortunate to have an incredible team here at Disney — individuals who really want our meeting attendees to have a tremendous experience. My challenge is to keep this powerful team motivated and excited about coming to work every day.

I love the fact that my job is different every day. The meetings business is ever-changing. Meeting planners have become increasingly professional. They are more focused on attendee experience, achieving results, and realizing a return on their meeting investment.

Being a mentor is very important to me at this point in my career. I get great joy out of helping people become successful and realize their potential. I love articulating the benefits of a convention sales and service career, and I work closely with students at Rosen College. My advice to those just starting out in the hospitality/meetings industry is to seek a variety of work experience, understand that you are always on the journey of learning, and to embrace change. There are times when things go great and times when they don't, but you pick yourself up and learn from it (I've applied that to my personal life as well). I love this industry. Life couldn't be better.

## Chapter 1: Introduction to the Convention, Meetings and Trade Show Industry

*Trade associations* are comprised of businesses that represent a specific industry; one example is the National Restaurant Association (NRA at www/restaurant.org). Trade associations typically hold educational seminars and conferences as well as state, regional, and national conventions (these large events are often held in conjunction with exhibits or trade shows).

*Professional and scientific associations* are usually nonprofit organizations that have been established to further a particular profession; a hospitality-related example is the Hospitality Sales & Marketing Association International (HSMAI at www.hsmai.org). Scientific associations typically focus on the sciences and engineering. These groups may have state and regional chapters as well as a national headquarters, and hold a number of different types of meetings as well as their national convention.

*Technical societies* are comprised of members in such areas as aerospace, broadcast technology, consumer electronics, and robotics. These groups may hold frequent meetings as new technologies are introduced. The Institute of Electrical and Electronics Engineers (IEEE at www.ieee.org) represents over 40 technical societies.

**Nonprofit Organizations.** Nonprofit organizations fall into three categories:

- Government agencies
- Labor unions
- SMERF groups

*Government agencies*, which include the Department of Commerce (www.commerce.gov), the Centers for Disease Control and Prevention (CDC at www.cdc.gov), and the Veterans Affairs Department (VA at www.va.gov), often hold off-site meetings for both their employees and the public. This business can be extremely lucrative for hotels, but government meetings follow a different solicitation process and hotel rates must fall within federal guidelines (we will discuss this market further in Chapter 6).

(A word of warning may be in order here. There is a love for acronyms among associations and governmental agencies that can drive the outsider up the wall. Each association seems to feel that the world is focused on it and that everyone knows what XYZ stands for. It also leads to crossed lines. Take "AMA": it can refer to the American Medical Association or the American Management Association, both prolific meeting holders. It takes a bit of caution. Listen carefully and take good notes. Take nothing out of context. Soon, you'll talk in acronyms, too.)

*Labor unions* are organized at four levels (local, state and regional, national, and international), with numerous meetings and annual or biannual conventions organized at each level. Business from unions for the construction, manufacturing, mining, and transportation fields, is generally the most lucrative, and these unions' large conventions typically include committee meetings, debates, speeches, and guest speakers.

The *SMERF groups* include social, military, educational, religious, and fraternal groups. This segment has become important to hotels due to the large number of room nights they occupy each year – especially during slack times. While SMERF groups are cost-conscious, they are also dependable. This niche is particularly steady – even during economic downturns – because, regardless of the economic situation, these groups continue to meet. Kay Summerville, TDM, CTA, the sales manager for the Plano (Texas) Convention and Visitors Bureau, says of the market:

So many [SMERF attendees] are people spending their own money, and that's sometimes their vacation. They always plan to do that [meeting], so they also go through with it.[3]

Von Harden, vice president of marketing at CE Educational Travel, adds:

There are only so many corporate groups you can target. But with SMERF groups, there are so many options. Talk to a general manager or director of sales who has recently lost some corporate business, and they'll tell you how important it is to have the SMERF market as part of your plan.[4]

A property that can offer discount rates—and is willing to assist the largely nonprofessional meeting planners—can find that SMERF groups may make a considerable impact on the property's revenues.

## Types of Group Customers

Since group meetings customers represent so many different types of organizations, from trade and professional associations to corporations and businesses to SMERF groups, you will likely work with different types of meeting planners with varying degrees of expertise. Meeting planners fall into four basic groups:

**Full-Time Meeting Planners.** Large national associations and corporations that look to convention revenues to financially support their organizations are most likely to staff full-time, professional meeting planners. These planners know exactly what is required to stage a successful event and will be thorough and timely in presenting information and instructions to the hotel.

**Single-Event or Part-Time Planners.** These meeting planners typically work for smaller companies or associations that do not have enough meeting activity to warrant a full-time meeting planner. The experience of these planners will vary; some will have little or no knowledge of the mechanics of running a meeting and will look to your hotel for assistance. It will be necessary to provide these planners with a timetable of the hotel's needs and deadlines and to assure them of your commitment to helping them stage a successful event. Other part-time planners have extensive knowledge of the meetings process. It is important, therefore, to ascertain the planner's knowledge and experience and to respond accordingly.

**Committees.** Many associations and nonprofit groups have committees that are involved in initial suggestions for meetings, screening of meeting sites, and the actual planning of meetings. As with single-event or part-time planners, the experience of committee members may vary and the hotel may be faced with multiple or conflicting decisions. You can minimize potential problems by suggesting that one person be put in charge and by offering your hotel's expertise in helping to make decisions.

**Third-Party Planners.** An increasing number of meetings are being booked by third parties, such as meeting management firms, association management companies, and travel agents. If this is the case, you will be dealing with an intermediary, not directly with the company, association, or nonprofit organization holding the meeting. Most of these third

## Meeting Planner Profile

Today's meeting planners spend thousands of hours a year planning events from simple training meetings to huge conventions involving thousands of participants and hundreds of exhibitors. It is an exciting and varied career, and one which is constantly evolving. So who is the "typical" meeting planner of today?

According to a survey conducted by *Meetings & Conventions* magazine, today's professional meeting planner fits the following profile:

- Female (83% versus 17% male)
- Works in a department with a dozen other people
- Has been at the same job for nine years
- Earns $77,000 a year (salaries range from $25,000 to $100,000 or more)
- 34% hold the Certified Meeting Professional (CMP) designation

Duties typically include: budgeting; site selection; negotiating with hotels, airlines, and vendors; program planning; trade show and exhibit planning; food and beverage selection; hotel and ground transportation arrangements; and post-meeting evaluation, including surveys of participants and an evaluation of the facility and service provided at each function.

In order to stay on top of market conditions, most belong to one or more professional associations, and find the following skills most useful for their profession: excellent oral and written communication and organizational skills; leadership qualities; flexibility; and the ability to handle pressure.

Joan Eisenstodt, a meeting manager with over 30 years of experience, suggests that you ask yourself the following questions to determine if you have what it takes to become a successful meetings professional:

- Do you like to plan parties, schedule your day, and so forth?
- Do you have a date book or personal digital assistant (PDA) that you update regularly and that includes everything you need to do for weeks or months in the future?
- Do you like to organize your bedroom, car, workplace, and so on? Is your idea of fun organizing a closet for someone?
- Are you very organized, almost to the point of obsession?

Joan Eisenstodt

---

parties are experienced planners, but there may be cases in which you will need to assist the intermediary in making decisions about the event. If problems arise, you should first deal directly with the intermediary; you must use discretion regarding contacting the group that the intermediary represents, only going to the group after exhausting all other avenues (and thoroughly documenting your attempts to resolve problems).

While the above profiles will help you determine how much assistance might be needed from the hotel, each group and each planner is different. All meeting planners, regardless of their level of expertise, expect you to get to know them, their group, and the purpose of their meetings so that you can best meet their needs.

## Types of Meeting Facilities

When the term "meeting site" is mentioned, hotels and resorts typically come to mind. Although downtown, suburban, and resort hotels host about 85 percent of all meetings, there is a wide variety of other choices. Smart meeting planners will select the type of hotel that best meets the needs of their meetings.

## Chapter 1: Introduction to the Convention, Meetings and Trade Show Industry

*Convention hotels*, which are either adjacent to or in close proximity to a convention center, are often selected for large groups of convention attendees, delegates and/or exhibitors at trade shows and large public events. Convention hotels are convenient, eliminating the hassles of scheduling shuttle service from other hotels, and they may also contribute to the group booking within its block because of their location.

Demand for convention hotels is increasing, and chains and venues have responded to the demand by adding more convention hotels to their portfolio. Marriott International, for example, offers new convention hotels in Washington, D.C.; Chicago; and, Austin and Houston, Texas. Hilton's newest entry is the Hilton Downtown Cleveland, while the Spokane Convention Center in Spokane, Washington, is also including a convention hotel, the Spokane Convention Center Hotel, in its expansion plans.

*Airport hotels* are excellent choices when the planner needs to get attendees to a central, convenient location, and these hotels are also sometimes chosen for one-day or overnight meetings (see Figure 1.4). Airport hotels offer the advantage of lower rates than comparable downtown hotels, and planners and attendees also save on transportation costs. Airport hotels often offer free Wi-Fi and hot breakfasts.

Today's airport properties offer more than the convenience of getting to a room quickly, however – the newest ones offer features and amenities that rival the finest luxury hotels. The 320-room Hilton Beijing Capital Airport Hotel and Conference Facility, which is located at Terminal 3, for example, includes four restaurants (including 32 private dining rooms), two ballrooms, and 21 meeting rooms, in addition to 24-hour shuttle service to Terminals 2 and 3, Wi-Fi in public areas, a luxury spa, and a state-of-the art fitness center.

**Figure 1.4. AIRPORT HOTELS.**

*This ad for the Hyatt Regency at the Dallas-Fort Worth International Airport promotes the time and cost savings of booking a property located not only near, but actually inside, an airport. Today's airport hotels typically offer business-class rooms and fine dining in addition to meeting space. Planners save money, as these hotels generally cost less than a downtown hotel, and attendees save time by getting to their rooms quickly and having easy access to meeting rooms.*
**Source: Courtesy of Hyatt Corporation.**

*Large motels and motor hotels* can be an ideal option when a number of attendees are within driving distance of the meeting site. Although meeting space and amenities may vary, most of these properties are able to handle smaller meetings, and most either have their own on-site restaurant or are adjacent to restaurants that provide private spaces for small food functions or meetings.

**Boutique (lifestyle) hotels**, which are generally small hotels offering unique architecture and décor, were designed to attract younger attendees. Their high-tech amenities, lobbies designed for socializing, and a hip vibe appeal to younger attendees, and they are also an excellent choice when a planner wishes to buy out an entire hotel to ensure privacy for a group. Because of their small size, boutique hotels generally offer meeting furniture that can be easily moved to the lobby or a rooftop.

**All-suite hotels** feature at least one bedroom and a separate living area (some also offer kitchenettes or full kitchens). Since meeting space may be limited, these hotels, which we will discuss further in Chapter 4, are often selected for board meetings, small training meetings, and meetings for smaller groups (usually less than 200 people). All-suites also appeal to groups that include families, as there is plenty of sleeping space and guests can save money by preparing their own meals. Many all-suites offer breakfasts as part of the room rate.

**Resorts**, which are often located in popular "playgrounds," such as beaches, in the mountains, and popular destination cities, including Orlando, Florida, and Las Vegas, Nevada, are a popular choice for annual conventions and incentive trips. Resorts are typically upscale and feature a wide variety of on-property entertainment and recreational facilities. A downside to resorts is that many charge a fee for the use of certain services and amenities, many of which are not used by the attendees (this concept will be discussed later in the text).

Resort fees are one reason that planners are increasingly using *all-inclusive resorts*, which offer complete packages that include guestrooms, all food and beverage, use of recreational facilities, and other amenities in addition to meeting space (additional charges may be added for golf, scuba diving, and high-end specialty drinks). While all-inclusive resorts used to be perceived as for the budget-minded and leisure travelers, that has changed as these properties have gone upscale, offering luxury suites, fine dining, and such amenities as 24-hour butler service for attendees.

Meeting planners can also look to non-traditional venues for both value and unique experiences for their attendees. **Conference centers** appeal to some groups, as they are designed specifically for meetings; state-of-the-art meeting rooms are situated away from high traffic areas to minimize distractions, and conveniently located breakout rooms are constantly refreshed. Because many conference sessions run for several hours, rooms are designed for endurance and comfort (see Figure 1.5). Another advantage is that meeting

*Figure 1.5. CONFERENCE CENTERS FOR BUSINESS AND PLEASURE.*

Boardroom meeting setup at Dolce Hotels and Resorts' Lakeway Resort and Spa in Austin, Texas. The property, a conference center that is a member of IACC, is not the traditional, institutional-like conference center of yesterday. Although it offers the dedicated meeting space long associated with conference centers, the Lakeway offers a fine-dining restaurant, bar, and lounge, as well as numerous resort amenities, including a spa, a marina for water activities, tennis, and easy access to four nearby golf courses.
**Source: Courtesy of Dolce Media Center.**

Chapter 1: Introduction to the Convention, Meetings and Trade Show Industry

> ### 🖥 INTERNET EXERCISE
> #### IACC Conference Centers
>
> Visit the website for the International Association of Conference Centers at www.iacconline.com. Navigate the site to answer the following questions:
>
> 1. What are the differences between conference centers and conventional hotels and resorts in each of the following areas:
>    - Focus and market segments
>    - Facility design
>    - Furnishings and equipment
>    - Food and beverage service
>    - Personnel
> 2. What are some of the industry *standards* and *guidelines* for conference centers?
> 3. What environmental initiatives are recommended to member conference centers?
> 4. What scholarships and awards does this trade association offer to students?

rooms can be booked on a 24-hour basis; if a meeting runs longer than expected, the group does not have to vacate or incur additional rental costs.

A major difference between conference centers and traditional hotels is *pricing*. Most conference centers offer their versions of a *Full American Plan* – a package price, available either per day or per person that includes guestrooms, meals, meeting rooms, basic audiovisual equipment, **continuous breaks**, and the use of other amenities, such as a library or computer center. This **complete meeting package** eliminates unexpected charges and is considered a real value by many meeting planners.

*Cruise ships* are a popular choice for incentive meetings, and, as with conference centers, the cost of food and beverages is included in the fee. Another benefit of a cruise ship meeting is that there is a captive audience, yet cruises appeal to attendees with families; cruises generally offer a variety of activities for passengers of all ages.

Other, more unusual, choices for meetings include camps and retreat centers, dude ranches, college and university campuses, arenas and stadiums, special event venues, and cruise ships. Accommodations, dining options, audiovisual equipment, and recreational amenities will vary widely, of course; arenas and stadiums and special event venues typically offer meeting space only, so other arrangements will need to be made for accommodations.

Today's meeting sites offer a wide variety of choices, advantages, and disadvantages. No matter what type of facility is selected by the meeting planner, however, the principles outlined in this text can be applied to all venues.

## Trends in the Meetings Industry

Today's trends are greatly impacting the meetings and conventions industry. To stay competitive in this lucrative market segment, hoteliers must stay abreast of changing technology, demographics, the changing tastes of meeting attendees, and methods to ensure they are getting the most from meetings and convention business. The following sections provide an *overview* of the trends that are impacting the meetings and conventions industry. Some of these trends have affected the way hotels reach and sell to meeting planners (these

19

Chapter 1: Introduction to the Convention, Meetings and Trade Show Industry

topics are discussed in the first half of this text); others relate directly to the service function, which we will discuss in greater detail in Chapters 10-18.

## New Technology

New technology has led to sweeping changes to nearly every aspect of selling to and servicing the meetings and conventions market. In this section, we will take a look at how technology has affected the sales and service process, including changes in how hotel facilities and services are promoted to meeting planners; the elimination of copious paperwork; streamlining the various aspects of a meeting; communications between the hotel, planners, and attendees; and facilitating the review process at the end of the function.

> **MORE ONLINE**
>
> Greg Oates, author of Social Tables blog, highlights the technologies Sheraton, Marriott, Hilton, IHG, and Fairmont are using to increase their group sales revenue worldwide. In this trends report you will learn:
> 1. How Hotels like Hyatt are Adopting Event Technology to Increase Meeting Sales
> 2. Why Marriott Considers Digital Media and Content Marketing, the New Power Tools of Meeting Sales
> 3. How Hotels With Minimal Meeting Space Are Still Winning Big Business.
>
> Use a search engine and type in "How Technology Is Increasing Group Revenue at Top Hotels," to view this excellent report.

**Using the Internet to Reach and Promote to Meeting Planners.** While most hotels have had websites for some time (and chain hotels may have both individual and chain sites), websites continue to be effective promotional tools, and they play an important role in reaching meeting planners and helping them to make decisions on where to hold their meetings. Maureen Callahan, vice president of communications and public relations at Destination Hotels & Resorts, explains:

> The meetings industry has been revolutionized by technology. Websites are now the ubiquitous solution for meeting research, planning, and booking. Current web technology allows access to detailed property data, interactive site tours, rate planning, site comparisons, and an experiential orientation to hotels and resorts. Web cams provide real-time views of properties, and, with the advent of Travel 2.0, planners can "chat" with other planners on key issues, gather information on meeting experiences at properties, and obtain referrals and recommendations. The business of planning and booking meetings is very transparent with these ever-evolving tools.[5]

Therefore, effective website design is critical. Sites need to be easily navigated, include all the information that a planner would need to make a decision (meeting room photos, sizes, capacities, catering options, special offers, and so on) – and provide a way for the planner to make contact with the property (a link to a request for proposal or contact information for key sales and service personnel). Because meeting planners of today typically use mobile devices such as smartphones and tablets, it is not enough to offer a standard website (see box titled "The Impact of Mobile Technology"). Properties are increasingly offering **mobile optimized websites** that allow the information on each landing page to fit on one page of the smaller screens of mobile devices. In most cases, properties include a link to these special websites on the homepage of their "regular" website.

> ### The Impact of Mobile Technology
>
> Mobile technology is consistently being integrated into the meeting experience:
>
> - Tablets are used by sales staff for interactive selling. Virtual tours can now be shared with meeting planners in their offices or with potential customers on the trade show floor. Not only is this more efficient, but it is a greener solution than offering printed promotional materials.
> - Mobile event apps developed for both the meeting planner and the attendee are becoming common. Hilton, Omni, Marriott, and Starwood all offer mobile apps that allow meeting planners to control their meeting space; planners can personally adjust meeting room temperatures and the volume of speakers from their smartphones or tablets. Banquet Event Orders (BEOs), group resumes, and interactive floor plans, preloaded in the app, assist with on-site operations, as do apps that connect the planner directly with a property liaison who can deal with any problems that might arise.
> - Digital Banquet Event Orders (BEOs) and meeting resumes are replacing printed staging guides that meeting planners formerly toted around in old-fashioned binders. Planners now have access to all their meeting details in the palms of their hands.
> - Attendees can also download event specific apps to their mobile devices. Event apps contain detailed information, such as the meeting agenda; speaker profiles; exhibitor lists; maps of the hotel, convention center, and local area; and interactive tools, such as audience response for real-time surveys, and networking capabilities for exchanging information with other attendees. In many cases, attendees can check-in or check-out without visiting the front desk; a code that can be entered into a check-in kiosk is e-mailed to their mobile devices.

In addition to web pages, hotels are gaining a presence on the Internet by participating on **social media** sites, such as Facebook, Twitter, and LinkedIn. Other properties set up their own Instagram accounts or YouTube channels to share photographs and videos to draw interest to their property. It is important to note, however, that these sites should not be considered as advertising avenues – they should be used to *build relationships* with potential customers. That does not mean that a property cannot promote a contest involving the property on a social media site, but the best use of social media is to provide information that is useful to meeting planners, such as meeting planning tips and information on the local area and upcoming events.

While a social media presence helps to familiarize potential guests with your property (clickable links to your sites should be included on your homepage), you can also take advantage of a number of opportunities to advertise over the Internet as well. The best places to advertise online include social media sites, websites frequented by meeting planners, such as association pages, and travel-related websites. There are a number of options for this advertising, including banner ads (which link to your hotel's website), display-type advertising, and sponsorships. We will discuss these options further in later chapters.

**Request for Proposal (RFP) and Communicating with Meeting Planners.** Most hotels that target the meetings and conventions business offer a request for proposal (RFP) link on their websites, as do the websites of third-party planners (we will discuss these firms later in this section). When a hotel accepts a request for proposal, technology is again used to share information with the planner and to help the planner get the word out to his or her potential attendees. While personal visits and telephone calls were once the primary ways of communicating with planners, many planners prefer to keep in touch via e-mails and texts.

**Sharing Meeting Information with Attendees.** Once details of the meeting have been confirmed, planners generally make reservations and program information available on the organization's website. Hotels may also design a special website for the meeting or include a link to the hotel's site on the organization's website.

Chapter 1: Introduction to the Convention, Meetings and Trade Show Industry

This is especially important for the reservations process. Hotels generally prefer that reservations be made through their own systems; this is an effective way to monitor the group's room block. Some organizations, however, use their own reservations process and send periodic payments (along with rooming lists) to the hotel. Since the group may incur fees if their room block is not filled, it is important that both the hotel and the planner closely monitor the progress of reservations.

**Eliminating Paperwork.** Even the simplest meetings involve a great amount of paperwork. In the past, planners had to carry huge binders filled with this information. Today, nearly all the details of an event are computerized, and they can easily be downloaded into the planner's mobile device, where they can be reviewed by a touch on the screen.

Technology has also made it possible to greatly reduce printing costs for meetings materials. Convention programs and meetings agendas, handouts, and promotional materials can be created on the computer (by either inputting or scanning) and viewed on the organization's link to the event, downloaded by attendees, or included in **mobile apps** that are also used to provide additional meeting information, such as a daily schedule. With computer applications, space is virtually unlimited – and content can be changed as required.

As mentioned previously, today's meeting attendees typically carry at least two mobile devices. These are most commonly a smartphone and a tablet or notebook, but may also include GPS devices, e-book readers (such as Kindle and Nook), personal digital assistants (PDAs), and others. Today, mobile devices can also be wearable; smartwatches and head-mounted displays are gaining in popularity.

**High-tech Assistance for Meeting Planners.** Technology has changed the way in which meeting planners make site selections, determine the optimal room settings for their functions, and manage their events. Site visits can now be made virtually, with some properties offering panoramic views of their facilities, and software can be used to place "furniture" into a virtual meeting room. Some apps also allow planners to use their smartphones to physically measure a room by tapping it against the walls.

Several hotels have developed content, such as property maps, a map of the exhibit hall, and area maps, that can be pre-loaded into the planner's own app for meeting attendees. Some chains also offer service apps, which allow meeting planners to immediately connect with their liaison for the meeting.

Technology also enables planners to closely monitor their group room block pickup, the number of attendees at food functions (badges or smartphones can be scanned at the door for admittance), and attendance at specific events in the program. Planners can also instantly communicate with attendees, make any necessary changes to the program schedule, and send follow-up surveys to their attendees.

> **WORTH WATCHING**
>
> Corbin Ball, a leading authority on technology in the hospitality industry, provides a short video on the impact of technology in the meetings industry. To view go to youtube.com and type in IAEE TV, Corbin Ball, Tech Trends.

**Meeting Room Technology.** Today's meeting rooms may be equipped with a number of flat screen monitors, touch screen meeting tables, and streaming or **video-conferencing** capabilities. Video conferencing, which is also called *teleconferencing*, has been used for some time, but new improvements include a higher quality sound and picture, instant replay, and "live projection" (projecting a close-up image of a speaker onto a large video screen to bring him or her closer to the audience). One of the most exciting innovations in video-conferencing is **telepresence**, which uses special studios and advanced audio and video equipment to give the impression that the participants are in the same room as participants in remote locations (see Figure 1.6).

*Figure 1.6 TELEPRESENCE: VIDEO CONFERENCING GOES HIGH-TECH.*

*Participants in a telepresence suite at a "hub" location interact with participants at a remote telepresence suite using high-tech video and audio. The immersion experience includes the projection of life-size images (at eye level) on the screens, and studios that "mirror" each other with half conference tables and matching décor, giving the impression that the attendees are in the same room.*
**Source: Courtesy of TANDBERG.**

**Video streaming**, in which content is transmitted over the Internet, is now being widely used. This has led to an increase in **hybrid meetings**, meetings that combine both remote and "live" content. Hybrid meetings are cost-effective, as speakers do not have to be flown in to the event, and they also make it easier to share the content of the meeting with those who could not attend. In many cases, the entire meeting is recorded for downloading, and absentees can view what they have missed by clicking on a link on the organization's website.

**Exhibit Hall Technology.** It is not uncommon today for exhibit halls to use both **beacon technology** and **near field communications** (NFC). Beacon technology uses a system of low-cost radio transmitters that use low-energy Bluetooth connections to transmit messages or prompts to a smartphone or tablet (the Apple version of the application is known as iBeacon). This technology is commonly used by attendees as a navigation and networking tool; exhibitors use it to track attendance to exhibit hall booths as well as for networking.

Near field communications (NFC) feature a short-range connectivity that enables attendees to use their smartphones to buy tickets or gain admittance to an event by simply tapping them on an entrance turnstile or reader. NFC is also used for networking; two smartphones are tapped together or the phone is tapped against a badge containing an NFC chip. NFC can also be used to help minimize theft; the NFC operates in a relatively small area (known as a *geo-fence*), and an alarm will sound when property is carried beyond the perimeter.

**Post-Convention Reporting.** Today's technology makes it possible to almost instantaneously view event expenditures, eliminating long waits for a bill at the end of the function. Point-of-sale (POS) terminals are common, and daily reports input into the hotel's computer system offer an up-to-date look at each event's attendance and financials. In addition, post-event surveys can be easily and conveniently completed and returned by meeting planners, providing the hotel with insight into what elements of the event went well and areas in which improvement can be made.

**Relationship Building.** New meeting formats and the increased use of technology have elevated the role of the facility's convention service manager. Convention service managers (CSMs) must work hand-in-hand with the meeting planner to determine the specific goals of the meeting and work with their service teams to successfully customize meeting setups, demonstrate an understanding of technological needs, suggest **bandwidth** requirements, recommend audiovisual enhancements, and offer creative, locally sourced food and beverage solutions to execute a unique event.

Devon Sloan, CMP, former director of events at the Hilton Tucson El Conquistador and now an event management specialist for the Hilton chain, says:

> We need to become a member of the client's team so we can better help each other, trust each other, support each other, and brainstorm with each other. If we can develop that kind of relationship with clients, the event logistics and planning will go so much better for both parties.[6]

While technology, including social media, e-mails and texts, and web presences, enables hotel salespeople, convention service managers, and meeting planners to share information and communicate quickly and efficiently, there is no substitute for personal interactions. Face-to-face meetings and telephone calls are an important part of the hospitality business. Jerry Wayne, former vice president of sales and marketing for the Greenbrier and now chairman of The Meetings Concierge, says:

> In my 30 years of sales and marketing experience, there has never been a substitute for personal relationships. In today's world of electronic communications, those relationships are declining. We are a people business, and those of us who have developed personal relationships with our customers will continue to have their loyalty.[7]

## Changing Demographics

As more millennials (those born between the early 1980s and the early 2000s) enter the business world and attend more meetings and conventions, they have become the driving force in changing the face of the meetings industry. More focused on technology and social interaction than attendees in the past, millennials are not content to just be part of an audience; they want to actively participate in and contribute to the program. This has resulted in an increase in "unconferences" and open space workshops that are participant-driven. And, since millennials are accustomed to receiving information in short bursts, meetings requiring long sessions are broken up by frequent participative learning opportunities.

These new meetings models have resulted in new setups designed to facilitate and encourage networking and connections between attendees. While traditional meeting setups (theatre-style, hollow square, and boardroom) are still being used for meetings, they are used in new, interactive ways. Heavy tables, for example, are being replaced by a combination of lightweight tables of varying heights. "Standard" seating may now include comfortable couches and club chairs, high stools that can be placed along the walls of the meeting room, and even beanbag chairs.

Meetings for millennials are all about flexibility – attendees want to be able to move tables and seating to enable them to break into small groups after a presentation. If hotels cannot provide this type of furniture, a larger number of breakout spaces will be required. These spaces, however, may not involve a large number of smaller rooms; breakout space can include the lobby or hallway adjacent to the meeting room, rooftops, and outdoor settings.

The influence of the millennials can also be seen in hotel lobbies. Millennials want a comfortable place where they can work and socialize, so many hotels have replaced their traditional lobbies with open spaces that feature comfortable seating, areas for working (individually or in a small group), food and beverage outlets, and entertainment. As mentioned earlier, millennials typically travel with at least two mobile devices, so the lobby should offer free Wi-Fi – and millennials also demand reliable Wi-Fi throughout the hotel (guestrooms, meeting rooms, and public areas, such as poolside). Another way to appeal to millennials is to offer opportunities, in either the lobby or other public areas, for them to socialize; coffee hours, nightly receptions, a nightly wine hour (Kimpton properties provide wines to guests at no charge), and free entertainment are popular options.

## Strategic Meetings Management

In the past few decades more hotels started using **revenue management**, which involves setting guestroom prices based on demand, with an eye towards maximum profitability. Today, groups are evaluated on their total *value* – not simply the number of guestrooms they will use or their total food and beverage spend for one event.

Meeting planners, too, are focusing more on the return on their investment (ROI) from their meetings. **Strategic meetings management (SMM)** programs are increasingly being developed to minimize costs, provide consistency throughout the organization, and offer an experience that will be educational and meaningful to attendees.

A good SMM program will clearly define the scope and breadth of the initiative (Is it for only one division of the corporation or association? Do the strategies apply to a specific type of meeting, such as a training meeting, or to all meetings held?).

Communication and involvement are the keys to SMM plans. Goals should be clearly defined and understood, input should be solicited on ways to cut costs and minimize risks, and any changes to the program should be immediately communicated to all levels of management involved.

Hotels can contribute to SMM programs by providing data on meeting spend and offering suggestions to reduce costs. In some cases, planners may opt to enter into agreements with particular hotels or chains to receive discounted rates for a promised amount of business.

## Complex Contracts

Because hoteliers are focusing more on the bottom line, meeting contracts are becoming more complex. Hotels are protecting themselves with attrition clauses, due diligence, and other measures to minimize losses from cancellations and other issues arising from group business. Meeting planners, on the other hand, want to protect themselves from exorbitant fees and penalties, resulting in a tension that did not exist in the days when space and service were the primary considerations.

> **WORTH WATCHING**
>
> Lisa Sommer Devlin, the foremost industry expert representing the hotel industry in meeting contracts, gives a short tutorial on negotiating contracts that are unambiguous, simple,( yet specific,) and free from complications. To view go to: hedtalks.connectplusathiltonworldwide.com (click on the "Driving Results" tab and scroll down to the "Contracts" video).

Jonathan T. Howe, the president and founding partner of Howe & Hutton Ltd., a law firm dedicated to solving the legal issues faced by meeting professionals and associations, and also the general counsel for MPI, says:

> Negotiations have taken on a new complexion. Contracts have gotten much more complex and extensive, and we have the whole request for proposal process now. There is a lot more counseling and active involvement by lawyers through the whole process — from the outset to final bill reconciliation.[8]

Many groups have hired attorneys to help them navigate the turbulent waters of complex contracts – and they may often present their own contracts for consideration by the hotel. While many hotels have standardized contracts that are personalized only with the details of each individual group (date, function room, banquet menu, and so on), there are still opportunities for negotiation. For example, if a planner fails to meet the minimum requirement for a food function, he or she can reduce or eliminate penalties by scheduling an additional food function (such as a buffet breakfast). It is important to remember that eliminating a risk, such as less guestrooms revenue, with a restrictive clause may negatively impact the hotel's future relationship with the group.

## Third-Party Meeting Planners

While hotel salespeople formerly dealt almost exclusively with corporate, association, and nonprofit meeting planners, third-party planners (either independents or meeting management firms) are becoming more prevalent in the industry.

Corporate downsizing, the increased complexity of negotiations, and increased use of Internet technology has resulted in many organizations looking *outside* their staffs for meeting planning services. Since these intermediaries are hired "out-of-house," a new industry buzzword— **outsourcing** —was coined. Corporations typically outsource their meeting planning to such intermediaries as travel agents, destination management companies, and incentive travel houses. Associations and nonprofits generally look to meeting management companies or association management companies to assist them with their meeting needs. Therefore, as a hospitality salesperson, your customers will not only be association or corporate executives, but also the meeting management firms that represent them.

These third-party planners act as liaisons, bringing their clients' needs for sleeping rooms, food and beverage, and meeting facilities to hotels. These firms can be broken down into several categories:

- Meeting management firms
- Association management companies
- Destination management companies
- Incentive travel houses
- Travel agents

**Meeting Management Firms.** *Meeting management firms* are private contractors (companies or individuals) who provide planning services directly to a client. Increasingly, planners are leaving their associations and corporations to set up shop as independents. Such planners are generally easy to work with because they are experienced. They function as intermediaries, and are paid a fee, which can vary. Some independent meeting planners simply assist corporate in-house meeting planners; others are responsible for the entire execution of the meeting. Interestingly, these companies often employ former hotel salespeople who know how to negotiate with hotels.

The largest of the **meeting management companies** are Experient Inc. (www.experient-inc.com), Conference Direct (conferencedirect.com), and Helms Briscoe (www.helmsbriscoe.com). While these third-party firms generate a tremendous volume of business, they are also costly to hotels. They make their money by charging fees for booking business, and, while they sometimes charge a flat fee to the meeting organization, most of their income comes from fees charged to hotels; a recent study found that these fees cost hotels $1.4 to $1.8 billion dollars annually!

Meeting management companies search out hotel sites and aid their clients in conducting meeting programs (the sidebar titled "Delegating Tasks" illustrates the services most often offered to meeting groups by third-party planners).

**Association Management Companies.** *Association management companies* work for smaller associations that do not employ a full-time professional staff. In most cases, employees of these firms work through the board of directors of associations to manage meetings and plan conventions and other activities. Often these firms provide management services for two or more associations. SmithBucklin (www.smithbucklin,com), the largest of the association management firms, manages the affairs, including annual meetings, for several meeting and event organizations.

**Destination Management Companies.** These firms offer convention and meeting services at the host city. **Destination management companies** may arrange for room accommodations, restaurant reservations, airport shuttle service, entertainment, technical services (teleconferences, audiovisual presentations, etc.), and special programs for attendees and spouses. The impact of these *local experts* is detailed in the box titled "The Growth of the Destination Management Industry."

### Delegating Tasks
What services do third-party planners provide for your organization?

| | |
|---|---|
| Facility research and selection | 51% |
| Planning entertainment, social and sports functions | 51% |
| Negotiating with facilities | 50% |
| On-site staffing | 49% |
| Destination research and selection | 48% |
| Transportation arrangements | 40% |
| Vendor research and subcontracting | 28% |
| Trade-show planning | 19% |
| Planning incentive travel programs | 13% |
| Negotiating with airlines | 8% |

Most destination management companies remain "behind the scenes," assisting the meeting planner with the details of the meeting. This type of firm knows the host city, and can provide in-depth information on the destination, both in terms of suppliers and extra convention activities (special sight-seeing tours, etc.). In Europe, a destination management company is generally called a **professional congress organizer.** Additional details of the services provided by destination management companies (DMCs) and professional congress organizers can be found in Chapter 16.

**Incentive Travel Houses. Incentive travel houses** deal directly with corporations, arranging incentive travel packages for companies that wish to reward or motivate their staffs or their customers. These packages are usually "first class" and involve an exotic or popular resort location. They typically include a number of "perks" and special amenities not commonly associated with regular hotel and travel packages. Chapter 6 provides an extensive discussion of the workings of the incentive travel market and the role **incentive travel houses** play in this segment of the meetings market.

**Travel Agents.** Some travel agents have expanded their traditional role of selling package tours, transportation, and guestrooms to offer meeting planning services to corporate accounts. Mega travel agencies, such as BTI Travel (www.btitravel.com) and American Express Travel (www.americanexpresstravel.com/Travel), which employs experienced "Destination Experts," plan everything from board meetings to trade shows.

---

### The Growth of the Destination Management Industry

Karen Gordon, Founder
Destination Management Alliance

After air travel allowed greater numbers of participants to attend conventions at a national level, ground operators began offering transportation and later "Ladies Programs" for the wives of attendees...Ground operators later added special events and themed parties to their list of services...As the role of these "local experts" grew, the industry began referring to them as Destination Management Companies, and these DMCs continued to expand their role in the meeting, convention, and travel industry...As corporate meetings and retreats became more common, many DMCs added additional services, such as motivational speakers, educational seminars, and personalized merchandise and gift items, making them a "one-stop shop" for meeting planning...Since the role of DMCs is to keep their city "fresh" in the eyes of repeat visitors, DMCs continually updated their services and style and, recognizing a need for regulation and standardization, created the Association of Destination Management Executives (ADME). This non-profit, non-partisan, international trade association defines DMCs as "Professional services companies possessing extensive local knowledge, expertise, and resources, specializing in the design and implementation of events, activities, tours, transportation and group logistics."...The growth from ground operator to destination management company in just over 30 years is only the beginning. With developments in technology, such as the World Wide Web, the average traveler is more educated than ever before, making the job of the DMC a continuous challenge to keep abreast of the ever-changing demands of the marketplace.

---

This transition came naturally, as travel agents were able to keep abreast of changing airline price structures and routes, and many corporate meeting planners are now turning to travel agents to arrange everything from transportation to rooms to meeting space. Since not all travel agents are experienced in meeting planning, corporate clients must carefully select those who have this expertise, and properties may have to work more closely with those who are just learning the meetings field. This association can prove extremely profitable, however, both in terms of meetings business and other individual and group bookings at the property.

## The Wellness Movement

Today's meeting attendees are far more conscious about nourishing body, mind, and spirit than attendees of the past. They are eating healthier, exercising more, and seeking ways to relieve stress and regenerate. Hotels are responding in a number of ways, including offering lighter fare and heart-healthy and gluten-free meals, providing in-room exercise equipment in addition to exercise facilities, and adding or upgrading spa facilities and services.

Recognizing the link between food and the alertness of attendees, meeting planners are opting for healthier foods, such as yogurt, granola and nuts, fresh and dried fruits, and do-it-yourself smoothie bars, instead of the traditional carb- and sugar-laden choices at refreshment breaks. Beverages are likely to include fresh juices and vitamin water along with coffee and tea. Banquet chefs are also developing "brain food" menus, replacing heavy foods with slow-release energy foods, including complex carbs (whole grain breads, pasta and vegetables) and lean meats. Food functions featuring tapas ("small plates"), which offer guests a larger variety of foods in smaller portions, are also becoming popular; guests are able to move about and socialize while enjoying a satisfying mini-meal.

Exercise facilities are also being used more frequently, and attendees expect the latest in equipment. Offering personalized training and individual or group classes also appeals to health-conscious guests, as do outdoor recreational opportunities, such as pools, tennis courts, and walking paths. Some chains, including Marriott and Hilton, also provide basic exercise equipment, such as yoga mats, hand weights, and resistance tubes, to guests who prefer to exercise in their rooms.

Spas have also become more popular, and some chains have added spa hotels to meet the demand. The Omni La Costa Resort & Spa in Carlsbad, California, one of the hotels in the chain's Spa Collection brand, features the finest in spa treatments and is also home to the Chopra Center for Wellness, a retreat that combines Eastern healing disciplines with Western medical techniques. Other hotels, such as the Renaissance Waverly Hotel & Convention Center in Atlanta, Georgia, have partnered with outside spa companies to provide services to their guests. Spa Waverly, which is operated by Village Health, provides a number of services, treatments, and amenities, including massages, facials, body scrubs and wraps, and fitness classes.

Taking the wellness concept to a new level, the InterContinental Hotel Group offers EVEN, a mid-priced brand that features a

> **WORTH WATCHING**
>
> The MGM Grand Hotel & Casino in Las Vegas has added Stay Well suites for health-conscious attendees. Go to www.youtube.com and search for stay well suites at the MGM Grand or go to www.youtube.com/watch?v=t9DA8vQs6R4.
> IHG's EVEN hotels are designed around wellness. To view a video on their innovative positioning, go to youtube.com and search for EVEN Hotels or go to www.youtube.com/watch?v=mFa4c7n7pxc.

> **MORE ONLINE**
>
> For great ideas about promoting a healthy meeting environment download the National Alliance for Nutrition and Activity's Tool Kit at: http:llcspinet.org/nutritionpolicy/healthy-meeting-toolkit.pdf or use a search engine and type in National Alliance for Nutrition and Activity's Tool Kit.

Chapter 1: Introduction to the Convention, Meetings and Trade Show Industry

1,200-square-foot (or more) athletic studio in the hotel lobby (the windows are frosted to enable guests to work out without being in public view). Guestrooms are also equipped with "training zones" stocked with yoga mats, balance balls, and other exercise equipment.

## Green Meetings and Social Responsibility

Social responsibility involves caring for both the environment and for the community in which groups meet. While many hotels, especially those in drought-prone areas, have practiced water conservation for some time, more attention is being given to such practices as eliminating waste materials and building environment-friendly hotels. Today's meetings may also involve caring for the community in which the meeting is held by including volunteer efforts in the meeting program.

**Environmental Responsibility.** Meeting planners and their attendees are increasingly seeking out hotels that are employing "green" practices. "Green meetings" place an emphasis on conserving natural resources (see Figure 1.7).

*Figure 1.7. PROMOTING GREEN MEETINGS.*

This ad for The Banff Centre, an IACC conference center in Alberta, Canada, promotes the property's commitment to green meetings — at no extra cost to the meeting planner. The ad also focuses on the property's unique location in an UNESCO World Heritage site teeming with natural wonders.
**Source: Courtesy of The Banff Centre, Banff, Alberta, Canada.**

There are several areas in which hotels can employ green practices:

- **Energy Efficiency and Conservation.** The use of efficient technologies for heating and air conditioning units, food service appliances, lighting, and transportation. The use of alternate forms of power, including wind power, solar power, and geothermal sources.

30

- **Water Efficiency and Conservation.** Conservation practices for linens. The installation of water-efficient toiletsand shower heads. The use of recycled water for landscaping.
- **Sustainable Food.** Increased use of organic and locally grown food items, reducing both the amount of pesticides and fertilizers that harm the environment and the amount of fuel used to transport food.
- **Recycling and Composting.** The recycling of such items as glass, plastic, metal, paper, ink and toner cartridges, and grease. Composting of food waste, either on property or through an outside composting service.
- **Education.** Making both property staff and guests aware of conservation efforts to enable them to actively participate in recycling and other programs. For example, meeting planners should be made aware of options to reduce paper, such as using electronic signs, online registration forms, and electronic note-taking, document downloads, and surveys.

In order to help keep up-to-date on conservation technology and products — and to get the word out about their green efforts — a number of hotels are joining associations that provide comprehensive guidelines and offer opportunities to promote green efforts. The Green Hotels Association (GHA at greenhotels.com/index/php), for example, offers a number of resources to help hoteliers. While the GHA does not certify hotels, the organization suggests that hotels take advantage of certifications offered by state and national organizations.

> **WORTH WATCHING**
> To view a video on environmental responsibility, go to www.youtube.com and search for Starwood Meetings — Education Series — Sustainable Meetings (or go to www.youtube.com/watch?v=d3hyQWi-uC8).

One of the most widely recognized of these is the Leadership in Energy and Environmental Design (LEED) designation, which was developed by the U.S. Green Building Council. Properties are evaluated in a number of areas, including both conservation practices and building design, and are awarded points that qualify them for one of four levels – certified, silver, gold, and platinum. A LEEDS logo can then be displayed to promote the property's commitment to the environment.

> **MORE ONLINE**
> To view the standards that were developed by the CIC/ASTM for green meetings, go to www.conventionindustry.org/StandardPractices/APEXASTM.

An important resource that is available to hoteliers is the environmental guidelines developed by the Convention Industry Council (CIC) and ASTM International (www.astm.org). These guidelines were welcomed by the conventions and meetings industry as they provide a standardized format for evaluating green meetings. Nancy J. Zavada, CMP, co-founder of the Green Meetings Industry Council and principal of MeetGreen in Portland, Oregon, welcomes the new standards:

> It was easy to talk green before we had standards. It was harder to be green because there was so little agreement about what "green" meant. Every planner, every sponsor, every vendor had their own definition. Now we have the same definitions whether you are in Portland, Oregon, Copenhagen, Singapore, or anywhere in between.[9]

**Corporate Social Responsibility and Team-Building.** In the wake of criticism over corporate excess, a growing number of companies are focusing on contributing to their host community while building bonds among attendees. In a recent survey by *Successful Meetings* magazine, 82 percent of planners said that they include corporate social responsibility (CSR) activities in their programs; 67 percent of these activities directly impacted the community in which the event was held.

As the popularity of these programs increases, many hotel chains are partnering with charitable organizations, such as impact4good (www.impact4good.com), or developing their own CSR programs. Fairmont Hotels & Resorts, for example, offers a "Meetings That Matter" program that includes activities ranging from assisting at the DC Central Kitchen in Washington, D.C., to assisting with trail cleanup at the Banff National Park. The Ritz-Carlton's program, VolunTeaming, incorporates both volunteer and *team-building activities*.

While team-building activities frequently involve outdoor, physical efforts, such as rock climbing and ropes courses, the volunteering option provides the opportunity for attendees to build bonds while giving back to the community in a number of ways. Activities often used for volunteering and team-building include working with such organizations as Habitat for Humanity, cleaning up a neighborhood park or river, building bicycles for needy children, and holding food and/or clothing drives.

## Summary

As you can see from this overview of the convention and meetings industry, there are a number of factors that must be taken into consideration after the decision has been made to solicit this lucrative market segment. To successfully compete for meetings business, you must have a working knowledge of the various types of meetings and the groups that typically hold them, be aware of the types of facilities that can best sell and service the various segments within the meetings market, and stay abreast of trends impacting the industry to enable you to develop effective strategies for attracting meetings business.

In the next chapter, we will take a look at the most important factor in successfully obtaining meetings business—planning—and learn how to successfully market a property. Subsequent chapters will detail establishing a sales office for maximum efficiency, outline specific strategies for reaching each of the subsegments of the meetings market, and discuss the issues most important to meeting planners today.

## Endnotes

1. EXPACT Convention Expenditure and Impact Study.
2. Amy Tiebel, "What Buyers Need to Know in a Seller's Market," *Convene*.
3. Nikki Gloudeman, "The Little Groups that Can: SMERF Groups Show Their Muscle," *Smart Meetings*, June 2011.
4. Ibid.
5. Maureen Callahan, "Confidence, Integrity, and a Competitive Spirit," *Meeting Planners Guide*.
6. Eric Blanc, "The Art of Developing Client Relationships", *hotelexecutive.com*.
7. "Leadership: A View from the Top," *HSMAI Foundation*.

8. "Expert Voices on 30 Years," *Meeting News*.
9. Fred Gebhart, "Setting New Standards," Meetings Focus, September 2013.

## Study Questions

1. Why is it important for hotel people to understand the differences between various types of meetings? After all, aren't all the definitions synonymous?
2. Distinguish between a congress and a conference, a symposium and a workshop, a trade show and a consumer show.
3. What three classifications of groups hold meetings and what are the characteristics of each?
4. Describe the different types of meeting planners. What kinds of meetings does each organize?
5. List at least three ways that technology is changing the way meetings are sold and serviced.
6. Define the term "millennials" and describe two ways in which this group is changing the meetings industry.
7. What is strategic meetings management (SMM)? How does it differ from revenue management?
8. Name the types of third-party meeting planners. How do these planners impact hotels?
9. Describe the elements of a "green meeting."
10. What are CSR activities? How do they benefit attendees and the community?

## Key Terms

**all-suite hotel**—A hotel that features rooms larger than typical guestrooms, with a living or working space separate from the bedroom(s).

**bandwidth**—The rate data is transferred from its original point of origin to a download at its destination. Different applications require different bandwidths; *effective bandwidth* is the highest reliable transmission a path can provide.

**beacon technology**—Low-cost radio transmitters that use low-energy Bluetooth connections to transmit messages or prompts to a smartphone or tablet. Commonly used to track attendance at a meeting room or exhibit hall and as navigation and networking tools.

**boutique (lifestyle) hotel**—A small, trendy hotel typically known for its unique architecture and décor. Frequently bought out by meeting planners to ensure privacy, attentive service, and a unique experience for meeting attendees.

**business center**—A facility that offers key equipment and services typically found in a business traveler's home office, including computer access, fax machines, and copy machines. Many offer secretarial and other services, such as shipping.

**complete meeting package**—An all-inclusive pricing plan (including lodging, all meals, and support services) offered at conference centers.

Chapter 1: Introduction to the Convention, Meetings and Trade Show Industry

**conference center**—A property specifically designed to handle group meetings. Conference centers are often located outside metropolitan areas and may provide extensive leisure facilities. May be certified by the International Association of Conference Centers (IACC).
**consumer shows**—Exhibitions that are open to the public; they usually require an entrance fee. Also termed a **public show**.
**continuous breaks**—Refreshment areas that are continually replenished while the meeting is in session. This allows attendees to break at will, in groups or individually, with the assurance that refreshments are always available to them.
**convention**—A meeting of delegates for action on a particular matter. Usually involves a general session and supplementary smaller meetings. Conventions are produced with and without exhibits.
**destination management companies**—Professional management companies specializing in the design and delivery of convention events, activities, tours, staffing, and transportation, utilizing local knowledge, expertise, and resources.
**"green" meetings**—Meetings that include practices, products, and services that are less harmful to the environment. Elements may include using less paper by employing electronic means to convey information, choosing recyclable products, and using meeting rooms that are built using natural materials and environmentally-friendly lighting.
**hybrid meeting**—A meeting that combines both live and remote elements, such as the downloading of a speech from the company president to a group of attendees in another location.
**incentive travel houses**—Full-time professional travel companies that make arrangements for companies that wish to offer incentive trips.
**meeting management companies**—Companies, representing another organization, that handle site selection, negotiations, and turn-key support for an event.
**mobile app**—A software program designed for mobile devices, such as smartphones and tablets.
**mobile optimized website**—A website that has been configured to enable each page of web content to fit on the smaller screens of mobile devices.
**near field communications (NFC)**—A short-range connectivity that enables attendees to use their smartphones to buy tickets or gain admittance to an event by simply tapping their smartphones on an entrance turnstile or reader. Also used for networking by tapping two smartphones together or tapping the phone against a badge containing an NFC chip.
**outsourcing**—Subcontracting a task or responsibility to a supplier to handle some aspect of an event.
**professional congress organizer (PCO)**—European term for a DMC (Destination Management Company). Local supplier who can arrange, manage, and/or plan any function or service an event.
**second-tier cities**—Smaller cities and suburbs of major cities that offer the meeting planner an attractive location and at the same time provide less costly accommodations and transportation.
**social media**—The tools and platforms that people employ to converse with each other and publish/share content online. These tools include blogs and podcasts as well as sites designed to share photos, videos, graphics, bookmarks, and other content.
**social responsibility**—Meetings that include a combination of volunteer and team-building activities.

**strategic meetings management (SMM)**—A program designed by meeting planners to get the best return on investment (ROI) for their meeting dollars while providing consistency and an optimal experience for attendees.

**telepresence**—A high-end form of video conferencing that uses studio-quality audio and video and life-size images of participants at other locations to make the video conference as much like a face-to-face meeting as possible.

**trade show**—An exhibition with displays, generally held within a trade industry or discipline. May be independent or in conjunction with a convention. Not open to the general public.

**video streaming**—Downloading content, such as remote speeches, videos, and other data, to the meeting room over the Internet.

## Industry Profile

## Chuck Kelley, Co-Owner

G7 Hospitality Group, Inc.

*A 1977 graduate of the University of Hawaii Travel Industry and Management School, Chuck Kelley began his 32-year-career with Marriott International as an assistant restaurant manager and had worked his way up to executive vice president for Marriott's Caribbean/Latin Region. During Kelley's ten-year tenure in that position, the region grew to 53 operating hotels and a confirmed pipeline of over 20 new hotels. Kelley is now co-owner of G7 Hospitality Group, Inc., a full-service hospitality advisory firm that specializes in "optimizing hospitality asset value, returns, and performance hotel operations." Also the author of several articles, he shares the following advice on positioning a hospitality property.*

## The Four-Pillar Imperative of Hotel Positioning

Positioning your property can be a matter of profit or loss. However, it's not as easy as it seems. Though the subject is discussed often, it's frequently misunderstood. To me, positioning means that you have identified your prime target markets, defined your competitive set, understand your product/service points of differentiation, and clarified guest aspirations.

The success of your positioning is not necessarily driven by a unique point of differentiation or a clever phrase. The success of your positioning is driven by the involvement and commitment of your entire operation. There are four pillars of a successful positioning:

1. **Involvement.** Representatives from all stakeholder groups need to be involved in defining your positioning – owners, senior management, department heads, line staff, and employees. You need to fully engage everyone to ensure a sense of ownership. You will be surprised at how insightful a frontline employee will be when asked his/her opinion. When you publish your key points of differentiation, you need real consensus and full support.

2. **Candor.** You must be candid about the strengths and weaknesses of your product and service. Without an honest evaluation, you don't have a good foundation for your positioning.

3. **Communication.** Too often, positioning resides in the Executive Office and is not communicated successfully. Once defined, you need to communicate your positioning across your entire organization. Explain the positioning, how it will be used and why it will benefit the individual and your hotel. Your communication must also be ongoing and frequent – a one-and-done philosophy won't work.

4. **Commitment.** Your positioning should be reflected in everything you say and do, your service standards, sales and marketing approach, human resource policy, and budgeting. Never neglect the back of the house. Your positioning should also be reflected in management communications, how employees communicate with each other, and how employees assist each other to deliver to customer expectations.

Positioning needs constant feeding to thrive. It needs to be used on a daily basis and revisited on a periodic basis. Positioning isn't static; it evolves. As your environment changes, your positioning may need to be tweaked. Clearly positioning is more critical as a competitive advantage in full-service commercial hotels and resorts.

Whether you are part of a large major brand or an independent, there is value in defining your positioning and leveraging your positioning to gain a competitive advantage. If you are willing and able, I can tell you from experience that there will be incremental RevPAR and market share benefits that will lead to incremental profits.

**Learning Objectives:**

This portion of your text covers the importance of developing a marketing plan in order to compete successfully in the meetings market. When you have studied this chapter, you will:

- Be able to explain the difference between sales and marketing, tell why marketing is essential to the success of hotels and restaurants, and describe the "Four P's" of marketing.

- Know the importance of a marketing plan and be familiar with the ideas, terminology, and steps associated with developing and implementing a marketing plan.

- Be familiar with such marketing concepts as market segmentation, positioning, and target marketing and be able to describe how marketers conduct marketing research.

- Be able to explain how objectives and action plans are developed as part of a marketing plan.

**Outline**

The Difference Between Sales and Marketing

The Importance of Marketing

The Marketing Plan

The Four Steps of the Marketing Plan

    Step #1 - Conducting Market Research

    Step #2 - Selecting Target Markets and Positioning the Property

    Step #3 - Establishing Objectives and Action Plans

    Step #4 - Reviewing and Monitoring the Marketing Plan

Putting a Marketing Plan into Action

Summary

Chapter Appendix:
Sample Marketing Plan

# 2 Developing Your Marketing Plan

In Chapter 1, we saw that the convention business is a potentially lucrative market segment that can be serviced by almost any type of property. But this does not mean that a hotel should just plunge headlong into attempting to capture all the convention business it can handle. Going after convention business without a sense of what the property can deliver may lead to costly mistakes, including misdirected advertising, fruitless sales calls, or, worst of all, poor service.

Tom McCarthy, past president of the Hospitality Sales & Marketing Association International and a leading trainer and consultant, advises:

> You definitely need a written marketing plan. When plans are verbal, they change frequently and confusion among the troops always results. Laying out your plan in writing for the entire year helps you to budget more accurately than making decisions as you go, but 75 percent of what I see in typical hotel sales/marketing plans is worthless — just filler to make the plan more important than it is.[1]

In this chapter, we present a practical step-by-step approach to developing a marketing program. The case study of the Rolling Green Resort will be used to explain key marketing concepts. Many of the figures and examples in this chapter are related to this case study, so it is important that you not only read the text but also review these examples (and the captions to each) for a better understanding of each application. The numerous illustrations are from actual forms used in the hospitality industry today. Therefore, you are not just learning theory — you will see exactly how marketing concepts are put into practice.

The marketing plan will be our base. We will refer to it often, so it is necessary to grasp the concept thoroughly.

## The Difference Between Sales and Marketing

Before we explore the foundation for convention sales and marketing, there is an important question that needs to be addressed: What exactly is **marketing**? Some people think that marketing and **sales** are synonymous. Others think that marketing is no different than the age-old sales and promotion concept; they consider the combination of sales, advertising, promotion, and merchandising to be marketing. Neither is correct.

There is a clear distinction between marketing and sales. The terms are not synonymous – sales and marketing are *not* equal; marketing is more than sales. Marketing is the combining, blending, integrating, and controlling of all the factors that have an influence on sales. Being market-minded is much broader than being simply sales-minded. Marketing is strategic and directive. It is goal-oriented, and the goals are concise and measurable. It is the groundwork, the research, the *plan* on which sales promotion is based (see box on the next page titled "The Difference Between Sales and Marketing").

In the recent past, the demand for hotel rooms was far greater than the supply; there simply were not enough rooms to go around. It didn't matter what type of rooms were built; the customer had no alternative choices. A marketing plan that was customer-oriented was not needed to sell the product.

But the hospitality industry of today is far different. The city that once had a single inn now has four or five new hotels, each of them unique. Where formerly the demand exceeded the supply, the reverse is now true in many markets.

Now the lodging industry is realizing that its problems are not unlike those of companies specializing in tangible products. Thus, many hotels are attempting to come to grips with what marketing means in an effort to apply marketing management principles. Hotels that wish to effectively compete must become marketing-oriented. The future belongs to those who are customer-oriented, those who are in the business of meeting the changing needs of the public -- not just in the business of maintaining hotel rooms.

### THE DIFFERENCE BETWEEN SALES AND MARKETING

| MARKETING | SALES |
| --- | --- |
| Focuses on market analysis, planning and control of changing market variables. | Focuses on field work and desk work to sell to the consumer. |
| Focuses on long-term trends and creating new products, markets, and strategies for future growth. | Focuses on short-term considerations—today's products, markets, consumers, and strategies. |
| Focuses on profit planning, including determining the optimum market segment mix. | Focuses on volumes and quotas, current sales, bonuses, and commissions. |

## The Importance of Marketing

Like other industries, the hospitality industry is subject to both controllable and uncontrollable variables that will affect sales efforts. External variables, such as weather conditions, fuel shortages, and airline strikes, are largely uncontrollable. Other market variables, however, are inherent to all properties and can be controlled through marketing strategies to attract and retain new and repeat business.

These controllable variables, called the **marketing mix**, consist of "Four P's"—product, place, promotion, and price. *Product*, in the hospitality industry, consists both of physical facilities—guestrooms, banquet space, meeting facilities, and recreational amenities—and of more intangible factors—such as service and the vacation or meeting experience itself. Since a large part of the hospitality product is intangible (you are often selling a property's atmosphere), most marketing strategies will emphasize *benefits* rather than the more tangible physical *features* offered by a property (this concept will be discussed in greater detail in the sales chapter of this book). *Place* refers to the accessibility of the products to its consumers. Hospitality products, of course, do not have to be distributed to the consumer; instead, the consumer must travel to them. This accessibility may be facilitated by marketing strategies which involve intermediaries such as meeting planners, tour operators, and travel agents.

*Promotion* includes both persuasion (getting the consumer to buy) and communication (developing a relationship with the client). In the hospitality industry, communication plays an especially important part in determining exactly what a meeting planner wishes to purchase and is just as important as the actual promotion of the property. *Price,* the fourth

Chapter 2: Developing Your Marketing Plan

factor, is one of the crucial concerns of the marketing mix. Since price is often an important consideration when dealing with the meetings market, this variable should be taken into consideration when establishing room rates for the varying market segments (see Figure 2.1).

Many large properties (250 rooms or more) employ a *director of marketing* to plan, direct, and control all of these factors. It is his or her job to establish programs, policies, and objectives to adapt to changing customer needs. The marketing manager must know and understand such concepts as capital markets, break-even analysis, and cost control, as his or her function includes establishing long- and short-range sales goals.

The marketing manager's job begins with planning. He or she must constantly plan new ways and activities to adapt to the changing needs of the customer while providing continuity to the hotel and improving its image and salability.

Figure 2.1. THE IMPORTANCE OF PRICE IN PROMOTING THE HOSPITALITY PRODUCT.

# Within Your Budget. Beyond Your Expectations.

At Marriott, we have a history of providing successful, risk-free meetings, at surprisingly affordable prices. You can rely on us to help plan your event, every step of the way. No matter what your particular needs. And you can be sure of working with professionals, who'll do whatever it takes to make your meeting special. So give us a call. And spend less than you bargained for, to get more than you bargained for.

**Marriott.**
HOTELS·RESORTS·SUITES
1-800-831-2878

*Many sources of group business, including associations, government groups, the SMERF market, and small corporations, are especially price-sensitive. This ad addresses the consumer's concern over price — while still promoting the services offered by the property at an affordable cost.*

# The Marketing Plan

While the fast-paced and ever-changing nature of the hospitality industry seems to be better suited to short-term sales efforts rather than long-term marketing strategies, there are many advantages to long-range marketing planning. Having a detailed, written plan creates an awareness of the problems and obstacles faced by the property and helps managers to think ahead to make better use of the property's resources. In addition, a written **marketing plan** sets responsibilities, coordinates efforts, and helps evaluate the results of marketing and sales efforts. As an added bonus, the research done in the early stages of developing the marketing plan can identify opportunities to increase revenues in some market segments and point out previously ignored segments.

To be most effective, a marketing plan should cover a *three-year period*. While many properties feel that a yearly marketing plan is enough, a twelve-month plan may restrict sales efforts to already established guest bases. Many corporations and associations make meeting commitments well beyond one year, and short-term sales goals may eliminate the opportunity to capture a larger share of the lucrative conventions and meetings business.

A three-year plan, of course, may be broken down into yearly segments with specific goals for each time period. Many convention-oriented hotels set a targetable plan with well-defined objectives and detailed action plans for the first year of the three-year cycle, and identify broad goals for years two and three. Periodic review of the plan is essential, especially if there are drastic changes in the economy or personnel. Periodic reviews enable advertising and sales efforts to be adjusted to adapt to these enviromental and property changes.

The marketing plan will serve as the property's "road map," and should include programs to attract business to each of the property's **revenue centers**—rooms, banquet facilities, meeting rooms, restaurants, the spa, and so on. Because these programs should complement rather than compete with one other, it is important to define specific objectives for each revenue center, and to be sure that these objectives—and strategies for attaining them—are understood by each staff member.

While the director of marketing is ultimately responsible for the property's marketing plan, many properties have recognized the benefit of a team effort in the development of effective sales strategies. In a marketing team or *sales committee* approach, representatives from each revenue center provide detailed information on the workings of their departments and offer specific strategies for review. As one consultant emphasizes, "None of us is as smart as all of us." This type of team effort not only gives the director of marketing better insights on how to best promote or improve day-to-day operations, but also provides an excellent way to sell the entire property.

For example, Tammis Anderson, former general manager of the Hassayampa Inn in Prescott, Arizona, actively involved all her department heads in the development of the inn's marketing plan. Every year, the department heads "retreated" off property for a few days to ponder the current year's results and the opportunities that might present themselves in the coming year. The department heads were then held accountable for agreed-upon goals, and they monitored the marketing plan to ensure that it was being executed, adjusting it periodically based upon changing market conditions. Anderson's marketing approach resulted in revenue increases in all of the property's profit centers.

# The Four Steps of the Marketing Plan

No matter what approach is taken, a marketing plan consists of four basic steps (see Figure 2.2):

- Conducting market research
- Selecting target markets and positioning the property
- Establishing objectives and action plans
- Reviewing and monitoring the marketing plan

To ensure a better understanding of these steps, we will be using the fictitious Rolling Green Resort as a case study (see " The Rolling Green Resort Case Study").

*Figure 2.2. THE FOUR STEPS OF THE MARKETING PLAN.*

```
                    STEP 1
                  Conducting
                Market Research

  STEP 4                            STEP 2
Reviewing & Monitoring     Selecting Target Markets &
  the Marketing Plan         Positioning the Property

                    STEP 3
            Establishing Objectives
                & Action Plans
```

*In today's highly competitive hospitality industry, it is essential to have a systematic approach for increasing sales. A well-developed marketing plan serves as a blueprint for the sales effort, and provides an effective sequence that minimizes wasteful effort. Marketing plan development, therefore, is a never-ending process. After one marketing plan cycle has been completed, results are evaluated and the process returns to the research portion of the marketing cycle to ensure that up-to-date sales guidelines and strategies are employed.*

## Step #1 — Conducting Market Research

Before you sell any product, you must know its strengths and weaknesses in order to determine how to best promote it. This is where the first step of the marketing plan, conducting market research, is invaluable. In selling the hospitality product, it is not enough to know what your property has to offer; you must also determine what competition you face and what trends in the marketplace may affect future sales and marketing efforts. In order to determine how to best position your property in the marketplace, it will be necessary for you to gather research information so you may conduct a:

- Property analysis
- Competition analysis
- Marketplace analysis

The findings from these three types of research will be used as the foundation to plan the most effective marketing strategies for your property, and will set the stage for the tar-

## The Rolling Green Resort Case Study

The Rolling Green Resort is a 320-room property located forty miles north of St. Louis, a metropolis of over three million people. Situated on the banks of the Pritchard River, it is in a renowned vacation area featuring high wooded hills, picturesque fruit and dairy farms, country estates, historic battlefields, and a national cemetery. A small community nearby, Forest Glen, serves as a shopping center for the approximately 1,200 rural residents of the valley.

The resort is about two miles off U.S.16, a main four-lane north-south highway that is fairly heavily traveled by tourists going south in the winter and north in the summer. This transient trade constitutes the bulk of the resort's business, which is good in the peak summer months and for a few weeks in the winter. But business is generally poor in the spring, fall, and late-winter months.

The Rolling Green Resort's revenues currently consist primarily of room sales to individuals and a minimal amount of banquet business—despite the fact that the property has an excellent dining room and boasts a ballroom that can accommodate 600 people on the second floor. Both the first-floor dining room and the ballroom overlook the river, and both feature charming outside patio/balcony areas. On the lower level, there are several rooms of varying sizes which are now being used only for storage.

Property recreational amenities include a large swimming pool, three lighted tennis courts, and riding stables. The resort is in close proximity to a number of riding, hiking, and biking trails, and bicycle rentals are available in Forest Glen. In addition, there is a small dock that is adequate for three or four small boats and can be used for fishing, although the resort does not offer any organized river activities.

The general manager of the resort is an elderly gentleman who knows the hotel business, but he is unable to come up with any ideas to increase occupancy. The property's board of directors has appointed you as their marketing manager, and it is your job to create a marketing plan that will meet the property's goals of attracting additional business—perhaps including the meetings market, which has not previously been targeted—and increasing occupancy during the property's slow periods.

---

geting of specific market segments and the development of marketing strategies designed to sell the property to each.

**Property Analysis**. A **property analysis** involves an honest appraisal of exactly what a property has to offer. Since this analysis will form the base of information from which virtually every marketing and advertising decision will be made, any error in judgment here will almost certainly result in mistakes in your marketing and advertising strategy. Charles Walhaven of Meetings.com explains the importance of a property analysis:

> Knowing what aspects of your meeting facility are most important to meeting groups is essential. The foundation of any marketing plan is the property analysis. A property analysis is a written, unbiased self-appraisal used to assess the strengths and weaknesses of your hotel. Know everything about your property – and experience it from a meeting planner's point of view. Your interaction with a planner will be more successful if you understand his or her objectives, format, and requirements, and if you are able to demonstrate exactly how your property can meet those needs. Your creativity and knowledge of your property's capabilities will help you meet the needs of your target markets.

In order to most objectively judge a property, input can be solicited from a variety of sources, including employees and guests. You might also try to picture the property as if you are seeing it for the first time—become a guest yourself and experience the property from a guest's perspective. Later, as you analyze other parts of the property, put yourself in the place of a meeting planner seeing the property for the first time.

## Chapter 2: Developing Your Marketing Plan

**Strengths and Weaknesses Analysis.** While it may seem superfluous, this analysis should always be done in writing (even if you feel you know the property inside and out), and should include all of the property's revenue centers. This analysis should *detail the property's strengths and weaknesses, provide columns for comments on areas that need improvement, and specify cost estimates and completion dates* (see Figure 2.3).

The first place to start the strengths and weakness analysis is with the property's physical appearance. Since customers, including meeting planners, form a negative or positive first impression from the appearance of the property, and appearance often plays a large part in sales promotion, a hotel with a neat eye-catching appearance (see Figure 2.4) is a step ahead of a more lackluster competitor.

First, the entrances, grounds, and exterior construction should be assessed with a critical eye for improvement. What is the overall general appearance? Is there ample parking? Are outside areas well-lighted and secure? The exterior of the property should be evaluated in terms of traffic flow, accessibility, eye appeal, and compatibility with local surroundings.

Next, make a detailed, room-by-room and facility-by-facility inspection. Are rooms clean and in good repair? What type of dining facilities are offered by the property? Are kitchen facilities modern and up to code? Do you have an on-premises lounge or nightclub? Does it offer entertainment—and what type? What is the condition of the property's common areas—are they clean, inviting, and well-lighted?

Put yourself in the place of the meeting planner. In terms of facilities, what do you offer? Location? Adequate transportation? Ample meeting space and up-to-date audiovisual equipment? Meeting rooms that are free from distraction? A highly trained staff? A well-lighted and secure environment that will make women attendees feel more comfortable?

Hotels vying for convention business should assess their function space and what equipment they have available or can obtain from local suppliers. It is wise for a hotel to prepare a printed list of its group-function business equipment, including the kind and quantity available and the locations of the specific pieces of equipment. This itemization can serve both as a selling tool when presented to a meeting planner and as an inventory list for the property.

In some cases, properties wishing to target a specific market segment, such as the meetings market, have designed special facilities to appeal to their target markets (see box titled "Facilities That Meet the Needs of the Meetings Market"). While this type of renovation may not be practical for all properties, the property analysis can give valuable clues as to what property modifications are needed to attract specific business.

And what about recreational amenities? Do you have indoor/outdoor swimming pools? Do you offer easy access to golf and tennis? Do you have an exercise facility? How good are your recreational amenities in relation to those of your competitors?

*Your inspection of the Rolling Green Resort has shown the exterior to be charming and in good repair, although the wide veranda could be made even more inviting with the addition of comfortable chairs. The guestrooms, ballroom, and kitchen facilities are modern and adequate, but you are determined to make better use of the wasted space on the lower level.*

*Your tour of the grounds has shown that the driveway to the property is in need of minor repair—and perhaps widening—and that parking facilities are minimal. The pool area is large and clean, but is probably underused; its size and convenient proximity to the kitchen facilities offer excellent possibilities for poolside food and beverage functions.*

In addition to taking stock of the physical aspects, the property analysis also takes into consideration such intangible factors as the property's reputation and quality of service. Reputation includes how the property is perceived — is it classified as an inn, hotel, or

Chapter 2: Developing Your Marketing Plan

*Figure 2.3. SAMPLE PROPERTY ANALYSIS FORM.*

## PROPERTY ANALYSIS - ROLLING GREEN RESORT

| AREA | STRENGTHS | WEAKNESSES | RECOMMENDATIONS |
|---|---|---|---|
| Exterior | Attractive and appealing, newly designed entrance | Lack of seating/relaxing area near entrance | Veranda entrance could be more inviting with addition of comfortable chairs |
| | Clean, good repair, freshly painted | Dumpster area visible from west wing | Construct fence to conceal trash area |
| Meeting rooms | Ballroom can accommodate 600 persons<br>Ballroom overlooks river | Rooms on main level are not utilized | Convert storage rooms to meeting and function space |
| Parking | Convenient to rooms | Driveway is in need of repair | Repair asphalt cracks in drive |
| | Lot has perimeter fence and landscaping | Perimeter fence is too low for security purposes | |
| | | Very narrow driveways at hotel entrance | Research feasibility of widening entrance |
| | | Difficult to enter driveway because of traffic | |
| Rooms | Comfortable, modern decor | Not entirely secure | Install stronger window locks |
| | Easy to keep clean | Little consistency in door locking systems | Install high-quality door latch mechanisms |
| | Cable television | Small bathrooms | Rent out less-desirable rooms last |
| | Easily accessible | | |
| | Refrigerator in each room | | |
| | Effective air-conditioning | | |
| Reputation | Friendly, clean hotel, modern, charming | Positioning is as an average facility | Use slogan or marketing strategy |
| | Courteous staff | More individual than group business | Involve hotel in more community support |
| | Moderate-priced rooms | Not a well-known property | |
| Location | Riverfront | Far from downtown and airport | Develop shuttle system for groups |
| | Accessible to expressway | | Billboard advertising on highway |
| | Popular vacation/resort area | Two miles off main road | |

To provide the best source of information possible about a property, a property analysis should be written out, and include an objective look at the property's strengths and weaknesses. This is only one of several pages in the Property Analysis. Similar comparisons should be done for every area that can affect the property's profitability, including restaurants, lounges, room service, catering, convention services, shops, recreational amenities, housekeeping, bell staff, reservations, and accounting and billing, as well as other influences, such as local attractions, pricing, and brand awareness. This type of analysis provides a means of taking stock of what the property has to offer, what areas need to be upgraded, and what steps can be considered to improve weaknesses. An estimate of the cost and completion date for each recommendation should be specified; some property analysis forms include columns for this information.

## Chapter 2: Developing Your Marketing Plan

*Figure 2.4.* **CONVENTION HOTEL CONSTRUCTION.**

The Mandarin Oriental, Las Vegas, the smallest of the three hotels at MGM-Mirage's CityCenter project and the only free-standing, non-gaming property on the Las Vegas Strip, was built exclusively to serve small, high-end groups. Promising to "set a new benchmark for service" in Las Vegas, the property will handle only one group (about 150 rooms and 400-600 participants) at a time, and the entire hotel staff, including a meeting concierge and butler, will focus on the group's needs.

    The Mandarin Oriental, Las Vegas offers 12,000-square-feet of meeting facilities, including a 7,650-square-foot ballroom, a divisible 810-square-foot event space, and a 20-person boardroom. All meeting spaces have outdoor balconies and floor-to-ceiling windows overlooking the Strip, offering planners the option of natural sunlight.

    Other hotels in the CityCenter complex that offer convention space are the ARIA, which has 30,000-square-feet of high-tech meeting space on three-levels, and the Vdara, which caters to smaller groups (under 150 people) with 10,000-square-feet of meeting space as well as the Sky Pool and Lounge that can accommodate groups of up to 1,500.

**Source: Courtesy of Mandarin Oriental, Las Vegas.**

## FACILITIES THAT MEET THE NEEDS OF THE MEETINGS MARKET

William Cox, the architect for the Boca Raton Hotel in Boca Raton, Florida, conducted a study to determine an ideal design and layout for function rooms at convention-oriented properties. His research showed that a different type of facility was needed for servicing groups than for catering to individual guests, and he recommended the following design guidelines to the Boca Raton management:

1. A large hall capable of seating and feeding at one time the total number of guests the house is designed to accommodate.

2. Meeting rooms for groups ranging in size from 20 to 100. The total area of these rooms should equal or exceed that of the banquet hall.

3. Large and small meeting rooms that can be partitioned easily and quickly to adapt to individual group requirements.

4. Built-in audio and visual aids in each meeting room, with individual control stations in each possible subdivision of the space. The speaker should be able to control lights, sound, and projection from a single station.

5. Stage facilities in the main banquet room for a single performer or production of musical shows.

6. Exhibit space with adequate electrical service, water, and gas. Another special requirement: doorways must be high enough and wide enough to accommodate a tractor-trailer.

Cox's recommendations can be applied by any property seriously considering the convention business.

Source: William Cox, "Design Guidelines for Convention Resorts" (highlights from a speech at a meeting of the American Hotel & Lodging Association's Resort Committee).

resort? Is it considered upscale, budget, or family-oriented? How would guests describe the atmosphere — relaxing, bustling, or business-like?

*As far as the Rolling Green Resort's reputation, it is perceived as modern yet charming, but —unfortunately—the property seems to be a well-kept secret. Aside from a directional sign on the highway, nothing has been done to promote the property. There is a definite need for you to get the word out.*

A property's location can also be a selling point. Is it within easy access to major highways or airports? Are there other historic or scenic attractions or major amusement centers close by? Are there annual events that draw people to the area?

*The Rolling Green Resort has the advantage of being located in a particularly popular vacation area—and can capitalize on a number of scenic attractions. Its location on the river can also be a selling point. Two drawbacks come immediately to mind—it is a considerable distance from the nearest airport, and, because of its location off the highway, may not be accessible year-round in inclement weather.*

**Business Status and Trends Summaries.** The last part of your property analysis helps you assess your property's current position in the marketplace by examining the property's sales

## Chapter 2: Developing Your Marketing Plan

history and current guest base. This part of your research, known as the **business status and trends summaries**, traces the property's past, present, and potential operating statistics, including sales patterns over a three- to five-year period (see Figure 2.5). Such analysis helps to track the "soft spots"—low business periods—inherent to hospitality sales, and can disclose sales areas that need improvement.

*Figure 2.5. THE BUSINESS STATUS AND TRENDS SUMMARIES.*

### MONTHLY OCCUPANCY AND AVERAGE RATE

| Month | 2014 Average Rate | 2014 Occupancy Percent | 2015 Average Rate | 2015 Occupancy Percent | 2016 Average Rate | 2016 Occupancy Percent |
|---|---|---|---|---|---|---|
| January | 69.00 | 50.5 | 74.50 | 46.7 | 86.70 | 59.6 |
| February | 61.50 | 52.4 | 71.00 | 52.6 | 85.45 | 62.0 |
| to Dec. | | | | | | |

### BANQUET FOOD AND BEVERAGE REVENUE (in thousands)

| Month | 2014 Food | 2014 Beverage | 2015 Food | 2015 Beverage | 2016 Food | 2016 Beverage |
|---|---|---|---|---|---|---|
| January | 7691 | 761 | 6541 | 531 | 14126 | 1646 |
| February | 10250 | 1614 | 4694 | 1911 | 17120 | 3361 |
| to Dec. | | | | | | |

### RESTAURANT FOOD AND BEVERAGE REVENUE (in thousands)

| Month | 2014 Food | 2014 Beverage | 2015 Food | 2015 Beverage | 2016 Food | 2016 Beverage |
|---|---|---|---|---|---|---|
| January | 15461 | 8761 | 18640 | 7640 | 21013 | 9641 |
| February | 20911 | 11411 | 22611 | 11311 | 23415 | 11421 |
| to Dec. | | | | | | |

### FUNCTION ROOM REVENUE (in thousands)

| Month | 2014 Food | 2014 Beverage | 2015 Food | 2015 Beverage | 2016 Food | 2016 Beverage |
|---|---|---|---|---|---|---|
| January | 1290 | 330 | 1700 | 410 | 2690 | 491 |
| February | 810 | 240 | 1423 | 467 | 2870 | 502 |
| to Dec. | | | | | | |

Figure 2.5 continues on the following page

*Figure 2.5 (cont. from preceding page) THE BUSINESS STATUS AND TRENDS SUMMARIES.*

### GEOGRAPHIC ORIGIN OF GROUP BOOKINGS

| Missouri | Number by City | Total by State | State Percent |
|---|---|---|---|
| Kansas City<br>Springfield<br>Joplin<br>Jefferson City | 51<br>36<br>32<br>24 | | |
| TOTAL | | 143 | 34 percent |
| etc. | | | |

### GROUP ROOM NIGHTS BY MARKET SEGMENT

| Segment | Jan | Feb | Mar | Apr | May | Jun | to Dec. |
|---|---|---|---|---|---|---|---|
| Corporate Group | | | | | | | |
| Insurance | 621 | 541 | | | | | |
| Computer | 29 | 59 | | | | | |
| Incentive | 43 | 122 | | | | | |
| Other | — | | | | | | |
| Association | | | | | | | |
| National | 330 | 461 | | | | | |
| State and Regional | 461 | 296 | | | | | |
| Other | 69 | — | | | | | |
| SMERF | | | | | | | |
| etc. | | | | | | | |

*This market research, which is also called an occupancy and activity analysis, traces the property's past and present operating statistics and aids in forecasting future activity. While most properties keep guestroom statistics, it is also important to monitor the activities of other revenue centers, such as restaurants and banquet operations, and to determine where the property's customer base is coming from — and when. Additional data that should be included in charts such as this one includes average rate by market segment, fair share and actual market share, restaurant and banquet covers, and check averages, all broken down by month, week, and day of the week. These statistics make it easier to develop effective marketing strategies to both existing and new markets.*

These charts show the history of occupancy and activity by month for all profit centers. Without this, it is difficult to determine objectives and action strategies for the coming year.

In addition to looking at room statistics, it is also necessary to determine the makeup of your property's **business mix**. How old are your guests? Are they singles, married couples, families? Middle-income, high-income? Sports-minded? Drinkers? This information, which is extremely useful in planning marketing strategies, can be obtained by designing a guest questionnaire and perhaps offering an incentive (a free dinner for two, a weekend at the property, etc.) to ensure guest participation. The box titled "A Guest History

## Chapter 2: Developing Your Marketing Plan

Analysis: A Valuable Key for Building Buisness" presented on the bottom of this page, explains how guest information can be obtained from guest registration cards.

This type of analysis of guest history and future prospect information is referred to as **consumer research**, and it can take many different forms. Theresa Choo, who was director of sales and marketing for the Conrad Centennial Singapore for 18 years, said part of her research included talking with her guests, an often overlooked source of ready information. She says:

> In the elevator, I introduced myself and tried to find out what the guest needed. I invited ten guests a week to have tea with me and asked them if what we were giving as value-added perks was actually what they wanted.[2]

Another key area for research is the **geographic origin study**. Not only is it important to know who your guests are, but also where they come from. Identifying **"feeder cities"** or "catchment areas" can result in a more effective use of time and money. The smaller the geographic areas used as categories, the better. It is more useful to know, for example, that a guest came from Chicago than to know that a guest came from Illinois. This breakdown by cities and even zip codes can help the property to direct advertising to those areas which are most likely to produce guests.

Geographic and zip code information can come from a number of sources, beginning with the guest registration card. Other sources of information include responses from advertising or direct mail campaigns. This information should be updated regularly to avoid having to deal with thousands of guest registration cards at one time and to ensure that the correct areas are being targeted.

---

### A Guest History Analysis: A Valuable Key for Building Business

Consumer research is an invaluable tool for both protecting a property's current customer base and for developing strategies to increase new and repeat business. While other guest market research, such as geographic origin, may be obtained from responses to advertising or direct mail campaigns or from post-departure guest surveys, one of your most valuable resources can be found in-house: *guest registration cards*. Guest registration cards are an effective way to determine the geographic origin of a property's guests, and offer a wealth of other information, including:

- The number and type of guests (individual business travelers, family leisure travelers, group commercial business, etc.)
- The source of the reservation (travel agent, meeting planner, guest direct, etc.)
- Reservation date (which will help to determine the lead time required)
- Length of stay
- Room rate and revenue generated (room, food and beverage, gift shop, valet, etc.)
- Personal information, including name, address, city, state, and zip code (a ready-made mailing list)

This knowledge helps a property to determine which market segments (and guests) are sources for the most business, and, by learning what zip codes are producing the most business, the property can direct advertising (or rely on repeat business and target other geographic areas).

By determining guest origins, patterns, and needs, a property can develop strategies and programs to increase potential business. If, for example, guest market research reveals that 80% of the property's business comes from within the state and that these in-state guests travel an average of three weekends a year, the property could consider quarterly mailings offering special packages to these guests to entice repeat business. A fishing tournament, a "Get-Away" weekend, etc., are just two examples of possible strategies. And, besides offering a great potential for repeat business, former satisfied guests are an invaluable source for building additional business through word-of-mouth advertising. Such referrals make it even more important to keep in touch with customers. It is costly to get guests the first time; it is vital to get their business again.

## Chapter 2: Developing Your Marketing Plan

**Competition Analysis.** In addition to analyzing your own property, it is of prime importance to know your competitors and evaluate their strengths and weaknesses in comparison with your own so you can emphasize your strengths in areas where you know competitors are weak. It is not enough to be *customer-oriented*; you must also be *competition-oriented*.

Generally, your competitors are comparable properties in the immediate area that offer similar facilities and room rates and service similar markets. In the case of large convention hotels, however, the nearest competition may be hundreds of miles away (for example, the Rosen Centre Hotel in Orlando might be competing with the Cloister Sea Island in Georgia for an East Coast meeting). Your own **competitive set** will usually include four to six properties that are the most important competition for your hotel. Two key forms that are used to assess competition are the competitive rate analysis and the competitive analysis need fulfillment by market segment (see Figures 2.6 and 2.7).

To completely and effectively assess your competition, fact sheets should be prepared to compare: guestroom and function room rental rates; banquet menu pricing; function room square footage and quality of meeting space; typical number of guestrooms allocated to groups (called the group room allotment); and services offered to meeting groups, e.g., audiovisual, airport shuttle, express check-in, and so on.

A **competition analysis** should be done at least quarterly, and information gathered from a variety of sources. The most useful source is a firsthand look at competitors. Walk the properties of competitors. For an even clearer picture, actually staying at competitors' properties is essential. Converse with their guests, talk with competitors' employees, pick up their literature, and study their advertising. Also, check your competitors' reader boards every day (some hotels display "welcome" messages on their outside signage; others have listings of the day's meetings on boards near the lobby or meeting areas of the hotel). Tracking your competition's meetings business provides an opportunity to prepare a game plan to

*Figure 2.6. COMPETITIVE RATE ANALYSIS.*

### COMPETITIVE RATE ANALYSIS

| Hotel / Rates | Rolling Green Single | Rolling Green Double | Rolling Green Suite | Arrowhead Conference Center Single | Arrowhead Conference Center Double | Arrowhead Conference Center Suite | Hilton Inn Single | Hilton Inn Double | Hilton Inn Suite |
|---|---|---|---|---|---|---|---|---|---|
| Rack | 84-92 | 94-102 | 130+ | 100-105 | 105-110 | 160 | 102-116 | 102-118 | 140+ |
| Corporate | 80 | 80 | 120 | 98 | 104 | 140 | 88 | 88 | 130 |
| Tour | 62 | 72 | — | — | — | — | 85 | 92 | — |
| Convention | 78-90 | 88-100 | 120+ | 85-100 | 90-105 | 140 | 88-98 | 94-104 | 130+ |
| Club Floor | 90 | 100 | — | — | — | — | 115 | 125 | — |
| Government | 68 | 78 | — | 85 | 90 | — | 85 | 90 | — |

*This form compares the rates of your property against those of the competition. Note that ALL types of rates are included — rack, corporate, convention, tour, club floor, and government. In today's technological market, rates comparisons should also be made for website rates and rates from Internet global distribution sites. In addition to benchmarking rates, hotels also gauge competitor activities in areas such as occupancies, group bookings, guest relations, promotional programs, use of advertising, selling methods, market penetration, and market segmentation mix. To monitor these areas, fact sheets are often prepared on each competitor. This comprehensive type of analysis can point out specific areas in which your property differs from the competition and can help you determine how to set your rates in order to better compete for specific market groups.*

51

## Chapter 2: Developing Your Marketing Plan

*Figure 2.7. COMPETITIVE ANALYSIS — NEED FULFILLMENT BY MARKET SEGMENT.*

### COMPETITIVE ANALYSIS
### NEED FULFILLMENT BY MARKET SEGMENT

| Needs and Wants of Target Markets | Rolling Green Resort | Hilton Inn | Arrowhead Conference Center | Comments |
|---|---|---|---|---|
| **Corporate Meetings Market** | | | | |
| AV equipment | 1 | 3 | 3 | Our acess to outside AV firms is limited |
| Security | 3 | 2 | 2 | |
| Training atmosphere | 2 | 2 | 2 | Our secluded location is a benefit to corp planners |
| Space on short lead time | 3 | 2 | 3 | |
| Soundproof meeting rooms | 2 | 2 | 1 | |
| Master account billing | 3 | 2 | 3 | |
| Efficient check-in, check-out | 2 | 2 | 2 | |
| Wake-up, message service | 2 | 2 | 2 | |
| Quality food service | 2 | 2 | 3 | |
| **Association Meetings Market** | | | | |
| Comp. room policy | 3 | 2 | 2 | We offer 1 comp for 40, rather than 1 comp for 50 rooms booked |
| Exhibit space | 1 | 3 | 1 | |
| Accessible location | 1 | 3 | 2 | |
| Overflow arrangements | 1 | 3 | 2 | |
| Assistance with housing | 2 | 2 | 2 | |
| Spouse programs | 2 | 3 | 2 | |
| Reasonable room rates | 3 | 2 | 2 | Key: 3 = superior |
| Recreational amenities | 3 | 1 | 1 | 2 = average  1 = poor |
| Convention coordinator | 3 | 2 | 2 | |

A competitive analysis can take many forms, including just a simple feature-by-feature comparison of the competitors' facilities with one's own. The most pertinent information can be gained by evaluating how one's property "stacks up" in specific market areas. This is one type of form used to compare the services offered to each market segment. Market segmentation is the practice of targeting segments of customers within the overall marketplace. Isolating target markets and determining how well your property fills the needs and wants of each segment is extremely helpful in finding your competitive advantages. Once determined, these advantages can be used to differentiate your property in the form of positioning. This form illustrates just two market segments. You should assess the needs and wants of all market segments you are targeting — the corporate individual traveler, the travel agent market, the incentive group market, the family market, and so on. The key is to find a "difference that makes a difference" to each targeted customer.

land these groups in the future. If it is not possible to check the competition's reader boards on a regular basis, a reader board service is offered by the Knowland Group (www.knowlandgroup.com).

You can also get literature from convention and visitors bureaus and your local chamber of commerce. Check the telephone directories, hotel chain directories, and travel guides to try to determine just what features are being promoted and to whom. Internet searches can also yield extensive information. Most convention hotels host Internet sites that you can access for a fast, comprehensive analysis of competitive properties. Smith Travel Research is another site that can be used to provide competitive intelligence and historical trends. For a fee, the firm will provide industry data customized to your local market and competitive set.

You can also monitor your competition by reviewing their social media sites, such as Facebook, Twitter, and Instagram, and checking customer reviews on such sites as TripAdvisor and Yelp. Most hospitality firms use social media to communicate with their customers and potential guests, so it is important to be aware of the types of content they offer (photos, videos, blogs, special offers, contests, and so on) and how often they are updating their sites. Review sites provide an opportunity to determine what problems customers are having with competing hotels to enable you to create both positioning and services to meet those needs. You should also keep abreast of what guests are saying about your own property; all posts – especially those that are negative – should be answered promptly.

Setting up Google Alerts is yet another way to monitor your competition. These notifications make it easy to see how often (and why) your competition is making news.

This analysis of the competition can help to point out market segments that are not being serviced at your property and can provide valuable clues as to how you can change your own marketing strategies to generate additional business.

*As far as the Rolling Green Resort is concerned, there is obviously no local competition for rooms, but this is a rare case in the hospitality business. In most locations — even small towns — there is at least one other competitor (and oftentimes many more) that may offer a different type of product or may target a market segment that your own property is overlooking. The Rolling Green Resort has identified the Arrowhead Conference Center and the Hilton Inn as competitors. Both are located in the outskirts of St. Louis.*

---

## 🖥️ INTERNET EXERCISE

### Marketing Intelligence

A number of firms, including the following, offer information that can be useful to the hospitality industry:

- Smith Travel Research (www.str.com)
- J.D. Power and Associates (www.jdpower.com)
- D.K. Shifflet & Associates (www.dksa.com)
- MMGY Global (www.mmgyglobal.com)
- PhoCusWright Inc. (www.phocuswright.com)
- PricewaterhouseCoopers (www.pwc.com)

Log onto the Internet, research one of these firms, and answer the following questions:

1. What services does the company offer?

2. How can the information it provides assist you in preparing a competition analysis?

**Marketplace Analysis.** The **marketplace analysis**, also known as a *situation analysis,* evaluates the environment in which the property operates (see Figure 2.8) and the property's operating status in that environment. The marketplace analysis identifies factors that can affect business, such as the cost of travel and government regulation, and also includes research on the environment around the property. This latter research can include the population and projected growth of the local community, the economic trends being experienced by local industry, the traffic counts for nearby highways and airports, recreational amenities and attractions in the area, and unique area activities — such as fairs, festivals, rodeos, etc. — that attract crowds. Not all of these factors will affect your property — the key is to recognize those that do impact you, and, where possible, capitalize or counteract them.

Data for the marketplace analysis can be found in census information, industry reports, periodic updates from the chamber of commerce, and even the local newspaper. Becoming involved in community affairs is another way to learn what is going on in the area and how trends may affect business.

*In the case of the Rolling Green Resort, the marketplace analysis may reveal that there is little going on in terms of population growth and projected changes in the economy. If you were to find out that a light industrial park was proposed nearby, however, that information would greatly impact your property.*

While the research phase of the marketing plan is very important, the crucial exercise is not to merely collect data but to *interpret* property, competition, and marketplace information. Bill Watson, former senior vice president of marketing for Best Western, advises that "researchers must put less emphasis on data and more on the interpretation of the data. They must work toward turning data into useful information. Collecting data for its own value is like collecting stamps. It's a nice hobby but it does not deliver the mail." The key is to "boil down" the statistical information gathered in order to select appropriate market segments and to help form strategies for reaching them.

*In the case of the Rolling Green Resort, for example, your research has shown that you could indeed service at least some portion of the meetings market if you were to formulate a plan to better utilize the "wasted" space on the main level. It may be viable to turn one or two rooms into attractive conference rooms, or to add a business center or other facilities — such as an exercise room or child-care center — to attract this additional business.*

As you can see, the research step of the marketing plan can be an involved and time-consuming process. Therefore, some hotels hire outside experts to assist with the research step of the marketing plan. Outside consultants provide an opportunity for you to get a fresh look at what the property is doing to maximize sales. When the Ritz-Carlton Kapalua on Maui wanted to validate its sales strategy, for example, it brought in David Brudney, a hotel industry consultant.

He reports:

> I spent an hour each with every member of the sales and marketing team and half a day with the GM; I spent a full day visiting the competition... Then I came back and did a report on why group business had dropped. I interviewed incentive houses and validated why incentive business had dropped.[3]

Brudney says his evaluation included questions dealing with account coverage, handling the SMERF market, and group sales strategy (whether proactive calls were made, how many sales calls were made, and how many site inspections were made). He also evaluated where leads were coming from, what hired parties the hotel was using to generate leads, and whether or not salespeople were receiving proper direction.

*Figure 2.8. THE MARKETPLACE ANALYSIS.*

## MARKETPLACE ANALYSIS

### Part I

| OPPORTUNITIES | EFFECTS ON BUSINESS |
|---|---|
| The St. Louis Airport is expanding and bringing in two new regional carriers. | Easier accessibility to the city. These airlines service several of our feeder cities. |
| The local college has made arrangements with several companies to hold seminars and workshops on electronics this spring and fall. | Possible room nights from students and instructors, and meeting space for meetings, classes, and seminars. |
| Archaeological dig in Majestic Canyon has uncovered an ancient Indian burial ground. An influx of scientists and historians have begun a major investigation of the area.<br>etc. | Possibility of room nights from those not wishing to sleep on-site, and day rooms from those who wish to shower and clean up after the dig. Also increased business in food and beverage areas. |

### Part II

| PROBLEMS | EFFECTS ON BUSINESS |
|---|---|
| The highway from St. Louis is scheduled to be repaired in May. | Guests will experience some travel delays during May. However, when construction is finished, the repairs and additional lane will make access to our resort easier and faster. Also a possibility of increased restaurant business from the workers. |
| A new Starwood W hotel has been proposed. Construction is to commence late next year.<br><br>etc. | This property is to be located midway between our property and St. Louis. If developed, this will be increased competition; and Sheraton is strong in the corporate market and has a good, established reputation. |

This marketplace analysis looks at the environment in which your hotel operates and assesses the effects of political, economic, sociological, and technological factors (these are often termed the "uncontrollable variables"). The marketplace analysis generally consists of two parts, one titled "Opportunities and Effects on Business"; the other titled "Problems and Effects on Business." These studies detail influences (both positive and negative) that may have an effect on your business and provide a way to determine how these opportunities and challenges can impact your property. You should use this environmental scanning to monitor your environment in order to design strategies that will help you avoid potential problems while taking advantage of the opportunities provided in your marketplace environment. This figure is abbreviated — you undoubtedly will identify several additional marketplace opportunities and problems that could impact your hotel in the immediate and long-term future.

Chapter 2: Developing Your Marketing Plan

---

> ### 💻 INTERNET EXERCISE
>
> #### Hotel Marketing Plan
>
> In this exercise, you will analyze a sample hotel marketing plan. Go to http://www.mplans.com/hotel_marketing_plan to see a complete example of a marketing plan for the Riverview Hotel.
>
> 1. What is the Riverview's positioning?
>
> 2. What market segments is the hotel targeting?
>
> 3. As you read through the marketing plan, do you feel there is redundancy (filler that covers the same topics repeatedly)?
>
> 4. Do you feel that the marketing and financial objectives are specific and measurable?
>
> 5. Is there a written action plan and budget for each market segment?
>
> 6. Compare the action plan in section four of the Riverside Hotel's marketing plan with the action plan of the Rolling Green Resort in the chapter appendix.

## Step #2 — Selecting Target Markets and Positioning the Property

How do you choose your **target markets**? The obvious first step is to target groups you are already serving. The information obtained from room reservation cards may show that a majority of your guests come from metropolitan St. Louis. If so, direct advertising there.

Next, chart the number of room nights you are currently selling to each market segment by month (see Figure 2.9). If you are realizing a high occupancy from associations or sports teams, for example, expand your efforts to those market segments.

You will also want to target markets that would be the most profitable to your hotel, not only in terms of rooms revenue but additional revenue from such sources as meeting space, food and beverage, and other property profit centers. **Segment profitability** is determined by analyzing the purchasing patterns of past customers. For example, your hotel may already be targeting sports teams, but what is the profit potential of targeting executives (both international and domestic) with unlimited expense accounts? When selecting target markets, you should keep in mind that a balanced guest mix is ideal. A full-service hotel, for example, will want to target several markets: meeting rooms may be used primarily by out-of-town convention groups during the week and by local groups on weekends, while the property's restaurant may serve local business clientele at lunch and hotel guests for dinner.

Marketing goals should be set and hotel salespeople should be trained to target business from potentially more profitable groups. If, for example, your hotel doesn't generate acceptable revenues in its profit centers from association meeting attendees, who tend to be more price-conscious, perhaps you should target other segments that tend to spend more freely on restaurant meals, recreational amenities, and gift shop items, such as business travelers on expense accounts.

Then, determine what other markets you may adequately service (see box titled "Selecting Target Markets"). A property such as the Rolling Green Resort would be an attractive destination for market segments such as honeymooners, business travelers, and families. Its location and atmosphere would be ideal for "murder mystery weekends" or special educational seminars or retreats.

## Chapter 2: Developing Your Marketing Plan

*Figure 2.9. STATE AND REGIONAL ASSOCIATIONS OCCUPANCY CHART.*

**TOTAL NUMBER OF ROOM NIGHTS FOR STATE AND REGIONAL ASSOCIATION MEETINGS**

KEY:
2014 ———
2015 — — —
2016 ■ ■ ■ ■ ■

Occupancy charting details the monthly room nights for a particular market segment (in this case, the state and regional associations market). All market segments should be charted in this way. Similar activity charting should be done for restaurants, lounges, and other revenue centers to facilitate assessment of market trends.

*In order to determine the most effective marketing strategies, properties should chart the number of room nights they realize from each market segment they serve. This occupancy chart for the state and regional associations market sub-segment provides such information as the number of guests and peak months of occupancy, and is useful to forecast trends and direct advertising.*

The property's guest mix should be reviewed periodically. Since the objective in selecting target markets is to create a mix of business that will generate the greatest revenue and produce the most profit, changes in strategy may be necessary during the course of the year. Defining and redefining markets is a continual process, and adjustments to the marketing plan are frequently required as conditions change.

## Chapter 2: Developing Your Marketing Plan

*The conventions and meetings industry has been shown to be a lucrative market segment that should be targeted. While the Rolling Green Resort is probably inadequate to handle large conventions, what other segments within the convention and meetings industry can it service? What specific needs of meeting planners does it meet? Your location away from the bustle of the city may be an inducement to St. Louis businesses wishing to hold training sessions in a quiet, yet convenient, location. And, many small meetings and seminars do not require large facilities — or even have a food function. Are there state or regional associations that can be targeted? SMERF groups? Other groups that you can adequately serve?*

*Due to its historic setting, the Rolling Green Resort might also appeal to historical societies, educational groups, and veterans' groups. And the nearby city of Forest Glen should not be overlooked as a potential source of business from wedding receptions, awards banquets, and other community functions. Perhaps the resort could promote regional activities, such as a dairy festival, or sponsor a sports team to attract visitors to the area.*

Once you have selected your target markets, you must then determine how to best *position* the property to each of them. **Positioning** refers to the perception of a property by the guest. It is a composite of the property's reputation, what it stands for, and how it differs from the competition. In short, it is the property's image or uniqueness — which gives you the wherewithal to sell it to your guests. It is not enough to promote a physical or nonphysical attribute that competing properties do not offer, however. Your positioning must be *meaningful* to your target markets – and offer a benefit that is meaningful to each of them. But you have to avoid the pitfall of trying to be all things to all types of customers. Kathleen A. Girard, former vice president of marketing at the Hotel Millennium in New York City, says:

> Knowing your product and how to position it is a fundamental key to success in the hotel business. You have to have a very strong identity from the moment you open your door, and you must not compromise it. Otherwise people get confused. You have to know who your audience is, who buys. Many hotels don't know who they are. They try to be all things to all people, and certain market segments clash. Conventions clash with the individual business traveler, for example. It's better to do a few things very well rather than do a lot of things in a mediocre manner.[4]

To effectively sell a property, your perception of it and your customers' perception of it must match (see box titled "Positioning Your Property"). An example of success in positioning is the Mercedes-Benz automobile. The name immediately conjurs up the image of a luxury car.

The property's positioning plays an important role in advertising. It enables you to create the advertising which will project the image you want for the property.

*You may, for example, wish to position the Rolling Green Resort as an attractive small meetings destination. Or, you may wish to "play up" the historical significance or the tranquility of the area to attract associations or retreat business.*

---

**WORTH WATCHING**

*Hotels* magazine posted an excellent three-part, multi-media series on the repositioning of Starwood's Le Méridien Chicago. Google "Repositioning Le Méridien Chicago" to view the complete series.

## Selecting Target Markets

The primary purpose of the research phase of marketing planning is to identify three to five priority needs for the property and ways to meet those needs. The study of the property, competition, and marketplace (the business status and trends summaries, in particular) assist the marketing team to identify areas needing sales activity and when specific business is needed.

Once a property's priorities are identified, market segments can be selected that can meet these priorities. Hotels are always looking for ways to improve their customer mix; they must periodically evaluate their customer mix in order to drop or replace low-rated segments and boost business from segments that are more profitable.

Noted industry marketing consultant Tom McCarthy suggests that properties ask the following five questions to best determine which market segments to target:

- Does the property meet the needs of this segment?
- How does the competition meet the needs of this segment? The number and quality of competitors in the area weighs heavily in determining whether or not to solicit a specific segment.
- Does this segment meet the property's needs? Look at the list of the property's needs and determine whether the segment will provide the kinds of business that will satisfy those needs.
- How much business is the property getting from this segment at present? If it is getting some business from this segment, there is likely to be more out there.
- How much time and money will it take to solicit this segment vis-a-vis its long-term potential?

In today's market, properties are being more selective, not only in regard to the market segments they are targeting, but even as to the particular customers they are booking. Transients pay higher rates than groups, so in periods of high demand, some meetings business is given "back burner" treatment. The type of group is also being closely scrutinized; those with substantial banquet business, for example, are of more value to hotels.

Barbara Best, former director of national accounts for Hyatt Hotels Corporation, says, "Smart hoteliers want to have a mix of business, but we are trying to learn how to best manage that mix." In periods of high demand, hotels can indeed be more selective—but their selectivity is often at the expense of the meetings industry. Lynn Tiras, president of International Meetings Managers in Houston, Texas, says, "Hotels are looking at the whole picture to see if a particular piece of business is of value to them, and they are turning away business that doesn't have enough food and beverage or whatever.

"In some cases I can understand it, like when they don't want to tie up all their meeting space for a group that may not need any sleeping rooms or F&B, but they are going way beyond what's reasonable in some cases too."

Obviously, a property must make sound business decisions, but it must be careful, too, not to jeopardize future business. Weighing out a property's priorities, current business relationships with the meetings industry, and market trends is essential to help a property to effectively manage its customer mix without jeopardizing future business.

To illustrate how these strategies are put into practice, let's go back to our case study of the Rolling Green Resort. The property's marketing team, for example, has decided not to solicit individual government business because the segment is too rate-conscious, and also determined that there is no substantial room night volume from the leisure sport fishing traveler. The marketing team instead decided on the following priorities and selected the marketing segments listed in the accompanying chart to meet the property's needs.

*Continues on next page*

Chapter 2: Developing Your Marketing Plan

| **Market Segments Targeted to Fill Priorities** ||
| **Priorities** | **Market Segments to Be Given Emphasis to Solve Priorities** |
| --- | --- |
| **Priority #1**<br>**Midweek Business**<br>**Year-Round**<br>This is our area of greatest opportunity for significant increases. We have some corporate individual travelers, but if this can be expanded and coupled with the corporate meetings market targeted, we will be able to create a strong corporate base to fill this need. | • Corporate Individual<br>• Corporate Meetings<br>• Intensive Training Meetings |
| **Priority #2**<br>**Shoulder and Value Season Group**<br>Early fall and late spring are our shoulder periods, with winter being the off season. The association market (particularly state and regional groups) have been our strongest in the past. We will concentrate our efforts in this market and also with the SMERF market to target groups into the shoulder and value seasons. | • State and Regional Associations<br>• Educational Groups<br>• Government Groups<br>• Religious Groups in Preparation for Christmas and Easter Pageants<br>• Medical Associations<br>• Veterans Groups |
| **Priority #3**<br>**Banquet Business**<br>Has not been pursued actively in the past. Efforts will be directed to maintain current customer base with increases in average check, banquet beverage revenue, and to target into the weekends. | • Local Corporate Groups<br>• Weddings and Bridal Fairs<br>• Reunion Business<br>• Civic Groups |

## Step #3 — Establishing Objectives and Action Plans

One of the attractions of the convention business is that it fills many rooms at a time — and business can often be controlled to fill those rooms at the most advantageous times, such as during the off-season or slow periods. To best take advantage of marketing opportunities, however, it is necessary to set specific objectives and develop plans to help bring about the desired results. And, since marketing goals cannot be met without sales, it is wise to look at each revenue-producing center and set goals for each.

**Marketing Objectives.** At the beginning of each year, research data should be used to set specific goals for each market segment. To arrive at these goals, certain questions need to be answered:

- When are the property's peak periods? In what months does business need to be increased?
- What revenue centers need more sales effort? Does the restaurant do more business during some months? Would offering family rates help to boost room occupancies?
- What market segments can be reached to increase business? What priority should each be given?
- What steps can be taken to generate additional revenues in each segment?

Marketing objectives should be set for each market segment, revenue center, and revenue-producing service (the property's laundry, valet parking, gift shop, and so on). These goals must be clearly defined *in writing* so that everyone involved gets the same information. In addition, the goals must be realistic yet challenging; if a property is currently experiencing an average occupancy of 65 percent, it is unrealistic to expect to set a goal of 100 percent — but the sales staff can shoot for a more reachable, yet challenging, goal of 80 percent during certain months.

Setting specific goals helps in the monitoring process. Room nights can be tracked and restaurant covers counted periodically to ensure that marketing goals are being met.

**Developing Action Plans.** Once objectives have been outlined, **action plans** must be developed to meet those objectives. Action plans spell out how you will use the marketing mix (price, promotion, product, place) to reach each target market. This is the real meat of the marketing plan. There should be detailed action plans for each market segment and revenue center, and, since action plans can be compared to "mini" marketing plans, they should incorporate the following six areas:

1. *A description of the market segments or types of business to be solicited.* Will the plan target business travelers? Local associations?
2. *A specific description of the target customer.* Good marketing plans define target markets narrowly. If the target segment is local associations, this portion of the action plan will include the names, addresses, and telephone numbers of local contact persons.
3. *Rates, special plans, or promotions that will be offered.* This should include any discounted rates for association groups, a possible free room for a tour operator, and special package rates (rooms, food service, entertainment) for groups.
4. *Specific objectives.* Here, the objectives are clearly spelled out. The plan should not just call for "increasing room occupancies," but rather should specify the room night and revenue goals by month for the entire year. These types of objectives enable the sales department to plan strategies to meet its goals.
5. *Action steps.* This portion of the action plan involves the actual steps that should be taken to carry out the marketing objective. Perhaps some promotional literature will be developed. An "open house" may be held to introduce the local meeting planners to your facilities. In the case of the Rolling Green Resort, you may plan an advertising campaign directed to those leisure travelers within a two-day drive of the property. A good marketing plan is full of dates and details.
6. *Budgeting.* It is not enough to simply set goals. Enough money has to be allocated to help achieve them. You should go through each strategy and action step to determine what each will cost.

## Chapter 2: Developing Your Marketing Plan

## Positioning Your Property

Branding is essentially the name recognition of your property by the public, and is critical to a property's success. Just as the "golden arches" are immediately linked to McDonald's, it is imperative for a property to establish a readily recognizable image in today's competitive hospitality industry.

One example is the Sensational Meetings program offered by Omni Hotel. The chain has uniquely positioned itself by not only offering meeting space, but also creating an environment for three types of meetings — energetic, challenging, and recognition. This is accomplished by offering innovative banquet menus as well as custom-tailored environments to meet the planner's goals for each type of meeting (the chain's program is explained in further detail in Chapter 13).

The chain, which won the top award for "Guest Satisfaction Among Upscale Hotel Chains" from J.D. Power and Associates, describes its positioning and advertising as appealing to both sides of the brain (emotional and logical). Christine Connolly, former director of corporate communications for Omni Hotels, said of the chain: "We try to fill a very unique niche between the luxury level and the simply upper scale. You get all or most of the services that you would see in a luxury hotel like the Ritz-Carlton or the Four Seasons, but at a price and at a rate that is sensible."

But positioning is more than just catchy symbols or logos. In today's competitive marketplace, proper positioning enables you to:

1. Identify possible competitive advantages.
2. Select the *right* competitive advantages.
3. Deliver your property's chosen position to carefully selected target markets.

To effectively position your property, the following factors should be taken into consideration:

- *Physical Attributes* — Is your property a "classic" hotel with a colorful history? Does it feature unique construction or features — formal gardens, waterfalls, etc.? How is it different from other properties in your area?
- *Service* — How efficient is your check-in and check-out service? How long is the wait at your restaurant? Do you offer specialized service needed by guests (computers, FAX service, children's programs, etc.)?
- *Personnel* — How are your customer-contact people perceived? Are they courteous and friendly? Can they communicate well and respond to guest needs?
- *Location* — Where is your property located — beachfront, mountain, mid-city, airport, etc.? Is it conveniently located (or, conversely, remote)? What aspect of your location gives you an advantage over the competition?
- *Image* — How is your property perceived by the public — luxury, family, business-traveler friendly? Do you have a distinctive image that differentiates you from your competition? Does your property live up to its perceived image?

Your property's projected image must effectively meet the needs and wants of each of your targeted market segments. You must find opportunities to determine and promote what each segment needs. What benefits do they seek? What needs are currently unmet — and what needs can be met or improved? What innovations are needed to attract unreached market segments? And, most important, are those additional segments worth going after?

## Chapter 2: Developing Your Marketing Plan

Action plans are specific and therefore require personalized attention. It is highly recommended that the action plans be assigned to specific individuals who can oversee their part of the total marketing effort, and dates should be specified for accomplishment. The chapter appendix provides a detailed description of how each of these six areas are applied in the Rolling Green's market segment plan for increasing corporate meetings.

**Budgeting.** Some properties base their marketing budget on what was spent the previous year. Rather, the marketing budget should be based on your strategies/action steps. Set goals for each market segment, identify what action steps are needed to meet these goals, and then determine how much money should be allocated. As was mentioned in the discussion on developing action plans, there needs to be a specific budget set for each revenue center and for each market segment (see Part VI of the chapter appendix). This type of fiscal planning ensures that there are enough dollars spent in the most effective areas.

While there are several types of budgeting, one of those most commonly used is **zero-based budgeting**. This method of allocating money is based on a "task method"; money is budgeted at levels to get the job done, but each expenditure must be justified. This approach assumes that the marketing department starts with zero dollars and that every expense is analyzed on the basis that it will yield more favorable results than spending the amount in another way (the box on the bottom of this page illustrates typical marketing expenses.)

Since this budget is based on the tasks that need to be done, *it can only be completed after an action plan has been developed*. In this way, the property can be sure that there has been enough money allocated to meet the objective. If, for example, you have determined that an extra six sales calls a month are needed in the St. Louis area, you can easily determine the amount of money needed to take care of that portion of the action plan.

> **WORTH WATCHING**
>
> View a short video on zero-based budgeting at youtube.com/watch?v=nG1ay-dg_HA.

Another advantage of this system is that once money has been committed to a certain department or market segment, there is some room for adjustment. If advertising costs less than estimated, for example, you may opt to increase advertising or divert the excess money into additional sales calls. In order to readily see what is available, however, a budget form must be developed that provides instant access to information (see Figure 2.10.). The budget

---

**UNIT-LEVEL MARKETING EXPENSES**

**TOTAL MARKETING EXPENSES**
Labor costs represented 58.6% of the unit-level marketing dollars spent

- 43.7% Salaries and Wages
- 14.9% Employee Benefits
- 2.2% E-Commerce
- 7.0% Advertising
- 4.6% Other Marketing
- 27.5% Selling

**Source:** Robert Mandelbaum and Gary McDade, "Marketing Might: Properties Continue to Invest in People and Technology," *Lodging Magazine*, April 2014, p. 27.

## Chapter 2: Developing Your Marketing Plan

*Figure 2.10. SAMPLE MARKETING BUDGET FORM.*

| NAME OF PROPERTY | | | | | | | | | | | | |
|---|---|---|---|---|---|---|---|---|---|---|---|---|
| Marketing/Sales Methods | | Last Year | | | | Next Year | | | | | | |
| Merchandising/ In-House Promotions | Actual Expenditures | Budgeted Expenditure | Variance | Budget | | Allocation by Target Markets | | | | | | Comments |
| a. Display Material | $___ | $___ | $___ | $___ | $___ | $___ | $___ | $___ | $___ | $___ | $___ | ___ |
| b. Special Events | $___ | $___ | $___ | $___ | $___ | $___ | $___ | $___ | $___ | $___ | $___ | ___ |
| c. Free Samples | $___ | $___ | $___ | $___ | $___ | $___ | $___ | $___ | $___ | $___ | $___ | ___ |
| d. Prizes | $___ | $___ | $___ | $___ | $___ | $___ | $___ | $___ | $___ | $___ | $___ | ___ |
| e. ___ | $___ | $___ | $___ | $___ | $___ | $___ | $___ | $___ | $___ | $___ | $___ | ___ |
| Subtotal | $___ | $___ | $___ | $___ | | | | | | | | |
| Travel Trade Marketing | | | | | | | | | | | | |
| a. Print materials | $___ | $___ | $___ | $___ | $___ | $___ | $___ | $___ | $___ | $___ | $___ | ___ |
| b. Travel/Trade Shows | $___ | $___ | $___ | $___ | $___ | $___ | $___ | $___ | $___ | $___ | $___ | ___ |
| c. Familiarization trips | $___ | $___ | $___ | $___ | $___ | $___ | $___ | $___ | $___ | $___ | $___ | ___ |
| d. ___ | $___ | $___ | $___ | $___ | $___ | $___ | $___ | $___ | $___ | $___ | $___ | ___ |
| e. ___ | $___ | $___ | $___ | $___ | $___ | $___ | $___ | $___ | $___ | $___ | $___ | ___ |
| Subtotal | $___ | $___ | $___ | $___ | | | | | | | | |
| Other Marketing Programs | | | | | | | | | | | | |
| a. Marketing seminar | $___ | $___ | $___ | $___ | $___ | $___ | $___ | $___ | $___ | $___ | $___ | ___ |
| b. ___ | $___ | $___ | $___ | $___ | $___ | $___ | $___ | $___ | $___ | $___ | $___ | ___ |
| c. ___ | $___ | $___ | $___ | $___ | $___ | $___ | $___ | $___ | $___ | $___ | $___ | ___ |
| Subtotal | $___ | $___ | $___ | $___ | | | | | | | | |
| TOTAL | $___ | $___ | $___ | $___ | | | | | | | | |

*A summary budget should be prepared combining the budgets developed for each of the market segment plans. This format is especially helpful when developing a marketing budget because it lists anticipated and actual amounts expended the previous year, provides a variance column, and allocates the current budget into targeted market segments. However, remember that while last year's budgeted and actual expenditures are useful for review, expenditures budgeted for the current year must take into account the tasks that need to be done when zero-based budgeting is used.*

form, when completed, is your most important budgeting tool. It not only specifies your original budget, but also breaks your budget down into spending for each market segment.

The use of computers in hotel sales offices has greatly facilitated the budgeting process. Computers can forecast based on previous and current expenditures, and provide instant printouts to let you know where you stand on dollars allocated for your marketing strategies.

## Step #4 — Reviewing and Monitoring the Marketing Plan

Despite the best planning, outside influences (an energy crisis, a natural disaster, etc.) or inherent weakness in the marketing plan (unrealistic goals, lack of provision for personnel turnover, etc.) make it imperative to periodically review the marketing plan. This evaluation should be done at regular intervals — each month, each quarter, or at the end of an advertising program — to ensure that marketing goals are "on track" and that money is not being wasted on strategies that are not producing the desired results.

John Hogan, former director of education and cultural diversity for Best Western International, says:

> Once the actions steps are reviewed and approved by the manager or owner, a follow-up system needs to be implemented. Each month, the

action steps need to be individually reviewed. Marketing and sales plans are only effective if managers, owners, and sales staff view the process as living and important. Regular reviews of tactics that do and do not work are essential to long-term success.[5]

Goals that have been clearly spelled out are easier to monitor and revise. For example, if specific goals have been set to increase room occupancies in the winter months by 15 percent or to cater an additional ten wedding receptions during the month of June, it is a simple matter to count room nights and banquet activity. Other types of monitoring can include the recording of room nights by market segment, charting and comparing room nights or restaurant covers before and after an advertising campaign, and determining what zip codes are producing the most business.

*In the case of the Rolling Green Resort, for example, you may have coded newspaper advertising to determine which cities are responsible for generating additional business. If you see that there is little response from the Chicago area, you may opt to channel advertising dollars being spent there into more lucrative areas, such as the St. Louis market, or try for a better response by advertising in travel guides or specialty magazines instead.*

*Before "scrapping" a part of the marketing plan, however, you must ascertain if the strategy was given enough time to work (as we have learned, some corporations and associations make booking commitments years in advance and a one-time direct mailing may not bring immediate results) and determine if there could be other reasons for a lack of response (inclement weather in the Chicago area, for example, may have prohibited people from traveling). Sometimes, all it takes is a little corrective action — such as targeting a market segment during a month in which it is more likely to book — for a strategy to bring about increased business. In other cases, an evaluation may show that a more effective marketing strategy is needed to reach a particular segment. Perhaps rooms are priced too high to attract a price-sensitive group, or a specific benefit offered does not have enough appeal. A periodic evaluation will point out these weaknesses and give the property an opportunity to either revise strategies or goals, or to focus its marketing efforts in other directions.*

This process of monitoring, evaluating, and correcting is the final phase of a marketing cycle that returns once again to the research stage in order to keep abreast of market trends and new ways to reach and retain business.

## Putting a Marketing Plan Into Action

The marketing plan is not developed to sit on a shelf collecting dust; it should be an integral part of sales and promotional efforts and referred to often. Once the marketing plan has been prepared, it should be distributed to each department, and its objectives and how to meet them explained to all of those who are involved in particular parts of the marketing effort. Juergen Bartels, past president of Westin Hotels, said of his chain's marketing plan, "It's not a dead plan, it's a lively plan; we work from the plan every day."

Since the marketing plan is the foundation for sales efforts, it is important that the entire sales team become especially familiar with the goals and objectives outlined. From these goals and objectives, sales goals and quotas are set and specific market segments are targeted. It is important that everyone on the sales team thoroughly understand their role(s) in the marketing effort, and utilize the research collected to position the property to appeal to potential sources of business.

The implementation of the marketing plan will impact everyone at the property, not just those in the sales department. Each department should be appraised of the sales department's goals—and the strategies for achieving these goals—and all departments should be made aware of the integral part that they play in the overall success of the property's sales efforts.

If a marketing team approach was used to develop the marketing plan, each department's representative can serve as a "team leader" to ensure that his or her department remains on track.

For long-term success, effective and complete communication between sales and operations is essential. The sales team has to "sell" internally to the rest of the hotel staff as well as to potential guests, so regular meetings should be held with such staff as front desk personnel, housekeepers, accounting staff, engineering personnel, cooks, wait staff, and so on. Topics for discussion can include how groups and individuals book at the hotel, how much time and effort it takes to get groups, how future and repeat business depends on service, how the operation staff's responsiveness is essential to total guest satisfaction, how the market is competitive, and how each staff member makes a difference in sales and service.[6] With this approach, line staff will understand how satisfied guests are the key to the property's profitability, which, in turn, results in additional compensation and benefits to them, and they will become willing participants in the property's overall marketing efforts. Another marketing textbook sums up the importance of having — and following — a good marketing plan as follows:

> A good marketing plan provides direction for an operation. It states where you are going and what you are going to have to do to get there. It builds employee and management confidence through shared effort and teamwork toward common goals. It recognizes weaknesses, emphasizes strengths, and deals with reality. It seeks and exploits opportunities. And, last but certainly not least, a good marketing plan gets everyone into the act.[7]

## Summary

Today's meeting planner has a myriad of choices, so competition for the meetings market has become fierce. Attracting and keeping customers requires a planned, carefully researched and thought-out effort, and a written marketing plan is a must for every hospitality establishment. In this chapter, we have discussed the four steps inherent to each marketing plan and how to implement the marketing plan.

Although the marketing effort will involve the entire staff of the property, the main thrust begins in the sales department. In the next chapter, we will discuss how putting together an effective sales team, implementing workable sales procedures and organizing an efficient sales office can help the property to remain competitive and meet its marketing goals.

### Endnotes

1. Tom McCarthy," Better Late Than No Plan At All," *Lodging Hospitality.*
2. "Marketing Research Includes Talking to In-House Guests," *World Hospitality.*

3. Harvey Chipkin, "The Sales and Marketing Audit: A Proven Way to Build Business," *HSMAI Marketing Review*.
4. *World Hospitality*.
5. John Hogan, CHA, CMHS, CHE, CHO, PhD, "Marketing Plans Must Be a 'Living Being': They Cannot Sit on Shelves!," hotel-online.com.
6. John Hogan, CHA, CMHS, CHE, CHO, PhD, "Everyone Should Know What the Sales Department Does," hotel-online.com.
7. *Marketing Leadership in Hospitality and Tourism, Sixth Edition,* Stowe Shoemaker, Robert C. Lewis, Peter C. Yesawich, Prentice-Hall, 2013.

## Study Questions

1. What is the difference between sales and marketing?
2. The marketing plan should cover what time frame?
3. List the four steps in developing a marketing plan.
4. Research should be conducted in what areas before developing action plans?
5. What factors should be considered when selecting target markets?
6. What is meant by zero-based budgeting?
7. Choose two lodging properties and assess how each has positioned itself in the marketplace. Include a discussion of the following factors: physical attributes, service, personnel, location, and image.

## Key Terms

**action plans**—The specific steps taken to achieve marketing objectives.

**business mix**—The variety or mixture of guests who stay at a property. For instance, business may consist of 20 percent association meetings, 15 percent corporate meetings, 15 percent SMERF groups, 40 percent leisure travelers, and 10 percent transient guests. Also called **customer mix**.

**business status and trends summaries**—Reports that assess the property's current position in the marketplace by examining the property's sales history and current guest base. Part of the property analysis.

**competition analysis**—An evaluation of competitors in order to identify their strengths and weaknesses in comparison to your own. Part of the market research step.

**competitive set**—A group of properties that are the most important competition for a hotel in a given market.

**consumer research**—Marketing research aimed at providing a profile of present and future guests.

**feeder cities**—Geographic areas from which business is derived, but where a company may or not have a property of its own. For example, Calgary, in Alberta, may be a feeder city for Vancouver, in British Columbia, Canada.

**geographic origin study**—Research identifying key feeder cities and the zip codes from which guests are generated. Part of the business status and trends summaries.

**marketing**—The practice of combining, blending, integrating, and controlling the factors that influence sales.

**marketing mix**—The combination of the Four "P's" of marketing — product, price, place, and promotion — used to achieve marketing objectives for a target market.

**marketing plan**—A written guide detailing sales, advertising, and promotion programs used to attract business to the property's revenue centers.

**marketplace analysis**—An evaluation of the environment in which the property operates. Assesses both opportunities and problems in the marketplace, and determines how they impact the property. Part of the market research step.

**positioning**—A strategy to develop a business's product and service as distinct in the minds of consumers. Positioning attempts to distinguish a firm from any of its competitors.

**property analysis**—An evaluation of a business's facilities, services, and programs to determine strengths and weaknesses. Part of the market research step.

**revenue center**—A hotel division or department that sells products or services to guests, thereby directly generating revenue for the hotel. Also called **profit centers**, these may include food and beverage outlets, room service, retail stores, recreational facilities, and other services, such as laundry services and valet parking.

**sales**—Direct selling efforts through face-to-face calls, telephone calls and mailings.

**segment profitability**—The profitability of a particular type of consumer or market segment, determined by analyzing the revenues generated through the sale of products and services to that type of consumer or segment.

**target markets**—Market segments that a property singles out as having the greatest potential, and toward which marketing activities are directed.

**zero-based budget**—A budget that starts at zero and requires planners to justify expenditures for each activity.

## Chapter Appendix

### Sample Marketing Plan

This excerpt from a hotel marketing plan illustrates a detailed market segment plan for the corporate meetings market. The Rolling Green Resort would prepare detailed action plans for each market segment and revenue center. This third step is the core of the marketing plan. The statistics gathered on the property, the competition, the marketplace, and the target customers in the first two steps might encompass more pages in the plan, but success is based on how well the action plans are developed and implemented.

As you read this action plan, note how complete and specific it is, providing a "road map" for the coming year. The strongest marketing plans result from the input of people from all areas of the property. Therefore, brainstorming sessions with key personnel are essential to developing effective action plans.

### Market Segment Plan

**Corporate Meetings**

**I. Description**

The Rolling Green Resort will aim at expanding its share of the corporate meetings market. Types of meetings sought will include: corporate sales, training and development, distributor and dealer, executive conferences, product presentations, stockholder, board and management meetings. Our property should target local, statewide, and national corporations who have yearly meetings in our area.

| | Number |
|---|---|
| **II. Target Customers** | |
| A. Present Local Files. | 98 |
| B. Priority Accounts — present high-volume accounts and those in the area not using us at present, but are known to produce high-volume business | 5 |

- Pritchard Data Services
- Harper and Associates
- Stewart Group
- Stubs Real Estate Investment
- Adam and Bre Corporation

C. St. Louis Prospects

- Companies of over 50 employees within selected SIC numbers in following zip codes: 63111, 63137, 63128, 63104, 63121     120

## Chapter 2: Developing Your Marketing Plan

|  |  |
|---|---|
| • Companies of over 100 employees within selected SIC numbers in all other zip codes within metropolitan area | 70 |

D. Tri-County-St. Louis Area (other than above zip codes)

All companies with 100+ employees plus the following companies if they have less than 100 employees:

|  |  |
|---|---|
| • Top 10 law firms, stockbroker-investment firms, leasing firms, relocation firms, insurance companies, advertising agencies, real estate main offices | 200 |
| • All branch and regional offices of Fortune 500 companies | 24 |
| • All companies of 50+ employees moving in from outside Montcalm County | 73 |

E. Kansas City, Springfield, Chicago (within one-day drive)

|  |  |
|---|---|
| • All manufacturing and insurance companies with 100+ employees | 55 |
| • All branch and regional offices of Fortune 500 companies | 62 |
| • MPI (Meeting Professionals International) and SCMP (Society of Corporate Meeting Professionals) members in these cities | 325 |

F. Four-State Region

|  |  |
|---|---|
| • Top 30 seminar companies | 30 |
| • Fortune 500 company home offices | 150 |
| • ASTD (American Society for Training and Development) members in the four-state region | 917 |
| Total Target Customers | 2026 |

### III. Rates, Special Plans, Packages, and Promotions

A. Seminar/Training/Corporate Group Package:
Available on selection of specific dates.
Minimum of 25 sleeping rooms include:

|  | Single | Double, Per Person |
|---|---|---|
| Room (per person) | $80.00 | $40.00 |
| Tax (7%) | 5.60 | 2.80 |
| Meeting Room | 4.00 | 4.00 |
| Continental Breakfast | 3.50 | 3.50 |
| Lunch | 7.50 | 7.50 |
| AM/PM Refreshment Breaks | 3.00 | 3.00 |
| All Food Tax (7%) | .98 | .98 |
| All Food Service (15%) | 2.10 | 2.10 |
|  | $106.68 | $63.88 |
| Above package including dinner |  |  |
| Dinner | 15.00 | 15.00 |
| Tax | 1.05 | 1.05 |
| Food Service | 2.25 | 2.25 |
|  | $125.00 | $82.18 |

B. Extended-Stay/Early Arrival

If stay is extended to include Saturdays, free unlimited use of the championship golf course and tennis facilities, along with free champagne brunch will be provided. For new bookings arriving on Sundays rather than Mondays, free welcome cocktail parties will be organized and tickets given to a local show or performance.

## IV. Objectives and Goals

Based on a review of our property, the competition, and the marketplace, we have identified fall and spring as our most important priorities for the coming year. The corporate market is targeted as one segment to fill this need. Our objective is to increase our corporate group rooms business from 6% to 10% of our total rooms business, and to increase our annual room sales revenue from $622,542 to $669,400 (7% increase) and increase average daily rate from $72 to $79 for this segment. Monthly targets are identified below:

| Room Nights and Revenue Goals From Corporate Meetings |||||||||||||
|---|---|---|---|---|---|---|---|---|---|---|---|---|
|  | J | F | M | A | M | J | J | A | S | O | N | D | Totals |
| Room Nights | 700 | 850 | 900 | 800 | 700 | 600 | 550 | 550 | 600 | 750 | 900 | 600 | 8500 room nights |
| ADR | 78 | 78 | 80 | 80 | 80 | 75 | 75 | 75 | 78 | 82 | 82 | 78 | $78.75 |
| Room Rev (000) | 54.6 | 66.3 | 72.0 | 64.0 | 56.0 | 45.0 | 41.3 | 41.3 | 46.8 | 61.5 | 73.8 | 46.8 | $669.40 |

## Chapter 2: Developing Your Marketing Plan

### V. Action Steps

#### A. Sales/Direct Mail

| Step No. | Method | Target Customers | No. | Details | Qtr. | Sales Days | Resp. |
|---|---|---|---|---|---|---|---|
| 1 | Telephone | Present local files | 98 | Survey their satisfaction over the telephone. Give comp one-night stays to any who were dissatisfied. | 1 | 5 | AH JM |
| 2 | Telephone | Priority accounts | 5 | Have contact with these accounts a minimum of once a month. Include entertainment at hotel, sporting events or other local activities to build relationship. | 1,2,3,4 | 20 | AH JM |
| 3 | Personal Blitz | St. Louis prospects and those in Tri-County St. Louis area | 287 | Personal visits by sales staff to outline our services and deliver small gifts such as a business pen. | 2,4 | 15 | TS AH JM |
| 4 | Phone Blitz | Planners in key feeder cities of Chicago, Kansas City, Springfield and Four-State Region | 1539 | Promote our package and familiarize the company with our product. | 1,3 | 25 | AH TS JM |
| 5 | Direct Mail | Previous corporate meeting customers | 250 | Send personal thank you letters for their past business and ask them to rate satisfaction by returning post-paid questionnaire. | 1 | 4 | AH JS |
| 6 | Telephone | Previous corporate meeting customers (not returning questionnaire) | 70 (est) | Survey satisfaction over the phone. Provide comp room night to any who were dissatisfied. | 1 | 3 | AH JS |
| 7 | Telephone | Tri-County St. Louis, Kansas City, Springfield and Chicago areas of over 100 employees | 340 | Call for initial qualification to determine if file should be set up (at least 30 room nights per year). Set up appointments. | 2 | 6 | JM TS |
| 8 | Direct Mail | ASTD members in Four-State region | 1000 | Promote our package and familiarize with our product special rates, etc. Mail-in response card enclosed. | 2 | 25 | TS JM AH |
| 9 | Telephone | ASTD members in Four-State region | 100 | Respondents to mailing. | 3 | 25 | JM AH |

#### B. Advertising

Media
The Trade Journal Magazine ( 2 col x 5 ")  12 times
Corporate Market Review (5 col x 8 ")  6 times
The St. Louis Directory — Annual

C. Merchandising
   Development of the following brochures and fliers:

   |  | Total |
   |---|---|
   | Meeting Planners Informational Brochure, 4p4c | 1,500 |
   | Hotel Fact Sheet (group) 8"x11" 2c | 1,000 |
   | Meeting Package 4p4c | 5,000 |

D. Public Relations and Publicity
   Contact local TV stations, major newspapers, and the
   Convention Authority announcing prominent corporate meetings.

E. Internet
   Add Facebook and Twitter links to property's website.   2,000
   Develop a blog offering advice to corporate clients.   2,000

## VI. Budget

A. Sales
   Dues and Subscriptions
   - The Trade Journal Magazine     $500
   - Corporate Market Review         350     $850

B. Advertising
   Media
   - The Trade Journal Magazine
     2 Col x 5" @ $800 x 12x        9,600
   - Corporate Market Review
     5 col x 8" @ $750 x 6x         4,500
   - The St. Louis Directory
     Annual                         1,000    $15,100

   Direct Mail
   - American Society for Training and
     Development (ASTD)                      $3,000

   Brochures and Fliers
   - Informational Brochures        1,650
   - Hotel Fact Sheets              1,200
   - Meeting Packages               2,400    $5,250
   Production costs (ads and brochures)      $5,000

   Other Selling Aids — Gifts for Blitzes    $6,000
                        Total Corporate      $35,200

**Summary**

Corporate meetings business is one of our priorities for the coming year. The estimated 8,500 room nights is 10% of total rooms business, and the $35,200 is 9.2% of the total marketing budget.

## Industry Profile

## *Kevin Buchanan, General Manager*

Hilton Garden Inn Providence Airport/Warwick

A 1994 graduate of Johnson and Wales University, Kevin Buchanan has served as the general manager of the Hilton Garden Inn Providence Airport/Warwick since the property opened in 2005. Over his 20-year career in the hospitality industry, Buchanan has been recognized with such honors as General Manager of the Year for Hilton Garden Inn and as the Rhode Island Hospitality Association Hotelier of the Year. Also employed by the Williamsburg, Virginia-based Newport Hospitality Group (NHG) since 2002, he was honored as General Manager of the Year. An active member of the Providence Warwick Convention and Visitors Authority for seven years, Buchanan also serves on the board of directors for the State Tourism Department for the city of Warwick, Rhode Island.

### The Sales-Focused General Manager

As general managers, we are responsible for leading everything at the hotel and delivering the results to contribute to its overall success. We help to drive sales and profitability as well as guest and team member satisfaction and ensure that brand standards are met. To achieve that mission, it is important that general managers are involved in sales and that they make sales a priority on a daily basis.

As a focused-service general manager, sales has always been a part of what I do on a daily basis. Supporting the sales team by meeting clients and picking up the phone and thanking them for their business goes a long way. Whether it is visiting key accounts, attending networking events with the sales team, or even prospecting potential business on a regular basis, the general manager must be a part of the sales department to the fullest. That means a lot of smart sales calls, entertaining, and, of course, networking events.

Sales is about building relationships – people do business with people they know, like, and trust – so it is important that the general manager is assisting the sales team and adding value and support for the department, not hurting a relationship that a sales team member has built. But sales involvement from the general manager plays an important role in relationship building for group business. Imagine a group that meets a general manager before making a decision – this could help the meeting planner make that purchasing decision because they would know the hotel has the ability to service the needs of their groups; the general manager can offer that reassurance. It doesn't hurt when groups are on property to make sure your presence is known.

**Learning Objectives:**

This portion of your text discusses how sales departments are organized. We will cover both the function and physical layout of a sales office, look at positions within sales and see how sales efforts are managed. We will also discuss how automation has changed the way hotel salespeople do business. When you have studied this chapter, you will:

- Understand the function of the sales office and how the sales office interfaces with other departments in the hotel.
- Be able to describe the various positions within the sales department and the duties of each.
- Understand how the director of sales manages the sales team in terms of standard operating procedures, conducting sales meetings, assigning account responsibility and evaluating the sales effort.
- Be familiar with the procedures used by sales offices to follow a sale through from prospecting to execution of the event and understand how sales office automation is being used to enhance the sales effort.

**Outline**

Sales Structures
- The Sales Office
- How the Sales Office Interfaces with Other Departments

The Sales and Marketing Staff
- Positions Within Sales
- Supplemental Sales Staff

Managing the Sales Effort
- Standard Operating Procedures
- Sales Meetings
- Assigning Account Responsibility
- Evaluating the Sales Effort

Sales Records and Filing Systems
- Hotel Filing Systems
- Control Books and Sales Forms

Sales Office Automation
- Advantages of Automation
- New Advances in Hotel Computer Systems
- The "Virtual" Office
- Additional Uses of Automation

Summary

# 3 Organizing for Convention Sales

Approximately 50 percent of the lodging industry's total receipts are derived from the meetings market, making it a prime target for many properties. But in today's highly competitive marketplace, it is simply not good enough to send salespeople out into the field to solicit meetings business. Tapping this lucrative market requires an efficient, organized sales endeavor.

Beverly W. Kinkade, former vice president of industry relations for Starwood Hotels & Resorts Worldwide, Inc., described the importance of a well-organized sales office:

> The role of the sales department in pursuing the convention business is vitally important. With today's competitive hotel environment, it is imperative to have sales policies and procedures in place to smooth the communication both within the sales office and other areas of the property. In order to reach occupancy and revenue goals, the sales office must not only be organized and staffed with enthusiastic, knowledgeable people but also have an efficient filing system, written operating procedures, and an effective system for monitoring both function room and guestroom bookings.

This chapter deals with how to organize the sales effort by creating a sales office — both the physical plant and the personnel in it — that maximizes a property's potential to sell to and service the convention and meetings market. We will also discuss some of the positions within sales, and see how sales efforts can be structured and managed for optimum results. We will also take a look at how today's technology has changed the sales function, including facilitating record-keeping, enabling the sales staff and their customers to communicate instantly, and maximizing profits through the use of revenue management software.

## Sales Structures

Two trends have greatly impacted the way hotel sales departments do business. First, acquisitions, mergers, and consolidations have occurred in the lodging industry at a record pace as companies realize the value of acquiring multiple brands and the cost savings from combining departments. Today, a handful of firms own nearly 100 brands. For example, the Waldorf Astoria Hotels & Resorts, Hilton Hotels & Resorts, Doubletree by Hilton, Embassy Suites, Hampton Inn, and Homewood Suites by Hilton are just some of the brands under the Hilton Worldwide umbrella. The InterContinental Hotels Group includes such brands as Holiday Inn Hotels, Crowne Plaza Hotels & Resorts, and Staybridge Suites, while Marriott operates the Ritz-Carlton, Courtyard, Fairfield Inns & Suites, and Residence Inn in addition to its Marriott Hotels, and Starwood Hotels & Resorts Worldwide includes such brands as St. Regis, Westin, W Hotels, and Sheraton.

To increase efficiency, these hotel companies are consolidating their operations and relying more on regional and national sales offices. Rather than having a dozen individual properties call on a potential client for meetings business, chains are assigning a single salesperson to represent every brand in the hotel company's portfolio to the client. While this practice has proven to be beneficial to the larger hotel chains, it has met with resistance from some meeting planners, who prefer to work with a salesperson who personally knows them and their business. This concept will be discussed in greater detail later in the chapter.

Second, marketing functions have increasingly been incorporated into sales. More hotels today are focusing on the overall bottom line, not just rooms revenue from meetings business. While rates, dates, and space are still important, more properties are evaluating a group's spending patterns and potential for revenue property-wide before booking them. This trend, called revenue management, has led to revenue management positions and departments within many sales offices, and revenue management is expected to expand throughout the industry. A detailed look at revenue management will be provided later in the chapter.

**Small Properties.** All hotels, whether they are large or small, should have some kind of sales department from which sales efforts are directed. At small properties, a salesperson usually handles all types of business. He or she may call on meeting planners, travel agents, tour operators, and other sources of potential business. Still smaller hotels may have to combine sales operations under another department—or even have the general manager direct the sales effort, with the GM often designating one day a week for personally making sales calls.

Regardless of size, every hotel has "non-sales" employees who could be recruited to assist in the sales effort. If a food service employee and two front desk people, for example, would each make five calls per week to qualify new prospects, fifteen calls per week -- 750 calls a year -- could be made by them!

**Large Properties.** Larger properties generally have a specialized sales staff and operate out of a separate sales office. It is best, if at all possible, to have full-time sales specialists for convention sales. In the largest organizations, the degree of specialization is carried still further, with salespeople assigned to market segments. One sales staffer may go after association business, another may be assigned to target corporate meetings business, another focuses on the nonprofit SMERF market, and still another focuses on incentive programs. Obviously, such concentration is practical only for chain operations. It is not essential to successful selling to break down the task so finely, but this should tell you that each segment of the market has its own appeal.

## The Sales Office

The sales office is often the first contact a client has with the property, and first impressions can make the difference between sales success or failure. To be effective, the sales office (and effort) must be properly organized. This organization should include both a sales philosophy as well as a physical office layout conducive to generating sales.

**The Function of the Sales Office.** As we have said, the sales office must be established and organized to enable it to meet the overall goals and objectives of the property's marketing plan. The sales department should be structured so that group business is not only solicited but also properly serviced, which means the sales office is given authority over other departments that will be involved in servicing group business (see Figure 3.1).

As this figure shows, sales efforts are always spearheaded by the property's general manager. A sales- and marketing-oriented general manager sets the tone for selling

Chapter 3: Organizing for Convention Sales

**Figure 3.1. TYPICAL CONVENTION HOTEL ORGANIZATION CHART.**

```
                         General Manager
                                |
                     Director of Sales
                        and Marketing
                                |
         ┌──────────────────────┼──────────────────────┐
   Reservations          Director of Sales       Director of
     Manager                                      Revenue
                                                 Management
                                |
         ┌──────────────────────┼──────────────────────┐
   Sales Managers         Convention             Banquet/Catering
                        Service Manager             Manager
```

*Organizational structures within properties vary, but this chart shows the typical management structure of a large convention hotel. In this example, the reservations manager, director of sales, and director of revenue management report directly to the director of sales and marketing. All three are sales-focused positions that are considered equal in terms of position level, and they will interact with each other on a regular basis. It is important to note that the director of sales is increasingly being given authority over other departments, such as banquets and catering, to enable the sales staff to deliver what it promised to clients.*

throughout the entire property as well as lending his or her expertise to the sales department. Hospitality consultant Carol Verret details several ways that the general manager can be instrumental in increasing sales:

- **Making a daily telephone call.** A call to a top account typically takes very little time, but clients are impressed when they hear from the head of the hotel. To make even more of an impression, the GM can provide his or her direct line to the client – and extend an invitation to call directly if the client encounters a problem at the hotel.

- **Stopping in during site inspections.** It makes an impact when the GM stops by while a salesperson is giving a tour of the property; a visit from the GM indicates that he or she hopes that the prospect will choose the property.

- **Going on sales calls to top accounts.** Accompanying a salesperson on a sales call to a top account that has not committed works wonders in negotiations. Prospects are usually so impressed to have the GM in on the negotiation that they're likely to be more open to the "boss" than they would be to the salesperson.

- **Providing the "GM close."** The personal guarantee of the GM can make all the difference in whether a sale is made. If the GM cannot be there in person, a short video of the GM indicting that he or she will make it right if the prospect is not satisfied in any way is extremely effective.

However the sales office is organized, it is crucial that all employees understand their roles in meeting the goals set forth in the marketing plan. Property salespeople should be professional, knowledgeable, and service-oriented. All property employees, whether they be field salespeople or the receptionist at the sales office, should be aware of their importance in the marketing effort. Walk-in clients, for example, should be greeted promptly and made to feel at home, and the receptionist or secretary should be able to answer any immediate questions a visitor or caller may have. This will demonstrate the property's commitment to customer service – and will also enable the salesperson to effectively respond to the client's request or concern.

Noted industry consultant and columnist Howard Feiertag suggests:

> Rather than just advise the caller that the salesperson is out, and passing the call on to voicemail, why not ask the appropriate questions the salesperson would ask? 'How may I help you?' works. Then record information that reflects the needs of the inquirer. A standard phone lead questionnaire sheet could be provided at the front desk for the type of information to be recorded on.[1]

**The Physical Layout of the Sales Office.** Both the location and the appearance of the sales office are important. Sales offices should never be hidden away in the basement or an unused guestroom; nor should they be located in "goldfish bowl" areas off the main lobby. Ideally, a property selling meeting and banquet facilities should locate the sales office adjacent to these areas.

The sales office should appear tasteful and professional, with a minimum of clutter, be well-lit and ventilated, and have comfortable seating and reading material available. Property information sheets and brochures, sample menus, complimentary letters from satisfied meeting planners, and perhaps albums of past events or news clippings about the property are informative — and good pre-sale tools. Sales office decor can also include photographs of guestrooms, banquet rooms, and the sales and managerial staff, as well as feature awards received by the property. This type of decor helps to familiarize the client with the property's facilities, and can also help to develop confidence in the property.

## How the Sales Office Interfaces with Other Departments

Before the hospitality industry became more marketing-oriented, the sales department was usually a separate entity responsible only for filling guestrooms and function space. Today, however, it has become imperative for not only the director of sales but also his or her staff to move into the mainstream of the day-to-day marketing operations of the property.

This is especially true in dealing with convention and group meetings business. In addition to ensuring that guestrooms are available, it is imperative that the director of sales and his or her sales staff work closely with a number of other departments, especially:

- Convention Services
- Banquets/Catering
- Revenue management

Chapter 3: Organizing for Convention Sales

**Convention Services.** As we will see in the second part of this book, a good convention services department is essential for repeat bookings. Meeting planners must be satisfied with meeting space, the handling of functions, the availability of equipment, and the service attitude of the staff in order to book repeat business or recommend the property to others (see Figure 3.2).

*Figure 3.2.* THE IMPORTANCE OF THE CONVENTION SERVICE DEPARTMENT

> You can't plan for everything.
> But with a little help you can get very close.
>
> **Crowne Meetings Director**
>
> If there's one thing we've learned from hosting thousands of meetings, it's the importance of having an expert you can rely on for all of your meeting needs. That's your Crowne Meetings Director.
>
> For your next event, count on the meeting experts at The Place To Meet.
>
> **CROWNE PLAZA**
> LEXINGTON
> THE CAMPBELL HOUSE
>
> THE PLACE TO MEET.
>
> 1375 South Broadway
> Lexington, KY 40504
> (859) 255-4281
> www.thecampbellhouse.net
>
> Book today call (877) 227-6963.

Crowne Plaza Hotels & Resorts, which positions itself as "The Place to Meet," developed a series of ads to promote the chain's commitment to successful meetings. In addition to ads that promote the chain's two-hour response to meeting inquiries as well as daily meeting debriefings, the series includes ads such as this one, which introduces the Crowne Meetings Director. These members of the convention service staff are experts in the field of meeting planning, which enables them to assist meeting planners with all of their meeting needs.
Source: Courtesy of Crowne Plaza Lexington, The Lexington House.

The convention service manager serves as the on-the-scene contact between the convention organizer and the hotel. He or she is the one who sees that all provisions of the contract are carried out, and is the one who must be prepared to cope with the requests — and emergencies — that come up as the convention nears and during the event itself.

This position is a very crucial one and should never be downgraded. The convention service manager must have sufficient stature and authority to cope with the unexpected (see Figure 3.3).

Sheraton, in recognition of the importance of convention services personnel, defines its convention and conference service professionals as follows:

> A Convention and Conference Service Professional is a diplomat, accountant, psychologist, juggler, mind reader, and goodwill ambassador with an impelling attention to detail. It's one of the most challenging and rewarding jobs in the hospitality industry.
>
> It's challenging because you get to wear so many hats. You deal with a lot of different personalities and a lot of demands are made on you. Details and deadlines define your workday.
>
> It's rewarding because you get to see a project through from start to finish, knowing that you helped make it all happen. You make meetings for two thousand or two dozen run like clockwork. And you make customers come back again and again, just because you did a good job.[2]

*Figure 3.3. THE COMMUNICATION ROLE OF THE CONVENTION SERVICE MANAGER.*

The convention service manager is the intermediary between the promises made by the sales manager, the expectations of the meeting planner, and the execution of the event by the hotel operating departments. The immediate conclusion from the chart below is that this individual must be very detail-oriented and tolerant of high degrees of stress during an event.

```
  SALES              CONVENTION           MEETING PLANNER
 MANAGER         SERVICE MANAGER

                 HOTEL OPERATING DEPARTMENTS
                       FRONT OFFICE
                       HOUSEKEEPING
                         CATERING
                    UNIFORM SERVICES
                        RECREATION
                         SECURITY
                        ACCOUNTING
                       RESERVATIONS
```

*The convention service manager acts as the on-site connection between a meeting group and the host property.*

**Banquets/Catering Department.** Although some people feel that the banquet/catering department does not belong under the authority of the sales department, control of all function space ideally should be overseen by one person — the director of sales. This eliminates confusion and communication problems, since choices must sometimes be made regarding who will get a function room on a certain night. This decision must be made with an eye toward the overall scheme of things, and this falls within the responsibility of the director of sales.

# Chapter 3: Organizing for Convention Sales

For the sake of argument, let's look at what would happen if this were not the case. This partial organization chart has the banquet manager reporting indirectly to the assistant manager. When a client requests banquet space, the banquet manager will book one of the hotel's banquet rooms. While this action seems efficient enough on the surface, the sales department often needs all of the banquet rooms should any convention group be booked.

This kind of a communication breakdown can happen with meeting rooms as well. If the banquet department booked a meeting room and the sales department unknowingly booked the same room for a training seminar, the hotel would be placed in an embarrassing position and would most likely lose business.

**Revenue Management.** With today's trend toward combining sales and marketing efforts, revenue management has become increasingly important to hotels. Properties that previously relied on the director of marketing and the director of sales to realize maximum profit potential are now creating a specific position dedicated to forecasting supply and demand and researching the potential profitability of groups.

> **MORE ONLINE**
>
> Additional information on becoming a revenue manager can be found at www.xotels.com/en/revenue-management/how-to-become-a-hotel-revenue-manager

Revenue management plays an integral role in the sales effort as it *manages* the demand created by marketing and captured through sales efforts. It is especially important today, as customers come from a wide range of channels. Without a thorough assessment of the factors affecting the bottom line – types of customers and their current and projected spending patterns, the rates charged by competitors, future trends, and so on — it would be virtually impossible to maximize revenue.

Swissôtel, for example, employs a revenue manager to decide price structure based on the date, season, day of the week, competitive situation, and the potential of the group.

---

### How to Become a Revenue Manager

As the hospitality industry moves from yield management to revenue management — and puts even more emphasis on the importance of revenue management's role in sales and marketing, the demand for qualified revenue managers is growing. No longer do revenue managers simply analyze booking patterns and make necessary adjustments or "crunch numbers" to compare performance from the current and previous years to tweak availability and rates; today's revenue managers are an integral part of a property's overall marketing effort. Although revenue managers must have excellent numerical and analytical skills, they must also be able to see the overall picture and be able to work with marketing and operations managers to ensure the best results for the property's bottom line.

Courses in revenue management are offered by several universities and organizations, such as the American Management Association, and online, including the eCornell online certificate programs. Seminars and webinars are also good sources of information and additional training.

A state-of-the-art computer system is at the heart of the revenue manager's decision-making process, and predictions can be made for weeks — even months — ahead. While the position is fairly new and can be expected to change, the HSMAI expects that the revenue manager position will be firmly integrated into hotel sales offices in the next few years.[3]

## The Sales and Marketing Staff

The sales staff is the first contact that many people have with a hotel. Corporate, nonprofit, and association meeting planners first establish contact with the hotel through the sales office. Their first impressions are formed by the warmth, personality, and efficiency of the sales staff.

### Positions within Sales

While the sales effort itself should be coordinated by one person, —the director of sales— there is a wide variety of positions within the sales department. While each individual on the sales staff is given certain responsibilities, it is important to remember that sales is a *team effort*. The efforts of each member must be coordinated with those of the others on the sales team for maximum results.

> **MORE ONLINE**
>
> "10 Things Successful Hotel Sales and Marketers Do Every Day" can be viewed at www.htrends.com/trends-detail-sid-80915.html.

**The Director of Sales and Marketing.** The director of sales and marketing spearheads the sales effort by setting objectives and monitoring action plans. He or she works closely with the director of sales to ensure that sales goals are being met and that the sales effort is kept within budgeted limits. To keep sales targets and goals on track, an effective director of sales and marketing must determine the day's priorities and follow through on their implementation, evaluate potential sales opportunities and check on the progress of these accounts, monitor the property's competitors, keep abreast of upcoming events and industry trends, and work closely with revenue managers.

**The Director of Sales.** The director of sales, who may be called the sales director or vice president of sales at some properties, is responsible for executing the marketing plan formulated and accepted by top management. It is his or her job to coordinate and direct the efforts of the sales staff. All sales promotional programs must be channeled through him or her for approval. He or she works closely with the general manager or director of sales and marketing to determine target markets and to set the budget appropriations for each market segment.

While the scope of this position is often argued, ideally the director of sales should be given all the authority necessary to ensure that sales goals are met. This may include becoming involved in a number of areas, including advertising and public relations, budgeting, and any other function of the hotel that directly or indirectly affects the sales effort. The salary for this position will vary depending on the type of hotel.

**Sales Managers.** Depending on the size and type of property, there may be a number of additional sales managerial positions. The *convention sales manager* is responsible for soliciting convention trade for the hotel (see Figure 3.4). It is his or her job to identify and

## Chapter 3: Organizing for Convention Sales

*Figure 3.4. SHERATON'S JOB DESCRIPTION FOR THE CONVENTION SALES MANAGER POSITION.*

| | |
|---|---|
| **Job Title:** | Convention Sales Manager |
| **Department:** | Marketing |
| **Reports to:** | Director of Sales |
| **Basic Functions:** | Reviews with Director of Sales the marketing strategy that will obtain maximum occupancy levels and average rate. Responsible for all convention group business related to the market segments as they relate to annual revenue projection. |
| **Scope:** | Sales manager will be the primary person for booking of long-term convention group business, with long-term being more than six months out. |
| **Work Performed:** | Initiate prospecting and solicitation of new accounts; manage current accounts to maximize room nights from the account in relation to the hotel marketing plan; responsible for administrative efforts necessary to perform the aforementioned. |

1. Quotas for this position are:

   | | |
   |---|---|
   | Room nights per month | 1200 |
   | Soft spot percentage | 20 |
   | Phone calls per week: | |
   |     Trace: | 20 |
   |     Prospecting: | 25 |
   | Personal calls per week | 10 |
   | New accounts per week | 10 |

   Individual to supply weekly, monthly, and annual reports supporting productivity standards.
2. Probe for customer needs: rooms, suites, desired dates, day of week pattern, program agenda, food & beverage requirements, and degree of flexibility in each of the aforementioned areas.
3. When available, obtain information on the group's past history, i.e., previous rooms picked-up, arrival/departure pattern, and double occupancy percentage.
4. Review availability of client's REQUIRED DATES AND ANY ALTERNATE DATES which should be offered. The dates presented to the customer should satisfy the customer's needs while allowing the hotel to maximize occupancy and average rate.
5. Negotiate with the customer: day/day of the week pattern, day-by-day room block, group rates (within guidelines as set by DOS, comps, and function space.
6. Tentatively block rooms and function space in accordance with office policy.
7. Confirm in writing all aspects of the meeting. Check to ensure they received the signed contract.
8. Upon receiving the signed contract, process definite booking ticket, definite function room outline, and credit application.
9. Oversee, manage, and track the way in which reservations are to be made.
10. Periodically contact the customer while in-house to be certain all is in order and going well.
11. Conduct an exit interview with the customer to determine their level of satisfaction and ask for additional business.
12. Send letter of appreciation to customer.

| | |
|---|---|
| **Supervision Exercised:** | Supervise and share one secretary with another individual. |
| **Supervision Received:** | Primary supervision from the Director of Sales. Initial training, and retraining as needed, also received from the Director of Sales, as well as direction as to room merchandising. |

*(continued)*

*Figure 3.4. (continued)*

| | |
|---|---|
| ***Responsibility & Authority:*** | Upon satisfactorily completing rooms merchandising and operational training, the individual will have the authority to make decisions and confirm dates, room blocks, and rates to the clients. |
| ***Minimum Requirements:*** | Bachelor of Arts or Science degree — preferably business, hotel, or restaurant administration. Individual must also be professional in appearance and approach. |
| ***Experience:*** | Minimum of two years' experience in hotel sales. |
| ***Sales Competencies:*** | 1. Ability to negotiate.<br>2. Accounts strategizing.<br>3. Ability to prospect.<br>4. Ability to judge profitablility of new business.<br>5. Knowledge of product.<br>6. Knowledge of competition.<br>7. Ability to make presentations.<br>8. Ability to organize and plan.<br>9. Ability to utilize selling skills.<br>10. Ability to overcome objections.<br>11. Ability to problem-solve and make decisions.<br>12. Ability to write effectively. |

*A job description is a detailed listing of the function and organizational relationship of each employee. This job description for the convention sales manager shows the many facets of this important job and details the qualifications required for the position. Note that under "Work Performed" both room night and activity goals are stated. Top salespeople like to have their efforts measured against predetermined goals. Quality of calls is more important than quantity; therefore, room night/revenue goals are most important. However, maintaining activity goals such as number of phone calls, personal sales calls, and new accounts per week leads to more room nights booked and more revenue.*

contact the associations, corporations, and fraternal organizations that could use the hotel for their conventions. Convention sales are generally made through personal visits, so the convention sales manager must build a relationship of confidence with the prospective client. Due to long lead times, a convention sales manager may need three to five years to get specific convention business.

The *convention service manager,* while not always considered an actual member of the sales team, works hand in hand with the convention sales manager. His or her job is to coordinate and service the conventions booked by the property. The convention service manager takes over after the sale has been made and begins to work out the fine details with the convention group. In addition, any problems that arise during the convention will be directed through convention services. The convention service manager must work closely with all departments, coordinating the efforts of the food and beverage department, the front office, and the banquet setup crew to see that things run smoothly in the exhibit area.

Since this is such an important position, as the convention service manager is ultimately responsible for the success or failure of a meeting, it has become increasingly common for CSMs to become certified. As we mentioned in Chapter 1, there are a number of certification programs available to ensure that CSMs provide the best in service to meetings groups. The "Best Practices" box on the next page details just one of these programs – the Meeting Maestros Program developed by Delta Hotels in conjunction with PCMA.

A *tour and travel sales manager* is responsible for developing group and charter business for the hotel. He or she works closely with travel agents, tour wholesalers, tour operators, and transportation companies. This person is generally instrumental in putting together tour packages and must have expertise in the pricing and promotion of group packages. The tour and travel sales manager may also put together group incentive packages.

## Chapter 3: Organizing for Convention Sales

Some properties may also employ a *director of advertising and public relations* whose job it is to coordinate all promotional materials and public relations and to make the final decision on advertising media (radio, television, Internet, social media, magazines, newspapers, billboards, direct mail).

**The Sales Staff.** The property's salespeople are the key to sales success. These are the people who prospect, set appointments, and make personal calls on prospective clients. They must be professional; knowledgeable about the property, the competition, and their markets; and possess excellent organizational and verbal and written communication skills. Today's sales professionals must also be computer-literate, as most hotels utilize computerized sales systems.

Ironically, the increased use of technology sometimes impacts relationships between salespeople and clients. The use of the Internet by meeting planners to research possible sites, take "virtual tours" of properties, and other technology (such as electronic transmittal of contracts) have sometimes minimized face-to-face contact between meeting planners and hotel salespeople.

This makes it all the more important for salespeople to commit to building long-term relationships with customers. **Relationship marketing** -- the building and maintaining of

---

**Best Practices**

### Delta Hotels and PCMA Team Up to Offer the Delta Convention Services Manager (CSM) Meeting Maestros Program

Delta Hotels, which has hotels throughout Canada, launched the Delta Convention Services Manager (CSM) Meeting Maestros Program, developed and sponsored by Delta Hotels and PCMA. The intensive three-day course focuses on the complex and changing role of the convention service manager, and features such topics as building client relations, adult learning, food and beverage, and technology.

All Delta CSMs are required to take the course, which centers on deliverables such as guaranteeing that all Delta CSMs will be PCMA-trained professionals, that meeting planners will be recognized on a personal level, and that Delta will deliver the fastest response in the industry. Sharon Bolan, the former director of learning and development for Delta Hotels, says:

> We wanted it to be known that if you're planning a meeting with Delta, you will work with someone who's trained specifically for that...We wanted everyone to be trained to the same standards. So it made sense that we would look for a [standardized] training program, and PCMA was able to customize it.

Darrin Stern, who helped develop the content of the course and facilitated it, says that the course was designed *by* meeting managers *for* meeting managers. According to Stern, one of the areas of the program that generated the most discussion among participants was the section on adult learning, specifically how a room setup affects learning.

Danny Champagne, former convention services manager for the Delta Centre-Ville, says:

> This three-day class made us realize what our clients are experiencing while they're at our property...I think that it brings new meaning to customer service for our clients. They already know that they are important to us, but the difference now is that they have the assurance that the convention services managers across Delta Hotels are devoted to their meetings and that we give guarantees to them in order to provide them with the level of service they deserve.

> ### The Importance of Relationships
>
> | How often does the relationship you have with a hotel salesperson influence where you place your business? | |
> |---|---|
> | Always | 11% |
> | Frequently | 43% |
> | Sometimes | 30% |
> | Occasionally | 11% |
> | Never | 5% |
>
> Have you ever switched hotel alliances to follow a hotel salesperson with whom you have an established relationship?
>
> Yes: 39%  No: 61%
>
> A key element in securing — and retaining — meetings business is building solid relationships with clients. *Meetings & Conventions* magazine recently polled hotel salespeople and meeting planners regarding how each felt about developing relationships. This chart shows that 84 percent of planners said that their relationships with hotel sales people "Always," "Frequently," or "Sometimes" influence where they book their meetings. Approximately 40 percent of planners surveyed have followed salespeople from one hotel company to another because of the importance of established relationships. Further, 65 percent said their relationship with a hotel's convention service manager is very important when selecting a site. This study clearly demonstrates the need for salespeople to focus on consultative and relationship-based selling and concentrate on building personal relationships with meeting planners. It is very likely that some of your prospects and your hotel's best customers are at the top of your competitors' hot prospect list, so it is extremely important to begin building a relationship at the very beginning — and giving a high priority to seeing that the relationship flourishes.
>
> Building relationships in a high-tech age is critical. Jack Schmidt, former regional director of sales and marketing for Destination Hotels and Resorts, observed: "What has happened is that the Internet and electronic distribution channels have driven people apart — we're doing business with machines and information, versus people today. And what that has done is depersonalize the sales process.
>
> It's more difficult to build relationships now because it's more difficult to get past e-mail and voice mail and even meet with planners. What used to be a relationship is becoming a transaction. New technologies have made us more efficient, but much less effective."
>
> Since building relationships gives salespeople an edge in capturing business as well as fostering future business, salespeople would do well to follow the example of the late Bob Keilt, who built and kept life-long relationships by being attentive and thoughtful, beginning with going to the airport to pick up important meeting planners who were in town for site visits. That personal touch and thoughtfulness, of course, left a lasting impression — meeting planners remembered Bob when making choices about properties and booking future events. His efforts paid off in a big way, enabling him to meet his primary goal: "I strive to develop such strong relationships with my accounts that I own their business."
>
> **Source:** Jack Buchanan, "A Meaningful Relationship: How Technology Affects the Connection Between Hospitality Marketers and Meeting Planners, *HSMAI Marketing Review.*

lasting relationships with customers -- is important in today's competitive environment (see the box above titled "The Importance of Relationships"). Meeting planners are more likely to feel comfortable with a salesperson who has performed well in the past, and may even take familiarity and trust into consideration over other factors, including price.

Unfortunately, meeting planners are sometimes unable to work with the salesperson who assisted with a past function. The turnover of sales personnel in the hotel industry is considerably higher than turnover in other industries. According to a recent Dartnell's Sales Force Compensation Study, the annual turnover in sales personnel in all industries is 14.1 percent; in the hospitality industry, turnover more than doubled at 30.5 percent. And the percentage may actually be considerably higher, as hotels do not consider transfers within the company as employee turnover. Greg Marshall, executive director and meeting planner for the Gift and Home Trade Association, has experienced problems with staff turnover first-hand. His take on the situation:

> From the time I signed the contract to the time the program was held, I had two different salespeople and four different convention service managers. It was like I was always starting from square one, educating the new person I was assigned about my group and the goals of our conference. Today, one of the first things I ask during site inspections is, "What's your staff turnover like?"[4]

Turnover is especially frustrating for meeting planners who have developed a good working relationship with salespeople and other property staff. Jackie Brave, a partner at Accenting Chicago Events & Tours, Inc, says:

> There has been so much turnover of personnel at hotels that it's hard to keep up with who is where. It's very difficult to create relationships with people who disappear at a moment's notice.[5]

The compensation structures employed by some hotels may be contributing to the problem. Some hotels opt to reward salespeople for performance, paying a commission rather than a salary, so there is a tendency for salespeople, especially younger salespeople, to opt for compensation from the generation of new business rather than commit to building relationships with current customers.

**Clerical Support.** To enable salespeople to handle the most important aspect of their jobs — selling — it is essential that a property employ a good clerical staff that can maintain careful and detailed records, make intelligent use of this data, and assist in follow-up. While responsibilities may vary from property to property, the main function of the clerical staff is to provide support at the home base and to handle walk-in clients in the absence of sales personnel.

It would be penny-wise and pound-foolish to foot the considerable expense of fielding a sales staff only to skimp on the support at home. The period of sales effort before signing a convention can be very long, and salespeople must be continually in touch with the meeting planner. With today's high cost of sales calls, a follow-up system of letters and phone calls generated by a well-trained clerical staff is essential. The clerical staff will also maintain careful, detailed records of your prospects' convention activities, personnel changes, and other data that may help win the sale.

## Supplemental Sales Staff

It is often impractical and uneconomical for hotels to cover all the market bases with their in-house staff. To gain representation nationwide, chain properties supplement their staffs' sales efforts with *regional and national sales offices,* while independent properties turn to *independent hotel representatives* to help them with regional and national sales efforts.

**Regional and National Sales Offices.** Many national chains are reorganizing their sales function from a property basis to a regional basis. Marriott, Hilton, and Starwood, for example, are merging sales departments from several properties into one central location. As this happens and the number of "unassisted" sales continues to grow as planners take advantage of Internet virtual tours and electronic transactions, individual salespeople in the future will only sell to their property's larger accounts, and sales staffs at the property level will be reduced in favor of regional sales reps (see box below titled "Marriott's New Sales Structure — Sales Force One").

One of the advantages of regional and national offices is their use of *corporate sales staffs* in regional sales offices. The **regional sales office** serves as an intermediary between meeting planners and individual properties by providing a central information point that directs meeting planners to the property that best fits their needs.

The corporate staff solicits business for any hotel in the chain, and there are a number of advantages in this approach. First, a customer who has experienced good service and a successful meeting in one hotel of the chain might be induced to stay within the chain for their next meeting. Even when convention organizers have to move around the country to increase attendance, they may be sold on staying within the chain. Secondly, it is easier for a meeting planner who is scheduling ten similar meetings in many parts of the country to book all of them at once with a single salesperson. Once a salesperson has broken through to close a sale, the way to booking additional locations is easier. Still another advantage comes into play when a meeting planner cannot get a free date at one hotel. The chain may be able to offer another hotel on that date, whereas an independent property loses out when firm dates cannot be met.

Several hotel chains, including Mandarin Oriental, Taj Hotels, Orient-Express, and Hyatt, have developed computer systems that link their convention hotels with their regional and national sales offices. These systems give instant electronic access to group

---

### Marriott's New Sales Structure: Sales Force One

J.W. "Bill" Marriott, the chairman and CEO of Marriott International, shared details about the chain's renovated sales structure in one of his recent blogs, which are designed to not only provide information and insights about the chain, but, most importantly, to develop relationships with the public. Below are excerpts regarding the purpose and workings of the chain's new sales strategy:

"The hotel business is a people business. It's about the one-on-one experience. And it's about building a relationship, anticipating needs, and selling our group customers the way they want to be sold.

"A few years after we opened a hotel in Lincolnshire, Illinois, I visited the property and asked them how the sales process was going. Well, the manager of the hotel said, "My sales manager went in to see a major client last week. When he walked into the office, there was the sales manager from the Residence Inn and the sales manager from the Courtyard. It seemed like all three of our brands were there to compete for the same piece of business. Of course, when I talked with our customer, he said, 'I don't like to be sold this way. Have one person represent Marriott for all your brands.'"

"So that's why we're rolling out what we call Sales Force One. That allows our sales people to create a one-on-one customer relationship and represent all our brands with an individual customer. This means our sales teams — no matter where they are — will have access also to the information about that particular customer, and our meeting planners will not have to continue to inform the latest sales person about who they are and how much business they give us.

"The new framework moves the majority of our salespeople out of individual properties and into centralized sales offices in metropolitan areas. Meeting planners have one contact person at the nearest regional office who helps place meetings among Marriott brands, including Marriott, J.W. Marriott, Ritz-Carlton, Renaissance, Courtyard, and Residence Inns."

**Source:** Bill Marriott blog (www.blogsmarriott.com) and Robert Carey, "'Sales Force One' Alters Marriott's Reps Structure," Meeting News.

Chapter 3: Organizing for Convention Sales

booking data, including availability, rates, and dates, and, in addition, track client histories and account activity chain-wide. With such information at their fingertips, many regional sales representatives are now empowered to block space, print out proposals for any hotel on the system, and book business on the spot. The hotel's director of sales is then notified by electronic mail for approval of the agreement. Regional sales offices also serve the properties within a chain's region by providing promotional materials and public relations.

While some meeting planners embrace the advantage of having their basic information and history available to multiple hotels throughout the chain, others are resisting the change. Many meeting planners prefer to work with an onsite salesperson, especially one with whom they have developed a personal relationship, rather than a regional salesperson who sells across all the brands within a chain. This is especially important to planners who want to be assured that "their" salesperson will be available to answer questions when the need arises. Planners appreciate a salesperson who builds sales by building relationships, rather than simply getting their business and moving on to sell to other groups.

**Independent Hotel Representatives.** Many hotels do not feel they can adequately cover all of their market bases with an in-house sales staff; they often supplement the staff with an **independent hotel representative**. These outside individuals or firms represent the property as a "long arm" of the sales department.

Because hotels have different needs, the services provided by independent hotel representatives vary widely. In some cases, the representative may be hired simply as a field

---

### INTERNET EXERCISE

### Independent Hotel Representatives

Independent hotels frequently look to independent hotel sales representatives or firms to assist in their sales efforts. These firms, which usually have offices in major cities such as Washington, D.C., Ottawa, Canada, and Chicago, have their own portfolio of clients and act as an extension of the independent hotel's sales office, much like the national and regional sales offices of the major chains.

Not only do representation firms field a staff of salespeople in key geographic areas, they also reach meeting planners at trade shows. Instead of buying a booth as a single entity, hotels can split the cost with other properties in the rep firm's portfolio. This is especially beneficial, as it can cost up to $20,000 to exhibit at some meeting planner trade shows.

The Ambrose Hotel's director of marketing, speaking of their representative firm, states:

> They are an adjunct to our sales effort. It's like having an additional arm that reaches farther than we could on our own and multiplies our efforts. They have enough representation to cover what we can't.

Log on to the websites of the following hotel sales representative firms:
- Associated Luxury Hotels International — www.alhi.com
- The Hyland Group — www.hylandgroup.com
- Preferred Hotel Group — https://preferredhotelgroup.com

1. Compare and contrast the companies. What are the strengths and weaknesses of each? Which firm do you think is best for a hotel targeting the meetings market?

2. How is each firm paid?

3. Explain how hiring an outside sales rep firm provides independent hotels with some of the same benefits of being a "brand," but without having to give up anything that made them independent in the first place.

salesperson, soliciting clients who are impractical for the hotel's in-house staff to reach. Other hotels may use larger representation companies, whose services include consulting, market analysis, advertising, and public relations in addition to sales.

Because of economics, independent hotel representatives usually represent more than one property. This causes many hotels to balk at the notion of being represented by such firms. Quite logically, they question having a competitor represented by the same firm. Hotel representatives answer this criticism by saying they represent properties of different sizes and market emphasis, not similar clients seeking the same clients.

Should a hotel use an independent hotel representative? If you can afford to field your own staff and it performs satisfactorily, that's fine. If you can afford only limited sales efforts, a representative may offer another dimension. What counts is the amount of sales generated.

A hotel should investigate the benefits offered by an independent hotel representative firm. Such firms usually specialize in a particular market, while overlapping to other sources of business. If your target market is the convention trade, be selective, and choose firms that actually specialize in this area. Since the majority of association and trade convention groups are headquartered in Washington, D.C., Chicago, or New York, your chances of reaching the convention market are greatly increased if your representative has an office in one of these locations.

There are a number of factors that you will want to consider in making your decision (see box below titled "How to Choose an Independent Hotel Representative"). In addition, you may wish to consult similar-sized properties that are using a representative you are considering. Ask them about the effectiveness of the representative, especially in regard to areas in which you feel you may have difficulties.

If you opt to go with an independent hotel representative, it is important to remember that these firms are generally hired on a contract basis, usually paid a fee, and receive a set percentage of the volume of business they directly book for the hotel. They must be given clear guidelines on what type of business the property is soliciting and what rates the property will accept.

In other words, the hotel representative should work within the framework of the property's marketing plan, and, as an extended member of your sales force, should be thor-

---

### HOW TO CHOOSE AN INDEPENDENT HOTEL REPRESENTATIVE

Choosing an independent hotel representative is not to be taken lightly. Take the same care in hiring a hotel representative as you would in hiring an in-house executive. Here are questions to help you to determine whether an individual or firm would be an asset to your sales operation:

1. How many hotels does the firm represent? Has it extended itself so much that it may not be able to meet your needs?
2. Does the firm represent competing properties? If so, how will this affect its handling of your account?
3. Does the representative specialize in the targeted markets you are seeking?
   Does he or she have knowledge of the group and convention business? Is the firm doing business with organizations you have targeted?
4. Does the firm have offices in the cities that are your major market areas?
5. Is the representative's staff knowledgeable about your type of operation?
   Does his or her staff have a hotel background?
6. How does the representative regard service? Do you want him or her to be an extension of your sales staff? Is he or she willing to be part of your team?
7. Can he or she deliver needed supporting services and advise you on brochures and other printed materials?

oughly familiar with the property's facilities, rates, and operating procedures. Personal visits and tours by the management should be encouraged. The representative should be given organization charts, operating manuals, and materials detailing charges for meeting rooms, guestrooms, and other facilities. Most importantly, the representative should be given a copy of the property's marketing plan — with specific objectives spelled out for him or her to meet.

In addition to hiring outside independent sales representatives, many independent hotels join global referral associations such as Preferred Hotels, World Hotels, Leading Hotels of the World, Relais & Châteaux, and Small Luxury Hotels of the World. These firms provide similar services as representation firms (personal selling, advertising, sales promotion, and public relations) as well as central reservations systems and loyalty rewards networks.

The selling point for many independent hotels is the reach realized from these firms' global reservation systems. Many independent hotels are family-owned and simply do not have the resources to open offices in Washington, D.C., Toronto, London, or Milan. Referral associations make a global presence possible — and provide association with other prestigious hotels within the group. Additionally, member hotels get access to discounts on goods and services due to the association's volume purchasing. These associations also provide valuable training and networking opportunities.

## Managing the Sales Effort

While hiring good salespeople, whether they be in-house staff or independent hotel representatives, is an important step toward achieving sales goals, the sales effort itself must be structured and managed properly for maximum effectiveness. Managing the sales effort involves a number of areas: the development of standard operating procedures (SOPs) for salespeople and convention staff; periodic sales meetings to discuss goals and problems; the prioritizing of accounts; keeping accurate records; and, most important, the monitoring and evaluating of progress.

### Standard Operating Procedures

An effective sales effort begins with standardized guidelines for each step of the sales and servicing process. Each salesperson should be made aware of the sales office's **standard operating procedures (SOPs)**. These are instructions explaining how recurring business activities should be handled.

Danielle Babilino, senior vice president of hotel sales at Wynn Las Vegas, explains:

Standard operating procedures provide a reference for our sales and catering personnel and are a great tool for training new salespeople. When procedures and policies are clearly defined in writing, communication is improved.

Each hotel salesperson should have a three-ring binder containing the property's standard operating procedures on their desk in order to keep everyone "on the same page" for consistent selling. Written SOPs presented together in a manual provide a constant reference for sales and banquet personnel, and are an essential training tool for new employees. Areas that might be included in a SOP manual include:

- Function book control and procedures
- Guestroom control book procedures
- Booking policies
- Rate guidelines for high and low demand periods
- Credit/deposit/cancellation policies
- Policies regarding VIP and complimentary rooms
- Meeting room rental fees and procedures
- Banquet and room reservation cut-off dates
- Convention service standards and procedures
- The organization chart and specific job descriptions for the sales department

The sales department's SOPs can be added to or amended as situations warrant, but it is important that each person involved in the sales effort be made aware of any changes. These written SOPs help to eliminate costly errors by ensuring that each member of the sales team follows the same procedures when booking and servicing groups.

## Sales Meetings

Just as written procedures are important, good communication is also essential to an effective sales effort. Sales meetings are an excellent way to ensure that all people involved in the sales effort have the same information and can help to eliminate potential problems by identifying and dealing with them early.

While the number and type of sales meetings may vary, the most commonly used meetings are *weekly and monthly staff meetings, weekly function meetings, weekly revenue management committee meetings, marketing team meetings, and periodic (usually annual or semi-annual) sales meetings for all employees.*

- Weekly and monthly sales or staff meetings are usually headed by the coordinator of the sales effort; this may be the director of sales and marketing, the director of sales, or the sales manager at larger properties, or the general manager at small properties. Held to discuss any changes in the sales or promotional effort, the progress on certain accounts, new and tentative bookings, sales goals, and potential problems, these meetings are usually attended by all sales personnel and the heads of any departments affected by the sales effort (convention services, banquet/catering, front desk, etc.). Since the mutual exchange of ideas and information is vitally important to any sales effort, these regularly scheduled sales meetings should also include a period of open discussion or a brainstorming session.
- Weekly function meetings generally include only the department heads involved in selling to and servicing the convention market. These meetings ensure that every area of the property is adequately covered when making commitments to groups, and help to ensure that specific business is understood and properly handled.
- Weekly revenue management committee meetings, which typically include the general manager, director of revenue, director of sales and marketing, director of sales, catering/food and beverage director, controller, reservations

manager, and front office manager, have grown in importance because the new reality is that not all revenue is created equal, necessitating that everyone work together to maximize revenues. It is no longer enough to simply book group business; managers must determine their clients' present and future value.

Today, pricing strategies are based on a calendar that forecasts high-, medium-, and low-demand periods. The objectives of revenue meetings, then, are to review the forecast calendar, and update it with new demand information, competitive influences, and reservations activity in order to reset or confirm pricing. Management can then inform the sales team of how much it can negotiate with meeting groups based on anticipated demand for the dates requested.

- Many properties hold an *annual or semi-annual sales meeting* for all the property's staff. The marketing plan—and each employee's role in it—is presented, and specific information, such as advertising and promotional efforts and their affect on individual departments and employees, is discussed. This benefits both employees and management, providing an opportunity to obtain ideas and suggestions from employees working in day-to-day operations.

## Assigning Account Responsibility

Keeping the sales staff abreast of current information and goals is only part of the management of the sales effort. It is the responsibility of the director of sales or other leader of the sales effort to ensure that accounts are being distributed and handled in the most productive and cost-effective manner for optimum results.

There are many variables in assigning responsibility. Some directors of sales feel that accounts should be assigned by market segment; if he or she has three salespeople, for example, one might be assigned to corporate meetings, one to association business, and one to the SMERF market. While this may seem practical on the surface, there may be a drastic imbalance within the market segments. The salesperson assigned to corporate meetings, for example, may end up with more accounts than he or she can handle.

The director of sales may see this imbalance, and assign two people to cover the property's most lucrative segment. This approach, too, may present problems, since most corporations find it more comfortable to deal with only one contact person at a property.

One solution is to *assign specific accounts, rather than market segments*, to each of the salespeople; one salesperson would be responsible for all the business generated by a particular organization. This type of account assignment is beneficial to both the salesperson and the client; it provides one contact person and helps to build rapport that may generate future business. If this approach is taken, it is important to distribute accounts with particular attention to the number of accounts, their geographic area, and the market segments into which they fall. In terms of numbers, it is usually considered best to assign accounts equally. If, for example, a property expects to target 900 accounts over the coming year, each of the hotel's three salespeople should be given 300 of them.

This number can vary based upon the location of the accounts. If, for example, a property can target a nearby industrial park, it is easier for a salesperson to handle these accounts than it would be for a salesperson to adequately cover accounts spread over a two-state area. In this case, the salesperson covering the local area can be assigned a larger number of accounts.

The market segment factor comes into play when determining just how much business will be generated by each account. A salesperson assigned to a large corporate account, for example, can expect to cover a great deal more business — meetings, award ceremonies, the annual convention, etc. — than a salesperson assigned to an association that stages just one annual convention. In this case, or in the case of the salesperson who shows particular expertise in servicing a specific market segment, accounts can be redistributed for the best results.

**Key Account Management.** Once accounts have been assigned, the typical salesperson may find that he or she is looking at 300 to 400 sources of potential business. Selling to and servicing these accounts will involve making sales calls, setting appointments, and following up — all activities that will generate a mountain of paperwork. So how does a salesperson decide how to handle the monumental task of effectively selling to his or her accounts? The solution is **key account management**.

Key account management involves prioritizing accounts based on their profit potential. This is important because, generally, 20 percent of a salesperson's accounts generates 80 percent of the business. Look at accounts individually to determine which ones have the highest potential for generating business and organize your time to sell and service these accounts. Key account management, then, involves ranking accounts. This is usually done on five levels:

- *Level 1* consists of all new and established accounts with a high potential for business. These are the accounts that will warrant your highest attention. As a general rule, a minimum of five personal calls and five telephone calls should be allocated to these accounts annually.
- *Level 2* consists of high potential accounts that are already providing a good share of business. Of course you want to continue to follow up on these lucrative accounts, but they don't require the same amount of personal attention and they can usually be serviced by four personal and four telephone calls annually.
- *Level 3* consists of new accounts with medium potential and established accounts that are not generating the medium potential expected of them. These accounts generally require three personal and three telephone calls each year.
- *Level 4* consists of accounts with medium potential providing an acceptable level of business. These accounts are normally followed up with two personal and two telephone calls annually.
- *Level 5* consists of low potential new and established accounts that do not warrant a great deal of time. These accounts require little more than token attention, such as a personal visit while on a sales trip to a more lucrative account or a telephone call after all other business has been handled.

The level of each account can be determined by preparing an account "spreadsheet" (see Figure 3.5) and by discussing questionable accounts with the director of sales. When setting account levels, however, remember that your priorities may change as your accounts and prospects change. Perhaps a company that had a low potential level because of its distance from the property may expand into your area, or an association that had previously met at another hotel chain may have become dissatisfied and is now looking for another meeting place. These scenarios, which are not that uncommon, show the necessity for qualifying each account (see box titled "Home Run Key Accounts") and for personally reviewing your accounts to determine how much time and effort should be spent to realize maximum sales potential.

## Chapter 3: Organizing for Convention Sales

*Figure 3.5. KEY ACCOUNT MANAGEMENT SPREADSHEET.*

**KEY ACCOUNT MANAGEMENT SPREAD SHEET**

| Name of account and key contact | # of times account was called on last year | # of times we expect to call on account this year | Estimate of room night potential from account |
|---|---|---|---|
| Stubbs Insurance<br>Mark Steward | 4 Personal calls<br>4 Telephone calls | 5 Personal<br>5 Telephone | 25 r.n. x 12 mo. @ $75 = $22,500<br>20 r.n. x 12 mo. @ $80= $19,200<br>30r.n. x 2 days x 4 @ $72=$17,280<br>125r.n. x3 days @ $75 = $28,125<br>Total          $87,105 |

*Prioritizing accounts can be accomplished easily if a salesperson takes a look at all of his or her accounts and judges them by the same criteria. A spreadsheet, such as this one, provides a place for necessary data and enables the salesperson to see the profit potential of each account at a glance. Since each of a salesperson's 300-400 accounts are assessed, the director of sales can review the spreadsheets with salespeople on a periodic basis (usually the end or beginning of a year) to reassess priorities.*

It is also important to note that the goals set for a salesperson will affect how he or she manages accounts. Most hotels measure sales productivity and provide salespeople with bonuses and incentives based on both the amount of revenue generated and the number of room nights booked. If salespeople were measured strictly by the number of room nights booked, there would be a tendency to book business at almost any rate rather than the highest possible rate. Some properties set goals for high and low periods. In this case, a fairly low priority account may provide the business needed during a slow period -- and help achieve an individual sales goal. It is also important to maintain a balance between maintaining good customer relations and prospecting for new customers. In some cases, salespeople will have sales goals based on business from current customers and business to book from new accounts. All of these variables must be taken into consideration to most effectively manage accounts for maximum benefit.

## Evaluating the Sales Effort

To ensure that the sales office is operating at top capacity, it is necessary to periodically review both the salespeople and the organizational structure itself. Salespeople should be monitored to determine if they are meeting their personal quotas. They should also be evaluated as to how they are using their general sales abilities — are they prospecting, developing concrete leads, following up? Do they have a good service attitude? Are they managing their time properly? These evaluations should be made at least quarterly to enable sales management to control small problems that could develop into major difficulties.

Doug Kennedy, president of Kennedy Training Network, suggests creating your own "scorecard" to monitor the progress of salespeople. Topics can include:

- **Salesperson availability.** Was the salesperson available on the first call?

- **Timeliness of first response.** If the salesperson was not available, did he or she call back the same day (if the call came in before 2:00 p.m.)?

*Figure 3.5. CONTINUED*

| | KEY ACCOUNT MANAGEMENT SPREAD SHEET | | | |
|---|---|---|---|---|
| | Estimate of food and beverage potential | Estimate of meeting room revenue potential | Total potential dollar value of account | Level of account priority (Level 1 through Level 5) |
| | 40% of Room Revenue = $34,842 | 4 Workshops - Complimentary function space<br>Product Showcase - 1.00 per square foot for exhibit hall = $10,000 | Rooms $86,105<br>Food & Beverage $34,842<br>Meeting Space $10,000 | Level 1 — High Potential Account |

- **Lead-tracking detail.** Did the salesperson take copious notes to show that he or she fully investigated the "story" behind the group function?

- **Timeliness of proposal/contract.** Did the salesperson respond with a proposal and/or contract within the standard time frame (typically one business day)?

- **Personalization of correspondence.** Was all correspondence (mail, email, or text) personalized?

- **Confirmation of receipt.** Did the salesperson confirm and document receipt of the follow-up correspondence?

- **Reinforcement follow-up.** Did the salesperson follow up to express interest after the proposal was confirmed?

- **Method follow-up.** Did the salesperson alternate between phone calls and e-mails? Did he or she follow-up at least three times unless asked not to by the client?

- **Long-term follow-up.** If a sale was not secured but the prospect could potentially generate future business, was the sales lead retraced to an appropriate future follow-up action step?[6]

### Home Run Key Accounts

In most situations, there are a few accounts on which you should concentrate, because these key accounts can have an immediate impact on your business. *Home run accounts* are those accounts that are likely to generate the greatest revenue.

To manage accounts properly, you must *fully qualify* the contact. Full qualification involves gathering all information necessary to place a dollar value on the account's potential business. For example, a corporation contact might state they average 25 room nights per month for their own executives, another 20 room nights for visiting clients, quarterly two-day workshops for 30 persons, and a large new product showcase annually, requiring 125 guestrooms for the three-day event. From this information, it is now possible to estimate the potential dollar volume the account represents for your hotel (see Figure 3.5).

New salespeople should be reviewed more frequently than quarterly to ensure that they are "on track." To assist in evaluations, each salesperson should maintain a **reader file**. This file contains copies of all correspondence and call reports generated by a salesperson. Each salesperson's reader file should be evaluated weekly by the director of sales.

The organizational structure of the sales office should also be reviewed to determine if the current structure make the most of the strengths of the staff and contributes to the property's bottom line. This involves taking a look at a number of factors. Are lines of communication open with both the sales staff and other departments on the property? Has authority been clearly delegated — and is the scope of that authority understood? Are duties and responsibilities being carried out? Is sales follow-up — correspondence, telephone calls, etc. — being handled properly? Is there an adequate support staff?

## Sales Records and Filing Systems

When selling, especially to groups, sales personnel need up-to-date information that is easily accessible. Vast amounts of client information must be documented and filed, if sales records are to be meaningful. It is important that the needed information can be located quickly. Therefore, every hotel sales department must have an efficient system in place for storing and accessing account information.

In this section, we will discuss how sales records are stored and some of the basic components of a hotel filing system. Later in the chapter, we will introduce various forms inherent to the sales function, show how computer technology is being used to manage the service function, and learn how technology is increasingly employed to enhance sales efforts and profitability.

### Hotel Filing Systems

The late C. Dewitt Coffman stated that "the maintenance of accurate and up-to-date file systems is the single most important mechanical operation of any sales department. Without minutely accurate file records, the sales department is without ammunition." Today's file systems are far more sophisticated than the manual systems used in the past, but they share some basic principles to ensure that hotel salespeople have the "ammunition" they need to properly sell to groups.

**Methods of Filing.** Although today's computerized systems allow salespeople to access accounts by a number of criteria, including account number, name, key word, and other specialized searches, some properties also keep hard copies of the paperwork generated in selling and servicing an account. An **account file** serves as the basic business record for the group, so it should include all the basic forms needed for the sales function as well as additional information, such as correspondence, past convention programs, and so on (Exhibit 3.6 on the next page shows the type of file used in a manual system; account-related materials are scanned into computerized files).

Files used by hotels are generally filed using one of three methods:

1. If *alphabetical filing* is used, accounts are filed by name order. This method is considered the easiest method of filing.

2. When the exact name of an organization is not known, *key word of the title filing* may be used. Files are identified by one or more words that describe the account (filing under "petroleum" or "oil," for example).

3. *Numerical filing*, in which accounts are assigned a designated account number, is commonly used with today's computerized filing systems, al though hard copy files can also be stored in numerical order.

*Figure 3.6. SAMPLE ACCOUNT FILE.*

**CLIPS**     **FILE FOLDER**

Front Sheet    Sales Reports

**Left Side**
- Front Sheet
- Booking Agreements
- Function Sheets

**Right Side**
- Sales Correspondence
- Call Reports
- Proposal Letter
- Contract or Letter of Agreement

Color-coded file folder labels are frequently used on account files to distinguish market segments.

Green..................................................................Corporate meetings
Red......................................................................Associations
Orange................................................................Incentive groups
Yellow..................................................................SMERF groups
Blue.....................................................................Tour and Travel

FOLDER — GENERAL MOTORS — GREEN STRIPE / FILE FOLDER LABEL
CORPORATE ACCOUNT NAME

*The account file is usually kept in a standard file folder and contains all of the group's information, including sales call reports, tentative and definite booking information, function sheets from past business, and correspondence generated relating to the booking. Information is placed in the file in chronological order (with the newest on top) and secured with clips to prevent loss.*

    Color-coded tabs are sometimes used on account folders for easy reference; a red tab can be placed on a large corporate account, for example, while an incentive group can be easily identified by a blue tab. And, to ensure that the sales staff can keep track of a file's whereabouts, a guide card detailing the name of the group, its file number, the date of removal, and the initials of the person requesting the file should be placed in the file drawer when a file is removed from the file cabinet.

    Any new information should promptly be placed into the file folder and/or scanned to be included in the computerized file. And, of course, computerized files should be backed up (to an external source) on a regular basis to ensure that the latest information is available in the event of computer problems.

**Elements of Filing Systems.** While filing systems will vary slightly from hotel to hotel, sales records always include the account file, a master card file, and a working file. The **master card** serves as a summary for the sales effort. It details such information as contact names and titles, addresses, telephone numbers, month or months in which the group meets, the size of the group, where it has met in the past, who makes the initial and final site decision, and other pertinent information.

The computerized version of the master card file enables the salesperson to instantly access the account and add an unlimited amount of material to each account file. The file can be broken down into several screens (or windows) that provide a variety of additional information: account history, name of contact person, etc. (see Figure 3.7). Using a computerized master card file eliminates the need to make copious notes on an index card, and necessary information is immediately available on a computer terminal.

After a group books into your hotel ("goes definite"), a **working file** is created. Unlike an account file, the working file contains only the information relevant to the event. This information typically includes room setups, banquet menus, guestroom blocks and any other specifics requested by the group. The departments involved in the execution of the event (convention services, banquets, reservations) are given direct access to this file. In a computerized system, the information is scanned into the working file. If a manual system is used, a hard copy file is created and materials are broken down and placed into the account file after the event.

If a manual system is used, it is also customary to set up a **tickler file**, also known as a *trace file*, *bring-up file*, or *follow-up file*, to remind salespeople keep in touch with account contacts through telephone calls, correspondence, or visits. Tickler files typically used dividers marked for each day of the month (index cards, correspondence, or other notes detailing the action to be taken were inserted behind the date on which the action was to be taken); accordion-style files with pockets designated by date were also sometimes used. After the action was taken, the reminder was removed from the file. This type of system eliminated reliance on memory and ensured proper follow-up.

Several computerized versions of the tickler file are available. Specialized hotel software, such as Delphi, not only reminds salespeople of important dates, but also offers additional sales tools. The computerized trace report shown in Figure 3.8, for example, breaks down the day's business into several categories. The salesperson can take advantage of this to prioritize his or her work and schedule each day to make the most of sales opportunities. But even salespeople who do not have access to hotel-specific software can utilize other programs, such as Microsoft Outlook, to help organize their work. The Outlook program features a daily calendar and task list, and today's salespeople also have the option of using reminders entered into the hotel's sales system or entered into their mobile devices.

## Control Books and Sales Forms

In addition to files, the sales office utilizes a number of control books and sales forms in selling to and servicing the group sales business.

**Control Books.** The "bible" of the sales department is the hotel's **function book**. A function book, which is an essential tool to eliminate **double bookings** and ensure that space is available for a group's events, consists of a page (manual system) or a screen (computerized system) for every day of the year. Function book entries include such information as:

- The name of the organization or person requesting space

Chapter 3: Organizing for Convention Sales

*Figure 3.7. COMPUTERIZED MASTER CARD FILES.*

This computerized version of the account master card enables the salesperson to instantly access the account — and add an unlimited amount of material to each account's file. The file can be broken down into several screens (or windows) which provide a variety of additional information — account history, name of contact person, etc. Using a computerized master card file eliminates the need to make copious notes on an index card — and the need to spend a great deal of time in locating the necessary information (it can all be done at the salesperson's desk).
**Source:** Delphi/Newmarket Software Systems, Inc., Portsmouth, New Hampshire. For more information, browse the company's website at www.newmarketinc.com.

- The contact person (name, title, address, telephone)
- Type of function
- Time required for the event
- Total time required (for setup, breakdown, cleanup)
- Number of attendees
- Type of setup required
- Rates charged
- Contract status
- Other remarks

There should be at least one section for each meeting or function room, with space to cover specific time periods in each day. To eliminate possible errors, only one person should be given control of the function book. This may be the convention sales manager, or, at properties with a large staff, the senior sales executive. Single-person control of the function book is essential; convention space cannot be sold efficiently without this control.

There may be instances in which the same space is desired by two groups. In this case, sales managers will try to determine the best "fit" for both the hotel and the group. Factors to be considered are the likelihood that the space will actually be filled, the estimated profitability of each group, the status of the group (regular client or new business), the likelihood of repeat business, the long-term profitability of each group, the possibility that one group would consider an alternate date, and the group's convention history.

In addition to controlling meeting space, it is also necessary to control guestrooms. Properties use a **guestrooms control book**, which is sometimes referred to as the *rooms control bible*, to ensure that an adequate number of guestrooms are available for the group. The guestrooms control book is used by the sales department to stay aware of the number of rooms it can sell, as hotels often stipulate a maximum *group allotment* — the number of rooms available for sale to groups — to ensure that a proper market mix of group, tour and travel, and individual guest business is maintained. Demand fluctuates by time of year and by day of week, so the group room allotment varies considerably. For example, the summer months are generally soft convention months, so a 400-room hotel might only do 25 percent of its business with meeting groups and 75 percent with individual travelers.

Although these percentages may be reversed in the typically busy convention periods of spring or fall, hotels rarely, if ever, will sell the entire hotel to convention groups. Individual corporate and leisure travelers are consistent year-round producers, and selling out to a convention will alienate travelers displaced by convention groups.

The guestrooms control book's format usually consists of monthly report pages or screens with space for the group's name and guestroom commitment by day. These forecast pages or screens provide projections for several years ahead. Some guestrooms control books also separate definite from tentative bookings on the screen.

As with the function book, one person should have control of the guestrooms control book, although information is shared with other departments.

It is extremely important for the hotel sales office and the front desk/reservations department to have good communication and contact with one another. Because both are booking business, it is imperative that room sales are not overlapped. Traditionally, reservations has reported to the front office manager, but reservations are increasingly being placed under the sales department in many convention-oriented hotels.

Most hotels have computerized their function and guestrooms control books (see Figure 3.9.). This method still provides control, since only authorized personnel can add or change information (while information is being changed, the system goes into a "read only"

*Figure 3.8. SAMPLE TICKER (TRACE) REPORT – COMPUTERIZED SYSTEM.*

## The Durham Resort
Morning Report for Ralph Johnson
September 21, 20XX

### Rooming List Due

| Group Name | Date | Day | Room Type | Agree | Block | Pickup | New Block |
|---|---|---|---|---|---|---|---|
| Mt. Hope Radiology Dept. | 2/ 2/xx | Wed | Run of House | 25 | 25 | _____ | _____ |
|  | 2/ 3/xx | Thu | Run of House | 25 | 25 | _____ | _____ |
|  | 2/ 4/xx | Fri | Run of House | 300 | 300 | _____ | _____ |
|  | 2/18/xx | Fri | Run of House | 25 | 25 | _____ | _____ |

### Deposits Due

| Group Name | Arrival Date | Trace Date | New Status/ New Trace Date |
|---|---|---|---|
| Acorn Dry Cleaning | 3/20/xx | 1/10/xx | _____  ___/___/___ |

### Verbal Definites - Contract Due

| Group Name | Arrival Date | Trace Date | New Status/ New Trace Date |
|---|---|---|---|
| Jacobs Wedding | 9/1/xx | 1/15/xx | _____  ___/___/___ |

### Tentatives - Decision Due

| Group Name | Arrival Date | Trace Date | New Status/ New Trace Date |
|---|---|---|---|
| Automobile Travelers Assn | 3/24/xx | 11/20/xx | ___/ ___/___/___ |
| Arizona Building Company | 4/30/xx | 12/20/xx | ___/ ___/___/___ |

### Leads - Decision Due

| Group Name | Arrival Date | Trace Date | New Status/ New Trace Date |
|---|---|---|---|
| Balloon Industries | 2/1/xx | 11/1/xx | _____/ ___/___/___ |

Source: Delphi Newmarket Software Systems, Inc., Durham, New Hampshire

*This report not only replaces the cumbersome manual tickler file, but also offers additional sales tools to the salesperson. The tickle or trace report, for example, breaks down the day's business into several categories. The salesperson can take advantage of this feature to prioritize work and schedule each day to make the most of sales opportunities.*

*Figure 3.9. COMPUTERIZED FUNCTION BOOK.*

## THE RIVERVIEW HOTEL

Date printed: October 1, 20__     Time printed: 11:59 AM

**DELPHI — Function Space Profile**     Page: 1

Report for Oct 1 20__ to Oct 31 20__

| Room Name | Time Period | We 1 | Th 2 | Fr 3 | Sa 4 | Su 5 | Mo 6 | Tu 7 | We 8 | Th 9 | Fr 10 | Sa 11 | Su 12 | Mo 13 | Tu 14 | We 15 | Th 16 | Fr 17 | Sa 18 | Su 19 | Mo 20 | Tu 21 | We 22 | Th 23 | Fr 24 | Sa 25 | Su 26 | Mo 27 | Tu 28 | We 29 | Th 30 | Fr 31 |
|---|---|---|---|---|---|---|---|---|---|---|---|---|---|---|---|---|---|---|---|---|---|---|---|---|---|---|---|---|---|---|---|---|
| WASHINTN | M/L/A/E | | | | D/D/D | D/D | D | | D | D | D | | | D | D | | | | T/T/T/T | T/T/T/T | T/T/T/T | | | | | | | | | | | |
| ADAMS | M/L/A/E | | | | T/T | T/T | T/T | T/T | | | | | | | | | | | DD | DD | | | DD | DD | | | | | | | | |
| JEFFERSON | M/L/A/E | | | | D | D | D | | VD | VD | VD | VD/VD | VD/VD | VD/VD | | | | | | | | | | | | | | | | | | |
| MADISON | M/L/A/E | | | | | | VD/VD | VD/VD | VD/VD | VD/VD | | | T | T/T | T/T | T/T | | | DD | DD/DD | DD | | | | T/T | T/T | T/T | | | | |
| MONROE | M/L/A/E | | | | | | | | | | | | | | T/T/T/T | T/T/T/T | T/T/T/T | | | | | | | | | | | | | | |
| JACKSON | M/L/A/E | | | | VD/VD | VD/VD | VD/VD | | | | D/D | D/D | D/D | | | | | | | | | | | | | | | | | | |

continued

*Many hotels are using computerized function and guestrooms control books to provide instant access to information by sales personnel, who must often provide an immediate answer regarding the availability of function space or rooms. These reports are very similar to the manual reports kept by some hotels. The main difference is that the computer generates these reports automatically by using booking information already entered into the system. These sample reports were generated by Delphi System, software specifically designed to meet the needs of the hotel industry. (continued on next page)*

mode until the information is updated). However, the information is readily available to salespeople, either in-house or from a remote location.

Before Hyatt Hotels updated their function books, Gordon Kerr, former communications technology manager at Hyatt Hotels Corporation, said:

> Each hotel kept this giant diary with function room bookings written in it. If a customer called Hyatt headquarters in Chicago to book a function room in San Francisco, for example, the manager of the San Francisco hotel had to be called to check availability. Customers eager to book space would wait hours, or even days, to receive a reply. By that time, many would-be customers had found space elsewhere. With the comput-

*Figure 3.9. (continued) COMPUTERIZED GUESTROOMS CONTROL BOOK.*

### THE RIVERVIEW HOTEL

Date printed: August 27, 20___      Time printed: 11:41 AM

**DELPHI — Group rooms Control Report for 20___ June**

| | 1 Sun | 2 Mon | 3 Tue | 4 Wed | 5 Thur | 6 Fri | 27 Fri | 28 Sat | 29 Sun | 30 Mon | Total Rooms | Total Guests | Ave. Rate | Room Revenue | Decision Date | RT | SRC | Stat | Date Entered |
|---|---|---|---|---|---|---|---|---|---|---|---|---|---|---|---|---|---|---|---|
| **DEFINITES for CORP.** | | | | | | | | | | | | | | | | | | | |
| D.E.C. | | | | | | | | | | | 500 | 500 | 124.00 | 62,000.00 | 8/27/96 | | TRB | D | 8/27/96 |
| Mass Bay Co | | | | | | | | | | | 200 | 200 | 118.00 | 23,600.00 | 8/27/96 | | TRB | D | 8/27/96 |
| I.B.M. | | | | | | | | | | | 90 | 90 | 125.00 | 11,250.00 | 8/27/96 | | TRB | D | 8/27/96 |
| Coastal Inc. | | | | | | | | | | | 15 | 15 | 128.00 | 1,920.00 | | | TRB | D | 2/13/96 |
| CORP. | 0 | 0 | 0 | 0 | 0 | 0 | 0 | 0 | 0 | 0 | 805 | 820 | 122.69 | 98,770.00 | | | | D | |
| **TENTATIVES for CORP.** | | | | | | | | | | | | | | | | | | | |
| Lotus Dev. Co. | | | 5 | 5 | 5 | 5 | | | | | 20 | 40 | 145.00 | 2,900.00 | 8/27/96 | | SB | T | 8/27/96 |
| Crimson Trvl | | | | | | 6 | | | | | 24 | 48 | 118.00 | 2,832.00 | 8/27/96 | | RWH | T | 8/27/96 |
| Eastern Inc. | | | | | | | | | | | 35 | 70 | 130.00 | 4,550.00 | 8/27/96 | | RWH | T | 8/27/96 |
| Lotus Dev. Co. | | | | | | | | | | | 15 | 30 | 121.00 | 1,815.00 | 8/27/96 | | RWH | T | 8/27/96 |
| Intel Corp. | | | | | | | | | | | 9 | 27 | 121.00 | 1,089.00 | 8/27/96 | | | | |
| Eastern Inc. | | | | | | | | | | | 4 | 4 | 145.00 | 580.00 | 8/27/96 | | | | |
| CORP. | 0 | 0 | 5 | 5 | 5 | 11 | 0 | 0 | 0 | 0 | 107 | 223 | 128.65 | 13,766.00 | | | | T | |
| **DEFINITES for Assoc.** | | | | | | | | | | | | | | | | | | | |
| Travel Assoc. | 25. | 25 | 25 | | | | | | | | 75 | 75 | 108.00 | 8,100.00 | 9/30/96 | | KL | D | 3/10/96 |
| N.A.F.E. | | | | | | | | | | | 30 | 60 | 127.00 | 3,810.00 | 8/12/96 | | CRW | DD | 8/12/96 |
| U.S.ASSOC. | | | | | | | | | | | 120 | 240 | 120.00 | 14,400.00 | 8/1/96 | | TS | D | 8/10/96 |
| U.S.ASSOC. | | | | | | | 7 | 7 | 7 | 7 | 63 | 126 | 112.00 | 7,056.00 | | | TS | D | 8/10/96 |
| U.S.ASSOC. | | | | | | | 5 | | | | 20 | 20 | 120.00 | 2,400.00 | | | | | |
| ASSOC. | 25 | 25 | 25 | 0 | 0 | 0 | 17 | 7 | 7 | 7 | 308 | 521 | 116.12 | 35,766.00 | | | | D | |
| **TENTATIVES for ASSOC.** | | | | | | | | | | | | | | | | | | | |
| Vets Assoc. | 2 | 2 | 2 | | | | | | | | 6 | 12 | 121.00 | 726.00 | 8/25/96 | | TRB | T | 8/25/96 |
| N.A.R.R.P. | 10 | 10 | | | | | | | | | 20 | 40 | 120.00 | 2,200.00 | 8/25/96 | | TRB | T | 8/25/96 |
| Data Systems | | | 6 | 6 | 6 | 6 | | | | | 48 | 96 | 131.00 | 6,288.00 | 8/25/96 | | TRB | T | 8/25/96 |
| D.P.A. | | | 10 | 10 | 10 | | | | | | 30 | 60 | 145.00 | 4,350.00 | 8/25/96 | | TRB | T | 8/25/96 |
| Mutual Assoc. | | | | | 3 | 3 | | | | | 24 | 48 | 131.00 | 3,144.00 | 8/25/96 | | TRB | T | 8/25/96 |
| Mont Ward Co. | | | | | | | | | | | 40 | 80 | 100.00 | 4,000.00 | 6/24/96 | | EP | T | 6/24/96 |
| Newsweek | | | | | | | | | | | 16 | 32 | 131.00 | 2,096.00 | 8/25/96 | | RWH | T | 8/25/96 |
| N.A.F.E. | | | | | | | | | | | 36 | 72 | 127.00 | 4,572.00 | 8/12/96 | | TRB | T | 8/25/96 |
| Int'l Assoc. | | | | | | | | | | | 8 | 16 | 118.00 | 944.00 | 8/25/96 | | TRB | T | 8/25/96 |
| Womens Assoc. | | | | | | | | | | | 4 | 8 | 110.00 | 440.00 | 8/25/96 | | TRB | T | 8/25/96 |
| Manufact. Assn | | | | | | | | | | | 48 | 96 | 127.00 | 6,096.00 | 8/25/96 | | TRB | T | 8/25/96 |
| N.A.T.C.O. | | | | | | | 45 | | | | 270 | 540 | 234.00 | 63,180.00 | 8/25/96 | | TRB | T | 8/25/96 |
| Dental Assoc. | | | | | | | | 2 | 2 | | 4 | 8 | 110.00 | 440.00 | 8/25/96 | | TRB | T | 8/25/96 |
| Central Assoc. | | | | | | | | | 30 | 30 | 60 | 120 | 120.00 | 7,200.00 | 8/25/96 | | TRB | T | 8/25/96 |
| US Yacht Club | | | | | | | | | 4 | 4 | 8 | 16 | 131.00 | 1,048.00 | 8/25/96 | | TRB | T | 8/25/96 |
| ASSOC. | 12 | 12 | 18 | 16 | 19 | 9 | 45 | 2 | 36 | 34 | 622 | 1244 | 171.58 | 106,724.00 | | | | T | |

*(Continued from preceding page) Tentative and definite bookings in the function book and guestroom control book are monitored on a regular basis. At the weekly sales meeting, discussion will center on booking activity and how to best manage the guestroom and function space inventory. The computerized function and guestrooms control books will help the sales team to look at business on the books and manage it for the benefit of both the hotel and meeting planners.*

erized system, Hyatt users can check availability and book function rooms at any connected hotel from any hotel in the network.[7]

Wendy Bonvechio, global account executive for Marriott International, says:

> Automation is very important to our business. A problem that has been completely eliminated is the inevitable double booking that occurred with the manual systems. With automation, the computer won't allow

you to double book. Our customers demand automation because it is quicker, makes us more efficient, and virtually eliminates mistakes. It's no longer an option, but a necessity in order to compete in today's market.[8]

**Sales Forms.** Once a sales commitment has been made, there are a number of forms used to follow the sale to the final execution of the function. The *tentative booking sheet* (or report) is used if a date has not been confirmed or if details have not been worked out.

In the normal sequence of events, a convention organizer may inquire about the availability of the property on certain dates. Requirements are discussed, but perhaps there are circumstances that must be resolved before setting a definite date. Perhaps board approval is needed or, in the case of a corporate meeting, a supervisor must be consulted. The meeting planner then asks for an **option** on the space, and a *hold* is placed on the room(s).

This means that the hotel has agreed to hold the space pending final confirmation by the client. Some properties are cautious about tentative bookings; they do not want to lose out on other business while protecting a tentative account that may not "go definite." That is why it is important to limit the length of the hold by designating an *option date.* An option date is the date by which the client must confirm the order or release the space. If this period is too long, the hotel has severely limited its freedom to seek another customer, but the date should be long enough to enable the client to secure the necessary approval. A typical first option agreement might read:

> This tentative room block is being held on a first option basis until [date]. Following this period, all space outlined above will become subject to availability unless prior arrangements for an extension have been made.

A *definite booking form* is used after business has been confirmed. It is processed when a contract or letter of agreement has been signed and when the business is scheduled for a specific date. The form includes a number of details needed to properly service the function, such as the number of attendees, setup requirements, etc. The date and details will be entered into the function book (and guestrooms control book, if required).

After the convention is booked, other forms may also be necessary. In some cases, details such as a date, room requirement, or guestroom figure may change. It is then necessary to complete a *change form* to ensure that these changes are made. There may be many times when a piece of business which was considered definite is cancelled. In such a case, a *cancellation form* must be filed. Since there may be a number of reasons for the cancellation, some properties follow up the cancellation form with a *lost business report* that details the reason for the cancellation.

Some properties use a general form that eliminates the use of several of these forms. And, in addition to these general sales office forms, salespeople also utilize a number of forms for their individual use to track their progress in selling to accounts. These forms will be discussed in Chapter 7, where we take a look at specific selling techniques.

## Sales Office Automation

Over the past several years, there have been dramatic changes in the way hotels do business. Today's advanced technology has eliminated much of the "drudge work" that was an inherent part of the sales effort. Paperwork that used to be done by hand (notes about sales calls and account requirements, for example), taking hours to prepare, update, and analyze, is now readily available by calling up a screen on a computer terminal. In this section, we will take a look at how the computer is drastically changing the face of the sales office — how it is not only helping to eliminate time-consuming paperwork, but how it is being used to personalize presentations, create lists of potential contacts, and forecast future demand for guestrooms and meeting rooms.

## Advantages of Automation

Hospitality industry professionals agree that up to 70 percent of a salesperson's time can be spent on non-sales activities, such as call tracing, checking the availability of rooms, blocking rooms and space — and simply running back and forth to filing cabinets to retrieve information if a manual system is used. The computer has changed all that. No longer is it necessary to search for lost files or prepare reports by hand; this data is readily available on individual computer terminals.

In addition, the computer frees salespeople from the office. If a salesperson is out making calls, information can be accessed by other salespeople or the clerical staff if immediate action is required. And, pertinent information (often in the form of reports) is instantly available to other departments requiring it (the banquet/catering department, reservations, etc.).

Computers make it easy to "personalize" important documents such as contracts and correspondence. They also simplify mass mailings, generating mailing labels (often by zip code or group type) in a fraction of the time it would take a secretary to sort through records and type labels to specified target groups.

In addition to direct mail, there are several programs that can help to manage e-mail marketing campaigns. ZDirect (www.zdirect.com), for example, offers programs to set up initial e-mails and follow-through with e-mail messages at specific intervals, whether or not there is a response. If an offer sent to meeting planners does not get a response, a follow-up e-mail is sent at a specific date; if a meeting planner shows interest, the initial e-mail is followed-up by an additional e-mail providing any requested information, and/or an e-mail to a salesperson to contact the planner. Hotel automated management systems such as these can also be used to generate surveys, reply to negative feedback, and direct potential customers to meaningful landing pages on the property's website.

Computers are also used to manage sales efforts and evaluate the progress of both the sales department and individual salespeople. Software for sales management includes Hotel SalesPro® (www.hotelsalespro.com), which is used by over 3,000 hospitality properties, convention centers, private clubs, and golf courses. The system's capabilities range from producing all sales-related documents; to tracking accounts by status, market segment, or other key value; and reviewing group rates by utilizing the group rate manager. These features not only improve response time, they also reduce the time spent on administrative functions and routine paperwork, allowing salespeople to spend more time selling.

## New Advances in Hotel Computer Systems

Hotels have been using computer systems for booking reservations for many years, but only recently have sales offices been automated to provide up-to-date information to salespeople and sales management. Tim Grover, regional director of sales and marketing for Starwood Hotels & Resorts Worldwide, states:

For any hotel sales force, automation is critical. Delphi (software for hotel sales and catering) controls more than 80 percent of the market; it is considered the 'Microsoft' of hotel sales and catering systems. They have a Windows-based version for managing sales contracts, group room blocks, and catering space. It is also user-friendly and can generate a variety of reports. Delphi software also functions as an excellent contact manager. Every conversation with a client about an event is documented and accessible to our entire sales team. And, finally, it helps us manage our revenue more efficiently. Knowing what's on the books at any given time for both room sales and catering is a valuable asset that benefits both the customer and the hotel.[9]

While there are dozens of firms that offer hotel sales and catering software, the leader in the market (as mentioned above) is Delphi, by Newmarket, Inc. Delphi Sales and Catering software is used by over 70,000 sales and catering professionals worldwide, and its influence continues to grow with the implementation of mobile apps; at the time of this writing, the latest version was Delphi 2015, which allows users to access N2GO on their mobile devices. Some of the components of the Delphi system include:

- **Sales Management.** A dashboard overview of the activities and progress toward sales goals by the property, its sales teams, and individual salespeople.

- **Account and Contact Management.** Allows for viewing and updating of accounts and contacts and for sharing this information with other properties within the chain.

- **Availability and Inventory Control.** Provides an in-depth look at the function book (Function Diary) and guestrooms control book (Group Room Control) to search for and book available space.

- **Business (Booking) Management.** Streamlines booking activity and the use of booking data.

- **Catering and Event Management.** Creates and manages such forms as the Banquet Event Order (BEO) and assists in the implementation of menus, pricing, and banquet checks (we will discuss this application further in Chapter 12).

Because the Delphi Sales and Catering system is used by so many hospitality properties, the company has created Delphi in the Classroom, a series of courses that can be taken by students to acquaint them with the program prior to seeking a position in hotel sales. A number of colleges and universities offer these courses to give their students a competitive edge (you can visit www.delphiintheclassroom.com to see the types of courses offered and the participating educational institutions).

Several other companies, including Cvent, offer certification programs. Cvent operates Cvent University, which provides training and certification to students enrolled in hospitality courses; professors have the options of making Cvent certification available through in-person workshops, self-guided online courses, and onsite courses. We will discuss Cvent in detail later in the text, but you can log on to www.cvent.com to learn more about the program.

In addition to providing easier access to account information, we have also seen how computers are being used to eliminate the large amount of paperwork generated by the sales department. One of the most important ways in which computers are being used, however, is to assist the sales department in organizing and analyzing information about meeting groups. Database management programs provide a way to keep a service history of all client bookings, including the expected and actual number of attendees, the number of guestrooms booked, the types of functions booked, average room rate and average check, etc.

Having this vast amount of information readily available makes it easy for salespeople to target specific groups. This data not only makes it easy for a salesperson to determine which groups meet in his or her area of the country, for example, but it also facilitates building relationships, as the salesperson can determine what factors are most important to each of these groups. This technique, which is called **database marketing**, is invaluable for serving both current customers and finding exactly the right customer mix for your property (see box below titled "The Hidden Opportunities with Database Marketing").

---

### THE HIDDEN OPPORTUNITIES WITH DATABASE MARKETING

Database marketing allows hotels to develop personal long-term bonds with customers. Sometimes called relationship marketing or loyalty marketing, this approach departs from the mass marketing that has long been used to reach meeting planners. Few industries maintain the information about their customers that hotels keep — files that not only indicate guest requirements but make it easy to identify customers for future communications. Every hotel has account files, including information on past groups and registration cards from individual guests. The most frequently asked question is, "How long do we keep these records?" A more important question is, "What can the information in these files do for us?" The history in these files is the foundation for database marketing.

As competition has heated up in the past five or ten years, hotel operators have scrutinized marketing expenditures more carefully than ever. What they have learned is that *it's five to seven times more expensive to acquire new guests than it is to retain existing ones.* Your best customers are those who have purchased recently, purchase frequently, and deliver the greatest contribution to revenue.

Guest folios, registration cards, and group history on meeting planners form the core of your database; they allow you to personalize service to meet guest needs, thereby improving the guest experience and reinforcing loyalty.

Hotels typically use database marketing to analyze travel and spending patterns of market segments. Database programs allow you to easily trace and maintain customer controls, call up any customer record quickly, generate call-back schedules, follow-up letters and mailings, as well as mail merge to individuals or a large number of customers.

Establishing relationships and a dialogue with customers is fast becoming a requirement for survival in the hotel industry. Whether a hotel continues to rely solely on its guest history system or decides to invest the time and money in a more sophisticated database system, one thing is certain: Hotel managers who know the most about customers and are able to harness resources for quick response to threats and opportunities will enjoy a tremendous advantage in the competitive decade ahead. If you cannot move quickly enough, your competitor across the street surely will.

**Contributed by Cindy Estis Green, former CEO of The Estis Group, a board member of the HSMAI Foundation, and co-founder and CEO of Kalibri Labs, LLC, a data modeling and consulting firm.**

## The "Virtual" Office

Besides eliminating much of the drudgery of keeping records and accessing the information necessary to sell to and service meetings business, technology is playing an increasing role in improving the efficiency of property salespeople. No longer does it take days to answer inquiries or check date availability. Nor do salespeople have to sell from their own property. Many of today's salespeople are using technological advances to create "virtual offices" — Armed with a laptop computer, tablet, or notebook, and their smartphone. Today's hotel salespeople are free to go where the business is — while still maintaining close contact with their home property. One of the earliest "personal digital assistants" (PDAs) was the BlackBerry, which provided features including a calendar, address book, task list, and memo pad. It also offered a Corporate Data Access feature that provided access to a property's customer relationship management (CRM) database and other pertinent corporate information.

Today, there are several models of PDAs available, but an increasing number of salespeople are using their smartphones for their sales efforts. Today's compact, sophisticated smartphones make it possible to talk to a client while surfing the web for information (or connecting to the hotel's sales department files via a dedicated web page), and a number of other features and apps can be downloaded to facilitate the selling process. Not only does the smartphone offer e-mail and texting capabilities, but it has also eliminated the need to carry an address book, a voice and/or video recorder or camera, and a translation device (several translation services can be accessed over the web).

The most popular smartphone models are equipped with voice command technology. Siri, which is advertised as a "digital assistant," is available on iPhone models 4S and above; it allows the salesperson to accomplish such tasks as sending text messages, scheduling appointments, adding calendar entries, and doing Google searches by voice command. Samsung began offering S-Voice on its Galaxy S3 models; billed as an "intelligent personal assistant," the voice commands are activated with a simple "Hi Galaxy." Google Now is available on Android 4.1 and above phones, and can be used for a number of search functions (weather, navigation, calculate and convert, answer questions). BlackBerry 10 Voice Control (available on Blackberry OS10 and above) offers the "basics" – making calls, sending emails and text messages, booking meetings and appointments, and changing Facebook status and making Tweets, as well as saving notes and memos in BlackBerry Remember.

These technologies have resulted in a growing number of hotel salespeople who work from their homes. Starwood, for example, estimates that about half of its 100 salespeople selling its Sheraton brand are home-based, and this trend is expected to continue.[10]

*Laptop computers* have been the main component of a virtual office. While they are portable enough to be carried in a briefcase, they provide the capability of tapping into the property or chain's computer system to check for room availability, rates, and other information needed by potential clients. Most are equipped with fax modems, enabling the salesperson to check availability, generate a reply or proposal for the meeting planner, and immediately fax the document to the customer. Smaller mobile devices, such as tablets and notebooks, are gaining in popularity. One drawback to using a mobile device is the size of the screen, so many hotels today are also developing a mobile presence that enables needed information to be easily read on the smaller screens (many properties offer both traditional and mobile websites for their customers, as well).

Swissôtel, a hotel chain with properties in the United States, Europe, Asia, and the Middle East, was one of the first hospitality firms to "go virtual." Their United States national account team was equipped with laptop computers and accompanying PDAs to enable salespeople to get immediate availability and rate information. The laptops were also used to send and receive faxes and, since they stored property photos and detailed information about guestrooms and meeting space, they were also used to create customized presentations for meeting planners.

Former Swissôtel president and CEO Andreas Meinhold said of the system:

> In a sense, Swissôtel has packed its bag and taken itself on the road using specially adapted laptops and connectivity links. Because our salespeople are tapped into the property-management system, they're able to operate out of their virtual office as if they were behind the front desk of any Swissôtel.
>
> Our account managers will be able to spend their time just selling, not focusing on administrative tasks. They can work when they want and where they want, and really spend their time focusing on our customers' needs.[11]

*Electronic mail (e-mail)* offers a number of advantages to salespeople. First is its speed. No longer does it take days to send correspondence to a client and wait for a reply. With e-mail, the salesperson can send off a message or proposal, get a reply, and respond to the reply within a short period of time (unlike telephone messages, e-mail can be directly responded to as soon as it is received; there is no need to talk to the home office, hang up the phone, and look for and dial the client's number). Second, although it is private, a number of the same messages may be sent to different contacts at one time (if a salesperson wants to get the word out about a new promotion, for example, the message can be generated once and e-mailed to several potential customers). Third, e-mail allows for flexibility. A number of messages — either the same or different — can be generated at one sitting and one or all can be sent at the same time. Conversely, an e-mail recipient can pick up all of his or her e-mail messages at once and respond as time and priorities allow. Last, but certainly not least, is the versatility of e-mail. E-mail communications can range from a short note requesting specific information to a large file of text and graphics; even software applications can be transferred via e-mail.

One disadvantage to e-mail is that meeting planners' inboxes are often filled with unsolicited messages. In order for your e-mail to be seen, you should include any pertinent information in its title ("The information you requested from the XYZ Hotel," for example). To eliminate e-mail clutter, some meeting planners prefer text messages. Text messages can be sent directly to one planner, but texting also offers the opportunity to reach several recipients simultaneously. Like e-mail, text messages offer the opportunity to insert pertinent data into texts, but they also have the advantage of going directly to the meeting planner's smartphone for immediate attention.

Former devices such as memo machines and electronic dictionaries and translators are increasingly being replaced by compact mobile devices that are equipped with all the tools necessary to do business. These advances can enhance efficiency and professionalism and give the salesperson more time do what he or she was hired to do — sell rooms and meeting space by going where the business is and focusing on the needs of potential clients.

Mike Mulcahy, the global account director for Dolce Hotels and Resorts, reflects on his "on the road" sales activity during his tenure as a sales manager for the Sheraton City Centre in Washington, D.C. Armed with his laptop and BlackBerry, he would spend four days a week soliciting meetings business in New York City. He felt that the arrangement was beneficial to both the hotel and the meeting planner, explaining:

> The bottom line is, I'm giving the planner more personal service by being here and meeting with them — there's nothing like being there and re-

## Chapter 3: Organizing for Convention Sales

viewing room availability on-screen with the client. And, not only that, but taking it a step further and generating the contract and having them sign before you leave. The level of immediacy is far greater.

## Additional Uses of Automation

In addition to automating sales records and enhancing the effectiveness of the property's salespeople, the computer and other facets of today's technology are being used to boost productivity and increase efficiency by:

- Generating daily, weekly, and monthly reports
- Providing rooms and equipment inventory
- Generating mailing lists, contracts, and proposals
- Personalization and yield/revenue management capabilities are also important additional uses of automation

**Personalization.** In terms of word processing, the computer age has also ushered in an age of personalization. Today's meeting planners want to be more than an account number. Computer databases make it easy to personalize correspondence and even routine contracts to meet this need.

Some of the advantages of using word processing, with a special emphasis on personalization, include:

- Letters need to be written only once and can be stored on file for future use.
- Spelling can be verified with the system's dictionary, and most systems offer a grammar check as well.
- Mailing lists for meeting planning organizations can be merged with in-house lists (duplicate entries are purged, resulting in a single, clean file).
- Standard paragraphs can be recalled for insertion into proposal letters and contracts.
- Information from a previous function can be used in a follow-up letter; for example, "Do you wish to use the Monte Carlo room for your awards banquet again this year?"
- Filing is done accurately, automatically, and quickly, eliminating the most hated clerical job in the office.

Simple mass mailings can be effectively personalized with the name of the contact person and his or her group. This information can be merged into a routine sales letter to give the impression of a personal touch. And, as with computerized sales records, this type of automation frees the sales department's clerical people to pursue other, more productive duties, such as setting appointments or following up on accounts for salespeople.

**Yield and Revenue Management.** Another vital use of the computer has been in the area of

---

**MORE ONLINE**

To download a free 65-page Revenue Management PDF Handbook, use a search engine and type in, Revenue Management Manual-Xotels.
The topics in this manual include Fundamentals of Revenue Management, Budgeting, Forecasting, Benchmaking, and Pricing.

market analysis. **Yield management**, which is based on the forecasted demand for function space and guestrooms, is becoming an increasingly important tool in filling both meeting rooms and guestrooms while increasing profitability for the hotel.

Although yield management has been used by airlines and cruise ships for a number of years (rates have long been based on the customer's willingness to pay), the hospitality industry was relatively slow to capitalize on this concept. Today, however, hospitality professionals can take advantage of a number of software programs designed specifically for the industry. One example is GroupREV® by Rainmaker, a program that calculates group pricing to ensure maximum profitability.

Today, most hotels constantly monitor their business mix (business travelers, leisure travelers, and the meetings segment) to maximize revenues. They can forecast what rates they want over certain days and determine how much group business they want to see over specific dates.

Fred Shea, former vice president of sales operations for Hyatt Hotels Corporation, says:

> A ceiling is put in place based on what we think the transient demand will be. But it is constantly being re-evaluated. As we get closer to the group block ceiling, we begin to re-evaluate whether the rate should go up or down, based on the overall demand we are getting.[12]

---

### 🖥️ INTERNET EXERCISE

**Hospitality Revenue Management Software**

IDeaS Revenue Optimization is one of the leading providers of hospitality revenue management software. Its system aids in forecasting and pricing group and meetings business. The company's website, www.ideas.com, is an excellent resource for increasing your understanding of the importance of revenue management:

- Click on the Tools & Resources tab to select On-Demand Webinars. Watch a webinar of your choice and report on the new insights you have gained about the application of revenue management.

- Click on the Success Stories tab and then on Optimizing Rates to see how hospitality properties are increasing their profits using revenue management.

- The future of hotel revenue management is discussed in a number of podcast conversations between Dr. Sheryl Kimes of Cornell University and the revenue managers of several hotel chains. Listen to at least one of these podcasts and report on what you have learned.

---

Savvy meeting planners who know a hotel's target business mix for the days of their meeting can leverage that information in deciding whether to place the business early and be guaranteed their desired meeting space or wait to see if demand falls off and they can get a better rate. They are also aware that past data is the hotel's internal tool for determining how much group business a property wants to sell over particular dates. If their group traditionally has a high profitability, it is looked on as a more favorable piece of business and the planner may be able to negotiate a better rate.

**Revenue management** takes yield management a step further by not only assessing a group's potential for rooms revenue but also looking at the group's projected impact on the

Chapter 3: Organizing for Convention Sales

property's overall bottom line. Kevin Kowalski, vice president of the Crowne Plaza brand, says that, with increased demand, hotels need to take a second look at their business mix to increase their profitability. He explains:

> We can concentrate more on getting group business that is better value-related, and less on SMERF [social, military, educational, religious, fraternal] groups, which generate less ancillary revenue.[13]

---

**Case Study:**

## The Breakers Adopts Automated Sales and Catering System

Founded in 1896 and listed on the National Register of Historic Places, The Breakers Palm Beach is one of America's legendary resort destinations. The 560-room, Italian Renaissance-style hotel is located on 140 acres of oceanfront property in the heart of Palm Beach, Florida. With the commitment of its original owners, The Breakers has invested $250 million over the past two decades in its ongoing revitalization and enhancement of its multi-faceted amenities — most recently, the dramatic transformation of the shoreline into a luxurious beachfront experience.

### A Reason for Change

For years, The Breakers Palm Beach relied on its own homegrown management system to manage its sales and catering processes. Jim Mostad, director of sales for the property, acknowledged that the program simply wasn't doing the job anymore. Because a significant percentage of The Breakers' revenue comes from groups and events, the hotel was in need of a solution designed to meet its intensive volume of meeting business. Additionally, the resort's sales, catering, and conference divisions comprised many moving parts that needed to be more organized and efficient while also continuing to provide the superior service the hotel's clients had come to expect.

In short, Mostad and his team needed to bring the resort into the next generation of technology and implement an entirely new sales and catering system. The Breakers chose the Delphi system for automating their sales, marketing, and catering processes, along with the company's Diagrams, a powerful design application that empowers the staff of The Breakers to quickly, easily, and accurately generate customized floor plans for meetings and events.

Response time between catering and sales is much improved. With the new system, a salesperson can send a draft contract to a customer instantaneously, allowing the resort and the customer to review it together. This feature pleases the customer and makes for a speedier process all around.

In addition to managing the day-to-day sales and catering operations, Mostad is excited about the ease in managing revenues using the automated system:

> Knowledge is truly power. Our automated system gives the sales team the information they need to work independently and take action right away. We can now better evaluate the resort's availability, giving us an overall convenience and ease of use we didn't have before. The Breakers can now access how they are doing by market segment at any given time. We now know what was booked and why; moreover, we can accurately assess the implications of taking business or booking an event. Predicting, forecasting, and knowing where the opportunities exist are extremely beneficial to The Breakers' bottom line.
>
> The system allows us to see where we stand, the actual business on the books, and truly have an understanding of where we are right now. This results in better forecasting, better selling strategies, and, ultimately, recognizing new opportunities for our property.

**Source:** Adapted from Newmarket International's website (www.newmarketinc.com). Photographs courtesy of The Breakers.

Revenue management takes into consideration the size of the group, its spending history (not just in terms of rooms, but overall spending at the property's other revenue-producing outlets, such as restaurants and recreational facilities), and future revenues for the hotel (additional bookings by the group and individuals, referrals, and so on).

## Summary

Organizing for sales is essential if a property is to capture its share of the lucrative meetings and convention market. In this chapter, we have discussed how sales are structured on a number of levels. We have detailed the importance of the physical layout of the sales office as well as the relationship of the sales department with other property departments that will be involved in servicing a group's business. We have discussed the various positions within sales, and introduced types of supplementary sales staff, including regional sales offices and independent hotel representatives.

Managing the sales effort at any level involves utilizing a number of forms to successfully follow up on business booked and to ensure successful execution of a group's events. We have looked at a number of these forms, including the function and guestrooms control books, as well as forms that enable salespeople to manage their time and enable them to focus on key accounts. We have also seen how the computer has changed the way in which salespeople do business, making it far easier and more efficient to reach and service their customers.

In many ways, technology has created an impersonal way of doing business. Salespeople benefit from the convenience and option of doing business 24/7, and the Internet is an important tool for prospecting and finding business. However, it is *personal service* that generally distinguishes one salesperson from another. The hospitality business is still a "relationship" business — the personal touch of interacting with meeting planners face-to-face or over the telephone is still the most effective means to book business. In the next three chapters, we will take a look at the primary sources of meetings business and see how sales efforts are specifically organized to sell to and service each segment.

## Endnotes

1. Howard Feiertag, "Stepping Up When the Salespeople Have Left the Building," *Hotel Management*, April 8, 2013.
2. Sheraton's Convention and Conference Service Standards Manual.
3. Lalia Rach, Ed.D., "The Current and Future Marketing Professional," *HSMAI Marketing Review*.
4. Peggy Swisher, Andrea Dole, Michelle Russell, "Driven by the Bottom Line," *PCMA Convene*.
5. Megan Rowe, "15 Things That Drive You Crazy and What to Do About Them," *Corporate Meetings & Incentives*.
6. Doug Kennedy, "How to Capture Group Demand," *Hotel News Now*, September 8, 2014.
7. Courtesy of Hyatt Hotels Corporation Sales Automation System, Datamation.
8. William Duncan, "Booking Streamlined by Next Generation of Hospitality Software," *Convene*.

# Chapter 3: Organizing for Convention Sales

9. "How Technology Is Refining Hotel Operations," *Convene*.
10. Beth Rogers, "Working at Home," *HSMAI Marketing Review*.
11. Laura Ross-Fedder, "Computers Empower Swissôtel Sales Staff," *Hotel & Motel Management*.
12. Cheryl-Anne Sturken, "As They See It: How Hotels Evaluate Group Business," *Meetings & Conventions*.
13. Ibid.

## Study Questions

1. How is the sales department perceived within the organizational structure of the hotel? Why is it necessary for the sales department to assume authority over other departments?
2. Identify the three departments that the director of sales and his or her staff must work most closely with. Why is it crucial that sales interfaces with these departments?
3. Sketch job descriptions for the various positions within the sales department. How will these vary between large and small properties?
4. What is an independent hotel representative? What considerations are important in choosing an individual or firm to effectively represent your property?
5. What are the key elements of a sales office filing system? Why is each important?
6. Discuss the importance of the function book and guestrooms control book. Why is it important that only one person control these books?
7. How has computer technology changed the sales office? How is automation being used to enhance the sales effort?

## Key Terms

**account file**—A standardized folder holding the information needed to serve a client.

**database marketing**—The process of using guest folios, registration cards, and group histories of meeting planners to develop relationships and dialogue with customers.

**double booking**—Reserving space for two groups to use the same space at the same time; neither can be fully accommodated as contracted.

**function book**—Master control of all banquet space, broken down on each page or screen by banquet rooms, with a page or screen for each day of the year.

**guestrooms control book**—A book or computer program used to monitor guestroom allocations to groups.

**independent hotel representative**—An individual or firm that acts as an addition to the hotel's internal sales staff.

**key account management**—Prioritizing of accounts based upon their individual profit potential.

**master card**—The summary of all the details of an account's business, including the organization's name, key decision maker(s), key contacts, addresses, telephone numbers, and e-mail addresses. Today's master cards are stored electronically to enable them to be accessed by members of the sales department, whether they are physically in the office or on the road.

**option**—Meeting space or guestrooms that are reserved by the meeting group but not yet under contract. A hotel extends a right of first refusal to either confirm or release the space if there is demand from another group.

**reader file**—A file containing copies of internal and external correspondence generated by a salesperson. Useful for reviewing the performance of the sales staff.

**regional sales office**—Sales offices for chain properties that are located in places other than the property. They help promote and sell individual properties.

**relationship marketing**—Marketing that views customers as assets and emphasizes retaining customers by nurturing and sustaining relationships with them.

**revenue management**—The practice of assessing a group's overall profitability on the property's bottom line. Not only is the group's impact on guestrooms and meeting space revenues assessed, but also its spending in other areas (from restaurants to retail) as well as its potential for future business.

**standard operating procedures (SOPs)**—Written instructions explaining how business activities should be handled.

**tickler file**—A reminder to make an important call, follow-up visit, or other sales activity on a particular date. Previously filed on index cards, these reminders are now entered into computer systems or stored in mobile devices.

**working file**—A file set up as soon as a booking is definite, containing information relevant to the event.

**yield management**—A technique used to maximize the revenue/profit of the hotel by basing prices for guestrooms and banquet space on supply and demand.

## Industry Profile

## Tom Costello, Founder and Former President

### Groups International and iGroup Advisor

Tom Costello has worked in the hospitality industry for over 20 years. In 2006, after serving as a regional manager at HelmsBriscoe, the global site selection leader for associations and corporations, he founded Groups International, a meetings and events management company. Costello later expanded the company's services to include iGroupAdvisors, a performance-improvement consulting firm, and he also co-developed iGroupPlanner™, a web-based meetings and events solution.

Costello, who is the author of Prepare for Liftoff – How to Launch a Career in Sales, also published a popular blog, The Hotel Advisor, which was read in 103 countries. Although he has returned to his real estate roots, serving as a commercial real estate investment advisor at Marcus and Millichap, Costello continues to contribute columns to leading hospitality publications and share his expertise with his "Mapping the Course" educational workshops.

## Prospecting for Association Meetings Business

Prospecting for new customers is a necessary function of the sales cycle…new customers generated as a result of prospecting can account for as much as 50 to 90 percent of your hotel's occupancy. No matter what channels you use for prospecting, you will need to make some general assessments that are associated with your territory, hotel, comp set, capabilities, etc. and then formulate a game plan associated with your assessments to make sure that your future calls or contacts will be quality ones and not "dialing for dollars." Here are seven assessments that need to be addressed:

**What is my territory or market segment?** If you are unfamiliar with your territory, you can find business using Google Earth. Simply type a zip code into the search field, hit the search button, type in "associations," then hit search again to see most of the larger associations located within that zip code (along with an address, telephone number, and a link to the association's website).

**Who are my competitors and how are they selling against my hotel?** If your hotel subscribes to an Online Reputation Management solution (such as ReviewPro, Revinate, or ReviewAnalyst), you can monitor your comp set and gather intelligence that will help you to better understand how your hotel compares against other selected hotels in your immediate market.

**How will I continually generate new prospects?** Mine your hotel's CRM system, ask for internal and external customer referrals, and referrals from other salespeople who call on your target market. Speak at functions that your prospects attend and attend networking functions, conferences, and trade shows where your prospects meet. Don't overlook social channels, such as LinkedIn, as a source for prospects and referrals.

**How much time will I be able to devote to prospecting on a regular basis?** If you are organized, you should be able to spend between 20 to 30 hours a week prospecting. Keep in mind that association prospects take time to cultivate, but view them as "career" or "home run" customers that will dramatically change your year when you land them.

**What are my prospecting strengths and weaknesses?** All of us have varying degrees of strengths and weaknesses. Find out what makes you tick and utilize resources that will help you to build on your strengths and help you to overcome weaknesses.

**What is the strength of my target list?** Create your own business directories and use search engines that are specifically designed to provide information about associations to add to your target list rather than relying on purchased lists.

**Do I conduct thorough research about prospects before I contact them?** The people that you will be contacting are more "sales savvy" than ever, so make sure you conduct research on your prospect and his or her company before you pick up the phone or send an email. You will have a much better chance of getting your foot in the door when you have a better understanding of your prospect's challenges and their corporate culture and are able to talk knowledgeably about them.

**Learning Objectives:**

This portion of your text takes an in-depth look at the association market. We will discuss the types of meetings held by associations, their typical patterns, requirements for meetings, how site decisions are made and by whom, and ways to reach this lucrative market segment. When you have studied this chapter, you will:

- Be able to explain the importance of conventions to associations and identify factors that association meeting planners consider when making a site selection.

- Be able to describe the different types of association meetings and know which characteristics of these meetings are most important when selling to this market.

- Be able to identify key association decision-makers as well as others who help to influence decisions regarding association meetings.

- Know the resources and tools available to help hotel salespeople to locate associations and research the types of meetings they hold.

**Outline**

Revenue Producers

Requirements for Association Meetings

Kinds of Association Meetings
- Annual Conventions
- State and Regional Conventions
- Conferences
- Seminars and Workshops
- Board and Committee Meetings
- Hybrid Meetings

Characteristics of Association Meetings
- Cycle and Pattern
- Geographic Restrictions
- Lead Time
- Kind of Sites
- Voluntary Attendance
- Convention Duration
- Price

Association Meeting Decision-Makers
- Association Director
- Association President and Officers
- Committee Chairperson
- Board of Directors
- Other Influences

Sources for Finding Association Business
- Directories and Databases
- Specialized Periodicals
- Hotel Records

Summary

# 4  Selling the Association Market

In the first three chapters, we've studied the importance of the convention business and the trends impacting it, the marketing plan (the cornerstone of sales) and the organization and operation of the sales office. In the next three chapters, we will take a look at the major meetings market segments in detail. In this chapter, we will take an in-depth look at the associations market; Chapter 5 will focus on the corporate meetings market; and, in Chapter 6, we will cover nonprofit organizations, the SMERF market, and special market segments, including incentive and medical meetings.

The two most prominent target markets, the association and corporate meetings segments, will follow a similar outline:

- What planners look for in selecting sites,
- The kinds of meetings held and the characteristics of each type,
- Key decision-makers, and
- How to locate sources for business.

Kathy Dixon-Leone, former senior vice president of sales for the Boca Raton Resort and Club, says:

> The association market provides a tremendous base of business, both in the meetings the market holds and the meetings it can generate through the exposure a property gains by hosting its corporate membership. If serviced properly, it can provide a base of business that can be the foundation of a property's success for years to come.

According to a Convention Industry Council study, associations spend more than $106.6 billion a year on meetings. It comes as no surprise, then, that hotel chains such as Fairmont, Four Seasons, Hilton, Hyatt, Marriott, and Starwood have convention properties in major cities and look to association meetings to fill 30-40 percent of their rooms annually. The historic Boca Raton Resort and Club attributes approximately 65 percent of its annual sales volume to groups and meetings; 40 percent of its sales from meetings are realized from the association market.

Associations business also benefits a hotel as it is virtually recession-proof. While corporation business is generally more lucrative – corporations generally pay a higher rate and spend more on food and beverage (and attendance is mandatory), they may also scale back or cancel meetings during economic downturns. Associations, however, maintain their meeting schedules; some have bylaws that set meeting dates and locations, others look to their larger meetings as a means of generating revenue (we will discuss that factor in the next section). Therefore, it is important to be knowledgeable about the kinds of meetings that associations hold – and learn how you can capture your share of this lucrative market.

## Revenue Producers

Its convention is of extreme importance to an **association**. It is the single largest source of associations' non-dues revenue (see box titled "The Principal Sources of an Association's

Income" below). According to *Convene* magazine's Meetings Market Survey, associations derive about 32 percent of their annual income from conventions and exhibitions. Membership dues range from twenty-five dollars or so to several thousand dollars annually in more affluent associations, but almost every association views its convention, meetings, and exhibits as prime sources of revenue.

**The Principal Sources of an Association's Income:**

- Other 30%
- Dues 30%
- Publications/Advertising 8%
- Conventions/Exhibits/Meetings 32%

Source: Recent Meetings Market Report by *Convene* magazine.

Associations earn money from conventions in several ways (see Figure 4.1 titled "Revenue Sources from Association Annual Conventions" on the next page). One is with exhibits. The group may rent the exhibit hall of a hotel or convention center for one to five dollars per square foot, depending on demand and season. The association then subleases the space to exhibitors for considerably more -- up to fifty dollars per square foot in some cases.

Registration fees at such events also add to the association's coffers. When a convention "package" includes a number of meal functions, it is not uncommon for the package to cost the delegate several hundred dollars. The hotel is paid only for the actual number of meal tickets collected or the number of meals the meeting planner guarantees, which adds more to the profits of the convention, since not every person attends every event.

Associations earn additional money from the advertising in their publications and programs. And when a participating company sponsors a segment of the program and picks up the tab, the association's costs are further reduced.

Thus, when you consider how important conventions are to membership retention and to revenue production, it becomes apparent that these events are absolutely essential for the well-being of an association. They constitute a major effort on an association's part, and they are planned and conducted as such.

## Requirements for Association Meetings

Site selection is crucial to the success of a convention. Mike Welch, former executive director of the Credit Union Executive Society of Madison, Wisconsin, said:

Chapter 4: Selling the Association Market

*Figure 4.1.*

### Revenue Sources from Association Annual Conventions

Association and independent meeting professionals reported that, on average, the revenue from association annual conventions came from the following sources:

- Other 2%
- Advertising Sales 3%
- Sponsorships/Grants 17%
- Exhibit Sales 25%
- Registration Fees 53%

Source: *Convene's* 23rd Annual Meeting Market Survey.

We look for good facilities, pleasant weather, an attractive location, and a city that's near the largest concentration of members. We also consider who else is going to be there and when. For instance, when our annual convention is taking place in a city, we don't want to go there for a seminar for a year or two.

Figure 4.2 on the next page details some of the other factors that meeting planners take into consideration when making a site selection. These considerations include:

- **Adequate meeting space.** The organizer is always concerned about your ability to house the general assembly and smaller sessions. He or she is interested in space for workshops and committee meetings, as well as your ability to handle food functions expertly without encroaching on the meetings.

- **Enough guestrooms.** Most convention organizers prefer to house the entire group in one hotel. Suites are needed in addition to singles, twins, and doubles. When a single hotel can't house the entire group, two or more hotels in close proximity are the most desirable.

- **Adequate exhibit space.** Exhibits mean money for the association and are an attraction for the members. Planners look for adequate exhibit space, located conveniently to housing. Hotels with exhibit facilities have an advantage. When larger exhibits require exhibition halls, the preference is for setups near the hotel. Delegates prefer not to travel between hotel rooms and convention areas.

- **An attractive location.** A location need not be a resort to attract different groups. Chicago attracts association business because of its central location, which is very important to many busy groups.

  Other groups may like to combine the show with other business. Your city may be in the heart of their business world. Attendance is also easier to stimulate if people don't have to travel too far. Easy driving distance may mean an extra ten percent registration. Many associations do like resort locations. You may be able to offer that, or perhaps you are located in great tourist country. Put simply, you have to offer something attractive to each group. It might be the draw of your city or destination, your proximity to a major airport, or your reputation for superior customer service.

- **Service.** Last, but probably most important, meeting planners look for service. They want some assurance that you have an experienced staff that is interested in doing a good job. Each convention event is a custom job and many things can go wrong. Convention planners live with such hazards and justly feel that your staff should have the expertise and the desire to keep the show moving. Service is what brings repeat and recommended business.

*Figure 4.2. FACTORS CONSIDERED IMPORTANT TO ASSOCIATION MEETING PLANNERS IN THE SELECTION OF A FACILITY/HOTEL.*

### Association Planners

| Factors Considered Very Important | Major Conventions | Smaller Assoc. Meetings |
|---|---|---|
| Number, size, quality of meeting rooms | 90% | 67% |
| Negotiable food, beverage, and room rates | 84 | 70 |
| Cost of hotel or meeting facility | 83 | 76 |
| Number, size and quality of sleeping rooms | 78 | 59 |
| Quality of food service | 70 | 61 |
| Availability of meeting support services and equipment, such as AV equipment | 54 | 43 |
| Availability of exhibit space | 53 | 28 |
| Efficiency of billing procedures | 50 | 52 |
| Previous experience in dealing with facility and its staff | 49 | 40 |
| High-speed Internet access | 47 | 46 |
| Assignment of one staff person to handle all aspects of meeting | 46 | 45 |
| Efficiency of check-in and check-out procedures | 42 | 39 |
| Meeting rooms with multiple high-speed phone lines and computer outlets | 38 | 38 |
| Proximity to shopping, restaurants, off-site entertainment | 28 | 19 |

Source: Recent Meetings Market Report by *Meetings & Conventions* magazine.

*Although the purpose of a meeting ultimately determines the facility selection criteria, this figure gives insight into general factors of importance to the association meeting planner. Negotiable rates and costs continue to be an important aspect of hotel selection for conventions and meetings.*

Chapter 4: Selling the Association Market

*Guest satisfaction is a major concern of meeting planners. This photograph from Shangri-La Hotels and Resorts emphasizes the chain's "Service with a Smile" promise.*
**Source: Photograph courtesy of Shangri-La Hotels and Resorts.**

## Kinds of Association Meetings

While we will primarily be discussing association meetings in the United States in this chapter, many associations have international chapters and hold meetings overseas. Companies such as the BestCities Global Alliance (www.bestcities.net) help U.S. associations organize meetings in such locations as Berlin (Germany), Bogota (Columbia), Cape Town (South Africa), Copenhagen (Denmark), Edinburgh (Scotland), Melbourne (Australia), Tokyo (Japan), Vancouver (Canada), and Dubai. Planners from other countries also hold their meetings outside their borders. According to a recent study by the International Congress and Convention Association (ICCA), the ten top destinations for international association conventions are the United States, Germany, Spain, France, the United Kingdom, Italy, Japan, China, Brazil, and the Netherlands.[1]

While we have already mentioned the importance of an association's annual convention, we will be taking a more in-depth look at this largest and most visible association meeting in this section. It is important to note that because of the planning involved in staging a successful annual convention, a number of other meetings, such as *board meetings* and *committee meetings*, may be required beforehand.

Other common association meetings include *state and regional conventions, conferences, seminars, and workshops.* These meetings are conducted throughout the year by most associations (see Figure 4.3 on the next page). These are all sources of good business for hotels. It is a rare property that cannot handle some kind of association business. You may not necessarily be able to handle the major events but there are many others that you can service.

124

*Figure 4.3. SUMMARY OF TYPES OF ASSOCIATION MEETINGS OTHER THAN MAJOR CONVENTIONS.*

| Type of Meeting | Average # Planned | Average Attendance | Average # Days Duration | Average # of Months Lead Time |
|---|---|---|---|---|
| Board Meetings | 3.4 | 28 | 1.8 | 5.6 |
| Training/Educational Seminars | 9.5 | 119 | 21 | 7.0 |
| Professional/Technical | 4.6 | 163 | 23 | 7.1 |
| Regional/Local Chapters | 6.5 | 153 | 1.9 | 6.1 |
| Other Meetings | 5.6 | 507 | 3.3 | 9.9 |
| Total/Average | 15.5 | 146 | 2.0 | 7.1 |

*The average association meeting planner works on over 15 meetings per year.*
**Source: Recent Meetings Market Report by** *Meetings & Conventions* **magazine.**

## Annual Conventions

Almost every association has an annual convention. The annual convention is a ritual in associations of all types—international, national, state, and regional.

Attendance varies, of course. Some conventions are truly huge affairs. The Chemical Society draws between 20,000 and 30,000; others have fewer than 100 attendees. The mean attendance is about 1,500 people. Conventions vary only in scale, maintaining similar philosophies and motivations no matter what their size.

Since 60 percent of all national meetings and trade shows have an average attendance of 300 or less, even small properties can take advantage of this lucrative market. And, small properties can benefit from the large conventions by making arrangements with neighboring properties to handle overflow business generated by large groups.

Exhibits are a major part of association meetings, especially trade and technical societies. Two-thirds of the annual association conventions are held in conjunction with a trade show or exhibit. These conventions attract an average of 265 exhibitors using an average of 56,000 square feet of exhibit space. Exhibits are a source of essential income to associations, and very important to exhibitors, too.

There are conventions without exhibits, of course, and it is also not unheard of for a convention to stage a major program with exhibits in one hotel and another program without exhibits in another. And sometimes, an event may be held in a city because of the presence of another convention with an exhibit.

Most conventions include a **general session**, (also called a plenary session) attended by everyone, along with a number of smaller meetings. These smaller meetings are often termed **breakout sessions**, where the group divides into smaller meetings, and **concurrent sessions**, where meeting sessions on different topics are scheduled at the same time. Sometimes, the general session runs concurrently with the exhibit hours; sometimes they run in tandem so as not to compete for members' attention.

It is a rare convention without food functions. Many groups sell a complete convention package for their event. The package includes registration fees and prepaid tickets to all food functions and special events.

You can see at this point that a convention, especially a large one, calls for a number of rooms of different kinds. Large rooms are needed for the general assembly, the exhibit, and the food functions; smaller rooms for committee and board meetings, workshops, and smaller food functions; and suites and similar rooms for hospitality centers.

Some associations also include an element of **social responsibility** at their conventions. Although corporations have been the driving force behind social responsibility (and often include team-building experiences in their programs), more associations are offering opportunities for attendees to give back to the community during their events. Some associations opt to hold their events on property, while others go out into the community to perform such services as refurbishing schools, parks, or playgrounds; planting a community garden; or, helping needy veterans or senior citizens.

Often a hotel cannot handle an entire convention because of its size, so several hotels may band together to sell an association as a team. The hotel business is odd in that strong competitors often become partners in a project, and both can enjoy additional business as a result. Even a piece of a convention event may be profitable, as well as giving the hotel a foot in the door for future business.

> **WORTH WATCHING**
>
> Jim Goodman, CMP, managing vice president – conferences & continuing education, the American Dental Association, explains how his association reaches out to communities at their annual convention at http://hedtalks.connectplusathiltonworldwide.com/#s-yGK8-5sqeN4.

There is another variation of the national convention—the exhibit without convention program. These events, often called *exhibitions*, *expositions*, or *trade shows*, sometimes are not even sponsored by an association but by individual entrepreneurs or companies. Many an exhibition becomes the focal point of the industry or trade it serves and gives exhibitors the opportunity to hold sales meetings and dealer meetings in conjunction with the event. Even if your property cannot house an exhibit, these events offer an opportunity for you to boost revenue through providing guestrooms and offering food and beverage service to attendees.

## State and Regional Conventions

While the national or international association convention is the prize for very large hotels, the state and regional convention can be targeted by hotel properties of all sizes (see Figure 4.4).

The major difference between a regional convention of a national organization and one staged by a state or regional association is sponsorship. A state association usually holds an annual meeting for its members within the state, although in recent years state organizations have ventured beyond state borders on occasion. Many national associations, even those with affiliated state chapters, hold regional conventions to supplement their national ones. Of interest is the recent growth in regional association meetings. When finances are short, many association members skip the big annual conventions, and attend smaller, shorter meetings that are closer to home. As a rule, the regional event is smaller than the national one both in attendance and size of the exhibit. Again, some regional conventions have exhibits and others don't. There is no rule of thumb.

The major difference, as far as hotel people are concerned, has to do with who makes the decisions about when and where the event will be held. The sidebar titled "State and Regional Association Planners Cite the Top Ten Attributes for Convention Site Selection"

*Figure 4.4. STATE AND REGIONAL ASSOCIATION MARKET AT A GLANCE.*

| | |
|---|---|
| Location | This segment of the association market is usually an offshoot of the national or international association. Groups usually rotate their convention among the major cities within the state or region and rely heavily upon local support for invitation. They meet four to six months before or after their affiliated national convention. |
| Facilities | While adequate meeting space and guestrooms, and food and beverage options play a big role in site selection, free parking is also an important consideration, as many attendees drive to these meetings. Because attendees are generally price-sensitive and balk at paying hefty parking fees, especially when meetings last for several days, planners look for hotels that already offer free parking, or they negotiate free parking or reduced parking rates that are included in the price of the program package. Most conventions require a ballroom for plenary sessions or banquets as well as several breakout rooms for seminars. |
| Price | Double occupancy is common, so hotels should consider a flat rate, perhaps a compromise between the single and double rates. Attendance is voluntary, so decision-makers are price-sensitive. They often will schedule their meetings during a hotel's off-periods and will schedule a Thursday arrival/ Sunday departure or Friday arrival/ Sunday departure. |
| Services | Preferred services include business services such as fax machines, office copiers, typing, and word processing. Other services include audiovisual equipment necessary for presentations and occasionally exhibit halls for table-top exhibits. |
| Decision-Makers | These groups usually do not have a paid staff or a permanent office, but rather are administered by volunteers and committees on a part-time basis. The local chapters frequently submit bids or invitations to host a regional or state meeting. Because volunteer staff changes annually, it is important to actively solicit and update files frequently to determine decision-makers. |
| Best Ways to Reach Market | Check the yellow pages under "Association" in all major cities (most are headquartered in a capital city due to lobbying efforts). Most states have an affiliate of the American Society of Association Executives (ASAE) and publish a list of their members. Local convention and visitors bureaus and chambers of commerce will normally supply a listing of professional associations in their area. Personal contacts and direct mail are the most effective means to reach the decision-makers. |

details some of the factors important in site selection. State and regional conventions are an important source of business for both large and small hotel properties (see Figure 4.5).

According to the *Association Meeting Trends* report, only ten percent of all state and regional conventions have an attendance of more than 1,000; 75 percent have less than 500 attendees, making this an ideal market for smaller properties.

Since chapters of national associations meet within the state or regional boundaries, it is a market that can be reached relatively easily. Sources for locating state and regional business include:

- Chambers of commerce and convention and visitors bureaus.
- The Yellow Pages of telephone directories for capital cities.
- Newspapers from capital cities or feeder cities.
- Online Databases and professional sites, such as LinkedIn

Chapter 4: Selling the Association Market

*Figure 4.5. MARKETING TO STATE AND REGIONAL ASSOCIATIONS.*

## Bavarian Inn Lodge
### & Conference Center
#### Downtown Frankenmuth

**Let us host your statewide or regional conference!**

360 Bavarian-Themed Guestrooms
Up to 500 Delegates - 10 Breakout Rooms
Advanced Audio/Visual Equipment

- 5 Indoor Pools (1 adult only)
- 2 On-Premise Restaurants
- 2 Phone Lines in Every Room
- Nightly Entertainment
- Walking Distance to Main Street
- Famous Frankenmuth® Chicken

Now Accepting RFP's online at frankenmuthmeetings.com

Contact our Professional Event Coordinators
1-888-775-6343 • Fax: (989) 652-3509

The Bavarian Inn Lodge & Conference Center in Frankenmuth, Michigan, America's largest Bavarian themed resort, is located in the heart of Michigan's "Little Bavaria." The property, which hosts about 300 groups a year, employs nine full-time staff members devoted to meetings and conventions. The property targets the statewide and regional conference market by promoting its meeting amenities, on-site facilities, and proximity to local attractions. In addition to print ads such as this one, the Bavarian Inn Lodge also reaches meeting planners at trade shows, and staff also works closely with local and state convention and visitors bureaus. To get the word out, the property also depends on the old and new: social media reviews and word-of-mouth referrals (each guestroom guide book suggests that guests recommend the property to a friend; about one-third of new guests have booked because of these recommendations, and several group bookings were made based on guests' satisfaction).

- The American Society of Association Executives (ASAE). Hotel salespeople can join such groups as the Washington Society of Association Executives (WSAE) or the California Society of Association Executives (CSAE) as allied members.

Once a group has been located, it is important to remember that in many cases the meeting planners may be committees or inexperienced planners and that lead time is usually fairly short. A property that shows a willingness to assist with meeting planning will gain an edge over the competition.

Another way to attract this market's business, which is an important source of revenue for off-peak periods, is to offer inexpensive room rates. Many attendees pay their own expenses, making room rates especially important to them. And, because spouses usually attend, a property that offers a single/double occupancy flat rate for these groups is especially attractive to this lucrative market.

## Conferences

Associations have become frequent stagers of conferences, primarily to supplement the annual convention program with a specific program made timely by new developments. The recent debates over stem cell research and national health care, for example, precipitated a number of conferences.

The number of conferences held within an industry varies, of course. They have become commonplace in the technical, scientific, and professional worlds. A breakthrough in an electronic process or medical treatment, or a change in corporate law or tax structure brings on a rash of conferences.

**State and Regional Association Planners Cite the Top Ten Attributes for Convention Site Selection**

| Attribute | Percent | Rank |
|---|---|---|
| Proximity of hotel to meeting facility | 71.4 | 1 |
| Capacity of meeting rooms | 65.6 | 2 |
| Hotel cleanliness | 62.8 | 3 |
| Number of meeting rooms | 61.6 | 4 |
| Quality of food and beverage | 59.8 | 5 |
| Banquet space | 59.0 | 6 |
| Complimentary meeting space | 57.3 | 7 |
| Meeting room rates | 56.7 | 8 |
| Friendliness of hotel personnel | 56.7 | 9 |
| Problem-solving skills of hotel personnel | 56.4 | 10 |

Source: Jeong-Ja Choi, Ph.D. and Carl A. Boger, Jr., Ph.D., "State Association Market: Relationships Between Association Characteristics and Site Selection Criteria," *Journal of Convention & Exhibition Management*, The Hawthorne Press, Inc.

## Seminars and Workshops

Closely allied to the conference, but on a more modest basis, is the seminar. Association seminars are usually tied in with training and continuing education, such as the training of apprentice craftsmen, the updating of scientific and engineering personnel, or the presentation of marketing developments within an industry. Such seminars are presented around the country to small groups. Such business is within the scope of almost any hotel property.

## Board and Committee Meetings

Association business regularly calls for smaller meetings. The board of directors may meet on a regular basis, not necessarily in the city of the association office. These meetings are often set in attractive locales as a way of encouraging outstanding people to serve on the board, since they are not paid. Attendance at board meetings may range from ten to twelve to up to two hundred. The hotel chosen for such meetings is in a prime position to sell the property for the national convention and for business emanating from the board members' own organizations.

Committee meetings may range in size from ten to fifty people and are held at varying rates of frequency. These events, too, can be serviced by hotels of any size as long as they are geared for meetings.

> **WORTH WATCHING**
>
> The value of adding virtual components to live meetings is explained at http://hedtalks.connectplusathiltonworldwide.com/#sAG003ddR-Y8 (click on the "Hybrid Live/Virtual Meetings" tab).

## Hybrid Meetings

Many association meeting planners today are turning to **hybrid meetings**, which combine a live program with a virtual component. Two common examples of a hybrid meeting include the audio or video streaming of a keynote speaker or a workshop presented at another location. But hybrid meetings can also include online chats or discussions, live blogs, and the uploading of educational content and event photographs for association members who were unable to attend the meeting in person.

Not only can associations generate revenue from their uploaded content presentations, but they can also stimulate interest in future meetings. Members who did not attend the event often realize the value of the face-to-face element of the program and register for the next event.

# Characteristics of Association Meetings

Association meetings of all types follow similar patterns; understanding these patterns will help you sell them intelligently.

## Cycle and Pattern

Conventions are held on a regular time cycle. The most common is annual, although about ten percent of associations hold two conventions a year and there are some that convene only every two years. The one-year cycle is often supplemented in a national organization with one, two, or even three regional conventions on a smaller scale.

Conventions most frequently begin on Sunday and run through Wednesday or begin on Thursday with a Sunday check out (see Figure 4.6). The reason for this pattern is the airfare savings realized with a Saturday night stayover. These Saturday night stayovers, required by most airlines to qualify for reduced airfares, have boosted the occupancies of many downtown hotels that previously saw weekends as their slowest periods. Meetings and conventions that previously began on Mondays have moved registration to Sundays whenever possible so attendees can take advantage of the lower airfares. Figure 4.7 shows Marriott's attempt to secure Sunday registrations.

A strong geographic pattern is also indicated. Jeff Sacks, CMP, vice president, strategic sales account management, at Experient, Inc., one of the world's largest meeting management companies, states:

> A smart organization will rotate its annual convention across the map. This strategy not only allows you to meet in all regions where your membership is based, but it also benefits membership growth and recruitment in addition to keeping the meeting fresh in terms of climate, attractions, time zones, and cost of attending.[2]

Most associations alternate between the East and West in site selection. The most popular variation calls for a Midwestern city every two years, with eastern and western cities alternating during the other two years. Typical examples follow:

|  | 2016 | 2017 | 2018 | 2019 | 2020 |
|---|---|---|---|---|---|
| *National Conventions* | | | | | |
| ABC Assn. | New York | Los Angeles | Washington | Denver | Boston |
| XYZ Assn. | Chicago | New York | St. Louis | Las Vegas | Milwaukee |
| *Regional Conventions* | | | | | |
| ABC Assn. | San Diego | Atlanta | Phoenix | Miami | San Francisco |
| | Cleveland | Kansas City | Cincinnati | St. Louis | New Orleans |
| XYZ Assn. | Los Angeles | Dallas | Philadelphia | Boston | Miami |
| | Atlanta | Seattle | San Diego | Detroit | Los Angeles |

The important factor is the area of the country, not the specific city. The pattern may call for a Midwest location, which could be St. Louis, Chicago, Cincinnati, or others. The Southeast could be served with Atlanta, Miami, Tampa, or Memphis. In Canada, Toronto, Quebec, and Halifax might be considered if the group is considering an eastern location. Much depends on the geographic interests of the association members. If there is no special interest factor, the site selectors attempt to provide an interesting place to serve as an additional attraction.

In order to attract and keep association business, several cities have banded together to provide a "one-stop shopping" option for meeting planners who rotate destinations. For example, Visit Baltimore (baltimore.org) in Baltimore, Maryland (East), the San Antonio Convention & Visitors Bureau (visitsanantonio.com) in San Antonio, Texas (Midwest), and the Anaheim/Orange County Visitor & Convention Bureau (anaheimoc.org) in Anaheim, California (West), have formed a tri-city alliance that allows the sponsoring entities and their member hotels to combine their resources and offer a consistent sales and service platform at all three destinations. One of this alliance's early successes was capturing the National Postal Forum, which scheduled its annual conferences in Anaheim in 2015, Baltimore in 2017, and San Antonio in 2018.

Figure 4.6. MONTHLY AND DAILY MEETING PATTERN OF ASSOCIATIONS.

**When They Are Held**

Rated by the *number of events*, these are the most active convention months in order of importance:
- October • May • April • June
- September

Rated by the *number of attendees*, these are the most acive convention months in order of importance:
- October • September • March
- February • January

**Starting Day of Meeting**

Percentage of total Market

- Sat 8.3%
- Sun 21.1%
- Mon 12.6%
- Tues 9.5%
- Wed 15.0%
- Thurs 17.5%
- Fri 16.0%

Source: By permission of *Successful Meetings* magazine.

# Chapter 4: Selling the Association Market

**FIGURE 4.7. CAPTURING SUNDAY MEETINGS BUSINESS.**

*Convention start and end dates are an important factor for hotel profitability. A Tuesday-Thursday convention, for example, is problematic for many hotels. To maximize revenues, hotels seek to book groups arriving on Sunday and checking out on Wednesday, and groups checking in on Wednesday and departing on Sunday. Sunday arrivals are especially important to city hotels, which traditionally see Sunday as the lowest occupancy day of the week. David Horowitz, of the Hyatt Regency Century Plaza in Los Angeles, states: "A Sunday arrival is much more valuable to us than a Tuesday arrival."*
**Source: By permission of Marriott Portland Downtown Waterfront.**

Figure 4.8 shows an example of tri-city alliance advertising for the cities of Pittsburgh, Pennsylvania (East), Milwaukee, Wisconsin (Midwest), and Portland, Oregon (West). Craig Davis, president and CEO of Visit Pittsburgh (www.visitpittsburgh.com), has stressed that cities must be similar in size, share a customer base, and rarely compete with each other for these alliances to succeed, as cities sharing these characteristics can offer comparable facilities and services as well as discounts for multi-year deals with an association.

The scheduling of regional events calls for a frank recognition that some members will not travel too far for the event. One association executive told us that his records show a hard core of regulars come to the convention every year no matter where it is held. This group is supplemented by members who come from within three hundred miles. Obviously, he holds regional conventions to keep his members involved. Perusal of the meeting pattern should show you when the group would next consider your part of the country.

## Geographic Restrictions

Many state organizations, as part of their constitutions, have limited site selections to within their own states. This is also true of regional associations. There may be further restrictions because of the narrow interests of the program or the nature of the association's business.

There has been some deviation from such rigid limitations in recent years. One device that association executives have used to break out of the pattern is a reciprocal agreement

**FIGURE 4.8. HOTELS TEAM UP TO OFFER DIVERSE LOCATIONS FOR ASSOCIATION MEETINGS.**

*This tri-city alliance print advertisement targets meeting planners who rotate their destinations. Formed by Visit Pittsburgh, Visit Milwaukee (www.visitmilwaukee.org), and Travel Portland (www.travelportland.com), the alliance provides benefits, including discounts realized from multi-year deals, to meeting planners while allowing participating cities to share promotional costs while generating association business.*

with another state organization. Thus a Colorado chapter might meet in Massachusetts one year and the Massachusetts chapter would meet in Colorado. This satisfies the political aspects of catering to local businesses while providing a novel site to stimulate attendance.

## Lead Time

Association conventions are planned well in advance, with a **lead time** of two to five years the norm for conventions, a lead time of one and a half to two years for state and regional events, and somewhat less than a year for other types of association meetings. Even decisions finalized two years in advance are the result of research and discussion that took up to five years. The larger the convention, the greater the lead time. Meeting planners are well aware that every hotel is not suitable for their convention. They want time to visit the site, check with past clients, and check other alternatives before making the decision.

This long lead time can be frustrating for the new hotel or the new hotel sales manager, but it is the pattern for associaton conventions. And the clear pattern enables you to decide when you can best propose your property to have the best chance of success.

## Kind of Sites

Association business does not all go to the same kind of property. This is hardly surprising, considering the many kinds of associations and societies and the many types of meeting events they hold. Requirements and preferences could scarcely be expected to be uniform, but it is a rare hotel property that cannot serve some sort of association event.

Meetings are held in various types of facilities, depending on the size, nature, and duration of meetings. Types of meeting facilities commonly used by associations include downtown hotels, airport hotels, suburban hotels, resorts, convention centers, conference centers, college/university campuses, and the association's headquarters (see box below titled "Types of Facilities Used").

The kind of site selected generally reflects the group's size, degree of sophistication, and members' affluence. Obviously, a 200-room hotel would not be considered for a 500-person convention, unless it is in cooperation with other hotels. The basic requirements must be met—an auditorium for the main assembly, exhibit space if needed, and support rooms for committees' and exhibitors' meetings.

Environmentally-conscious associations also look for properties that can host *green meetings* (see Chapter 1). Hotels with eco-friendly facilities and energy and water conservation, recycling, and composting programs, are especially attractive to these planners, as is the availability of organic and locally grown foods.

We have discussed geographic considerations. Add to that ease of transportation and how the association executive feels about it. It is hard, for example, to find a more accessible

| Types of Facilities Used | For Conventions | For Other Association Meetings |
|---|---|---|
| Downtown hotels | 62% | 68% |
| Resort hotels (not including golf resorts) | 24% | 36% |
| Suburban hotels | 15% | 36% |
| Suite hotels | 12% | 13% |
| Airport hotels | 8% | 22% |
| Golf resorts | 7% | 14% |
| Gaming facilities | 5% | 5% |
| Residential conference centers | 3% | 9% |
| Nonresidential conference centers | 1% | 6% |
| Cruise ships | 1% | 3% |

*Association planners prefer downtown hotels. Average room rate paid by association attendees is $177. Two-thirds of major association conventions involve exhibits, utilizing an average of 56,000 square feet. Note: Totals exceed 100% due to multiple responses.*
**Source: Recent Meetings Market Report by *Meetings & Conventions* magazine.**

place than the hotels near O'Hare Airport at Chicago. If the executive believes that such a site would draw more attendance, he or she may choose it.

There are other geographic factors involved. Planners may also wish to choose other locations to provide a new "flavor" to their meetings. Many associations, especially those that are price-conscious, opt for **second-tier cities** – smaller cities or suburbs of larger cities. Examples of second-tier cities include Milwaukee, Wisconsin; Hamilton, Ontario, Canada; and, Charlotte, North Carolina.

Second-tier locations benefit attendees by providing experiences not offered by larger cities; attendees may be able to go white-water rafting, for example, or visit unique attractions. For the

*Downtown properties are commonly used for association meetings.*
**Source: Photograph courtesy of Hyatt Regency, Calgary, Canada.**

planner, second-tier cities are not only more economical, they may offer better service; larger cities often service a great deal of meetings business at one time, but the staffs of hotels and other meeting sites in smaller cities sometimes have only one meeting to service. The meeting planner gets undivided attention and attendees are warmly received.

Another option for attracting attendance is holding a meeting in a **walkable city**. A walkable city is a location that hosts the meeting in or near the hotels providing lodging for the event (see Figure 4.9). Fine-dining restaurants, entertainment, shopping, cultural activities, and other attractions are also available within walking distance.

Walkable cities include New York City, San Francisco, Boston, and Chicago. Smaller cities, including Oakland, California; Indianapolis, Indiana; and Austin, Texas, are also considered pedestrian-friendly. The important factors to consider are ease of getting to and from the meeting site(s), the safety of attendees' routes, and the appeal of nearby options (a younger group would likely be more interested in nightlife, for example). Walk Score (www.walkable.com/cities-and-neighborhoods) provides an annual ranking of the top ten U.S. cities for walkability, and the site also rates cities across the U.S., Canada, and Australia based on transit and bike scores as well as walkability.

Walkable cities benefit meeting planners by eliminating the hassle of contracting and scheduling bus or shuttle service – as well as eliminating the cost of these services. Since most attendees pay their own expenses, they also appreciate saving money on taxis or other transportation at the meeting site, and they also benefit from not being tied to a shuttle schedule. Walkable cities also provide the opportunity for attendees to schedule personal activities, such as a dinner with friends at an off-site fine-dining establishment, and they are also attractive to fitness-minded attendees, who enjoy walking, and attendees from Europe, where walking is commonplace in many cities.

Many convention organizers want the vacation element working for them. How many extra registrations can a site such as Toronto or Las Vegas or Colorado Springs draw? That's the name of the game. There are many ways to enliven a regularly scheduled convention. Good, stimulating programming is the ideal way, but it's very hard to execute. It is often easier for planners to stage the event at a lovely resort and keep their people happy by exposing them to "the good life."

Chapter 4: Selling the Association Market

**Figure 4.9. AD STATING THE PROXIMITY OF CONVENTION CENTER AND HOTEL.**

# INDY HAS MORE CONNECTED HOTEL ROOMS THAN ANY U.S. CITY*

### ELIMINATE TRANSPORTATION COSTS AND MAKE PLANNING EASY.

**#1 CONVENTION CITY IN THE U.S.** - USA TODAY

*Indy*

* 4,700 rooms connected by skywalk to 749,000 sq. ft. of exhibit space under one roof.

VisitIndy.com/Meet

This ad promotes the proximity of the Indiana Convention Center in Indianapolis to hotel rooms, meeting sites, restaurants, nightlife, shopping, and attractions. While this ad promotes the city and the convention center, individual properties that are within walking distance to the meeting site and other attractions can use with this type of advertising to appeal to meeting planners who wish to keep their groups within close proximity while still offering attractive entertainment choices for non-meeting time.
*Source: Visit Indy (www.visitindy.com), the official tourism site of Indiana.*

Sports also play a role in site selection. Golf, tennis, swimming, and boating are factors considered by convention planners as they analyze the interests of their people. Some fervent golfers on the board may very well swing the decision to a property with a famous golf course and favorable climate.

## Voluntary Attendance

It should be clear by now that the association convention planner has to *attract* members to the annual event. One might think that business and professional interests would suffice as a magnet. Undoubtedly they do draw a certain number, but there are an indeterminate number of fence-sitters. Should they go this year or should they skip it? This is where site attraction plays such an important role, and the meeting planner is aware of it.

The option to attend is the member's own. He or she may demand that both business needs and vacation desires be satisfied. If your property or region has tourist attractions, you should make sure that these are all part of your presentation. Whether it is the opera at the Lincoln Center or shopping at Saks Fifth Avenue in the Big Apple, exploring the winding streets of Quebec City (the only fortified city in North America), or white-water rafting in Vancouver, British Columbia, a hotel's attraction is more than just its decor and facilities. Learn what positive aspects of your property you can project. Sales may depend on it.

As a bonus, records show that spouses come too when the site is attractive. That results in double-occupancy revenues and longer stays. Vacations with tax-deductible expenditures also help turn out the members.

## Convention Duration

The average duration of a convention is three to five days (see Figure 4.10). This is generally true for national events, although smaller affairs may last only two or three days. Seminars, committee meetings, and the like can last just a day or two. Most conventions with exhibits meet no fewer than three days. There is quite a lot of additional business to be picked up as a result of such conventions, as many exhibiting firms hold sales meetings just before the event. This is true, too, for the association's board of directors and many committees. Look also for small associations among delegate groups that meet each year at the major convention.

**Figure 4.10. AVERAGE DURATION OF ASSOCIATION MEETINGS.**

**Length of Meeting**
(Percentage of Total Market)

- 3 Days: 36.2%
- 4 Days: 22.6%
- 2 Days: 16.5%
- 5 Days: 12.8%
- 6 Days: 4.5%
- 1 Day: 4.4%
- 7 Days: 2.0%
- 8 Days: 1.0%

Source: By permission of *Successful Meetings* magazine.

## Price

Your rate schedule is an important consideration for the association executive. We refer to your guestroom rates, not so much to your charges for meeting rooms, food functions, etc., although they will be reflected in the overall registration fee and charges for individual events. Guestroom rates must be aligned with the kind of people expected to attend. This is where the full range of hotels comes into play.

Many a convention organizer sticks with the traditional downtown hotels because of price. The older properties, built years ago at lower costs and with lower mortgages, often can offer lower rates. That means nothing to some associations. But to others, it can mean the difference between choosing your property and rejecting it. Even if price is not always the most important factor for a site selection, it is a rare planner who does not mention price. This is especially true for associations with price-sensitive attendees who must also budget for travel costs to the location as well as lodging and additional food and beverage costs.

Here, too, some study of where the group has met before will help. If its history discloses successful years at places such as the Fairmont in San Francisco, the Plaza in New York, and the Four Seasons in Ottawa, you can feel pretty sure that the convention organizer wants the best places for his or her people and that they are accustomed to paying the price. On the other hand, one convention organizer said that her people were middle-level employees who traditionally paid their own way to the convention. When she booked at a more expensive place, she invariably received an increased number of complaints from members.

There is no one right price level. It must suit the group you are trying to sell. Or, more accurately, it must suit the picture the association executive has of his or her people.

# Association Meeting Decision-Makers

Selection of the convention site—both city and hotel—is a two-step process. The meeting planners first step is screening all suggestions and solicitations; the second is the final approval. We have separated the two because not all people are active in both phases.

## Association Director

Almost every association employs an executive to help with running the association. The title may be executive secretary, executive vice president, or executive director. Usually, he or she is the administrator of the association, and a very important person to hotel people.

Your sales effort starts with this decision-maker. A well-run sales staff of a hotel or convention bureau will treasure a file on each association and its key people; the list always starts with the executive director (see Figure 4.11).

The executive director is a key person for the initial screening of suitable convention sites and swings great influence over the final selection as well (see box "Former Executive Directors Speak Out About How Sites Decisions Are Made"). After all, this executive enjoys a continuity in office that the elected officials do not have. The elected officials may serve for a year or two and then pass on the reins to the next team. But the executive director continues in office, and does so with the backing of the key members of the association.

The executive director doesn't work alone, however, especially in larger organizations. Since most of the administrative work has nothing to do with the convention activities, the executive director often has a staff member specifically assigned to convention

*Figure 4.11. TYPICAL JOB TITLES OF ASSOCIATION DECISION-MAKERS.*

| Job Title | Association Planners |
|---|---|
| Executive Director/Conventions/Conference Planner/Coordinator/Manager/Director | 43% |
| President/Executive Vice President | 20 |
| Meeting Planner/Coordinator/Manager/Director | 8 |
| Assistant to Executive | 1 |
| Treasurer | 3 |
| Director of Education | 3 |
| Marketing Director/Coordinator/Officer | 1 |
| Board Member/Program Director/Member Services | 1 |
| Other | 20 |
| Total | 100% |

Source: Recent Meetings Market Report by *Meetings & Conventions* magazine.

planning. In the largest organization, this person may have a staff as well. This convention planner thus is another person you should consider as very important when you make your presentation. He or she reports to and works closely with the executive director. Often the executive appoints a site selection committee to do **site inspections**. This group visits cities and hotels and is responsible for securing convention space arrangements for the association.

Small associations that cannot afford a full-time executive may choose to hire the services of a **multiple-association management company**. These organizations function as the executive and office staff for a number of associations that otherwise would have to make do with volunteers. In this way, the associations enjoy professional management at costs they can afford.

---

### Former Executive Directors Speak Out About How Site Decisions Are Made

**Garis Distelhorst, former CEO, National Association of College Stores:**
"Our process is collaborative. The meetings staff screens proposals and prepares a list of four or five cities. At that point, my role is to determine if there are any that wouldn't work and to suggest any destination not on the list that we might want to do additional research on. We try to follow an East/West/Central rotation. We focus on second-tier cities that are going to treat our meeting as a big deal...."

**Ron Moen, former Executive Director, American Association of Orthodontists:**
"Preliminary screening is the responsibility of the director of meetings. Actual site reviews of two or three cities on the short list are conducted by the director, myself, and the member of the board who will be president in the year that the meeting will be held. A committee of the board rubber-stamps our recommendation...when it's unanimous...."

**Dan Weber, former Executive Vice President, Institute of Food Technologies:**
"The recommendation comes to me. I visit cities in the running and make the site decision. While it ultimately goes to the executive committee for approval, in 30 years they've never failed to ratify a selection."

Source: Drs. J. Dana Clark, Catherine Price and Suzanne Murrmann, "Collaborative 'Buying Centers': How Associations Choose Destinations," *Convene*.

## Chapter 4: Selling the Association Market

There are approximately 500 association management companies in business today, managing the affairs of over 800 national associations and more than 1,000 state and regional associations.

If an association employs an association management company (AMC), you may find yourself dealing with one man or woman responsible for several convention bookings. The advantage to you is that when selling to these organizations you are not talking about a group coming back in four or five years. One of their clients may be interested in your property later in the same year. Many of these management organizations specialize in one or two industries. If your hotel's history shows a concentration of certain types of associations, such as automotive or computer groups, it would be wise to link with those association management organizations that represent these types of associations.

The trade association representing association management organizations is called the Association Management Companies Institute (www.amcinstitute.org). The AMCI holds an annual meeting and trade show, and is an ideal target market for smaller lodging properties.

In addition to "traditional" AMCs, some associations now utilize the services of firms that offer single components, such as hotel rate negotiations, logistics at the meeting site, and so on. Using these firms, which basically function like third-party planners, not only frees up association staff for other duties (such as planning the meeting or convention program), but the association also benefits when it comes to negotiating hotel rates. Since smaller associations have little bargaining power due to their infrequent meeting schedules, outsourcing this task to a firm that handles negotiations for hundreds of associations can make an enormous difference when it comes to hotel rates. HelmsBriscoe, for example, is

---

### 🖥 INTERNET EXERCISE

### Multiple Association Management Companies

Many small associations cannot afford a full-time association executive to manage their groups. These smaller associations, therefore, often contract with a multiple-association management company that will serve each association as needed, including selecting convention sites and planning conventions at an affordable cost.

These multiple-association management firms have organized their own trade association, the Association Management Companies Institute. Log on to their website (www.amcinstitute.org) to answer the following questions:

1. What is a multiple-association management company and who do these companies serve?

2. What specific services does the AMC Institute offer to its members?

3. Are hotels allowed to join the organization as associate members?

*SmithBucklin Chairman & CEO Henry S. Givray speaks to executive Boot Camp participants about leadership.*

Next, log on to the websites of Talley Management Group, Inc. (www.talley.com), SmithBucklin (www.smithbucklin.com), and Eisenmann & Associates, Inc. (www.eisenmanassociates.com), three of the largest multiple-association management companies, to answer the following questions:

1. Approximately how many associations does each represent?

2. What services does each provide?

the largest single source of group business for such chains as Hilton Worldwide, InterContinental Hotels Group, Marriott International, and Starwood Hotels & Resorts.

There is generally no cost for some negotiated services, such as room rates (firms receive commissions from hotels and from other service providers), and the fee for other services is comparable to the cost of the task if handled by the association (the difference is that services can be contracted on an as-needed basis, which is especially important to associations that have a limited staff). Convention management companies work either for a negotiated fee or for a percentage of the registration fees as an incentive to stimulate attendance. Such management firms obviously are important. They influence site selection and are also the people who work with the hotels to execute the meeting.

## Association President and Officers

The power of the president varies greatly among associations. As mentioned, the president usually serves for a year or two. He or she may serve as an honorary figurehead or may flex a great deal of muscle. You really have no choice but to pay a lot of attention to this key person. In almost all cases, keep in mind that he or she shares in the initial screening of a selection site and is certainly in on the final decision.

When you build your files on association personnel, take notes on the vice presidents and secretary/treasurers as well. These officers are often future years' presidents. A recent study suggests:

> It is not uncommon in associations to have a new chairperson every year. Often, this chairperson has substantial power over staff and other members...Such power may include the ability to affect the list of sites initially being considered and one that is eventually chosen as the convention location in the future. Because of the lead time necessary to plan major conventions or trade shows, many of these meeting sites are picked years in advance. At the same time, many associations also know in advance who the association president will be in any given year. Either tradition or bylaws regulate much of the decision power on site selection to the person who will be president during the year of a particular convention. Therefore, marketing strategies not only need to be aimed at the current chair or president, they need to identify and court future leaders. A long-term relationship between the hospitality marketer and the association chair(s)-to-be can impact how they use their influence in your favor for the year they are in power.[3]

## Committee Chairperson

Certain committee heads get involved in the initial suggestions and screening. This depends on the nature and structure of the organization and the subject of the event. Commitee chairpersons definitely are a factor in site selection for seminars dealing with the committee's subject matter.

You can see that a fair number of hands get involved in creating the original list of proposed places and in the preliminary screening to narrow down the choices. If you are eliminated in the final selection, it may mean loss of business that year, but you may well be in line for a booking when the cycle brings the association back to your part of the country.

> **Profile of Association Meeting Planners**
>
> - 75% are female; the average age is 50.
> - Spend an average of 60% of their professional time on meeting planning activities.
> - Have been arranging meetings for 13 years.
> - Decision-making responsibilities include: selecting hotels (87%); selecting locations (78%); setting budgets (78%); planning entertainment (76%); trade show/exhibit planning (66%); and planning meeting agendas (58%).
> - Approximately one-quarter have earned profession certifications, and the majority hold membership in a meeting planning association such as MPI, ASAE, or PCMA.
>
> Source: Recent Meetings Market Report by *Meetings & Conventions* magazine.

There may also be some consolation prizes in the form of selection for lesser events such as committee meetings or seminars.

## Board of Directors

The selection list is usually presented to the board of directors, who make the final selection. It is worth emphasizing that the recommendations of the executive director usually are accepted. Some get their way all the time; some must deal more politically and tactfully. But the executive director remains the single most important person you must sell to get association business. He or she may not rule autocratically, but they manage to get their own way most of the time. You may lose the business at the directors' meeting, but without the support of the executive director, you never even get that far. Generally, *all* the finalists have won the director's approval.

## Other Influences

It is common practice in many scientific and technical societies for local chapters to make an **association bid** for the national event. That is not to say they *bid* in the sense of offering money. Rather, they request the honor of playing **local host** to the national group and offer their efforts to make the convention a success. This is especially true with international societies; an invitation from a national chapter is required before a location is considered.

Hotel salespeople are aware of this practice. There are cases in which a local delegate to an international congress has been approached by a convention bureau or hotel. An appeal is made to his local pride and to any other emotions that can be brought to bear. It is not uncommon in such cases for the bureau or hotel to bear the costs of the delegate's travel, a hospitality suite, and the presentation to the board. It is wise to assure the delegate that the bureau or hotel would supply clerical support to enable the delegate to fulfill his role of host.

It doesn't always require such effort. Appeals to local delegates or chapters often bring results merely because of civic pride and a willingness to help local businesses. Look around your city and make friends with people in local association chapters. At the very least, you may pick up a banquet or one-night meeting.

It is important when you enlist the aid of local members to impress upon them that you and your establishment are fully capable of handling the business. They may very well feel uncertain about the wisdom of getting involved and perhaps fear the embarrassment of a debacle at the national convention. But then you have to convince any prospect at any level that you and your staff are competent and interested in doing a good job. Those are the two key points you must make over and over — that your staff has the *expertise* and the *desire* to do whatever must be done to execute the meeting properly.

## Sources for Finding Association Business

Fortunately, associations can be readily located. The national ones seem to be clustered in a relatively few cities. The Washington, D.C. area is home to more associations (4,000) than any other city, with New York City (2,400) and Chicago (2,000) placing second and third. Other major U.S. headquarter cities include Austin, Indianapolis, Los Angeles, Milwaukee, Oklahoma City, Philadelphia, and Richmond. In Canada, sources for association business can generally be found in Ottawa and in the capitals of the provinces.

### Directories and Databases

While print directories are on the decline, due to their cost and the inability to update information on a frequent basis, there are still several print resources that can be used to locate association decision-makers. One example is *Encyclopedia of Associations: National Organizations of the U.S.*, which provides information on more than 25,000 membership organizations; entries include: the organization's complete name, address, e-mail address, and/or website; the primary official's name, title, and telephone number; the association's founding date; the purpose of the association; dues; and data on the association's national and international conferences. This volume, which is published annually by Gale (www.gale.com), is part of the Gale Library Directory, which also offers online databases of this book and its other publications, including *Encyclopedia of Associations: Regional, State, and Local Organizations*, and *Encyclopedia of Associations: International Organizations*. The online versions may include more data than the print version (especially if several months have passed since the publication date), and individual entries can be printed, e-mailed, or downloaded; also, entries of online versions include direct links to the organization's website and e-mail addresses (when available).

> **MORE ONLINE**
>
> AssociationExecs.com (www.associationexecs.com) provides information on over 45,000 association executives in 16,000 associations as well as 400 association management firms. Entries are updated daily, and planners listed can be contacted by email directly from the site. A subscription is required to access data, but a free trial is available.

Another publication that is available in print and online is the *National Trade and Professional Association Directory*, which features listings of over 20,000 association executives in 7,800-plus organizations. This resource is available for purchase on the Associationexecs.com (www.associationexecs.com) and Association TRENDS™ (www.associationtrends.com/store) sites, and online access can be purchased for the Associationexecs.com online version. Both sites also offer the *Association Meeting & Event Planners CD Directory* and have customizable mailing lists available for purchase.

One of the largest sources for association information is Meeting Planner Lists (www.meetingplannerlists.com), a service offered to its membership by the Hospitality Sales & Marketing Association International (HSMAI) (www.hsmai.org). This database, which includes information on over 50,000 meeting planners, offers customized searching for national and state and regional associations by such criteria as location, group size, type of facility desired, and so on (see Figure 4.12). Members of the HSMAI receive 100 free searches annually, and members and exhibitors at HSMAI events receive a ten percent discount on additional searches. Annual student and faculty memberships are available (at $70 and $100 respectively), while hotel/associate memberships cost $385 per year.

## Chapter 4: Selling the Association Market

**Figure 4.12 SAMPLE OF INFORMATION PROVIDED BY DIRECTORIES.**

| | | | CALIFORNIA – HUNTINGTON BEACH | | ■ TYPE OF MEETING | † NO. MEETINGS PER ANNUAL | † MONTHS HELD | ★ NO. OF DAYS | ★ NO. OF ATTENDEES | O TYPE OF FACILITY |
|---|---|---|---|---|---|---|---|---|---|---|
| | ASSOCIATION | MEETING PLANNERS | CONVENTION BOOKINGS | | | | | | | |
| | UNITED STATES LIFESAVING ASSN (USLA) PO BOX 366 HUNTINGTON BEACH, 92648 714-536-5283/FAX: 714-374-1500 | BILL RICHARDSON (Pres) *Speaker  Exhibit Space* | 05/93 Florida Keys 11/93 Chicago 05/94 Seattle Booked 6 mos in advance | | C | | | 3 | B | DAR |
| | WESTERN ECONOMIC ASSN INTL (WEA) 7400 CTR AVE # 109 HUNTINGTON BEACH, 92647 714-898-3222/FAX: 714-891-5715 | ELDON J DVORAK (Exec Vp) VERONICA M DVORAK (Dir Of Conf) | 06/91 Seattle 06/94 Vancouver 07/92 San Francisco 07/95 San Diego 06/93 Lake Tahoe   Far East Booked 1 yr in advance   South Pacific OC | | C M | 1 | | 3-4 | E | DRC |
| | WYCLIFFE BIBLE TRANSLATORS (WBT) P O BOX 2727 HUNTINGTON BEACH, 92647 714-969-4600/FAX: 714-969-4861 | RON OLSON (Assoc Dir) GERALD ELDER (Treas) *Speaker* | OC | | M | 12 | V | 3 | A | |
| | THE ELECTRICAL MANUFACTURING & COIL WINDING ASSN INC PO BOX 278 IMPERIAL BEACH, 91933 619-575-4191/FAX: 619-575-5009 | CHARLES E THURMAN (Exec Dir) *Speaker* | 10/91 Boston 10/93 Chicago 09/92 Cincinnati 09/94 Chicago 06/93 Hong Kong   Far East Booked 2-3 yrs in advance OC | | C M | 2-3 | | 3-4 3 | E A | AC |
| | AMERICAN COLLEGE OF TRIAL LAWYERS (ACTL) 8001 IRVINE CTR DR STE 960 IRVINE, 92718 714-727-3194/FAX: 714-727-3894 | ROBERT A YOUNG (Exec Dir) | Booked 2-3 yrs in advance | | | | | | | |
| | INTERIOR DESIGN EDUCATORS COUNCIL (IDEC) 14252 CULVER DR SUITE A331 IRVINE, 92714 714-551-1622 | CANDEE ERWIN (Exec Secy) *Exhibit Space* | 04/92 Alexandria | | M | 6 | 4 | 4 | C | D |
| | MOTORCYCLE INDUSTRY COUNCIL (MIC) 2 JENNER ST SUITE 150 IRVINE, 92718 714-727-4211 | PAMELA AMETTE (Vp) CATHY WILSHIRE (Asst Prog Dir) *Speaker* | 02/94 Cincinnati 02/95 Cincinnati Booked 2 yrs in advance | | C M | 1 | 10 | 1 3 | A U | C C |
| | MULTI LEVEL MARKETING INTL ASSN. (MLMIA) 119 STANFORD CT IRVINE, 92715 714-854-0484/FAX: 714-854-7687 | DORIS WOOD (Pres.) *Exhibit Space* | 09/91 Toronto 08/92 Orange County   Canada 02/93 Orange County   Europe   Far East Booked 3-5 mos in advance OC | | C M | 4 | 1, 4, 7, 10 | 4-5 2-3 | B U | AR |
| | NATIONAL ASSN OF NAMEPLATE MANUFACTURERS (NAME) 17300 RED HILL AVE STE 100 IRVINE, 92714 714-261-9588/FAX: 714-261-2594 | JAMES A KINDER (Exec Vp) LINDA BRADY (Dir Of Educ) *Speaker  Exhibit Space* | 03/93 Naples 10/94 St Louis 09/93 New Orleans 03/95 Palm Springs 03/94 Scottsdale   Mexico   Caribbean Booked 2 yrs in advance OC | | C M | 1 | | 1-2 4-5 | D B | D DR |
| | NATIONAL MIDAS DEALERS ASSN (NMDA) 14795 JEFFREY RD STE 202 IRVINE, 92720 714-551-1289/FAX: 714-551-0621 | MYRON P GORDON (Exec Dir) FRANK MAGLIOCCO (Assoc Exec Dir) *Exhibit Space* | 10/91 Las Vegas 09/94 Boca Raton 11/92 New Orleans 10/93 Colorado Springs  Canada Booked 2-3 yrs in advance OC | | C M | 10 | 1, 2, 3, 4, 5, 6, 7, 8, 9, 10, 11, 12 | 4 1-4 | C U | DR A |

■ TYPE OF MEETING  (C) Convention Data  (M) Smaller Meetings & Seminar Data
† MONTHS HELD  (1) Jan (2) Feb (3) Mar (4) Apr (5) May (6) June (7) July (8) Aug (9) Sept (10) Oct (11) Nov (12) Dec
  (P) Spring (S) Summer (F) Fall (W) Winter (V) Various
★ NUMBER OF ATTENDEES  (U) Under 50  (A) 51-100  (B) 101-200  (C) 201-500  (D) 501-1000  (E) 1001-5000  (F) Over 5000
O TYPE OF FACILITY  (D) Downtown  (A) Airport  (R) Resort  (C) Convention Center

This is a typical entry from Meeting Planner Lists (www.meetingplannerlists.com/association.aspx), which offers information on over 17,000 state and national associations and 40,000 association meeting executives. A useful feature in this directory is the type of facility used; this information can help salespeople to target their sales efforts to associations that typically use their type of property. Other lists of meeting planners are available to members of such organizations as the Association of Meeting Professionals (AMPS) (see www.ampsweb.org for more information) and the Destination Marketing Association International (DMAI) (www.destinationmarketing.org).

> ### 💻 INTERNET EXERCISE
> #### Links to Meetings-Related Websites
>
> Listing your property with online meeting directories is a cost-effective method of reaching meeting planners. The web sites listed below allow meeting planners to search for hotels and send out requests for proposals (RFPs). Hotels listed generally pay the site a commission for each RFP that results in a booking. These sites also offer the opportunity for hotels to purchase banner ads and priority listings. The volume of RFPs from these sites continues to grow as meeting planners see "online shopping" as one of the most desirable ways to research hotels. Log on to the following web sites to answer the questions that follow:
>
> - Cvent (www.cvent.com)
> - Meeting Broker (www.meetingbroker.com)
> - Lanyon Star Cite™ (www.lanyon.com/solutions/starcite)
>
> 1. Which online marketplace focuses on smaller groups?
>
> 2. Which site is affiliated with the Destination Marketing Association International (DMAI)?
>
> 3. Which is the lead management program for Newmarket International and has partnered with Cvent, Worktopia, and StarCite to send leads directly to hotel users of their Delphi sales and catering software?

The Destination Marketing Association International (DMAI) (www.destinationmarketing.org) also offers a large database to its membership (student and educator memberships are available). For many years, this information was kept confidential, but the organization later made its historical and demographic meeting information available through its member bureaus. These meeting profiles include such invaluable information as the decision-maker, history of past meetings, start and end dates, registered attendance, number of guestrooms used, number of meeting rooms used, square footage of exhibit space, and definite and tentative future bookings. Today, the DMAI offers empowerMINT, which is described as "an industry-wide, collaborative marketing initiative whose mission is to connect planners to DMOs." The database contains over 168,000 meeting histories as well as information on over 96,000 meeting planners, 30,000 meeting organizations, and 148 participating destination marketing organizations (DMOs).

There are far too many other sources to list here, but you can visit your local library's reference section to check for publications, and many libraries are also participating members of database services, such as Reference USA (referenceusa.com). You can also do an Internet search for association membership listings, especially those in the fields that your property wishes to target. And, you can also find — and connect with — meeting planners on such professional sites as LinkedIn (www.linkedin.com).

Most meeting planners are eager to verify information for these databases on their organizations' meetings for two reasons. First, this history provides them with information useful in negotiating with hotels. Second, planners recognize that database information allows hotels to target their prospects, eliminating misdirected efforts and reducing the number of cold calls from suppliers that do not have enough rooms and/or meeting space for their meetings.

Databases provide a valuable service in building your prospect file for sales campaigns. One subscriber to databases says, "We feel it is an innovative way to find pre-qualified profiles and a really efficient way to pursue business. By receiving the profiles, we save hours of time that would otherwise be spent on cold calls."

## Specialized Periodicals

There are a number of periodicals that serve the market. Some go only to association personnel; others are distributed to both association and corporate personnel. Their advertisers are hotels, convention bureaus, airlines, and other suppliers in the convention industry.

*Associations Now* is published monthly by the American Society of Association Executives. Its circulation consists of the members of this prestigious organization (over 21,000 association executives). The list is available for rental for direct mail under specific circumstances. The Association Directory & Buying Guide lists members with their addresses and telephone numbers, which makes it most useful. Vendors may join the society as associate members.

*Association News* (www.associationnews.com) is a monthly magazine directed to state and regional associations. If this is your target market, you might consider advertising in this publication (the print and digital editions have a circulation of over 80,000 association executives and meeting planners).

*Convene* is published ten times annually by the Professional Convention Managers Association (PCMA).

*Meetings & Conventions* is a monthly publication whose circulation also contains association personnel. Its circulation is available for rental for direct mail. Advertisers get a reader service card system plus a sales lead service in the association and corporate fields.

These are prominent publications but not the only ones. For a comprehensive list of trade publications directed to the meetings industry, visit www.conventionplanit.com. Click on "News & Resources," scroll down and click on "Industry Resources," and then click on "Publications" to reach the "Trade Publications" page (click on the "Trade Publications" link below the search box to see the listings of these resources). Many of these publications offer free subscriptions to those involved with the convention and meetings industry. Information as to the particular segment each serves should be obtained from the publishers. Begin today to advance your knowledge by submitting your information and subscribing to publications of interest.

## Hotel Records

If you are newly assigned to a hotel convention sales staff, one of the first things to do is to closet yourself with the function books and other records from the past few years. Much can be learned from them. Identify your most lucrative association accounts and determine why they are your best producers — and how you can find similar business. How many groups met in your house but never returned? It is amazing how many times business is lost because no one followed up and pressed for more business.

Your hotel records will also offer clues to personnel changes. If a group didn't return, a new executive director could offer another chance. You could call and indicate that his group had met successfully at your hotel in the past and perhaps persuade the group to book again. You also should try to find out where the previous director is now located. After all, he or she selected your hotel previously and may be amenable to doing so again. No sales staffer should rely on a past customer's memory to bring him or her back. Sales life is not that easy. You must go after business.

Learning about a hotel's customer history is important, but that doesn't mean that a salesperson has to spend valuable sales time poring over files. Industry expert Howard Feiertag, who has written articles for *Hotel & Motel Management* magazine for over three decades, states:

Time needs to be set aside, perhaps even on a daily basis, for someone to get back into the old files to do some prospecting. This is not a difficult task. In fact, salespeople need to get someone else to do the prospecting so that sales staffers can better spend their time in actual selling to the prospects that are being developed.[4]

Keep in mind that the easiest prospect is a satisfied past customer. Referrals and recommendations from satisfied planners are excellent ways to prospect for new business. Don't wait for details of a planner's event to sit dormant in your property's records — planners are happy and motivated upon the completion of a successful event; that is the time to ask for referrals. Potential prospects who have been introduced through a referral will have a much greater close rate — 50 to 90 percent higher. When meetings go well, you have excellent prospects for repeat business. If they do not go well, it is imperative to find out why. It could be something that you must prevent from happening with other clients, or it may be something that you have already corrected and you could then press for business. Some of the best business relationships result from clearing up past grievances, many of which could have been eliminated in the first place had sales executives better understood the needs of association meeting planners. To minimize problems with members of this market segment, some hotel chains are offering specialized training to their sales personnel (see "Best Practices" box).

Hotel records may also lead to other prospects gleaned from local small bookings. A dinner meeting handled solely by the banquet manager may indicate only a local chapter. But this small bit of business of dinner for twenty or so may be just the Trojan horse you

---

**Best Practices**

### Marriott Hotels & Resorts and PCMA Team Up to Help Hotel Sales Executives Think Like Association Meeting Planners

The Certified Association Sales Executive (CASE) Marriott/PCMA Program is an intensive nine-week course designed exclusively for hotel sales executives who sell to the association market. Louis Nicholls, senior account executive for Marriott International and a CASE graduate, says:

> This course specifically targets issues that pertain to our industry and our day-to-day roles in it.

The CASE program, which is open to all Marriott employees involved in association sales, gives the sales executives the opportunity to "get inside the heads" of their association clients through a combination of online learning, instructor-led training, and first-hand experience with association personnel. Jessica van der Gaast, a senior account executive at the San Francisco Marriott, who had never been on the association side of meeting planning, says:

> I had the opportunity to observe the roles and responsibilities for each staff member of the association, sit in on important meetings, and observe first-hand the decision-making process and structure of the organization. I had one-on-one discussion time with each staff person, including the executive director, and learned about current technology and changes in society in terms of how they affect the organization and its strategic planning.

Through this course, hotel salespeople get a real sense of how associations operate in terms of structure and timing issues. This understanding helps them to see associations as valuable business and be able to offer solutions to help this segment meet their objectives.
**Source: Ginny Phillips, "Creating a Niche," *Convene*.**

need to penetrate the state or national parent organization. Much can be learned from the members themselves. At the least, a follow-up phone call will increase the chances for more local business.

It is important to realize that much association business must be cultivated over the long haul, so don't get discouraged. The road to that major booking may have to go through many minor bits of business before you score the big one, or before scoring at all. Maintain a good follow-up system; keep after target associations, and you'll get your share.

## Summary

In this chapter, we have discussed the importance of the associations market to hotels and identified some of the factors that hospitality firms need to consider if they wish to target this market segment. It is essential to know the types of meetings that associations hold, the characteristics of these meetings (cycle and pattern, geographic restrictions, lead time, kinds of sites desired, and price considerations), and to determine the key decision-makers and how to reach them. A hotel that "does its homework" can attract business that will fill rooms and bring revenue to the property's other facilities in what would normally be slack months, and may generate significant repeat business from association meeting attendees.

In the next chapter, we will discuss the corporate meetings market. While some corporate meetings may seem similar to those held by associations at first glance, there are major differences to consider that will enable your property to target this primary source of meetings business.

## Endnotes

1. "Top 10 Global Destinations for Associations," *Meetings & Conventions*, June 2014, p. 18.
2. Jeff Sacks, CMP, "Site Selection," www.pcma.org/templates/Conferon/charts/Ch2_1.htm.
3. J. Dana Clark, Michael R. Evans, and Bonnie J. Knutson, "Selecting a Site for an Association Convention: An Exploratory Look at the Types of Power Used by Committee Members to Influence Decisions," *Journal of Hospitality & Leisure Marketing*.
4. Howard Feiertag, "Prospecting for Clients and Booking Groups Made Easy," *Hotel Management.net*, posted on January 13, 2014.

## Study Questions

1. Conventions are extremely important to associations for financial reasons. Explain why.
2. What kinds of meetings do associations hold? What type of facilities are best suited to each?
3. How do state and regional association meetings differ from the national

# Chapter 4: Selling the Association Market

association meetings?
4. Identify the monthly and daily meeting patterns of association meetings.
5. Attendance for association conventions is voluntary. How important is price to association executives? What implications does this have on a hotel's sales efforts?
6. What individuals in the association make the site selection decision?
7. List sources for locating associations.

## Key Terms

**association**—A group of people joined together for a common purpose.
**association bid**—A regional chapter requests the honor of hosting a national convention.
**breakout session**—Small group sessions within the meeting, formed to discuss specific topics.
**concurrent session**—Meeting sessions on different topics scheduled at the same time.
**general session**—The main meeting attended by the majority of the association members. Also called a **plenary session**.
**hybrid meetings** – A meeting or event, such as a tradeshow, that combines a "live," in-person component with a "virtual" online component. Hybrid meetings offer the advantage of bringing the event to members who cannot be there in person and enable the event to be shared with members at a number of locations simultaneously.
**lead time**—The time between the booking of the meeting and the actual meeting date.
**local host**—A group of local people that carries out the strategies and policies established for the organization of an event held in their geographic area. Also called an **organizing committee**.
**multiple-association management companies**—Firms that function as the executive and office staff for a number of associations.
**second-tier cities** – Smaller cities and suburbs of major cities that offer the meeting planner an attractive location while providing less costly accommodations and transportation.
**site inspection**—Tour of the property conducted by representatives of the association or corporation in order to determine whether the hotel is suitable to host the meeting/event.
**social responsibility** – Meetings that include a combination of volunteer and team-building activities.
**walkable cities** – Cities that offer hotels, dining, shopping, cultural activities, and entertainment in close proximity to the meeting site. Choosing a walkable city not only stimulates attendance, but it also cuts costs by eliminating the need for bus or shuttle services.

## Industry Profile

# Tina Edmundson, Global Officer/Senior Vice President Luxury and Lifestyle Brands

### Marriott International

*A graduate of the University of Bombay, India, Tina Edmundson enrolled in the master's program at the Hilton School of Hotel Management at the University of Houston to pursue her interest in hotels. Edmundson's experience includes serving as general manager of the Westin in Philadelphia before beginning her career in the luxury segment with the creation of the W brand and the repositioning of the St. Regis brand. Moving to Marriott International in 2008, she served as senior vice president and global brand leader, lifestyle brands before being named to her current position.*

## The Road to a Career in Luxury Brands

One thing I say to young people on my team is: 'If you're going to be in this business, then it is really important that you run a hotel.' What I wanted to do, quite frankly, was run hotels. My plan was to be a general manager and hopefully have some area role where I had multiple hotels. If your career ambition is to have a big job in a corporate environment, you have to understand the business you are in. That means being responsible for the P&L for a hotel, and I've done that. Then, I think my experience in sales, revenue management, and brand management helped a lot at Starwood, particularly in the luxury and lifestyle space.

For those graduating from hotel school, it's crucial to remain open to trying a variety of experience. Just because you are great in the F&B area doesn't mean you shouldn't try sales. Exposure is the name of the game.

My job now is to elevate the presence of Marriott's luxury and life-style portfolio. That portfolio – Edition, Autograph Collection, Renaissance, Moxy, the Ritz-Carlton, Ritz-Carlton Reserve, JW Marriott, and Bulgari Hotels – has close to 450 hotels with a pipeline of 200 more. This involves making sure Marriott understands where each brand is in the cycle and that each has the support to stay distinctive, relevant, and deliver on the brand promise.

Luxury is about finding what's authentic; it's not all about the show anymore. It's about coming away from an experience feeling like you've had this really meaningful sort of authentic experience and having it less stuffy. The culture Ritz-Carlton has is wonderful, and it's really hard to create. It's our jobs to protect what's special and to protect the magic with Ritz-Carlton.

Friendly but not familiar is really where the next generation is going. The data we see when we do research around it really talks about that. What resonates with this generation is honesty and integrity. You're looking for what feels right – not necessarily what looks very polished and put together. You really want to make sure you never have a cookie-cutter mentality.

Technology is also playing a large role in service. At Moxy, for example, it's much about a self-service, do-it-yourself environment. We've really done our homework to understand what the target guest is looking for and designed the spaces and experience to actually show that. The most important thing is free Wi-Fi, so we want to make sure we're delivering on that. Then it's being tech-enabled to make sure all of their devices can connect and they are not searching for plugs. These things sound small until you don't have them, and then it's the biggest deal ever.

We also manage social media in two ways. One is from a customer-care perspective, which is a response to anything people may say across channels. The other is the push of information on various channels, and each brand has its own voice to be quite authentic.

**Learning Objectives:**

This portion of your text takes a look at the corporate meetings market. We will discuss the kinds of meeting held by corporations and what factors are considered in staging corporate meetings, the key decision-makers for company meetings, and how to locate sources of corporate business. When you have studied this chapter, you will:

- Be able to identify factors that corporate meeting planners consider when making a site selection.

- Be able to describe the types of meetings held by companies and tell how these meetings differ from meetings staged by associations.

- Know the characteristics and requirements for company meetings of all types.

- Be able to identify key corporate decision-makers and detail ways in which sources of business can be located.

**Outline**

Requirements for Corporate Meetings
Kinds of Company Meetings
- National and Regional Sales Meetings
- New Product/Dealer Meetings
- Professional/Technical Meetings
- Management Meetings
- Training Meetings
- Stockholder/Public Meetings
- Incentive Meetings

Characteristics of Company Meetings
- Small Meetings
- Time Cycle
- Lead Time
- Geographical Patterns
- Kinds of Sites
- Attendance
- Duration
- Exhibits
- Meeting Room Requirements
- One Meeting, One Check
- Multi-Booking Potential

Corporate Meeting Decision-Makers
- Full-time Meeting Planner
- Company President
- Marketing and Sales Executives
- Advertising and Sales Managers
- Other Corporate Executives
- Passenger Traffic/Corporate Travel Managers
- Procurement (Purchasing) Managers
- Training Director
- Meeting Specialists/Third-Party Planners

Sources for Finding Corporate Business and Decision-Makers
- Special Meeting Publications
- Trade Directories, Publications, and Databases
- Trade Associations
- Convention and Visitors Bureaus
- Lateral Referral and Account Penetration

Summary

# 5 Selling the Corporate Meetings Market

Today's corporation is a complex organization. The geographic marketing range has grown to the point that most companies now market nationally or internationally. The structure of larger companies is more detailed and multifaceted than ever before. Modern executives who received their training with such companies in mind are keenly aware of the vital need for *communication*. Meetings remain a most basic form of communication within companies. As a hotel salesperson you are concerned solely with those company meetings that take place off company premises, and there are enough of them to satisfy any enterprising hotel sales staff.

If the association convention business represents the best-known and most visible segment of the meetings field, corporate meetings offer the greatest potential for growth. You must, however, keep up with the latest trends to be ready to meet the needs of this market. Today's corporate meeting planners are shifting their focus in terms of meeting locations as well as the size and "flavor" of their events. A recent survey by StarCite, a leader in meeting management, meetings procurement, and online event registration, showed that 70 percent of meeting planners are meeting closer to home and that 43 percent are changing the ambience to reflect backlash against what appears to be corporate excesses.

The new "normal" environment calls for meetings that are sensible, practical, and responsible — with an emphasis on value, convenience, and service.[1] This means that companies are meeting closer to home (with regional rather than national meetings) or in less expensive second-tier cities. Corporate meetings are also getting smaller due to budget cuts, and may include virtual components, such as teleconferencing and "webinars," to save on travel costs.

Corporate meetings are also more likely to be more strategic and practical. Certain elements, such as elaborate meal functions and big-ticket entertainment, are being scaled down or eliminated as companies seek to be more fiscally responsible. In response to this trend, a new industry buzzword, **strategic meetings management**, has been coined to reflect how corporate meeting planners strive to prove to their bosses that meetings and events can be strategic assets to their companies.

Corporate business may not seem as visible as association meetings, but business meetings are held far more often, and they generate higher revenues from guestrooms and food and beverage. Since company meetings are varied and are controlled by a wider variety of personnel, they are harder to dig out. But they offer a great deal of group business potential that no hotel should ignore.

Fortunately, hotel marketing people do not have to decide which segment of the market — associations or corporations — to sell. The two are a digestible mix, and a successful property enjoys its share of both kinds. The ratio of each really reflects upon the kind of property you have, what you are equipped to handle, and where you are located. While some hotel features and benefits appeal to both markets, there are significant differences (see Figure 5.1). Examine your hotel with an eye to what corporate meeting planners want and the kinds of meetings they hold.

---

**MORE ONLINE**

To learn more about SMM, log onto www.mpiweb.org/portal/research. Resources include: SMM Research; SMM Resource Library; Meeting Design; Articles, Blogs & Videos; Education; and, Discussion. You can also find a number of other sites that offer advice on SMM by using a search engine.

## Chapter 5: Selling the Corporate Meetings Market

*Figure 5.1. COMPARISON OF ASSOCIATION AND CORPORATE MEETING GROUPS.*

| FACTOR | ASSOCIATION | CORPORATION |
|---|---|---|
| Attendance | Voluntary | Mandatory |
| Decision-making | Decentralized; often commitee | Centralized (usually one person) |
| Meeting Focus | Primarily educational and networking opportunities held in conjunction with trade shows | Training, team-building, or incentives |
| Hybrid Meetings | Increasingly used for general sessions to engage both on-site and market to off-site members | Limited usage, teleconferencing is more common |
| Strategic Meetings Management | Not widely used | Defining and identifying ROI on meetings is high on the list of priorities |
| Room Block | Must track reservation pickup closely | Stable |
| Spouse Attendance | Common | Seldom |
| Exhibits | Frequent; heavy demand for hospitality suites | Less frequent |
| Site Selection | Need to build attendance with attractive location | Seek convenience, service, and security |
| Location | Look for hotels close to the destination's convention center and cities with attractions and shopping within walking distance | Purpose of the meeting is determinant in city and venue choice |
| Geographic Pattern | Rotate geographically | No set pattern |
| Lead Time | Long (usually two to five years) | Short (often less than one year) |
| Billing Format | Individual Folios | Master Account |
| Risk of Cancellation | Minimal | Higher; penalty clauses and advance deposits are common |
| Arrival/Departure | More likely to have early arrivals | Few early arrivals or departures |
| Convention and Visitors Bureau involvement | Frequently utilize convention bureaus, especially with citywide conventions | Seldom contact convention bureau |
| Attrition Concerns | Over 50% of association meeting planners cite attrition as a major issue in contracts | Only one in four corporate planners mention attrition as a concern |

*If you pursue a career in convention sales and services, you must have an understanding of the critical differences between association and corporate meetings. This knowledge will be vital when responding to a request for proposal (RFP) or selling to meeting planners face-to-face.*

Chapter 5: Selling the Corporate Meetings Market

## Requirements for Corporate Meetings

The factors that make a hotel attractive for association events hold true for most corporate meetings too. Keep in mind that corporate meetings vary a great deal in size, scope, and purpose. It is important, therefore, to match the planner's needs with the hotel's facilities.

**Quality food service.** Food and beverage functions are major contributors to the success or failure of corporate meetings. Long after other meeting details are forgotten, corporate attendees remember an elegant banquet, a unique refreshment break, or an unusual theme party.

Hotels can increase the comfort level in this area by having staff that assures the meeting planner of the property's attention to all the details of food and beverage functions. Mark Beaupre, former food and beverage director and executive chef for the JW Marriott Orlando Grande Lakes and currently food and beverage director at Marriott's Orlando World Center, always meets with meeting planners beforehand and says:

> The idea is to build relationships, especially if the meeting is, say, three years away. I assist the sales managers, and that really adds to the comfort level of the person responsible for the event. By the time the group gets here, I have talked with and e-mailed him or her many times. During

---

### STRATEGIC MEETINGS MANAGEMENT

Many corporations today view their meetings as an investment, and they are setting up Strategic Meetings Management Programs (SMMP) to ensure that their meetings are providing a good return on that investment (ROI); some corporations use the term return on event (ROE). Today's corporate meeting planners, therefore, have much more to consider than booking a site and guestrooms; they must become strategic thinkers and financial strategists to prove to management that the meeting was both justified and meaningful to attendees.

No longer does a corporate planner select a property based solely on location or type of facilities offered; they must select a hotel that meets management's objectives in terms of bottom-line value. One of the strategies to ensure that meetings business will be handled properly and cost-effectively is to select specific properties or chains that meet the corporation's requirements. Large international companies, such as Siemens, Pfizer, and Best Buy (as well as a growing number of other businesses), opt to enter into **preferred vendor agreements** with hotel brands. These agreements spell out the specific terms of the relationship between the corporation and the hotel supplier, and many larger corporations draft their own meeting contract and stipulate their rules and expectations from their preferred hotel. Because of the volume of business large companies control, they are able to include favorable contract language for food and beverage, guestroom pickup, and attrition, yet they receive lower rates and other special treatment.

If you are a salesperson from an independent hotel who wishes to approach a large corporation that has preferred vendor agreements with chains such as Marriott, Hilton, or Starwood, you'll first need to contact the correct person at the corporation to discuss how you can become part of the preferred hotel program. Many have strict SMM programs which restrict meetings to those on their preferred hotel program, and they only use specific Internet companies, such as StarCite or Cvent, for distribution of their requests for proposals.

Before you try to get your foot in the door, reviewing a corporation's preapproved contract will help you to determine if you are able to work with their specific clauses. Additionally, knowing how a corporation's meeting planning department is structured is helpful prior to making contact. Such factors as whether the department is centralized or decentralized, if it utilizes a third-party planner, and their experiences with previous hotels can help you to properly plan a sales approach…or move on to more promising business.

the event, every evening I sit with the planner over a glass of wine, and we talk about that day and the one to follow.[2]

*Crown Room Banquet Setup.*
**Photograph courtesy of the Hotel del Coronado, San Diego, California.**

Corporate meeting planners consistently rate quality of food service as very important in choosing a hotel or facility (see Figure 5.2). The planner of today is continually encouraging the staff to surpass a previous year's convention program. To gain its share of repeat business, a hotel must continue to upgrade menus, contribute to the uniqueness of each event, and create an occasion that will be long remembered.

> **WORTH WATCHING**
>
> Sean Moon, managing editor of *Corporate Meetings and Events*, discusses food trends. Use a search engine and type in - Top five food trends in the corporate meetings and event industry

**Adequate meeting space.** It is hard to hold a meeting efficiently if the meeting rooms are too small—or too large (although surplus area may be screened off). When you go after corporate business, discuss room requirements in detail. The main room may need support from a number of small rooms. If your layout shows these nearby, you have a strong selling point. The traffic flow pattern of the meeting is very important.

In addition to adequate meeting space, most of today's corporate meeting planners require "high tech" equipment and Internet access in both meeting rooms and guestrooms. Since most corporate meetings are about productivity and businesspeople most generally come to these meetings armed with their laptops and mobile devices, hotels that wish to capture this market segment must offer such services as High-Speed Internet Access (HSIA) and/or Wi-Fi- wireless technology that allows attendees to log on to the Internet using radio frequencies (wireless technology is commonly offered in lobbies and other public areas as well as in meeting rooms and guestrooms).

The Internet is frequently used for demonstrations and business applications at corporate meetings, and attendees tap into the Internet to maintain productivity while on the road, including keeping in contact with customers via e-mail. In some cases, hotels are charging a daily fee (which can be a separate charge or included in the room rate) for both wired and wireless Internet access, or are "bundling" these services with other amenities, such as a continental breakfast and newspaper for Concierge Level service. Meeting planners (and guests), however, are increasingly insisting on free Internet and Wi-Fi services, and hotels are responding by offering these services at no charge.

155

## Chapter 5: Selling the Corporate Meetings Market

Still other hotels offer **business centers** for guests requiring Internet service or other office-related needs, such as faxing, copying, and shipping. Some business centers offer secretarial services and tech support, while others are self-service (see box titled "Hotel Business Centers").

Sheraton Hotels & Resorts has changed the concept of the traditional business center by providing a space for guests to meet, connect, and relax just off the lobby. Its Link@Sheraton program, which offers all the services of a traditional business center, also provides individual working spaces, community tables, entertainment options (big screen televisions, games, books, and so on), and food and beverage service. The concept has met with enthusiastic reviews from guests and from hotel management – it increases both guest satisfaction and food and beverage revenues.

> **WORTH WATCHING**
>
> Google Link@Sheraton Youtube to view a number of videos of the facilities and services included in Link@Sheraton locations around the United States.

Figure 5.2. FACTORS CONSIDERED IMPORTANT TO CORPORATE MEETING PLANNERS IN THE SELECTION OF A FACILITY/HOTEL.

| Factors Considered "Very Important" | Corporate Planners |
|---|---|
| Number, size, and quality of meeting rooms | 82% |
| Negotiable food, beverage, and room rates | 82 |
| Cost of hotel or meeting facility | 81 |
| Quality of food service | 75 |
| Number, size, and quality of sleeping rooms | 74 |
| High-speed Internet access | 55 |
| Availability of meeting support services and equipment, such as AV equipment | 54 |
| Efficiency of billing procedures | 51 |
| "Green" practices at the facility | 51 |
| Meeting rooms with multiple high-speed phone lines and computer outlets | 49 |
| Assignment of one staff person to handle all aspects of the meeting | 48 |
| Previous experience in dealing with the facility and its staff | 45 |
| Efficiency of check-in and check-out procedures | 43 |
| Availability of exhibit space | 39 |
| Provisions of special meeting services, such as pre-registration, special equipment, etc. | 37 |
| On-site recreational facilities (swimming pool, tennis, spa, etc.) | 37 |

Corporate austerity programs, coupled with a greater awareness of the size of meeting expenditures, have caused corporate planners to rank the cost of a hotel or meeting facility and negotiable food, beverage, and room rates high on their list of factors for site selection. The quality of food service, which was formerly their first priority, moved to fourth place on their list.
**Source:** Recent Meetings Market Report conducted by *Meetings & Conventions* magazine.

**Service.** Companies meet for good reason, and they don't want problems. They want service — good service. They want what was promised, and on time. The reward is repeat business. Except for incentive programs, corporate meetings promise the most repeat business. Many planners mention good service first when asked what they look for in a meeting site.

**Enough guestrooms.** No company likes to split up at a meeting, chancing the "loss" of attendees during the walk or cab ride to the meeting site. They prefer to house everyone under one roof. This is a difficult problem to overcome if you can't offer it but your com-

> ## HOTEL BUSINESS CENTERS
>
> Technology has revolutionized today's hotel guestrooms, which increasingly feature high-speed wireless Internet service, fax machines, media hubs, and other amenities, such as large desks (often stocked with office supplies) and ergonomic chairs. Wi-Fi is commonly offered in hotel common areas.
>
> Despite these innovations, many business travelers still have a need for additional services, such as copying, printing, and shipping. Hotels have responded to this need by offering business centers equipped with computers, scanners, printers, copy machines, and other office equipment. Equipment offered varies greatly, as does other services offered and costs for the use of the center's amenities.
>
> At some hotels, business centers offer secretarial services and tech support. Other hotels simply provide equipment, which can be accessed with cash, credit card, or a pre-paid card that can be purchased through the hotel.
>
> The costs of investing in a business center can be quite high, of course, so some hotels turn to companies such as Hotel Internet Services (HIS), which offers the Bizcenter™ System. Hotels can purchase, rent, or enter into a revenue-sharing agreement with the company, which provides self-service office equipment and tech support to such chains as Best Western, Comfort Inn, Crowne Plaza, DoubleTree, JW Marriott, LaQuinta, Radisson, and Wyndham Hotels & Resorts.

**Source: Photograph courtesy of Crowne Plaza Hotels.**

petitor can. Hotels combine presentations to large groups but the first choice is invariably a single hotel housing all attendees.

**Convenient location.** Location is very important to the corporate meeting planner. Travel means company money. Time spent traveling and at the meeting itself means time off the job. That's a prime factor. A convenient location is a strong sales asset. Company planners use downtown hotels, airport hotels, and suburban locations, especially for regional meetings and training sessions.

**Attractive location.** Business officials have a clear image of their company, and they want to meet in a hotel consistent with that image. This does not necessarily mean a posh place, but it does mean an attractive place. Boutique (lifestyle) hotels are often a popular choice (see box titled "Boutiques (Lifestyles) Attract Corporate Groups").

For incentive trips, it goes without saying that the hotel and the area must have tourist attractions. The basic concept is to reward those who meet targeted goals. The prize selected must stimulate extra effort. The approach for incentive meetings is quite different from that of sales meetings, but the two are often intertwined. A working sales meeting requires solely a *suitable* hotel site; an incentive meeting requires a most *desirable* one.

**Security.** Corporate meetings are private affairs to a far greater extent than most conventions. The discussions are not meant for the ears of people outside the company, and, because of the increasing competition in the marketplace — especially in the computer and

## Boutiques (Lifestyles) Attract Corporate Groups

In the mid-1980s, nightclub entrepreneur Ian Schrager introduced the first boutique hotel, a trendy, small property that featured chic décor, plenty of natural light, and lobbies and bar areas designed for socializing. Typically small (150 rooms or less), boutique hotels were originally built to appeal to a young, hip crowd by offering the "comforts of home" in an upscale, yet relaxed atmosphere that was enhanced by attentive service and the "gadgets" and facilities that were an essential part of their everyday lives.

It wasn't long before the meetings market discovered boutique hotels. Attracted by their small size, which offered both personalized service and attention to their group as well as security for meetings, meeting planners increasingly began buying out boutique hotels for their meetings.

Sarah Clark, former vice president of corporate communications for the Preferred Boutique arm of the Chicago-based Preferred Hotels and Resorts, said:

*Source: Photograph courtesy of InterContinental Hotel Group.*

> A buyout gives a group tremendous focus throughout every aspect of the meeting. The entire staff is dedicated to the group, and the property is always available for their enjoyment.

Lindsey Ueberroth, president and CEO of Preferred Hotels & Resorts, adds:

> One of the advantages that boutiques have is that they can offer much more flexibility and personalized service than a big hotel can. The management at a boutique tends to be hands-on, so you're working with the general manager of the hotel, not just the sales and catering managers.

In addition to the increased flexibility and the unique guest experience offered by boutiques, Jacques-Olivier Chauvin, former CEO of Relais & Châteaux, a Paris-based company that represents upscale boutique properties worldwide, said of the security issue:

> We've seen a significant growth in executive retreats, board meetings, and events for luxury goods and car launches. If a group is staying in a large hotel, there's a risk that confidential information will be disclosed. With a buyout, the property is secure because it's just you.

The growing popularity of boutique hotels did not go unnoticed by the large hotel chains. Starwood, which was first to jump on the boutique bandwagon with its W Hotels, now also offers the Aloft and Element brands. The InterContinental Hotel Group launched Indigo, Choice Hotels offers Cambria Suites, and Hyatt serves boutique customers with its Hyatt Place brand.

Sources: Jennifer Nicole Dienst, "All Yours: Buying Out a Small Luxury Hotel," *Meetings & Conventions,*; Tony Bartlett, "Lofty Lifestyle: New Boutique Brands are Transforming the Hotel Scene, *Meetings West*; and Steve Bjerklie, "Big Fish, Little Pond," *Smart Meetings*.

other high-tech fields, security has become an even more important issue for corporate meeting planners. If your property understands this need for additional security and can offer viable solutions, you will have a far greater chance of securing corporate meetings business. Mary Kay Hokanson, a meeting planner for Allianz in Minneapolis, has one particular clause that she's very careful about including in her meetings contracts:

> We always request that no other financial services institution is holding a meeting at the hotel the same time we are. Our independent producers sell

a variety of products and we want their meeting to be a total Allianz experience.[3]

Folding vinyl partitions and meeting rooms right off busy lobbies leave corporate planners cold, as does unrestricted access to meeting rooms and areas in which equipment and displays will be stored. In some cases, the planner may even worry about communications sent to the property's fax machine or the security of the property's phone system.

If you hope to handle this type of high-level meeting, you must be prepared to answer these concerns. First, offering a layout of the traffic pattern of the property can be an asset if the group's meeting and storage facilities will be isolated from the main flow of traffic. Second, you may offer additional security measures, such as assigning one or two trusted employees to freshen meeting rooms and watch over unoccupied facilities. Third, the business may be so attractive that you will want to go to the extra expense of hiring outside security guards or setting up a dedicated fax line for the group. If the company will be the only group meeting in the hotel at that time, you have an additional selling advantage. This is an asset for small properties, turning what may be considered a liability (small size) into a positive attraction. This is also a strong selling point for resort properties; the remoteness of a location may be an additional sales point for the security-conscious client.

Some companies opt to *buy out* the entire hotel to ensure that their group has the exclusive usage of a property's meeting rooms, banquet facilities, guestrooms, and even recreational facilities. Of course, not all properties are conducive to this type of security measures; smaller hotels, such as the boutique hotels mentioned in the "Boutiques (Lifestyles) Attract Corporate Groups" box, are ideal for a buyout, but larger properties, including resorts, are also a possibility during a slow season. In some cases, the group may be lucrative enough to warrant turning away additional corporate or leisure travel business.

## Kinds of Company Meetings

Corporate meetings business has been increasing more rapidly than any other market. Hundreds of thousands of meetings are held all over the world throughout the year, and the spectrum of meetings attended is broad. Among the prevalent types of company meetings are:

- National and regional sales meetings
- New product introduction/dealer meetings
- Professional/technical meetings
- Management meetings
- Training meetings
- Stockholder/public meetings
- Incentive meetings

Each will be considered in detail, but Figure 5.3 summarizes several key characteristics. The most widely attended meetings are for sales and marketing purposes and training, each type totaling over 12 million attendees. On average, the highest attendance is at new product introduction meetings (163 attendees) and the lowest is at training meetings (73 attendees) and management meetings (42 attendees). The average number of off-premises meetings planned yearly by corporate planners is 19.4.

The kinds of companies holding meetings are diverse. Insurance, banking and investment groups, automotive and other industrial and manufacturing concerns are just a few of

## Chapter 5: Selling the Corporate Meetings Market

*Figure 5.3. SUMMARY OF TYPES OF CORPORATE MEETINGS.*

| Type of Meeting | Off-premise Meetings | Average # Planned | Average Attendance | Average # Days | Average # of Months Lead Time |
|---|---|---|---|---|---|
| Management Meetings | 205,276 | 6.2 | 42 | 2.2 | 3.5 |
| Group Incentive Trips | 75,628 | 3.8 | 130 | 5.0 | 8.2 |
| Training Seminars | 302,512 | 10.0 | 73 | 2.5 | 3.7 |
| National/ Regional Sales Meetings | 226,884 | 6.7 | 94 | 2.7 | 3.8 |
| Professional/ Technical Meetings | 118,844 | 6.2 | 89 | 2.3 | 5.3 |
| New Product Introductions | 32,412 | 3.3 | 163 | 2.1 | 3.7 |
| Stockholder Meetings | 10,804 | 1.8 | 79 | 1.7 | 5.2 |
| Other Meetings | 108,040 | 12.3 | 183 | 2.3 | 9.1 |
| Total/Average | 1,080,400 | 19.4 | 78 | 2.7 | 5.5 |

*Note that the average lead time for corporate meetings is less than one year, the attendance is generally less than 100 persons, and the duration of most corporate meetings is two to three days.*
**Source: Recent Meetings Market Report by** *Meetings & Conventions* **magazine.**

the prospects for the corporate meeting business. It would be more difficult to find any sizable organizations that do not hold meetings — and lots of them.

## National and Regional Sales Meetings

The best-known company meeting, and one of the largest sectors of the corporate meetings market, is the **sales meeting**. The nature of a national sales organization makes it a natural for meetings. These events are scattered throughout the country. With new products and new sales developments appearing all the time, there is constant need to meet face to face with the sales team, at every level. There are national sales meetings with everyone present, meetings of regional sales managers, and regional sales meetings run by regional sales managers.

In addition to national and regional meetings, many companies today have offices in countries around the world – and, conversely, overseas companies may have offices – and, therefore, the need to hold meetings – in North America. International meetings may differ slightly from domestic meetings in terms of types of hotels used (first-class properties are often a priority) and logistics (travel arrangements, requirements for food and beverage, and so on are often different for international meetings). If a property hosts international meetings, special training is provided to its sales and service staff to ensure that these meetings are adequately serviced.

In order to save money and maximize company productivity, many firms today are combining meetings or holding different meetings back-to-back at the same property. When companies use the same hotel for back-to-back meetings, they not only save on hotel rooms, food and beverage expenses, and on-site staff costs, but they can also save money by using the same off-site venues, entertainment, speakers, production equipment, and ground transportation. In some cases, companies will combine a large sales meeting with smaller meetings either the day before or the day after the "main event." In other cases, companies use the same facility for both training meetings and incentive trips. David Lutz, past president of the Twinsburg, Ohio-based meeting planning firm, Experient, says:

> We're seeing it [combining meetings] happen to a much greater degree than ever before, and we're seeing it across industry segments.[4]

Attendance at national sales meetings averages about 150 for three to four days. Regional sales meetings are smaller, averaging 65 in size over two to three days.

The reasons for the sales meetings are many, often dealing with several objectives. The annual sales meeting may involve new product introduction, new company policy and suggested sales techniques to overcome problems, or it may simply be a morale builder and stimulator to cap a successful year and to start work on the next one. Sales meetings come in all sizes, at any time of the year, and all mean good, regular, repeat business for hotels.

Sales meetings are generally staged and controlled within the sales and marketing departments of each division of a company.

## New Product Introduction/Dealer Meetings

Sales executives often hold national and regional events to meet with dealers or distributors. New product introduction is very important in these meetings too. The introduction of new sales and advertising campaigns calls for carrying the message out to the hinterlands. The very heart of the sales and marketing philosophy is to sell your own staff first and then your distributors and dealers and their staffs, and to work them up to new levels of enthusiasm. This approach results in many meetings around the country and possibly international locations.

As in the case of sales meetings, **dealer meetings** can be very small, such as a cocktail reception for a dozen or so one evening, or great affairs involving thousands and running three to five days. The Ford Motor Company spent several million dollars for a live Broadway-type stage show, combined with a multimedia presentation, at the large Las Vegas Convention Center. The affair called for several days of rehearsals and two weeks of back-to-back charter flights from all parts of the country. The production was worthy of any on Broadway, yet had a run of only two weeks. If the objective of the meeting is achieved, the meeting is a success and the cost accepted as necessary and worthwhile.

Dealer meetings, in addition to being attended by sales personnel, also attract top company management, stockholders, and the press. Since these meetings are often "gala affairs," they provide an excellent opportunity to "show off" the property and book additional business from both company personnel and "outside" attendees. There is no better sales presentation than a successful execution of a meeting on premises. This is the opportunity to display your hotel at its best.

## Professional/Technical Meetings

The need to update technical personnel increases every year. The volume of technical development and innovation is hard to envision. In only the last 100 years — just four generations — man has created the automobile, the airplane, the computer, the spaceship, and the laser. An engineer or scientist cannot afford to stop learning or he or she will soon be obsolete. To give you some idea of the scope, General Electric employs over 30,000 engineers worldwide, representing an enormous investment in technical talent that requires constant updating. It is a resource that needs to be safeguarded against personnel obsolescence.

Company **professional/technical meetings** often take the seminar and workshop formats. Independent consultants, educators, and even vendors are invited to demonstrate and lecture.

## Management Meetings

Just as sales and technical personnel meet, so do all levels of executives. Far-flung organizations mean that there is a need even at the top for executives to get together for discussion.

Such meetings may be regular events, such as board meetings, or may be called in response to a special situation. These are usually small meetings, but they call for the finest in accommodations and service. An important characteristic of such meetings for hotel salespeople is that each attendee is a potential customer for meetings within his or her own division or company.

**Management meetings** most commonly last for two days and follow no special locations rule, ranging from convenient downtown or airport locations to remote resorts and lodges.

## Training Meetings

Training of personnel on all levels is an important activity of the larger corporations. Companies may conduct training in technical skills such as welding, machinery repair, and maintenance. Training sessions are required whenever computer systems are installed or updated. Sales personnel receive training, as do executives.

About half of training directors conduct programs off company premises. These **training meetings** are held on a regular basis and usually run about three days. Attendance is usually small. Most training groups number fewer than 100, and most are nearer 60. Groups of ten to 15 are not at all rare, so even small hotels can handle these meetings.

That is not to say that training directors are satisfied by just any facility; they have firm criteria. They do, however, deal with small groups that are easily accommodated. They want meeting rooms with permanent walls instead of screen dividers, rooms good for audiovisual use, easy access to meeting rooms without distraction from other hotel activities, and prompt service for food

Source: Courtesy of the Emirates Academy of Hospitality Management and Jumeriah Hotels.

functions, such as refreshment breaks and lunches. Well-lighted and well-ventilated rooms with adequate space for either classroom or U-shaped seating (there is often a preference for extra-wide 24- or 30-inch tables), and guestrooms with well-lighted work space (desks or large tables) are especially attractive to planners of training meetings.

Training directors do not need prestigious locations and impressive surroundings. They are more likely to choose hotels that are convenient to airports, highways, and parking. Training directors have no need to change locations to stimulate attendance or interest. They make excellent customers because they tend to come back to hotels that have worked out well. Dependability, reasonable prices, and good service all count a great deal toward repeat business.

Many hotels and motels have done well with this kind of business, to the point of having almost permanent commitment of certain meeting rooms and a constant use of a minimum number of guestrooms by a single company. Chains find this to be good business, too, as many national companies rotate similar training sessions to several cities around the country.

Regular business bookings can also be picked up when personnel become acquainted with a property while attending a training session.

An odd characteristic of training meetings is the frequent reluctance to use the term *training*. At lower levels, employees look for training and will regard it as an added benefit; they frequently stick with an employer that offers it. But sales and middle-level managers at times resent the thought that they *need* further development. The situation is dispelled by tact, so don't be surprised to see *workshops, seminars, management development, or simply meetings being booked by training directors.*

Another type of training meeting that is promoted under a different name is the *corporate retreat*. Corporate retreats are typically held for small groups to foster relationships and team-building, and they may include challenges and strategic games to enhance communication and problem-solving skills. In most cases, a remote location is chosen, but that does not mean that participants are deprived of "creature comforts." Many corporate retreat packages offer deluxe accommodations, meal functions, and a number of recreational options (see Figure 5.4).

The position of training director has broadened in many companies over the years. Today, you may find your key decision-maker under a title reflecting involvement with *human resources.*

## Stockholder/Public Meetings

Companies find it necessary at times to hold meetings for non-employees. These typically fall into the category of **stockholder/public meetings**. The annual stockholders meeting can range from a mere formality attended by a handful to a fairly active one-day event involving a goodly number, with lunch and refreshment breaks. These meetings seem to vary with the economic climate.

Public relations and industrial relations departments also hold meetings and exhibits to tell their stories. They, too, add their bit to the growing number of corporate meetings.

## Incentive Meetings

Each year, as millions of people exceed their business goals or quotas, many are rewarded by a trip — trips that collectively mean close to $8 billion to the travel industry. Up to 45

Chapter 5: Selling the Corporate Meetings Market

*Figure 5.4. ATTRACTING THE CORPORATE RETREAT MARKET.*

## Cowboy Ethics Bootcamp at the Alisal

A unique corporate retreat designed to boost morale, raise standards and rejuvenate the spirit of integrity. Join us as we team up with renowned author and speaker Jim Owen to create the first-ever "Cowboy Ethics® Bootcamp".

PACKAGE INCLUDES:

- Studio accommodations for four days and three nights
- Welcome basket (includes book "Cowboy Ethics")
- Welcome reception- meet James Owen "Cowboy Ethics" author
- Breakfast, lunch and dinner, including wine with dinner
- Private winemaker's dinner
- Three workshop sessions with James Owen
- Free time for golf, tennis, lake activities, spa activities, horseback riding & more
- Taxes and service charges

Package Price:

$2,250 single occupancy all inclusive.
$3,000 double occupancy all inclusive.
10 room minimum.

THE ALISAL
Guest Ranch and Resort

1054 Alisal Road
Solvang, CA 93463
1-800-425-4725
sales@alisal.com

Corporate retreats are usually held for small groups at remote locations, such as the Alisal Guest Ranch and Resort in the Santa Ynez Valley in Solvang, California. The property's accommodations include 73 studios or two-room suites, none of which include a television or telephone in order to enhance the retreat atmosphere (participants' messages are delivered by staff members). Also included in this particular retreat's package are a welcome basket and reception, three meals daily, workshops, and free time for recreational activities, including golf, tennis, lake activities, and horseback riding. Team-building activities, such as a ropes course, mini Olympics, and other strategic games, can also be added to the program.
**Source: Courtesy of the Alisal Guest Ranch and Resort.**

percent of that figure is spent on hotels alone. Meetings are included in 85 percent of all incentive trips, and those meetings are called **incentive meetings**.

Incentive travelers may be suppliers, dealers, customers, salespeople, or other employees. They must qualify in some way to participate.

What do incentive customers want? Above all, they look for first-class service.

| Group Reward Travel | |
|---|---|
| Percentage of corporate planners who arrange incentive trips | 33% |
| Average number planned | 3.8 |
| Average number of attendees | 130 |
| Average duration | 5 days |

**Source: Recent Meetings Market Report by *Meetings & Conventions* magazine.**

Companies offer these trips as rewards to top performers, so they want them treated in a special way.

For hotels that can deliver what these customers want, the benefits are substantial. First, bookings are guaranteed. This means easy forecasting and a break-even factor that's minimal compared to other markets. Second, incentive participants typically make use of all hotel facilities, such as restaurants, bars, and room service. Third, incentive meetings mean high-dollar revenues. Average room rates are usually higher, with double occupancy most common, and they spend more on banquets than do many other meeting segments. Although incentive meetings are unique to corporations, they are so important that an in-depth look at this segment's needs – and ways to capture incentive business – is included in Chapter 6.

## Characteristics of Company Meetings

Any meeting should have a clear objective, a logical attendance group, and a site and structure to suit the event. When we discuss characteristics of company meetings, keep in mind that we are talking about many different *kinds* of meetings — all sizes and shapes, instigated by many causes, planned and executed with rare exceptions by a variety of people.

But this very difficulty in describing a "typical" meeting should be most encouraging to hotel staffs. It is a most unimaginative hotel salesperson, or a particularly primitive hotel property, that cannot come up with some part of this market that can be sold and serviced well. This is the time to ignore what facilities you may lack and concentrate on what you *have*. Select that portion of the market that you can target and call your own. Think in terms of your own sales campaigns and the kinds of hotel properties that can handle the situations discussed in this chapter.

### Small Meetings

As we mentioned in the introduction to this chapter, a number of factors, including a fluctuating economy and public scrutiny of events deemed as corporate excesses, has resulted in companies scaling back large events and booking smaller meetings. According to a recent Meeting Planners Intention Survey conducted by PCMA, American Express, and Ypartnership, 52 percent of meetings booked had an attendance of 100 or less, while 67 percent of meetings planned were for fewer than 50 attendees.[5]

This trend is good news for small and mid-size lodging facilities, boutique hotels, and conference centers, which can easily serve this excellent market. And larger hotels, such as Gaylord, are attempting to capture a share of small meetings business with a hotel-within-a-hotel concept. Major chains such as Hilton and Marriott are also reaching out to the small meetings market, offering convenient, online tools that make it easier for corporate meeting planners to book their small meetings on a 24/7 basis — without having to deal with a hotel salesperson.

Since small meetings account for 86 percent of Hilton meetings worldwide — and 55 percent of guestrooms for 25 or less are booked less than ten days out – the chain introduced Meetings Simplified™ to offer personalized services for meetings with less than 50 attendees, and Hilton also launched e-Events™, which offers online planning and booking tools for events requiring 25 rooms or less, at a number of its brands (see Figure 5.5). Booking online allows planners to book direct, providing quick access to guestrooms and meeting

## Chapter 5: Selling the Corporate Meetings Market

space while avoiding detailed contracts. Bob Brooks, former vice president, global culture and strategic initiatives, for Hilton Hotels and Resorts, says:

> We developed e-Events to address the growing needs of people to plan, book, and manage their events online at their convenience. Our research continues to reflect the ongoing trend of many first-time planners — primarily GenX and GenY users — who drive the online booking process. With the majority of today's consumers Internet savvy, our goal is to make online bookings of events and meetings as commonplace as online airline bookings.

Once an event is booked online with e-Events, customers have immediate access to additional online booking tools and resources that al-

*Figure 5.5. BOOKING SMALL MEETINGS ONLINE WITH HILTON'S e-EVENTS.*

The e-Events online booking and planning tool, which is offered by hotels in The Hilton Family, including Embassy Suites Hotels, makes it easier for planners to book their events and manage their small meetings at a time that is convenient for them. Online booking is growing in popularity, and allows planners ready access to information — without the need of calling a hotel directly and dealing with a hotel salesperson.
**Source: Courtesy of Embassy Suites Hotels, a member of The Hilton Family.**

166

low them to manage their rooming list and create a customized page for their event. In our effort to continue enhancing e-Events, Hilton has also introduced customized menus.

Marriott's QuickGroup booking option, which can be accessed from the chain's website (www.marriott.com), offers online booking for event space and catering for groups needing between ten and 25 rooms for up to seven nights at participating Marriott, Renaissance, JW Marriott, Courtyard, Residence Inn, SpringHill Suites, Fairfield Inn, and TownePlace Suites. Meeting planners have instant access to meeting space floor plans and dimensions, and several electronic tools are available — including space and budget calculators, online rooming and group lists, web pages for groups, and step-by-step meeting guides — to assist meeting planners on a 24-hour basis.

## Time Cycle

Corporations tend to meet midweek and throughout the year (see Figure 5.6). Company meetings seem to follow a demand schedule instead of the fixed-time cycle that is common with associations. A meeting is planned and executed as need arises. After all, a company meeting doesn't require the time needed by associations to build attendance. A simple directive from the top brass is all that is needed to ensure that everyone will attend the meeting.

*Figure 5.6. WHEN CORPORATE MEETINGS ARE HELD.*

**By Quarter**

| | |
|---|---|
| Jan, Feb, Mar | 25.9% |
| Apr, May, Jun | 24.9% |
| Jul, Aug, Sep | 25.3% |
| Oct, Nov, Dec | 23.9% |

**By Days of the Week**

| | |
|---|---|
| Weekdays (Mon-Fri) | 59.8% |
| Weekends (Fri-Sun) | 16.8% |
| Weekdays+Weekends (Mon-Sun) | 23.5% |

The beauty of corporate meetings is their consistency. Corporations meet regularly throughout the year and generally follow a mid-week pattern.
**Source: State of the Industry Report by *Successful Meetings* magazine.**

## Lead Time

The planning period for company meetings is relatively short, rarely longer than a year. In the case of incentive trips, some consideration about general area may be made some eight

## Chapter 5: Selling the Corporate Meetings Market

months to a year in advance, and, in the case of great numbers, the time may stretch to two years. But that is still much shorter than the lead time for many associations meetings.

The annual sales meeting is usually planned eight to twelve months prior to convening. Corporate structure in this decision-making is simple. Some middle-level person, or perhaps two, will suggest, investigate, and screen properties and pass along the recommendation to one executive who generally makes the final decision. In some companies, one person does it all, which certainly can shorten lead time. There are many variations, of course.

Most other company meetings have a very short lead time -- less than three months is becoming typical. Due to changes in the economy, the introduction of new products and companies, mergers and acquisitions, and breakups or expansions, businesspeople meet more often on short notice (see box titled "Shrinking Lead Times"). Short lead times are especially prevalent in the technology and pharmaceutical industries due to product breakthroughs. Nearly every company meeting planner can recall instances when it seemed like the meeting was needed for the next day. Situations may also arise that require staff to get together immediately; these types of meetings are commonly referred to as *crisis meetings*.

---

### SHRINKING LEAD TIMES

According to a study by *Meetings Today*, 74 percent of all corporate meetings can be classified as short term, having a turnaround time of 90 days or less. Rich Del Colle, manager, global accounts at HelmsBriscoe, and former travel procurement manager at Hewlett-Packard, explains:

> Today's pace has picked up from 10 years ago. Before, business used to be five days a week, but now it's 24 hours a day, seven days a week. That's what people expect, and you need to keep customers happy and get your products out there.

Another contributing factor is the increased use of technology. Internet virtual tours of properties, electronic requests for proposals, and instant communications through e-mail and fax have enabled corporate planners to act more quickly. Technology has replaced the numerous telephone calls, letters, and in-person site inspections formerly inherent to corporate meeting planning, and hotels that wish to capture their share of this market must have the technology and flexibility to respond to today's corporate needs.

#### How Short Is Short Term?
**What was the turnaround time for short-term meetings last year?**

- Don't Know/No Answer: 5%
- Less Than 30 Days: 31%
- 30-60 Days: 36%
- 60-90 Days: 28%

Source: Meetings Today Survey of Corporate Meeting Buyers

It is too late to start selling your property at that point. If you had been in there selling, or had enjoyed some business from that company before, you might get a chance at this business. Certainly, there is no time for anyone to shop around. The situation calls for fast action and the meeting generally goes to a place the company has used before or to some wide-awake salesperson who had been in there pitching at the time.

It is such types of corporate business that must fill the gap when the convention function book is less than filled. The unexpected sales meeting, the crisis that calls for facing dealers or distributors, the new modification for which service personnel must be trained — all these bring opportunities for business meetings. These are meetings executives don't discuss when you talk to them. You must sell them on the idea of using your facility when the need next arises, and hope you made enough of an impression that they'll remember.

## Geographic Patterns

There is no general geographic pattern for company business. To begin with, there is often no reason to vary sites to attract attendance, as in the case of associations. When the vice-president of sales calls a meeting in Chicago or Montreal at the first of the month, it is not surprising to find the sales staff in Chicago or Montreal at that time.

There is also no reason not to go back to the same hotel if it performed satisfactorily. The main reason for another selection may very well be mere boredom on the part of the meeting planner or his or her boss. It really depends on the kind of meeting. The annual meeting, with much hoopla and singing of the company song, may call for a variety of sites from year to year, but the hastily organized meeting doesn't. In fact, a strong case can be built for repeating at a hotel proven dependable by the last meeting, or at least for some hotel that had been pushing for the business.

Training directors, in particular, prefer to deal with the same hotel on a consistent basis. Some feel that with only small meetings to offer, they reach the status of *important customer* only through the promise of repeat business. Most training directors feel the need for distraction-free, classroom-type isolation, with a good supply of audiovisual equipment and service. Once having worked out such an arrangement with a suitable facility, they are understandably loathe to change.

There is some geographic factor involved, but it is the most obvious one. An Atlanta hotel obviously will have a better chance at getting a regional sales meeting for a staff covering the southeastern states than will a hotel in Boston or St. Louis. Time, the cost of transportation, and convenience are all factors affecting the geographic location.

Imagine the assignment given to the company meeting planner to arrange for a series of regional meetings for an international sales staff. He or she might plan to use hotels in New York, Chicago, Seattle, Los Angeles, Atlanta, and Toronto – or there may be a need to book the meeting in Europe or the Far East. If you have a hotel in any of these general areas, geography will work for you and give you a chance at the business in your sector. But the planner is also free to meet in Ottawa instead of Toronto, in St. Louis or Milwaukee instead of Chicago, in Boston or Philadelphia instead of New York.

This is where selling comes in. The hotel sales staffer must present the hotel positively and turn what might be a liability into an asset. If Kansas City is less glamourous than New York, it is more centrally located. If your property is not downtown, it offers fewer distractions, easier access by automobile, and free parking. If it is downtown, it offers more opportunities for entertainment. A salesperson should concentrate on the property's positive factors instead of being haunted by its shortcomings.

Company meetings, unlike many association meetings, rarely have regulations against meeting anywhere. The company president or board may favor some types of sites and frown on others in keeping with the image they want to project, but that's not the same as restrictions written into a constitution or bylaws.

## Kinds of Sites

What kind of hotel does a company prefer? The answer has as many variations as there are companies and kinds of meetings (see Figure 5.7). A meeting planner should select a site to benefit from its locale and the hotel's attractions. The hotel that would be good for an incentive trip or annual dealer meeting may not be the wisest choice for that crisis meeting or training session.

For a successful sales and marketing career, help your customer achieve the kind of meeting he or she wants. Try to get those meetings that go well in your establishment. Let the ones that get away be those that really should be held in some other type of hotel.

**WORTH WATCHING**

To view a short video providing insight into how corporate planners select the appropriate site and venue for corporate events, visit www.corporatemeetingsnetwork.ca/vreports/five-tips-for-selecting-a-venue-or-site-for-your-next-meeting-or-event.

**Figure 5.7. TYPES OF FACILITIES USED BY CORPORATE MEETING PLANNERS.**

| Facility | Percentage |
|---|---|
| Downtown Hotels | 75% |
| Resort Hotels | 48% |
| Suburban Hotels | 45% |
| Convention Centers/Hotels | 45% |
| Airport Hotels | 29% |
| Golf Resorts | 27% |
| Suite Hotels | 20% |
| Gaming Facilities | 18% |
| Residential Conference Centers | 11% |
| Cruise Ships | 9% |
| Non-Residential Conference Centers | 8% |

Total is greater than 100% due to multiple mentions.

Meeting planners, who typically pay an average daily room rate of $184.00, prefer downtown hotels, followed by resort hotels and suburban hotels. The key selection criteria is generally the purpose of the meeting.
**Source: Recent Meetings Market Report by *Meetings & Conventions* magazine.**

Give careful thought to the kind of meetings most suitable for your hotel. Is yours a downtown hotel? Then stress its convenient location, especially when some people participate in only part of the program. Comfortable and familiar, the downtown hotel is a frequent choice.

Is yours a suburban hotel/motel? It offers easy access by auto and free parking. Stress its informal atmosphere. Will the meeting be the only one in the house? That is considered by many corporate planners to be so important that it may be the very factor that swings the business to you.

Airport location? The obvious advantage is convenience when air transportation is used, plus all the features of the suburban hotel. Once small properties, airport hotels come in all sizes today.

Resort? This is the obvious choice for incentive meetings, but is also often chosen to get away from the distractions of the city. Resorts in the off-season offer excellent rates, charm, exclusivity, industrial security, physical beauty, and a good image.

> **WORTH WATCHING**
>
> To see a video of the state-of-the art SilverBirch Conference Centres in Canada, which offer all-inclusive meeting packages, go to www.youtube.com/watch?v=7eMjfgPbfps

Conference center? As mentioned in Chapter 1, conference centers are growing in popularity with corporate meeting planners, and many major hotel companies, including Marriott, Hilton, and Sheraton have noticed this shift and are becoming key players in the conference center segment. While the few conference centers of past decades had a "going back to school" stigma, today's state-of-the-art facilities are often the choice of corporate planners looking for high-tech presentation equipment and locations that minimize distractions (see box titled "Re-branding Conference Centers").

Boutique (lifestyle) hotel? Many corporate groups prefer full buyouts of these hotels for the privacy offered.

All-suite hotel? These are often chosen by planners looking for meeting space for small groups. Many attendees, especially women business travelers, appreciate having a sitting area separate from the sleeping room, which enables them to more comfortably entertain colleagues in their rooms. All-suites also provide the advantage of all attendees being housed in the same type of room, and these hotels usually offer free breakfasts and cocktail hours in the lobby.

Extended-stay all-suite hotels are ideal for employees who need to stay at a particular location for some time as well as for the relocation market, as they provide "all the comforts of home." While these hotels are primarily booked for one corporate traveler, some meeting planners see them as an inexpensive alternative to multi-day room rates at local hotels, so many extended-stay properties now offer expansive lobbies or small meeting rooms to attract meetings business.

These are but a few benefits and characteristics of each type of property. You should be able to add others and to present your property positively as the one that best fits the meeting planner's event.

## Attendance

One characteristic of corporate meetings that makes them popular with hotel people is the predictable attendance. Whether attendees come alone or with their spouses, attendance is nearly always mandatory. A rooming list submitted before the event is usually accurate. Barring mishap or illness, no-shows are minimal. Nancy Holder, an award-winning meeting

Chapter 5: Selling the Corporate Meetings Market

## Re-Branding Conference Centers

*Dolce Seaview Resort*

Andy Dolce founded Dolce International, which would grow into a chain of 26 unique properties in the United States, Canada, and Europe. Committed to an environment that reflected his clients' need for environments that inspire creativity and learning, Dolce elevated the meeting and conference model, offering luxury services not found in typical conference centers and pioneering the Complete Meeting Package (CMP), which offers assistance to meeting planners with all the details of their meetings at an all-inclusive package price.

Each of the unique properties in the chain is geared toward business travelers, with wireless high-speed Internet access in meeting rooms, public spaces, and guestrooms; a 24/7 technology help desk; fully equipped business centers; and in-room business amenities; but each also provides upscale guestroom amenities, such as luxury bed linens and pillows, fine dining restaurants, and fitness facilities that range from spas to championship golf courses. Teambuilding/group activities can also be included in a group's agenda.

Despite the special services and amenities offered at the chain's properties, meeting planners felt the term "conference center" was too confusing — they thought of conference centers in terms of meeting space only. In response to focus groups held with planners, Dolce International became Dolce Hotels and Resorts. This change enabled the chain to more accurately reflect the services and amenities offered to hotel guests — and it was also adopted to appeal to leisure and transient business as well as the meetings market.

*Dolce Hayes Mansion Banquet Setup*

Conference centers typically capture a mere 10-11 percent share of the meetings market business, while approximately 90 percent of this segment opts for hotels and resorts when booking meetings. Dolce says:

> We've been fighting for that 90 percent the last 20 years. We figured it is best to join them, to change our image and call ourselves hotels and resorts. Our tagline is, "Meet with Inspiration."

Meetings are still the chain's core business (eighty percent of its $350 million revenue is meetings related). The company's goal, however, is a 70/30 percent business/leisure mix with a higher level of occupancy, and the chain also has plans to double in size over the next five years.

**Sources: Roger Carey, "Seizing the Moment,"** *Successful Meetings*, **photographs courtesy of Dolce Hotels and Resorts.**

planner who organized the meetings department at R.J. Reynolds Tobacco Company/RJR Nabisco, says:

> In corporate planning, if you book 200 rooms, you're going to use 200 rooms, unless there's an emergency. In other areas of planning (associations), you have to convince people to come. In the corporate world, if the CEO tells you to show up, you're going to show up.[6]

While attendance at corporate meetings is mandatory, one problem associated with corporate meetings is the risk of cancellation of the entire event. Poor financial returns or unexpected delays may result in a corporate official changing or cancelling the meeting. For this reason, most hotels now require nonrefundable deposits and have included stringent cancellation clauses in their contracts with corporate groups (cancellation clauses are explained and illustrated in Chapter 9).

Care should be taken to get a VIP list. It can be embarrassing to everyone to have the fledgling sales trainee assigned to the fine corner room and the vice-president of sales in a minimum single. If no VIP list is submitted, bring up the subject yourself and help your customer create one. If no need exists for him or her, fine. But check it out and at least flag a few names for preferred treatment. Those executives' comments may determine whether you get the group again.

## Duration

Most corporate meetings are short. Some are limited to a single day and others may run as long as five days, but three days are about the most common. Arrival on the previous evening is popular so that the meeting can start early the next morning. Cocktail receptions and/or brisk action at the hotel bars add to the profits to be derived from corporate business.

Take care to coordinate the final day meeting program with your policy on check-out time. Plan ahead. If you can't gracefully extend the normal check-out time, perhaps you can arrange to check all the luggage with the bell captain or arrange for all luggage to be placed in just a few rooms before the check-out deadline. If you don't look ahead and decide how you will cope with the many requests at the last minute (or even with the entire group checking out late without even discussing it with you), your staff will be forced to improvise. And they may not always handle it as you would like.

Bring the matter up with the meeting organizer even if he or she doesn't. State your policy and suggest how to arrange matters. You can arrive at an agreed-upon arrangement. At the very least, you have alerted the planner to a potential problem.

## Exhibits

The exhibit is a trademark of the association for the most part. Corporate meetings, however, frequently have exhibits too. It is not uncommon, for example, for such meetings to display new products or to use live presentations on a grand scale. Thus you can expect requests for stage facilities and exhibit space when servicing corporate events.

| Corporate Trade Shows | |
|---|---|
| Percentage of planners involved in trade shows | 53% |
| Average number planned | 9.1 events |
| Average number of attendees | 1,210 |
| Average duration | 3.3 days |

Source: **Recent Meetings Market Report** by *Meetings & Conventions* magazine.

The most recent *Meetings & Conventions* Meetings Market Report found that roughly 50 percent of corporate meeting planners plan trade shows for their companies. While the average number of attendees (1,210) is less than the number of attendees at association trade shows, the average duration of the show is similar (about three days). Therefore, meeting groups that hold trade shows in conjunction with their meetings are potentially very profitable for your hotel.

## Meeting Room Requirements

There is a need for large and small meeting rooms, varying from event to event. Some meetings call for small committee-type rooms. In many training setups, the main group breaks into units of as few as ten people who meet separately for awhile, then reconvene in the main meeting room. Most meeting organizers prefer such *breakout* rooms to be right at hand.

If your hotel has such rooms in the same wing of the building, you have an edge when you solicit such business. It leaves something to be desired if the group has to huddle around a few tables in different parts of the main meeting room. It certainly is difficult to attract such a group under those circumstances if the competition can offer more suitable arrangements.

With corporate meetings, there is little likelihood that meeting rooms will have to be changed at the last minute. Association meetings, on the other hand, have higher attendance and the program often features concurrent meetings (several topics covered at the same time in various meeting rooms). The more popular topics may draw a larger audience than anticipated, requiring the meeting room setup staff to bring in extra chairs or make other arrangements (which may include moving the meeting to a larger room).

## One Meeting, One Check

It is nice for a hotel to have most group business paid for with one check. That's one appeal of corporate business. Many companies pay all the expenses for their employees; others have different guidelines. Discuss with the meeting planner what he or she will approve for payment on the master account and what the individual must pay for upon check-out. Your front desk must be informed. Your credit manager may want to do some homework on the customer-corporation and may propose a schedule of payments, beginning with a deposit. As a general rule, corporate business is paid for en masse.

## Multiple-Booking Potential

Hosting company meetings offers the opportunity to promote other business. Each person attending the meeting has sampled your hotel. If the impression is favorable, you may become the first choice whenever that person stops in your city on business trips. Or you may benefit from recommendations to others both in and out of the organization. Remember that most association boards include businesspeople who hold their own organizational meetings.

Help to execute a smoothly functioning meeting and you can pick up future business from the company as well. What appears to be a single meeting may be repeated in several parts of the country. This is a great situation for hotel chains. One person may order meetings in a number of locations, and that person may handle the logistics of all those meetings. There is often enough flexibility in the designation of the cities to be used that a chain may sell dates in a number of different properties.

The appeal to the meeting planner is achieving the status of a more important customer, and he or she has only to explain his or her needs once and have them duplicated in different hotels.

Surprisingly, however, chain loyalty is not a trademark of corporate meetings. A survey of corporate meeting planners conducted by *Meeting & Conventions* magazine determined that only 25 percent of corporate meeting planners used the same hotel chain for the majority of their meetings.

What does this mean to a single-location hotel? In order to compete with a chain effort, the individual hotel must present a good case for being the best choice in the city. Ideally, that image would be so strong that a meeting planner normally using a chain for the entire group of meetings would break that pattern when it comes to your city.

Many wise hotel salespeople cooperate with their counterparts in independent hotels in other cities. They try to get the meeting planner to buy from independents as often as possible, and make it easy for that to happen by recommendations and the passing of the sales lead to each other. Independent hotels in different cities recognize that they function as true allies in the sales competition with chains. This concept has helped in the development of the hotel representative who, with a stable of independent hotels, can offer the same kind of "one-stop shopping" as the chains.

## Corporate Meeting Decision-Makers

No sales effort succeeds unless it is directed at the person or persons with the authority to make the decision. The convention sales picture is no different. Your story may be a good one, but it will be to no avail unless it is told to the right person.

Who is the *right* person? Not only does it vary from company to company, but it may vary from year to year within the same company. But some titles do keep coming up and they certainly represent a starting point for sales penetration (see Figure 5.8).

To find the decision-maker, you have to ask the right questions. "Who coordinates your meetings?" is not a good question; the person who coordinates the details of a meeting may not be the actual decision-maker. It is far better to ask, "Who is responsible for deciding which hotels your company uses for meetings?" With this approach, you will be able to make immediate contact with the decision-maker or recommender rather than having to deal with one or more "go-betweens," saving valuable time and effort.

*Figure 5.8. MEETING PLANNERS' CORPORATE POSITIONS.*

| Job Title or Position | Corporate Planners |
|---|---|
| Corporate Executive Management | 24 % |
| Meeting Planning/Convention Management | 30 |
| Sales/Marketing | 11 |
| General/Other Management/Administration | 17 |
| Other | 18 |

Many corporations do not have professional meeting planners. Therefore, in prospecting for business, it is wise to know the common job titles for corporate decision-makers. These are summarized above.
**Source: Recent Meetings Market Report by *Meetings & Conventions* magazine.**

Another approach, which may require slightly more time and effort, but which may also prove profitable, is to start at the top of the company and work downward. While speaking with the president of a company may not result in an immediate booking, this contact can prove valuable in two ways: you won't be referred to someone below the decision-making or recommending level, and a referral "from above" is a great door-opener.

Once the key contact is determined, you should pay attention to tomorrow's decision-makers. As the account is worked and information is secured on the organizational structure, "star performers" should be identified and relationships with them cultivated. Knowing the people who are likely to succeed present decision-makers can pay dividends in the future.

## Full-Time Meeting Planner

When companies have centralized meeting planning activity, you deal with a full-time meeting planner. Hopefully, this should make your job easier because you deal with an experienced, knowledgeable pro who knows what he or she wants and how to go about getting it.

It is easier to deal with someone who knows what he or she wants. It can protect you from overlooking something in the arrangements. Both parties want the same thing — a smoothly run meeting — and it helps if both parties are expert. Build a reputation for competence and fair dealing and you are on your way to a successful sales career in the convention field.

The organization that represents corporate meeting planners is Meeting Professionals International (www.mpi.org). Membership is comprised of 18,500 members representing 86 countries.

## Company President

Smaller companies seldom have enough meeting activity to warrant a full-time meeting planning employee. In many such companies, the decision-maker is the president or some counterpart, such as a partner or chairperson. It is understandable that the president of a large corporation such as General Motors will not be involved in such decisions, but the president of a company employing several hundred people might get involved in the national sales or dealer meeting. Never worry about making contacts too high up the corporate ladder. If he or she isn't involved personally, a president is seldom hesitant about naming the right person. And the recommendation of the president does you no harm when you deal with subordinates.

Administrative assistants to company presidents are also influential in meeting site decisions. Hyatt and the International Association of Administrative Professionals (IAAP)

---

**Profile of Corporate Meeting Planners**

- 72% are female; average age is 48.

- Spend an average of 53% of their professional time on meeting planning activities.

- Have been arranging meetings for 13 years.

- Plan most of their meetings (58%) for 50 or fewer people.

- Duties include: selecting hotels (88%), selecting locations (81%), planning entertainment (72%), setting budgets (70%), planning meeting agendas (51%), arranging for transportation (air, 54%; rental cars, 42%) and trade show/exhibit planning (51%).

- Only 19% are Certified Meeting Professionals (and only 4% are Certified Meeting Managers), but 28% are members of Meeting Professionals International (MPI).

Source: Recent Meetings Market Report by *Meetings & Conventions* magazine.

(www.iaap-hq.org) determined that meeting and event planning is an administrative professional's second most time-consuming office activity; 81percent of administrative assistants plan four off-site meetings annually.

## Marketing and Sales Executives

Marketing and sales executives are key people. The exact title may be *vice president, sales,* or *marketing director, or manager* or *product manager.* They may operate on a regional, national, or even international basis. The bulk of corporate meetings involves the important areas of sales and marketing, so it makes sense to zero in on these people.

Such executives don't join meeting planning societies. They don't think of themselves as meeting or convention planners. But they do plan many of them, or, more accurately, are involved with planning them. They call the meetings, control the kind of meetings they want, and most often have the most important voice as to where and when they will take place. That makes them very important people for you to contact.

## Advertising and Sales Promotion Managers

One step down the corporate ladder is the *advertising* or *sales promotion manager.* One person may carry both titles because the work is interrelated. In addition to usual duties, such middle executives frequently handle meeting planning functions. There is no relationship in such assignment to the size or type of company. If the company does not have a full-time meeting planner, the task is assigned to some departmental or divisional manager, and since it involves marketing activity, the advertising or sales promotion manager is often selected.

At the very least, such middle managers get involved in the initial screening of a site and the planning and execution of a meeting. They could be your first hurdle. You need them to recommend your property. In some cases, that is sufficient; in others, the final selection is made by their boss — the vice president, director, or manager of sales and marketing. Some people freely admit when their authority is limited, but some find it too painful to do so.

It helps you to know who the final decision-maker is, but you have to pay attention to the level that screens, too, or you may never get to the final selection stage. Make sure that your presentation summarizes your strong points very clearly so that they may be passed along accurately in discussion with others.

## Other Corporate Executives

Not all meetings stem from marketing divisions. Other executives get involved with staging meetings and therefore influence site selections. They carry titles such as *manager of corporate relations, public relations, industrial relations,* or *communications.* Such personnel may very well be active in sales and marketing, too. Corporate organization charts seldom indicate anyone as meeting specialists, yet many executives are. The executive in charge of meetings may have that assignment for a period of time and then it may pass on to another. The role of meeting planner is often a part of the career path for upward-bound middle management.

## Passenger Traffic/Corporate Travel Managers

Many companies maintain a travel desk, which handles arrangements for employee business travel. When plane or hotel reservations are needed, they are requisitioned through the passenger traffic personnel. Traditionally, these corporate travel planners were responsible for booking hotel rooms and travel for individual corporate executives, and commonly negotiated with hotels and travel providers for a *commercial rate*, a lower rate guaranteed to their personnel.

Increasingly, however, because of consolidation of the meetings and travel departments at a number of corporations, the responsibilities of corporate travel planners have expanded to include planning meetings. These personnel, therefore, not only negotiate for rates for guestrooms but also for meetings space and food and beverage functions.

Membership in the Global Business Travel Association (GBTA) (www.gbta.org), an organization of corporate travel managers, once consisted of corporate travel planners who dealt primarily with individual travel for their personnel. Today, 94 percent of GBTA members are involved in planning meetings for their corporations. In order to better assist corporate travel planners, especially those new to the meeting planning area, the GBTA offers training classes and joined the Convention Industry Council (CIC) to provide additional opportunities for the education of their membership.

The Global Business Travel Association (GBTA) has branches in 60 different countries on six continents; in Canada, the organization is called the Global Business Travel Association – Canada, while in Asia, it is referred to as the Global Business Travel Association – Asia Pacific. The latter organization sponsors an annual trade show in August. A similar organization for corporate travel planners, the Association of Corporate Travel Executives (ACTE), is a global association of over 60,000 travel executives in 82 countries. ACTE also hosts a trade show as well as educational conferences. The shows of both of these organizations are well-attended by hotels seeking to build corporate group travel business, especially since the position of corporate travel manager is expected to grow in scope.

## Procurement (Purchasing) Managers

Another answer for companies that wish to cut costs by consolidating their meeting and travel departments is to structure meeting planning within the procurement (purchasing) department. The involvement of the procurement department in meeting planning is changing the nature of planner/hotel relationships. While hotels traditionally have dealt directly with the meeting planner (who answered to his or her company or organization regarding the meeting budget), the procurement department is increasingly involved in the decision-making process – from selecting hotel sites to approving menus and costs for food functions.

> **WORTH WATCHING**
>
> Jill Harrington, a globally-respected meeting executive, offers tips for hotel salespeople on how to work with corporate procurement specialists. Using a search engine type in: Jill Harrington, Selling to the purchasing specialists.

While meeting planners generally have some knowledge of the nuances of meeting costs, such as paying more for guestrooms or food functions to enable them to receive free meeting space, for example, procurement managers often look at buying hotel rooms and services in much the same way that they look at purchasing other commodities; in other words, they want to get the best price possible. And this doesn't mean strictly in terms of rooms or meeting space; procurement managers also look for the best values in such products and services as audiovisual equipment, decorators, and so on, which can result in decreased revenues for the hotel. A recent survey of meeting planners by *Successful Meetings* determined that nearly 60 percent of planners say procurement departments have input on how event budgets are spent.

This trend has not only resulted in increased competitiveness among hotels, but has also affected the way in which salespeople do business. The decision-maker for a corporate meeting may now be the procurement manager, and the salesperson dealing with this decision-maker has to be able to prove the value of what his or her hotel has to offer. This can include explaining everything from the quality of the hotel's food to its reputation for high service standards to something as intangible (but important) as the experience of the attendees.

Fred Shea, senior vice president of convention sales and services for VisitOrlando, says:

> Our sales managers have to show price value, but not just price, because dates and rates are all online, right there for the customer to see. We are training our people how to do a better job of making that procurement customer understand the value that goes back to them, both in service and actual attendee experience.[7]

## Training Director

Training directors use a wide variety of hotel types. Airport and other suburban locations are popular because of ease of access and parking. Small resorts and boutique hotels are used in the off-season, especially when executive development programs call for more prestigious sites. With lower budgets, training directors make good use of secondary hotels, off-season rate breaks, and all-cost packages.

Training departments usually handle their own meetings, even in cases where the company already has a setup for sales meetings. You may sell the sales department for their meetings but still have to sell another group for training sessions.

Training directors' requirements do not differ from those of most small meetings, but they are less likely to be permissive about such things as audiovisual equipment, permanent dividing walls, low-hanging chandeliers, and nearby distractions in the hotel. Actually, these specifications are similar to those that any good meeting planner would want (see Figure 5.9).

## Meeting Specialists/Third-Party Planners

Just a few years ago, nearly all corporate meetings were planned by in-house departments. Due to downsizing, many companies, like associations, are looking outside their own organizations for meeting planning services. Some of these **third-party meeting planners** only get involved in larger meetings. Others select hotels, airlines, destination management companies, and other meeting services. They conduct site searches, negotiate rates on behalf of the companies and associations they represent, and assist in conducting meetings and conventions. Travel organizations are called in at times, especially for incentive programs. These organizations are important sources of business.

Chapter 5: Selling the Corporate Meetings Market

*Figure 5.9. ADVERTISING TO PLANNERS OF SMALL MEETINGS.*

This ad promotes the meeting space at the luxury boutique hotel, The Miami Edition, which is part of a partnership between hospitality innovator Ian Schrager and Marriott International. The ad promotes the hotel's 8,400 square-foot ballroom, 3,200 square feet of pre-function space, three meeting studios with natural light, and the 2,400 square-foot La Vista Event Terrace. Additional information about the hotel, which would appeal to planners of upscale meetings, can be viewed at www.editionhotels.com/miami-beach/meetings-and-events.
**Source: Courtesy of The Miami Beach Edition.**

As mentioned in the opening chapter, third-party companies have become prominent sources of meetings business. According to a Future Watch survey by Meeting Professionals International, about 20 percent of events are outsourced to these kinds of planning firms. Third-party planners such as Experient, Inc. (www.experient-inc.com) and HelmsBriscoe (www.helmsbriscoe.com) have developed such strong relationships with some meeting planners (association and SMERF as well as corporate) that the corporate planner and the

> **Generating Sales from Third-Party Planners**
>
> Roger Helms, Founder & CEO
>
> HelmsBriscoe
>
> Scottsdale, Arizona
>
> We are an international travel and meeting planning company that plays "matchmaker" between companies looking for hotel rooms and meeting space and the venues that can meet these needs. We're a wonderful resource for meeting managers because we free up their time to focus on content and the delivery of the meeting's message. We also offer them the advantage of our volume purchasing, which means better pricing and more lenient contracts (hoteliers favor us because we provide business they weren't reaching and we save them the cost of setting up sales offices in markets we've penetrated).
>
> In 1992, while working as a sales and marketing executive with the Registry Hotel Corporation, I spotted a void — and the opportunity to act as "resource firm to the conference industry." That same year, I teamed with Bill Briscoe, a 14-year Registry veteran, and HelmsBriscoe was born.
>
> Since that time, we have grown to become the largest purchaser of group hotel rooms in the world. We have a network of nearly 1,000 associates, most former seasoned hotel salespeople, in over 30 countries. We work with hotels throughout the world on a daily basis and are compensated by the hotels that pay us a placement fee based on room revenue. Our company represents clients ranging from fraternal organizations holding reunions to large corporations launching new products — anybody who plans meetings. We started as a very small boutique company and have been fortunate to maintain this great culture and sense of communication and community as we grew the organization. The dedication and passion of our associates, as well as the technology to communicate globally, has made this possible.
>
> As is always the case with the future, the only constant is change. Staying ahead of industry trends and client needs is a key component of our company's success. The difference between a good company and a great one is that some will learn nothing and some will learn a great deal and become better and stronger. I'm proud to say that I believe HelmsBriscoe fits into this latter category.

third-party planner work together as a team, particularly when it comes to hotel site selection.

Hotel chains now focus their efforts on deriving their business from the biggest clients and have justified this approach based on the rationale that 80 percent of group business comes from 20 percent of their clients. Therefore, third-party leads will grow in importance.

Steve Armitage, senior vice president of sales and managing director-sales at Hilton Hotels Corporation, says:

> We want to increase our market share with key accounts, and the more business we get from an organization, the better positioned we can be to partner with them on the rates they need for an event to be successful.[8]

Third-party companies make their money by charging a management fee to the meeting groups they represent or by charging the hotel a commission on the room rate. Obvi-

**MORE ONLINE**

The Knowland Group has prepared a white paper for hotel professionals who wish to work with third-party planners. Log on to www.knowlandgroup.com and scroll down and click on the "Whitepapers" tab, then scroll to "Understanding, Selling to, and Working With Third Party Planners" to access this resource.

> ### 🖥 INTERNET EXERCISE
>
> #### Third-Party Meeting Planners
>
> Corporations often outsource their meeting planning to third-party meeting planning firms. These firms will take site inspection trips and negotiate meeting contracts for their clients. Because they represent several companies and bring a large volume of business to hotels, they claim to be able to negotiate a better meeting package than a company could get when acting alone. The salespeople who work for these third-party firms are independent contractors, and many have worked in hotel sales positions and have their own corporate meeting contacts.
>
> Log on to the websites of the companies below and answer the questions in this exercise:
>
> - Experient - www.experient-inc.com
> - ConferenceDirect - www.conferencedirect.com
> - HelmsBriscoe - www.helmsbriscoe.com
>
> 1. What services do each of these companies offer?
>
> 2. What are the benefits for hotels that partner with these firms?
>
> 3. How are each of these companies paid — by the meeting planner or are they paid a commission by hotels for booking business?

ously, hotels would prefer that these third-party planners secure their fee from the groups they represent, but, recognizing the volume of business provided by third-party planners, many hotels are willing to pay commissions.

Many smaller associations and corporations have limited bargaining power when negotiating with hotels. But when they outsource their meetings to a large third-party planner they often realize the advantage of volume savings. To get more personal attention -- and perhaps greater concessions from hotels -- it is likely that more planners will turn to third-party meeting management companies to locate and negotiate facilities for their meetings.

## Sources for Finding Corporate Business and Decision-Makers

It's a great big business world out there, and while you may be eager to just get out there and knock on doors, that isn't the recommended use of time. Tom McCarthy, a veteran of hotel sales, believes prospecting should be more calculated:

> A salesperson might have a territory that includes 35,000 companies. If a salesperson can qualify 20 new prospects a week, it doesn't take much figuring to determine that the salesperson can qualify about 1,000 accounts a year.
>
> Wouldn't it make more sense to work with a list broker and pick 1,000 companies in advance that would be assigned to the salesperson (based on proximity, size, and type of business), rather than just telling the person to "hit the bricks"? Do we think the person will call on the best 1,000 out of the 35,000 by chance?
>
> Here we are working with computers and sophisticated software and still living in the 19th century when it comes to the most basic principles of prospecting.[9]

In today's competitive environment, prospecting for new business is essential, but going up and down the street knocking on doors is not the way. Once you know the kind of corporate executives you want, there are a number of ways for you to reach them effectively.

## Special Meetings and Business Publications

The corporate meetings business is served by several publications that have literally done your job of sorting out those executives interested in meetings. It is hardly a surprise, therefore, to find that advertising appearing in these publications seems to be an industry rundown of the leading convention hotels. These magazines also offer advertisers sales lead services, providing the names of, and data about, likely prospects.

Leading publications include *Corporate & Incentive Travel*, *Corporate Meetings & Incentives*, *Meetings & Conventions*, *The Meeting Professional Magazine* (published by MPI), *Smart Meetings*, *Successful Meetings*, *Financial & Insurance Meetings*, *Meetings*, *Incentive Magazine,* and *Prevue*. Most of their circulation is to readers in the corporate area, and all have Internet sites for instant access.

There are other publications of interest to hotel marketing people, although they do not specialize in conventions; they either deal with related editorial subjects or reach the executives likely to make meeting decisions. Most relevant is *Sales and Marketing Management*. As its name implies, the publication is directed to sales and marketing executives who are frequently involved with meetings.

General business publications can be considered as well. Although these publications are not directed specifically to executives who are involved with meeting decisions, their circulations reflect profiles similar to those of meeting planners. Hotels with adequate advertising budgets can promote their meeting facilities in such publications as *The Wall Street Journal*, *Bloomberg Business* (formerly known as *Bloomberg Businessweek*), and *Fortune*.

## Trade Directories, Publications, and Databases

It is possible to develop sales leads by working your way through a specific industry. If your records indicate meetings of similar companies, it may be that industry is a fertile field for more business. The insurance industry, for example, is a prolific meeting group. There is even an association of meeting planners solely within that field. Other individual trades and industries may offer names of companies similar to those that have met in your hotel.

*The Dun & Bradstreet Million Dollar Database* (www.dabdd.com), which was formerly available in directory form but is now posted online only, lists the largest businesses in the United States and Canada and their officers. Hotel salespeople can search by specific companies or by specific industries.

*Standard & Poor's Net Advantage* (www.netadvantage.standardandpoors.com) is a similar database that lists over 60,000 companies and provides addresses and basic information on key personnel, number of employees, and revenues.

*Meeting Professionals International Membership Directory* is available to members and allied members of Meeting Professionals International (MPI) (www.mpi.org). To obtain a copy of this guide — the best-known source of corporate meeting planners — hotel people must join the organization along with a meeting planner.

*Best Insurance Reports,* published by A.M. Best Company, (www.ambest.com/BIR) lists some ten thousand executives of insurance firms. A.M. Best Company also offers extensive online information that can help hotel salespeople identify principal officers and get company names and addresses at www.ambest.com.

The *Corporate Meeting and Event Planners Directory* lists more than 14,000 meeting planners in the United States and Canada. Listings include key information such as addresses, telephone numbers, websites, when and where meetings are held, number of meetings, average meeting length, and the type of facility used. This directory is also available on a disk that can be purchased at www.meetingplannerlists.com.

## Trade Associations

If you feel that specific industries might be worth following, call on the executive directors of their trade associations. *You should be calling on them anyway for their own association business*, but they can also be a prime source of leads. They can pinpoint the larger companies in the trade and those in your part of the country. Their trade directories could be a good source of leads and a good addition to your mailing list.

Another effective way to find meeting planners is to visit Internet sites that provide membership information and search services. One of the largest is MPIWeb, the website of Dallas-based Meeting Professionals International. MPI has more than 71 chapters in 86 countries, including 30 in North America, and you can click on "MPI Chapters" to find chapters in specific geographical areas. The site offers a free search service (a hotel salesperson does not have to be a member or associate member of MPI to use the search feature) that allows you to select such items as "Meeting Consultant/Independent Planner." By entering a specific city and state, you will be provided with a list of updated names and contact information.

This is just one of the many sites available on the Internet. LinkedIn (www.linkedin.com), a business-oriented, professional networking social media site, allows salespeople to reconnect with past and present business contacts. Hoover's (www.hoovers.com) offers an online directory that provides information on 32 million companies. This directory lists the names of key decision-makers in various industries, allowing a hotel salesperson to build customized lists of prospects. Tools such as this directory and other directories available online are great tools for reaching the corporate market, allowing you to expand contacts at companies you are presently doing business with and identify other potential customers in the same industry. Online directories offer varied services, such as access to financial data and the ability to download reports or lists; some charge subscription fees.

Steve Tremewan, former director of marketing at the Radisson Resort and Spa Scottsdale (Arizona), and current director of sales marketing at Lake Arrowhead Resort and Spa (California), says:

> We used to do research at the library and subscribe to all the local newspapers in our target markets. But now we are able to do most of our research on the Internet.[10]

He still reads local newspapers in his property's major target areas, but their online versions rather than printed publications, to determine if new businesses may be coming to town as well as what conferences and meetings are scheduled to be held. He also uses these and other online sources to find contacts in market segments that his property wishes to target.

Many meetings are held in the principal locale of the sponsoring company. It makes sense, therefore, to study directories of businesses within your city, state, or area of the country. Chambers of commerce could also supply such lists.

The local library, chamber of commerce, and state industrial commission are also excellent sources for local leads. Most offer publications that list businesses according to North American Industry Classification System (NAICS), developed by the federal government. In many cases, your property may already have a breakdown of businesses booked by NAICS code; this makes it particularly easy to target other businesses from the same category.

Don't neglect to solicit the local branches of national organizations. You may be told that meeting decisions are made at the national headquarters, but don't ignore the local firms. It is common for a corporate meeting planner to ask a local district manager about a suitable hotel in the area. The order may come from corporate headquarters, but the important input could come from your own area.

In addition, local branches often hold meetings of their own, albeit smaller ones. Local dealer meetings, training sessions, and regional sales meetings are often within the responsibility of the regional sales manager. Going after the regular commercial business of a branch sales office may give you a chance at some group business as well.

---

### INTERNET EXERCISE

### Garnering Sales Leads from Cyberspace

There are a number of websites that allow meeting planners to conduct detailed property searches on the Internet. Four popular sites are:

- Cvent — www.cvent.com
- Convention Planet — www.conventionplanet.com
- Knowland Group — www.knowland.com
- Lanyon StarCite™ — www.lanyon.com/solutions/starcite

Log on to each of these sites to answer the following questions:

1. Which site offers the greatest number of facility listings for meeting planners to consider?

2. Which site requires members to pay a listing fee to be included on the site?

3. In your opinion, which of these three sites would meeting planners find to be the most user-friendly?

4. Which site(s) offer a solution section for hotels and for procurement managers?

5. "Insight: Lead Generation for Group Business" is a landing page on which site?

6. Which site offers a reader board service to assist hotels in lead generation?

---

## Convention and Visitors Bureaus

Many hotel salespeople are also finding that working with their city's convention and visitors bureau can be an excellent way to build corporate business. While CVBs formerly dealt exclusively with associations business, many are now targeting smaller corporate markets and can provide leads for your property.

Just a few years ago, the Destination Management Association International (DMAI) held its first Destinations Showcase event in New York City to promote CVB services to corporate planners. While many corporate decision-makers had not previously used CVBs, interest in using them as "one-stop shopping" venues has increased. If a corporate meeting planner is interested in booking space in Orlando, for example, he or she need make only one call to the CVB; the CVB will respond with information on only those hotels that meet the planner's needs.

Properties can also find additional leads by participating in the destination marketing efforts of CVBs. Many of them participate in trade shows promoting their destination city, and participating properties may either send salespeople to meet with show visitors or make promotional materials available at the CVB's booth (selling with CVBs is explained in detail in Chapter 7).

## Lateral Referral and Account Penetration

Many hotel people are content when they get meetings business from a large corporation. But hosting company meetings offers the opportunity to promote even more business. Just help to execute a smoothly functioning meeting and your hotel will have an edge on the competition when it comes to additional business from the firm.

Some companies are so large that employees in one division have little or nothing to do with those in other sectors. If your meetings business comes from a product manager in one division, give serious thought to following up with everyone who has the title of product manager in that and other divisions of the company.

> **WORTH WATCHING**
>
> Joe Nishi, managing partner at Meeting Encore Limited in Toronto, Canada, discusses how the relationship between a hotel salesperson and a meeting planner is a key component in the world of corporate meetings at www.corporatemeetingsnetwork.ca/Vreports/the-power-of-relationship-2/.

The operating structure of the company may be uniform throughout, and if the product manager in one instance has the meetings responsibility, it is likely that others would too. If not, the manager will likely be able to point you to a decision-maker. Your case is stronger if you can get a recommendation from your original product manager customer. Even if he or she doesn't know the others personally, an endorsement from someone within the firm should open some doors.

Such lateral referrals and complete **account penetration** of all sectors of a large firm is the sign of a successful hotel sales manager. Think of the large companies in your area as a multi-divisional entity simply loaded with business potential. To ensure that you have reached all potential decision-makers and other influential staff members, you can employ a technique called **account mapping**. Neil Salerno, CHME, CHA, founder and owner of the Hotel Marketing Coach, explains:

> An excellent technique to penetrate larger corporate accounts and get more of their business is account mapping. Place the name of a decision-maker on a chart. Now, add who your contact reports to and who reports to them. If you don't know, find out and contact the additional staff members. Once they have been contacted, add them to your chart and continue the process. The end result should be a virtual organizational chart of the company. This chart or map will ensure that you are doing business with every mover and shaker in that company.[11]

This will also help your prospects for business in other companies. You will gain an insight into corporate structure that will help you analyze other companies in the same industry. The structures are generally similar. It certainly provides you with a good starting point by knowing the titles you are seeking. Understanding the corporate setup and who most likely has the meetings chore gives you a big leg up to penetrating and selling corporate business.

Other opportunities await at the property level. Local suppliers, such as your produce wholesaler, dairy operator, insurance agent, and other suppliers of products and/or services, are potential sources of meetings business. Even if a property's suppliers do not require meeting space for themselves, many belong to trade, professional, or civic organizations or social or religious groups. The property's suppliers, then, could very well be in a position to recommend the property as a meeting site for future meetings of their respective organizations.

One industry consultant advises:

> Look through the newspaper for announcements of meetings being held at competitors' properties — and try to get them for their next meeting. Look through the business section of the newspaper and trade journals for companies moving to town and for promotions or honors given to officers of companies. All of these are good lead opportunities.[12]

Employees at your hotel are also good sources of meetings business. Many employees belong to organizations (bowling teams, garden clubs, the P.T.A., religious groups, etc.) that meet regularly or have need of function space for special occasions such as installation dinners, awards nights, and other events. Property employees could very well influence the choice of "their" property for those events.

## Summary

In this chapter, we have taken an in-depth look at the corporate meetings segment, which is typically viewed as the most profitable group market segment. Not only does this segment often pay higher rates for rooms (despite meetings held during slow seasons), but it also can add to the hotel's bottom line with food and beverage, audiovisual, and recreation revenues. We have discussed the kinds of meetings held by corporations and the characteristics of the various company meetings. We have determined who the key corporate decision-makers are likely to be and how to find them. This lucrative market segment is becoming increasingly important to hotels, and hotel salespeople who understand the requirements of corporations and can match these requirements to their properties can successfully target the corporate market. In the next chapter, we will take a look at the third segment of the group meetings market, the varied nonprofit groups.

## Endnotes

1. John Anderson, "In Front of the Curve, *Smart Meetings*.
2. Terence Baker, "Coffee With...Mark Beaupre," *Meetings & Conventions*.
3. www.meetingsnet.com/financialinsurancemeetings/mag insurance_leveraging_smallmeetings_spend_0509/index.html.

Chapter 5: Selling the Corporate Meetings Market

4. Marshall Krantz, "Combo Meetings: Seeking Efficiencies," *Meeting News*.
5. Macie Schreibman, "Small Meeting Myths," *Smart Meetings*.
6. Michael Adams, "Career Jumping," *Successful Meetings*.
7. Cheryl-Ann Sturken, "Making Inroads," *Meetings & Conventions*.
8. "Hilton Makes Fast Progress Absorbing Promus," *Meetings News*.
9. Tom McCarthy, "Get Your Sales Management Ready for the 21st Century," *Hotel and Resort Industry*.
10. Cheryl-Ann Sturken, "Making Inroads," *Meetings & Conventions*.
11. Neil Salerno, "Are You Being Out-Hustled by Your Competition? How to Dominate Your Hotel's Market Set," www.hotelmarketingcoach.com/are_you_being_outhustled_by_you.htm.
12. Howard Feiertag, "New Sales Teams Often Miss Opportunities," *Hotel & Motel Management*.

## Study Questions

1. There are many similarities between association meetings and corporate meetings, but there are also clear distinctions. Contrast the two considering lead time, attendance, and kind of site required.
2. Company meetings come in many sizes and shapes. If you were the sales manager of a small property with limited meeting facilities, what types of company meetings would you target?
3. Discuss the multi-booking potential of corporate meetings.
4. As with associations, finding the key decision-maker within a corporation is of utmost importance. Why is this problem so acute in the corporate meetings market? List probable decision-makers within the corporate structure.
5. What role do local chapters or business offices of regional, national, or international corporations play in the determination of meeting sites?
6. Discuss how hotels are upgrading guestrooms with extra services and "perks" to meet specific business traveler needs.
7. List the major sources for finding corporate meetings and tell how each is used to develop a client base.

## Key Terms

**account mapping**—Determining the arrangement of and relationships between various company personnel to ensure that a salesperson has made contact with every potential decision-maker or influential staff member.

**account penetration**—The process of determining new sources of business within an organization.

**business center**—A facility that offers key equipment and services typically found in a business traveler's home office, including computer access, fax machines, and copy machines. Many hotel business centers offer secretarial and other services, such as shipping.

**dealer meetings**—Meetings held on a regional and national basis for dealers and distributors. Usually held to introduce new sales and advertising campaigns and new products.

**incentive meetings**—Meetings held during incentive trips given to employees, distributors, and dealers as a reward for top performance.

**management meetings**—Relatively small meetings consisting of top management, often requiring upgraded accommodations and services.

**preferred vendor agreement**—A legal document drafted between an organization and a specific vendor for that organization. This contract spells out the terms of the relationship to ensure that both parties understand expectations, and it can lay the ground work for legal recourse should any problems arise.

**professional/technical meetings**—Meetings held in order to update the company's technical personnel, usually taking the form of seminars/workshops.

**sales meeting**—Often a meeting dealing with such company objectives as product introduction, sales policies, company goals, and a discussion of sales techniques; or held to boost morale.

**stockholder/public meetings**—Meetings for non-employees.

**strategic meetings management**—A return on investment program implemented by corporations to bring accountability, consolidation, collaboration, and cost-consciousness to the meetings management process.

**third-party meeting planners**—Outside individuals or firms that handle meeting planning for companies. Services may include site selection, negotiations, and assisting in all phases of staging the meeting.

**training meetings**—Meetings held to update personnel in new company policies, methods, or procedures. Usually fairly small in size.

## Industry Profile

## Burt Cabañas, Founder, Chairman and CEO

### Benchmark Hospitality International

A graduate of Florida International University with a bachelor's degree in hotel and restaurant management, Humberto "Burt" Cabañas established Benchmark Hospitality International in 1980, after buying the former Benchmark Management Company from The Woodlands Company, where he was senior vice president. Burt had previously been the director of operations for The Stouffer Corporation, overseeing the financial performance of six hotel and resort properties, and the director of operations at the Doral Hotel and Country Club in Miami. A founding board member and past president of the International Association of Conference Centers (IACC), Cabañas received the organization's Mel Hosansky Distinguished Service Award in recognition of outstanding service to both the IACC and the conference center industry, and he has been selected as one of the "25 Most Influential People in the Meetings Industry" by MeetingNews.

## Tips to succeed in the Meetings Industry

I wanted to start an independent management company with an entrepreneurial spin, not the anti-chain, but a company that looked at individual properties as their own brand with unique personalities and unique services. As for the employees, I wanted to train our service staff to move up into management. It's worked. Today, 33 percent of our 700 managers have risen from service ranks. Always remember that you are only as good as the people who work for you. I didn't build Benchmark on my own. I just happened to be the orchestra leader.

Fifty percent of our growth in the next ten years will be internationally, with the majority of that growth being in Central and South America. We have an office in Santiago, Chile, and Tokyo. We are breaking ground in Panama. We are planning another facility on the west end of Panama and another in Patagonia.

E-commerce has been the biggest change I've seen. The ability for customers to shop and understand everything there is to know about our properties on the web and take virtual tours has been huge. People aren't just relying on 800 numbers and chains anymore. The second biggest change has been the increased variety in properties.

Decisions are made to stay at various places because of the destination qualities and because of meeting space. But what takes that meeting from being one that merely got through the agenda to one that is memorable and makes the meeting attendees think, which then reflects on the quality of the company, has to do with the people you have managing that effort.

One of the things that evolved out of Benchmark is a balance of living, learning, and leisure. When you ask me who the most successful meeting planners are in generating great meetings, I'd say it's those who effectively create that balance that allows people to learn, allows people to meet other people, and allows people to test their physical abilities. These are the best aspects of a hotel, a resort, or a learning environment/conference center.

Don't be afraid to take risks. If you are adverse to risks, work with someone who isn't. Make a strategy of taking risks. Push the edge of the envelope with regard to customer service.

**Learning Objectives:**

This portion of your text introduces you to the third major source for meetings business, nonprofit organizations. Also included in this chapter is a discussion of incentive meetings, insurance meetings, and medical meetings. When you have studied this chapter, you will:

- Be able to identify the types of nonprofit organizations that provide extensive meetings business and explain how to sell and service government agencies, labor unions, incentive meetings, insurance meetings, and medical meetings

- Be able to identify SMERF organizations and describe the types of meetings they hold and the factors that influence site decisions.

- Be able to summarize how to sell and service government agencies, labor unions, incentive meetings, insurance meetings, and medical meetings.

**Outline**

Nonprofit Organizations

The SMERF Groups
- Social Groups
- Military and Other Reunions
- Educational Meetings
- Religious Meetings
- Fraternal Meetings

Government Agencies

Labor Unions

Incentive Meetings

Insurance/Financial Service Meetings

Medical Meetings

Summary

# 6 Selling Other Markets

This chapter introduces the third major source for meetings business: nonprofit organizations, including SMERF groups, government agencies, and labor unions. Also included is a discussion of three other major meeting segments: incentive meetings, and insurance/financial service meetings, both of which are prominent types of corporate meetings; and medical meetings, which is a type of association meeting.

Lyn Matthew, CHSE, CMP, states:

> The remaining group market segments, commonly referred to as SMERF (Social, Military, Educational, Religious, and Fraternal), as well as government, union, medical, insurance, and incentive markets are by far the most diverse and challenging... Meeting needs vary widely...Research is critical in determining which groups can best be served by your property...Since a property can be perceived in many different ways by targeted prospects, it is important to communicate the benefits that highlight the planner's needs and wants...The astute sales executive must carefully match property capabilities with the needs of the conference planner. By selling the benefits of the property relative to the conference needs and wants, the sales executive has the opportunity to become a top producer while at the same time satisfying the needs of the meeting planner and paving the way for future bookings.

**CONVENTION INCOME SURVEY**

**Average expenditure per delegate per stay by convention type.**

**Average length of stay is 3.48 days.**

- Social $626
- Educational $690
- Trade Show $796
- Medical $916
- Religious $423
- Military $387
- Social Services $483
- Government $514
- Veteran $572

*This chart illustrates the average expenditure per delegate per stay for the SMERF groups that we will discuss in this chapter. Medical groups and trade shows have the highest average expenditures, while military and religious groups are the most price-conscious and spend the least money. While most of the SMERF groups fall below corporations and associations in terms of convention expenditures, these groups typically meet during months in which corporations and associations are not holding group meetings and conventions, making them a very attractive source of business for hotels.*

The "Market at a Glance" boxes in this chapter give a "snapshot" of these groups. They identify each segment's key characteristics, including location requirements, facilities commonly used, price range, services needed, typical decision-makers, and the best ways to reach each market. This will enable you to identify the group(s) best suited to your property and develop strategies to capture their business.

## Nonprofit Organizations

Although many organizations cannot be termed associations, they are structured in similar fashion. They have members, are nonprofit, and were created to accomplish some common purpose. Some, such as the Red Cross and the Boy Scouts and the Girl Scouts, promote charitable causes. In addition to meetings business, these types of organizations, which exist through fund-raising, may be excellent sources of business for your banquet department. Others of this category include political clubs and parties, which need hotel meeting accommodations for their regular conventions and frequent meetings. Still others include social, military, educational, religious, and fraternal (SMERF) groups; government agencies; labor unions; and medical groups, which will be discussed in greater detail in this chapter.

Selling to these organizations is much the same as selling to trade associations, although it is difficult to find a central source that identifies these organizations, since they are so varied. The records of a convention or tourist bureau may be of some help, and there are also directories from which a list of nonprofit meeting groups can be compiled. The *National Directory of Nonprofit Organizations* for example, can be accessed on the Gale Group's website (find.galegroup.com/gd/help/GDLeDirNDNOHelp.html), or you can do an Internet search for other listings of nonprofits.

Another particularly good avenue for reaching nonprofit, cost-conscious groups is the Hospitality Sales & Marketing Association International's MEET shows, which include MEET Mid-America, MEET West, and MEET National (you can get information on these shows at www.meetconference.com). Named the most popular meetings events in an online survey conducted by *Meetings & Conventions* magazine, these events include a 650-booth trade show as well as seminars for planners and hospitality suppliers, and meeting planners can attend both the trade show and educational program free of charge. Most planners attending these shows are not members of traditional planner's associations such as MPI or PCMA; they are volunteer meeting planners or those whose titles don't imply meeting planning. These people plan such events as hobby conventions, military reunions, educational, religious and fraternal meetings, and government meetings.

Once you have determined which of these groups you can best service (some groups look for all-inclusive packages that cover guestrooms, meeting rooms, and meals at one rate, for example), you can start by soliciting local chapters of national groups. Generally, most nonprofit organizations are staffed by permanent employees and volunteers, and overseen by a board of directors. Site selection processes will vary, but recommendations are usually passed along to a board of directors for a final selection. Lead time tends to be shorter than that of most trade associations; a lead time of one to two years is most common.

Since most local committees are made up of volunteers, it is a good policy to assure them of your aid should they succeed in getting the national organization to schedule its event at your property. If you offer to extend help for the chores associated with being the host chapter, this may encourage them to push for consideration of your locale as a meeting site.

As a further selling point, don't be reluctant to point out the many economic benefits to the community when a convention is held there. Research has indicated that delegates to regional and state conventions account for expenditures of about $190 a day for three or four days.

Once you are past the local chapters and have penetrated the national organization, you will usually find that there are experienced meeting planners on the staff. Some of these national organizations do a great deal of convention work. They will work with you in the manner of association staffs, especially if you have been successful in getting the local chapter to request the position of host chapter.

## The SMERF Groups

One of the most important subsegments in the nonprofit organizations market are the **SMERF groups** (see box titled "The SMERF Market at a Glance"). This acronym represents the collective group of **S**ocial, **M**ilitary, **E**ducational, **R**eligious, and **F**raternal groups. These groups, though typically price-conscious, are economically viable to properties (large and small) both because of their sheer numbers and their ability to fill "soft spots," as most meet during the typically slow summer months (see box titled "Typical Monthly Meeting Patterns").

While we will take a closer look at each of the SMERF categories in the following sections, there are several characteristics that the SMERF market shares:

- Dependable; meet during good and bad economic times.

- Generally meet on weekends or during off-peak periods and shoulder seasons to save money.

- Cost-conscious; attendees generally pay their own expenses.

- Prefer walkable, family-friendly cities with nearby entertainment and attractions; often choose second- and third-tier cities for their affordability.

### The SMERF Market at a Glance

- Many SMERF meeting planners work part-time or are volunteers.
- SMERF attendees tend to stay together in the hotel for food and beverage. Many groups have up to three meals in the hotel.
- Attendees bring their families. While one member is in meetings, other family members are visiting attractions.
- 32% plan one to three off-site meetings a year; 27% hold up to 10 off-site meetings annually.
- Attendance projections are reliable and less likely to be affected by economic downturns.
- 70% of SMERF meeting planners report attendance of less than 500 persons; 50% reported that attendance at their largest event was less than 500.
- 43% have meeting budgets of less than $100,000.
- A little over half of SMERF annual events include a trade show or exhibition.

**Types of Facilities Used by the SMERF Market:**

| | | | |
|---|---|---|---|
| Urban/Midtown Hotels | 65% | Convention Centers | 29% |
| Suburban Hotels | 44% | University Facilities | 20% |
| Conference Centers | 36% | Arenas/Stadiums | 7% |
| Resorts | 32% | | |

Sources: Patricia Sherman, "SMERF Events," *Expo*, and Howard Feiertag, "SMERF Business Ideal to Help Fill Weekend Room Nights," *Hotel & Motel Management*.

**TYPICAL MONTHLY MEETING PATTERNS**

This chart shows the monthly convention meeting pattern for both association and corporate business. Note that business is usually slower in the months of July and August. Targeting SMERF groups, which normally meet in these months, can help increase business over these "soft spots."

- Look for cities with easy access to freeways; ideally within driving distance of home or in close proximity to an airport.
- Likely to choose destinations or hotels where their group will be given personalized attention and where attendees can engage with local citizens and have cultural options. These groups are loyal to hotels and cities where they are treated like "the big fish in a little pond" (see Figure 6.1).
- Sometimes use non-traditional venues, such as universities, colleges, stadiums or arenas, conference centers, camps, and retreat centers. Dedicated conference centers are increasing in popularity due to the convenience of being able to keep the group together in one location, usually at an all-inclusive rate.
- Planners often need extra guidance in executing the event, so many rely on convention and visitors bureaus (CVBs) or destination management organizations (DMOs) to assist with hotel selection and the logistics of the meeting.

Hotels that wish to attract this market must assure the planner that they will provide extra support for the event and offer contracts that are easy to understand – with no hidden fees or attrition penalties. Although most groups prefer to have a single hotel liaison, such as a personal conference service manager, support staff should be readily available to assist with last-minute needs. Some hotels develop or provide apps that instantly connect meeting planners with their liaison or support personnel.

## Social Groups

People are avid "joiners," and there are groups for almost every interest. Just looking through the "Groups and Organizations" listing in a local telephone directory may yield such prospects as chess clubs, ethnic groups (Italian-American clubs, etc.), garden clubs, and bowling leagues. These organizations may be local, or they may be part of a regional or national organization. No matter what their size, these social groups should not be overlooked as potential sources of business. Since most SMERF meetings are not driven by business needs, but rather by social and personal ties, they are generally more recession-

# Chapter 6: Selling Other Markets

**Figure 6.1. ADVERTISING TO THE SMERFS**

Who do you thinks gets the most attention? There are advantages to being a big fish in a little pond.

Smaller cities really appreciate a sporting event coming to their community. You'll receive over-the-top personal service and find affordable destinations. Wilmington, Ohio, is such a place. Located in the middle of Cincinnati, Columbus and Dayton, we've hosted events to include tennis, softball, baseball, gymnastics, equine, soccer, football and wrestling.

Let us show you how you should be treated. Call today.

Clinton County Convention & Visitors Bureau
877-4-A-VISIT  www.clintoncountyohio.com

*Many meeting planners in the SMERF market are in-experienced, or they may feel that their group is overshadowed by bigger business. This ad reassures planners that their meetings are important to them – and that their group will receive personalized service...and be welcomed by the community.*
**Source:** *Courtesy of Clinton County [Ohio] Convention & Visitors Bureau.*

proof than other types of meetings. Even a small local group may require meeting space or can generate meals business, while large groups can be an excellent source of banquet and convention business. Many social clubs hold awards banquets or fund-raising functions, or can be a source of business for annual events such as Christmas parties and installation ceremonies. Groups such as garden and craft clubs often host local shows or fairs, which not only result in meeting space sales, but may bring in out-of-town business and generate publicity for your property. Most social group decision-makers are inexperienced in meeting planning. Louise Hurlbut, former vice president of marketing for Groople, an agency that specializes in group online travel arrangements, says:

"These groups are often run by volunteers or by people who may not handle an event from year to year. So when you're dealing with a less experienced audience, you may need to help them through the process by providing them the tools that make it easier for them to find the appropriate facilities and travel arrangements for their group."

## Military and Other Reunions

The reunions market, which consists of family, class, and military reunions, is a rapidly growing market segment. Reunions of all types have different needs than conventional meetings. While association and corporate events are primarily about business, reunions focus more on sharing memories, fun, and visiting tourist attractions; a minimal amount of business is conducted. This segment is an excellent source of flexible weekend business.

**Military Reunions.** Military reunions are held by thousands of groups: large, national organizations, such as the Veterans of Foreign Wars of the United States (VFW), Disabled American Veterans, and the American Legion; umbrella organizations for a particular branch of service (the Air Force Association, Fleet Reserve Association, Marine Corps League, and National Guard Association, for example); and groups that have served together in battle (WWII, the Korean conflict, Vietnam, Iraq, and Afghanistan) or on the same military base, unit, or ship. As you can see, this market is highly fragmented – and these groups rarely work together – but military reunions are a viable target market as attendees spend over $15 billion annually for air travel, hotels, food, drink, and entertainment during their reunions.

Military reunion business has several notable characteristics (see box titled "The Military Reunion Market at a Glance"). For the most part, reunions are held from April to October, and occupancies run from Thursday or Friday through Sunday (the average length of stay is 2.5-4 days). Most groups meet annually or bi-annually during the same season of the year, although dates are flexible. Reunions may be held in different cities to promote interest.

Most military reunions include a welcome reception on Friday, a Saturday night banquet, and a breakfast buffet on Sunday; a memorial service and a short business meeting are also included during the reunion. Most groups request one or two large rooms that can seat the entire group for the banquet and for socializing, as military meetings are all about camaraderie and sharing stories. Ted Dey, founder and vice president of sales, Armed Forces Reunions, Inc., says:

*Social groups meet to share common interests, and, depending on the type of group, can prove to be an excellent source for meeting rooms business as well as food functions.*
**Source: Photograph courtesy of Loews Hotels.**

| | **The Military Reunion Market at a Glance** |
|---|---|
| **Location:** | Family and/or military-oriented destinations that can offer a combined vacation/reunion. Past destinations have included San Diego, California, Daytona Beach, Florida, Branson, Missouri, San Antonio, Texas, and Norfolk, Virginia. Almost any city with popular local attractions or a good climate, however, can compete for this market. |
| **Facilities:** | Programs usually consist of a short business meeting, a memorial service, and a Saturday night banquet. Requirements include limited audiovisual equipment, but there must be enough banquet space to seat the entire group and their spouses at one time. A hospitality room is usually required. |
| **Price:** | Since many attendees are on fixed incomes, this group is very cost-conscious. Properties that offer low rates, free or low-cost meeting space, or discounts to local attractions are especially inviting. Free or discounted parking is also appreciated. |
| **Services:** | Properties targeting this group can expect to assist with the planning of functions, as many military reunions are planned by nonprofessionals. Some groups will also require special meal menus. |
| **Decision-Makers:** | Contact must be made with each individual military unit or group to determine the decision-maker. |
| **Best Ways To Reach Market:** | Join THE Reunion Network, and advertise in THE Reunion Network News. Other advertising opportunities include *Reunions, the Magazine* and *Military Reunion News*. Find contacts through the *Military Reunion Handbook*, and purchase lists or labels from Service Reunions National Registry. Attend military reunion training conferences and organize fam trips for military reunion planners. |

The hospitality room is the reunion. That's where it happens. The ideal hospitality room would be one that's large enough to accommodate tables of memorabilia and where attendees are allowed to bring their own liquor.[2]

Room occupancy is usually 75 to 150 per night, although this can go higher for larger reunions. Since many attendees are on fixed incomes and are paying their own way, they are extremely price-conscious. Attendees often share rooms with spouses or friends. Since spouses have a strong voice in the decision to attend, a hotel with planned spouse programs often has an edge over the competition. One meeting reunion planner states:

> All of the men have something in common, but almost none of the women do. If you do the job right, the wives will send the check in the day the registration notice arrives.[3]

As veterans age, there is an increased need for special services for attendees with physical problems, including those using wheelchairs and walkers or the hearing-impaired. There may also be the need for special menus to accommodate some of the older attendees.

More family members, including children, are attending military reunions, and there has also been an increase in reunions for military personnel from the Vietnam and later wars, including the Gulf War and Afghanistan. Therefore, a hotel that can also accommodate all age groups is appealing – if it is affordable.

Ideal sites for military reunions include cities in close proximity to a former base, home port, or other military facilities. Popular choices include Norfolk and Virginia Beach, Virginia; Jacksonville and Pensacola, Florida; San Antonio, Texas; Colorado Springs, Colorado; and San Diego, California. Reunion groups also prefer locations that are close to other attractions, including military museums, historical sites, theme parks, beaches, shopping and entertainment, and so on. These groups often include tours to these sites in their programs (some groups charter buses for day trips).

Other sites are chosen for their uniqueness – especially if there is a military connection. The Hangar Hotel in Fredericksburg, Texas, for example, was built to resemble a WWII hanger, and inside décor, which is reminiscent of the 1940s, includes model planes, airplane memorabilia, and a history of the USO. Adjacent to the property is a diner that serves popular fare from the 1940s and an Airport Conference Center with 1940s touches. A nearby park provides numerous recreational amenities for attendees and their guests.

In the past, military reunions, which typically draw 100 to 300 people or more, were planned by nonprofessionals. Because of the rising demand, however, several resources were developed to assist inexperienced meeting planners. Some firms, such as Military Reunion Planners (http://militaryreunionplanners.com/), provide complete military reunion services – from site selection to registration to event and tour planning. Other firms, including Your Military Reunion Connection (YMRC) at http://ymrc.net/, provide training and offer advice to meeting planners. The YMRC offers suppliers an opportunity to meet with planners at YMRC Marketplace events. Unlike traditional trade shows, these events do not use booths; instead, attending planners have 15-minute meetings with exhibitors. The advantages of this type of arrangement are that the hotel saves on booth shipping and staffing costs (exhibitors bring only their business cards and collateral material), but the downside is the limited time spent with each planner (and many planners may not be interested in what your property has to offer).

Several other organizations, including The Alliance of Military Reunions (www.allmilitaryreunions.org) and the Reunion Friendly Network (reunionfriendly.com), provide assistance to planners of military reunions – and can be an excellent way for hotels to find and contact military reunion planners. The Alliance of Military Reunions offers informative seminars, fam tours, and informational publications to members and publishes an online member directory and listing of reunions. The Reunion Friendly Network's support includes weekly "Salute" newsletters, and the organization also publishes *Reunion Friendly Network Magazine*, in which military-friendly hotels can advertise. Back issues of the magazine can be viewed on the RFN site, which also includes a list of upcoming reunions and events, including its ConFAMS, which provide hotels with the opportunity to meet with planners in locations across the country.

Other publications that can be useful to reach this market are *Reunions Magazine* (reunionsmag.com) and the *VOB Business Directory* (www.veteranownedbusiness.com), which offers banner ads on its website; advertising can be custom-tailored for specific cities, counties, and states to maximize cost-effectiveness.

## Class and Family Reunions

Class and family reunions differ from military reunions in terms of size, meeting frequency, and types of programs. Recreational amenities are considered very important, and there may be several food and social functions but little in the way of meeting space is needed. Like military groups, however, these groups pay their own way, and usually provide a good number of double occupancy rooms.

Source: Photograph courtesy of Pifemaster Productions.

Class reunions are the largest in terms of numbers of events and number of attendees. However, attendees stay an average of just one night in a hotel. Family and military reunions, on the other hand, draw fewer people but the attendees stay for a longer period of time -- an average of two nights in the case of family reunions and about three nights at military reunions.

Although most family reunions are hosted by nonprofessionals, there is a growing number of trained class reunion meeting planners. The National Association of Reunion Managers (NARM), whose website is www.reunions.com, is an organization that offers meeting planning training and networking. Another professional organization, the National Coalition of Black Meeting Planners (NCBMP) (www.ncbmp.com) hosts an annual conference at which hotels can exhibit. According to the NCBMP, African-Americans can be an excellent source of reunions business if your hotel is located in a city with points of interest relative to black heritage (museums, entertainment, and so on), and your property is sensitive to the issues faced by African-Americans.

Other ways to target the class and family reunions market are to advertise in *Reunions Magazine* and other reunions publications, and to work closely with your local convention and visitors bureau or chamber of commerce. These organizations are often contacted by individuals or groups wanting information about "reunion-friendly" hotels (see Figure 6.2).

The Internet is an excellent source for advertising and finding leads. There are a number of sites that offer opportunities to purchase ads targeting the *family reunion* market. Classmates.com (www.classmates.com/reunions) and Great Reunions (www.greatreunions.com) are two of the largest *class reunion* planning sites. Both offer advertising opportunities – and also post a listing of upcoming reunions. These leads can be useful in attracting future reunions business, especially if your hotel is located in close proximity to the school or university.

## Chapter 6: Selling Other Markets

*Figure 6.2. REUNION-FRIENDLY HOTELS.*

This ad for the Holiday Inn, San Diego Bayside, promotes an experienced staff who can assist the planner in organizing a "perfect event" as well as special reunion amenities, such as special reunion rates, a complimentary hospitality suite, and a welcome letter and gift of chocolates in each room.

## Educational Meetings

The educational meetings market is an excellent market segment for filling rooms during slow summer occupancy periods. Elementary, high school, and college teachers and others affiliated with academic programs are prime sources of convention business. They hold a number of meetings, and every state has a teachers' association of some sort as well. In addition, most states have continuing-education requirements that necessitate periodic seminars and classes for teachers.

Most educational meetings are relatively short (sometimes lasting only a day), and meeting planners look for accessibility and value. Since most attendees come at their own expense, they are extremely price-sensitive. Sometimes, costs are kept low by using connections to venues or partnering with alumni-owned businesses that have ties to meeting-related businesses. Another avenue to lower cost is "add-on" events; offering other (usually smaller) events in addition to a larger meeting may help the planner to negotiate better rates with hotels and other meeting venues.

Properties that are located close to major transportation arteries or an educational center (college, university, etc.) and can offer reduced room rates are especially attractive. Conference centers are another popular choice for educational meetings. Educational groups, especially those at the college and university level, are familiar with the campus concept; in fact, this is the most likely segment of the SMERF groups to utilize these facilities. Conference centers offer a dedicated environment which allows a planner to keep the group together in one place. Another advantage is the all-inclusive rate; with a complete meetings package (CMP), attendees don't have to worry about additional expenses. These CMPs can be customized for groups that have specific requirements or don't require all the services offered by the conference center.

Since this market is so diverse, there are many potential contact persons. Cooperative extension services often sponsor seminars, and the state director is the decision-maker (a county agent's directory is an excellent source of contact names). Alumni offices and divisions of continuing education at local colleges and universities are sources of leads for meetings business, and admissions offices can provide transient business from visiting parents and prospective students. Other leads can be obtained through the administrative offices at a local educational institution or board of education. Personal contacts and referrals are often available from college professors and teachers who belong to professional associations.

An excellent resource for locating national and state educational associations is www.officialusa.com/stateguides/education/associations.html. This web page provides links to educational associations in all 50 states as well as to such national organizations as the National Education Association, the National Association of State Boards of Education, and the American Association of School Administrators. You can also do an Internet search to find other resources.

Hotels can also reach this market by advertising in educational publications, purchasing banner ads or a sponsorship on an educational group's website, and advertising on sites such as Cvent (www.cvent.com/rfp/hotels). This site features over 1,000 destinations and more than 218,000 event venues, and is often used by price-conscious planners as they can compare details on various aspects of their meetings, from minimum food and beverage requirements to attrition clauses, in one convenient location. Many hotel chains exhibit at the annual Travel, Events and Management in Sports (TEAMS) conference and expo. This convention provides networking opportunities and one-on-one appointment sessions. Information on upcoming events can be found at teamsconference.com.

## Religious Meetings

Religious groups are an excellent source of business for gatherings both small (board meetings, committee meetings, seminars, and workshops) and large (area and regional meetings and conventions). Large conventions of 10,000 to 45,000 attendees are a common annual occurrence. The last survey by the Religious Conference Management Association (RCMA) shows that religious meetings have grown by 195 percent over the last decade. A property that understands the unique needs of religious groups can take advantage of this opportunity to fill "soft spots" — most groups meet over a three-day to one-week period during the summer months (see box titled "Religious Meetings at a Glance").

Most large religious meetings are "family affairs," and meeting planners tend to choose locations that are family oriented (Orlando, Anaheim, Indianapolis, Toronto). They also look for walkable cities – and especially appreciate having a choice of inexpensive restaurants within close proximity to the hotel or other meeting venue. Many families arrive a few days early and stay a few days after the meeting to make the most of their vacation. Mike Blackwell, former festival coordinator for the United Church of God, speaking of his Branson, Missouri, meeting, says:

> Many of our members make this their family vacation. All ages attend, so we have to have a destination with something for everybody.[4]

There has also been an explosion in religious meetings for youth and young adults. Student retreats in the summer, for example, can attract hundreds or even thousands of attendees, and youth events are also scheduled between Christmas and New Year's day be-

Chapter 6: Selling Other Markets

> ### Religious Meetings at a Glance
>
> **Attendance:** Consists of hundreds of organizations from dozens of denominations throughout the United States and the world; may range in size from small board meetings to mega-conventions of up to 75,000 (see photo). May consist of clergy, lay people, or both; are often family affairs.
>
> **Location:** Favor family-oriented cities such as Orlando, Anaheim, and Atlanta. Also prefer second-and third-tier cities, generally in the South or Midwest, such as Birmingham, Branson, Indianapolis, and St. Louis. Mark McCulley, CMP, former conference director for the Worldwide Church of God evaluated each city for facility size and quality; affordability of hotel and convention facilities; area attractions and amusements; friendliness of the city; and overall entertainment value of the region.
>
> **Facilities:** Need a wide selection of meeting and convention space — small meeting rooms for seminars, workshops, and meetings; large convention halls to hold large crowds. Often require numerous breakout rooms and have many, often simultaneous meal functions.
>
> **Services:** Restaurant availability is a high priority. According to April McWilliams, former V.P. of Sales for the Greater Birmingham CVB, "Whenever people finish up with a meeting, they're always hungry. They want a place to eat, so it's important that hotels or centers have restaurants open for them, even if it's just for pie or coffee." Some religious groups will require special menus as well (i.e., Jewish Kosher foods).
>
> **Price:** Middle- to low-budget hotels are preferred, since most pay their own way. Double occupancy is the norm. Property-offered discounts and complimentary transportation are valued. However, the once-pervasive image of penny-pinching religious meeting attendees is no longer valid. Anne Hamilton, vice president, resort and sales services, for Disney Destinations, states, "Disney World has 25 resorts at four price points and religious meeting attendees stay at all of them."
>
> **Decision-Makers:** Most national events are planned by professional meeting planners. Local and regional events are planned by a committee or the leader of the organization.
>
> **Best Ways To Reach Market:** The RCMA (Religious Conference Management Association) is a national organization representing over 250 denominations and religious organizations. They publish a monthly magazine, *Religious Conference Manager*, and a membership directory.
>
> *Religious groups, such as the Promise Keepers, a men-only ministry based in Boulder, Colorado, generate over 7,200 conventions and meetings internationally and represent 30 million nights of hotel accommodations annually.*

cause students are out of school. Meeting planners generally look to "fun" locations, such as proximity to an amusement park or the beach, for these attendees.

Religious meeting attendees often make up for their lack of alcohol consumption in food consumption. D'Wayne Leatherland, former senior administrative coordinator - meeting/event services for the Church of the Nazarene, states:

## Summary of Types of Religious Meetings

| Type of Meeting | Total Attendance | Average No. of Days |
|---|---|---|
| Convention/Conference | 10,871,566 | 4.0 |
| Board | 121,449 | 2.3 |
| Committee/Seminar | 626,571 | 2.2 |
| Retreat | 465,729 | 3.4 |
| Other | 1,804,442 | 2.8 |
| Total | 14,889,757 | |

**Types of Meeting Facilities Used**

| | |
|---|---|
| Downtown Hotel | 17.2% |
| Conference Center | 16.6% |
| Suburban Hotel | 12.8% |
| Camps/Retreats | 11.2% |
| Resort Hotel | 11.1% |
| Convention/Civic Center | 11.1% |
| Airport Hotel | 10.5% |
| College/University | 7.6% |
| Cruise Ship | 1.9% |

*Downtown hotels are the top choice of religious meeting groups, with conference centers the second most popular option. While only about five percent of religious groups need more than 3,000 sleeping rooms, the majority require exhibit space.*
**Source: "RCMA Survey,"** *Religious Conference Manager.*

> Our meetings history supports the claim that our group likes the "f" in food and beverage.[5]

He suggests that hotels convert bars into ice cream parlors or coffee shops during his group's meetings, turning lost alcohol revenue into food revenue.

Most religious meeting attendees pay their own way, so they are price-sensitive and usually opt for double-occupancy rooms, but religious meetings can be profitable to a hotel because they do not displace corporate or association business. Because these groups are value-conscious, religious meeting planners negotiate lower rates by booking on holidays and weekends and seeking shoulder or valley periods. Vaughn Hall, former director of convention sales and marketing for the Santa Clara, California Chamber of Commerce/Convention and Visitors Bureau, says, "We've targeted the religious market because our weekends are slow and it's a good filler market for us."

There is another very good reason to target this market. Many religious groups do community service projects when they visit a city. Most religious groups, in fact, are committed to giving back to the community in which they meet, and they usually reach out to other partners in the city – from the mayor's office to local businesses – in order to determine which projects would be most beneficial. In Indianapolis, for example, 2,000 meeting attendees helped local neighborhood associations rehabilitate ten houses and clean up city parks. Other groups reach out to the homeless, sort books for libraries, and collect needed items, such as supplies for babies and needy school children.

Other requirements for religious meetings include large meeting rooms, smaller meeting rooms for break-out sessions, and audiovisual equipment, as hybrid meetings are often used to stream meeting activities to members unable to attend or to stream messages from church leaders to attendees. These groups also generally have a longer lead time for their meetings than corporations. It is worth it, however, to accommodate their business, as these groups are extremely loyal to hotels and destinations willing to work with them.

Many of the large religious meetings are planned by professional meeting planners, many of whom belong to the Religious Conference Management Association (RCMA). This group was founded in 1972 and has over 800 meeting planner members and 2,100 associate members that represent hotels, convention bureaus, and other suppliers. RCMA members are responsible for over 7,200 meetings a year, and represent more than 300 denominations and religious organizations.

Other organizations that serve this market include the Christian Meetings & Conventions Association (www.christianmeeting.org), the Christian Management Association (www.christianmanagementassociation.org), and Rejuvenate (www.rejuvenatemeetings.com). Hotels and other travel suppliers can join these associations as associate members and advertise on their sites and in their publications; the RCMA publishes *Aspire Magazine* quarterly and an *Aspire* newsletter bi-weekly, *Rejuvenate Meetings Inspiration* is published bi-monthly by Rejuvenate, and the CMCA publishes the quarterly *Good Newsletter*. Advertising, of course, should appeal to the needs of this market (see Figure 6.3).

There are also several other ways to reach this market. A growing number of religious meeting planners are using the services of third-party planners, such as ConferenceDirect and Experient, Inc., to be able to concentrate on the content of their programs rather than the logistics. Hotels can contact these firms to inquire about being put on a preferred supplier list. Another avenue is to join forces with a faith-based business. The Westfields Marriott Washington Dulles in Chantilly, Virginia, for example, partnered with the region's leading Christian radio station, WAVA-FM, and doubled its weekend religious meetings business. Louis Nicholls, the hotel's former director of sales and marketing, says:

> In exchange for trade-outs on F&B, meeting and sleep space, we got radio time that has proven to be a powerful business builder.[6]

There are also several trade shows at which hotels can exhibit and meet with religious meeting planners. RCMA's EMERGE, the organization's national convention, uses a hosted-buyer program that sets appointments for qualified meeting planners to meet with hotels and other suppliers. To qualify to have their expenses reimbursed, buyers must hold meetings in multiple locations and utilize a minimum of 50 room nights in peak periods at least once annually, and keep appointments with 14 exhibitors over the two-day tradeshow. The RCMA also hosts four Aspire Regionals annually; although a smaller show, hotels receive appointments with approximately 50 faith-based planners. Suppliers can also attend all of the sessions, and they receive three meals and can attend breaks.

Rejuvenate Marketplace is another annual trade show that features three days of sessions and training as well as a hosted-buyer trade show. At their appointments, planners can place RFPs and secure dates with hotel exhibitors. Planners pay a deposit that is refunded if they keep all their appointments.

The CMCA hosts a Spring Showcase for religious meeting planners. Hotels can meet with planners and receive favorable publicity by becoming a sponsor of the event. The organization is also expanding its efforts to become a clearinghouse of information for both planners and suppliers.

## Fraternal Meetings

**Fraternal organizations** can be broken down into two categories: college fraternal groups or "The Greeks," which are the familiar college campus societies; and fraternal service groups, such as the Benevolent Protective Order of Elks, the Fraternal Order of Eagles, the Lions Clubs International, Shriners International, and Freemasons, to name a few.

*Figure 6.3. ADVERTISING TO THE RELIGIOUS MARKET.*

### Religious Meetings – A Specialty of The Victorian Condo Hotel & Resort!

**The Victorian Condo Hotel Resort and Conference Center** is a favorite destination for those planning church seminars, youth group trips, and couples retreats.

Our **condominium suites** offer floor plans and decors for 1 to 8 people in a condo, with separate living, sleeping, dining, and private balconies to overlook the Gulf of Mexico.

**The Victorian Resort** offers two swimming pools, one heated year round, tennis court, fitness center, picnic areas and more.

**Our staff** has the expertise to meet your expectations for meeting facilities and to provide options for your groups' outings to the Island's world class attractions.

**For groups of 12 to 300**, The Victorian provides over 10,000 square feet of indoor and outdoor meetings areas.

#### THE VICTORIAN
CONDO·HOTEL
RESORT & CONFERENCE CENTER

6300 Seawall • Galveston • TX • victoriancondo.com
www.facebook.com/galvestonvictorian • kallen@viccondo.com
888.804.1420

This ad appeals to several of the needs of the religious market. The hotel offers condominium suites that accommodate up to eight people (religious meetings attendees often share rooms to save money), on-site meeting space, and recreational amenities.
**Source: Courtesy of The Victorian Condo Hotel Resort and Conference Center.**

**College Fraternal Groups.** National fraternities and sororities on college campuses across the country, typically meet during the summer months at events planned by a paid executive. The activities of this vast market are coordinated by three major groups: the North American Interfraternity Conference (NIC), which represents 48 fraternities; the National Panhellenic Conference, the female counterpart of the NIC; and the Fraternity Executives

Association (FEA), whose membership is made up of paid executive officers from a number of fraternities (see box titled "Sources for Reaching the Fraternal Market").

Sidney Dunn, executive director of FEA, says of this segment:

> They meet frequently: an annual business session, generally once a year for leadership education, board meetings, alumni events, and regional meetings, sometimes at campus facilities. When I was a fraternity executive, I would plan as many as 14 meetings a year. In some cases, the frequency of events can be used as negotiating leverage during a site search; that is, the right deal will encourage the group to regularly use the property...Generally, fraternities and sororities meet in the summertime, and, due to the need for lower rates, will opt for southern tier cities and the warmer cities in Arizona, Texas, and Florida, where summer business is generally slower. They aren't able to meet as much in the northeast and upper Midwest cities because summertime there is popular for tourists."[7]

The size of most general membership meetings, held during the months of June through August, ranges from approximately 150 to 800 or more. Multiple-occupancy rates are high, since spouses or fellow students often share rooms. Meeting agendas typically include a banquet lunch, so properties wishing to service this market must have ample facilities to seat the entire delegation at one time. Lead time is typically two to three years.

In addition to general meetings, sororities and fraternities hold educational retreats and leadership training institutes, which are usually held during the school year to train

---

### Sources for Reaching the Fraternal Market

#### Fraternal Executives Association

**Attendee Profile:** College fraternity executives (executive directors and national presidents) from the top college fraternal organizations in America.
**Program:** Fraternity-related suppliers from the hospitality industry can socialize with executives and participate in a trade show.
**Contact:** Fraternity Executives Association, 1750 Royalton Drive, Carmel, IN 46032-9620; (317) 496-2411, fax: (317) 580-9299; e-mail: fea.inc@gmail.com; website: fea-inc.org.

#### National Panhellenic Conference

**Attendee Profile:** College sorority executives (executive directors and national presidents) from the top women's fraternal organizations in America.
**Program:** Geared mainly toward hospitality industry suppliers, the best opportunity for business development occurs during the trade portion of the event.
**Contact:** National Panhellenic Conference, 3901 West 86th Street, Suite 398, Indianapolis, IN 46268; (317) 872-3185, fax: (317) 872-3192; e-mail: npccentral@npcwomen.org; website: www.mpcwomen.org.

#### North-American Interfraternity Conference

**Attendee Profile:** National fraternity executives and college fraternity advisors from throughout the country.
**Program:** Mainly fraternity related; the trade show portion of the event offers the best opportunity for business development.
**Contact:** North-American Interfraternity Conference, Inc. 3901 West 86th Street, Suite 390, Indianapolis, IN 46268-1791; (317) 872-1112, fax: (317) 872-1134; website: www.nicindy.org.

newly elected officers. While some of these meetings are held on college campuses for cost-effectiveness, properties that can offer discounted rates may be able to capture some of this business.

Other possibilities for business include national board or council meetings, which usually consist of the governing boards of sororities and fraternities. Since group size is small, (ranging from six to 125 people), and meetings are shorter, these meetings are often held on weekends (usually during the months of October and February). Airport facilities and properties close to the campus can often draw this type of business.

A subsegment for special consideration is African-American fraternal organizations. These groups have annual or biennial conventions of 2,000 to 20,000 people. Besides generating high attendance, the advantage of servicing this market is that the membership is

# No Matter Which Fraternity You Belong To, You Belong Here.

We may not have a secret handshake, but at Marriott, we know the secret to success when it comes to hosting fraternity functions. No matter what the occasion, we'll provide risk-free meetings at a surprisingly affordable price. In fact, you can rely on us to plan your event every step of the way. No matter what your particular needs. And you can be sure of working with professionals who are pledged to making your meeting the best it can be. So give us a call. And you'll see why Marriott is right where you belong.

**Marriott.**
HOTELS·RESORTS·SUITES

1-800-831-2878

generally older and more affluent than the typical collegiate fraternity member. Alumni chapters play active roles in these organizations, and attendees tend to have more disposable income than their college counterparts — which translates to higher entertainment, catering, and alcoholic beverage revenue for hotels.

In addition to the traditional Greek societies, there is another group of professional or honorary societies that should also be included in this category. Some examples include Alpha Omega, a professional dental fraternity, Sigma Delta Chi, a professional journalism society, and Delta Epsilon Sigma, a scholarship honorary society. Some of these host large conventions, meeting on an 18-month rotational basis in the months of August and December. The December conventions, held between Christmas and New Years Day, are an excellent way to fill this traditionally slack time. These groups can be reached through related professional associations or through contact with the American Society of Association Executives (ASAE), since many of these meeting planners belong to that association.

**Service Fraternal Groups.** Service groups also hold a number of meetings and special events throughout the year. While many of these groups (such as the Elks, Shriners, the American Legion, and Freemasons, for example) have their own meeting facilities, they can be excellent sources of business for special occasions, including fund-raising events and annual functions such as Christmas parties. Service groups may also play host to regional and national conventions or generate rooms business from out-of-town guests attending local functions.

Both fraternal and service groups' regional and national meetings are usually family affairs and are often presented to delegates — who pay their own way —as a vacation-convention combination. Planners, therefore, look for recreational amenities as well as value.

Some service organizations have special needs. Lions Clubs International, for example, strives to serve people with sight challenges, and more than five percent of the attendees at the group's annual meeting are blind. Renee Aubin, convention division manager for Lions Clubs International, says the group must look for a destination that doesn't require a lot of walking yet has enticing activities close by for the group's multi-national attendees. She found that "Montréal excels as an easy multilingual destination with a compact downtown and tantalizing pre- and post-convention tourist opportunities." She adds:

> It was one of the best cities, with its housing package and diversity.[8]

There are a number of ways to reach this lucrative market segment. Sororities and fraternities can be reached by contacting college campuses and their alumni associations or by contacting the national governing groups mentioned in this section. Service groups may be found in local telephone directories or through chamber of commerce listings.

To solicit this market on a larger scale, you may wish to consider participating in three events held by major fraternities and sororities. The Fraternal Executives Association (FEA) holds its annual conference and vendor trade show during the first two weeks of July, while the North-American Interfraternity Conference (NIC) holds a larger event during the first week of December. While this event also includes a trade show, it is less hotel-specific than FEA's event. The National Panhellenic Conference (NPC), which is held in October, also features a trade show and gives vendors the opportunity to meet with the executives and staff members of 26 attending sororities.

# Government Agencies

Another frequently overlooked — but potentially lucrative — nonprofit market segment is government meetings business (see the box titled "The Government Meetings Market at a Glance"). This market segment spends over $18 billion for meeting expenses annually, with $3 billion spent on food and beverage and $5 billion on lodging.[9] It can be an excellent source of conventions business, especially when agencies deal with business groups. The Department of Commerce, the Department of Veterans Affairs, the Department of Justice, and the Department of Labor are just four examples of government agencies.

It is difficult to generalize about the kind of business that comes from government agencies. It varies a great deal, as does interest in different parts of the country. Meetings may range from large conferences with international dignitaries to training meetings for small groups; hybrid meetings are often used to save time and money. Some meetings are held only once, so it is difficult to get an accurate meetings history from this segment.

When you are trying to attract government meetings, you will find some similarities to corporations – you will deal with a strata of executives, you can expect many small meetings (often on short notice), and meetings are generally held on weekdays (lodging is typically required from Mondays through Thursdays). Most government meetings are training meetings, so you may work with a training officer, contract specialist, or procurement officer in addition to a meeting planner, and, since planners operate on tight budgets, they look for discounted rates and free services (such as complimentary shuttle service and meeting space). Accessibility is also important, so if your hotel is near an airport or other transportation hub, you have an advantage.

So how is government business different from corporate business? Government business at all levels – federal, state, and local – operates under specific guidelines, and hotels that wish to attract this market must meet these criteria. First, government employees must adhere to a strict **per diem** allowance – a fixed amount for each day of travel outside the office. The per diem, which must cover lodging, meals, and taxes, is adjusted yearly and varies by city. A complete listing of per diem rates can be found at www.gsa.com (click on the per diem tab to search for amounts by city and state or zip code, or do a statewide search by clicking on the interactive map). Although government employees often use their own money to supplement the per diem, if your hotel can offer a meetings package of rooms and meals (including tax), you will be more likely to attract this market.

In addition to per diems and government payment schedules (some agencies can take up to 45 days to pay), government business also differs from corporate business in the way it is contracted. Government contracts are awarded through the General Services Adminis-

### Factors Important for Government Meetings

When asked to rank the most important critetria for selecting a hotel, government meeting planners responded:

| | |
|---|---|
| Rates | 100 |
| Location | 83.3 |
| Attrition Policy | 56.6 |
| Free WiFi | 50.0 |
| Service | 44.4 |
| Meeting Room Technology | 33.3 |
| Amenities | 22.2 |
| Chain Hotel | 16.1 |
| Guestroom Technology | 11.1 |
| Recreational Facilities | 5.6 |

Source: 2015 Meetings Focus Trends Study.

tration (www.gsa.gov), which oversees all procurements made by the federal government. There are two primary ways that the government solicits for business: Invitation for Bids (IFB); and, Requests for Proposals (RFP). In the IFB procedure, sealed bids are mailed or hand-delivered to the requesting government office by a pre-set bid-opening date. During the bid opening, all prices are announced and the contract goes to the lowest bidder. The RFP is a confidential method of selection, and the government is free to negotiate with a supplier that meets government standards (the property selected must prove that it can provide the contracted services, both physically and financially).

To participate in government bidding or to have your property listed with FedRooms® (www.fedrooms.com), a government lodging service that matches properties that meet safety and per diem requirements with government meeting planners, your property must be certified and registered. Hotels can become FEMA certified and placed on the National Master List (NML) by completing an online application at usfa.fema.gov/hotel/main/hotelFaq (scroll down to the registration form link).

In order to bid, certified hotels can register free of charge with the System for Award Management (SAM) at www.sam.gov/portal/SAM/##11 (click on the Register/Update Entity tab; assistance is also provided under the Help tab). You can also apply to be included in the "Specialized Conference Facilities" category of the GSA Schedule. The lengthy application process includes a review of corporate and financial information, past performance, commercial practices, and proposed government rates, but this option provides five-year, renewable, pre-approved, pre-negotiated contracts to government meeting planners. Properties on the schedule must adhere to the Federal Travel Regulations and offer complete

### The Government Meetings Market at a Glance

**Location:** Preferred locations are those that are easily accessible. Cities to which airlines offer direct flights and discounted fares are given priority. Government planners must be sensitive to the public appearance of booking a resort or elegant location.

**Facilities:** Preferred facilities offer double-double guestrooms and reasonably priced restaurants. Most meetings involve training, so quality meeting rooms and audiovisual support are prime concerns.

**Price:** Generally are cost-conscious. Planners must deal with a strict bid process and sparse per diems. Hotels bidding for this business must know how to fit within government per diem guidelines; rates quoted must include taxes.

**Services:** All "low-cost" or "no-cost" services that the property can provide are solicited by planners, i.e., free shuttle van from airport, complimentary coffee breaks, and waived meeting room rental. This market requires flexible payment schedules, as the government is often slow in paying. Hotels must also be flexible with dates; lead times can be short when meetings cannot be scheduled until funds are allocated.

**Decision-Makers:** Meetings are planned at the local, state, and federal levels. Key contacts include the agency director, training officer, contract specialist, and procurement officer.

**Best Ways To Reach Market:** Join the Society of Government Meeting Professionals to make connections and obtain leads. This organization has an annual tradeshow, and it also publishes *Government Connections* magazine, providing an opportunity to advertise to government meeting planners. Apply for your hotel to be listed in FedRooms' database of FEMA and ADA-certified hotels and in the "Specialized Conference Facilities" category with the GSA. Subscribe to *FedBizOpps* (formerly the *Commerce Business Daily*) to search for bidding opportunities and possible contacts. Participate at tradeshows with your local convention and visitors bureau and ask for referrals from local government offices and the chamber of commerce.

meeting packages, which include guestrooms, meals and refreshment breaks, meeting rooms, audiovisual equipment, full-service business centers, and dedicated meeting staffs.

Because of the complicated procedures and forms needed to be considered for government business, help is available from a number of sources, including the "Vendor Support Center" tab on the GSA's website. Several organizations have also established programs to assist hotels in navigating government waters. HSMAI, for example, recently partnered with Federal Hospitality Solutions to launch a Government Insider program that provides comprehensive training and resources to hotels that wish to solicit government business.

Hotels can also turn to third-parties to assist them with government business. Courtesy Associates (www.courtesyassociates.com), a conference and event management firm owned by SmithBucklin, offers a consulting service to help hotels that want to be added to the GSA Schedule. The Federal Contractor Registry (FCR) (www.federalcontractorregistry.com) also assists hotels and other suppliers to register, and it also provides leads for government business.

There are several sources for locating government business, including government-related websites, publications, and contacts with members of professional government meeting planners' societies and state and local governments (see "The Government Meetings Market at a Glance" and the "Five Steps to Capturing Government Meetings Business" boxes). In addition to advertising on these sites and in these publications, direct mail can also be used to reach government meeting planners (be sure to include your government rate

---

**Five Steps to Capturing Government Meetings Business**

1. **Become FEMA certified.**
   Hotels that wish to do business with the U.S. government must be certified by FEMA (Federal Emergency Management Agency). You can become certified by logging on to www.usfa.fema.gov/applications/hotel and clicking the "Register" link. The form can be filled out online or you may download a PDF version. If you are unsure if your property is already FEMA approved, you can use the website's search tool to determine your current status.

2. **Register your property in the federal government's database, System for Award Management (SAM).**
   Hotels that wish to be considered for government business must be listed with the System for Award Management. The registration form can be accessed at www.sam.gov.

3. **Determine and be able to comply with government per diem rates.**
   Per diem is the allowance that the government pays for daily lodging (including taxes), meals, and incidental expenses in any given city. These rates are tied to local markets, and they change periodically. To determine current per diem rates for your area, log on to www.gsa.gov/perdiem.

4. **List your property on government-related websites.**
   Business Partner Network, accessible at www.ccr.gov, is an official vendor service for the U.S. government; registration with the System for Award Management will make your hotel's information available to government meeting planners. You can also list your property on www.fedtravel.com. This website provides information on FEMA-certified hotels that offer government contract rates.

5. **Join organizations for government meeting planners.**
   Joining one or both of the following organizations can provide opportunities to network with government decision-makers. Each organization also offers education on ways to capture the government meetings market.

| | |
|---|---|
| The Society of Government Meeting Professionals (SGMP) | The Society of Government Travel Professionals (SGTP) |
| 908 King Street, Suite 200 | P.O. Box 158 |
| Alexandria, VA 22314 | Glyndon, MD 21071 |
| (703) 549-0892 | (202) 241-7487 |
| www.sgmp.org | sgtp.org |

sheet and endorsements from other government groups that have met at your property). Working with conventions and visitors bureaus can be advantageous as well.

Dan O'Neill, vice president of strategy and sales at the Bloomington Convention & Visitors Bureau of Minnesota, says:

> Our message to government planners is we are a value destination with affordable amenities, and we have the resources to promote your event without additional cost to you. There wasn't that relationship with government meeting planners at one point; now they're seeing the benefit of working with us. Our services (providing hotel sourcing, transportation arrangements, even venue selections) have been available, but with regulation changes they are even more relevant.[10]

While capturing government meetings business can be challenging and time-consuming in the beginning, it is certainly a segment that warrants attention. The help available – both from the government and from third-party sources – will make it easier for you to take advantage of the opportunities to tap into this multi-billion-dollar market.

## Labor Unions

Despite a decline in private sector union membership (6.6 percent in 2014 compared to 24.2 percent in 1973), the public sector is comprised of 35 percent of union workers, and the labor unions meetings market is still so important that many properties employ sales personnel to specifically target this category. There are over 150 unions in the United States and a similar number in Canada, and most hold meetings fairly regularly. In addition, most unions stay with a property with which they have been satisfied, providing an excellent opportunity for repeat business.[11]

Union meetings, which are usually held only at hotels that are unionized, fall into three general categories: national conventions, regional conferences, and executive and committee meetings.

*National conventions* are usually held every two years, with site locations shifting between eastern and western regions. National conventions typically generate:

- High spouse attendance
- High per-person expenditures
- A number of social programs
- Several sponsored functions, providing good food and beverage revenue

Because of their size, national conventions are held at large properties that can provide the rooms and meeting space needed to accommodate the delegates and their spouses. The general session, which typically takes on a political atmosphere, is the focal point of the convention and is usually attended by all of the delegates. Sophisticated audiovisual equipment is often required, as is media accessibility, since prominent political speakers are often part of the program.

In addition to the large amount of space needed for the general session, sufficient space is needed for the various social functions in the program. These may range from banquets for the entire contingent, to breakfast meetings for key leaders, to a number of hospitality suites.

*Regional conferences* are usually held in central locations. Meetings typically last two to three days and draw attendances of 200 to 500 delegates. As in the case of national conventions, meeting planners seek out properties that can accommodate all of their delegates and offer sophisticated audiovisual equipment.

*Executive and committee meetings,* which number as many as four a year, are usually held in the union's headquarters city. Since participants are key union people, attendance is smaller (15 to 20 people). These meetings are important to a property, however, as the success of a small meeting may lead to the booking of larger meetings and conventions.

Contact persons for union business include the general secretary of a union for national conventions and the secretary-treasurer for executive and committee meetings. Most unions also have branches, called local unions or simply locals, in cities across the country. These locals can also be sources of business, as they have their own governing bodies; at the very least, they can offer information on union events. Meeting planners are professional and well-disciplined, and the selling process must include a sense of trust based on personal relationships and the ability to meet the meeting planner's needs. Directories that can be helpful in locating labor union business include the *Directory of U.S Labor Organizations* and the *Directory of Labour Organizations in Canada* (this directory is available online at www.labour.gc/ca). Information on labor unions can also be found with an online search.

## Incentive Meetings

While incentive travel is a part of the corporate meetings market, this important market segment is sufficiently different to deserve special mention, especially due to its growing impact and importance to resort properties.

What is **incentive travel**? It is a travel award — often a deluxe tour package — offered as motivation to employees and customers to put forth extra effort and meet criteria established by the program sponsors. Since the trip is a reward for meeting or exceeding performance expectations, incentive meeting planners seek first-class accommodations and service, and look for locations that offer good weather, sightseeing, recreational facilities, entertainment, and a choice of restaurants (see Figure 6.4).

> **WORTH WATCHING**
> 
> Shane Watkins, event project manager for Alfa Insurance, talks about the value of effective incentive trip programs for attracting and retaining talent at http://hedtaks.connectplusathiltonworldwide.com/#sPhaa0w0ENE.

The economic environment has a great impact on the degree of incentive travel. When times are tough, it becomes critical to motivate employees and customers. Incentives have been proven to increase employee and distributor participation in moving products and services. Travel incentives, which are recognized as effective motivators, have been used to improve morale, reduce turnover, and, in the case of group incentive trips, build teamwork. They have also been used to get dealers to concentrate on specific brands and to increase purchases.

Incentive travel includes both group trips and individual incentive travel. Most group trips last five days to a week (occasionally longer), and have an average attendance of 105 people to ensure that everyone involved gets special attention. Typical per-person costs for a group incentive trip average about $3,600.

Individual incentive travel accounts for about 35 percent of incentive travel. In some cases, a specific location is offered as a reward; in other cases, the recipient is given a choice

## Chapter 6: Selling Other Markets

*Figure 6.4. FACTORS IMPORTANT TO INCENTIVE TRAVEL PLANNERS WHEN SELECTING GROUP DESTINATIONS.*

| Factors Considered "Very Important" | Group Incentive Trips |
|---|---|
| • Climate | 92 % |
| • Sightseeing, cultural, or other extracurricular attractions | 82 |
| • Safety and security of destination | 81 |
| • Availability of hotels or other facilities suitable for meetings | 78 |
| • Affordability of destination | 75 |
| • Glamorous or popular image of location | 71 |
| • Ease of transporting attendees to and from location | 64 |
| • Transportation costs | 62 |
| • Availability of recreational facilities, such as golf, tennis, swimming, etc. | 56 |
| • Distance traveled by individual attendees | 50 |

Total is greater than 100% due to multiple mentions

*Since incentive travel is largely motivational — a "reward" for a job well done — incentive travel planners have different requirements than general corporate meeting planners. Interestingly, while climate is ranked number one on the list, the safety and security of a destination is now also a top concern.*
**Source: Recent Meetings Market Report by *Meetings & Conventions* magazine.**

of several locations. The trip is further customized by a choice of activities that fit the lifestyle of the recipient.

It is important to note that most incentive awards include a guest. In many cases, winners travel with their spouse – and it has become increasingly common for the recipient's family to accompany him or her on the trip. Having additional guests not only contributes to increases in the double-occupancy of a property, but it is also a factor in increased spending. The award winners will often spend their own money on "extras," such as gift items, recreation, and entertainment options not included in the award package.

Obviously, incentive trips call for the best in accomodations and a desirable vacation setting. All the tourist attractions come into play here — be it a natural attraction, an ideal climate, excitement, or even some tie-in with the industry or company. The experienced incentive planner will analyze his or her people carefully to decide what type of site and program will draw the greatest number of people (see box titled "Top Hotel Criteria"). It may be a big-city trip, a trip abroad, a cruise, or an exciting visit to a playground such as Las Vegas or Hawaii. When families are accompanying the award winner, the planner will usually look to a family-oriented city, such as Orlando or San Diego. If the attraction is adventure travel, upscale mountain or beach resorts or exotic locations are typically selected. Other incentive trips may be planned around specific interests of the group; a trip to a world-class spa would be favored by attendees interested in wellness, for example. And, in addition to domestic trips, 32 percent of American planners sponsored incentive programs outside of the United States.

### Top Hotel Criteria

1. Safety/Security
2. Service
3. Reputation
4. Meals/catering/restaurants
5. Beach/pool
6. Proximity to cultural attractions
7. Number of rooms
8. Spa
9. Shopping
10. Golf

Source: "The Incentive Travel Buyers Handbook," a special advertising section in *Successful Meetings*, December 2014, p. 60.

## Incentive Meeting Trends

- **Customized Itineraries.** To accommodate today's multi-generational work force, group trips must include something for everyone, and the planner must find the right balance between group events and free time. Individual incentive travelers are often given a choice of locations or they can choose from various activities at a designated destination.
- **Family-Inclusive Itineraries.** Many incentive travel winners include their spouses and families on their trips, so family-oriented destinations with activities that appeal to both adults and their children are increasingly being chosen. Venues that can provide children's programs are especially attractive.
- **Adventurous Activities.** Adventure travel is growing in popularity, and sharing adventures is a great way to create bonds between co-workers and family members. Typical adventure incentive trips may feature white water rafting, windsurfing, kayaking in Costa Rica, snorkeling in the Galápagos Islands, or hiking in the Swiss Alps.
- **Off-the-beaten-path Locales.** Incentive planners are always looking for new, exciting destinations, and out of the way locales are especially suited to team-building or just relaxing and recharging.
- **More Cruises.** Cruising remains a popular option, both for adults and their families. Upscale hotels and resorts located near departure ports or airline hubs can capture a share of this business.
- **International Destinations.** Incentive trips to major European cities, such as London, Paris, and Rome, are popular, as are trips to resort locations in the Caribbean and Central and South America. Trips to far-flung locales, such as Australia, New Zealand, the Far East, and South Africa are also gaining in popularity.
- **Social Responsibility.** Many incentive group travel trips include an opportunity for participants to give back to their host community. Activities vary widely, but many companies see social responsibility projects as an important (and rewarding) way to build employee relationships while making a difference in the lives of the people or organizations they assist.

Lead times for incentive meetings typically range from six months to a year for domestic trips and up to a year or more for international incentive events. Much less is called for in the way of meeting space for incentive groups than for a convention or conference. For most group trips, only one large room that can accommodate the entire group is needed, although some trips may include a hospitality suite. Planners typically use the room for social group activities, such as rallies, an awards banquet, or a networking breakfast, in order to give attendees plenty of time to enjoy the vacation aspect of the trip.

Almost any resort property should be able to handle this type of business. If your property could be considered a candidate for incentive travel, you would greatly benefit by developing a marketing strategy to reach incentive travel planners.

*Incentive meeting participants are increasingly looking to be pampered at resort spas. Studies by the International Spa Association suggest that spas are viewed as a means of escaping pressures and getting re-energized.*
**Source: Photo courtesy of Banyan Tree Phuket (Thailand), one of the luxury properties in the Banyan Tree Hotels & Resorts chain.**

There are a number of ways to reach this market segment. Contacts and leads can be developed through the Society for Incentive Travel Exellence (SITE). SITE has dozens of chapters throughout the world, and the association's website (www.siteglobal.com) includes a search engine that enables planners to search hotel partners by type and location. SITE also publishes an annual directory of incentive travel executives and hosts two annual trade shows: IMEX, which is held in Europe, and IMEX America, which is held in

## Chapter 6: Selling Other Markets

> ### INCENTIVE TRAVEL HOUSES
>
> E. F. MacDonald is generally regarded as the innovator in incentive travel. Working as a stock boy in a luggage factory, he observed an NCR representative picking up merchandise. He learned the luggage was intended as incentive prizes for dealers. He conjectured that if luggage could be used as an incentive, so could travel. From this was born the specialized incentive travel agent. E. F. MacDonald (now Carlson) was soon joined by other firms. Creative Group, Inc., Maritz Travel, Peak Performance, and others have moved in to capture a share of this growing market. At one time, incentive travel was planned exclusively by the company, but the tremendous growth in incentive travel created a demand for full-time professional incentive travel companies (houses). These organizations fall into three basic categories:
>
> 1. *Full-service incentive houses* — These organizations offer clients a wide range of services, from program planning and development to implementation. This type of firm handles both travel and merchandise fulfillment, and offers specific measurement criteria, promotional materials, and sales campaigns based on each company's goals.
> 2. *Travel fulfillment companies* — These organizations handle the travel planning while the corporate clients design and operate their own incentive programs.
> 3. *The travel agency with an incentive division* — This type of firm does not offer marketing services, but has personnel that specialize in incentive trips.
>
> These companies see to the details of the incentive program. They negotiate with airlines and hotels and then package the transportation, lodging and meeting accommodations, meals, tours, and entertainment. They often prepare the promotional literature and may even get involved in setting the goals of the program. Before the group arrives, the agent visits the site and reviews with the hotel the arrangements for servicing the group. The agent sees the group through its stay, serving as the liaison between the group and the hotel. In essence, then, the agent serves as a bona fide meeting planner, seeing to the needs of the group he or she represents. Minneapolis, Chicago, and St. Louis are the locales of the top incentive travel companies in the country. Large hotel chains and convention bureaus often schedule an "incentive house blitz" to these cities to solicit these companies.

Las Vegas; both are hosted-buyer shows, providing scheduled appointments for hotels to meet with qualified incentive travel planners. Another incentive travel trade show, IBTM America, is held annually in June. Organized by Reed Travel Exhibitions, the show's format includes both hosted-buyer appointments and an exhibition.

The international marketplace (primarily Europe, Asia, and Canada) has also become an attractive area. Convention bureaus and hotels can attend key international shows such as the Asia Meeting and Incentive Travel Exchange (in Singapore), and the European Incentive & Business Travel & Meetings Exhibition (EIBTM), held in Barcelona, Spain. You can also attend the Incentive Travel Exchange (ITE) show in Las Vegas, and locate Canadian trade shows at 10times.com/canada/travel-tourism/tradeshows.

Still another option is dealing with **incentive travel houses** (see box titled "Incentive Travel Houses"). While repeat business from groups is rare because destinations are varied each year, incentive travel houses, which represent several different companies, can provide repeat potential; they often will return different groups to a property that they have successfully dealt with in the past.

Advertising is yet another way to reach this market. Unlike ads to corporate meeting planners, which stress a property's professionalism in handling meetings, incentive travel ads must stress the desirability of your location and the recreational and entertainment amenities available. Trade publications for reaching incentive planners include *Corporate & Incentive Travel*, *Incentive*, and *Prevue*, and you can also advertise on the websites of these publications and on the websites of other incentive-related associations and firms, such as the Incentive Marketing Association (IMA) (www.incentive marketing.org).

## Insurance/Financial Service Meetings

The financial services industry is comprised of four segments: banking; financial/asset management; venture capital; and, insurance, the largest of the subsectors. Although financial services and insurance companies fall into the corporate market category, these firms deserve special attention because they spend more money on meetings than any other industry. According to a recent economic impact study by Financial & Insurance Conference Planners, companies in this industry hold 47 conferences, 20 strategic events, and 23 sales/training meetings annually. The largest meetings have about 500 participants, who on average use 252 guestrooms at a rate of $248 for 3.5 nights; smaller meetings typically have 40 attendees, who on average use 29 guestrooms at a rate of $160 for two nights.

In addition, insurance and financial services meeting planners anticipate an increase in incentive, sales, and training meetings in the future, as these companies are consolidating and merging at a significant pace. A recent study reports that one in three have acquired another company within the last two years. These mergers mean more meetings because field forces and home offices must learn each others' culture and practices.

There are over 6,000 insurance companies in the United States and Canada, and each holds a number of meetings annually. These range in size from 20 attendees at small workshops, to conferences of 200, and major conventions of 1,000 or more. These national conventions are the largest, held annually for three to five days and planned a minimum of a year in advance.

Regional meetings are smaller and held more frequently than national meetings, and tend to be sales-oriented. While expenditures per person are typically less, resorts are considered for this type of meeting. Convenience and accessibility are the important factors in site selection; lead times average six to nine months.

Local meetings are usually held in hotels, and are primarily training seminars and board meetings. Local meetings may have a lead time of as short as two weeks, and proximity to the home office is a prime consideration in site selection, as is quality of service and facilities.

Although the insurance industry sells two basic types of insurance, life insurance and casualty insurance, most business comes from the life insurance segment. Life insurance companies employ large sales forces, and they have regular training meetings and conferences. This segment also holds a large number of incentive meetings to keep its sales staff motivated.

Whether large or small meetings are planned, this group is not overly price-conscious, and the availability of recreational amenities often plays a role in site selection. The agenda of a small meeting usually calls for business meetings in the morning and afternoon, and scheduled recreational or social activities in the evening. At larger meetings, business sessions are held in the morning, recreational activities are offered in the afternoon, and social functions figure prominently in the evening. Since spouses are usually invited to large regional and national meetings, the availability of spouses' and guests' programs is an added plus when attempting to solicit insurance company business.

Meetings for the other three segments of the financial services industry are similar to those of insurance companies – they hold training meetings, conferences and conventions for members of their firms, stockholder meetings, and even incentive events – but there are several differences. First and foremost, while these groups are not overly cost-conscious (they prefer to use top-tier hotels), they are sensitive about how their meetings are perceived by the public. They want to avoid being perceived as extravagant, so they have eliminated the word "incentive" from their vocabulary, and they often require meeting venues to sign confidentially agreements (not only regarding the content of their meetings, but also regarding the group being there at all); when signage is used, it is likely to feature a generic name, such as "2016 Executive Council" rather than using the company's name.

In addition, planners are under increasing pressure to justify the meeting's value. They are now booking during "shoulder" periods rather than peak months, and financial planners are more likely than insurance planners to book at conference centers instead of hotels (especially for meetings with educational content, such as review of new government regulations, fluctuations in financial markets, and so on) because of the all-inclusive rate. If a financial firm that does business with the government books with a hotel, the property must meet the guidelines for government business that we discussed earlier in this chapter. A hotel located in one of the "capitals of finance," such as New York City, San Francisco, London, Hong Kong, or Tokyo, is also attractive to this market.

To solicit this lucrative market, you should start at the company's home office. There may be a number of decision-makers within the company (see box titled "Insurance/Financial Services Company Decision-Makers"). Many large insurance/financial companies have their own travel departments, often staffed by five to seven meeting planners. When selling to this market segment, it is important to remember that even the persons responsible for the meeting planning in smaller companies are highly skilled professionals who are good negotiators and they demand the same quality in their suppliers.

Because insurance/financial companies plan numerous similar training and sales meetings over a large geographic area, they often look to hotel chains for one-stop shopping for meeting sites. Sharon Chapman, CMP, CMM, of Berkshire Life, says:

> **WORTH WATCHING**
>
> Angela Zaltsman, founder of A to Z Event Management, Inc., discusses the planner/supplier relationship and provides tips on how to build new relationships and maintain existing ones. Use a search engine and type in: Angela Zaltsman, Challenges facing the event planner/supplier relationship, video.

> Hotel-chain national sales offices are a real time-saver. I can go through one contact rather than call each individual property, and the national sales offices understand my business. They can tell me if a property I'm thinking about will fit my needs, make other recommendations, and find the best value.

As in other meeting market segments, third-party planners are increasingly being used by the insurance/financial industries. Approximately one-third use incentive travel houses and/or meeting management companies to assist in site selection and program planning.

When targeting insurance/financial meeting planners, a professional, well-prepared, and sincere approach is the best, whether you are reaching them through direct sales or advertising. There are several magazines that can be used to reach this market, including *Insurance & Financial Meetings Management* (www.themeetingmagazines.com/insurance-financial-meetings-mananagement/), *Business Travel News* (BTN) (www.businesstravelnews.com), and *Meetings & Conventions* magazine (www.meetings-conventions.com). Other publications of interest to the financial services segment include *American Banker*, *Bloomberg BusinessWeek*, *Global Finance*, *Institutional Investor*, *Mortgage Banking*, *Pensions & Investments*, and *The Wall Street Journal* (the ad in Figure 6.5 appeals to the needs of this market).

Insurance/financial meeting planners typically conduct their own site inspections, and detailed letters of agreement are important to them. The better you understand their

## Insurance/Financial Services Company Decision-Makers

A recent survey by the *Financial & Insurance Meetings* magazine determined that the principal job titles for insurance company decision-makers were:

| Job Title | Insurance Planners |
|---|---|
| Vice President | 28% |
| Director of Meetings | 26% |
| Marketing/Administrative Executive | 25% |
| Meeting Planner | 16% |
| President | 5% |
| | 100% |

Statistics from the survey also revealed that:
- 80 percent were female;
- their average age was 44;
- planners had an average of ten years of experience;
- there were approximately five persons in their department;
- 79% host golfing events (typically three annually);
- 69% rate a spa facility at their meetings as important or very important.

The meeting planning department typically resides in the marketing/communication division of the company.

---

needs for each meeting and demonstrate how your property can meet the high standards of the meeting planner, the better chance you will have in securing their business.

Most insurance/financial services executives and meeting planners belong to trade associations, the two most well-known being Meeting Professionals International (MPI) and the Financial & Insurance Conference Planners Association (www.ficpnet.com). The Life Insurance Marketing Research Association (LIMRA) (www.limra.com) is also a key life insurance trade organization (its members write more than 90 percent of all life insur-

**FIGURE 6.5. SAMPLE AD FOR THE INSURANCE/FINANCIAL MARKET**

**TIME IS MONEY - save both**

Hyatt Regency DFW is the perfect location for financial services meetings. Our airport location reduces transportation costs and our world-class business hotel delivers everything you need for a memorable meeting. Book now with offer code DFW123 and get extra value with a free suite, guest internet and Double Hyatt Gold Passport® points.

Call 972 615 6504
or visit hyattregencydfw.com

**HYATT REGENCY**

HYATT REGENCY DFW
2334 International Parkway
DFW Airport, TX 75261

Planners of financial meetings are often pressured to find the best value for their meetings. This ad appeals to their need to save both time and money while providing an up-scale environment for their attendees.

*Source: Courtesy of The Hyatt Regency DFW.*

ance). Allied membership is available in most associations serving this market, and this would be a worthwhile investment in gaining insurance groups meetings business.

## Medical Meetings

While the medical meetings groups may fall into a number of categories (corporate, association, and nonprofit), this dynamic and rapidly growing segment merits additional attention (see box titled "Medical Meetings at a Glance").

| | Medical Meetings at a Glance |
|---|---|
| Location: | Meetings are normally attended by an average of 200 people, although the larger meetings may have an attendance of 30,000 or more (both the Radiological Society of North America and the Greater New York Dental meetings draw over 50,000 attendees). They require a large meeting room and a number of smaller breakout rooms. The nature of the meetings is best suited by a quiet location in close proximity to a medical facility. Most meetings travel from city to city, other meetings are sponsored by associations. National association meetings are usually held in a vacation location to draw the most delegates. |
| Facilities: | Most medical meetings require high-tech audiovisual equipment for presentations and for streaming data or holding videoconferences. Most association meetings require exhibit space as well as meeting rooms and banquet facilities. |
| Price: | This group is not overly price-conscious, but as they join managed care organizations they are given a budget. Professionals in the medical field need these meetings in order to gain certifications and stay current in their practices. Hotels must be able to provide billings that break down the expenses for each attendee. |
| Services: | Free Wi-Fi for the attendees' mobile devices; a business center or accessibility to photocopiers and other needed equipment. A health club is an excellent selling point. |
| Decision-Makers: | The decision-makers are experienced professionals in associations. The newer meetings are coordinated by hospitals and managed health care organizations. The managed health care facilities are also requiring doctors to attend certain seminars in order to stay abreast of the latest medical developments. |
| Best Ways to Reach: | Many medical meeting planners are members of PCMA and receive *Convene* magazine. There are also a number of Internet sites that have listings of medical meetings. The Healthcare Convention and Exhibitors Association (www.hcea.org) sponsors a number of medical meetings and conventions and offers a meetings search feature on its site. Other sites include Doctor's Review (www.doctorsreview.com/meeting), which has a database of over 2,500 medical meetings that are searchable by destination and specialty, and EMedEvents (www.emed.events.com), with a searchable database of over 25,000 medical meetings worldwide. You can also work with local convention and visitors bureaus and get leads from hospitals and medical professionals in your area. |

Today's ever-changing technology and treatment breakthroughs, the development of new drugs, and healthcare reforms make it mandatory for medical professionals to keep abreast of how the latest trends impact their profession. It is estimated that medical and healthcare groups currently hold over 35,000 meetings annually, and this number is expected to grow dramatically for a number of reasons:

- Medical professionals must stay current on new treatments, potential cures, and the latest surgical procedures and medical techniques, while pharmaceutical professionals must stay abreast of the availability of new drugs as well as any changes in regulations relating to dispensing medications.
- Modern advances such as robotic surgery, immunotherapy, and implantable brain chips that allow paralyzed patients to regain control of their limbs are changing the way medicine is practiced. Trade show exhibitors and product demonstrations provide opportunities to introduce medical professionals to the latest technology.
- Doctors and other healthcare professionals must earn Continuing Medical Education (CME) credits to maintain certifications. The most popular places to earn CME credits are forums sponsored by medical societies, associations, universities, and private providers.
- The constant emergence of new medical specialties (and subspecialities) has spawned a number of new medical organizations. This trend will create additional continuing-education needs.
- Globalization has also impacted the medical profession. Record numbers of international attendees have been reported at the medical meetings held in the United States, and more American medical professionals are attending meetings abroad.

Medical meetings, like government meetings, are subject to strict regulations. There are more than 80 industry codes and guidelines that impact both healthcare professionals and the pharmaceutical segment of this market. The Physician Payment Sunshine Act requires that payments and gifts made to physicians and teaching hospitals by medical device and pharmaceutical companies be reported to the Centers for Medicare & Medicaid Services (CMS) to be made available on their database (www.cms.gov). The AdvaMed Code of Ethics on Interactions with Health Care Professionals, established by the Advanced Medical Technology Association, focuses on the interests of patients by defining appropriate activity between health care professionals and AdvaMed member companies. Although voluntary, most firms in the pharmaceutical field adhere to PhRMA Codes (guidelines established by the Pharmaceutical Research and Manufacturers of America, PhRMA). Meetings in both the medical and pharmaceutical fields must also be in compliance with state laws and the provisions of the Patient Protection and Affordable Care Act (ACA), which is commonly referred to as "Obamacare." Under the provisions of the ACA, pharmaceutical planners are now required to document and report every item valued at ten dollars or more for each attendee. This data, which includes such items as meals, hotel room nights, cab rides, and airline tickets, is posted on a government website that is open to the public. Failure to comply with this regulation can result in fines and even jail time.

Because of the complicated regulations, today's medical meetings planners must be more like "medical paralegals" to ensure that guidelines are met. In order to facilitate their jobs, the Convention Industry Council (CIC), at the suggestion of the International Medical Meetings Professionals Association (IMMPA), offers a CMP-HC certification program for those in this specialized market segment. The program is a subspecialty of the CMP program; only those who hold a current CMP certification are eligible to earn certification. Pat Schaumann, the founder of IMMPA, says:

> Meeting professionals in the healthcare segment face the stiffest and most complex government regulations of any industry. With required reporting and transparency, understanding compliance is critical for anyone involved in healthcare meeting management.[12]

Assistance is also available to both planners and hotels that provide products and services to the healthcare industry. Meeting Professionals International (MPI), in association with St. Louis University (SLU), now offers a Healthcare Meeting Compliance Certificate to hotel salespeople who complete a four-hour program that covers such topics as understanding the various regulations affecting the industry and learning how to create the right environment for healthcare meetings.

Most medical meetings are small (the majority have 200 or less in attendance) and are usually held in sites close to major medical facilities (such as Rochester, Minnesota, home of the Mayo Clinic; Cleveland, Ohio, site of the Cleveland Clinic; and, Houston, Texas, whose Texas Medical Center represents nearly 50 different medical entities, including 14 hospitals); other attractive locations include intellectually-oriented cities, such as Boston, home to the Massachusetts University of Technology (MIT), and Harvard University. While most meet during peak periods (fall and spring), some groups also meet during traditional "soft spots" (summer and winter months). And, since many medical groups plan several meetings a month, there is a great potential for repeat business.

Medical meetings require a high level of presentation. Technical presentations, in which demonstrators can interact with the audience and take questions from all over the world, are sometimes done via satellite. One medical meeting planner explains:

> We show live surgeries on a big screen...our camera work allows for close-ups and instant replays...busy physicians are drawn to medical meetings with new techniques and new knowledge.[13]

**WORTH WATCHING**

You can take a virtual tour of The Oquendo Center, a dedicated medical meeting facility in Las Vegas, at www.oquendocenter.org/facility. While The Oquendo Center does not offer guestrooms, it partners with local hotels to provide accommodations for medical meeting attendees.

Requirements for medical meetings also include several breakout rooms for small group discussion and WiFi service to keep the group connected via their mobile devices. For larger medical meetings, exhibit space with adequate electrical outlets will be needed. The Center for Exhibition Industry Research reports that nearly 25 percent of all exhibitions are medical or healthcare shows. Since most meetings are technical meetings, medical groups prefer to meet in a quiet location; a meeting booked near rooms used for a college reunion or a bowling league will lose future business.

One difficulty with medical meetings is that the amount of function space they require is incredibly high relative to the number of guestrooms typically used. Therefore, they are sometimes not a good piece of business for a hotel, particularly during high-demand periods. Meeting planners have responded to this dilemma with a space-saving technique that is becoming increasingly used for medical and scientific group meetings: **poster sessions** rather than formal verbal presentations. Presenters use computerized presentations or horizontal corkboards to display a summary of their findings, experiences, or opinions instead of giving an oral presentation from a platform.

In terms of food and beverage, because most medical meetings planners operate under a strict per diem guideline, hotels must be able to provide healthcare-appropriate menus that provide variety to attendees. Because food costs in some locales, such as New York City, can greatly exceed what planners are allowed to spend for meals, hotels have responded by offering room and meal packages. These packages can include the room and a single meal, such as breakfast or dinner, or a full day of meals along with lodging. These packages make it easier for the planner to break down the per-person expenditures that are required to be reported.

A sub-segment of the medical meetings market that warrants additional attention is the multibillion-dollar pharmaceutical industry. Pharmaceutical companies primarily hold meetings to introduce new products to their sales staffs and to doctors who are likely to prescribe the latest medications. While pharmaceutical meetings are similar to other medical meetings in that they often have short lead times due to the latest breakthroughs, there are also two other major concerns that must be taken into consideration when targeting this sub-segment.

> **MORE ONLINE**
>
> The Knowland Group offers a free whitepaper titled "Understanding Pharmaceutical Terminology & Events" on its website, www.knowland.com. Click on the Support tab and then the Whitepapers tab and scroll down to view this informative resource.

The first is *security*. Since the pharmaceutical industry is an extremely competitive industry, with companies striving to be the first to introduce new products, a hotel that can offer complimentary paper shredders and secure storage in meeting venue offices has an advantage over another property that cannot do so. Some pharmaceutical companies also insist on a non-compete clause — requiring that the hotel not book simultaneous meetings for two or more pharmaceutical companies.

The second consideration is *image-oriented*. Pharmaceutical companies must operate under spending guidelines issued by the Pharmaceutical Research and Manufacturers of America (the PhRMA Code) as well as the Affordable Care Act. A meeting for doctors, therefore, cannot be booked at a five-star hotel, which gives the impression that doctors are being bribed to prescribe the company's products. This does not mean, however, that pharmaceutical meetings cannot be booked at desirable locations offered by such chains as Hilton, Loews, and Sonesta. The key is to be able to offer an upscale meeting at a moderate price.

KSL Resorts, a collection of distinctive resorts that includes the Hotel del Coronado, on Coronado Island near San Diego, The Vail Mountain Lodge & Spa in Colorado, and the Miraval Resort & Spa in Tucson, Arizona, trains its entire staff — from sales, catering, and convention services to hotel operations — in the nuances of pharmaceutical meetings. One topic covered by the company's Pharmaceutical Expertise Program, for example, details an option for getting around the luxury-image issue — individuals are charged for spa services rather than having them charged to the master account. The program also provides information on which companies are competitors, which eliminates the problem of booking two competing groups at the same time, while still being able to service the meetings of two or more non-competitive groups.

Hotels that wish to attract medical meetings can attract planners by offering value and being flexible in terms of pricing (both rooms and meals) and billing. In addition to the room/meal packages mentioned earlier, many properties offer flat rates for meals and/or rooms, enabling the planner to apply the costs equally to all attendees. Working with a convention and visitors bureau can ensure that all attendees receive the same type of room at the same rate. It is also helpful to have a staff that understands the terminology and needs of this market.

It is fairly simple to reach this lucrative and growing market segment. The typical medical meeting planner is an experienced professional; most belong to the Professional Convention Management Association (PCMA), a trade association originally formed for medical meeting planners and now open to all association planners. This association holds an annual meeting in January, and is an opportunity for hotel salespeople to interact with planners. A large meeting for the pharmaceutical meetings market is Pharma Forum; infor-

Chapter 6: Selling Other Markets

mation is available at cbinet.com (click on the Conferences tab). You can also locate medical meeting planners on the Internet at sites including www.medilexicon.com/medicalassociations.php and www.omnimedicalsearch.com/associations.html. You can also place print ads, such as the one shown in Figure 6.7, in medical periodicals and journals, and on websites dedicated to healthcare professionials. Working with a convention and visitors bureau is also a good strategy; many target the medical meetings market since the economy is not a factor for these groups – they must meet as needs arise.

**Figure 6.7. ADVERTISING TO MEDICAL MEETING PLANNERS.**

This print ad, which appeared in Medical Meetings magazine, attracts medical meeting planners with a catchy headline (the medically related "Intensive Care"), and promises a "clinically-tuned" solution to meeting needs.
**Source: Courtesy of Ojai Valley Inn & Spa.**

## Summary

In this chapter, we have detailed the types of meetings held by nonprofit organizations and specialized segments of the corporate meetings market. We have seen how nonprofits, though largely price-sensitive, can add to a property's bottom line by filling typically slow periods and providing potential repeat business. And we have seen how other segments, such as labor unions and incentive travel, can be lucrative for specific types of hotels. In this chapter, as in the two previous chapters, we have determined:

- Each segment's characteristics and needs.
- The kind of meetings they hold.
- What they look for when selecting a property.
- The decision-maker for each market segment.
- How to locate key sources of potential business.

These crucial factors are essential in determining what type(s) of group business your property can handle. In the next two chapters, we will see how these factors also play a key role in determining the most effective ways to sell and advertise to each segment of the meetings market.

## Endnotes

1. Beth Rogers, "SMERF: A Multi-Billion Dollar Market Worth Pursuing, *HSMAI Marketing Review*.
2. Larry Keltto, "Tailor-Made Meetings," *Association Meetings*.
3. Fred Gebhart, "Reunion Meetings," *Meeting News*.
4. Patricia Sherman, "SMERF Events," *Expo*.
5. June Norman, "Moving Toward the Mainstream," *The Meeting Manager*.
6. "How SMERF Planners Take on the Site Selection Challenge," *Association Conventions & Facilities*, August 1, 2014.
7. Ruth A. Hill, "Faithful Market," *Meetings South*.
8. Larry Keltto, "Tailor-Made Meetings," *Association Meetings*.
9. www.ustravel.org.
10. Cheryl-Anne Sturken, "Government Attendees: Endangered Species?" *Meetings & Conventions*, March 2014, p. 39.
11. "The Shrinking American Labor Union," *The New York Times*, February 7, 2015.
12. "Progress Report: The Meetings and Events Industry's First Healthcare Meetings Certification Coming in 2013," *Medical Meetings*.
13. Joseph Dabrian, "The Changing Pulse of Medical Meetings," *The Meeting Professional*.

## Study Questions

1. What are SMERF groups? Why are they an important market segment? What SMERF market segments show the most potential for future growth?
2. How does dealing with government agencies differ from dealing with other meetings groups? What types of hotels are best-suited for the various types of government meetings?
3. What types of meetings do labor unions typically hold? What factors are important to planners booking labor union meetings?
4. What makes the incentive market different from the corporate market in general? What types of properties are best-suited to handle this market segment? What types of amenities would you stress if you were trying to attract the incentive market?
5. What are the characteristics of insurance/financial meetings? What types of hotels might be most attractive to this type of business?

Chapter 6: Selling Other Markets

6. Cite several reasons why the medical meetings market segment is likely to grow.
7. Who are the key decision-makers for each of the segments discussed in this chapter? How can each type of meeting planner most effectively be reached?

## Key Terms

**fraternal organizations**—Groups in which membership is based on common personal interests rather than on common work or career responsibilities.

**incentive travel**—Travel financed by businesses as an employee or dealer reward for outstanding performance.

**incentive travel houses**—Full-time professional travel companies that make arrangements for companies that wish to offer incentive trips. Usually represent several different firms.

**per diem (means per day)**—The fixed amount of money given to government representatives for each day of travel away from home. Government employees have a fixed amount of money that they can spend per day on food, beverage, and lodging.

**poster session**—Display of reports and papers, usually scientific, accompanied by their authors or researchers. Can also refer to a session dedicated to the discussion of posters shown inside the meeting area. When this discussion is not held in a special session, it can take place directly between the person presenting the poster and interested delegates.

**SMERF groups**—An acronym for the nonprofit organization market segment made up of social, military, educational, religious, and fraternal groups.

## CHAPTER APPENDIX

### TIPSHEETS

The Knowland Group is a provider of meeting and group data and has published a number of white papers to assist hotels. Knowland's Glossary of Terms and White Papers may be viewed at www.knowland.com, under the Resource tab. The following two tipsheets offer insight into the group characteristics and booking patterns of both Military Reunion Groups and Pharmaceutical Planners, and are provided courtesy of the Knowland Group

Chapter 6: Selling Other Markets

## Top 10 Tips for Working with Pharmaceutical Planners

1. **Understand The Four Main Rules and Regulations.** These include PhRMA codes, AdvaMed codes, The Sunshine Act (PPSA), and State Laws. The end of a meeting is just the start of a long reporting process, which requires compliance with laws, regulations and guidelines.

2. **Understand Their Pain.** As a vendor, understand the level of reporting and detail they may need from you to parallel their due diligence on regulations.

3. **Make Billing Process Pharmaceutical Friendly.** Use a tool that allows them to see their per attendee charges in real time which reduces the amount of work in the event of an audit.

4. **Provide Detailed Reporting.** You should be able to give planners the data they need about the meetings they have with you. This may be more in detail than other customers may demand, but pharmaceutical planners may need minute-by-minute breakdowns!

5. **Be Highly Responsive To Their RFPs.** Pharmaceutical planners are looking for RFPs that are fully addressed, responded to quickly and completely. Sometimes the booking windows are very short and they need answers fast.

6. **Offer Pharmaceutical Friendly F&B Menu.** Make sure you are able to provide menu offerings that meet and address the pharmaceutical codes, rules and regulations that are also health conscious.

7. **Be Flexible When Negotiating Contracts.** Planners look for flexibility and growth potential as well as limited liability when numbers shrink. Make sure you offer full disclosure of other groups in house, offer at least a year for rebook clauses, and consider waiving fees like Resort and Housekeeping.

8. **Know Pharmaceutical Vocabulary.** Be educated on the lingo, the types of meetings, and the language of pharmaceutical meeting planners. Make sure that everyone who interacts with the meeting planners is educated in this as well.

9. **Review Your Own Policy.** Take a good look at your policies, billing, and contracts. How pharmaceutical-friendly are you? Make changes as needed.

10. **Get The Buy In From The Top.** Make sure that you have top-level support for pursuing this market segment so that you don't have to get case-by-case exceptions made. Talk to your General Manager about having pharmaceutical-friendly policies in place as a standard.

## Top 10 Characteristics of "The Ideal Hotel" For Military Reunion Groups

1. **Reasonable Room Rates.** Price is one of the most important factors considered by military reunion groups. Most of these groups look for $100 a night or less when booking.

2. **Flexible Food and Beverage Rates.** While some military reunion groups have higher budgets for F&B than others, flexibility in pricing will make your hotel ideal. Many groups would like to supply their own alcohol for the events.

3. **Reasonable Local Transportation Costs.** Many of these groups prefer hotels that offer complimentary transportation to and from the airport. Again, these groups are very cost conscious when it comes to selecting an event space.

4. **Hospitality Suites Available.** Most of these groups have a hospitality suite as a main focus and gathering place for the group. Many have a cash bar component and want F&B services such as simple snacks available.

5. **Free Meeting Room Rental.** Short meetings such as a Board of Directors meeting are usually held during the group's time at the hotel. They typically last only a few hours, so the ability to use a meeting space free of charge is important to them.

6. **Knowledge Of The Military Reunion Market.** Hotels that seem to have knowledge and expertise of the military market will win their business over others. Acknowledging the specifics of their military service (what battle they fought in, base location, etc) will make a significant impact.

7. **Detailed Information On Your *Destination*.** These groups are open to meeting in most destinations, but it is up to you to sell your location to them. Highlight important activities such as landmarks (military or historic), shopping (outlets), and other things to do in the area.

8. **Responsiveness To Special Needs.** These groups are a very unique segment. With members of all ages and backgrounds, and some with physical handicaps, it is important to understand how to accommodate people of all types.

9. **Relationship To Military Background.** Depending on the exact reunion group, the hotel's location can be a deciding factor. Many groups look for hotels near the unit's former base, near other military facilities, or near the location that they fought.

10. **Recommended By A Friend Or Colleague.** This market is primarily relationships based. Usually, one person is responsible for selecting the location, and they take word of mouth recommendations very seriously. Since they rely on word of mouth, a good review from one planner to the other is valuable.

## Industry Profile

### Doug Baarman, Senior Vice President/ Team Director

ConferenceDirect

A graduate of Ferris State University in Michigan, where he received a Bachelor of Science degree in hospitality management, Doug has built a team of over 35 active meeting professionals who have placed over $330 million in revenue for their customers in hotels around the world. He previously had a successful career with the Marriott chain, serving as director of sales/director of national accounts for JW Marriott. During that time, Baarman headed contract training for Marriott salespeople, and he led a field sales team focused on new business development. He then moved to Gaylord Entertainment, where he served as director of sales and helped to establish the pre-opening team for the largest hotel ever built in the Washington, D.C. area, before joining ConferenceDirect. Baarman brings expertise from both sides of the industry to his position as an independent hospitality professional; his first job was on the "buyer's side" — serving as an account executive for National Trade Productions, where he was responsible for exhibit sales targeting the government and government contractor markets. He is also a successful life coach, teaching individuals how to move from being employees to independent business owners.

### Nine Tips to Better Networking in the Hospitality Industry

Below are nine quick tips about networking that I have been given by my mentors and learned from (sometimes painful) trial and error:

1. **Get out of your office.** Sitting at your desk will not help improve your networking skills or enable you to grow your business.
2. **Get involved.** Join organizations within your industry and become an active member of the organization on a committee or in a leadership role. Get involved with organizations or causes you have a passion for and enjoy.
3. **Create your own personal brand.** Who are you, and what can you do for the person you are speaking with?
4. **Refine your "elevator" speech.** Be able to articulate (in 20 words or less) what you do and your value proposition. Let everyone know what you can do for them.
5. **Give referrals.** Understand the needs of others and offer referrals.
6. **Ask for referrals.** Do not be afraid to ask anyone if they know of anyone who can benefit from your product or service.
7. **Understand and become active in social networking.** Join such sites as LinkedIn, Facebook, and Twitter, and consider writing a blog.
8. **Attend hospitality industry events.** Attending hospitality events enables you to meet great people, ask questions, share experiences, and learn from one another. Bringing people together is a great way to get things accomplished – nothing can replace a handshake, a smile, and face-to-face conversation. Hospitality industry events power global businesses and represent all sectors of the industry and are a great way to stay current with the industry and continue to build your expertise.
9. **Follow-up with everyone that you meet.** Keep in touch with the people you meet through networking. They may be excellent sources for future business.

These tips have helped me grow as a professional, and they helped me grow my business. It was scary at first to no longer have a brand name behind me, but now I am pleased that people know me for who I am, what I have accomplished, and what I can do for them in the future.

Note: Doug shares his expertise with industry professionals on his two blogs: www.hospitalitylifestyles.com and www.meetingplannerplaybook.com.

**Learning Objectives:**

This portion of your text discusses direct selling to meeting planners. In the chapter, we will cover personal sales calls, telephone sales calls, and the other most commonly used methods of selling to planners. When you have studied this chapter, you will:

- Be able to describe the six steps of a personal sales call and be able to explain why each is important.

- Know how to most effectively use the telephone to sell to planners, handle inquiries, and follow up on your accounts.

- Be able to detail other methods of direct selling, including sales blitz selling, trade show selling, selling with convention bureaus, site inspection selling, and familiarization tour selling; and know the advantages and disadvantages of each.

**Outline**

Personal Sales Calls: Mastering Consultative Sales
- Step #1: Pre-Call Planning
- Step #2: Opening the Sales Call
- Step #3: Getting Prospect Involvement
- Step #4: Presenting Your Property
- Step #5: Handling Objections
- Step #6: Closing and Follow-Up

Telephone Selling
- Telephone Techniques
- Screening Prospects
- Setting Appointments by Phone
- Telephone Sales Call Follow-Up
- Handling Inquiries
- Telemarketing

Sales Blitz Selling

Trade Show Selling

Selling with Convention and Visitors Bureaus

Site Inspection Selling and Familiarization Tours

Summary

# 7 Selling to the Meetings Market

The size and diversity of the meetings market makes it a viable target market for all types and sizes of hospitality properties.

There are two basic ways to reach this lucrative market: *selling* and *advertising*. In Chapter 8, we will discuss how to advertise to meeting planners. In this chapter, we will take a look at how the sales process is changing and provide an in-depth look at the most effective ways to sell to meeting planners.

Selling to the meetings market has changed dramatically in recent years. The Internet has changed how event planners search for hotel information and how they book their meetings, leading to changes in how salespeople do their jobs. Some of these important changes include:

- "Cold calls" are increasingly becoming "warm calls" as salespeople turn to the Internet to research their prospects before making contact with them. Sites such as LinkedIn enable salespeople to study the profiles of meeting planners – and contact them via email — before making a sales call. Busy planners often prefer email and text messages to an unannounced visit.
- Today's meeting planners are increasingly expecting salespeople to become resources for them. They appreciate creativity and "thinking outside the box," so many salespeople develop blogs to provide suggestions and "insider tips" for their destination. Collaboration and consultative sales – salespeople working together with the planner as a team – are also becoming the norm (we will discuss these practices in greater detail in this section).
- Because of the growing partnerships between salespeople and planners and the use of technology to qualify and book customers, today's sales managers typically focus on building customer-hotel business relationships and have strategic oversight (along with the hotel's revenue manager) of the performance of accounts on the regional and global level rather than simply overseeing day-to-day sales operations.
- Today's salesperson is likely to work with more than one decision-maker, so he or she must focus on what his or her property can do for the customer rather than simply offer information on rates, dates, and meeting facilities. In some cases, meeting planners rely on third-party firms, such as Experient, Helms-Briscoe, and ConferenceDirect, to handle their meetings business. In this case, a salesperson must research the type of hotels that the clients of these third-parties use, and inquire into being placed on a preferred hotel list.
- More and more corporations are relying on strategic meetings programs (SMMs) for cost-effectiveness, so today's salespeople must learn the rules and regulations formulated by the SMM programs, which were designed for greater efficiency and cost savings.

# Personal Sales Calls: Mastering Consultative Sales

The most effective tool in convention sales, or any other kind of sales, is the personal sales call. This type of face-to-face selling works well with both professional and occasional meeting planners. The personal sales call offers the opportunity to present your case in a detailed manner, to answer questions immediately, and to read the reaction of the prospect so you can gain a better understanding — and take remedial action if necessary.

Roy Stone, senior vice president, sales and marketing for Accor Hotels, believes that even with so much media attention given to social communities, text messaging, and digital channels, the personal sales call is still the most effective method to reach meeting planners:

> You can make telephone calls, send e-mails, and Skype, but nothing beats sitting down across from a person and demonstrating that you are interested enough to be there and that you want to listen to them. Body language is so important, and you don't get that any other way except meeting someone face-to-face.
>
> Obviously, in today's fast-changing world, it's critical that you efficiently drive your share in the online environment, but the sales function must be there taking its place in your toolbox.[1]

In today's competitive environment, salespeople have to do more than simply sell meeting space and guestrooms; they must become *consultants* who identify customers' needs and provide solutions by adopting selling methods tailored to potential meeting customers. Although **consultative selling** is a low-pressure form of personal selling, it is a highly effective sales strategy and well-suited to hospitality sales. The focus here is to build relationships — not just get an immediate sale, but to create and keep long-term clients.

Collaboration now rules the sales process, so providing insight and working together with the planner for the long-term mutual benefit of both parties is crucial in developing a relationship of trust. In a recent speech, Bob Gilbert, president and CEO of the Hospitality Sales & Marketing Association International (HSMAI), said:

> Today, the art of sales is about collaboration. A salesperson solves problems, provides advice, and works together with the buyer. It is a long-term, team approach, solving problems through planning and analysis. What's driving this is that the buyer is more educated, engaged, knowledgeable, and sophisticated than ever before. Their behavior transforms all market segments.[2]

To respond to this trend, consultative salespeople's calls must be interactive. They must ask more questions to enable them to provide insights and advice to their prospects and customers. And, they must offer customized rather than generic solutions to possible problems, and work together with the planner to implement these solutions.

The personal sales call consists of six essential steps (see Figure 7.1). Each of these steps is vitally important in presenting your

**WORTH WATCHING**

HSMAI America's board member, Jack Horne, senior vice president, sales, Hyatt Hotels Corporation, is interviewed about "Insight Selling" at www.hsmai.org/knowledge/multimedia.cfm?ItemNumber=5044 (can also be viewed at www.youtube.com/watch?v=DktxYTvfNvM).

## Chapter 7: Selling to the Meetings Market

*Figure 7.1. THE SIX STEPS OF A SALES CALL.*

```
                                          Step 6
                                       Closing and
                                        Follow-up
                                  Step 5
                                 Handling
                                 Objections
                           Step 4
                         Presenting
                        Your Property
                    Step 3
                 Getting Prospect
                   Involvement
              Step 2
            Opening the
             Sales Call
        Step 1
        Pre-call
        Planning              THE SIX STEPS OF A SALES CALL
```

*The sales process is a systematic series of actions that directs the meeting decision-maker toward a buying commitment.*

property effectively to the meeting planner, and we will cover each of them in the following sections.

## Step #1: Pre-Call Planning

While getting out there and selling is the best way to ensure that you will generate meetings business for your property, there is another — quite logical — step that should always precede the selling process: *pre-call planning*. While this planning (and the research inherent to it) may seem time-consuming and tedious, the keys to effective selling are:

- Knowing your property
- Knowing your competition
- Knowing your prospect

*Knowing your property* can help your sales effort in two ways. First, you will know exactly what you have to sell. You will know your property's strengths and weaknesses — and how to showcase or downplay them as needed. Second, and just as important, knowing basic facts about your property will give you the confidence you need for making a sales call. You won't have to worry about what questions a prospect will ask — you will already have the answers to most of his or her concerns (how many rooms are available, the size and capabilities of meeting rooms, audiovisual equipment available, etc.).

William R. Tiefel, former vice chairman of Marriott International, Inc., and chairman emeritus of The Ritz-Carlton Hotel Company, LLC, advises salespeople to:

> Learn as much as you can about the business through a variety of jobs. It's a mistake to go right into sales and then try to learn by osmosis, or by

working a week here and there and think you really know the hotel. The best-prepared salespeople are those who have product knowledge. I don't think you get as much from a training program as you do when you experience something long-term. We (Marriott) have a myriad of sales schools and activities for people at different levels in the organization, which is great. But I still think the basic concept of knowing the product is important.[3]

Since it is virtually impossible to memorize every detail about your property, many hotels prepare a **property fact book** to assist their salespeople (old and new) to know enough about the property to properly present it. Figure 7.2 provides a beginning outline of the key elements in a property fact book. Every salesperson should know these important facts. This information can be updated as necessary and serves as an excellent tool for the selling process.

It is also important to have firsthand knowledge about your property. You should experience your property from a guest's perspective. Stay in a guestroom, sample your property's restaurants and room service, sample the property's recreational amenities, and become familiar with the layout of meeting rooms. Additionally, spend time at your hotel's front desk to observe the check-in and check-out process, visit the housekeeping department to learn about procedures and amenities, and learn how the food and beverage department handles functions from refreshment breaks to large banquets. Not only will your interaction with other departments add to your knowledge, but it will be invaluable when tailoring presentations to your target markets.

*Knowing your competition* can also help you to better sell your property. If you know a competitor's rates are slightly lower than yours, for example, you may expect a prospect to raise an objection about price— and you can be prepared to justify your additional cost by pointing out your property's special amenities, free parking space, or some other feature that the meeting planner may perceive as well worth the rate difference.

Fred Shea, former vice president of sales at Hyatt, says:

> Our hotels always want you to know what they're up against because, hopefully, they know the strengths and weaknesses of hotels in their competitive set and can sell against that. If, as a hotelier, I'm bidding in a vacuum, I'll give what I think is our best bid, but if I knew that a competitor had more services to offer, it may compel me to do different things.[4]

To fully understand your competitors, it is advantageous to personally experience their hotels. Were the competition's facilities clean and inviting? Was the front desk staff courteous and helpful? Were meeting rooms clean and away from heavy traffic areas? Did the other guests you encountered seem to be happy with their stay – or did they have complaints about the facilities or service? Your personal experiences will be invaluable in helping you to differentiate your hotel and its services when you are making a presentation to potential clients.

The third phase of pre-call planning, *knowing your prospect,* is essential for tailoring presentations to meet the needs of meeting planners. David Scypinski, senior vice president of Conference Direct, believes that hotel salespeople must know the customer as never before:

> It's not enough to know your customers' products, services, and objectives. You have to know everything about their business and industry. Hotel salespeople should understand how the organization they are trying

to book makes money and how large their budget is...there's no substitute for knowing your customers' organization, business needs, and objectives.[5]

*Figure 7.2. OUTLINE FOR PROPERTY FACT BOOK.*

| GUESTROOM INFORMATION | RESTAURANTS & LOUNGES | MEETING AND BANQUET FACILITIES |
|---|---|---|
| **Priority I**<br><br>Number of rooms<br>Number of singles/doubles/suites<br>Size of rooms — square footage<br>Number of floors<br>Phones in rooms<br>Fire alarms/detectors in rooms<br>Handicapped rooms<br>Non-smoking rooms<br>Amenities in rooms<br><br>**Priority II**<br><br>Room rates<br>Check-in/check-out times | **Priority I**<br><br>Seating capacity<br>Number of tables and types<br>Atmosphere/interior design<br>Non-smoking sections<br>Dress requirements<br>Pricing by restaurant<br>Restaurant positioning<br><br><br><br><br>**Priority II**<br><br>Menu style/theme<br>Types of food by restaurant | **Priority I**<br><br>Location of meeting rooms<br>Square footage/seating capacity<br>Utilities available<br>Exhibit space<br>Meeting room rental rates<br><br><br><br><br>**Priority II**<br><br>Function room furniture<br>Audiovisual capabilities |
| **Priority III**<br><br>Customer mix<br>Average occupancy by day of week<br>Average length of stay by segment<br>Sales budget<br>Profitability by segment<br>Group check-in/check-out procedures<br>Front desk staffing | **Priority III**<br><br>Entertainment<br>Reservation policy<br>Cocktails available<br>Wine cellar/list<br>Food served in lounge<br>Special promotions<br>Opening/closing times | **Priority III**<br><br>Banquet seating capacities<br>Banquet menu<br>Theme parties<br>Outside services<br>Types of banquet specialties<br>Beverage service<br>Banquet staffing levels |

*New salespeople cannot learn everything about a property in their first week. To help them gain knowledge in a logical order, questions about each area (guestrooms, restaurants and lounges, meeting and banquet facilities, etc.) should be arranged by priorities. At the end of week one, a salesperson should master all Priority I questions; and each week thereafter, master another priority level. The director of sales should assign the responsibility of updating and maintaining the property fact book to one specific person in the sales department.*

Many properties — even those that utilize mailing lists to develop new sales leads — send out surveys or make telephone calls to gather information about potential prospects (see Figure 7.3). And, don't forget the benefit of obtaining information right under your own roof; talk to meeting planners currently using your property and ask them about potential leads (and their requirements).

Once you decide that a prospect is indeed a valid one, you must make contact to try to sell. Sales calls in which you initiate the contact without any degree of interest indicated by

*Figure 7.3. SAMPLE SALES PROSPECT CARD.*

| | |
|---|---|
| Date of Contact _____ | Trace Date _____ |
| Name of Contact _____ | New Prospect ☐ Yes ☐ No |
| Company Name _____ | Type of Business _____ |
| Address _____ | Telephone _____ |
| _____ | Fax _____ |

Prospect's estimated sales potential:

    Room nights _____

    Meetings/Banquets _____

    Dollars _____

Facilities/services needed:

_____

_____

_____

Background information on prospect and company:

_____

_____

_____

Salesperson's Name _____

To make the most of a sales call, it is helpful to have some basic information about the needs of a prospect. A sales prospect card can help the salesperson to determine how to best structure his or her presentation to appeal to the needs of the client.
**Source: Used with permission of the Grand Traverse Resort, Traverse City, Michigan.**

the prospects are called **cold calls**. The anticipated percentage of success in these cases is understandably lower than when you are dealing with past customers or recommendations. It is often a problem just getting in to see the right person.

    While the primary purpose of cold calls is to find the name of the decision-maker and to determine prospect needs, these types of calls are often not well-received by meeting planners. Harlan Didrickson, a former manager, of executive and administrative services at Skidmore, Owings & Merrill, LLC, a Chicago-based architectural firm, says:

> I work in an almost constant state of chaos, so cold calls are very irritating. They're a waste of my time, and I find them rude.[6]

Didrickson's opinion is shared by 51 percent of 235 meeting planners surveyed by *Meeting News*. Receiving cold calls was the top complaint among respondents, whose other "pet peeves" include salespeople who don't ask if a planner has time to talk, repeated contacts (especially after they have told a salesperson they are not interested), and salespeople who go over the meeting planner's head by asking to speak to upper management. That does not mean cold calling should be eliminated. For maximum effect, you should "do your homework" and target your efforts, rather than rely on a "hit-or-miss" strategy. There is a wealth of information available today that can help you to research prospects with the highest potential for business. It is a waste of both the planner's and the salesperson's time, for example, if a small hotel calls a planner who books only with large hotel chains. And, by being aware of the organization's busiest times, you will avoid making a bad impression by calling on them when they are focused on important business, such as a stock holder's meeting or a large meeting or convention.

You can increase the efficiency of such efforts if you precede your visit with some sort of preliminary campaign. You might send your convention facilities brochure to the contact person, along with a personal letter. Follow up with another letter if you hear nothing within a few weeks. Then call for an appointment. If you fail to get an appointment, try again.

Your most effective calls will likely be **appointment calls**, where you have prearranged a visit with the prospect, but don't completely rule out calling without an appointment. When you are already in the area for another appointment, a cold call is worth a try.

---

### Advice for New Hotel Sales Professionals

David Brudney, ISHC

David Brudney & Associates

Carlsbad, California

Today's hospitality sales professionals must deal with a much more sophisticated, knowledgeable, and demanding meeting planner. Never has it been more critical for sales directors and managers to know their "stuff" and share their knowledge; to master the art of people-connecting; and to respond quickly and accurately at all times.

If you are new to hospitality sales, you most likely are a member of a new generation of salespeople. Therefore, you need to understand that in order to be successful — and, more importantly, to sustain that success over the years — you need to balance time spent on the computer against time spent on the telephone and out on personal sales calls.

Your generation of sales professionals is the most tech-savvy of any generation in the history of the hospitality industry. You are masters of the Internet. You fully expect information to come customized and instantly. History? That's all about yesterday. What's important today is today.

You may expect instant success from your efforts in selling room nights and F&B events, and become impatient when you find that you can't close a piece of business quickly via e-mail and text messaging.

From day one you will need to begin mastering the "high-touch" aspects of direct selling: selling on the telephone and selling when making outside sales calls, selling at trade shows, on fam trips, and anywhere you find yourself face-to-face with potential clients. Remember always that you live by *relationships* with support from technology.

You new generation of sales pros must not fail to learn that one-on-one sales, on the telephone and at clients' places of business, will always be the cornerstone to professional selling.

What is the best advice I can give to the new generation of hospitality sales professionals? It is all about relationships. Build and maintain solid relationships that will support you for the life of your sales career.

Cross-index your prospect list geographically. Mixing cold calls with your appointments will increase your number of sales calls. Cold calls sometimes work, but even if you cannot get in to see the right person at that time, you stand to lose little except a few minutes' time. Sales success, to use an analogy from baseball, is accomplished not so much from achieving a high "batting average" as from your total number of hits. More "turns at bat" (sales calls) mean the chance for more "hits" (sales).

Once you have completed the research phase of your pre-call planning, assemble the materials needed to make an effective presentation. A well-organized and professional **presentation book** should include only that information pertinent to each prospect's needs. Fumbling through too many materials in a sales kit may result in a loss of presentation momentum. Most sales kits contain basic information such as a general property information sheet, a meeting and banquet room information sheet, a convention brochure and other visual aids, including color photographs, a map of the property, etc. Many properties also include third-party endorsement letters, also called *testimonials*, which are letters of recommendation from meeting planners who have used the properties' facilities. If these are used, however, they should be relevant to your prospects. A letter from an association meeting planner praising your theme party, for example, would have little significance for a corporate meeting planner wishing to hold a training session.

Today, a growing number of salespeople have replaced traditional presentation books with virtual presentations on their laptops or mobile devices. These virtual presentations include all the components found in a presentation book, including forms and testimonials, but they have the advantage of allowing a planner to "see" a panoramic view of the property (we will discuss virtual tours in more detail in the site inspection section of this chapter). In many cases, virtual content includes information and graphics for all the property's market segments; presentations can be custom-tailored using only the files and screens appropriate to the potential customer. When a virtual presentation is used, the salesperson should still carry the most requested collateral materials – a business card, convention brochure, room layouts, and so on – to leave with the meeting planner.

If your property targets a number of market segments, you should consider preparing a presentation book or visual presentation tailored to each of those segments. While incentive and tour groups can be adequately served with glossy brochures and information on local attractions, meeting planners require "working documents." Your presentation book for meeting planners should include meeting space layouts on white, uncoated paper to allow the planner to easily make notes during a site inspection. These diagrams (ideally one per page) should include all specifics for meeting rooms, including anything that impacts the usable square footage of the room. You may also want to include specifications for alternative room setups.

Additional "must haves" in a presentation book or visual presentation for meeting planners include large, detailed area maps with clear driving directions (these should be designed to enable the planner to fax or otherwise duplicate them), audiovisual price lists, parking information, transportation information (such as airport shuttles, hotel shuttles to nearby destinations, and so on), dining outlets (including types of cuisine, and hours of operation), detailed summaries of guestroom types and amenities, and business center information.[7]

## Step #2: Opening the Sales Call

Selling is essentially helping someone to buy. Open your sales call in such a way that it puts the customer at ease so that he or she can build rapport with you. Your opening should

## Chapter 7: Selling to the Meetings Market

consist of an introduction, a statement of the purpose of your call (and its benefit to the prospect), and a bridge statement that leads into the actual presentation. You can start by introducing yourself and your property ("Good afternoon, Mr. Jones. I'm Dan Merrill from the Golden Gate Resort in San Diego, California."), while offering a brief but firm handshake. You may also wish to add a few words at this time to show your interest in the prospect. For example, "I've heard so much about what your firm has been doing in the area of microcomputers, and I'm looking forward to hearing more about your innovative uses of

---

### 💻 INTERNET EXERCISE

**Invaluable Advice from Seasoned Hospitality Professionals**

In the box titled "Advice for New Hotel Sales Professionals," David Brudney says it is crucial for successful hospitality sales professionals to share their knowledge with the next generation of salespeople. Brudney is one of a number of experts in the hotel sales field to share his expertise on a website (www.davidbrudney.com).

To bolster your knowledge with the help of seasoned hotel pros, log on to the following websites:

- Corbin Ball – www.corbinball.com
- Howard Feiertag – www.hotelmotel.com (type "Howard Feiertag articles" in the search box)
- Brenda Fields – www.fieldsandcompany.net
- Dr. John Hogan – www.hotel-online.com (type "Dr. John Hogan articles" in the search box)
- Neil Salerno – www.hotelmarketingcoach.com
- Steve Steinhart – hotelsalescoach.com

Read at least two articles by these experts that relate to the sales skills covered in this chapter. What additional tips have you learned from these articles?

---

microchips." But take care not to get so immersed in discussion about the company that you neglect your objective.

As soon as possible after the introduction, state the purpose of your call. Can you offer the prospect additional meeting space or are you there to try to win back former business? After stating your purpose, you should present a benefit or two that will give the prospect a reason to listen to you. Once you have stated your property's benefits, lead into the body of the sales presentation with a bridge statement. This statement basically asks the prospect for permission to continue, and is usually in the form of a question: "Would you be interested in learning how other associations used one of our theme parties to increase attendance?" or "May I show you just a few examples of our state-of-the-art audiovisual system?" If the prospect gives a positive response, you have the green light to continue. If the prospect is not interested, thank him or her for their time and ask for an appointment in the future.

### Step #3: Getting Prospect Involvement

Involve the prospect in the sales process to determine his or her needs. Do it by asking questions, and always ask *before* making your presentation. Two types of questions are generally used: close-ended questions and open-ended questions.

**Close-ended questions** require a specific reply. These include such queries as, "How many training meetings do you stage each month?" or "What is your average attendance at your annual convention?" **Open-ended questions**, on the other hand, give the prospect an opportunity to express his or her feelings. Open-ended questions such as, "Why do you think last year's meeting was so successful?" or "What factors are most important to you in selecting a resort?" will provide clues into what is important to the prospect and can help you to adjust your sales presentation to meet those concerns.

Effective questioning is among the more critical aspects of selling. Decide what information you need from the prospect in advance, and use it as a checklist for asking questions during your sales call.

> **MORE ONLINE**
>
> Information on "The 10 Ways to Fully Uncover a Group's Overall Needs" can be found at www.knowland.com/content/industry-resources-tipsheet (click on the Tipsheets tab to view the article).

Take notes when questioning. Prospects appreciate the fact that you are taking time to write down their concerns which encourages them to give additional information. Additionally, your notes become the basis for your presentation as well as a part of your sales file when trying to book the client's next meeting.

Don't forget that the most important skill in gaining client involvement is *listening* to the client's responses. Sal Dickinson, president of Dickinson Associates, a consulting firm to hotel sales executives, stresses that successful salespeople are active listeners who relate to the prospect's needs and desires. He says:

> Get to know your prospects' needs better than the competition by being a better listener. Do your due diligence and research well. Knowledge is power, and the more you know, the more effective you'll be...Come armed with solutions, not features, and spell out how what you have will be valuable and make life easier.[8]

## Step #4: Presenting Your Property

While every salesperson should have a prepared and rehearsed sales presentation that addresses the needs of each market segment, you increase your chances of a sale if you custom-tailor this general presentation for specific clients. Most clients are really interested only if what you offer will benefit them. Rather than being a product-seller, become a problem-solver; always present your property's features as benefits to the client (see Figure 7.4).

Your presentation should directly address the client's needs — and should include visual aids such as pictures, charts, and graphs to enable the planner to envision how your property will work for his or her meeting. Many salespeople today use more sophisticated visual aids — such as a DVD brochure or online video — but the important factor is how these presentations relate to the client.

Tom McCarthy, CHME, CHA, past president of Hospitality Sales & Marketing Association International, suggests that each hotel create several five- to six-minute introductory presentations (with pictures) that can be used at a prospect's office, a one-minute presentation to introduce your hotel over the telephone, a presentation to use on a tour of the hotel, and presentations to overcome the most frequently raised objections. Salespeople should then rehearse these presentations before actually giving them to prospects.[9]

When presenting, use testimonial letters and publicity reprints to increase your credibility. Prospects are more likely to believe the good things their peers and unbiased reviewers have to say about your property than what a salesperson might say. Third-party endorsements from meeting decision-makers in the same market segment as your prospect are best; use association-related letters when selling to association meeting planners, corporate letters when presenting to corporate decision-makers, and so on.

## Chapter 7: Selling to the Meetings Market

*Figure 7.4. TURNING FEATURES INTO BENEFITS.*

| Feature | | Benefit |
|---|---|---|
| All of our breakout rooms are adjacent to the room where your general session will be held | SO THAT | no time will be wasted between sessions and you will be able to keep your meeting on schedule. |
| We offer 24-hour room service | SO THAT | those attendees who must check-in late may still enjoy a late meal in the comfort of their room. |
| Every room has a desk | SO THAT | your meeting attendees will have plenty of room to review and work on handouts they receive during the daily meeting sessions. |
| We have a health club and spa | SO THAT | your trainees can relax and unwind after a day of intensive educational meetings. |

| Benefit | | Feature |
|---|---|---|
| Those attendees who check-in late may still enjoy a late meal in the comfort of their room | BECAUSE | we offer 24-hour room service. |

*Salespeople who present only features rely on their prospects to interpret how those features can benefit them. Instead, salespeople should try to influence the interpretation by always linking features with benefits and explaining to prospects how the features will benefit them and enhance their meetings. To assist you in thinking "benefits," the words "so that" can be used to tie the two. The selling sentence can also be reversed, using the word "because" to link the benefit to the feature.*

Once your presentation is completed, make a transition statement (which can be as simple as asking, "Do you have any questions?") that may lead to a close — or to what is often the next phase of the sales call, overcoming objections.

## Step #5: Handling Objections

It is a rare meeting planner who will not have some questions or objections. It is important, therefore, to anticipate the most likely areas of concern and to be able to respond immediately.

The most common objections involve concerns over price or product, or simply a lack of interest. *Price* objections ("Your competitor has cheaper rates") can often be overcome by pointing out a compensatory benefit ("Perhaps. But our meeting package includes free meeting and function space as well as free golf and tennis facilities."). Whenever possible, try to get the focus off price ("Putting price aside for the moment, do you have any other concerns?").

**WORTH WATCHING**

You can view a series of brief, to-the-point videos by Jill Harrington, the former CEO of the Society of Incentive Travel Executives and now president of salesSHIFT, at:
- Unsolicited Sales Calls From Hotel Salespeople – www.salesshift.ca/cold-calling-from-the-buyers-perspective/
- Do Your Sales Calls Matter? – www.salesshift.ca/do-your-sales-calls-matter
- Why Salespeople Irritate – www.salesshift.ca/why-sales-people-irritate
- What Salespeople Should Stop Doing – www.salesshift.ca/sales-people-should-stop-doing-this-once-and-for-all

*A major advantage of personal sales calls is immediate feedback and two-way communication. Research conducted by* Meetings News *found that 85 percent of meeting planners affirmed their preference for face-to-face contact when asked, "What is your preferred method of professional networking?" And, a recent survey by the Hospitality Sales & Marketing Association International (HSMAI) found that hotel salespeople believe that person-to-person sales provides the best return on investment of all selling and advertising methods.*
**Source: Photograph by Alan Cresto. Courtesy of Loews Hotels.**

This tactic may work if you can demonstrate how your property meets the client's needs so well; then, price diminishes in importance.

*Product* objections ("Your property may not be as attractive to our attendees as the new resort in your area") may be handled in a number of ways. Try restating the objection and offer a positive response: "I gather that you don't feel our property is modern enough. Although we are an older property, our rooms and meeting space have been completely renovated and we offer all amenities found at new properties in our area. Clients tell us our property has a great deal of character and charm."

*Lack of interest* objections ("We are happy with our present hotel") can be overcome by finding out why the client is satisfied and offering comparable —and additional — benefits. Or, you may point out that a change of site may prove to be stimulating to the attendees. A change in site could then be considered acceptable to the planner; and you offered an alternative without the implication that the prospect's selection of the previous property was a mistake in any way. If nothing changes the client's mind at that time, it is still a good practice to ask to be considered for a meeting or function in the future. There are many factors that may come into play at some future date that may open the door for you.

Although objections are generally a part of a sales presentation, a salesperson should not fear them; instead, objections should be viewed as an opportunity to help a planner to make a buying decision. To do so, you must listen to the prospect and empathize with what he or she is saying. Ask questions when necessary to ensure that you understand the needs and concerns of the prospect. Engaging in this type of dialogue – rather than simply pushing for a sale – allows the planner to express his or her concerns and makes it easier for the salesperson to respond to specific needs. Most importantly, this type of interaction is the first step in building a consultative relationship with the client.

When handling objections, it is vital that you *never* knock your competition. At best, this is unprofessional; at worst, the meeting planner may feel that your words reflect on his or her judgment — and you may lose any possibility of booking a sale at that time or in the future.

## Step #6: Closing and Follow-up

While many salespeople enjoy presenting their product, some hesitate when it comes to asking for the sale! The skill of closing, however, can be learned, and can be more comfortable when salespeople realize that clients *expect* to be asked to book at the property.

There are two types of closes: trial closes and major closes. **Trial closes** are used to elicit responses from the client, and are generally used to build an "agreement staircase." In other words, the salesperson periodically asks for a positive client response ("Don't you agree that our audiovisual equipment will greatly enhance your training sessions?" or "Don't you think our ballroom would make an elegant setting for your awards banquet?" or "Don't you find our golf course to be one of the finest in the state?"). Positive responses, repetition of benefits by a client, and positive nonverbal signs (frequent smiles, the client leaning forward, etc.) are excellent indicators that the salesperson can proceed with his or her major close.

*Many hotel salespeople have a specific room they use when making their sales presentations. One salesperson told us, "I always use our boardroom when closing. It overlooks our fountains, waterfalls, and the golf course. If prospects are hesitant, I point out the view and ask if their board wouldn't appreciate the scene."*
**Source: Photograph courtesy of Fairmont Chateau Lake Louise, Banff, Alberta, Canada.**

---

### When to Ask for Business

There are several points in a sales presentation when it may be appropriate to ask for a client's business and close the sale:

- Any time the customer indicates an appreciable amount of interest.
- Any time the customer begins asking questions about your product. Try a close immediately after you answer the question.
- After making a strong point about your product.
- After answering an objection.
- When your customer agrees with you on a major point.

**Source: HSMAI CHSE Study Guide Excerpt.**

---

The **major close** is the question or statement that asks for the sale. It should be attempted as soon as the client has reached a peak of excitement, and should elicit a commitment. This close should be as direct as possible ("May I reserve space on a definite basis?"), and after making it, you should stop talking and give the client a chance to respond. Avoid the temptation to keep talking — you may inadvertently say something that brings up concerns the client had not previously considered!

Once your call is completed, leave as soon as is politely possible. And, whether you have made a sale or not, always follow up your sales call promptly with a thank you letter. This gesture shows your commitment to customer service and may result in future sales.

# Chapter 7: Selling to the Meetings Market

If a commitment has been made, follow-up is even more important. You will want to service your client with frequent post-sale contacts, including keeping him or her informed on the progress of preparations for the function. Find out the client's preference for communicating — by phone, fax, e-mail — through their assistants. It is also important to check with the planner during the function. Arlene Sheff, CMP, a former senior meeting and event planner for The Boeing Company, said this of one of her meetings:

> I never saw the salesperson once on site. I spoke to him on the phone several times before the meeting, but while the meeting was going on, he never came by even once to see how things were going. If a hotel salesperson wants my repeat business, they need to track me down and check on my meeting. It's all about building a relationship with me.[10]

Contacting the client after the function to ensure that all went according to plan is also essential. Never assume that a lack of complaints means that the client was satisfied. Follow-up is the key to building long-term relationships. Remember: customers don't care how much you know until they know how much you care.

This type of commitment leads to customer rebookings and word-of-mouth referrals for additional business.

## Telephone Selling

One of the problems with personal calls is that they are getting increasingly expensive. Many properties are cutting down on the expense of personal calls by stepping up their use of the telephone, especially as a tool to screen prospects and to set appointments with clients.

Although telephone calls should not be a substitute for as many personal visits as you can manage, you should become proficient in using the telephone as a means to increase customer contact, screen prospects to make personal calls more effective, and offer immediate assistance to clients in the event of urgent situations.

### Telephone Techniques

Since using the telephone is much more impersonal than talking face-to-face with a prospect, it is important that you and your salespeople develop techniques to make the most efficient use of this sales tool. As with a personal sales call, *preparation* is the key.

Start by doing your research. Find out as much as you can about the company and the people you will be contacting. There is a wealth of information on the Internet regarding companies, their key staff members, and the

> **WORTH WATCHING**
>
> You can watch telephone customer service videos by Nancy Friedman, President of Telephone Doctor© Customer Service Training, a popular keynote speaker and author, at the following sites:
>
> - Essential Telephone Skills – www.youtube.com/watch?v=E5_JmqsK8_c
> - Best Customer Service Training – www.youtube.com/watch?v=sUXegFI0930
> - Customer Service – Listening and Questioning – www.youtube.com/watch?v=6Z2Hy1OpP2A
>
> View additional telephone etiquette and technique videos by typing "Nancy Friedman Telephone Doctor" in the search box at www.youtube.com. You can also sign up for Nancy's free customer service newsletter at www.linkedin.com/in/nancyfriedmanspeaker or on her website at www.nancyfriedman.com.

products or services they offer. This data will help you to pre-screen businesses, prepare a custom-tailored telephone inquiry, and can help to "break the ice" when you make your first call (offering a word of congratulation on a company achievement, for example, can be the first step in building a relationship with a prospect).

Before making a call, you should have an outline of what you are going to cover. A clearly typed topical outline will help you maintain control of your thoughts and maintain a logical flow in your conversation. You can even use a prepared presentation — as long as it doesn't sound "canned." Along with your outline or presentation, you also want to keep pertinent backup information — room rates, function room sizes and capacities, availability, and so on —at hand so that you never have to fumble while searching for it. Also, keep paper and pencil handy to jot down notes or to remind yourself of information requested by the client.

Using the telephone involves the mastery of several simple techniques. Always hold the receiver slightly away from your mouth and speak slowly and distinctly. Immediately identify yourself and your property. Put your personality into the call — be cheerful yet professional — and always be willing to listen to the prospect's views. Don't be reluctant to ask the prospect to spell his or her name if it isn't clear. Few people mind repeating or spelling their name. Above all, smile – a smile and enthusiasm are contagious.

## Screening Prospects

The telephone makes it easy to prequalify prospects before making appointments for personal calls. The Kingsmill Resort in Williamsburg, Virginia, employs a sales assistant to use the Internet and the telephone to determine prospects' meeting plan profiles. The sales assistant obtains the decision-makers' names, contact information, meeting frequency, length of meetings, arrival and departure dates, number of attendees, type of property preferred, and any other information needed to qualify a group. Profiles are then turned over in a written report to the appropriate salespeople. Letting a sales assistant do the screening allows salespeople to spend 100 percent of their time selling. Many properties use sales lead services, often referred to as *tip sheets,* to analyze information about convention and meeting planners. All of these names will not be high-priority prospects; they must be scanned to determine those who best fit into your marketing plan. But, since other hotels are receiving the same tip sheet, you must take quick action after an initial screening. Since you already have basic information about each lead, you can tailor your telephone calls to these prospects.

Other prospects can be interviewed directly by salespeople, who will enter information that could be helpful in a sales presentation on a **call report** (see Figure 7.5). This form can help the salesperson to determine the needs of the prospect — if the prospect represents viable business. In some cases, marketing surveys are conducted by members of the property's clerical staff, while large properties and chains may have an entire department that surveys potential prospects (see the telemarketing section later in this chapter). Training clerical staff specifically in telephone techniques pays dividends.

## Setting Appointments by Phone

Since cold-calling is less effective than calling on prospects who are already interested in what the property has to offer, the telephone is a useful tool for setting appointments for sales presentations.

*Figure 7.5. SAMPLE CALL REPORT.*

## RED LION HOTELS

### CALL REPORT

FIRST CALL
REPEAT CALL
FILE NO.

COMPANY / ORGANIZATION:
STREET ADDRESS
CITY                    STATE                    ZIP
CONTACT:                                PHONE:

DOES YOUR COMPANY HAVE MEETINGS?   ☐ NO   ☐ YES   HOW OFTEN?
SIZE                         CONTACT
WHEN IS YOUR NEXT MEETING?           WHERE
DO YOU NEED GUEST ROOMS?   ☐ NO   ☐ YES   HOW MANY
WHO MAKES THE RESERVATIONS?
DO YOU NEED OUT OF TOWN RESERVATIONS?   ☐ NO ☐ YES  WHERE?

DO YOU HAVE SUCH THINGS AS:
- CHRISTMAS PARTIES
- AWARDS BANQUETS
- OTHER

ARE YOU OR ANYONE ELSE IN YOUR
COMPANY AFFILIATED WITH AN ASSOCIATION?

COMMENTS:

SALESPERSON                           DATE

FORM NO. 001-S47 (4/86)

*Call reports are used by salespeople to survey the needs of a potential contact and to trace the follow-up on each account. At some properties, surveys are taken by support staff and the names of qualified prospects are passed on to the salespeople for follow-up.*

One of the most challenging tasks in using the telephone to set appointments is getting by the intermediaries — the receptionist, secretary, administrative assistant, etc. — to reach the decision-maker. The intermediary is often your contact person in determining who

**247**

makes the decision for holding meetings and can be your best friend — or worst enemy; his or her response and level of assistance can make the difference between whether you get an appointment or not! These people can be an added source of information, too. It is important, then, to build rapport with support people. They should always be treated with respect, and, for best results, should be told the objective of your call — and how it will benefit their boss.

There are a number of techniques that can be used to get past these "gatekeepers." If you have done your homework, you can appeal to a need and offer a solution. Perhaps you have read that the company is about to hold a new product launch; you can then appeal to the need for additional rooms for the expected guests, mentioning that you can offer a special rate or perks to pique the interest of the gatekeeper. Another effective technique is to create a personal connection with the gatekeeper and other employees in the organization. You may have met another staff member at a networking event, for example, and your mention of that connection may open doors. Or perhaps you have read about a special accomplishment by the meeting planner. Expressing your interest and admiration goes a long way in developing rapport with the gatekeeper.

Meeting planners are usually busy and their time is scarce, so you should remember that the objective of your call is usually to simply set an appointment — not to make a sale. Once you have reached the decision-maker, the telephone appointment call involves three steps: opening the call, the presentation, and setting the appointment (see Figure 7.6).

## Telephone Sales Call Follow-up

It is just as important to follow up on your telephone calls as it is on your personal calls, especially since a telephone call does not leave as lasting an impression as a personal visit. Since you are either looking for information or an appointment when you make telephone contact, you should take the time to write a friendly note thanking the prospect for his or her time or confirming an appointment date.

Use this further contact as an additional pre-sale tool. Along with a professionally typed letter, include requested information (room rate sheet, menus, etc.) or some hotel brochures to familiarize the prospect with your property before you arrive. Then, a few days later, you can call the prospect to verify that they received your materials.

This type of follow-up not only keeps you in the prospect's mind, but also demonstrates your property's commitment to customer service. Meeting planners, especially those who are nonprofessionals or those with limited experience, are more likely to choose a property that has demonstrated its willingness to work closely with its clients.

## Handling Inquiries

In today's high-tech world, many meeting planners prefer doing business via e-mail. Today, Hilton (as well as other hotel chains) equips its salespeople with laptops and mobile devices to enable them to read and respond to e-mails and text messages quickly, as timing is critical for clients with short-term meetings, and the hotel that responds first often gets the business. Larry Luteran, senior vice president group sales and industry relations for Hilton Worldwide, says:

> Speed to market is critical now. A good response time used to be two days, then it was 24 hours, and now it's a few hours.[11]

## Chapter 7: Selling to the Meetings Market

*Figure 7.6. SAMPLE SCRIPT FOR A TELEPHONE APPOINTMENT CALL*

There are three steps in making a telephone appointment call once you have reached the decision-maker: opening the call; the presentation; and setting the appointment. Sample statements include:

### Opening the Call

"Hello, Mr. Stubbs. My name is Diane Street, sales manager of the Oakbrook Hotel, the new hotel just down the street from your offices. Since we are neighbors and so convenient, I thought you would be interested in hearing about our hotel and the affordable meeting package we have just designed for local businesses."

### The Presentation

"Mr. Stubbs, from my research, I've learned that you schedule intensive training meetings lasting two or three days with several evening working sessions. We have developed a 24-hour meeting program for companies with needs such as yours. The program reserves your meeting rooms on a 24-hour basis so that you will not be inconvenienced with removing training materials each evening and resetting equipment the next morning. In addition, our copying equipment is available to you 24 hours a day for any timely additions or changes in your handout materials."

### Setting the Appointment

"I know you'll be impressed with our state-of-the-art meeting rooms and our convention service staff who will assist you in staging successful training meetings. When could we meet for lunch to discuss your upcoming employee development seminars?

"Would you prefer the beginning or later part of the week? Is 11:30 or 12:00 most convenient for you?

"Great. I'll see you Thursday at 12 noon at our concierge desk. I'll have my name tag on so you can recognize me.

"Thank you for your time, Mr. Stubbs. I'm looking forward to meeting with you personally. Have a good day."

Source: Photograph courtesy of Swissôtel.

Note that the salesperson clearly identified herself and her hotel, stated the purpose of her call, and explained how the prospect would benefit from an appointment, appealing to his need for convenient meeting facilities. Note that in setting the appointment, she asked forced-choice questions, giving the planner a choice between two positive alternatives.

---

Inquiries about your property also come via requests for proposals on the Internet or your hotel's website; by fax, telephone calls, or mail; and from walk-ins. Walk-ins should always be immediately referred to a hotel salesperson; other inquiries require an immediate follow-up by telephone (see Figure 7.7).

A large number of properties use voice mail systems. While these systems are convenient, many planners are put off by them. They want a timely response, so sales department phones should be answered by a live person. Not only does this show that a property is interested in the planner's business, it provides the opportunity for the salesperson to determine the prospect's needs.

A recent survey by *Meeting News* found that meeting planners' chief complaint about hotel salespeople is their failure to respond to inquiry calls, requests for proposals (RFPs), and e-mails in a timely manner. Quality Track International, a leading provider of group sales mystery shopping services to the hospitality industry, conducted an independent test on 750 hotels and found that 28 percent of new group sales are lost, ignored, or abandoned. Meeting group sales are a significant source of revenue for most hotels, yet over one-fourth of initial customer contact inquiries go unanswered!

## Chapter 7: Selling to the Meetings Market

*Figure 7.7. CROWNE PLAZA'S GUARANTEED RESPONSE TO MEETING INQUIRIES.*

"We'll get back to you later" is not in our vocabulary.

2-Hour Response Guarantee. Only from Crowne Plaza.

Kathryn Unagst
Crowne Meetings Director of the Year
Crowne Plaza Hilton Head Island Beach Resort

Unlike other hotels, we don't just promise to be responsive. We prove it to you. In fact, we guarantee that we'll respond to your Request for Proposal within two hours, or we'll give you 5% off your total master account. And to make sure your whole meeting runs like clockwork, we'll also give you a Crowne Meetings Director—your one point of contact to take care of everything. So share your plans with people who share your sense of urgency. The meeting experts at Crowne Plaza.

CROWNE PLAZA
HOTELS & RESORTS
THE PLACE TO MEET.

Book today: crowneplaza.com/meetings, 1-800-MEETING or call a hotel directly.

For complete details, visit crowneplaza.com/meetings. © 2005 InterContinental Hotels Group. All rights reserved. Most hotels are independently owned and/or operated.

*In today's competitive marketplace, it is essential that hotels make immediate responses to inquiries. This ad for the Crowne Plaza Hotels & Resorts promotes the chain's 2-Hour Response Guarantee, which promises to respond to a Request for Proposal within two hours or the chain will take 5% off the group's master account.*

Inquiry calls should be handled like sales calls. Whether the call is answered by a salesperson or the sales staff, it should be answered quickly (within three rings) and professionally, and voice tone should be friendly but efficient. Interest should always be shown to the caller – the call should never be regarded as an interruption – and the caller should be asked if he or she can be put on hold or transferred to another person or department.

No matter what their source, all inquiries should be followed up by a phone call. Salespeople are not simply order takers. During the call, the salesperson should ask enough questions to be able to present the property effectively. By getting to know the prospect and his or her needs, even if the property cannot handle the business at that time, a relationship has been built and there is a greater potential for future business.

If a salesperson is out of the office or busy with other duties, there should always be someone who is available and trained to properly handle the inquiry; it leaves a very bad impression for a call to be relegated to voice mail. In large sales offices, a secretary or another salesperson may take the call; in a smaller sales organization, another staff member – perhaps a front desk clerk or even the general manager — should answer. No matter who takes the call, it is important that all pertinent information is written down and passed along to the salesperson as soon as possible.

## Telemarketing

Besides individual telephone calls, the hospitality industry is making extensive use of **telemarketing** — large-scale telephone qualifying and research — to identify potential prospects. While the larger chains have used telemarketing for some time, the practice has become more widespread. Smaller properties have found that telemarketing can be an invaluable tool to reach prospects before sending salespeople out on expensive sales calls.

Telemarketing falls primarily into two basic categories: qualifying and market research. When a property simply wishes to obtain information, smaller properties can utilize additional staff — secretaries, front desk personnel, etc. — to assist in a telephone effort. It should be noted, however, that this type of "telephone blitz" is not true telemarketing — which is a specialized program backed by technology which offers instant access to information.

For large-scale efforts, a professional telemarketing staff is trained to work from prepared scripts. Using such a script, an experienced telemarketer may reach 50 or more prospects a day, either to obtain information or to present the property and close a sale. Reduced sales budgets have caused many properties to increase telemarketing efforts, especially to reach prospects in distant areas that you cannot get to economically.

A good telemarketing script must be short enough to keep the prospect on the line, but long enough to get the desired information or sale. It should also be specific, with benefits to the client spelled out early. It should be structured to draw the prospect into the conversation and offer the opportunity for him or her to become involved by expressing views and needs. When attempting to make an actual sale, follow the same steps as you would in a personal sales call.

Telemarketing is also used for market research, to determine exactly what meeting planners are looking for. Such information is used to upgrade facilities and services, making it easier for salespeople to present the property as meeting the needs of meeting planners.

No matter what type of telemarketing program is implemented, is it essential that it be as disciplined as any other form of selling. The staff should be thoroughly trained, and there should be clear-cut goals and follow-up to ensure that goals are being met.

Chapter 7: Selling to the Meetings Market

# Sales Blitz Selling

A **sales blitz** focuses on contacting potential clients in a concentrated area over a brief period of time (usually three days), and is an effective tool for both reaching and qualifying new business (see Best Practices box titled "Hyatt's CRUNCH Time Maximizes Sales Blitz Success"). A sales blitz may consist of simply "cold calling" on businesses and associations in an area, but unannounced, random sales calls on meeting planners are usually not a good idea. Planners often feel such calls are intrusive and discourteous. Instead, hotels should carefully plan and identify prospects prior to a sales blitz -- and, ideally, send prospective clients a letter advising them of the coming visit.

> **MORE ONLINE**
>
> Plan B Consultants, Inc. organizes sales blitzes for numerous hotels. To view "Sales Blitz Success Tips," go to www.planbconsultants.com/2011/06/hotel-sales-blitz-success-tips/. There are also a number of sites that feature articles on sales blitzes. Google "Sales Blitzes: A Look at the Benefits of Team Efforts."

Other sales blitzes may be more elaborate. A new property, for example, may wish to use the sales blitz technique to introduce itself to the community; the blitz would serve as a way to invite potential clients to attend a special property presentation. If a sales blitz is used to introduce a new property or to promote a special property presentation, however, extensive planning is needed. The program may include audiovisual presentations, property tours, and food and beverage functions. In many cases, notables such as local or national celebrities or political figures are invited to stimulate interest and lend credibility to the

---

**Best Practices**

### Hyatt's CRUNCH Time Maximizes Sales Blitz Success

When the Hyatt chain sought to jump-start its sales efforts, it organized a program called CRUNCH TIME, which stands for: Close tentative business; Refer new business; Unite our forces; Network our clients; Clean up data base; and Have fun. The program translated into a massive 12-day sales blitz that involved more than 600 corporate and property salespeople targeting 40,000 potential customers.

The program, which included incentive prizes for top performers in a number of categories (number of calls made, revenue, referrals, and so on), was kicked off when corporate headquarters sent lists of clients to be called on to individual hotels and regional offices. The lists were generated to minimize possible overlaps, and were followed up by electronic CRUNCH Grams to stimulate interest in the program and keep salespeople up to date on the campaign's progress (salespeople sent in their results every three days).

CRUNCH Time resulted in a total of 36,219 contacts made by 566 employees. Nearly 2,200 of these calls led to business closings, generating $30 million in bookings, including a single $600,000 piece of business and several bookings of approximately $500,000 each. In addition, some 1,250 referrals were sent property to property, which would likely result in additional business.

Not only did the program generate sales and sales leads, it also led to camaraderie in the sales force, and CRUNCH Time was deemed so successful that the chain planned to repeat it at least annually and expand the program to targeted segments with Catering CRUNCH and Corporate Traveler CRUNCH.

property. No matter what type of program is planned, however, its ultimate purpose should be to demonstrate a property's ability to handle meetings business. It is of obvious importance, therefore, to get as many of the prospects as possible to attend the event and receive the special presentation.

Still other properties join up with their local convention and visitors bureau to conduct a sales blitz. In this case, several entities are involved (the CVB, area hotels, destination management companies, and area attractions) in a coordinated sales effort to attract a specific market. In Orlando, the CVB has entered into a partnership with the Rosen College of Hospitality Management, and students make prospecting calls for the bureau.

Whether a sales blitz will lead to a property presentation or will be used simply to survey potential clients, most properties begin planning several weeks in advance. Sales letters are often sent out to prospective clients to advise them of the coming visit. This strategy leads to "warm calls" — contacts with planners who have some idea of what the property can offer. Proper preparation is important, as it will result in the sales blitz participant getting in to see more prospects and create an atmosphere conducive to selling.

When planning a sales blitz, a city directory is used to map out specific target areas. Providing each participant with a list of prospects in a concentrated area greatly reduces the traveling time involved, enabling a sales blitz participant to make 75 to 90 calls over a three-day period.

In most cases, the sales blitz is used simply to collect information, qualify prospects, or invite prospects to a special property presentation, so it is not always necessary to tie up the property's sales staff in a sales blitz effort. Some properties hire a temporary sales blitz staff or utilize sales-oriented college students for blitzes over break periods.

Each person involved should clearly understand the purpose of the blitz, including how many calls he or she is expected to make and what questions he or she can answer (if using an outside blitz team, participants are usually instructed to refer contacts to a member of the property's sales staff). For training and communication purposes, the sales blitz organizer may want to schedule daily pre-blitz meetings in the morning, set up a schedule of check-in phone calls (either made or received by participants), and hold a recap meeting at the end of each day. Participants should also be advised of any prizes or recognition offered for outstanding performance in such areas as most calls made or most revenue generated.

Sales blitz participants should be given an adequate supply of survey sheets (see Figure 7.8) and collateral materials, such as property business cards, convention brochures, and low-cost specialty items imprinted with the property's name and telephone number to keep the property's name in front of the prospect.

A great deal of effort is put into a sales blitz, so proper follow-up is important to maximize results. It is wisest to evaluate the results of a sales blitz on a daily basis. This enables the sales manager to determine if there are any leads that should be followed up immediately, to make any changes in strategy (if, for example, there seems to be considerable interest in one geographical area, some participants can be redirected to that location), and, in cases where incentives are offered, reward the day's most successful participant (thereby motivating the other participants).

## Trade Show Selling

Trade shows provide an opportunity for a property to reach meeting planners (see Figure 7.9). One of the advantages of trade show participation is that you will meet people who are buying. Anne Marie Spatharakis, senior account executive for the Renaissance Hotel in Washington, D.C., extols the advantages of trade shows:

# Chapter 7: SELLING TO THE MEETINGS MARKET

Trade shows are great places for big sales to happen. Calling on customers individually takes a lot of time and effort, but at shows you have everyone either buying or selling, so there is a collaborative spirit where quality matches are made.[12]

*Figure 7.8. SAMPLE SALES BLITZ SURVEY SHEET.*

## Sales Blitz Survey Sheet

Organization_____

Address_____

_____Zip_____Phone_____

Contact_____Title_____

Contact_____Title_____

1. How many meetings do you have a year?_____ When?_____
   Size_____ Who plans them?_____

Contact_____Title_____

When is your next meeting? _____

Where are meetings usually held? _____

2. Do you have incoming visitors that require sleeping accommodations?

   Yes_____ No_____ How many per month?_____

   If yes, where are they housed?_____

   Do you reserve the room? Yes_____ No_____ (If not, who does?)

   Contact_____Title_____

3. Does your organization plan such things as:

   ___Christmas Parties?          ___Retirement Dinners?
   ___Award Dinners?              ___Other Social Events?

   Are you the organizer, or is there a social chairman?
   Yes____ No____ Contact_____

4. Are you, or any of your associates, affiliated with any other organizations or associations that might have need for meeting or banquet space? Yes____ No____

Name_____Contact_____

Comments:

Taken by: _____Date Taken_____

Source: Howard Feiertag, "Blitzes and Sales Calls: Indispenable Selling Tools," *HSMAI Marketing Review.*

*During a sales blitz, survey sheets are used to record prospect information. Once qualified, the prospects with the highest potential for business will merit additional contact. Besides this vital information, additional questions might include: "Who else is involved in decision-making?" and "How are meeting sites selected?"*

Another advantage to trade show selling is the relatively low cost. While trade show participation requires effort and expense, it can be cost-effective. According to the Center for Exhibition Industry Research, the average dollar amount to close a sale from a trade show lead is $625, while it costs $1,117 to close a personal sales call. And, if your convention bureau is exhibiting in a trade show, it may be possible for your property to share booth space and expenses with them. In addition to these benefits, trade shows also provide excellent opportunities to see what your competition is doing!

There are also some disadvantages to selling through trade shows. First, there is the initial cost and transportation of a property's display; these expenses are especially prohibitive for small properties that must compete with the elaborate displays of larger competitors. Secondly, your competition is likely to be participating in the same show and wooing the same target markets you are trying to attract. And, lastly, your booth time may be taken up by a number of meeting planners who will not generate business for your property.

> **MORE ONLINE**
>
> To see a comprehensive list of meetings industry tradeshows, go to http://conventionplanit.com/savedate_n.php.

*Figure 7.9. SAMPLE OF TRADE SHOWS FOR REACHING THE MEETINGS MARKET.*

| Exhibit Shows | Number of exhibitors | Usual attendance | Type of Tradeshow |
|---|---|---|---|
| 1. American Society of Association Executives Annual Meeting & Expo | 800 | 5,000 | T |
| 2. ASAE Springtime | 800 | 5,000 | T |
| 3. Religious Conference Management Association Annual Conference | 688 | 1,250 | HB |
| 4. Meeting Professionals International Annual Meeting | 350 | 1,700 | HB |
| 5. Health Care Convention & Exhibitors Association Annual Meeting | 130 | 600 | T |
| 6. IAEE Expo! Expo! | 125 | 1,000 | T |
| 7. HSMA's MEET | 900 | 3,500 | T |
| 8. DMAI's Destinations Showcase | 300 | 1,150 | T |
| 9. IMEX Incentive Meetings Show | 3,000 | 7,000 | HB |
| 10. IBTM World | 4,000 | 9,300 | HB |
| **Key: T= Trade Show    HB = Hosted-Buyer Show** |||| 

Thirty years ago, the only major industry trade show for the meetings industry was the American Society of Association Executives Expo. Today, there are a number of shows aimed at different segments of the meetings industry. Above is a brief listing of national and regional exhibit shows, and recent attendance figures. When selecting a show at which to exhibit, keep in mind your primary target markets and plan your trade show strategy specifically for these markets. Although hundreds of exhibit shows are produced annually, you will want to participate only in the shows that attract buyers from the market segments your property wishes to target.

## Chapter 7: Selling to the Meetings Market

One way to ensure that your property makes the most effective use of trade shows is to exhibit at a show that offers a **hosted-buyer program**. This concept, which began in Europe but is now gaining popularity in the United States, connects qualified buyers with hospitality sellers though the show's organizer, who uses sophisticated software to match the needs of these buyers with the facilities and services offered by hotels and other hospitality organizations and firms. Appointments between buyers and exhibitors are set before the show begins, allowing hospitality participants plenty of time to custom-tailor their presentations to these pre-qualified buyers.

The concept benefits meeting planners, as they will spend time with suppliers who are already familiar with their needs; they can also schedule time to visit other exhibits that may be of interest, such as booths for an independent hotel or a destination that might be considered for a future meeting. In many cases, buyers have their expenses (travel, lodging, and so on) paid by the show's organizer; these expenses are passed along to participating hotels, convention and visitors bureaus, and other meeting suppliers with whom the planners will meet. Other trade show organizers offer more limited "perks," to buyers, such as a comp badge to the trade show. Even though hotels may incur extra costs if buyers' expenses are passed along to them, participating in a hosted-buyer show can be extremely cost-effective as there is no need to qualify prospects; exhibitors get one-on-one face time with qualified buyers who have already expressed an interest in what the exhibitor has to offer.

To make the most of trade show selling, planning is again the key (see Figure 7.10). A pre-show action plan identifying potential clients and a strategy for contact and follow- up is an excellent way to ensure that the maximum benefit is derived from trade show participation. Strong potential business should be targeted, and your representatives should find out where these planners are staying; this enables your reps to see planners that don't make it to the property's booth. It is best, therefore, to allow at least two days to make calls before the show opens and to allow at least one day after the show to follow up on new local contacts made through the show.

Both your booth and personnel should adequately reflect your property's image and professionalism. Personnel should always be friendly, courteous, and informative, and the booth should be arranged in a manner that involves the prospects. Rather than setting tables across the booth, it is more effective to place tables along the sides and back to draw people into the display. Giveaway materials should be kept to a minimum; it is a mistake to offer too many giveaways. Most meeting planners prefer to "travel light" and do not wish to be overwhelmed by too many materials. It is far better to show a video brochure and/or give live presentations at scheduled times. These can be enhanced by one or two pieces of concise, informative material accompanied by your business card.

No matter how simple or elaborate your display, it is important to always remember your purpose: selling. It is important to qualify prospects. If your property is a resort, for example, it would have little appeal for a meeting planner seeking airport hotels at which to hold training meetings. While you shouldn't discount these prospects entirely — they may have contacts who can use your property or may have use for your property at a later date — it is important to deal primarily with meeting planners who offer a high potential for business for your property. In other words, you must quickly qualify prospects to determine how much time you should spend with them. A survey sheet or questionnaire is an excellent way to determine if a booth's visitor is a good

> **WORTH WATCHING**
> 
> Jeff Hewitt of the Savannah Convention Bureau explains the advantages of Meeting Planners International's Hosted Buyer shows at www.meetings-conventions.com/videos.aspx?playlistid=1448988&videoid=92298824.

*Figure 7.10. EXHIBITING AT TRADE SHOWS.*

> ### Exhibiting at Trade Shows
>
> #### Before
>
> - When choosing trade shows, ask show management for a rating ratio of meeting planners to salespeople.
> - Contact previous exhibitors; ask about attendance and quality of prospective buyers. Set measurable sales and qualified-lead goals.
> - Use pre-show promotions. Target important prospects by mail or phone. Arrive early to make sales calls in the area prior to the show.
> - Be prepared with meeting planner kits for distribution at the booth.
> - Meet with the sales team to clarify team objectives, and set individual goals. Train salespeople with written sales scripts. Role-play different sales situations — using a sales brochure, qualifying prospects, and securing information from prospects.
> - Design a custom lead form to qualify your prospects.
>
> #### During
>
> - Set up the booth in advance and assign salespeople to no more than three-hour-shifts before a break.
> - Ask quick, qualifying questions to help determine interest. Be courteous and friendly but discontinue discussion when the visitor is not a prospect.
> - Smile; act and look knowledgeable; stand, don't sit; don't smoke, eat, or drink in the booth.
> - Use prospect's business card to take notes of specific needs for follow-up.
> - Schedule sales team meetings before and after each day of the show to discuss problems and solutions and to coach the sales team.
>
> #### And After the Show
>
> - The sixty days after the show are most critical. Assign responsibility for following up on leads and appointments; establish deadlines for follow-ups.
> - Review exhibit objectives to see if goals were attained. Each dollar invested should return ten dollars in sales.
> - Use the telephone, mail, and e-mail to follow up. Make sure all your leads are followed up within 48 hours after the show and your results will soar.
>
> Used with permission of Howard Feiertag, CHSE, CMP.

*To make the most of trade show exhibiting, the above list details what to do before, during, and after a trade show.*

prospect. If he or she is unlikely to have a need for your property, be polite but brief and move on to a better-qualified prospect as soon as possible.

Trade show selling is not complicated if you have set clear-cut goals for before and during the show and have established guidelines for follow-up. The contacts made at a trade show should be followed up as quickly as possible after the show to keep your property fresh in the contact's mind. This interest and demonstration of your property's commitment can result in both business from your trade show contacts and referral business in the future.

## Selling with Convention and Visitors Bureaus

Even if you represent a large property with extensive convention facilities, a local convention bureau can be an invaluable partner in selling to the meetings market, even serving as an

## Chapter 7: Selling to the Meetings Market

### DESTINATION MARKETING

Over a century ago, in 1895, Detroit hotelier Milton J. Carmichael presented an idea of promoting the city as a whole to help build individual hotel business. The concept proved to be so successful that the Detroit hoteliers created the nation's first convention bureau. Before long, the idea spread to other cities, and today hundreds of such bureaus exist around the world.

The convention and visitors bureaus' primary objective is *destination marketing* — promoting their respective areas as a whole to attract meetings and convention business. To do so, convention and visitors bureaus engage in advertising campaigns, participate in trade shows, and offer a number of services to meeting planners, including general destination information, centralized housing of convention delegates, and registration services.

Once given a meeting's requirements — dates, rates, and space — bureaus go to work for planners. The bureau usually arranges site inspection visits. After a group is booked, the bureau's focus shifts from marketing to service.

While the scope of services offered by bureaus depends largely on staff size and budget, some bureaus have become very innovative. The Chicago Convention and Tourism Bureau utilizes its in-house telemarketing department to help planners build attendance at conventions. Using a prepared script and a database of the convening group's members, the bureau's staff makes up to 2,500 calls free of charge. This service is credited with increasing convention attendance in the Windy City by as much as 16 percent. With each additional attendee representing an average of $800 in spending, such effort benefits both planners and local businesses.

**GOOD SPORTS**

Play is serious business. That's why we renovated our 13,000 seat arena, cultivate lush, green fields and keep plenty of rinks on ice.

Whether you seek the swish of the net, the crack of the bat, or room to run, you'll find the perfect facility in Providence/Warwick, Rhode Island. We know good sports.

Look for us at TEAMS to learn more about Rhode Island.

**PROVIDENCE THE CREATIVE CAPITAL**

Providence Warwick Convention & Visitors Bureau • 401-456-0200 • www.GoProvidence.com • sports@GoProvidence.com

Hilton Providence   Providence Biltmore — A Rhode Island Tradition Since 1922 —   THE WESTIN PROVIDENCE

extension of your property's sales staff. Bill Snyder, past president of the Anaheim Convention and Visitors Bureau, states:

> A Bureau's function is to bring conventions, trade shows, and tourists to its respective area. A secondary objective is, of course, to offer those services which necessarily follow the attraction of conventions, trade shows, and tourists.
>
> A Bureau should be the nucleus for the sales effort in the visitor industry for that community and should also represent the point of "one stop shopping" for any prospect or client contemplating holding a convention

or trade show in that city. A Bureau must be impartial in its representation of its facilities if it is to be successful.[13]

Convention and visitors bureaus (CVBs), which may also be referred to as destination marketing organizations (DMOs), are structured in different ways. Some are membership organizations to which hotels, transportation companies, restaurants, and local merchants turn to organize efforts to bring in convention business. Others are funded through **room taxes** and work to promote general tourism. In some cases, they operate exhibition halls that were built with public funds.

The convention bureau's sales office is set up similarly to a hotel sales office, but on a larger scale. Its job, sometimes called **destination marketing**, is to sell the city, bring conventions to the area, and to make the group's stay productive and enjoyable (see box titled "Destination Marketing"). CVBs primarily use print advertising, television spots, and participation in trade shows to promote their areas. And, like hotels, they are increasingly making use of social media and technology to attract meeting planners. CVBs use such sites as Facebook, Twitter, and YouTube to reach planners and provide a means for planners

---

### INTERNET EXERCISE

### Destination Marketing

Log on to the website of the Destination Marketing Association International (DMAI), the membership association for Convention and Visitors Bureaus, at www.destinationmarketing.org. Navigate the site to answer the following questions:

1. How do convention bureaus help meeting planners?

2. If convention bureaus don't charge for their services, how do they make money?

3. What resources and benefits are available for student members of this organization?

4. DMAI maintains the Meeting Information Network (MINT), an online database that contains profiles of more than 40,000 events conducted by more than 20,000 organizations. How can this extensive database help hotels to garner leads and qualify prospects?

---

to promote their events to increase attendance (this practice is known as "delegate boosting"). A number of CVBs have also developed apps to showcase their locations. These apps, which are available for iPhones, iPods, and iPod Touch, include Tourism Vancouver, Visit Denver, and Boston USA. While content varies, apps almost always include an overview of the city or area and its attractions, and some may offer calendars of events and, as in the case of Boston USA, a means to purchase tickets to local attractions.

When a bureau receives a letter or phone call from a meeting group saying the city has been selected for its convention, the bureau sends out a **convention lead form** to local hotels (see Figure 7.11). Many bureaus now distribute this information electronically, sending leads to selected hotels via the Internet. The hotel may then contact the group. Because CVBs are experts in arranging logistics for meetings, some planners see them as an extension of their own staff; one meeting planner said that she couldn't imagine a meeting without her external team at the CVB.

In addition to providing leads to area hotels and convention support firms, the bureau also assists in executing conventions, often supplying registration clerks, guides, spouses' program personnel, and so on. Most important for hotels, most convention bureaus also provide a housing bureau for placing delegates in the city's hotels when large conventions are booked.

If your area has a convention bureau, it most likely is a member of the Destination Marketing Association International (DMAI). If so, you are fortunate, because DMAI of-

*Figure 7.11. SAMPLE CONVENTION LEAD FORM.*

---

# SAN FRANCISCO
## CONVENTION & VISITORS BUREAU
1390 MARKET STREET, SAN FRANCISCO, CALIFORNIA 94102

### CONVENTION LEAD FORM

Date: xxx

**TO** All major hotels

**FROM** Matt Miller

**GROUP** XYZ CORPORATION

**CONTACT** Mr. John Jones **TITLE** Convention Manager

**ADDRESS** 6000 K Street N.W.

**CITY** Washington, DC 20097 **PHONE** (202) 123-4567

**ATTENDANCE** 500 **NO OF ROOMS** 350

**EXHIBIT SPACE NET SQ FT** 4000

**REQUESTED DATES** February 3-6, February 10-13, 2017
arrivals 2/2 or 2/9; departures 2/7 or 2/14

**MEETING REQUIREMENTS**

| | |
|---|---|
| 2/2 or 2/9 | 6 p.m. reception for 300 people |
| 2/3 or 2/10 | 8 a.m. breakfast for 150 |
| | 12 noon lunch for 500 |
| | 9:00-5:00 general session for 500 theatre style |
| 2/4 or 2/11 | 9:00-12 noon 5 workshops for 100 each theatre style; afternoon free |
| 2/5 or 2/12 | 9:00-12 noon general session for 500 theatre style |
| | 12 noon reception & lunch for 500 |
| | 2:00-5:00 5 workshops for 100 each |
| 2/6 or 2/13 | 9:00-12 noon general session for 500 theatre style |
| | 7 p.m. reception & dinner dance for 500 people |

San Francisco is definite; hotel selection within three months

**Please copy the Bureau on all your correspondance**

**History**

| | | |
|---|---|---|
| 2015 | New Orleans | 476 registered; 327 rooms used |
| 2016 | Las Vegas | 498 registered; 319 rooms used |

---

*This is an example of a form sent by the San Francisco Convention & Visitors Bureau to hotels in the city, advising them of an upcoming convention. Note that the form includes the group's requirements (number of rooms, types of functions that will be held, room space requirements, etc.) to enable hotels to decide if they can realistically service the business.*

## Chapter 7: Selling to the Meetings Market

> ### 🖳 INTERNET EXERCISE
>
> ### Virtual Site Inspections
>
> Interactive, 360-degree, and 3-D virtual site inspections are now available on the websites of some hotels. For example, Starwood Hotels has rolled out a virtual event planner that allows meeting planners to view photos of sample event setups (including classroom, theater, cocktail, and banquet setups) that they can customize. Details can be modified — from linen color and the placement of tables and chairs to adding a stage or dance floor. Other hotels offer virtual tours that are less interactive, allowing only a 360-degree pan around empty rooms.
> Visit the websites below and assess each from a meeting planner's perspective:
>
> - www.radisonblu.com/hotel-berlin (click on the Virtual Tours tab)
> - www.rosencentre.com/photo-gallery/virtual-tours
> - www.biltmorehotel.com/resort/tour.php
>
> 1. Do you think virtual site tours can replace physical site inspections?
>
> 2. What considerations important to event planners cannot be shown in a virtual site inspection?
>
> 3. Search the Internet and find other hotels or convention centers that offer virtual tours on their websites. What features do you find most appealing and why? If you could design a virtual site inspection, what features would you include?

fers a wealth of detailed, confidential information to assist you in your selling efforts. Each DMAI member receives and files reports dealing with convention performances and characteristics of all associations that convened within the member's city. This data includes promised attendance and actual attendance figures, prices paid, concessions granted, and almost everything else you would want to know about a prospect. When you track a convention over a period of five years, a pattern emerges that enables you to decide whether or not you have a good chance to get such business — and how to go after it.

In addition to maintaining records on major associations and corporations, bureaus also subscribe to key association and corporate publications, such as the *Encyclopedia of Associations,* and make them available to local hotels for research. These types of publications are invaluable in securing the meetings market, but are often too expensive for individual properties to purchase.

The most important facet of working with convention bureaus, however, is the advantage of pooled resources. The convention bureau serves as a coordinator when the size of an event makes it mandatory to present the sales proposal as a group and to house the delegates in a number of hotels. And, since the convention bureau's function is to promote the area as a whole, its efforts — exhibitions at trade shows, print advertising, and direct mail efforts — will directly benefit your property and serve as an additional marketing resource in helping you to obtain business.

## Site Inspection Selling and Familiarization Tours

One of the best ways to show exactly what your property has to offer is to invite the meeting planner to visit it personally to experience your facilities and services for themselves. This can be done in two ways: on an individual basis *(site inspection selling)* or in a structured

## Shopping Around
How many hotels do you usually visit before booking?

- One: 44%
- Two: 32%
- Three: 15%
- Four or more: 9%

Source: Art Pfenning, "Site Visits Still Key," *Meetings & Conventions*

group setting *(familiarization or "fam" tours)*, offer a number of planners the chance to experience what the hotel has to offer.

Many meeting planners will not book a site unless they have had the opportunity to see it personally. In a recent survey conducted by *Meetings & Conventions* magazine and NTM Research, 90 percent of all planners reported that they personally visit potential meeting sites before making a final decision (see sidebar titled "Shopping Around").[14]

Therefore, a **site inspection tour**, at which prospective clients are invited to personally tour your hotel, is an ideal sales situation. Site inspection selling is most effective if the following guidelines are followed:

- Always schedule a visit when the property is busy. This will give the planner an opportunity to see your efficient service in action — and will give credibility to your claims of excellence.
- Don't be too busy, however, to devote time to the planner. He or she should be greeted like a guest, and should have the opportunity to meet those people with whom he or she will be dealing (the catering manager, convention services manager, and so on).
- Alert the staff of the impending site inspection. If possible, post a photograph of the meeting planner and provide pertinent information to enable employees to greet the planner by name. Some properties establish guidelines for employee involvement in their SOPs; if your property has such a standard operating procedure, make sure that all staff is aware of their roles in the site visit and what questions they are authorized to answer for the planner.
- A welcoming note from the general manager upon the planner's arrival and a brief visit with the general manager sometime during the visit are good gestures. Many planners indicate they can tell a lot about how a hotel is run by meeting the general manager.
- Feature only those items of interest to the planner. Don't waste everyone's time showing your state-of-the-art audiovisual equipment to a planner whose focus will be social functions or recreational activities.
- Train a number of staff personnel to serve as "tour guides" in the event a salesperson is away. These staff members should be able to answer questions — and sell features as benefits. It is also helpful if they can offer supplemental material, such as photographs of past successful events, third-party endorsements, and so on, to capture the planner's interest.
- Remember the purpose of suggesting a site inspection: selling. Knowing your property, competition, and prospect are keys. Follow the six steps of personal selling discussed at the beginning of this chapter. Laura Anevedo, a former meeting planner for Alder Droz, Inc., says:

> My favorite part about site inspections is being able to visualize my next meeting taking place at the prospective property. Usually the salesperson is putting his/her best foot forward in order to capture the busines and is

really excited about showing off the property. If the salesperson has done homework on my past programs, he/she can really be influential in my ultimate decision to book a program at that property.[15]

Many of today's meeting planners, especially those who plan a number of small meetings, do not have time to personally tour every hotel that can potentially stage their meetings. Hotels are responding by offering *virtual site tours*.

Virtual site tours generally include a panoramic view of the property's exterior, guestrooms, meeting rooms, banquet facilities, recreational amenities, and nearby attractions. These features may be presented in a series of static photos that are put together as a slideshow or video; audio may be used to enhance the presentation. These tours are even more realistic when a 3D element is used, and now a 4D format is being used by the Marriott chain. First introduced at the New York Marriott Marquis, the "Get Teleported" presentations featured such locations as Boston, Dallas, London, Maui, Hawaii, Washington, DC, and Dallas, and offered content ranging from "flyovers" of the city's skyscrapers to a "visit" to Maui's beaches. While these presentations were primarily focused on a destination to offer planners a look at the location before deciding to visit there, multi-media presentations are increasingly being used by individual properties to attract business.

While some hotels already offer photographs and moving images of their guestrooms and their meeting facilities on their websites, it is much more effective for a hotel to combine this sales tool with an actual telephone call with a salesperson. In this way, the salesperson can determine the planner's needs and steer him or her to specific features of interest as well as answer any questions that might arise.

If a hotel targets several market segments, it should consider tailoring virtual tours to individual segment needs. Some hotels create a "bank" of digital photographs to enable them to present features most important to a potential client. Whether these photographs are presented online or e-mailed to the client, you will capture far more business if a "live" representative from the property walks the prospect through the presentation.

**Familiarization (fam) tours** require more planning than individual site inspection visits, and, since they can be expensive for the property, involve qualifying prospective visitors. Michael Smith, former director and vice president of convention sales for the Portland, Oregon Visitors' Association, states:

> We do not invite people just because they happen to plan meetings. Unless they are seriously thinking of meeting in Portland, they are not invited. Our members need to know that the people we are bringing in are legitimate and the trip is an investment.[16]

Qualified meeting planners may be contacted either by mail or telephone, and should be given a reasonable lead time to make plans (four to six weeks is the norm). If a group tour, planners invited should have similar professional needs. One planner stated:

> I hate to go on fams where everyone is an association planner and I'm the only corporate planner. They show you everything from an association standpoint, and there's a big difference between the needs of an association meeting planner and a corporate meeting planner.

The property should let attendees know exactly what the fam tour involves: its duration; what is included (meals, transportation, etc.); and whom the invitation includes (spouse, other members of the selection committee, etc.). When the meeting planners arrive for the tour, they should be greeted individually and given a schedule of events. Events

## Chapter 7: Selling to the Meetings Market

should be planned to show prospects exactly what the property can offer (see "Best Practices" box titled "Sheraton San Marcos Qualifies Prospects For Fam Tours"). Staff members usually handle property tours, although an outside person (a member of the local convention and visitors bureau, for example) may conduct off-property tours of the area's leisure and cultural activities.

As with individual site-inspection selling, property salespeople should try to get a meeting commitment before the guests leave the property. If this is not possible (in some cases, for example, the planner must report back to the site selection committee), the fam tour should be followed up as soon as possible. Many properties include a questionnaire in their follow-up letter, asking what the participants liked and disliked. This type of questionnaire not only can assist the property to plan better fam tours, but can also be used to provide insights into the needs, likes, and dislikes of the individual participants.

Fam tours not only bring business from the participants, but can influence their peers as well. Today, a number of properties are using technology to make their fam tours available to a wide audience of meeting planners. A fam tour, marketed to a specific segment of planners, can be recorded and made available on a CD or DVD and/or posted on the

---

**Best Practices**

**Sheraton**

### Sheraton San Marcos Qualifies Prospects For Fam Tours

George Mittler, former director of sales at the Sheraton San Marcos in Chandler, Arizona, also believes in qualifying prospects, and achieved remarkable results from his semiannual fam tours. He explains:

> "At the Sheraton San Marcos Resort, we have found the formula to successful fam trips. After spending $40,000 on our two semiannual fam trips, we booked $900,000 in business as a direct result of the trips. Resorts generally strive for ten times the return on the money invested in a fam tour, but we consistently come back with more than 20 times the investment. In fact, on every fam tour we've organized in the past two years, we've booked business while meeting planners were still on-site.

> "Competition in our area is stiff, so you have to develop a niche. Ours has been to go above and beyond what the competitors offer. We sell service and successful meetings. We train our people, and everybody from the general manager to the busboys sells the resort. Our philosophy of involving the entire staff as salespeople is the reason we convert so many fam trippers into clients.

> "To fascinate the fam trippers, we stage three major events while they're here: a 'Meeting Planners Invitational Golf Tournament,' 'Dinner in the Desert,' and a '50s Night' or a 'Casino Theme Night' dinner-dance. The whole point of these extravaganzas is to demonstrate to planners how the San Marcos can plan and carry out theme events.

> "Since it costs about $400 to $500 per person, not counting airfare, to host fam-trip guests, we pre-qualify fam trippers. The days of 'Come eat my shrimp and drink my booze' are long over, so we make sure these people are qualified. To cut costs, we also co-sponsor with a local airline."

Source: From correspondence with George Mittler.

## Summary

As you can see, personal selling — whether it be an individual effort, such as a face-to-face sales call or telephone call, or a strategy to sell to groups at a trade show — plays a key role in booking meetings. In this chapter, we have looked at the six steps of a personal sales call, examined how the telephone is used in selling to the meetings market, and discussed other direct sales tools, including the sales blitz, trade show selling, selling with convention and visitors bureaus, site inspection selling, and "fam" tours.

But direct selling is not the only way to introduce your property to meeting planners. In the next chapter, we will see how *advertising* can supplement your sales efforts. We will take a look at how this sales tool can work hand-in-hand with personal selling to help generate lucrative meetings market business for your property.

## Endnotes

1. Yeoh Siew Hoon, "Don't Forget the Power of the Sales Call," *Hoteliers: Hospitality, Hotel & Travel News.*
2. From the keynote speech by Bob Gilbert at the HSMAI's 10th Annual Asia/Connect Conference, September 3, 2014, and posted on the HSMAI website.
3. "Interviews With Marketing Leaders," *HSMAI Marketing Review.*
4. Rayna Katz, "Planners as Honest as Relationships Dictate," *Meeting News.*
5. "A New Approach to Selling," *The Meeting Professional.*
6. Rayna Katz, "Planners, Sales Reps Often Out of Sync," *Meeting News.*
7. Joan Barker, "Stand Out in the Crowd," *HSMAI Marketing Review.*
8. Robert Gilbert, "Mastering the Basics," *Lodging.*
9. Tom McCarthy, "Don't Forget to Rehearse," *Lodging Hospitality.*
10. Becky Cumming and Melina Legos, "Squaring Off," *Successful Meetings.*
11. Rayna Katz, "Hilton Eases Buying Process Via Package of Web Enhancements," *Meeting News.*
12. Ruth Hill, "Lost and Found," *HSMAI Marketing Review.*
13. From correspondence with Bill Snyder, past president, Anaheim Convention and Visitors Bureau.
14. Art Pfenning, "Site Visits Still Key," *Meetings & Conventions.*
15. "In the Trenches," *Meetings in the West.*
16. Suzanne Miller and Ross Weiland, "Planners Want Better Fam Trips," *Meeting News.*

## Study Questions

1. Identify the steps in making a personal sales call. Why is each important?

# Chapter 7: Selling to the Meetings Market

2. List the steps in making a telephone appointment call. Why is follow-up especially important after making telephone contact? What kind of follow-up can be done?
3. In what other ways is the telephone used to sell to and service customers?
4. What is a sales blitz? Why can a sales blitz be a cost-effective sales tool?
5. What is a trade show? How can a property make the most of its trade show exhibit?
6. What are the advantages of working with a convention and visitors bureau to secure business?
7. What is a "fam" tour? What steps should a property take to ensure that a "fam" tour is successful?

## Key Terms

**appointment call**—A prearranged appointment with a prospect to introduce the features and benefits offered by a property. During this visit, the salesperson may or may not attempt to close the sale.

**call report**—A document, usually resulting from some personal contact, that provides general information about an account (address, contact person, etc.) as well as remarks on the needs of the group and any action steps that can be taken to sell the hotel's products and services to the group.

**close-ended question**—A question requiring a specific answer that often can be given in just a few words.

**cold call**—A fact-finding call on a prospect with whom there has been little or no previous contact; often made without a definite appointment. Sometimes referred to as **canvassing**.

**consultative selling**—A customized sales presentation approach in which the salesperson is viewed as an expert and serves as a consultant to the prospect. This involves identifying the prospect's needs and recommending the best solution for meeting them — even if that solution does not include the salesperson's products or services.

**convention lead form**—Information sheet used by convention and visitors bureaus to circulate announcements about meetings to hotels, destination management companies, and other potential suppliers.

**destination marketing**—Promotion of a particular location as a meeting site and/or tourist attraction.

**familiarization (fam) tour**—Free or reduced-rate trip given to meeting planners, travel agents, travel writers, and other sources of potential business to acquaint them with a property or destination, and to stimulate the booking of an event.

**hosted-buyer program**—A trade show program that brings qualified buyers and exhibitors together on an appointment basis. The show organizer typically picks up the cost of travel and hotel expenses if the buyer is qualified and accepted into the program; a property benefits by having face-to-face meetings with potential buyers who have been "matched" to their products and services with the use of sophisticated computer software. This arrangement enables sellers to prepare "custom-tailored" presentations for interested buyers and maximize their trade show selling time.

**major close**—A question or statement at the end of a sales presentation that asks for a definite commitment on the prospect's part.

**open-ended question**—A question that gives a prospect the opportunity to express his or her feelings and knowledge.

**room tax**—Tax placed on hotel/motel room rentals. Generally all or part of the revenues generated from these taxes are used to finance the operation of convention facilities. Also called a **bed tax** or **occupancy tax**.

**presentation book**—Sometimes called a **sales kit**, this sales tool provides detailed information on a property's facilities and services. Materials should include floor plans, photographs of rooms and creative banquets, sample menus, complimentary letters from satisfied guests, and favorable press comments. In some cases, special presentation books are prepared as handouts for meeting planners visiting the property on fam tours.

**property fact book**—A summary of what a lodging property has to offer, including: number and types of guestrooms; room rates; booking policies; food service available, including menus, seating capacities, and hours of operation; descriptions, layouts, and capacities of meeting and banquet facilities; recreational facilities; and area amenities. The property fact book is used as a tool for salespeople, enabling them to translate the property's features into benefits.

**sales blitz**—Concentrated canvassing by several sales representatives of a selected geographic area over a specific time period in order to gather information on potential leads.

**site inspection tour**—Prospective customers visit the property and are given a tour that showcases such features as guestrooms, meeting facilities, food and beverage facilities, recreational amenities, and other property services, such as valet parking, shuttle service, and other services that may give the property an edge in the site-selection process.

**telemarketing**—The systematic use of the telephone for marketing or sales purposes.

**trial close**—A statement or question posed by the salesperson during a sales presentation that seeks to evoke a positive response from the client.

**virtual site tour**—An online panoramic view or video presentation of a property's facilities. Designed to give viewers a lifelike 3-D view of property features, virtual tours may consist of a collection of panoramic images that are played in sequence to simulate a moving video, or models may be used in place of real life images.

## Industry Profile

### Ed Griffin, Jr., former Executive Vice President/CEO
Meeting Professionals International

Ed Griffin, Jr., the president of Ed Griffin Consulting Group, has had a distinguished career serving public and private sector associations for over three decades. In addition to his 13-year tenure as President/CEO of Meeting Professionals International (MPI), he has also been Executive Director of the Greater Dallas Restaurant Association, President/CEO of the Florida Lodging Association, and Executive Director of the Kentucky League of Cities. Griffin has also been a member of the board for a number of associations, including the American Society of Association Executives and the Kentucky Society of Association Executives. An honorary lifetime member of the National Speakers Association, Griffin's areas of expertise include marketing/branding, legislative advocacy, political consultation, growth management, and organizational development.

### Advertising from a Meeting Planner's Perspective

Every day, I am buried under piles of advertising and direct mail. And every day, I hear planners say that advertising in our industry goes to waste. We need the information, but who wants to wade through this fluff? Like other CEOs and meeting pros, I try to keep up with what's happening, but I find I clip only the most important material.

Planners *do* want to hear from suppliers, and good advertising *will* affect a planner's decision. Good advertising can even be educational. It creates awareness and tells us about options, and shows us who's savvy and aggressive enough to develop appropriate marketing programs in good times and bad.

Studies conducted by the American Business Press have proven that advertising in business publications is an effective form of advertising. It is also one of the least expensive "cost per contact" in terms of providing customers with useful information.

Advertising wins when the meeting planner understands both the benefits and the unique qualities of a product or service. The hotel must explain how the product will satisfy the planner's needs. In order to do that, the advertiser must know what's important to the planner. Planners want to know about such things as room capacities, pricing, guarantees, restrictions, and value seasons. It is essential for your messages to be direct, simple, and concise – with copy directed specifically at the planner (with a view to planner benefits rather than product features).

Advertising is not a frill. It's a bona fide necessity in this highly competitive industry. Our industry is catching up with the sophisticated techniques of niche marketing, long used in consumer markets, and more mature business-to-business arenas. Wasted marketing dollars are a thing of the past.

At the same time, planners are trying to maximize their dollars in making effective decisions on site selection, transportation negotiations, and increasing attendee satisfaction. They're reacting to facts about how a conference or convention could be produced more effectively at a lower price.

With increasing time pressures, planners need information that's relevant. The key is focus – focus on benefits, focus on dollars, and focus on the customer. Marketing to meeting planners is a blend of many refined techniques, but the root of its success is good advertising.

**Learning Objectives:**

In this chapter, we will discuss the types of advertising most commonly used to reach the meetings market. We will also detail how to plan an advertising strategy and discuss how public relations and publicity can be used to project a positive image of your property to meeting planners. When you have studied this chapter, you will:

- Be able to describe how hospitality firms use print media and technology to advertise to the meetings market.

- Understand the purpose and types of collateral materials commonly used.

- Be able to explain how to conduct a direct mail campaign.

- Know the factors involved in planning an effective advertising strategy.

- Be able to describe how public relations and publicity enhance a property's image.

**Outline**

Print Advertising
- Trade Magazines
- Hotel Directories

Using Technology for Advertising
- The Internet
- E-mail Advertising
- Fax Transmissions

Collateral Materials
- Brochures
  - Printed Convention Brochures
  - Electronic Convention Brochures
- Other Collateral Materials
- Specialty Items

Direct Mail Advertising

Planning an Advertising Strategy
- Reach, Frequency, Timing, and Consistency
- Exchange Trade Advertising
- Cooperative Advertising and Strategic Partnerships
- Advertising Agencies

Public Relations and Publicity

Summary

# 8 Advertising to the Meeting Planner

Advertising can play a key role in your sales effort, since its primary function is to generate interest in your property. Advertising supplements your sales effort. Advertising makes prospects aware of your property before you make a sales call, while publicity and public relations help to keep your hotel's name in the minds of current and potential customers (and lend credibility to your sales and advertising efforts). Advertising is an invaluable tool for targeting meeting planners who have not previously been reached and offers additional information to those who are aware of your facilities.

When a property advertises, its message is seen by a vast audience, generating potential leads that can be followed up by the sales staff. Marketing efforts, then, should be supported by an advertising, public relations, and promotional strategy that is carefully planned and executed.

One of the benefits of advertising is that it, like sales presentations, can be "tailored" to meet the needs of potential customers. For example, properties can target the corporate segment, whose meetings are often staged by inexperienced planners, with one type of ad, and target the association segment, which looks for a desirable location as well as meeting planning assistance to increase attendance, with an ad promoting those benefits (see Figure 8.1).

While there are a number of media available, including newspapers, trade magazines, travel guides, direct mail, collateral material, outdoor advertising, radio, television, and the Internet, not all are used to reach meeting planners. Outdoor advertising (signs, billboards), radio, and television, for example, do not reach a targeted audience, so these options are a haphazard way to reach meeting planners. Newspapers can be used to reach meeting planners, but newspaper ads cannot match the quality of magazine ads – and newspapers, unlike magazines, are generally thrown away rather than being passed on to additional readers. If you do opt for newspaper advertising, you need to take steps to ensure that your ad will be seen by planners – place your ad in the business pages to reach corporate planners, the society pages or entertainment pages to attract planners looking for a venue for a banquet or special event, or consider special interest sections, such as a winter sports section, supplementary entertainment sections, or a section on your area's history or attractions (a planner may wish to hold a meeting or reunion to coincide with an interesting event to build attendance). You will have to make very specific choices based on your target customers, marketing goals, and budget.

It is important to note that traditional advertising is increasingly being replaced by *digital advertising*. It is a rare property that does not have a website to promote their facilities and services. Traditional brochures have often been replaced by virtual tours online or on DVD, and e-mail campaigns have cut the cost of direct mailings – and allow for a faster response. In addition, hospitality firms are turning to social media to engage with current and potential customers and build name recognition. We will discuss this increased use in technology in greater detail later in this chapter, but it remains important to have a firm grasp of advertising basics. Your Internet ads will be much more effective if you follow the strategies used for print ads, and a successful e-mail marketing campaign can be developed by using the basic direct mail techniques discussed later in this chapter.

270

*Figure 8.1. SAMPLE PRINT AD.*

**I want** someone to make me look good with my board, attendees and exhibitors.

Ask about
**Wyndham Meeting Rewards**

Earn up to 25,000 miles
$500 event credit
Palm™ m515 and more

**WHAT'S YOUR REQUEST?**℠ Do you want enough coffee to keep 300 people on the edge of their seats? Or someone to take care of the things you haven't even thought of yet? We'd like to hear about it. Tell the meeting managers at Wyndham your idea of the perfect meeting and they'll make it happen – and give you a special reward when it's over.
Call us or visit our website. **1.888.WYNDHAM** www.wyndham.com

WYNDHAM PHOENIX   602-333-0000
50 East Adams Street • Phoenix, Arizona 85004
one block west of Phoenix Civic Plaza Convention Center

**WYNDHAM PHOENIX**

*This print ad for the Wyndham Phoenix appeals to the personal needs of association meeting planners, who answer to a board, attendees, and exhibitors. Promising the services of a skilled professional to ensure that the meeting planner stages a successful event, the ad also promotes special rewards for booking a meeting at the hotel. This ad includes all the successful elements of a print ad: a headline (promoting a benefit), a photograph, copy to support the benefit in the headline, and a logo and contact information at the lower portion of the ad.*

## Print Advertising

One way to reach meeting planners is through **print advertising**. Most meeting planners look for information. Advertising in printed media most likely to be seen by meeting planners can increase your property's chances of generating meetings business.

While some properties advertise in such newspapers as the *Wall Street Journal* and magazines such as *Fortune* and *Time*, which are often read by meeting planners, the most promising print media in which to advertise is **trade magazines.** We have included a number of these magazines in the following section, and you can refer back to Chapters 4, 5, and

6 to see other magazines used to reach corporate, association, and nonprofit meeting planners.

## Trade Magazines

Magazine advertising offers several advantages. First, ads can be printed in color and photographs reproduced with good quality. Second, many magazines have a long reading life. Back issues of some magazines are kept and reread, and are often passed on to others, giving ads a longer life. Third, and most important, magazine advertising gives the hotel an opportunity to key its convention promotion efforts to a select group of readers.

Once you have opted to use print advertising, you will need to develop effective print ads. Good print ads don't just happen. They are carefully thought out and targeted toward a specific audience (see Figure 8.2).

The most effective ads follow the AIDA principle, which focuses on *attention, interest, desire,* and *action*. To attract *attention*, your ad must stand out from the rest. In most cases, this is done through the use of a **headline** or eye-catching illustration. If an illustration is used, it must tie in with the copy of the ad. Whenever possible, use *color* to attract attention. If your budget prohibits using full-color ads, even a property with limited funds can use black plus one other color to draw attention to key points.

To keep the reader *interested*, your **body copy** should be specific and to the point. Don't be reluctant to use plenty of white space and large or bold type for easy readability. Use bulleted lists for key points. Keep the copy simple, using short sentences and words that are easy to understand. Make your ad quick to read and easy to comprehend.

> **WORTH WATCHING**
>
> Steve Bartolin, the former president and CEO and now chairman of The Broadmoor, explains the property's unprecedented guarantee to meeting planners dealing with an economic downturn at meetingsnet.com/video/broadmoor-guarantee-meeting.

To build *desire*, the text should present your features as benefits and tell the reader why your property is different. If you offer special services to meeting planners, tell them so — and offer this as a benefit to them. The print ad in Figure 8.3, for example, promotes the unique guarantee offered to meeting planners who booked meetings at The Broadmoor in Colorado Springs.

In an unprecedented move, the hotel promised to waive all master account fees if a meeting or incentive program didn't meet the planner's expectations for value, service, facilities, and quality. The ad appeared in several major magazines, including *Corporate & Incentive Travel, Successful Meetings,* and *Insurance & Financial Meeting Management,* as well as on several websites in addition to The Broadmoor's own site.

You may also want to include photographs of your expertise in action. But don't make the mistake of including a photograph of an empty room — nothing looks more sterile. Portray action by including people in your meeting or function room photographs.

Last, but certainly not least, you will want to create an ad that stimulates *action* on the part of the reader. Since the primary purpose of your ad is to generate a response, offer a way to do so. Today, most properties include their website and e-mail addresses and a toll-free number to encourage prompt responses. Reply cards can also be included in your ad, and several magazines offer a directory of advertisers (respondents check the ads of interest on a reply card inserted into the magazine and information is sent to them). Peter Warren, past president of the Hotel Sales & Marketing Association International and owner of one of the leading hospitality advertising firms, says:

**Figure 8.2. EFFECTIVE PRINT ADS BOOST THE BOTTOM LINE.**

This ad, part of the "Omni Understands" campaign, promotes the chain's multi-year/multi-program contract that enables meeting planners to book multiple meetings – over several years, if required – by negotiating just one contract. This eliminates the need for planners to negotiate the terms for each of their meetings and allows them to devote their time to actually planning their meetings.
**Source: Courtesy of Omni Hotels & Resorts.**

# Chapter 8: Advertising to the Meeting Planner

*Figure 8.3. PROMOTING A UNIQUE BENEFIT IN PRINT ADS*

While it is important for every hotel to offer a benefit that differentiates them from the competition, this is especially important in the luxury segment. The Broadmoor, an upscale meetings property in Colorado Springs, Colorado, offered a benefit never before offered to meeting planners: "The Broadmoor Guarantee." The offer was clear and simple: "Your meeting is exceptional. Or it's free. Period."

No other U.S. hotel has matched the Broadmoor's offer, as many hoteliers are fearful that clients will take advantage of guarantees and revenues will be lost. But when a hotel guarantees its product, it sends a message that the property is confident in its products and services.

**Source: The Broadmoor, Colorado Springs, Colorado.**

The purpose of your ad should be to begin the process of "awareness, interest, desire, then action." A mistake made by some clients is to expect the ad to do everything, so they try to make their ads into brochures. Because a one-page ad cannot tell the whole story, entice them to visit your website where they can find a more compelling story, or call an 800 number for more information.[1]

Always be sure your ad includes your property's name, address, and your **logo**. It is highly effective to have ads that are readily identifiable, and, since your logo is distinctly yours, it should be used in all media efforts (it generally appears toward the bottom of the ad).

Once you have developed the components of your ad, you will have to decide on how you want it positioned in the magazine. Magazine space is sold in a variety of sizes (see Figure 8.4). You will have to determine which size and placement will work best for your ad. Choices that can enhance readership include:

- Three single-page ads that appear on consecutive right-hand pages.
- Two single-page ads that appear on right-hand pages in different sections of the same issue.

*Figure 8.4. MAGAZINE SPACE OPTIONS.*

| Full Page | 2/3 Page Vertical | 1/3 Page Vertical / 1/3 Page Square | 1/4 Page Vertical / 1/4 Page Square |
|---|---|---|---|
| 1/2 Page Vertical | 1/2 Page Horizontal | Island 1/2 Page | 1/6 Page Vertical / 1/6 Page Horizontal |

The standard magazine page is 7x10 inches. Tabloid publications are larger. A popular tabloid size is 10x14 inches, but tabloids do vary in dimension. The ad sizes offered by tabloid publications are, of course, a full tabloid page, a junior page (which is usually 7x10 and is positioned like the half-page island in a magazine), and smaller ads that usually follow the sizes and designations of the magazine format like above. There are many variations and combinations that can be used; for example, two 1/2 page horizontal ads running across two facing pages. These shown are the most common and universally accepted by publications. "Bleed" is the term used when the ad extends beyond its usual border out to the very edge of the paper. Most publications make an additional charge for bleed ads.

*Magazine ad space is sold by the page or fraction of a page, and ads can be positioned in standard layouts in a variety of ways. These are some of the sizes and placements most commonly used.*

- A two-page spread.
- A full-page ad on a right-hand page.
- A full-page ad on a right-hand page with a strip (one-column) ad on a left-hand page.

Other magazine advertising options that heighten readership include the use of **gatefolds** (oversized pages or portions of pages added to a regular page) and inserts, which can range from a simple business reply card to a full-page color section bound into the magazine. Keep in mind that magazines charge extra for these options – and for certain ad positions, including the back cover, the insides of the front and back covers, and the center spread (a double-page spread in the center of the magazine).

The positioning of your ad is important. Studies have shown that the reader's eye is drawn initially to the upper part of the right-hand page. For an ad smaller than a full page, the position on the upper right-hand page might mean more readership. It is even more preferable to have your ad positioned in the editorial section of the magazine; when possible, ask that your ad be the only hotel ad on the page. The magazine's placement of your small ad next to competing ads may reduce its efficiency. Sometimes you can negotiate to avoid such circumstances; sometimes an additional fee will guarantee it. Good position, facing editorial copy, will help your ad do the job.

The size and frequency of your ad is largely dependent on your budget. While some properties can afford full-page color ads, other properties have to opt for smaller ads if they are to place them frequently. Ads are like sales calls; frequency is important. Your prospects may require several exposures to your advertising before they respond. Advertising gurus advise you to run ads at least every other month throughout the year. If, in your eyes, a publication doesn't warrant six ads a year, perhaps you ought to rethink your decision to advertise in it at all. Frequency is important for effective advertising.

You can get information on the circulation or audience of print media from a number of sources, including **publisher's statements** that list the publication's circulation, subscription rates, distribution, and other pertinent information, such as the type of readership they serve. The publisher's statements also include a *circulation audit*. These audits, usually performed by a third party, are more reliable than research statistics from the publication alone, as they break down circulation by qualified (paid) circulation and non-qualified circulation (free issues that are sent to advertisers, sample copies, and so on). The fact that the numbers look good on a publisher's statement doesn't necessarily mean that the publication will meet your needs, however. If a publication is unfamiliar to you, it is a good idea to ask for a sample copy or a list of current advertisers; its editorial content may not match your image or its pages might be cluttered with the ads of competitors. Additional information concerning publisher's statements can be found on the website of the Standard Rate and Data Service at http://next.srds.com (click on the For Agencies and Marketers tab). The SRDS researches newspapers, magazines, and broadcast media, and it offers educational tools for students.

## Hotel Directories

Meeting planners who use hotel directories are looking for *facts*. Printed hotel and business directories list property information in a standard format, giving a planner the opportunity to "comparison shop" a number of factors, including location, facilities, transportation, and price. Most directories also provide for the insertion of a small photograph, and some also offer the opportunity to purchase a larger ad for your property.

Print directories are not usually published on a monthly basis, so you have a "one-shot" chance at reaching meeting planners. Additionally, there are few print directories today that are published nationally; most cover only a particular city or region. These directories, often published by convention and visitors bureaus, chambers of commerce, or tourism-related firms, can be useful to help you reach planners in your immediate area, but your advertising may not be seen by planners in key target cities.

Today, most of the "traditional" hotel directories have been replaced by online versions. The *Hotel & Travel Index*, which was used by the industry for decades, for example, is now part of Northstar Travel Media's online catalog (www.northstartravelmedia.com/Data-Products/Hotel-and-Travel-Index/), and a number of other directories can be found on several sites, including www.travelweekly.com/Hotels (a searchable database of *Travel Weekly*), issuu.com/search?q-meeting+planner+guide, and www.hotel-d.com. Hotels can also get listed on other sites that are accessed by meeting planners, such as www.meetings-conventions.com/meeting-facilities/, a facilities search service of MPI, and Convention Bureaus (www.conventionbureaus.com); this site offers both free listings and a premium package (no competitors' ads on the property's listing page) for hotels. Since many meeting planners turn to CVBs when planning an event, this can be an excellent way to get your property's name before this market.

Directories vary widely in scope; some include thousands of worldwide listings, while others list only the properties in a single chain (these generally include links to each individual property website). Most online directories also sell advertising space in addition to providing listings (we will discuss the various types of ads later in this chapter). There are several advantages to online advertising, including being able to provide much more information than is possible in a print ad (it is not uncommon to find mapping features and links to virtual tours and the property's website, for example), information can easily be updated, and your ad can be readily accessed on a 24/7 basis.

## Using Technology for Advertising

Over the past few years, a number of new technologies have made a difference in how hotels market themselves to the meetings market. While print advertising is still used to get a property's message out, these new technologies make it even easier for a property to reach new and existing customers and to interact with them in exciting new ways.

*Digital marketing* brings the techniques of traditional marketing to digital channels, but it is a unique vehicle because it is based on the psychology of sales – an understanding of customer behavior. In today's connected world, meeting planners are digitally empowered. They are typically relying less on their desktop computers and becoming multi-device users; most carry at least two devices – the two most common being smartphones and tablets – making it easy for them to access information whenever it is convenient for them. Therefore, today's planners are more likely to make meetings decisions based on their own research; they are no longer dependent on the aid of property salespeople to make meeting decisions.

Although meeting planners may not rely on hotel salespeople for site selection and other meeting decisions, digital marketing is an important tool to keep in touch with customers. With digital marketing, communication is instantaneous. Because of the advantages and increasing use of digital channels, the Hospitality Sales & Marketing Association International (HSMAI) has created a Certified Hospitality Digital Marketer (CHDM) designation, and dozens of articles on the topic can be found with an Internet search.

In order to most effectively compete for a planner's attention, hotels today are developing **content marketing**; this means providing information that will make the jobs of meeting planners easier while establishing your property as one they can trust – and use for future meetings. These planners are not likely to be viewing your site or reading an e-mail from your property solely to see advertisements or news of special promotions; they are looking for valuable information that will help them to execute a successful meeting. This information may include news about local attractions and transportation options as well as meeting planning tips and suggestions for memorable events.

To make the most of content advertising, it is important to know what is foremost on the minds of your meeting clients. This can be done by creating surveys or simply asking for suggestions. You can also involve clients in the content process by asking them to share their photographs and experiences – not in the context of helping you to create content, but to put them in the spotlight. Once you have developed a strong content marketing approach, you can use it in a number of ways to reach current clients and attract potential business.

The most commonly used Internet strategies include creating your own website, optimizing your website for mobile users as well as for search engines, advertising on other websites commonly used by meeting planners, and interacting with planners (and their groups) through social media. Since there are so many options available, it is especially important to develop a strategy for your Internet marketing – and to budget adequately for associated costs (you can view a typical digital advertising budget at www.hebsdigital.com/blog/the-smart-hoteliers-guide-to-2015-digital-marketing-budget-planning).

> **WORTH WATCHING**
>
> When Le Méridien Hotels, a Starwood brand, introduced its re-branding campaign, "Destination Unlocked," it created a short video offering an inside view of the creative process. Use a search engine and type in: youtube, Le Meridien brand design refresh. Note that the You Tube page for the video includes links to numerous social media sites to enable viewers to share the video with their social networks as well as the Comments feature for viewers' input.

Create a yearly plan for both general Internet marketing and social media marketing to ensure that funds are allocated for designing (or updating) your website, purchasing domain names or paying fees for hosting services, paying pay-per-click or premium position charges, funding the cost of developing ads and videos, and paying for site maintenance. You may also have to budget for additional staff and/or outside firms to monitor your sites, especially your social media sites, and you will need to develop methods of tracking your Internet campaigns to ensure that you are getting the most value from your online efforts.

## The Internet

The Internet is the heart of digital marketing. According to the recent Meetings Market Report, some 99 percent of association planners use the computer to help plan meetings, and other benefits cited from using the Internet include its 24-hour availability, a wealth of up-to-date information on potential meeting sites (not only locally, but also around the world), and the ability to "interact" on most sites (RFPs and booking options are usually readily available).

Using the Internet also saves time and money while making a planner's job easier. Cathi Shurety, meetings and events coordinator for Aluma Systems in Concord, Ontario, Canada, says:

The Internet definitely makes it easier for me to do my job. Now when a department comes to me with a meeting request, I can come up with a list of potential venues based on their criteria within half a day. Before the Internet, we mostly looked at local venues. Now I can easily inspect properties anywhere in the world.[2]

It is a rare property today that doesn't have its own website, and e-mail, instant messaging, and videos are other avenues used to promote hospitality products and services and build relationships with meeting planners. In the following sections, we will take a closer look at the Internet options that are most commonly used to attract business and build and maintain relationships with your clients and potential customers.

**Property Website.** Every property, whether large or small, should have an Internet presence in order to reach potential customers who turn to the web to research lodging properties and book rooms and meeting space. Websites should provide an overview of your hospitality products and services, and they can also be used to quickly get the word out about special promotions, rate changes, personnel changes, expansions, and other news of interest that will help in making a meeting site decision. Therefore, even if your property is part of a chain, you should still have your own site to offer additional information about both your facilities and the local area.

According to a recent Meetings Market Report by *Meetings & Conventions* magazine, two-thirds of the meeting planners surveyed access individual hotel websites to make meeting site decisions. The following website elements were considered "extremely useful" by both association and corporate planners: floor plans; meeting space specifications; maps/directions; destination information; photographs; virtual tours; meeting management tools; facility search; special dates/rates; and video.

Websites should be designed to be visually appealing, but before we get into website content, it is important to mention that easy navigation is critical. Your website is of little value if your property cannot be found or if planners find it difficult to quickly access needed information (if that is the case, they are likely to look elsewhere). In order to ensure that you will reach as many meeting planners (and other target markets) as possible, you will need to employ two strategies: search engine optimization and a mobile optimized website. **Search engine optimization** involves using key words and phrases that will bring your name to the attention of people using search engines. Categories of key words include your property's type (resort, boutique hotel, dedicated meetings facility), nearby attractions (beaches, recreational opportunities, popular shopping districts), and physical location (your property's name would appear in such destination searches as "hotels near Vancouver, British Columbia" or "hotels near Denver International Airport").

> **MORE ONLINE**
> Additional information and examples showing the difference between mobile optimized and mobile compatible websites as well as suggestions on how to create an effective mobile optimized site is presented at blog.leonardo.com/mobile-compatible-vs-mobile-optimized-whats-the-difference.

Most search engines will also display results from other sources in which your name is mentioned, such as online news releases, online travel agency sites and travel reviews, and even social media posts. There are a number of firms that offer search engine optimization services to ensure that your property achieves its maximum online presence.

A **mobile optimized website** is a *separate website* designed specifically for the smaller screens of smartphones and tablet computers. A mobile optimized website is differ-

## Chapter 8: Advertising to the Meeting Planner

ent than a *mobile compatible website*, which offers content that can be read on a mobile device, but it is a mistake to try to squeeze your regular web content into the reduced screen space – the result will be poor both visually and in terms of navigation.

Since a recent study conducted by Google found that 61 percent of shoppers will leave a website if it is not optimized for their mobile devices, it is important that every property that wishes to attract meeting planners, who typically use at least two mobile devices, have a mobile optimized website. An ideal mobile optimized website is generally ten to 15 pages of content, with each page designed to fit entirely on the screen of a mobile devise. Mobile users typically spend less time on the web than when using a desktop or laptop, so be sure to maximize your content, including only the most pertinent details.

Also important for your mobile site are location-based mobile services (such as mapping and directions based on mobile GPS capabilities) and check-in and check-out capabilities (many planners and meeting attendees prefer to use their mobile devices to check in on the way from the airport). Although some properties have developed **mobile apps** to enable guests to make reservations or check in, many industry experts feel that it is more cost-effective to allocate funds for the development of mobile websites rather than apps. Many hotels today include a link to their mobile site on their primary web page.

> **MORE ONLINE**
>
> Read more about effective hotel website design at www.hotelnewsnow.com/article/15054/6-tenets-of-good-hotel-website-design.

Hotel websites will vary significantly, depending on the property and the services it promotes, but all websites feature a "home page" at a specific "address" on the web. The home page typically includes the property's name, logo, and a "menu" of information from which to select. If a chain services a number of market segments, it is best to provide links to information of specific interest. The Marriott chain, for example, includes a Meetings & Events tab on its website, the InterContinental Hotels Group offers information for both professional and occasional meeting planners on its website (see illustration in this chapter), and the Hyatt chain promotes its online meetings management tools both on its website and with print advertising (see Figure 8.5).

The best, most effective homepages are visually attractive and should project the company's image or positioning. As with other advertising, the first step is to attract attention, and the homepage should also feature navigational links (text, an icon, an image, or some combination) to direct planners to site content that showcases your meeting facilities and other items of interest. Links should include other features and tools that will assist planners, including meeting guides, special offers and promotions, links to your social media sites, and, most importantly, a way to communicate with your hotel, including Request for Proposal (RFP) forms and links to direct e-mail contacts with key hotel personnel, such as the convention service manager, food and beverage manager, and so on. Most hotel websites consist of more than one page. Additional pages, called **landing pages**, can be categorized as *reference* (information) or *transactional* (business/customer engagement, such as obtaining an e-mail address or making a booking). Having multiple landing pages enables targeted segments to access pertinent information quickly; having categories will also result

> **WORTH WATCHING**
>
> Industry expert and strategist Greg Oates shares five tips for hotel marketers to better share their story. Use a search engine and type in: youtube, Leonardo blog, five tips on telling your story visually online.

Chapter 8: Advertising to the Meeting Planner

in more hits when a potential customer is using a search engine.

Your landing pages should not only contain information, but also visuals that appeal to specific segments. If you are marketing to corporate meeting planners, for example, be sure your visuals include photographs of your meeting facilities and special dining setups as well as a link to a RFP. Other visuals, such as slide shows and virtual tours may also result in a booking decision, as can featuring your local area and nearby attractions.

Research has shown that 360-degree virtual tours are one of the most effective sales tools to attract the attention of meeting planners. Virtual tours can feature panoramic photographs put together into a slide show, a video presentation (with or without audio), or a combination of both. These tours are most effective when they show a variety of room setups as well as representations of successful events. And, you don't have to limit your virtual tours to your website; many hotels have created YouTube channels that feature videos of the property and its personnel as well as meeting planning tips (include links to your YouTube presentations on your website and your social media sites).

Most sites now offer the opportunity for planners to search for specific meeting criteria. The planner enters specifics and the computer will search for a "match" for his or her requirements within the chain. And, as we have said earlier, RFPs are usually available. But sites should also include a direct link to the property sales office or reservation system as well as pertinent e-mail addresses and your property's toll-free and fax telephone numbers.

Two excellent examples of hotel websites designed specifically for meeting planners were developed by the Marriott and Hilton chains. Marriott provides a Meetings & Events tab on its main website, www.marriott.com, that provides links to other landing pages, including a Meeting & Event Overview, Business Meetings, and the chain's Convention & Resort Network. The chain has also introduced a Meetings Imagined™ program with its own dedicated website (www.meetingsimagined.com). The chain interacts with customers by encouraging them to share their ideas and upload photographs of their events. The Meetings Imagined™ program is a perfect example of the content marketing that we discussed earlier in this chapter.

The home page of the Hilton chain (www.hilton.com) offers both a Meeting & Events tab and a link to the chain's meeting planning services. The Meeting Resources tab on the link takes planners to such landing pages as Meetings Simplified™, which offers a

*Figure 8.5. ONLINE MEETINGS MANAGEMENT TOOLS.*

**MEETINGS AND INCENTIVES AT YOUR FINGERTIPS.**

resorts.hyatt.com

Your complete online planning tool, featuring:

- Searches based on activities, space, rooms, locations and other options
- Robust high-resolution photo galleries for use in presentations and program brochures
- Planning resources and incentive checklists
- Fact sheets, detailed floor plans and capacity charts
- Links to additional destination information

For more information, visit resorts.hyatt.com.

HYATT RESORTS

*Hyatt Resorts promotes its online meeting tools in print ads such as this one. Features include photo galleries for use in event brochures, checklists, fact sheets, and detailed floor plans.* **Source: Courtesy of Hyatt Resorts.**

## Chapter 8: Advertising to the Meeting Planner

*This website for InterContinental Hotels Group provides information of interest to both professional and occasional meeting planners. Note the links to customer service, featured offers, and a meeting and event guide in addition to a search feature that enables planners to find potential meeting sites in the chain by city, state, and country.*
**Source: Courtesy of InterContinental Hotels Group.**

meeting package as well as several "add ons" (breakfast, lunch, and dinner options; healthy and fun break options to enhance energy; and, an LCD projector and screen or monitor).

**Meeting-Related Websites.** Another way to reach meeting planners browsing the Internet is to link your property to meetings-related sites, such as a CVB site, city site, the site of a meeting planner service provider, or the sites of other firms to which planners turn for information. If you are targeting the association market, linking to a CVB site is extremely important; a recent survey indicated that three out of four association meeting planners use CVB sites to plan their meetings.

Web directories are also popular with meeting planners, so they are an excellent resource for hotel Internet marketing. When PCMA's *Convene* magazine publishes its annual directory every August, its addresses of national and international convention and visitors bureaus, conference and convention centers, hotel chains, hotels and resorts, convention services, and airline and car rental agencies are also available online. Contacting and linking with one of these entities is likely to increase your chances of reaching prospects looking specifically for meeting services.

You can also list your property on such meeting service sites as www.cvent.com, conventionplanit.com, sitevisit.com, and a host of others, which compile lists of databases of properties interested in hosting meetings and group business. These services help planners to narrow down choices by filtering such aspects as location, size, and facilities and then provide electronic RFP forms to send to hotels identified as meeting their requirements. Robert Bennett, Senior Vice President – Supplier Market for StarCite, whose technology is used by HelmsBriscoe, says:

> The number of inquiries and leads distributed from our sites has increased 428 percent in the last two years.[3]

A property can also advertise on a number of other sites likely to be viewed by meeting planners. One option is to purchase a listing or advertise in an online directory, such as Hotels.com (www.hotels.com) and KAYAK (www.kayak.com), or on travel review sites, such as TripAdvisor (www.tripadvisor.com) and Yelp (www.yelp.com). Research has shown that meeting planners often visit travel review sites to compare properties.

There are several ways to advertise. **Banner ads**, which take web surfers to your website when clicked on, can be positioned at the top of the screen above content or in other positions on a website. Two other types of website ads that are sometimes used are pop-up and pop-under ads. **Pop-up ads**, which open a new window over the content being viewed,

---

## 🖥️ INTERNET EXERCISE

### Property Websites

A growing number of today's meeting planners turn to the websites of convention hotels to compare venues before making meeting site decisions. The four websites listed below have won awards from the hospitality industry for their effective online messages to meeting planners.

Log on to the following sites and go to the meetings and/or convention areas of each to answer the following questions:

- Hyatt Regency Chicago (www.chicagoregency.hyatt.com)
- InterContinental Toronto Centre (www.torontocentre.intercontinental.com)
- Saddlebrook Resort (www.saddlebrook.com)
- Sheraton Vancouver Wall Centre (www.sheratonvancouver.com)

1. Which sites offer the option of e-mailing a request for proposal (RFP)?

2. Which hotels offer "e-mmediate response" to meeting inquiries, promising instant group date and rate availability?

3. Which sites provide a virtual tour of the property's meeting rooms?

4. Which sites offer a link to the bios and achievements of key meeting staff members?

5. Which websites explain their program for sustaining a natural environment and their "green" policies?

6. Identify the sites that provide testimonials from past clients and guests.

7. Which sites offer links to social networks such as Facebook and Twitter?

are often a source of annoyance for web users, who dislike having a browsing session interrupted (Google has banned them, and there are a number of programs that block pop-up ads). A **pop-under ad** is less intrusive, as it opens a new window under the content being viewed; the ad is not displayed until the browser closes the content window. Yet another option is a *sponsorship*, which usually involves a financial contribution or the donation of a product or service. In many cases, sponsors receive a clickable listing or banner ad in return for their sponsorship; other sites may simply feature your logo (along with the logos of other sponsors).

There are several ways in which Internet advertising can be purchased. First, you may purchase space for your banner ads on a websites frequented by meeting planners, including the sites of meeting planner associations and travel-related sites. There are usually additional costs for some ads due to their size as well as ad placements on a web page. You can also opt to use a banner ad placement service, such as DoubleClick (www.google.com/doubleclick) to place ads for you.

The second way to purchase Internet advertising is on a **pay per click** (also called cost per click) basis. Using this method, properties pay the publisher (usually the website owner) a contracted amount for each time their ads are clicked upon. An advantage of this type of advertising is that it is easily measured; the results accurately reflect the number of times an ad has drawn attention and interest, rather than simply being seen. Some website publishers use adware, a software application that monitors Internet sites visited by browsers and then matches advertising content to them on a variety of sites, including their home pages, on their social media sites, and even in their inboxes. It is important to note that adware is often viewed negatively (and programs are available to block adware).

Fees and requirements for Internet advertising vary – as does the effectiveness of some ads. In order to make the most of Internet marketing, many properties are also turning to another Internet resource, social media, to maximize their exposure and create goodwill.

**Social media** has exploded over the past few years as more people join online networking communities where they share information, photographs, videos, and music. While there are opportunities to advertise on social media sites, social media should NOT be considered an *advertising distribution* channel. Instead, social media should be viewed as a very important *customer engagement* channel that provides a convenient way to network and build relationships with meeting planners.

Social media sites such as Facebook, Twitter, and LinkedIn are excellent vehicles to interact with current and potential customers, both as an individual representative of a property and as a property as a whole. Salespeople can use their individual profiles and accounts to create a network of contacts, while properties can create a presence by developing interactive pages, starting or joining social media groups directed toward meeting planners, and sharing helpful videos and information over such social media channels as YouTube, Pinterest, and Instagram. Hotels that share tips, information about their local area and attractions, and other information of interest (and encourage reader input) have the most success with social media.

While face-to-face communication is most preferred, social networking sites allow salespeople to build and maintain relationships with meeting planners. Salespeople often use social media sites to stay in touch with contacts. If a salesperson is attending a trade show, for example, he or she might alert contacts about being there and try to arrange for a meeting at the event.

Hotels can use social media to send out bulletins and audio or video messages regarding an upcoming event or promotion. Social media has become such a part of today's business culture that a trainer and consultant to the hospitality industry said:

Gone are the days when the salesperson booked the business, handed it over to conference services, and pretty much disappeared. The salesperson needs to have a system of communicating with their clients going forward — that can be a periodic newsletter to client groups, blogs that are uploaded to the salesperson's profile on social networks, and/or pushing out an occasional light communication on Twitter!

Use a flip camera to take videos of an event at the hotel or hotel team members doing something unique, like towel sculptures on the bed. Post it on YouTube and your social network pages, and send the link to clients. Touching accounts and contacts in non-intrusive ways helps keep that person in your tribe.[4]

When you create a presence on social media sites, you have the potential to be seen by millions of viewers, as people who "like" or follow you have networks of friends who are also part of networks – and Google and Bing now include posts and tweets in their search results. To be effective on social media, however, you must avoid simply promoting your product and instead focus on building a community. This takes a constant, consistent effort. It is not enough to post once a month; you must keep abreast of current conversations and topics to keep your posts relevant. You can further enhance your social media pages with photographs and videos, and by featuring special offers or holding contests.

As with advertising, your social media should be directed toward the groups you are targeting. Since LinkedIn is the social media site most often used by meeting planners, you will want to concentrate your efforts there.

> **MORE ONLINE**
> - "The Hotelier's Guide to Boosting Group Business with Social Media" by Junvi Ola, an eBook made available by the Cvent Supplier Network, can be read at www.luxuryhotelassociation.org/?wpdmdl=3548.
> - A guide to developing an effective profile on LinkedIn is presented on topdogsocialmedia.com/linkedin-training-creating-the-perfect-profile.

Most prominent meeting planner associations have groups that you can join on LinkedIn, and meeting planners can also be reached through meeting-related groups, such as Event Planning & Event Management, Global Hotel Sales & Marketing Professionals, Hotel Industry Professionals Worldwide, I-Meet, Linking Hoteliers, Luxury Hotel Sales & Marketing Manager's Club, Meetings Industry Network by Cvent, and MPI's Meeting & Event Discussion Group. A LinkedIn member can join up to 50 groups at once, providing an excellent opportunity for your property to maintain a presence and build an excellent reputation by offering information useful to meeting and event planners.

Rodahl Leong-Lyons, Hyatt's vice president of sales - America, says:

> Hyatt is increasingly focused on connecting with planners where they already spend their time, particularly online. We strive to be a resource to them and will continue to connect with planners through our LinkedIn Hyatt community.[5]

Meeting planners also look to travel-related social sites such as TripAdvisor and Yelp, to make site selection decisions. These sites, which feature reviews from people who have experience with specific hotels, should be carefully monitored as part of your social media effort. Respond to posts about your property promptly – especially if the review is negative; in that case, offer your apologies – and an opportunity to "right" the situation – to make a positive impression on a meeting planner. You will want to avoid "canned" responses, however (always personalize your answers) – and it is far better to have a particular person or member of a team, such as a customer service representative, answer the post; avoid having the property "respond", as it is far more effective for posters to relate to a person, not an entity.

Your staff and the meeting planners you serve can also play an integral part in your social media efforts. Encourage them to post photos and reviews on social media sites or have your staff include property updates on their personal social media pages. Another effective way to connect on a personal level is through a **blog**, a personal online journal that can also feature photographs, videos, and links to pertinent sites. J.W. "Bill" Marriott was a pioneer hospitality industry blogger, posting some 250 "Marriott on the Move" blogs in his first five years of blogging. His blogs, which can be viewed at www.blogs.marriott.com, offer insights on a variety of hospitality topics and include an e-mail sign-up feature as well as links to properties within the Marriott chain. Blogs that you create yourself can be shared on social media sites and other blog sites, such as The Huffington Post (www.huffingtonpost.com), BuzzFeed (www.buzzfeed.com), and WordPress (https://wordpress.org). The latter site offers free templates for bloggers, and most blog sites feature searchable categories, including "travel."

The channels and techniques for social media often change, so it is important to stay current with social media site trends, especially those sites frequented by meeting planners. At one time, for example, MySpace was the predominant social media site until its members flocked to Facebook, and today's social media sites are continually adding new features that will better help you to reach your targeted audience.

## E-mail Advertising

According to the most recent Meetings Market Report conducted by *Meetings & Conventions* magazine, 89 percent of meeting planners use **e-mail** for planning purposes. Hoteliers who want to get the word out about their products and services have found e-mail an inexpensive and effective way to advertise. Compared to traditional direct mail advertising, e-mail is highly economical and almost instantaneous. Bakulesh "Buggsi" Patel, president and CEO of BHG Hotels, says:

We still do direct mail, but we're finding e-mail to be an extremely effective use of our time and money. The Internet is changing the way properties go to market. It's the medium that everyone who is looking ahead is looking to leverage.[6]

As with other advertising, however, planning is needed before sending out e-mail messages. First, using e-mail requires building a database of qualified prospects. Second, content must be developed that will appeal to your various targeted segments. And, last but certainly not least, e-mail must be welcomed by your prospects.

### The Peabody Orlando's E-Mail Marketing Success Story

The Peabody Orlando significantly increased its share of group meetings by developing an e-mail strategy based on e-mail lists of qualified prospects and select third-parties. The campaign, which was held for a 90-day period, highlighted the unique meeting spaces and services provided by the hotel and included a special offer for planners to visit the property. The campaign resulted in over 5,000 meeting planner visits to the hotel's website, over 100 meeting RFPs submitted, ten site visits scheduled, and significant new group business from new markets, including the booking of a large group from the West Coast, an area where the property wished to gain a greater market presence. And, the campaign was extremely cost effective — resulting in a 47:1 ROI.

## Chapter 8: Advertising to the Meeting Planner

Time and privacy are important to planners, and sending "spam" -- the electronic equivalent of unsolicited "junk mail" -- may drive potential customers away. Today's successful e-mail marketers are using **permission marketing** to ensure that their messages make a favorable impression. This strategy involves asking a planner's permission before sending an e-mail about your property. You can create an *opt-in form* on your website to enable meeting planners to enter their e-mail addresses if they wish for you to send updates on your property. When meeting planners share their e-mail addresses with you, they are giving you permission to contact them in the future. Since 80 percent of your meetings business generally comes from 20 percent of the meeting planners with whom you communicate, it is critical to send regular (but pertinent) e-mails to planners who have expressed a willingness to hear from you.

In order to cut through e-mail clutter, be sure to include a subject line that will identify you or your hotel and give the reader a reason to open the e-mail. For example, subject lines such as "A Special Offer from the XYZ Hotel" or "The Information You Requested from the XYZ Hotel" are far more likely to be read. Since meeting planners are looking for helpful, pertinent information, you should create targeted e-mails for specific types of planners (a planner for an association has different needs than a corporate planner or the planner of a military reunion). All types of planners, however, are generally interested in special offers, updates on facilities and services, and a monthly property newsletter.

> **MORE ONLINE**
> Additional tips for developing effective e-mails are presented at hospitalitycontentstudio.com/make-your-hotels-emails-worth-opening/.

E-mails should be kept as short as possible. Include links to your website, newsletter, or an online video to save on space while providing additional information (many e-mails also include links to the property's social media sites). If you need to communicate about several topics at the same time, use bulleted points to draw attention to the different aspects of your message.

It is highly effective to create a sense of urgency. A limited time offer is more likely to generate a response – but all e-mails should ask for a response – and provide a way to do so (special telephone number, dedicated landing page on your website, and so on). Don't make the mistake of simply suggesting that the planner contact you at his or her convenience; instead, offer to contact the planner on a specific date or include dates and times when you will be available to take his or her call.

Keep in mind that the majority of meeting planners today use tablets and smartphones, so your e-mails should always be optimized for mobile devices. Avoid embedding large blocks of copy that can be unreadable on smaller mobile screens, and provide links to the mobile optimized version of your website.

> **WORTH WATCHING**
> Do an Internet search for #AskDJV-Episode 10: Email Marketing Strategies That Drive Business to view Lodging Interactive's short video on the topic. You can also view additional videos by searching for "email marketing strategies" on the web.

E-mail advertising typically yields responses up to 15 times greater than those generated from direct mail and also has the advantage of doubling as a lead qualifying tool. Hoteliers are also seeing the value of e-mail as a new way to communicate with customers on a regular basis. You can also communicate with contacts and customers via text messages. Text messages have the advantage of going directly to the planner's smartphone, instead of possibly being overlooked in a full inbox. And, like

287

e-mail, they can contain a great deal of information if links to optimized web pages or videos are included.

E-mail and text messages are seen as an effective way to nurture customer relations by demonstrating the hotelier's commitment to staying in touch and serving the planner's future needs. As we have mentioned previously, it is important that all advertising, including e-mail campaigns, are integrated into your property's marketing plan. Adequate funds must be allocated for your e-mail efforts (whether single e-mails or e-mail campaigns) and your e-mails should be targeted to build or boost business during slow periods to make the most of this advertising strategy.

## Fax Transmissions

While many meeting planners prefer to get information via e-mails and text messages, fax (facsimile) transmissions are still used to provide meeting planners with up-to-date information on new products and services. Faxes provide a copy of the original document — a letter, proposal, advertisement, special announcement, etc. — and are advantageous in that they are instantaneous, do not get lost among e-mail clutter, and many meeting planners make them a priority to read. There are two ways in which fax transmissions are commonly used: fax-on-demand and broadcast fax.

**Fax-on-demand** offers the latest in property information directly to a meeting planner via a special fax number. This information can be accessed at any time, even when the sales office is closed, and can be updated as required to supply the latest information.

**Broadcast fax** provides simultaneous transmission of information to a database of interested or qualified prospects. Special announcements, changes in services offered, or other information can be sent to a number of planners at once.

Will technological developments such as the Internet, e-mail, text messages, and fax transmissions, replace personal site visits or diminish the role of the hotel salesperson? A recent study by Meeting Professionals International (MPI) and PlanSoft Corporation found that while technology is a useful tool for initial screening, it cannot replace in-person visits to investigate space for meetings. The large majority of respondents to the survey say that personal contact and building relationships are still essential to the meetings process.[7]

## Collateral Materials

**Collateral material** is supplementary advertising pieces used along with direct mail, magazine advertising, and other promotional efforts. This includes a vast array of promotional materials such as convention and rack brochures, newsletters, postcards, menus, tent cards, matchbooks, and many other items.

The greatest distinction between collateral material and other advertising devices is the directness of collateral pieces. Collateral material is specific and is usually directed right to the decision-maker.

### Brochures

Perhaps one of the most familiar collateral materials is the brochure. Most convention hotels use two brochures: a standard *rack brochure,* which is directed to the leisure market, and a *convention brochure.* As with other advertising, the focus of these brochures will differ widely. The rack brochure usually promotes rooms, restaurants, and recreational amenities and is targeted to leisure travelers and travel agents. The convention brochure, on the other hand, provides detailed information regarding function space, food and beverage service, and convention services and is targeted to meeting planners.

Most properties offer convention brochures in two formats: printed and electronic. While some meeting planners request a standard printed brochure, an increasing number of them prefer to get property information online. We will discuss these two types of brochures in the following sections.

**Printed Convention Brochures**. The convention brochure may be prepared in a number of ways. It can be a standard three or four-fold type, loose-leaf pages bound in an attractive cover, or presented in booklet style. Whatever style you choose, remember that it should fit in with your property's overall advertising and project your property's image. In addition, no matter what type of brochure is used, it should always contain pertinent information.

When planning a convention brochure, whether for print or for the Internet, start with the assumption that your prospect has never seen or even heard of your hotel, and certainly has never been informed of its convention capability. Image yourself as a meeting organizer looking for a suitable hotel for your next event. The information you would want should be presented clearly and concisely. A common complaint from planners is the lack of good, accurate descriptive material from hotels.

A brochure will give the planner enough basic data for preliminary planning. The box titled "Basic Convention Brochure Information" provides guidelines to create an effective print or electronic brochure.

---

### BASIC CONVENTION BROCHURE INFORMATION

Your property's convention brochure should provide all the information a meeting planner needs to make a decision on a meeting site. Effective convention brochures should include most — if not all — of the following information:

- Your property's name
- Your property's address and, when possible, an area location map detailing proximity to airports, major highways, and area attractions
- Your property's telephone number (a toll-free number encourages responses) and name of contact person, if applicable (convention services manager, convention coordinator, etc.)
- Your property's website address, pertinent e-mail addresses, and your fax number
- Photographs, diagrams, or *complete* descriptions of exhibit space (dimensions, scaled drawings, floor load, ceiling height)
- Audiovisual equipment available
- Other meeting services available (free WiFi, videoconferencing, business center, clerical/registration help, and so on)
- Special services and facilities (photographic services, flowers, entertainment)
- Banquet and beverage arrangements
- Theme party arrangements
- Guestroom information (descriptions, floor plans, room block policy, reservations, rates, arrival/departure information)
- Special procedures (billing procedures, shipping and receiving procedures, signs and notices policy, etc.)
- Recreation and amenities (hotel attractions, spouse entertainment, area attractions)
- Transportation (parking facilities, shuttle service, tours, taxis, public transportation)
- Other general information (climate, dress, gratuities, the availability of room service, etc.)
- References from past conventions
- Checklists and planning guides for the meeting planner

---

*This checklist may also be used for an electronic brochure on the Internet. A website is an ever-evolving marketing tool on which electronic brochures can be updated whenever the need arises.*

The larger meeting rooms should be diagrammed, if possible, or at least described adequately. "Large" is not a very accurate phrase. How many people will the grand ballroom accommodate? In what sort of setup (auditorium-style offers greater capacity than seating at round tables, for example)? A good brochure will give enough information so it can be used as a tool by meeting planners to narrow down a field of contestants for meeting functions.

One of the primary sources for ideas for preparing a convention brochure is, of course, existing pieces. Begin collecting brochures. There are some excellent ones in the field. Start a reference file of brochures you admire for one reason or another. They'll give you many ideas you may want to incorporate into your own brochure.

The best brochures show scaled outlines (blueprints) of all major rooms. One meeting planner stated:

> I like to receive a meeting planner's kit, not general information about the hotel. I need to see a floor plan with specific seating capacities. It takes time and it's expensive for a hotelier to send out information; it should be useful.

The brochure need not be so utilitarian that it fails to present your property in a good light. A facility is not chosen merely for its ability to house the event. The beauty of the structure and surroundings, the convenience of the location, and the expertise of the staff are all important. But such data should not be included at the expense of basic facilities information.

Design your material to enable your contact to present your case completely and favorably. Good brochures will work for you in sales presentations and mailings, at trade shows, and through intermediaries such as convention bureaus, airlines, and convention specialists.

**Electronic Convention Brochures.** Today, printed brochures are being increasingly replaced with *electronic brochures* that can be accessed on a property's website (and sometimes on additional Internet sites, including YouTube and Facebook) or sent via e-mail or text messages. These online brochures are available as downloadable PDF files or, more commonly, as video productions offering "virtual tours" of the property and its facilities. For example, the Bellagio in Las Vegas offers a number of downloadable PDF brochures, including several for meeting planners; brochures include "Convention Sales," "Meeting Facilities," "Convention Policies & Procedures," "Catering Sales Policies," and a meeting planner guide (these can be viewed at www.bellagio.com/download-brochures/). Meeting planners can look through the pages and use a zoom feature to enlarge details of interest. And, because these brochures are available on the property's website, all a planner has to do is click on the Meetings & Groups tab and scroll down to contact the convention sales department or access a SpeedRFP.

The Broadmoor, which has opted for the video approach, has developed segmented video brochures that cover recreational amenities and dining options as well as meetings and events facilities (www.broadmoor.com/video-gallery). It also offers virtual tours of each of its event spaces at www.broadmoor.com/virtual-tours.

Meeting planners have expressed a preference for online brochures, as they can be viewed on as "as needed" basis and there is no need to file printed material away. Advantages to the property include lower costs, as there is no need to budget for printing and postage costs, and online brochures can be easily updated to provide the latest information on special offers, changes to facilities or staff, and so on. As with printed brochures, the

Chapter 8: Advertising to the Meeting Planner

information and photographs in your online brochures should be pertinent to meeting planners.

In addition to making brochures available for viewing on the Internet, some properties produce DVD (digital video disc) brochures. DVD's are both inexpensive and versatile, and a DVD can show a property's selling points in a way that no printed piece can (see Figure 8.6).

As with online brochures, a DVD brochure can show the property at various times of the year, and is an excellent resource for the meeting planner who is unable to visit the property in person. DVD brochures can show a property at its best, in a variety of setups (setups should be shown for both meeting rooms and banquet facilities), and can also show other important selling points, such as seasonal attractions.

Most DVD brochures are fairly short, running four to six minutes in length, and must present the property's best points in that short time. Many properties, therefore, enlist the services of a firm that specializes in hotel electronic brochures before attempting to shoot

*Figure 8.6. CONVENTION AND PROPERTY BROCHURES ON DVD.*

*Many hotels today supplement their printed convention brochures and property information sheets with DVDs. These virtual presentations enable hotels to provide panoramic tours of the properties' facilities and services at various times of the year. When creating a convention brochure on DVD, however, it is not enough to simply show off meeting and function rooms; meeting planners must be provided with pertinent information, such as room dimensions, room capacities, and banquet menus, that are commonly found in printed convention brochures.*
**Sources: Courtesy of The Broadmoor in Colorado Springs, Colorado; the Fontainebleu Hotel in Miami Beach, Florida; and Gaylord Opryland Hotel & Convention Center in Nashville, Tennessee.**

Chapter 8: Advertising to the Meeting Planner

> ## 💻 INTERNET EXERCISE
>
> ### Digital Convention Brochures
>
> Today, many hotels supplement their printed convention brochures with DVDs and online information. However, some hotels fail to include the detailed information that meeting planners require when they develop their electronic presentations. Meeting planners, for the most part, prefer a brochure that is "long on facts and short on pictures."
>
> One meeting planner states:
>
> > I used to have a file cabinet full of convention brochures. Now I depend on the Internet to provide what I found in traditional sales kits — photos, menus, floor plans with room dimensions.
>
> Log on to the following hotel electronic brochure sites to answer the questions below:
>
> - MGM Grand Hotel – www.mgmgrand.com/meetings/
> - Snowbird Meeting & Conference Center – www.snowbirdmeetings.com
> - Woodcliff Hotel and Spa – www.woodcliffhotelspa.com (click on the Meetings & Events tab)
>
> 1. Compare the three brochures. Which is "long on facts and short on pictures"? Which do you think is most useful to meeting planners?
> 2. Evaluate each brochure based on the checklist titled "Basic Convention Brochure Information" provided earlier in this chapter
> 3. Do you feel these brochures could substitute for a printed convention brochure?

one on their own. This may cost slightly more, but the benefits of the expertise of the professional firm (and high-quality shooting techniques) are worth the additional time and expense.

As with other types of advertising, DVD presentations should project the desired image for your property and should meet the needs of meeting planners by offering pertinent information. The detailed floor plans mentioned above are an excellent selling point, as are interviews with key convention services personnel, a "tour" of the property (preferably when there are groups in-house), testimonials by satisfied clients, and so on. Many properties opt for professional assistance when creating their first DVD, especially if it will be used in conjunction with an Internet marketing program.

## Other Collateral Materials

In addition to brochures, collateral materials may include such diverse pieces as postcards, fliers, maps, menus, tent cards, and newsletters (see Figure 8.7). These materials not only serve to keep your property's name and its features in the prospects' minds, but also can be used by salespeople to enhance their sales presentations.

As with brochures, all other collateral pieces should be carefully planned and integrated into the property's overall marketing and advertising strategy. All pieces should be attractively designed and, as in print advertising, list the benefits offered by your property as well as its features. Most importantly, printed collateral materials should be targeted to the conventions market (separate newsletters should be developed for the meetings market and the leisure travel segment, for example).

Chapter 8: Advertising to the Meeting Planner

*Figure 8.7. SAMPLE HOTEL CHAIN NEWSLETTER.*

The newsletter is an excellent — and relatively inexpensive — way to convey property information to meeting planners. Newsletters may be produced at the property level or as part of a chain's effort to introduce its properties to meeting planners. Newsletters typically contain such features as property statistics, articles and/or photographs of successfully staged events, personnel profiles, special offers, and general meeting information. Newsletters are typically used in convention kits, enclosed with sales letters, or used in direct mail campaigns, and many are also sent via e-mail or are accessible on the website of the property or chain.

## Specialty Items

Collateral materials also include **specialty items** (sometimes called **premiums**) that are marked with the property's name and toll-free number. These may include such inexpensive items as matchbooks or keychains, or "signature" items, such as glassware, plush toys, or sportswear featuring the property's logo.

Chain properties have the advantage of ordering specialty items from the chain's catalog at greatly discounted rates. But even small properties can take advantage of this advertising tool — which, according to the Specialty Advertising Association (SAA), boasts a recall factor of up to 40 percent even after six months. It is fairly easy to find suppliers of specialty items, and costs can be kept down by ordering in quantity and staying with the same imprint.

Select items that reflect the image of your property, not necessarily the cheapest. It is far more cost-effective to choose items, such as a desk calendar or coffee mug, that a planner is likely to use daily to keep your property's name on his or her mind.

## Direct Mail Advertising

Another popular tool in the promotion person's kit is **direct mail advertising**. Direct mail can be used to screen prospects, follow up on advertising leads, and make a printed sales presentation in great detail to many prospects at once — at far less cost than for print or broadcast advertising. Direct mail pre-selects the client and reaches him or her personally and privately.

Unfortunately, there are also disadvantages to direct mail. The cost of direct mailings has increased over the years, especially due to increasing postal rates. Another disadvantage of direct mail is that pieces frequently end up in the wastebasket. An efficient program that will overcome these difficulties, however, can be produced at almost any budget level.

One factor in the success or failure of direct mail is ensuring that you are advertising directly to your target market. A direct mail campaign is only as good as the **mailing list** used. If your hotel does not have a mailing list, start one immediately. Begin by compiling a list of planners who have met in your hotel in the past. Keep in mind that we are a mobile business society and lists must be updated frequently. Expect many returns and changes of names and addresses after each mailing, and remember to budget for postage due on returned pieces. It is vital to delete the undeliverables and note the changes of addresses on your list so that expensive printing and postage are not wasted in subsequent mailings.

As we have discussed, there are also several directories and a number of publications that supply the names, addresses, and phone numbers of most association, corporation, incentive, fraternal, and other meeting planners. It is also possible to rent names from the circulation lists of suitable magazines.

Convention bureau notices from past years can also be a source of prospects for your mailing list, since major citywide conventions are channeled through the bureau. Groups that have met in years past may hold smaller meetings that you may be able to attract. The convention bureau list might also show some groups have a repeat pattern for the city. These groups should be given a high priority in your sales campaign.

It is a good policy to develop two lists: a *general* one of all prospects you feel reasonably sure are relevant, and a *preferred* list of screened prospects and past customers. You will probably mail more frequently to the second list than to the first.

Before sending any mailings, you should also decide on a follow-up method. Ideally, your direct mail efforts will give you a list of "hot" leads to follow up. The list of new leads generated through direct mail will be wasted if these prospects are not attended to promptly. You may wish to have follow-up literature readily available, or forward responses directly to your salespeople for an immediate personal contact.

Direct mail should be carefully planned for maximum results. The direct mail campaign must be integrated into the hotel's overall sales objectives, and mail pieces should blend with the property's other media advertising.

Some of the most commonly used direct mail pieces include sales letters, surveys, and postcards, but more creative and elaborate visual aids may also be used (see Figure 8.8). When deciding what types of materials would be most effective to use, several factors must be considered, such as the purpose of the mailing, its scope, and the costs involved.

**Figure 8.8. DIRECT MAIL "NOVELTIES".**

The Skamania Lodge promoted its world-class meeting facility, which is located in the Columbia River Gorge Scenic Area, an area teeming with outdoor wonders, with a mailing of hand-carved and painted Chinook salmon (along with campaign literature) to approximately 2,500 meeting planners. The creative, award-winning campaign generated 23 group bookings, resulting in 1,237 room nights, rooms revenue of $212,774, and food and beverage and other revenue of $108,129.
**Source: Courtesy of the Skamania Lodge, Stevenson, Washington.**

**Writing Better Sales Letters.** *Sales letters* are the meat of any direct mailing. Their function is to convince and to sell. Time does not permit a salesperson to make personal calls on every prospect, so the message must be communicated through the written word.

It is effective to use well-written personal letters, with convention brochures as enclosures. Seemingly personal, individually typed letters can be produced using your in-house word processing system or local letter shop services. If you want to create more ambitious direct mail programs, use your advertising agency or local creative services agency to produce the mailing pieces. But don't underestimate the power of personal letters addressed to a person by name. The high cost of brochures and postage make it advisable to polish your techniques (see box titled "Writing Effective Sales Letters").

Many properties find that a number of mailings must be used to achieve best results. A one-time mailing is not too effective unless it is a birthday or holiday greeting or an answer to an inquiry. Direct mail *campaigns*, then, should be a part of your direct mail efforts.

---

### WRITING EFFECTIVE SALES LETTERS

Effective letter writing is a skill than can be developed. Here are a few fundamental techniques that should be used:

- Use the correct titles of hotel personnel and the person with whom you are dealing.
- Be informative but brief. Stick to the facts.
- Be yourself; write like you speak. Write as if the client were with you in the office.
- Emphasize key points by underlining them or using bold-faced lettering.
- Avoid using computer-generated form letters that do not address specific needs.
- *Always ask for the sale* — and provide a means for the client to respond (a reply card, toll-free number, etc.).

Keep in mind that you should always write in the client's language; avoid the use of hotel terms that may confuse or mislead. Don't give the sales copy second billing in direct mail pieces. Be specific, and make your correspondence meaningful and convincing.

---

When using more than one mailing, the frequency, as well as the content, is important. There is no hard and fast rule, but the maximum interval between mailings is considered to be about two months. Obviously, multiple mailings must never be the same. The first letter must be an attention-getter. Its content must be appealing and retain the reader's interest. Future mailings should be built around the theme presented in the first one, but the information and point of the letters should be different. In some cases, you may want to build on each letter sent. The point of your message may be the same, but the content should be stated differently and creatively or the reader's interest is sure to wane.

## Planning an Advertising Strategy

As you can see, there are a number of ways to reach meeting planners, and you must develop a strategy that will work best for your property. Developing such a strategy, of course, means working within the marketing plan — and budget — established for your property, and structuring your efforts accordingly.

Some of the factors you will want to consider in devising your strategy include whom you wish to target, what media you will use, and how much money you can spend.

Chapter 8: Advertising to the Meeting Planner

Many properties prepare a media chart (see Figure 8.9) to plan advertising placement and expenditures over the course of a year. Annual planning is much more effective than last-minute, haphazard efforts. When you plan on an annual basis, keep in mind that you can

*Figure 8.9. SAMPLE HOTEL MEDIA CHART.*

Client number: BM100-3  
Media: MEETINGS  
MEDIA SCHEDULE 01/01/__ THRU 12/31/__

| Publications | January | February | March | April | May |
|---|---|---|---|---|---|
| **Association Management**<br>Pub Number   Issued   Circulation<br>AS700-6A   Monthly   21,120<br>96 Rates   15th of 2nd Month<br>Publication Total   $8,372.50 | | | | Page 4/C<br>$4,186.00<br>Or Pg 4C | |
| **Business Travel News**<br>Pub Number   Issued   Circulation<br>BTN15-8A   Bi-Weekly   51,046<br>Jr Pg or 1/2SPD   3 Weeks Prior<br>Publication Total   $34,000.00 | | | Jr Pg 4/C<br>$6,800.00<br>Mtgs Today<br>22 +BRC | Jr Pg 4/C<br>$6,800.00<br>Mtgs Tday<br>19 | Jr P4\C<br>$6,800.00<br>Mtgs Tday<br>10 +BRC |
| **Corporate & Incentive Travel**<br>Pub Number   Issued   Circulation<br>C0605-6A   Monthly   49,698<br>One Month Prior<br>Publication Total   $4,764.00 | | Page 4/C<br>$4,764.00<br>DSTNTN<br>Colorado | | | |
| **Executive Memo**<br>**Colorado Soc. Of Assn Executives**<br>Pub Number   Issued   Circulation<br>COSAE-6A   Monthly   250<br>One Month<br>Publication Total   $12,605.50 | | | | Page BW<br>$500.00 | |
| **Executive Update - GWSAE**<br>Pub Number   Issued   Circulation<br>EU478-6A   Monthly   9,000<br>33% DSCNT<br>Publication Total   $12,605.50 | | | | | Page 4/C<br>$3,740.00<br>SPGNTME<br>PK |
| **Forum (CSAE)**<br>Pub Number   Issued   Circulation<br>For 10-9   11X/Yr<br>½ SPD or Pg   6 weeks Prior<br>Publication Total   $6,262.37 | | | | Page 4/C<br>$1,789.25 | |
| **Incentive**<br>Pub Number   Issued   Circulation<br>IN150-6A   Monthly   40,281<br>15th, 2 Months Prior<br>Publication Total   $39,467.80 | | | | Page 4/C<br>$4,911.30<br>+BRC | Page 4/C<br>$4,911.30 |
| **Insurance Conference Planner**<br>Pub Number   Issued   Circulation<br>IN500-6A   Bi-Monthly   7,451<br>1st of Month Preceding | | | | | Page 4/C<br>$2,622.25<br>Incentive |

All listed rates are based on applicable rate card as of the date of preparation and are subject to change.

*In order to plan an effective advertising strategy, many properties prepare an annual media chart that lists such data as name and type of publication to be used, size of ad (or length of spot), and advertising expenditures, both for production and space costs. This approach provides an at-a-glance overview of the property's advertising, controls budget commitment, and can also be used to measure the effectiveness of advertising. This sample shows data from January- May; a complete chart would extend through December. Note that this chart covers advertising in publications only; a similar chart would be developed for other advertising efforts, such as Internet ads and promotions and direct mailings.*

297

schedule your advertising expenditures to match your property's fiscal or budget year. Publications compute frequency discounts on a consecutive twelve-month period. You can, if it suits your purpose, schedule your advertising from March 2016 through February 2017, for example. Also, it is helpful, if you can manage it, to set aside a sum for special situations that crop up during the year.

## Reach, Frequency, Timing, and Consistency

When planning your advertising strategy, whether it is print, Internet, or direct mail (or any combination of these), four key factors should be taken into consideration: reach, frequency, timing, and consistency.

**Reach** refers to the number of different individuals who are exposed to your message during a specific period. This, of course, is determined by the media you select. When targeting the conventions market, for example, you are focusing on a smaller number of specific prospects than if you were targeting the transient market. You should select the media that will be most effective in reaching them (a specialized trade journal, for example) rather than opting for indiscriminate media (a television spot). You are interested in how many potential customers you can reach for each dollar spent.

**Frequency** refers to the number of times your target audience sees or hears your message. As with sales calls, advertising is rarely effective on a "one-shot" basis; it is usually necessary to expose your prospects to your message on a frequent basis — and often in a number of ways, such as the combination of trade journal advertisements and direct mail efforts. It is beneficial to expose your prospect to your message a number of times.

**Timing**, then, is an important factor. Some properties prefer to advertise or send out mailings on a *continuing* basis, timing their advertising to appear once a month, for example. There are times, however, when you can take advantage of a *pulsing* approach. Pulsing is used to promote business over slow periods. A property, for example, may wish to offer special rates during its valley periods of early fall and mid-winter, and would advertise over a predetermined time prior to these periods. Similarly, *flighting* (advertising only when managers feel it necessary, with no regular pattern) can be used when it is necessary to promote special packages or events. Perhaps the area will be host to a local festival or special event; advertising can promote the property's participation or proximity to the action.

Most convention publications run special editorial sections throughout the year dealing with meetings in certain geographic areas, such as a city or state, or specific types of properties, including golf resorts, airport hotels, conference centers, etc. Editors and publishers will usually supply the schedule of such features for the full year. When you plan your advertising, you might be able to take advantage of such targeted sections by placing your ad in them while still maintaining your objectives in timing and frequency. There are additional advantages to appearing in editorial sections describing your specific area.

No matter what approach is used for timing, **consistency** in advertising is vital. Your advertising must develop distinguishing characteristics — a logo, special colors or design, etc. —to stand out from the rest. Your prospects should be able to identify your property's ad at first glance.

Not only should your advertising have distinguishing characteristics, it should also be consistent with and supportive of other elements in your marketing plan. This approach, called **integrated marketing**, ensures that your advertising and marketing activities have a common focus for both your marketplace in general and specific market segments in particular.

Since the purpose of your advertising is to become known and patronized, your advertising strategy should also include a program of follow up and monitoring and evaluation. *Follow up* is extremely important, especially in the conventions and meetings market. Most planners are "comparison shopping" and if they have responded to your ad or mailing it is likely they have responded to others. Your prompt handling of an inquiry will demonstrate your commitment to provide efficient service.

At the very least, inquiries should be followed up with a personal letter and information that was requested. Whenever possible, especially if the respondent has included his or her telephone number, make a personal call of thanks and request an appointment. This can lead to an immediate sale.

To develop the most cost-effective program, however, you must carefully *monitor and evaluate* your program periodically. Determine which ads or direct mail pieces seem to attract the most interest; check to see which publications are generating the most leads; and monitor the number of conversions from inquiries. Also, take steps to determine the actual cost per conversion from each type of inquiry. If your ad series is costing $35,000, for example, but you have only generated $15,000 in business, take another look at your ad program.

## Exchange Trade Advertising

To cut advertising costs, many properties have looked for alternatives, such as trading out goods and services or sharing advertising expenditures. **Exchange trade advertising** is an arrangement in which the hotel exchanges its services (rooms, food, beverage, use of recreational amenities, etc.) for advertising. Such arrangements are also referred to as *reciprocal advertising*, *barter advertising,* and *trade-out advertising,* and can be very worthwhile as long as the hotel fully understands the procedure. It is important to realize that exchange trade advertising is not free; there is a cost to the hotel, and this cost must be budgeted, just as print and Internet advertising costs are. Remember, whether you are paying cash or exchanging services, your hotel's advertising efforts must be directed to your target markets. If you are trying to build group meetings business, for example, a trade exchange with a billboard specialist would not be the wisest use of your money.

Exchange trade advertising does offer some real advantages to a convention hotel, and its possibilities should be investigated. As with any advertising strategy, there are factors that should be considered and guidelines to follow in order to utilize this type of arrangement for your maximum benefit (see box titled "Making the Most of Exchange Trade Advertising").

The use of exchange trade advertising does require increased recordkeeping, but it also affords yet another benefit — the opportunity to build relationships with media firms. A friend in the media can be a real asset when it comes to editorials and publicity about your hotel (and the hotel is in a position to extend extra courtesies to the media's important clients). In the final analysis, exchange trade advertising can be mutually beneficial if a fair arrangement is negotiated.

## Cooperative Advertising and Strategic Partnerships

**Cooperative advertising** also provides an additional way to save on advertising costs. In a cooperative arrangement, several properties — or a property and several related entities,

> **MAKING THE MOST OF EXCHANGE TRADE ADVERTISING**
>
> Consider these recommendations for negotiating exchange trade agreements:
>
> 1. Consider some variations on the "one-for-one" arrangement, especially when a publication or website domain holder approaches you. You could receive $1.50 or $2.00 of advertising for every dollar of hotel facilities, especially if food and/or beverage are included in the arrangement. When such is the case, point out that food and beverage represent an out-of-pocket cost to you, whereas available publication space or radio and TV time ordinarily does not.
> 2. Consider these limitations, all of which mean money in your pocket: For commercial hotels and motels, (a) rooms only, and then only during periods when you don't expect to be at capacity, or (b) food only, rather than food and beverage. For A.P. (American Plan) or M.A.P. (Modified American Plan) resorts, the room portion only.
> 3. Bring your advertising agency into the picture and require the publication or website to pay the customary 15 percent commission. Your ad agency will undoubtedly handle the placement of the advertising, and if it receives the commission, you will not be required to pay it.
> 4. Include as a condition of your reciprocal deal that your facilities are limited to use by certain individuals (publisher, key executives, employees), and secure in advance a list of those persons.

such as a convention and visitors bureau, an airline or car rental company, or local area attractions — advertise together to both save on costs and maximize results.

Cooperative advertising, which we mentioned in previous chapters, can be used as either a "one-shot" promotion, or, as is done more commonly, in an advertising campaign that promotes the services and attractions available in an area. This type of advertising provides meeting planners with more information and options, and can also prove beneficial to your property. If your property has limited meeting facilities, for example, you can advertise with a full-service meeting hotel, offering your rooms to accommodate meeting overflow.

**Strategic partnerships** are another form of cooperative agreement. These alliances are relationships between independent parties or chains that agree to cooperate in advertising but still maintain their separate identities. A common example is several hotels combining forces with each other (and often the city's CVB and/or other attractions) to offer a "one-stop shopping" alternative to compete with larger cities (see the "Best Practices" box titled "Hilton Hotels & Sheraton Hotels Form a Strategic Partnership to Capture Meetings Business in New York City").

One of the most unique and far-flung strategic alliances is the Energy Cities Alliance, which is comprised of: VisitAberdeen in Scotland (www.visitaberdeen.com); the Abu Dhabi Convention Bureau in the United Arab Emirates (abudhabi-cb.ae); the Calgary Telus Convention Centre in Alberta, Canada (www.calgary-convention.com); and, Region Stavanger in Norway (www.regionstavanger.com/en). These alliance members, which are connected in some way to the energy industry (including such areas as fossil fuels, green energy, and energy-related academic research), jointly fund the alliance, which has its own website; energycitiesalliance.com. Alliance members offer a number of services to planners, including bidding support with local vendors, hosting receptions with local dignitaries, referrals to local speakers, marketing support, and event promotion to build attendance.

Gillian Taylor, former manager/advisor of the Abu Dhabi Convention Bureau, said:

> We have greatly benefited from the Energy Cities Alliance, particularly with business intelligence and lead sharing. The WorldSkills Interna-

tional Competition alone will bring 7,000 skilled, trained youngsters, teachers, and trainers from 52 countries.[8]

---

**Best Practices**

**Hilton**    **Sheraton**

**"Hilton Hotels & Sheraton Hotels Form a Strategic Partnership to Capture Meetings Business in New York City"**

Hilton New York, Sheraton New York, and the Sheraton Manhattan, which are about 150 feet from one another in mid-town Manhattan, have 100 meeting rooms, more than 225,000 square feet of meeting space, and a combined total of 5,000 guestrooms. They can also accommodate up to 425 exhibits. Although they are competitors, the three hotels took advantage of an opportunity to market their combined facilities to appeal to meeting planners.

The three hotels created NY 5000, a partnership geared to a joint sales and marketing effort. Christopher Perry, former director of marketing and sales for Hilton New York, said:

> We wanted to offer an alternative for conventions that need 1,400 rooms or more on a peak night. We are ideal for events that want to come to New York, would like to stay with two or three hotels, and prefer not to use the convention center. It saves them money on transportation and creates better networking opportunities. We also have a consistency of product and service, including food and beverage.

Although meetings customers negotiate independently with each hotel in order to protect any proprietary information, the hotels have jointly developed a presentation, designed collateral materials, and developed a website (ny5000.com; now www.nycandcompany.org/meetingplanners/ny-5000), and salespeople regularly meet and make pitches for NY 5000 business when appropriate.

While the three hotels had previously been averaging about eight large meetings jointly, they added four additional large group bookings in the first year of the formation of NY 5000.

**Source:** Harvey Chipkin, "Success Stories That Inspire," *HSMAI Marketing Review*.

---

Alliances offer the advantage of consolidating efforts (at a lower cost to each participant), and these joint efforts may reach meeting planners who may not have considered an alternate location. When considering forming an alliance with other hotels or areas, however, you will need to research the benefits of such relationships versus results you could achieve on your own.

## Advertising Agencies

Since developing an overall advertising plan or creating a single ad campaign within a workable budget can be a complicated process, many hospitality firms seek assistance from **advertising agencies**. Advertising agencies can be extremely helpful in making media decisions that will cut through media clutter and make the best use of your advertising dollars.

There are several types of advertising agencies: full-service agencies, à la carte agencies, creative shops or boutiques, and media-buying services.

*Full service ad agencies* generally employ a full-time staff and are usually structured into four departments: the creative department handles the development and production of ads; the media department selects specific media and places the ads; the research department serves as the firm's marketing arm; and the business department handles the agency's business affairs. These agencies may be independent operations or may have branches or affiliates that can provide coverage wherever their clients' products are sold.

*Á la carte ad agencies*, also known as *modular services*, are usually full-service agencies that offer selected services on a negotiated-fee basis. A property may use this type of ad agency for a one-time production of ads or their placements.

*Creative shops* or *boutiques* offer creative services on a free-lance, per-job basis. These agencies are usually staffed by free-lance artists and writers and may develop into full-service agencies as their client bases grow.

**Media-buying services** do not offer creative services, but specialize in buying print space and airtime. This type of agency can prove useful to hospitality firms with in-house advertising departments.

Many convention hotels have found it advantageous to use advertising agencies, but it is extremely important that when a hotel uses an advertising agency that both are in agreement as to the direction of the advertising campaign. Naturally, a hotel is more familiar with its strengths than the outside agency. The hotel must communicate its positioning and goals to its agency representative to ensure that the advertising creates the image a property wishes to project and is aimed at its target market(s). To ensure that the property and the agency can work well together, it is important to select an agency carefully (see box titled "Selecting an Advertising Agency"). A properly functioning agency offers you an experienced and objective view of your property's promotional efforts. One advertising executive says:

> We're concerned not just about creating and placing [clients'] advertising, but helping them with their in-house promotions in all of their market segments; developing new segments; motivating their salespeople; building their collateral; redesigning Web sites; and managing direct mail promotions...We truly want to become the client's marketing partner, and not just its [ad] studio.[9]

---

### SELECTING AN ADVERTISING AGENCY

Before you select an advertising agency, you should evaluate your property's needs. Will you need full services or just assistance in placing your own promotional material? How would an advertising agency be utilized — as a supplement to your in-house advertising department, occasionally as needed for research or production, or as an extension of your advertising and sales effort? How much can you afford to spend on outside services?

Once you have established guidelines, informal meetings should be held with representatives of agencies of interest to you. Each representative should provide answers to the following questions:

1. How long has the agency been in business? Does it have a proven track record in the hospitality industry?
2. Does the agency represent competitors? If so, how will this affect the handling of your account?
3. What services can the agency provide? Does it offer full creative services? market research? media placement?
4. Who will be assigned to your account? How much time can he or she spend learning about your property and its needs? In the event "your" account person is not available, who will be assigned to handle your account?
5. How will costs be handled? Is the agency willing to work within the property's budget?

## Public Relations and Publicity

While advertising is a powerful method of reaching target markets, you can do more to keep your hotel's name before your potential customers. Advertising and e-marketing coupled with public relations and publicity can form a stronger combination to reach planners.

**Public relations** is a broad term that encompasses a number of methods of communicating favorable information about a property. Its purpose is to create a positive image about the property. Loews Hotels, for example, began a model program -- and won an award -- with its Good Neighbor Policy. This community outreach program seeks to address a number of concerns, such as homelessness, illiteracy, and environmental preservation, and mobilizes not only the chain's properties but meeting planners as well. The hotel's contracts include an offer for meeting planners to donate surplus products and materials to a local charity. Donations have ranged from clothing to items from food shows to basic supplies (poster board, masking tape, etc.) that are donated to area preschools.

> **WORTH WATCHING**
>
> Annie Buckley, former public relations manager at the Ritz-Carlton, Dubai, offers insight into hotel public relations.
> Use a search engine and type in:
> youtube, Annie Buckley, Ritz-Carlton.

As with advertising, a good public relations plan must be developed — and people trained to implement it. While every employee — from general manager to front desk personnel to a valet attendant — plays a role in developing and maintaining a positive image for the property, it is essential that a professional public relations person or staff be employed to oversee the property's efforts in this important area. Small properties may employ one person or work with an outside public relations firm. Large properties may also utilize an outside public relations firm or hire a multi-talented public relations staff. In either case, public relations people or firms will be called upon to perform a variety of duties, including acting as the property's spokesperson, contacting the media about the property, maintaining contacts with past guests, and so on.

One of the public relations staff's most important responsibilities is dealing with the media to obtain favorable publicity for the property. **Publicity** is the gratuitous mention of your hotel in newspapers, magazines, and over the airwaves. When you advertise, you pay for space or airtime and control what is said about your hotel and its services. And, with advertising, many readers or listeners may be apprehensive about whether you can or will deliver on your promises. Publicity, however, which comes from an impartial third party, lends credibility to a property.

In the hospitality industry, there are many opportunities to generate good news. Some of it just happens — a celebrity stays at the property, the property wins a prestigious award, a trade magazine does a story on a particular area, and so on. Much of it, however, is created — the hotel sponsors a festival, for example, or creates innovative theme parties. Or, the property can get its name in the news through its expansion and renovation programs or the involvement of its staff members in community affairs.

Meetings magazines — one of your best resources for reaching meeting planners — are always interested in stories of interest to meeting planners. Innovative meeting techniques, reports on new methods used to service successful meetings, renovations programs that will impact the meetings industry (the opening of additional facilities, etc.), and personnel changes are all of interest. Some magazines publish "Meeting Calendars" that list major meetings and their venues; these are an excellent vehicle for free listings for your property.

To enhance your chances of being featured in a meetings magazine, consider inviting travel writers from the major magazines (*Convene*, *Meetings & Conventions*, *Successful Meetings*) and from magazines directed toward your target markets to stay overnight and experience your property firsthand. This is an excellent way to reap the benefits of editorial coverage — and the resulting publicity.

Make a strong effort to get photographs of meetings in progress at your property. Meetings magazines are always looking for such illustrations. In addition, the organization sponsoring the meeting may use your photographs in their own publicity efforts, giving you additional exposure at the same time. It is not by accident that hotel lecterns carry the hotel's logo prominently across the front panel so that all photos of the speaker show the logo as well.

Trade magazines, such as those listed in earlier chapters, are spearheaded by an editor who makes the decisions about the subjects of articles and when they will run. They also have a managing editor who coordinates the makeup of the magazine. These people should be on your mailing list to receive publicity materials (press releases, newsletters, personal letters and invitations, etc.), as should editors of major newspapers in your property's target

> **WORTH WATCHING**
>
> In order to make information readily available to the press, Starwood Hotels & Resorts launched its Starwood Media Centre, a multi-lingual online news service that offers information in seven languages. You can see a video promoting this multi-lingual, online news service at www.youtube.com/watch?v=OwQbcFrup4c.

---

### 🖥 INTERNET EXERCISE

**Providing Media Information Electronically**

Today, many media representatives prefer to receive news releases and story ideas via e-mail or from a property's website. Therefore, you should always include a link for the press on your site.

Electronic press kits typically include all the elements found in a printed press kit — fact sheets, biographies and photos of key personnel, the property's brochures, photographs (both interior and exterior shots), mention of awards received by the hotel, and current news releases. Both past and present news coverage can usually be accessed by links to the publication, and the electronic format provides an excellent vehicle for showing video of the property and events staged there. Many hotels and chains offer an image gallery of photographs that can be accessed and used by the media (galleries typically require registration).

Log on to the websites of the following hotels to answer the questions below:

- Hotel Del Coronado — hoteldel.com (scroll down to "Press Room" tab)
- The Sanctuary at Kiawah Island — www.kiawahresort.com (scroll down to "Press Room" tab)
- Swan-Dolphin Hotel — swandolphinmedia.com

1. How thorough are the press kits of each hotel? Do their press kits cover all of the areas mentioned in the introduction to this Internet Exercise?

2. Are both high- and low-resolution photographs available for downloading by the media for use in news stories?

3. Review the current news releases from each of these sites. Identify releases directed to the meetings market.

markets. The news generated about your property must meet their requirements of editorial interest, timeliness, and accuracy to be considered for publication.

Almost all properties send out **press releases** about events of importance. Press releases are usually printed on stationery with the property's logo and name, physical address, web and e-mail addresses, and telephone number; they include basic information (time, place, and other pertinent details) and the name of a property contact person. In today's high-tech world, the computer is increasingly being used to get the word out about a property. Instead of traditional press releases, e-mails and text messages, often with attachments that include photos or video, are increasingly being sent to the media.

Press releases should always be sent well in advance of a deadline, but it is important to note that there is no guarantee that your material will be featured — or that it will be presented as written. You are not paying for space and you have no control over editorial content or its presentation.

It is important, then, to plan your press releases to ensure the maximum coverage possible. Since your press releases will be aimed at meeting planners, consider those events and personnel changes most likely to get them thinking about your property. The development of a state-of-the-art audiovisual system, for example, is of interest and is likely to make it to trade magazines. As is news of expansions (again, think how you can best word your release to appeal to the meeting planner — present a benefit in your copy), personnel changes (especially if the staff member is well-known in the meetings field), and special events held by your property — your innovative execution of an elaborate function will appeal to other meeting planners.

In addition to press releases and promotional material to send to respondents, most properties with a planned public relations and publicity strategy prepare a **press kit** to both introduce the property to the news media and to provide back-up information. Press kits generally feature a property information sheet, the property's brochures, biographies of key personnel, and, when available, previous press clippings. Press kits should be updated as necessary and targeted for your property's market segments; a press kit for meetings magazines, for example, would contain different material than a press kit directed to travel writers.

In addition to press kits, both individual properties and chains have developed "media only" websites that offer immediate access to press releases, photographs, logos, hotel specifications, dining and entertainment options, and other information. Content is continually updated, and many "user-friendly" sites offer the option for members of the press to cut and paste a press release (or a portion of it) directly into their news stories.

A good public relations and publicity plan does not just seek to get your property's name in the media. To be effective, *the plan should be integrated into the overall hotel marketing strategy, targeted toward specific market segments, and scheduled to coincide with the property's slow periods.*

## Summary

As you can see, a good advertising strategy coupled with a carefully planned public relations and publicity plan can greatly enhance the sales effort and actually "pre-sell" the property by creating awareness and a positive image in the meeting planner's mind. These tools can help the salesperson to close a sale and begin the second phase of his or her job — helping to coordinate the meeting planner's function. In the next chapter, we will take a look at what happens after a meeting planner commits to a property. We will discuss how nego-

## Endnotes

1. "Ad Agencies Are Your Marketing Partners," *HSMAI Marketing Review*.
2. Anne Dimon, "Are You E-Planning Savvy?" *Meetings & Incentives*.
3. "StarCite, PlanSoft Give Planners Faster Response from Hotels," www.hotel-online.com.
4. "Key to New Business Development in 2010 & Beyond," *Hospitality Upgrade*.
5. *Lodging*, February 2013, p. 37.
6. Marty Whitford, "You've Got Mail," *Hotel & Motel Management*.
7. Lauren Shababb, "In-Person Inspections, Please," *Successful Meetings*.
8. Lisa A. Grimaldi, "Sister Cities," *Meetings & Conventions*, June 2014, pp. 45 - 46.
9. "Ad Agencies Are Your Marketing Partners," *HSMAI Marketing Review*.

## Study Questions

1. What is print advertising? What elements should always be included in print ads? Where can print ads be placed to effectively reach meeting planners?
2. Why is the convention brochure an important sales tool for the meetings market? What information should be included in a convention brochure?
3. Why is direct mail an effective tool for reaching meeting planners? What are the elements involved in an effective direct mail campaign?
4. Why is it necessary to plan an advertising strategy? What factors should be considered?
5. What are exchange trade and cooperative advertising? What are the advantages and disadvantages of each?
6. Why do some properties use advertising agencies? What factors should a property consider when selecting an advertising agency?
7. What is the difference between public relations and publicity? How can each be used to enhance the property's advertising efforts?

## Key Terms

**advertising agency**—A firm that provides advertising and marketing services to clients. Types of advertising agencies include full-service agencies, á la carte agencies, creative shops or boutiques, and media-buying services. Ad agencies may be paid by receiving a commission from the media or a predetermined fee from the client.

## Chapter 8: Advertising to the Meeting Planner

**banner ad**—An ad placed on another firm or organization's web page, such as the site of a business- or travel-related entity. Commonly linked to the advertiser's site, banner ads are the dominant form of web advertising.

**blog**—Personal or corporate online journals that offer reporting and/or opinions about people, things, and events. Blogs are designed to allow readers to post responses or comments, so the most successful blogs generate a high degree of interactive dialogue.

**body copy**—The main text of an ad.

**broadcast fax**—A function that transmits fax messages to a large number of pre-selected recipients.

**brochure**—A printed folder containing descriptive or advertising material; rack brochures target individuals, while convention brochures target meeting planners.

**collateral material**—Supplementary advertising materials, including brochures, tent cards, key rings, matchbooks, postcards, and video brochures.

**cooperative advertising**—A pooling of marketing dollars by several tourism businesses for promotional purposes in order to increase market impact and/or reduce costs.

**consistency**—In advertising, refers to the design of advertising messages for a similar look or sound to enhance audience recognition and greater cumulative impact.

**content marketing**—Providing information to clients that will make their lives/jobs easier while establishing your property as one they can trust and return to with their business.

**direct mail advertising**—Advertising sent via mail to prospects' residences or places of business. Contains copy to motivate the reader to purchase a product or utilize a service and usually includes a means to respond.

**e-mail**—Electronic mail messages sent via computer.

**exchange trade advertising**—An arrangement in which the hotel exchanges rooms, meals, recreational amenities, etc. for advertising space or time. Also called **reciprocal advertising, barter advertising,** and **trade-out advertising.**

**fax-on-demand**—A function that provides an immediate response to information requests via fax transmission. In most cases, information is requested through a toll-free number.

**frequency**—The number of times advertising appears in print or on the air.

**gatefold**—An oversized page or portion of a page added to a regular magazine page.

**headline**—The most prominent part of a print advertisement. Used to get attention, it usually promotes a promise or benefit.

**integrated marketing**—Marketing activities with a common focus on the marketplace or a specific customer segment. The execution of each individual component is consistent with, and supportive of, each of the other elements in the marketing plan.

**landing page**—A single website page that is reached via an Internet search or a link on a website or a social media page. Most hotels have multiple landing pages to ensure optimum search engine results.

**logo**—A unique trademark, name, symbol, signature, or device used to identify a company or other organization. Used in advertising, for promotion, and for image building.

**mailing list**—A collection of names and addresses of past and potential customers to which mailings are directed. Generally maintained on a computer.

**media-buying service**—A type of advertising agency that does not offer creative

## Chapter 8: Advertising to the Meeting Planner

services but instead specializes in purchasing print space and radio and television time for their clients.

**mobile app**—A software application designed to run on smartphones, tablet computers, and other mobile devices. Hospitality uses include apps to keep a meeting planner in touch with the hotel's staff during an event and apps that display additional information regarding menu items and beverages.

**mobile optimized website**—A website that is designed specifically for a smartphone or a tablet. Navigation is efficient, with quick loading and the capability to display content on the smaller screens of mobile devices.

**pay per click**—An Internet advertising option in which a publisher, usually a website owner, is paid a contracted amount each time an advertisement is clicked on. Also known as *cost per click*.

**permission marketing**—An e-mail marketing campaign in which messages are sent only to those who have requested (opted-in) to receive specific types of information.

**pop-under ad**—An advertisement that opens in a new window under the window in use. The ad appears after the content window is closed, so users are not interrupted while viewing content.

**pop-up ad**—An advertisement that opens in a new window over content currently being viewed, partially or totally obscuring the content. Considered annoying and intrusive, pop-up ads are prohibited on the Google search engine.

**press kit**—News releases, fact sheets, photographs, news clippings, and other materials, often attractively packaged, designed to give the news media background information about a property.

**press release**—A prepared statement, usually one or two pages, released to the news media regarding a hotel, one of its products or services, an individual, or a special event. Designed to be newsworthy, can be "For immediate release" or prepared to be released at a specified time or date. Also called a **news release**.

**print advertising**—Advertising appearing in print in such media as newspapers, magazines, and directories.

**public relations**—The systematic effort of a company to create a favorable image in the minds of various segments of the population.

**publicity**—One facet of public relations, it comprises the gratuitous mention or exposure a company receives from announcements, events, and press releases.

**publisher's statement**—A statement by a publisher that includes information about circulation (broken down by paid subscriptions, number of copies available at newsstands, circulation of regional editions, and so on), subscription rates, advertising rates, mechanical requirements for ads, and deadlines for submitting ads.

**reach**—The percentage of different people or locations exposed to a media message at least once during a specified period of time.

**search engine optimization**—The use of key words and phrases to ensure that the content of a website is picked up as many times as possible by search engines.

**social media**—The term used to describe the tools and platforms that people employ to converse with each other and publish/share content online. These tools include blogs and podcasts as well as sites designed to share photographs, videos, graphics, bookmarks, and other content.

**specialty items**—Supplementary advertising items, such as coffee cups, T-shirts, beach towels, and so on, that bear the name of the business and other advertising and contact information. Also called **premiums**.

**strategic partnerships**—Relationships between independent parties that agree to advertise cooperatively but still retain their separate identities.
**timing**—In advertising, refers to the scheduling of ads.
**trade magazine**—A publication, such as *Financial & Insurance Meetings* magazine, that targets a specific industry or profession.
**video brochure**—A short video (typically four to six minutes) that presents a property's products and services and is designed to be viewed off-site.

## Industry Profile

### Andria Goldin, President
Meeting Knowledge, LLC

*Over her two-decade career in the hospitality industry, Andria has focused on developing the strongest communication connection possible between meeting planners and hotels. Andria previously served as sourcing manager for Maritz Travel, where she sourced, contracted, and managed national sales and marketing meetings at major hotel venues across the country, and as purchasing and global sourcing manager for Boehringer Ingelheim.*

## Keys to Successful Contract Negotiations

I've been in the meetings planning business for a long time. To me, sourcing (identifying and engaging properties that are right for my meeting) is the most exciting part of planning a meeting because concept and creative is still in development. However, it seems the hotel-meeting relationship has fundamentally changed. Where is the hospitality in contract negotiating? We seem to have lost that dual partnership, the "we are in this together" feeling. The new art of negotiating now becomes which contact will prevail – the client's or the hotel's.

Dennis Noonan, vice president of sales and marketing for the Nemacolin Woodlands Resort in Farmington, Pennsylvania, told me that "hotel sales managers don't have half the negotiating power they used to have. Salespeople have become the middle person to the marketing director, and everything goes back to the revenue management program."

Since the struggle seems to be in the RFP process, during which a lot of properties simply plug in the needs of a meeting and respond with rooms and rates, Noonan prefers to have a conversation with the client prior to presenting a proposal to communicate three key points:

- Is the Woodlands Resort right for the client?
- What is the client's meeting history?
- Does the client understand the contract process before the RFP process begins?

Noonan feels this is where creating the hotel relationship and trust begins. "Otherwise", he says, "I am just a piece of paper with a rate." Noonan also prefers conversation rather than e-mail, even though communications between planners and suppliers are usually conducted through e-mail and texting; there is very little telephone interaction, resulting in a lot of back-and-forth messaging. Real-time dialogue allows for a better exchange of ideas.

The best negotiations are often the most personal, although that can prove challenging, given the constraints of many modern-day, digital sourcing request-for-proposal tools. It helps when meeting planners are forthcoming with their requests. Planners should share their wish list from the "get go;" they shouldn't use "nibbling" negotiation (adding one request after another). The sales manager can't go to bat for planners if they don't have all the information needed; and, since each new request has to be considered and approved, the "nibbling" approach extends the negotiation process unnecessarily.

## Learning Objectives:

This portion of your text introduces the factors that must be considered and the necessary steps that need to be taken when negotiating contracts for functions with meeting planners. When you have studied this chapter, you will:

- Know how to negotiate contracts with meeting planners that benefit both the hotel and the group.

- Be able to describe the various areas that are included in a typical hotel contract.

- Know the importance of standardizing contracts and be able to detail how multiple-meeting contracts are negotiated.

## Outline

Negotiations
Letter of Agreement/Contract
- Names of Organization and Hotel
- Official Dates
- Number and Kinds of Rooms
- Rates/Commisions
- Arrival/Departure Pattern
- Meeting Space
- Complimentary and Reduced-Rate Rooms
- Prior Visits
- Working Space
- Registration Control
- Exhibit Space
- Food Functions
- Refreshment Breaks
- Liquor
- Gratuities and Service Charges
- Audiovisual Equipment
- Union Regulations
- Master Account and Credit Procedures
- Method of Payment
- Termination/Cancellation Clauses
- Damage Clause: Liquidated or Mitigated Damages
- Attrition Clause
- Arbitration/Dispute Resolution
- Warranty of Authority
- Insurance/Indemnification
- Other Contract Matters

Contract Standardization
Multiple-Meetings Contracts
Summary

# 9 Negotiations and Contracts

In today's competitive market, hotels largely book business based on its maximum profitability. With the growth of individual business and leisure markets, which tend to pay higher rates than the group meetings segment, properties have become stricter in terms of room rates and contract negotiations for meetings business. But wise hoteliers know that their relationship with planners is equally if not more important. David C. Scypinski, senior vice president at ConferenceDirect, says:

> The most successful salespeople take a long-term approach to negotiating contracts by looking to develop an agreement that benefits both the hotel and the customer. A one-sided contract may bring in much-needed revenue in the short-term, but may make it impossible to re-book the business. And in this business, as in any other, the key to profitability is repeat business. This is not to say you shouldn't seek to negotiate the most profitable contract possible; but you should be professionally aggressive in your negotiations, looking to balance the financial goals of your hotel and the customer's objectives.

Today, negotiations between hotels and planner have changed because of an emphasis on revenue management. Most hotels that derive 20-40 percent of their business from meeting groups have a revenue manager who has input into the value of a particular piece of business. This adds another layer to sales — salespeople must sell to the meeting planner and then sell the value of the meeting to the revenue manager. There is nothing more frustrating than for a salesperson to build a relationship with a planner and then have to turn away the group's business.

While the sales department is responsible for determining the client's needs, the revenue manager's job is to balance those needs with the hotel's objectives, especially in the areas of guestroom rates and food and beverage revenue. Prior to extending a proposal, salespeople meet with the revenue manager to discuss and qualify all potential groups. Group histories are analyzed on how each meeting will impact profit centers within the hotel. If the group will displace transient business, for example, will it provide enough ancillary spending to offset the loss of transient business? Does the group require excessive meeting space that will prevent the hotel from booking other groups? Is the group flexible with their dates?

In order to determine the value of a group, the following variables are taken into consideration:

- Stay pattern – season, day of the week, and length of meeting.
- Mix of sales – targeted transient and group business on dates requested.
- Room inventory – group business already booked for the stay pattern in question.
- Group's guestroom and food and beverage budget.
- Guestrooms to meeting space ratio.
- Acquisition costs – is the booking direct or through a third-party, to which a ten percent commission will need to be paid?
- Brand loyalty – does the group have a history of booking with the hotel brand?

Revenue managers work in tandem with the hotel's sales department to ensure that the goals of both the group and the property are met; if a group wants to meet during a peak period, for example, the revenue manager may suggest alternate dates that will enable the hotel to work within the group's budget. Although this is a collaborative process, the ultimate decision usually rests with sales. A recent survey conducted by MeetingsNet determined that the property's director of sales is the ultimate decision maker on meetings business 60 percent of the time, while the revenue manager has the final say only 16 percent of the time.

> **WORTH WATCHING**
> 
> Barb Bowden, former vice president/ general manager of The Orlando Peabody, discusses the changing role of revenue managers in contract negotiations at www.hsmai.org/knowledge/multimedia.cfm?ItemNumber=5045.

Gus Vonderheide, vice president global sales – Americas for Hyatt Hotels Corporation, concurs:

> Although revenue managers play a very significant role at our properties, they're just part of the process. Directors of sales still make the ultimate decision on whether to accept the group or not.[1]

Today's hoteliers must negotiate contracts that provide optimum benefits to both the property and the planner. In this chapter, we will see how contracts are negotiated, the areas of concern taken into consideration and included in the contract to ensure the successful execution of a function, and detail how hotels use specific clauses to protect themselves financially.

## Negotiations

Negotiations involve two or more parties coming together to reach an agreement for their mutual benefit. This process should be viewed as a friendly, problem-solving partnership, not as a fearful or uncomfortable situation. Negotiating can result in a win-win situation for both your property and the meeting planner when handled properly.

Since knowledge is power (for both parties), good negotiation skills begin by researching three key areas: your product, your competition, and the prospect.

Product knowledge begins by studying the *property fact book*. It is nearly impossible to effectively sell features and benefits or to demonstrate how your property is best equipped to meet the prospect's needs without thorough knowledge of your property (see Chapter 7).

In addition to knowing your property's features, you must also understand *when* your property needs group business, the optimum guest mix, and the average daily rate for each market segment. The bargaining position of meeting planners will vary depending on your hotel's level of business, which can be divided into three categories:

- *Peak* — this is the period when demand for a property and its services is highest and the highest prices can be charged. Also called "high season."
- *Valley* — this period, also known as the "value season" or "low season," characterizes times when demand is lowest. Reduced prices are offered to meeting planners during valley periods to attract business.

## Chapter 9: Negotiations and Contracts

- *Shoulder* — this period falls between a peak and a valley. Rooms are available and a mid to high rate can be charged. The shoulder period is the time when many properties concentrate their sales and marketing efforts.

You must know as much about your competitors' products as your own in order to successfully sell against them. When negotiating, emphasize the strengths of your property where you know the competition is weak (this information is available from the property's Competitive Analysis Charts, which we discussed in Chapter 2).

Being a good negotiator means learning as much as possible about the buyer. There are several factors to consider when evaluating your prospect's position:

- **Budget.** Knowledge of the meeting planner's past and present budget gives you an indication of how much he or she may be willing to spend on similar events, and if price is a major concern.
- **Purpose of the meeting.** Every property has its appeal. If a meeting is for training, a small suburban property can offer the group the option of being the only meeting in the house, which pleases some planners.
- **Dates.** When is the meeting scheduled? How flexible is the group? Do your competitors have the preferred dates open? You are negotiating from a position of strength when you know your competitors don't have the desired dates open.
- **Arrival/departure pattern.** Determine the group's arrival and departure pattern to determine how well the group will fit in with business you have already booked. A Tuesday to Thursday meeting schedule may be problematic, for example, if you have already booked a group that arrives on Sunday and departs on Wednesday. In such a case, you could try a little suggestive selling to the meeting planner: "Yes, we do have some rooms available on Tuesday. However, if you can come in just one night later, we can offer a nice discount. Would you consider that?"
- **Hot buttons.** What are the meeting planner's key concerns and what are the most important buying factors? Is it the availability of special services, such as express check-in/check-out, extra staffing at the front desk, or special meals? Key concerns tell you what to emphasize and also give clues to the importance of price. Obviously, planners who mention VIP service and extra amenities as crucial to their meeting are going to be less price resistant.
- **Past problems.** Did the planner experience problems with another property? If poor food service is mentioned more than once, then price may not be as important a consideration as quality food at next year's event.
- **Group food and beverage revenue.** What is the group's past propensity for spending on food and beverage, theme parties, hospitality suites, and so on?
- **Group history.** Find out what properties the group has previously used to enable you to compare what you have with what other properties offered. What has been their spending history at previous hotels with regard to various profit centers (food and beverage, shops, spa, recreation, and so on)?

How far back should the group history go? Three years' worth of history should be reviewed. The foremost resource in this area is the Destination Marketing Association International's (DSMAI) empowerMINT program, which evolved from the DSMAI's original Meeting Information Network (MINT) initiative. MINT was developed as a shared repository of information (collected by convention and visitors bureaus) about association and corporate meetings. You can learn more about this program at www.destinationmarketing.org/topics/empowerment.

- **Rooms to function space ratio.** What is the guestroom-to-meeting space ratio? Groups that are function-space intensive may not be a good fit.
- **Decision deadline.** Your hotel's negotiating position will be affected by how quickly a decision must be made. Your negotiating strategy will be different when dealing with a planner who must make a decision immediately versus a planner who does not have to decide on a site until sometime in the future.

When negotiating, it is essential to look at the **customer's lifetime value**. Sometimes, hotels will under-price to gain new customers or be generous to existing customers in order to retain them over the long term. Trade-offs are a part of negotiating; if you sell value, you can avoid making **concessions** that will impact the property's bottom line. A concession is *not* a compromise; any possible concessions should be carefully reviewed and analyzed as to their impact on the property's profit margin *before* entering into negotiations. In most cases, concessions are not negotiated dollar-for-dollar; salespeople must be trained to negotiate concessions with the least impact on hotel profitability. It is a wise strategy for hotels to prepare a concession calculator that spells out the concessions commonly requested, their cost to the hotel, and their value to the client.

> **WORTH WATCHING**
>
> In an HSMAI Insight Interview, Brian Keenan, former vice president of sales for the MGM Grand (now vice president of development at MGM Resorts International), discusses the challenges of negotiating in today's economy at www.youtube.com/watch?v=3LyXOLhK5AM.

In a recent study by Cvent, hotels ranked their top ten amenities to negotiate: discounted sleeping rooms; discounted meeting space; meeting room Wi-Fi; discounted menu prices; in-room Wi-Fi; allowable attrition; sleeping room upgrades; discounted audiovisual; discounted parking; and late check-out times. Meeting planners, on the other hand, ranked the amenities that were most important to their attendees as: free Wi-Fi/Internet access; round-trip airport transportation; free parking; late check-out; meal service; early check-in; fitness center access; business center access; welcome reception; and beverage service. Other concessions that a hotel may consider include changes to the group's cut-off dates and attrition rates.

Some of these concessions are costly to the hotel; in the case of the length of a cut-off date, for example, the earlier the cut-off date, the more time the sales team and the revenue manager have to adjust selling strategies to maximize revenues. The value of this concession, however, varies depending on the season (during peak periods, a 45-day cut-off is preferred; if demand is slow, a 30- to 21-day cut-off may be agreeable). The same is true of free or discounted meeting room rental; if there are no other groups forecasted for the time period, this concession does not make a large impact on revenue – the room would be unused anyway. The same applies to room upgrades; the group sees a suite (which can be used for VIP guests or a hospitality suite) as an added value, as some suites are priced as high as $1,000. The hotel, however, is not losing $1,000 if the room will be unoccupied at the time of the group's meeting – and is building goodwill in the process.

Other discounts can be trickier. As we mentioned earlier, concessions are rarely dollar-for-dollar. A salesperson needs to take profit ratios into consideration before offering a concession (see sidebar titled "Industry Profit Margins"). Food and beverage discounts, for example, should be carefully weighed; it is often more cost-effective to offer a discount on rooms or free meeting space instead of offering concessions on food and beverage.

Successful negotiating is a give-and-take process — the end result is that both parties are satisfied. The planner can look forward to a successful meeting within budget, while your hotel benefits from a profitable piece of business and from the positive relationship that may lead to additional business in the future.

**Industry Profit Margins**

- Retail/Misc Depts -15%
- Recreation/Spa - 15%
- F & B Outlets - 19%
- Group F&B - 38%
- Rooms - 77%

*A hotel's foremost profit center is its guestrooms; group food and beverage generates less than half of the revenue of guestrooms. Therefore, an event requiring a large amount of meeting space in relation to the number of guestrooms required is often undesirable.*
**Source:** Meeting Sites Resource (www.meetingsites.com). Used with permission.

# Letter of Agreement/Contract

While contracts are now the norm, the word *contract* frightens many people — people who readily enter into an agreement made formal by a letter. Most businesspeople would not dream of drawing up a contract without legal counsel, but will sign a letter that lists the terms of an agreement. For all practical purposes, a letter of agreement and a contract function the same way, the difference being one of semantics.

A **letter of agreement/contract** should include, in simple language, all arrangements that have been negotiated and agreed to. The contract should be straight-forward, free of "legalese," and clear to anyone who reviews it. If necessary, diagrams or examples should be included so that both parties have no questions regarding the terms of the contract. This protects the client and the hotel, but it also does something else of extreme importance. By itemizing all matters to be covered, the letter of agreement is essentially a clearly stated checklist of what is expected of either party. This is vital, because most misunderstandings reflect a lack of communication and a lack of experience by either the hotel executive, the client, or both.

The letter of agreement/contract should cover each point clearly in a separate paragraph or clause, and each topic should have its own header. Each point should be documented. Nothing should be left to verbal agreement. The parties who negotiated the deal may no longer be employed by the hotel or the client when the convention actually takes place. In any case, memory is decidedly fallible. Everything should be included *in writing*.

## Chapter 9: Negotiations and Contracts

This will eliminate many misunderstandings when the time comes to settle up the accounts, and even prevent malfunctions during the meeting itself.

It is also sound practice to contact a hotel that was previously used as a convention site by the group. This contact can be made by using an **inquiry questionnaire**, which asks a group's former hosts to critique the group for the benefit of a prospective host property (see Figure 9.1). This information is helpful intelligence data to use during negotiations.

*Figure 9.1. INQUIRY QUESTIONNAIRE.*

**U.S. Grant Hotel**
AN ATLAS HOTEL
Post Office Box 80098
San Diego, California 92138
(619) 232-3121

Dear Colleague:
The U.S. Grant Hotel is working with: _____

We understand this group met with you. At your convenience we would sincerely appreciate receiving the following information:

1. 
   | Date | | | | | | | | |
   |---|---|---|---|---|---|---|---|---|
   | Original Room Block | | | | | | | | |
   | Actually Used | | | | | | | | |

Meeting Requirements (Program if available):

2. 
   | | Persons | Set-up |
   |---|---|---|
   | General Session | _____ | _____ |
   | Breakouts | _____ | _____ |

Catered Functions:

3. 
   | | No. of Functions | Persons |
   |---|---|---|
   | Breakfast | _____ | _____ |
   | Lunch | _____ | _____ |
   | Dinner | _____ | _____ |
   | Receptions | _____ | _____ |

4. Comments: _____

Thank you in advance for your cooperation. We will be happy to reciprocate at any time.
Sincerely,

_____
Signature

*It is sound practice to track the historical performance of meeting groups. A questionnaire such as this one requests a post-convention critique from hotels used by the meeting group in the past. This information is extremely valuable in negotiations, as it gives the hotel an early sense of whether the group meets its commitments. While it is acceptable practice for competitor hotels to exchange basic information on groups (such as rooms blocked, actual pickup, percentage of double occupancy, number of food functions, and the like), it is a violation of antitrust law and a criminal offense to exchange pricing information (such as room rates or banquet charges).*

Chapter 9: Negotiations and Contracts

> **MORE ONLINE**
>
> An excellent example of a RFP from the National Association of School Psychologists can be viewed at www.meetings-conventions.com/News/Features/The-Comprehensive RFP/ (scroll down to the "here" link).
> You can also view guides for meeting planners on what should be included in a RFP at www.conventionindustry.org/StandardsPractices/APEX/RFPWorkbook.aspx (click on RFP Workbook and scroll down to link to download the workbook) and at meetings.zentila.com/8secrets-download (registration is required for this free download).

Cooperation of this kind is commonplace among hotels. Such inter-hotel conversations will not only make you aware of possible pitfalls with a group, but can also keep you abreast of current practices and trends throughout the hotel industry. Some discretion should be exercised not to make inquiries from a hotel — or a hotel within a chain — that is in a position to make a last-minute bid to book the business. But with some care, past sites of the group could be valuable sources of helpful data.

Before offering a letter of agreement (contract), most hotels send out a **proposal letter** to meeting planners after either a site visit or receiving a RFP. All RFPs should be personalized to the group and spell out exactly what the hotel can do for it. This does not mean listing your features and benefits (you should avoid doing so in your proposal letter). Instead, proposal letters should include most of the information that will be included in a contract, just not in as much detail. Many hotels, including the Destination Hotels & Resorts chain (www.destinationhotels.com), make detailed contract clauses and other pertinent meetings information available on their websites to help planners to make a decision.

The proposal letter should reflect the personality of the hotel and never give the impression that the planner is being sent a form letter. Instead, the salesperson needs to write a proposal letter as if he or she were speaking to the prospect. This is an excellent way to build rapport and demonstrate that the salesperson is personally invested in the planner's meeting.

In addition to mentioning property meeting rooms that would work well for the planner, it is effective to add photographs or perhaps a convention brochure, a banquet menu, and testimonials from satisfied planners of similar meetings if you are sending the proposal letter by mail or via FedEx or some other carrier (a proposal sent in this manner is particularly effective to respond to a site selection committee – especially if your proposal letter is professionally printed and is in an attractive binder). An e-mail proposal letter can include links to photographs or videos of meeting rooms, past events, testimonials, and even a personal message from the salesperson or the general manager.

Be sure your proposal letter reflects a professional image – avoid misspellings and grammatical errors – and do not include hotel jargon. Your copy should reflect the hotel's attention to detail and focus on its *investment* in the group, rather than using such common terms as price, rate, charge, fees, and expenses; when the term *investment* is used, it gives the impression that the group can expect to get something of value in return.

Your proposal letter is often the first step in a mutually beneficial relationship with the planner and his or her group *if* you *ask* for the group's business – and provide a way for the planner to respond. Proposal letters should include the salesperson's contact information (telephone and cell numbers, e-mail address); e-mail proposals can also include a link to the sales department's landing page on the hotel's website. And, once you have made contact, be sure to follow-up; you will have a better chance of actually closing the sale if you keep in contact with the planner by whatever means is best for him or her.

A proposal letter is normally initiated from a site inspection or a **request for proposal (RFP)** from a meeting planner. A written RFP from a planner includes the group's desired dates, guestroom and meeting space requirements, and the group's meetings history.

## Chapter 9: Negotiations and Contracts

Since planners often send out a RFP to several hotels at the same time, your response should be timely. Planners expect to receive information on availability and pricing within a day or two of their request.

It is important to respond to every RFP quickly, but this has become more difficult as planners increasingly turn to the Internet to send RFPs to properties, either through links on the property's website or via third-parties, such as Cvent, StarCite, ConventionPlanit.com, and Zentila. A recent M&C Research survey showed that 95 percent of meeting planners use online RFPs – and 52 percent of them are for 100 or more room nights. However, only 36 percent research properties that fit their needs before sending online RFPs; 47 percent send exploratory online RFPs, while 34 percent send online RFPs to narrow down their options midway in the site selection process.

While some third-party firms limit RFPs to six to eight per client, some planners now send 25-30 RFPs simultaneously. This practice has created an avalanche of *electronic spam*, and has put a burden on salespeople, who must respond to every electronic RFP (e-RFP) and lose valuable selling time in the process. This is a big problem, especially since the conversion rate on e-RFPs is typically two to three percent.

There are several ways hotels are handling the situation. First, since it is unlikely that hotels can add staff to address RFPs, many use the triage system; research is done on the organization and RFPs are prioritized based on such factors as the overall revenue a group can provide, requested dates and flexibility, special requests and comments, and the source of the lead. If a group is not a fit for the hotel, it is still necessary to respond, however.

Many properties have turned to technology to help with the process. There are several software programs that can analyze the group and others that create custom proposals based on the information the group has provided. Two of these programs include Cendyn's eProposal® (www.cendynarcaneo.com/proposal) and ACTIVE MarketView 3.0 (formerly StarCite® MarketView), which enables hotels to process e-RFPs up to 70 percent faster. The Hyatt chain has used QuickBook for some time to check pricing and availability and respond to the e-RFP within 15 minutes.

Whether or not a RFP results in a sale, a customized response is an effective sales tool. Smaller groups (under 100 rooms) will appreciate that the hotel took the time to tailor a response, and they may give greater consideration to the hotel for future meetings. Larger groups, which generally have professional planners or use third-party firms, should receive a quick response that answers all their questions thoroughly and puts an emphasis on the desired outcome of the meeting. Remember, however, that there is a lack of direct interaction with the salesperson when e-RFPs are used. It is important, then, that salespeople pick up the phone (ideally) or send a follow-up e-mail after sending out a RFP (e-mails are more effective if video links are used to "introduce" the planner to the salesperson or the property). And a handwritten thank you note should always be sent when a sale is made.

> **WORTH WATCHING**
>
> Heather Allison Smith, former director of sales and marketing at The Ritz-Carlton Lake Tahoe and now director of sales and marketing at The Ritz-Carlton & JW Marriott Los Angeles, discusses challenges to hotel sales productivity due to the avalanche of Requests for Proposals in an HSMAI Insights interview.
> Go to youtube.com and type in: HSMAI Insight, Heather Allison, Ritz-Carlton

Should the group accept your proposal, you should send a letter of agreement along with a note of thanks. It is customary for this letter to be sent in triplicate, and to request that it be countersigned by a responsible person from the association (or other sponsoring organization) and returned. As explained, this constitutes a legal contract whereby both parties have agreed to the terms and arrangements. An alternative to the triplicate-copy method might be a letter or an e-mail from the meeting planner stating that the letter of agreement is correct and accepted.

When sending out contracts or letters of agreement, it is important that the contract be dated. This is extremely important during the negotiation stage, as it ensures that the most current version of the contract will be signed by each party. When it comes to signing, however, the hotel salesperson or another hotel contact should not sign the contract before the meeting planner does. If someone at your property is the first to sign, you do not have the chance to correct anything or change your mind about a point once the buyer has signed (the signatures of both parties constitute a binding legal document). The best policy is to send three originals, asking the buyer to sign two and return them to you and keep the third for his or her files. Then, once the signed originals are received, you can sign both originals and send one back to the meeting planner.[2]

Do not be in a rush to sign the returned contracts. You will want to carefully look them over and initial any changes that may have been made. The customer will also have to initial those changes for them to be binding.

It is worth repeating that a soundly written letter of agreement helps both parties execute a successful meeting and prevents misunderstandings by stating exactly what is to be done, by whom, and at what price. Be sure that there are no "surprises" – each aspect should be reviewed with customers in order to protect your business relationship.

Since nothing is part of the agreement that is not included in the contract or letter of agreement, it is essential that certain information be recorded. Details on essential information and commonly negotiated points are covered in the following sections.

---

### 🖥️ INTERNET EXERCISE

#### Electronic Requests for Proposals

Approximately 15 years ago, the first online request for proposal (RFP) debuted on the website of the Radisson Miyako Hotel San Francisco. Today, virtually every hotel website has some means for meeting planners to request a RFP online. In fact, hotels are on RFP overload, but all RFPs require prompt attention. To ensure that action is taken immediately, Crowne Plaza guarantees a response within two hours or a 5 percent discount will be applied to the final master account.

Visit the websites of the hotels listed below to view the RFPs for each:

- InterContinental Boston – www.intercontinentalbostom.com (Click on "Meetings & Events" tab and then on the "Request for Proposal" option)
- Rosen Plaza – www.rosenplaza.com (Click on "Contact Us" and then "Meeting and Proposal Request Form").

Read through each of the RFPs and answer the following questions:

1. Which of the RFPs do you think is the most meeting planner friendly? Why?
2. Compare the hotel RFPs with the Request For Proposal template recommended by the Convention Industry Council (CIC). This template can be viewed at www.conventionindustry.org/StandardPractices/APEX.aspx (click on the "Requests for Proposals" tab and scroll to "Single Facility RFP;" the RFP can be downloaded in either a MS Word or PDF format).

---

## Names of Organization and Hotel

Most letters of agreement or contracts begin with an introduction, known as a **preamble**, that clearly specifies the parties entering into the contract (parties should be identified by name, and the addresses and contact information for both should be listed), a statement of intent by both parties to enter into the contract, and the name or a designation of the event. The preamble also includes the official performance dates of the event (see below).

## Official Dates

It sounds basic, but make sure the exact dates of the event are specified (this includes dates for move-in and move-out as well as the dates for event functions). These dates, which are often referred to as the *official dates*, should include not only the date and day, but also the beginning and ending times for each event. This protects the hotel from tying up a room beyond an official cutoff time (you don't want a breakfast ending too late to set up the room for a luncheon or training session later in the day).

## Number and Kinds of Rooms

Specify the number of guestrooms to be held, spelling out the number of suites, single, double, and twin rooms. Sometimes a client will want the location of the rooms specified, such as pool-side, ocean view, or in a quiet wing of the hotel. If you agree to it, specify the number of rooms in each requested area.

Many hotels present the sleeping room block in a table format, such as the one illustrated on the following page. This table shows the dates and days of the week, the specific breakdown of room-suite types, rates, and the number of rooms contracted for each night.

Also include a reservation **cutoff date.** Attendees who make their reservations after the cutoff date are not guaranteed a room or the negotiated convention rate. If this is the case, attendees must pay the "market rate" for available rooms. A typical clause might read: "*A cutoff date of thirty days prior to the opening of the convention is established. This cutoff date is May 1, 20___. After this date, any of your unused room commitment will be released to the general public. After the cutoff date, we will continue to accept your group's reservations on a space-available basis.*"

Meeting planners may ask that the hotel continue taking reservations from attendees at the negotiated group rate (rather than the prevailing rate) after the cutoff date if rooms are still available. Hotels are usually reluctant to continue to offer group rates, especially in high-demand periods, when they are able to sell rooms at higher rates than the group rate. For one meeting planner, this meant that the negotiated $224 per night block rate skyrocketed to $429![3]

Experienced meeting planners, in anticipation of late attendee registration, will often ask for a contract provision allowing them the option of increasing their room blocks beyond the cut-off date at the group rate. Based on room availability, your hotel might agree to do so, perhaps increasing the group's room block up to ten percent at the group rate.

It is important to note that although the number of guestrooms blocked for the group is spelled out in the contract, hotels will sometimes "hedge their bets" by forecasting the actual room pickup at less than the number contracted. This process is termed a "blind cut" in the industry because the number is not shared with the group.

Hotels base a blind cut on a review of the group's meeting history as well as economic conditions in the marketplace. Since blind cuts can be dangerous, particularly during peak periods, it is always best to share your concerns openly with the planner. If you lack confidence in the group's ability to pick up the number of rooms contracted, convey your concerns to the planner and renegotiate a room block commitment to a more realistic level.

Specify any individual deposits required and the method by which room reservations will be made: by mail; over the Internet; through a third-party housing company; by rooming list; through the Housing Bureau of the Convention and Visitors Bureau; to the hotel directly; or to an "800" number. Also specify who is to handle the receipt of the reservations – the hotel, the convening group, or a third-party housing company.

| ROOM TYPE(S) | ROH | RCST | EXEC | STAFF | Contract |
|---|---|---|---|---|---|
| ROOM RATE | $260 | 1500 | 260 | 165 | |
| Monday, 10/20 | | | | 7 | 7 |
| Tuesday, 10/21 | | | | 7 | 7 |
| Wednesday, 10/22 | 3 | | | 7 | 10 |
| Thursday, 10/23 | 46 | 1 | 5 | 7 | 60 |
| Friday, 10/26 | 46 | 1 | 5 | 7 | 60 |
| Saturday 10/27 | 46 | 1 | 5 | 7 | 60 |
| Sunday, 10/28 | | | | 7 | 7 |
| (2) Executive suites will be at $425 ||||||

Key: ROH – Run of House
RCST – Ritz-Carlton Suite
Exec – Executive Room

*A group's room block should be defined in a table format, with the days and dates down the side. Types of rooms and rates should be noted on the lines for each day, and you may also want to add columns for the number of arrivals and departures on each day of the event.*
**Source: Courtesy of the Ritz-Carlton, Lake Las Vegas.**

## Rates/Commisions

Specify clearly the rates for each type of accommodation. If a range is agreed to, list rates from the lowest to the highest. If a flat rate (all guestrooms at the same price) is negotiated, state it clearly. If rooms are to be priced differently in different sections of the hotel, it may be wise to list such rates separately. And when listing rates for suites, be sure to note that the suite includes a parlor and a number of guestrooms, such as a parlor and one bedroom or a parlor and two bedrooms.

Many large conventions are planned well in advance, and most hotels will not quote firm room rates more than a year out. In this case, a formula for establishing future rates will need to be negotiated. Often, a "percentage off rack rate" is used to establish a future rate. For example, if the hotel's current rack rate is $150 per night and the current convention rate is 20 percent less ($120), this percentage would be used to determine room rates at the time of the meeting (attendees would get 20 percent off the rack rate in effect at the time of the meeting). Other formulas used to establish future rates might be to specify a maximum percentage increase from current rates or to tie the future rates to the **Consumer Price Index**.

Applicable taxes should also be spelled out. In most cases, attendees will be required to pay the state sales tax and any applicable room taxes. If service charges and gratuities are also assessed, these, too, should be listed to avoid any unpleasant surprises.

In addition to negotiating with meeting planners, it has become increasingly common for third-party meeting planners to be involved in negotiations. As we discussed in earlier chapters, firms such as Conference Direct, Experient, and HelmsBriscoe are often contracted by groups to negotiate and book hotel rooms, food and beverage, and meeting rooms. Because of the volume of business these firms book, they are paid significant fees, which are sometimes collected as commissions from hotels.

Any contract, therefore, should specify the terms and conditions under which any **commissions** will be calculated and paid. It is important that all parties involved clearly understand which rates and packages are commissionable and how the commission will be calculated (commissions on some package plans, for example, are paid only on the rooms portion negotiated, while other commission plans pay commissions on the total plan). The contract should also include to whom and when the commission will be paid.

## Arrival/Departure Pattern

It is important that you know the group's **arrival/departure pattern** – the dates and times that meeting attendees will arrive and depart. If 400 rooms are being held, it is unlikely that all 400 room occupants will arrive on the same day. You should develop a **flow chart** to reserve rooms in accordance with the agreement. The agreement, for example, might call for 100 rooms for arrival on Monday, January 10, 200 rooms for arrival on Tuesday, January 11, and the remaining 100 rooms on Wednesday, January 12. It is also wise to indicate the breakdown of the rooms into singles, doubles, twins, and suites. You may find arrival dates easier to secure than check-out dates, but these too are of great importance to you.

Since all hotels strive to maximize occupancy, a loss of revenue can result if a group's guests leave early. Many hotels combat this problem by charging an **early departure fee** to any guest who checks out earlier than the original departure date indicated on his or her reservation. Contracts, therefore, should clearly spell out the reasons and amounts of early departure fees — and these, in turn, should be clearly indicated to the group's membership on printed meeting materials (registration forms, housing forms, and so on) and on the group's web page.

Clauses regarding early departures may be negotiated, of course; if a guest leaves as a result of an emergency, for example, the fee is waived. Or, a clause may allow a guest to change his or her departure date at check-in without penalty (the early departure fee would only be charged if the guest checks out before the verified date). Other contracts contain clauses that waive early departure fees for certain attendees, such as the organization's staff members, VIPs, and speakers.

## Meeting Space

The experienced convention planner will want you to hold all your meeting rooms and public space until he or she has firmed up the program and the resultant traffic flow pattern. If the event is far in the future and if it will not occupy the entire hotel, this may be difficult. You need public space to sell other meetings. Keep in mind that while eye-catching events are the big ones, most meetings do not fill the hotel; usually there are several in the house at once. The second or third meeting in the hotel at the time, albeit smaller ones, represent important income, as well as opportunities to serve repeat customers.

How much of your meeting space to hold is a point to be negotiated, but it is reasonable to hold all rooms that might possibly be used for the event. A date must be set by which the program will be completed to the point that unused public space can be released. If you agree to hold rooms without setting an option or **release date**, you may find yourself unable to use them to solicit other meetings or banquets.

Many meeting planners prefer specific meeting rooms to be named in the contract. This limits your flexibility. If possible, avoid naming the specific function rooms and include a clause to indicate how and when meeting space may be released. For example:

*We have reserved function space based on the requirements described to us. The meeting group will provide the final program to the hotel nine months before the meeting. At that time, all space not being used will be released back to the hotel. The specific names of the function rooms will be furnished to you when you are ready to print your program. This allows time for attendance figures to be well established.*

Meeting space is extremely valuable to your hotel; without adequate meeting space for groups, you reduce your ability to maximize occupancy and revenue. Groups and transients are both part of the hotel's overall room demand. Groups book well in advance, so hotels can generally offer them lower rates for a guaranteed block of rooms. The booking cycle for transients is much shorter (a week or two) and they pay higher rates. Depending on demand, a hotel's group room allotment differs daily throughout the year.

An important metric that meeting hotels use when negotiating with groups is the **guestroom-to-meeting-space ratio**. This ratio varies from hotel to hotel, but convention hotels are typically built with 100 square feet of meeting space for every guestroom they commit to group business. For example, if a 400-room hotel designates 150 rooms for leisure, transient, and individual business travelers, it would have a maximum group allotment of 250 guestrooms and 25,000 square feet of meeting space.

Consider a 400-room hotel with a **group ceiling** (targeted number of group rooms) of 300 rooms over a given period and an expected transient demand of 100 rooms. The property is effectively a 300-room group hotel. Revenue is lost if the hotel assigns all its meeting space to a 200-room group, as that leaves no meeting space for the remaining 100 group rooms.

Meeting groups that are space-intensive but light on guestroom usage, however, should not be immediately dismissed by hotel sales. Jody Brandes, senior meeting planner for Genentech, a San Francisco-based pharmaceutical firm, says her meetings are complicated due to an unfavorable ratio of guestrooms to meeting space. She explains:

> Like many pharmaceuticals companies, we're a space hog and want a lot of breakouts, even for meetings of 100 room nights on peak. To make properties more willing to provide lots of meeting space without charging very high room rates, I alter certain meeting elements to drive RevPAR while getting something of value in return.
>
> We are more generous with our food and beverage; we upgrade to the omelet station rather than doing a continental breakfast, and we often keep our final-night dinner on property. And, I provide meeting histories that show we've done all this before. Plus, I emphasize that our attendees spend a lot of time in the bars and lounges on property, and spend across the retail, spa, and other outlets.[4]

Groups that need extensive meeting space but not a great deal of sleeping rooms should be encouraged to schedule their meeting to coincide with other events that do not require a lot of meeting space but fill guestrooms, such as a citywide convention or incentive program. In these cases, hotels will tend to have the needed meeting space available without tying up guestrooms needed for other groups, making space-intensive groups a perfect fit.

## Complimentary and Reduced-Rate Rooms

It is commonplace in the convention industry for hotels to supply some complimentary rooms, but the number varies a great deal. A hotel may be more generous if the meeting is scheduled during an off-time of the week or season. A more successful hotel may be tougher when it comes to concessions.

In most cases, hotels offer complimentary rooms based on the number of guestrooms used. A very common rule of thumb is one complimentary guestroom for every 50 guestrooms utilized and one complimentary suite for every 100 paid room nights. The hotel's policy should clearly be spelled out, as in the sample clause below:

*We will be pleased to furnish one complimentary guestroom for every fifty room nights utilized. The complimentary commitment will be provided on a cumulative basis for the length of the meeting. The hotel offers a choice of accounting procedures for complimentary rooms. A bottom-line dollar credit on the Master Account will value each unit at the daily average guestroom rate generated by the group, or guestrooms/suites can be reserved on a complimentary basis to arrival.*

Notice that the clause above specifies that comps are calculated on a *cumulative* rather than on a per-night basis. Many meeting planners prefer that rooms be calculated in this way. That is, if a group used 45 guestrooms on the first night and 55 on the second night, a cumulative computation would result in two comp room nights; if the comp rooms had been based on a per-night basis, only one comp room would be earned for the second night. No matter what formula is used to calculate comp rooms, it should be clearly spelled out; hotels should specify if complimentary rooms are based on all nights of a group's stay, including early arrivals and late departures, or only calculated during the official dates of the convention.

A hotel and a client may also agree to a number of reduced-rate rooms. This is usually done for staff members, VIPs, speakers, and performers, and, of course, is subject to negotiation. The contract should clearly specify the number of rooms that will be reduced, the rate for each, and, perhaps, the designated occupants.

If charges are to be made for meeting rooms, rates should be specified for each room. As with comp and reduced-rate guestrooms, these charges are usually based on the number of guestrooms used. The contract should specify the guestroom requirement and detail how meeting room rates will be assessed based on room pick-up.

## Prior Visits

A hotel often will not charge for guestrooms used by the meeting organizer and his or her staff during visits to the hotel before the event to make preliminary arrangements. This is often done on a *space-available* basis. It is wise to set a specific limit on the number of rooms made available for this purpose.

## Working Space

Offices, press rooms, and similar working space should be discussed. If a charge is to be made for them, specify the rates. If no charge is to be made, specify this clearly, but also spell out the maximum number of rooms to be used for this purpose. Many meeting planners insist upon indicating the location of such rooms to make sure the locations are convenient to the meeting sessions.

## Registration Control

In the case of association conventions, hotels usually agree to clear all requests for accommodation from people of that particular industry with the convention organizer. You need to do this in order to credit the association with the total number of rooms used in conjunction with the convention. All such rooms should be applied against the guaranteed number of rooms. In addition, a convention organizer often wants to control the use of suites as hospitality centers or even as setups that circumvent the exhibit itself and its booth space and decorating costs.

## Exhibit Space

If a charge is to be made for the exhibit hall, say so clearly and state what is to be included in the charge. Items to be considered are hours the exhibit is to be open, electricity, air conditioning or heat, carpeting, and the number of tables and chairs. List what the hotel is to furnish and what must be contracted for with a show decorator.

Secure exact dates for the exhibition from the meeting planner, including beginning and ending times that include an allowance for the move-in and move-out of the exhibits. Many hotels provide forms for the meeting planner to verify dates and times for both the exhibit and exhibitor move-in and move-out.

Some hotels charge on the basis of the number of booths sold by the association. The charge is usually a per-booth rate by day for the duration of the convention, including move-in and move-out days. However, this ties the hotel's rental income to the show manager's ability to attract exhibitors; hotels, therefore, normally levy a flat charge. A fee of two to five dollars per square foot for each exhibit day is quite common.

## Food Functions

Meeting planners will not expect you to establish menu prices today for a meeting three years in the future. Most realize that, because of rising costs and daily fluctuations in market prices, catering managers usually won't quote firm menu prices until six months out. But a meeting planner has to make budget projections, so expect experienced planners to negotiate a fixed percentage off the printed menu prices in effect at the time of the meeting or to attach a current banquet menu to the contract and negotiate that prices won't increase by more than a certain percentage each year.

Specify how much notice you require for guarantees on food functions. Most common is 48 hours advance notice, but many hotels have increased their guarantees to 72 hours. If you need more time, and you may over weekends, negotiate it and include it in your letter of agreement. Menus have to be priced and approved. Most hotels will agree to set tables for a percentage above the number guaranteed in order to accommodate additional guests. Many set for an additional five percent, others hold it to three percent, and still others base the percent on the number of persons to be served. For example, a typical contract might include points such as the following:

*A 48-hour guarantee is required on all meal functions. Your catering manager must be notified of the exact number of attendees for whom you will guarantee payment. For functions scheduled on Sunday or Monday, the guarantee must be received by noon on the preceding Friday.*

*The hotel will set up as follows:*

| | |
|---|---|
| *20-100 persons set* | *5% over guarantee* |
| *101-1000 persons set* | *3% over guarantee* |
| *1001 persons and over* | *1% over guarantee* |

*In the event a guarantee is not received, the original estimated attendance count will be prepared and billed.*

---

### APEX Contracts Report

To assist hotels navigate contract issues, the Convention Industry Council (CIC) offers *APEX Contracts Accepted Practices*, an educational paper that is part of its APEX (Accepted Practices Exchange) initiative. Like other APEX guidelines, the report was developed by a seven-member panel, but there were some major differences from typical APEX offerings, which typically provide templates to help standardize hospitality industry practices.

Tyra Hilliard, a veteran attorney, speaker, and meetings consultant, was the chair of the APEX contracts panel. She says:

> Contracts are meant to be negotiated. This is an educational document, it's not meant to take the place of a negotiation. It's meant to help people understand contracts better so that they can negotiate better.

The panel determined that it was not possible to develop a "standard" contract for a number of reasons, "including the large and multifaceted industry with many different types of vendors, customers, facilities, and requirements, and also because legal considerations and fostering competition would prevent creation of such a document." Rather than suggesting a format for a hotel contract (although the paper includes an outline with a suggested order of clauses), the *APEX Contracts Accepted Packages* paper provides an alphabetical listing of 24 different clauses typically found in hotel contracts, explains the purpose of each clause, and details the factors that should be taken into consideration before including each type of clause in a contract.

To view the complete *APEX Contracts Accepted Practices* paper, log on to the CIC's website, www.conventionindustry.org. Click on the APEX tab and then Accepted Practices. Scroll down to APEX Contracts Accepted Practices.

Sources: APEX Contracts Accepted Practices, Convention Industry Council; Corrie Dosh, "CIC Prepares to Issue Educational Paper About Meetings Contracts," *Business Travel News*,.

---

When a salesperson quotes food and beverage prices, he or she will note a "price, plus, plus." The price is the price per person and the **plus, plus** represents taxes and service charges added to the per person charge. The actual percentages will vary depending on state sales taxes and property service charges. For example, a Carmel Valley, California, hotel might quote a per person rate for a reception as $25.00 ++. The total price would then be $31.88 — $25.00 plus $1.88 (7.5 percent sales tax) plus $5.00 (a 20-perent service charge). Keep in mind that tax rates can vary, even within a state; in California, for example, local cities and counties can charge up to an additional 2.5 percent for a total sales tax of 10 percent. Be sure to advise the planner of these additional taxes – and add them to the contract.

Many hotels have added **food and beverage minimum clauses** to their contracts. As the name suggests, groups are required to purchase a minimum dollar amount of food and beverage during a meeting or conference. These clauses do not sit well with planners, especially since the contract language holds the group responsible for making up any difference between the contracted amount and the amount actually spent. And, the minimum amount does not include taxes, service charges, and group spending in hotel restaurants and bars.

It is important to keep in mind that food and beverage is a major profit generator for hotels – in many cases, hotels realize a 40-50 percent profit on food functions. But food and beverage minimums may vary, depending on the season, the cost of food, the demand, and the size of the group. In peak season, for example, a dinner may cost $150 per person, while it may be priced at $125 (or even lower, as it is far more cost-effective to plan for a larger group) during a non-peak period. While hotels are sometimes willing to offer discounts on food functions during these times (or if other business warrants them), they want to ensure that no revenue is lost due to overbuying or overstaffing. That is where the minimum food and beverage clause comes into play.

If a group agrees to a $20,000 food and beverage minimum, it will have to pay the $20,000 — whether or not it meets the required amount. Most groups will want to avoid a shortfall, so planners will want to compare the hotel's prices against their budget. In some cases, this can be advantageous to them. A savvy meeting planner may see that his or her costs amount to $25,000, which is $5,000 above the minimum food and beverage contracted. If the planner agrees to the $20,000, he or she can ask for a *tiered contract* – asking that any excess be applied to concessions that are valuable to the group. For example, the planner may tell the salesperson, "I agree to your F&B minimum, but if we spend at least the minimum, I want to unlock these additional concessions" (concessions can range from upgrades to suites, waiver of the banquet room charge, additional A/V equipment, and so on).

If a planner sees that there will be a shortfall, however, he or she has several choices. First, the shortfall can be overcome by adding more food or beverage – ordering a breakfast buffet with an omelet station rather than a continental breakfast, upgrading to a fancier (or custom) menu at dinner, or providing alcohol at a reception that would usually feature a cash bar. The options not only have the advantage of meeting the minimum, but they also create a memorable experience for attendees.

Second, a planner can ask for a F&B minimum on a per-person basis. This option eliminates the problem of having to pay for attendees who have left early or arrived late and are not partaking in scheduled food and beverage functions. A third option is to ask for a complete meetings package (CMP), which offers a fixed price per attendee.

If the planner still comes up short, there may be no other recourse than to pay the resulting charges. Since food and beverage damages are based on net profit, however, many planners object to paying full costs; after all, the hotel has not incurred any charges for the cost of the food or cooking and serving it. Therefore, they often insist on clauses based on *liquidated damages* (that is, costs based on the amount after the profit margin is taken into consideration). Although terms and discounts may be negotiated, a typical clause may read:

*In the event that the F&B Minimum is not met, the group will pay the profit difference estimated at 40% of the unmet F&B Minimum.*

Some hotels may add "plus tax" to these clauses, but this can only be done if the tax is actually required by law. In most states, a tax can only be imposed if an item was actually sold.

## Refreshment Breaks

It is amazing how many arguments stem from refreshment break arrangements. Many meeting organizers think in terms of coffee shop standards. They do not understand the conditions under which the hotel operates. As a result, much resentment is evidenced, and it is

Chapter 9: Negotiations and Contracts

---

### 🖥 INTERNET EXERCISE

#### Evaluating Contract Templates

The Institute of Electrical and Electronics Engineers offers a number of sample contracts. Use a search engine and type in: ieee-templates of contracts and legal documents. You will be able to view contract templates developed for negotiations with the following chains and hotels:

- Disney (FL)
- Disney (CA)
- Fairmont
- Hilton
- Hyatt
- IHG
- Marriott
- Starwood

Download a copy of the group meeting contract for one of the above hospitality entities and identify the following clauses in the contract:

- Arbitration and Dispute Resolution
- Attrition
- Cancellation
- Complimentary and Reduced-Rate Rooms
- Gratuities and Service Charges
- Guestroom Pickup Review
- Indemnification
- Master Account and Credit Procedures
- Termination

Use the information found in these clauses to answer the following questions:

1. What clauses were developed to ensure the organization is getting the lowest group rate?
2. How much slippage does the contract allow before attrition charges are assessed?
3. What information is the hotel required to provide in the post-meeting report?

---

important to explain all that is involved when the hotel supplies refreshment breaks. Spell out the costs and labor required for all refreshment breaks. Include prices for cakes, soft drinks, and juice, too. It is important to the hotel that its clients have faith that the hotel charges are fair.

## Liquor

Spell out the hotel's policy on liquor service. Most hotels prohibit meeting planners from bringing in food or liquor from outside the property. State your policy on this matter clearly so that no misunderstandings arise during the meeting. A typical contract clause might state:

*No food or beverages of any kind will be permitted to be brought into the hotel from the outside without the written permission of the hotel. The hotel reserves the right to assess a service charge for any food and beverages brought into the facility in violation thereof. If any alcoholic beverages are to be served on the premises (and/or elsewhere under the hotel's alcoholic beverage license) the hotel will require these beverages to be dispensed by hotel servers and bartenders. The hotel's alcoholic beverage license requires the hotel to (1) request proper identification (Photo ID) of any person of questionable age, and refuse alcoholic beverage service if the person is either under age or proper identification cannot be produced, and (2) refuse alcoholic beverage service to any person who, in the hotel's judgment, appears intoxicated.*

If you charge by the bottle, an arrangement should be made for inventory control and credit given for unopened bottles after the convention. It is important both for the hotel and the client to identify the person authorized to tally the inventory with your staff. The credit could be issued at that time.

## Gratuities and Service Charges

Gratuities and service charges should be discussed in advance of the meeting and should be spelled out in the letter of agreement. Most meeting planners view gratuities as part of convention costs, and even though a touchy area, no problems should arise if guidelines are clearly established at the outset. For example, a gratuity clause might read:

*Bellperson gratuities of $3.00 per person round trip are mandatory on group arrivals. Room attendant gratuities of $1.00 per room, per night, are optional, but suggested.*

A service charge statement might read:

*All catered food, beverage, and related service charges will be subject to the current sales tax. Each catered function will automatically reflect a service charge of 17 percent.*

Note that the above clause specifies that the service charge is taxable. Taxes on service charges may vary from city to city, and the amount of tax (if any) on the service charge should be clearly spelled out in the contract.

---

### THE CONVENTION INDUSTRY COUNCIL

The best customers are the ones who really know their business. And they like to do business with vendors who know theirs. It is amazing how rapidly and steadily the convention business grew, with very little done to expand areas of knowledge and expertise. In 1949, four associations – the American Hotel & Lodging Association, the American Society of Association Executives, the Hospitality Sales & Marketing Association International, and the International Association of Convention & Visitors Bureaus – came together to establish a new organization to develop commonly accepted trade standards. Today, that organization, which is known as the Convention Industry Council (CIC), is comprised of 33 organizations (about half representing seller groups and half representing buyer organizations) and boasts a membership of more than 103,500 individuals and 19,500 firms and properties involved in the meetings, convention, and exhibitions industry.

The CIC of today still adheres to its original four basic objectives:

1. to bring about a sympathetic understanding and acceptance among these organizations of the responsibility of each to the other.
2. to create a sound and consistent basis for handling convention procedures and practices through a program of study and education.
3. to conduct educational and activities of mutual interest to participating organizations.
4. to acquaint the public with the fact that conventions are essential to industry and to the economy of the community and nation.

Through the years the Council has been the educational leader for the industry. Tools and programs developed by the CIC to support the industry and meet its challenges include:

- Publishing industry reference materials, beginning with the *Convention Industry Council Manual*. This resource presents detailed responsibilities of each of the three groups involved in a convention – the sponsoring organization, the hotel, and the convention bureau – and how they are interrelated. The manual, now in its ninth edition, contains useful checklists, forms, and an industry glossary.
- Creating the Certified Meeting Professional (CMP) certification program.
- Spearheading the Accepted Practices Exchange (APEX) initiative to develop accepted practices for the industry.
- Recognizing pioneers of the industry through the Hall of Leaders program.

## Audiovisual Equipment

Some hotels supply audiovisual equipment from their own inventories; others use local dealers. In either case, it is important to show the rate structure for equipment and services, or to indicate that it is the convention staff's responsibility to make its own arrangements. You may prefer to supply the names of local service companies that deal directly with, and bill to, the client. Some hotels will accept the local dealer's bills and rebill the convention. It is important, then, that there be a clear understanding as to who has the responsibility to provide the necessary equipment so that the client receives the service needed.

## Union Regulations

Convention organizers are accustomed to union help and regulations, but you should list the basic workday, rates, and overtime charges. You should also state any out-of-the-ordinary union requirements in your labor contract. Making your client aware of them eliminates much aggravation.

Many astute meeting planners will not sign confirmations or agreements without first checking out union conditions. The hotel has a responsibility to alert the meeting planner to the possibility of local labor contracts terminating before the meeting, any likely labor rate increases, or possible labor disputes.

## Master Account and Credit Procedures

The meeting planner will have a master billing account. He or she must furnish the hotel with a list of people authorized to sign for charges that are to be placed on the **master account**. The client must also indicate which charges the convention organizer will pick up for such people as speakers and performers. The client may choose to pay the room rate only and let the individuals pay all incidental charges. In the case of a corporate meeting, the arrangement may have to be clarified for each attendee. Make it clear that the master account will have to be verified and initialed before the client leaves after the meeting.

Before extending credit to a corporate group or an association, hotel sales executives frequently request a completed credit application (see Figure 9.2). Calls also may be made to colleagues at properties where the group has met previously. These references, combined with Dun and Bradstreet credit checks, are used to determine the credit limit extended to the meeting group.

## Method of Payment

Specify how and when the group's bill is to be paid. Most contracts include a payment schedule that details the amounts due on specific payment dates. This schedule should also include any penalties for late payment as well as discounts that are available for early payment of the master account (in some cases, discounts are offered on a graduated scale – the earlier the account is paid in full, the higher the discount; if there is a cut-off date for discounts, this should be spelled out in the contract). If you require a deposit, say so and give the date that it is due. Also negotiate any additional sum to be paid, as well as the final payment.

## Chapter 9: Negotiations and Contracts

*Figure 9.2. APPLICATION FOR DIRECT BILLING.*

**MARRIOTT'S Camelback Inn**
RESORT GOLF CLUB & SPA
P.O. BOX 70 • SCOTTSDALE, AZ 85252 • (602) 948-1700

### CREDIT APPLICATION

Direct billing privileges are not automatically extended. To apply for direct billing privileges, please complete and return this application to the hotel. Should you have any questions regarding the status of your application, please call the Credit Manager at (602) 948-1700, ext. 7715 or your Sales Representative.

Name of Group: _____

Address: _____

City: _____ State: _____ Zip: _____

Telephone: _____ Date(s) of Event: _____

**References:**
Hotel Reference: _____ Contact: _____

Address: _____ Phone: _____

Date(s) of Event: _____ Amount Billed: _____

Hotel Reference: _____ Contact: _____

Address: _____ Phone: _____

Date(s) of Event: _____ Amount Billed: _____

Bank Reference: _____ Officer: _____

Address: _____

Telephone: _____ Account #: _____
(please indicate the acct. # from which payment will be drawn)

Items to be Billed: (Please check)
- All Room Charges ( )
- Some Room Charges ( ) please specify
- Restaurant Charges ( ) please specify
- Banquet Charges ( )
- Recreational Facilities ( )
- Other ( ) please specify
- Other ( ) please specify

Estimated Value _____

I have completed this application in behalf of this group and believe all information contained to be correct. I understand that the extension of direct billing privilege is conditional upon our agreement to pay our account in full within thirty days of receipt of the hotel's statement.

Signed: _____ Date: _____

Title: _____

Accounting Department Approval _____

*Many hotels do not automatically issue credit to new clients. Meeting groups that do not have a credit history with the hotel must fill out a credit application form. Note that both hotel and bank references are requested on this form.*

Most convention organizers prefer to go over the master account before they leave the hotel, but some hotels cannot have it ready that quickly. It is a common practice to leave some portion of the account unpaid, should there be some items that require negotiations or that aren't ready for final accounting. But most hotels do insist that the master account be approved by the client before leaving, while all matters are fresh in the mind and the staff is available for consultation. A statement such as the following might be included:

*The hotel will be expending money immediately in labor and services to ensure the most successful meeting for you. Therefore, it is our policy to ask for 75 percent of the master account to be paid prior to your departure from the hotel. The remaining 25 percent will be direct billed.*

## Termination/Cancellation Clauses

A **termination clause**, sometimes termed a force majeure or Act of God clause, should be included in the agreement for cases when either party might cancel because of circumstances beyond its control. Termination means that both parties are excused from performance without liability. For example, the hotel should not be held responsible for nonperformance in the event of a strike, lockout, fire or failure of heat, light, power or natural disasters. Planners might terminate if there is a change in ownership, hotel chain affiliation, management company, or bankruptcy proceedings by the hotel. Other forces beyond the control of the group or the facility that would apply include weather events, large-scale disasters, or civil unrest. You can view a sample termination clause at meetings-conventions.com/article.aspx?id=39278.

The next paragraph after the termination clause should be the **cancellation clause**. *Cancelling* a contract is not the same as *terminating* a contract. Termination means that neither party has any continuing obligation to the other. Cancellation means that one party elects not to perform, which ordinarily requires the payment of damages. Many conventions are planned a number of years in advance, so occasions do arise that call for a cancellation of the event. The cancellation clause should spell out what it will cost the hotel and/or the group if either party should cancel for reasons not identified in the termination clause.

Cancellation clauses in hotel contracts often establish cancellation fees on a sliding scale, with the amount increasing the closer the cancellation is to the anticipated date. Planned food and beverage functions might also be factored into the scale. Since cancellation fees are based on lost profits, not lost revenues, the percentage of revenue received by the hotel cannot exceed its profit margin (generally 70-80 percent for sleeping rooms and 30-40 percent for food).

Recently, the Hyatt chain implemented a new standardized contract, which was most notably changed in the area of cancellations. Hyatt now uses a graduated formula for cancellation damages; the closer to the group's scheduled arrival date a meeting is cancelled, the more the group's damages increase. In the event of a cancellation between the time the contract is signed and two years before the meeting date, the charge is 40 percent of rooms revenue and 15 percent of food and beverage and meeting room minimums. Meetings cancelled within six months of the meeting date carry the heaviest charges: 80 percent for rooms; 40 percent for food and beverage and meeting room rentals. If it is the hotel that cancels, it pays the same fee to the group. Because Hyatt either owns or manages under contract all its 120-plus properties, it has little trouble applying the new contract (with its penalties) uniformly.

Currently, cancellation clauses seldom provide mutual accountability; there is often no recourse offered to the group if the hotel cancels or does not perform as contracted. Meeting planners, understandably, find this practice to be unfair, and they are increasingly insisting on a "Breach by Hotel" paragraph in their contracts. For example:

*Failure by the hotel to provide guestrooms, function space, and/or services as agreed, or any breach of any representation by the hotel, shall render the hotel liable to the group for all direct and indirect damages, attorney fees, and costs incurred by the group on account of such breach.*

## Damage Clause: Liquidated or Mitigated Damages

To protect themselves in the event of cancellation, most hotel contracts include either a **liquidated damage clause** or a **mitigation of damage clause**. A liquidated damage provision is an agreement by both planner and hotel in advance as to the penalty for cancellation. Damages are collected upon cancellation. With a mitigation of damages clause, the penalty is not predetermined — the hotel must wait until the convention dates actually pass and then prove its actual loss. Tracking and reporting the use of space and then computing actual losses following a cancellation is inconvenient, difficult, and requires waiting much longer to recover damages, so most hotels prefer a liquidated damage clause.

| LIQUIDATED DAMAGES | MITIGATED DAMAGES |
|---|---|
| Amount agreeed upon in advance of breach | Actual damages proven after breach |
| • Predetermined | • Must wait until dates pass |
| • Risk on hotel | • Risk on group |
| • No proof problems | • Hard to prove/calculate |

*Liquidated damages are a compromise that reduces risks to both parties. The hotel is not required to prove its actual loss and no proof of mitigation is required.*

A liquidated damage clause allows the parties to agree in advance as to the amount and method for calculating damages that might be paid in the event of cancellation. Generally, the amount of liquidated damages is less than what a hotel might have received from mitigating damages, but it is a "sum certain." The liquidated damage clause sets the limits of damages well in advance of the meeting. If the hotel resells some of its rooms, there is no reimbursement to the meeting group.

A liquidated damage clause is generally stated in a sliding scale tied to a percentage of anticipated profits and/or to a specific dollar amount. The amount would be low for cancellations two or three years out and higher for cancellations closer to the meeting date. For example:

*Under the terms of this Agreement, the Hotel is reserving for your use the room block and public space requirements described herein. In the event these reserved facilities and related services are not used, the Hotel will experience significant monetary losses.*

*Notwithstanding any other provision of the Agreement, you shall have the right to cancel this Agreement without cause upon written notice to the Hotel at any time prior to the event and upon payment of an amount based on the following scale:*

| | |
|---|---|
| *Notice and payment received on or before (15 percent of total anticipated profit)* | *12/15/16 - $183,060* |
| *Notice and payment received on or before (30 percent of total anticipated profit)* | *11/15/17 - $366,120* |
| *Notice and payment received on or before (70 percent of total anticipated profit)* | *11/05/18 - $854,280* |
| *Notice and payment received after (100 percent of total anticipated profit)* | *11/05/18 - $1,220,400* |

## Chapter 9: Negotiations and Contracts

---

### Computing Damages

The difference between liquidated damages and mitigated damages is that mitigated damages are *actual* charges, and liquidated damages, while predetermined, are less than actual damages. For example, assume a hotel books a group needing 200 room nights at $100 per night; the estimated room revenue for the group would be $20,000:

| | |
|---|---|
| Group Rooms Blocked: | 200 Room nights |
| Group's Average Rate: | $100 |
| Profit Margin for Guestrooms: | 70 percent |

What happens if the group cancels? With a *mitigated (actual) damage clause*, the hotel would be entitled to 70 percent ($14,000) of the lost revenues. The hotel collects only 70% of lost revenues because damages are based on *lost profits*, not on lost revenue. Lost profit is defined as gross revenue minus variable expenses.

Hotels track profit separately for each revenue-producing department. The industry average profit margin for guestrooms is 70 percent. Catered food has an average profit margin of 35 percent, while alcohol has an average profit margin of 80 percent.

If the cancellation clause spelled out *liquidated damages*, both the meeting planner and the hotel might agree to a penalty of 20 percent of lost profits if the group were to cancel. In the above case, the damages would total $2,800.

| Mitigated (Actual) | Liquidated |
|---|---|
| $20,000 x 70% = $14,000 | $20,000 x 70% = $14,000 |
| | $14,000 x 20% = $ 2,800 |

With a mitigated damage clause, if the hotel is able to resell 50 of the cancelled rooms, it would credit $3,500 back to the meeting group:

| | |
|---|---|
| 50 rooms resold @ 50 x $100 x 70% = $3,500 | $14,000-3,500 = $10,500 |

---

Carolyn Colton, former vice president and associate general counsel for Marriott International, cautions that in calculating a liquidated damage amount the hotel should consider other profit centers beyond sleeping rooms. She says:

> When a group cancels an event, the hotel also experiences substantial damages in lost food and beverage/banquet sales and/or lost fees for use of function space. In addition, the hotel suffers losses in other aspects of its business, such as lost restaurant and gift shop sales, movie purchases, and room service.[5]

Most meeting planners will favor a mitigation of damage clause. Such a clause requires the hotel to try to minimize its damages by working to find business to replace the business lost by cancellation. Hotels that agree to mitigate damages must wait until after the meeting dates have come and gone before determining damages and then are faced with the difficulty of computing damages.

It is common for meeting planners to request that a combination of both clauses be included in the contract. David Scypinski, senior vice president of Conference Direct, warns against this. He says:

> **Include a liquidated damages clause or a mitigation clause, but never both.** Mitigation is the process of reselling your hotel's loss brought about by a cancellation or through attrition. Mitigated damages can only be collected *after* the dates of the cancelled event. Liquidated damages, on the other hand, are damages collected immediately upon cancellation.

Obviously, the best cancellation clause includes a liquidated damages proviso, which is what you should negotiate. Sometimes a customer will insist on a mitigation clause. *Reason:* Both the liquidated and the mitigated clauses discount the amount of revenue you'll be able to recover; if you include both clauses, you'll be penalizing your hotel twice.[6]

In summary, when liquidated damages are specified in the contract, there is no room resale provision. The hotel is not required to mitigate damages (do the best it can to resell guestrooms and meeting space). The law is very clear that if the parties to a contract agree to a liquidated damage clause, the injured party does not have to prove its loss — or whether it was able to mitigate its loss. Even if the hotel resells the rooms in question, the meeting group must pay the hotel the negotiated fee, as the hotel is accepting an amount that is less than the actual damages.

## Attrition Clause

Attrition is not the same as cancellation. Attrition refers to under-performance — the difference between contract commitments and actual guestroom pickup, food and beverage spending, and meeting room usage by the convening group. If a meeting group or hotel cancels an event, no rooms or services are used. **Attrition clauses** are included in contracts to compensate a hotel for its losses if a group fails to meet its contractual commitment.

**Guestroom Attrition.** In the past, it was industry practice for hotels to accept the risk of low pickup by agreeing to hold a block of rooms for a group until a specific cutoff date (generally 30 days). After that date, the unused rooms reverted to the hotel for resale with no additional liability to the group.

Although some hotels still adhere to this practice, most, especially in periods of high demand, have altered their contracts to include attrition clauses. An attrition clause allows the hotel to collect damages if the actual sleeping rooms used are significantly fewer than the group's **block**, the number of rooms originally reserved for the meeting. Guestrooms that are used are referred to as **pick-up**; unused rooms are known as **slippage.**

Attrition clauses protect hotels from excessive losses due to slippage by shifting the risk of low pickup to the meeting planner. The hotel attempts to sell the rooms remaining after the cutoff date, but the meeting planner is liable to pay for any rooms left unsold. John Foster, an attorney specializing in meeting law, states:

> Slippage clauses are making planners a little sharper in their forecasting. You're better off in today's climate to underbook your convention than overbook. It's always easier to go back to the hotel and ask for more rooms than to decrease your block.[7]

---

### Split Contracts

Some hotels offer a **split contract**, which is a firm contract with an added tentative contract, to meeting planners. For example, if a planner wants to reserve 200 rooms but doesn't want to be responsible for a large attrition rate, the hotel might offer a split contract that holds the group responsible for a firm ten percent attrition rate on 140 of those rooms. The added tentative contract would specify that the group could confirm or release the remaining 60 rooms 90 days prior to arrival. If the group determines that registration is not proceeding as anticipated, they may refuse the tentative contract, allowing the hotel ample time (90 days) to sell the 60 rooms to another group. The split contract option tends to make attrition more palatable to the planner and is beneficial to both parties.

## Chapter 9: Negotiations and Contracts

The number of rooms for which a planner must pay attrition is negotiable. Kristy Sartorious, former director of sales for Wyndham Hotels in Dallas, says that they allowed a group twenty percent attrition off their room block before penalties were assessed. In contrast, Westin Hotels adjusts the percentage from city to city and by type of property: resort versus downtown.

For example, the Westin St. Francis in downtown San Francisco allows a ten percent slippage, while the Westin La Paloma Resort in Tucson allows only five percent. The reason for the difference is that downtown properties can more easily resell rooms to business travelers, while resort hotels primarily rely on vacationers.

Attrition fees are generally based on a sliding scale: the fewer the rooms occupied, the greater the penalty (see Figure 9.3). Attrition fees are best negotiated as an exact dollar amount, and should provide several option dates to review the room block with an agreed-upon percentage of reduction. For example:

*Figure 9.3. ATTRITION LIABILITY CALCULATOR.*

### Attrition Liability Calculator
**MINIMUM COMMITMENT (I.E. 80%)**

|  | 26-Jun | 27-Jun | 28-Jun | 29-Jun | 30-Jun | 1-Jul | 2-Jul | 3-Jul | 4-Jul | 5-Jul | Total |
|---|---|---|---|---|---|---|---|---|---|---|---|
| Contracted Block | 20 | 40 | 80 | 120 | 80 | 40 | 20 | - | - | - | 400 |
| 80% commitment | 16 | 32 | 64 | 96 | 64 | 32 | 16 | 0 | 0 | 0 | 320 |
| Your group's actual pickup | 10 | 20 | 40 | 60 | 40 | 20 | 10 | 5 | 0 | 0 | 205 |
| A. Per night liability | 6 | 12 | 24 | 36 | 24 | 12 | 6 | -5 | 0 | 0 | 115 |
| B. Rooms available for sale in hotel* | 0 | 10 | 25 | 40 | 10 | 6 | 10 | 10 | 0 | 0 |  |
| Liability (lesser of A or B) | 0 | 10 | 24 | 36 | 10 | 6 | 6 | -5 | 0 | 0 | 87 |

Room Profit Percentage (100%, unless negotiated to be lower) **75%**

TOTAL LIABILITY
Single Room Rate $200.00 x 87
Room nights X 75% = $13,050

*Total hotel rooms minus comp rooms, unavailable rooms and all rooms sold that day.*

This spreadsheet lists a group's daily contracted room book (across the top from left to right). In this example, the hotel allows a 20 percent attrition rate, so the minimum guarantee is found by multiplying each day's room block by 80 percent. The per-night liability is determined by subtracting the actual pickup from the minimum required pickup.

Row B lists the hotel's total number of rooms available for sale for each night of the meeting, and the group is required to pay only for lost profit at 75 percent for each night. For example, on June 26, the hotel's rooms were sold out, so the group did not have any liability on that day. Adding the totals across, however, shows that the group owes the hotel an attrition fee for 87 rooms. At a room rate of $200 per night, the group's total attrition fee amounts to $13,050.

**Source:** From the *Experient Guide,* published by *Convene* magazine. Used with permission.

*The Hotel agrees to hold ample inventory to accommodate the rooms reserved in your group rooms contract. In doing so, the Hotel may be put in a position to turn away other groups that may request rooms for the same dates. Therefore, the Hotel limits the amount of attrition or reduction in the contracted room block.*

*From one year to nine months prior to arrival, the group will be allowed to reduce their room block by twenty percent without penalty. For reduction over twenty percent, a fee of ___ dollars per room will be assessed. From six months to three months prior to arrival, the group will be allowed to reduce their room bock by ten percent without penalty. For reduction over ten percent, a fee of ___ dollars will be assessed.*

**Food and Beverage Attrition.** In addition to attrition fees for sleeping rooms, some hotels are requiring planners to pay fees for meeting space and food and beverage that are not picked up because the group did not meet its guestroom commitment. A food and beverage attrition clause might read:

*The number of catered food and beverage functions and the attendance figures for such functions have been taken into consideration in establishing the room rates for this convention. Should any food and beverage functions be cancelled, the Group will be responsible for 50 percent of the estimated food and beverage revenue lost, based on the minimum catering prices in effect at the time of the meeting multipied by the number of scheduled attendees.*

In order to avoid attrition fees resulting from low guestroom pickup and under-attendance at food and beverage functions, many hotels and meeting planners negotiate an **audit clause** that provides the means for gathering information and verifying the group's actual performance.

Audits generally consist of reviewing records both prior to and during an event, and they help meeting planners to plan for future events as well as resolve any disputes that may occur during an event. For example, if a hotel determines that a group has picked up less than 80 percent of the contracted room block, an audit may be conducted to determine how many attendees were actually staying in the hotel — but not in the group's contracted block. This would involve comparing the group's list of attendees with the hotel's in-house guest list. If it is determined that the group's actual attendance (including rooms booked outside the block) met the attrition requirement, attrition damages would not be assessed.

If audit clauses are used, they should be specific and detail how audit information will be used to resolve any discrepancies. The contract should specify when audits will take place, who will conduct the audits (hotel staff, meeting staff, outside auditor), what elements will be audited (room block versus room pick-up, food and beverage commitments versus actual covers, ancillary revenue, and so on), and who will pay for the audit if any costs are involved.

**Meeting Room Attrition.** A meeting room (function space) rental attrition clause might read:

*The hotel is currently holding function space based on the attached Schedule of Events. Should it be necessary for you to cancel or reduce the estimated attendance by more than 25% of any of the major functions listed on the Schedule of Events, the hotel will be entitled to liquidated damages based on the following scale:*

> *More than 60 days to 120 days prior to the scheduled date: An amount equal to one-half (1/2) of the estimated food & beverage profit based on the minimum estimate of the total cost of the function.*
> *Less than 60 days prior to arrival date: An amount equal to 75% of the estimated food & beverage profit based on the minimum estimate of the total cost of the function.*

These attrition clauses clearly spell out what is required of the group and the specific damages that will be levied should the group fail to live up to its contract. Many meeting planners are vocal against these clauses, claiming that attritition clauses force them to look into a crystal ball. Richard Granger, a former meeting planner for Allmerica Financial and now assistant vice president of conference and travel services for the Hanover Insurance Group, Inc., explains:

Five years ago you didn't see attrition clauses. Now you're lucky to be permitted ten to fifteen percent shrinkage. Attrition clauses are not only tougher, but broader. They used to cover only room slippage, but now include food and beverage costs too.[8]

Hotels, citing their need to be financially accountable, feel that such clauses are justified and prevent the unethical practice of meeting planners overestimating room counts to obtain additional concessions.

Smart hoteliers try to smooth over an adversarial negotiating climate. Most hoteliers agree that "attrition is painful," and they want to keep attrition situations to a minimum. While hotels are reimbursed some damages with attrition, they would prefer to have guestrooms occupied by guests who spend money in gift shops and lobby bars and on room service.

Meeting planners see attrition fees as money down the drain, and hoteliers realize that good will is lost when they have to ask for attrition fees. In the spirit of compromise and looking to the value of future business, hotels are now favoring **rebooking clauses**. A rebooking concession would allow the meeting group to apply a specified percentage of the attrition fees to a future meeting at the hotel. A sample clause might read:

*Hotel agrees to apply 25% of paid attrition fees toward a similar-sized meeting that takes place within one year.*

Since markets may change due to the economy (with sellers' markets favoring hotels and buyers' markets advantageous to the planner), there must be a willingness to work together and be flexible with policies and procedures in order to build long-term relationships.

## Arbitration/Dispute Resolution

**Arbitration** is the most commonly used form of **dispute resolution** (other means of resolving contract disputes include mediation and litigation). Arbitration clauses are often used because arbitration provides an efficient, timely, and relatively inexpensive alternative to litigation, which is both time-consuming and expensive due to crowded court calendars and the costs of a trial. An arbitration rather than a court action is usually in the best interests of both the hotel and the meeting planner. A typical arbitration clause might read:

*Any controversy or claim arising out of or relating to this agreement, or the breach thereof, shall be settled by arbitration in accordance with the Rules of the American Arbitration Association, and judgment upon the award rendered by the Arbitrator may be entered by any court having jurisdiction thereof.*

## Warranty of Authority

The principles of agency law specify that if both parties are authorized to sign a contract for a meeting, the contract is still binding on both the hotel and the meeting group if one or both of the signers is no longer with their employer. A warranty of authority clause states that the signers have been granted authority by their respective organizations to enter into an agreement. Such a clause is especially relevant given the turnover of both hotel salespeople and meeting planners and in light of the considerable time frame between the signing of the agreement and the execution of the event.

A warranty of authority clause might read:

*The Group Name and the person signing this Agreement on its behalf represent and warrant that the undersigned person is an authorized and appointed agent of the Group Name, fully empowered to bind the Group Name to all provisions contained in the agreement, and that no further action is required on the Group Name's part to enter into this agreement.*

*This agreement shall be binding upon the Group Name and its successors and assigns.*

## Insurance/Indemnification

Most hotels stipulate that the meeting group must agree to carry adequate liability insurance that protects the hotel against claims arising from the group's activities conducted in the hotel during the convention. In doing business with associations and trade shows, a hotel incurs specific liability in its relationship with trade show exhibitors. Although exhibitors sublease hotel space from the association or trade show, the hotel should require the exhibitor to sign a "hold harmless" or liability agreement that confirms that the hotel is not responsible for damages or theft of material or equipment. Some hotels extend this to deny accountability for accidents occuring in public areas that are not the result of negligence by the hotel.

Convention hotels also request that a copy of the meeting group's exhibitor contract be submitted to the hotel's convention services department prior to its printing and distribution. The reason for this is to ensure that the meeting group and the hotel are protected.

An insurance clause might read:

*The group acknowledges that the hotel and its owners do not maintain insurance covering property brought into the hotel by exhibitors and that it is the sole responsibility of the exhibitor to obtain insurance covering such losses. The group shall give written notice of such to any exhibitors. The group is responsible for submitting to the hotel an executed release of liability from each exhibitor.*

Indemnification is a word found in many meeting contracts. To indemnify means to protect. An **indemnification clause** (hold harmless clause) provides mutual protection. The hotel and the meeting group indemnify each other. A typical indemnification clause might read:

*Each party agrees to indemnify and hold harmless the other from any and all loss, damage, or expense (including attorneys' fees) arising from the negligence or willful misconduct of the indemnifying party, its agents and employees in the performance of its duties and responsibilities under this agreement.*

This clause states that each party will be responsible for its own negligence and that each party agrees to hold the other party harmless if the actions of one party cause the other party to be sued or suffer loss.

## Other Contract Matters

In addition to the topics covered above, meeting planners may have other concerns, or events may have special requirements. In these cases, additional clauses covering these issues are often added to completed, written contracts as **addendums**, additions that must be signed by both parties for the addendum to be a binding legal document.

Some of these additional clauses may cover such topics as:

- Americans with Disabilities Act requirements
- Overbooking and relocation of "walked" guests
- Construction/Renovation

*Americans with Disabilities Act (ADA) requirements* may be an important aspect of events at which attendees may be visually or hearing impaired or have mobility issues. Under the ADA, both the hotel and the meeting planner are responsible to ensure that guests with disabilities can have equal access to the facilities. Generally, the hotel is responsible for public areas, guestrooms, and restrooms, while the meeting planner must ensure that function room layouts are adequate and special needs are accommodated (a sign language interpreter for the deaf, large-print materials, and so on).

An ADA clause should clearly spell out the special needs that must be addressed, and such clauses may also require that the hotel be in compliance with the ADA and that it is committed to accommodating guests with disabilities and special needs.

*Overbooking and relocation of "walked" guests* are covered in clauses to establish the requirements for the hotel to make alternative arrangements and/or pay damages when it is unable to honor a booked reservation. In some cases, the hotel will offer several alternatives, such as booking the "walked" guest at a comparable hotel at no charge, providing monetary consideration, or offering special services, such as complimentary shuttle service to the guest for each day he or she is displaced from the hotel. Other considerations may be providing an upgraded room at no extra charge when the guest can return to the hotel and crediting the room toward the group's block.

*Construction/Renovation clauses* may be included if an event is scheduled far in advance of the signing of the contract. These clauses generally stipulate that the hotel and its facilities will be in the same or better condition as they were when the contract was signed, and they detail damages if facilities are under construction or substantially altered when the group convenes. In most cases, the clause will specify that the hotel will notify the group of any changes in the condition of the premises — especially changes that may affect the portion of the facility to be used by the group. As with other clauses, the construction/renovation clause specifies each party's obligations in the event that changes will disrupt the contracted event.

## Contract Standardization

To facilitate the formerly time-consuming process of contract negotiation and to meet the requests of meeting planners for more consistency when dealing with properties, the hospitality industry has responded with an important trend: the standardization of contracts and other meetings-related paperwork. Following the introduction of the Marriott Meetings Network a number of chains have developed their own standardized forms and services (see box titled "Contract Standardization").

Standardized contracts, which are most prevalent in the area of small meetings due to their short lead time, essentially provide a heightened degree of communication by standardizing language and covering all relevant issues, and most meeting planners are very receptive to them. The manager of corporate event planning at McGraw-Hill in New York, says:

> If I receive a contract that is not that customer friendly, I have to run it by the legal department and it delays the signing of the contract. In the past, it was nightmarish. Now I'll approve some of the contracts on sight.[9]

> **Contract Standardization**
>
> In response to meeting planners' needs for consistency when negotiating with hotels within its chain, Marriott developed the Marriott Meetings Network after two years of intensive customer research. This computerized system enables properties within the chain to standardize contracts and eliminates the need for meeting planners to update contracts.
>
> Chains including Hilton, which was a leader in standardization, Hyatt, Ritz-Carlton, Renaissance, Omni, and Westin all offer standardized contracts and meeting forms, and some chains also work with their customers to develop pre-approved meeting contract templates that planners can fill in with the specific details of their meetings. The IEEE (Institute of Electrical and Electronics Engineers), for example, offers standard templates of contracts that were negotiated with several North American hotel chains, including Disney (Florida and California), Fairmont, Hilton, Hyatt, InterContinental Hotels Group (IHG), Marriott, and Starwood.
>
> Third-party meetings firms, such as Experient and HelmsBriscoe, have also negotiated contracts with major hotel chains as well as independent hotels and resorts; these contracts can be customized for specific groups to speed up the negotiation process, and the group also benefits as a result of the bargaining power of these firms. Because hotel contracts tend to favor the hotel, some groups have developed their own contracts, either with the advice of a legal professional or by using meeting contract software. While it is likely that hotels will adhere closely to their standardized contracts, going to the negotiating table with a contract that has been pre-approved by the group helps to save time in the negotiating process, as these documents detail the specific needs of the group and specific requirements or clauses can be inserted into the hotel's standardized contract where warranted.

There are drawbacks, of course. Some meeting planners, especially independent ones, prefer to use their own forms. Their point of view is that every event is unique and no one form can handle all individual group needs. But their perspective is being overshadowed by the sea of planners who welcome not only standardized contracts, but other standardized forms and services as well — event resumes, banquet event orders (BEOs), billing procedures and computerized access to such areas as rooming lists. Diana Johnson, conference administrator for 28 events in different cities across the nation, says:

> Once you've read the standard BEO you know the format. You know right where to look to find the same things; meeting setups, guarantee policies, set menus. You don't have to scrutinize it as much.[10]

The standardization of these previously time-consuming pre-convention documents and procedures enables both the meeting planner and the convention staff at individual properties to concentrate on servicing the event and offers yet another benefit besides saving time and money — meetings clout. Jack Breisacher, former vice president of group sales for Renaissance Hotels and Resorts, explains:

> After all, the customer is often spending a few hundred thousand dollars with us, and all they want to know is how much money was spent in each area. Then they'll take that information to a property next year and say, "Here's what we did, and based on that, here's what we need at this time." It becomes a solid negotiating tool.[11]

## Multiple-Meetings Contracts

Negotiating multiple-meetings contracts is becoming commonplace in the hospitality industry. These contracts, which schedule business over a period of one to several years, have grown in popularity -- especially with corporate meeting planners, who laud them as time- and cost-saving (see Figure 9.4). A planner from a healthcare organization, for example, says she signs a multiple-meetings contract with a major hotel chain for her group's 200 educational seminars held every year around the country. The contract guarantees a price that is a percentage off the rack rate at each hotel and saves time, eliminating the need to negotiate separate contracts.

*Figure 9.4 PROMOTING MULTI-MEETING AND MULTI-YEAR MEETINGS CONTRACTS.*

*Today, many chains are offering multi-meeting and multi-year contracts to meeting planners to facilitate the negotiating process. Rather than having to negotiate for each meeting or event – or worry about costs for future meetings — planners can sign a single contract and concentrate on the job of planning their programs. This ad for Starwood's Convention Collection promotes the benefit of booking "across years, properties, and destinations" at several of the chain's brands.*
**Source: Courtesy of Starwood Hotels & Resorts.**

> **Best Practices** — Marriott
>
> ### Marriott Contracts with MetLife for 15 Incentive Meetings Over a Two-Year Period
>
> MetLife, a large insurance company that previously held its meetings in a number of different hotels, signed a deal with Marriott International to book 15 incentive meetings into the chain's Marriott, J.W. Marriott, and Ritz-Carlton properties across the country over a two-year period. The deal, which represents 15,000 room nights, came about because MetLife's recognition programs represent some of the company's biggest meetings, and the company's management felt that these meetings were too important for a "cookie cutter" approach.
>
> In addition to the benefits of a meetings consolidation plan that would both save money and create consistency, MetLife gained major clout as a potential client when it put all 15,000 of its room nights on the table to potential hotel companies. Bob Pizzute, AVP, former conference planning and event services manager at MetLife in New York, says:
>
>> When we took an enterprise approach to meeting planning, where all of our distribution channels come to one source for meetings, we became a much larger player in the market.
>
> Negotiations for the actual terms of the contract took months, as there were hundreds of details to be worked out, including space, rates, and concessions. Jeff Calmus, CMP, vice president – global event management for MetLife, said:
>
>> Rates were different based on the time of the year and availability, but we had developed concessions that every hotel agreed to.
>
> The successful deal benefited both parties, as MetLife got as good a deal for a 220-room-night program as for a 3,800-room-night program, and Marriott not only benefited from the large piece of business but may see additional income, as Pizzute says he will go to hotel chains with future RFPs. The win/win negotiation between the parties on their first multiple meetings deal (and Marriott's successful execution of the meetings for which it contracted) will likely result in the chain being a strong contender for MetLife's future business.
>
> Source: Alison Hall, "Big Deal," *Insurance Conference Planner.*

Another advantage for the meeting planner is meeting clout; a hotel is usually more open to making concessions for a planner who schedules a great deal of business. Judi McLaughlin, CMP, managing director at HelmsBriscoe, the leading meetings and group rooms procurement company in the hospitality industry, states:

> In many companies, meeting planning is fragmented and decentralized. One of our clients found that it used 29 different properties in Chicago in one year for some 70 meetings. Through consolidated planning, the company has named ten preferred hotels in that city.
>
> The benefits to the company are guaranteed discounts in pricing, overall agreement to standard contracting terms and conditions, increased efficiencies throughout the planning process, and better quality meetings. And the preferred properties are certain to see a dramatic increase in their market share of the company's business.[12]

There are, of course, some disadvantages for meeting planners, including the difficulty of accurately predicting meeting attendance (unless attendance is mandatory); future developments, such as company downsizing or mergers; or being "locked in" by contracts. In the last instance, the meeting planner is bound by the previously negotiated multi-meetings contract and cannot take advantage of opportunities that arise when other properties can provide the same services at a lower rate.

> **WORTH WATCHING**
>
> Watch a short video of Yolanda Radochia, director of event services at 1105 Media, explaining how multi-year agreements have benefited her organization at hedtalks.connectplusat hiltonworldwide.com (click on the "Driving Results" tab and scroll down to the "Multi-Year Agreements" video).

For hotels, multiple-meetings contracts offer the advantage of guaranteed business, but there is also a major disadvantage: perhaps another group comes along that would generate more rooms or food and beverage revenue for the property. If the space is tied up, the property has no recourse but to let the new business go. It is imperative, therefore, that hotels consider multiple-meetings contracts carefully, weighing the proposed multiple-meetings business while maintaining a degree of flexibility in these contracts, especially those that are a year or more out. Other factors, such as the history and stability of the group or possible business developments on either the part of the group (a possible merger in the group's future, for example) or the property (perhaps the obtaining of new, more lucrative business) should also be considered before entering into multiple-meetings contracts.

## Summary

If doing business by letter of agreement/contract seems complex and detailed, think of this format as a checklist or order form. Arranging for a convention requires more than ordering a certain number of guestrooms. Your letter of agreement shows you, the hotelier, what the client expects and also shows the client his or her responsibility. It works out well when thought and time are given to each detail.

The first letter of agreement/contract may be the hardest to write. After you get it polished, save it as a sample. It will save much work if that polished letter and its various clauses are individually stored in a word processor file so that they may be used when you are formulating new contracts or letters of agreement.

As you can see, the hotel industry is working hard to deal with meeting planners on a highly professional basis and to make the process of securing profitable meetings business easier through the development of "win-win" contracts and the standardization of meetings-related services.

In the next section of this book, we will take a look at the various areas involved in actually executing the meetings and conventions secured through excellent salesmanship and effective negotiating.

## Endnotes

1. "The Dealmakers," *Meetings & Conventions*," May 2012, p. 47.
2. Howard Feiertag, "We're Into a Seller's Market Again, So Watch Those

Contracts," *Hotel & Motel Management*.
3. James Goldberg, "Seller's Market Means Tougher Terms," *Corporate Meetings & Incentives*.
4. Rob Carey, "Navigating the New Market: Planner Strategies for Successful Hotel Negotiation," *Meetingsnet.com*.
5. Carolyn Cotton, "Liquidated Damage Provision Reflects Compromise on Hotel's Part," *Convene*.
6. Correspondence with David C. Scypinski, senior vice president of industry relations, Starwood Hotels.
7. Mary Ann McNulty, "Be Prepared for a Slippage Clause," *Meeting News*.
8. Melinda Legis, "Killer Contracts," *Successful Meetings*.
9. Kenneth Hein, "Standardization Efforts Paying Off," *Meeting News*.
10. Ibid.
11. Ibid.
12. Alison Hall, "Fewer Suppliers, Better Deals," *Corporate Meetings & Incentives*.

## Study Questions

1. Distinguish between a proposal letter and a letter of agreement (contract).
2. What elements should be considered when developing a contract?
3. What is the master account? In what ways is this account billed?
4. What is a damage clause? An attrition clause? What is the difference between a termination clause and a cancellation clause? How extensively are each of these clauses used?
5. What is the Convention Industry Council? What groups make up its membership and what is their role in the convention industry?
6. What are standardized contracts? What types of properties typically use them? What are the pros and cons of using standardized contracts?
7. What are the advantages and disadvantages of negotiating multiple-meetings contracts?

## Key Terms

**addendum**—An addition to a completed written document. Must be signed by all parties involved in the contract to become part of a legally binding document. Sometimes called an **amendment**.

**arbitration**—The settling of a disagreement by the review and decision of an arbitrator rather than using the courts.

**arrival/departure pattern**—Anticipated date and times of the arrival and departure of a meeting group's members.

**attrition clause**—Allows the hotel to impose damages if the actual guestrooms used are significantly less than the rooms blocked. Can also apply to food and beverage and meeting room rental. Hotels will often include an allowable attrition amount (20 percent), holding the group liable for the contracted and room block and/or food and beverage minimum minus the allowable attrition amount.

**audit clause**—A clause that allows one or both parties in a contract to perform audits to measure and validate certain aspects in the terms of the contract. Audits ideally should take place through the term of the contract to avoid potential problems from arising.

**block**—The number of guestrooms reserved for a group.

**cancellation clause**—Provision in the contract that specifies damages that apply for both parties should either party terminate the agreement. A cancellation is a breach of the contract. There is often a sliding scale that indicates fees owed based on when the meeting cancels. For example: 31-90 days prior to arrival, group owes 75 percent of room revenue and 50 percent of food and beverage minimum; 0-30 days prior to arrival, group owes 100 percent of room revenue and 100 percent of food and beverage minimum.

**commission**—A fee or percentage paid to a sales representative or an agent for sales one has made or services rendered.

**concession**—Items the hotel offers complimentary or at a reduced cost to "sweeten the deal." Concessions are not automatic; hotels should base their decisions on the overall value of the event and offer concessions when the meeting planner exchanges something of value to the hotel. Meeting planners may include preferred concessions in the initial RFP, making the sales manager aware of the planner's expectations and the group's needs. Also called *special incentives* or *upgrades*.

**Consumer Price Index**—An index that compares the changes of the costs of basic goods and services with the prices previously set in a fixed-base period.

**customer lifetime value**—The value of profits expected from a customer's future purchases. A corporation or association meeting planner who is satisfied and books several meetings with your property over his or her buying lifetime is more valuable than a one-time purchaser. If the satisfied customer refers other meeting planners, the value would be even greater.

**cutoff date**—The designated date when the buyer (upon request) must release or add to their function room or guestroom commitment. After this date, the hotel may release any remaining guestrooms that have not been utilized in the contracted block and sell the guestrooms at a higher rate. A standard cutoff date is 30 days prior to arrival, but many hotels will work with planners to extend the contracted guestroom rate after the contracted cutoff date.

**dispute resolution**—The means by which the parties entering into a contract agree to resolve any disputes. These means may include mediation, arbitration, litigation, or other ways to resolve problems.

**early departure fee**—A set fee charged to a hotel or conference center guest who checks out earlier than the original departure date originally agreed upon.

**flow chart**—Indicates the arrival and departure pattern of the meeting participants.

**food and beverage minimum**—The total amount of catered events (not including service charge and sales tax) required by the hotel based on meeting space and dates being held.

**group ceiling**—The maximum number of guestrooms that can be allocated to groups on a particular day. Sometimes referred to as the hotel's **group room allotment**.

**guestroom-to-meeting-space ratio**—The relationship between a group's room block and the amount of meeting space requested by the group. Generally, groups that require a high number of guestrooms and limited meeting space are preferred by hotels.

**indemnification clause**—Contract clause that specifies compensation for injury, loss, or damage. Also referred to as a **hold harmless clause**.

**inquiry questionnaire**—Questionnaire requesting a post-convention critique from hotels used in the past by specific meeting groups.

**letter of agreement/contract**—Letter from the buyer accepting the proposal. No legal agreement/contract exists unless both parties have accepted the hotel's proposal.

**liquidated damage clause**—A contract clause that specifies in advance the exact amount of money parties agree to pay in the event of breach of contract.

**master account**—One folio for the group on which all charges are accumulated. Also called the **master folio**.

**mitigation of damage clause**—A contract clause that requires parties to determine damages after the dates of the canceled event. Mitigated damages are actual damages.

**pick-up**—Number of guestrooms actually used out of a room block.

**plus, plus**—Addition of taxes and service charges to the standard prices charged for food and beverage. Designated on a catering contract and a BEO by the notation "++."

**preamble**—An introductory statement at the beginning of a contract. Identifies the parties involved, a statement of intent to enter into a contract, the name of the meeting or event, and performance dates. Also called a **recital** or **background** in some contracts.

**proposal letter**—A letter sent by the hotel before the letter of agreement or contract that spells out exactly what the customer will receive.

**rebooking clause**—Provides for a portion or all attrition or other group liability to be applied to a future meeting or meetings (the hotel will often designate a set time limit – such as within one year — in which the new business has to be booked). Groups often ask that a rebooking clause be included in the contract to minimize their losses.

**release date**—The date beyond which the hotel is free to rent the unused function space to other groups.

**request for proposal (RFP)**—Action initiated by the meeting planner for an offer or bid for hotel services.

**slippage**—The number of guestrooms not used from the original reserved block.

**split contract**—Combining a firm contract with a tentative contract, such as requiring a room block pickup of 400 rooms but allowing the group to hold another 100 rooms until an agreed-upon date without any liability to the group. This type of arrangement is typically negotiated in cases where exact attendance is uncertain to help to minimize attrition fees.

**termination clause**—Contract clause that limits liability should the convention be prevented due to circumstances beyond either party's control. Sometimes referred to as an **Act of God clause** or a **force majeure clause**. When a contract is terminated, neither party is considered in breach of the contract.

# Chapter 9: Negotiations and Contracts

## Industry Profile

### Paul Ruby, CMP, Associate Director of Catering & Event Management

Sheraton Dallas Hotel

Paul Ruby is a highly experienced event professional with nearly three decades of event and hotel experience. Ruby's career has also included positions as the Director of Catering Services for Sheraton and Director of Catering/Convention Services and then Convention Manager for Westin. In 2009, he brought his expertise to the Sheraton Dallas, which is one of the largest meeting venues in the city (the hotel offers over 230,000 square feet of ballrooms, boardrooms, and entertainment suites). A member of the Board of Directors of the Event Service Professional Association (ESPA), Paul has received ESPA President's Award as well as other awards and recognition for his contributions to the industry.

## The Importance of the Convention Service Manager During the Sales Process

The partnership between sales and the service team has been evolving over the past few years. Event service managers are increasingly being integrated into the pre-contract process, particularly during the meeting planner's site visit. The importance of having the hands-on expertise of an event service manager involved from the very beginning helps solidify the property's partnership with the planner.

It's critical to begin building a relationship between event services and the planner as soon as possible and showcase a property's sales/service partnership to the planner. At the Sheraton Dallas, we are seeing more planners asking for the event service manager to be involved on site visits, and our sales team is being more proactive — even scheduling event service manager participation with planners who do not request it.

During a site visit, an event services manager sees and feels meeting details from a different perspective than a sales manager does. On a site tour with the planner, the sales manager and I can begin to get into the "nitty-gritty" of the event, which prompts more questions from the meeting planner. Many times, new ideas arise as the planner asks questions and really begins to picture their event coming to life in our meeting space. Planners embrace the detailed property and service knowledge a convention service manager brings to the table.

In addition to more direct client contact at the site visit level, our sales team often reaches out to event services during the Request for Proposal phase for photos of similar events, floor plans of previously booked meetings of similar size, client testimonials, and overall brainstorming ideas, all of which support the success of the property's proposal. Requests for Proposals do not reflect the personal touch that is often key to making an event successful, so the sooner we are able to begin connecting person to person and building rapport, the better off we all are in the process.

Event service manager involvement early on helps close the deal and also sets us apart from other venues that may not incorporate an event service manager prior to signing the contract. In today's world, it is not about sales versus services, it is how we work together and take the best care of the customer. The sales and event service teams that win business and earn repeat business are the teams that have figured out how to align their efforts and help each other throughout the entire process.

**Learning Objectives:**

This portion of your text looks at the role of the convention service manager and his or her staff in ensuring that the property delivers all that was promised to the meeting planner. When you have studied this chapter, you will:

- Know the importance of servicing convention groups and be able to identify how the convention service function and the role of the convention service manager has developed.
- Be able to describe the duties and responsibilities of a property's convention service manager in meeting planning, execution, and the evaluation of group events.
- Be able to describe how group business is turned over to the convention service department and how the salesperson's involvement varies at different properties

**Outline**

Service Is the Key

Who Services?
- The Convention Service Manager
- Increased Recognition
- Convention Service Staff
- Convention Service Managers at Convention and Visitors Bureaus

The Transition

An Overview of the Service Function

Summary

Chapter Appendix: Convention Service Checklist

# 10 The Service Function

Securing a convention is only the beginning; once business has been booked, you must deliver what was promised. How a convention goes out of a hotel is equally — or even more—important as obtaining the group's business. A hotel salesperson does not sell just guestrooms, meeting space, and complicated audiovisual equipment—his or her most important product is reassurance; reassurance that the hotel is capable of handling the group's business. To a great extent, the meeting planner's job depends on how well the hotel does its job.

Hard work and many dollars are invested in advertising and promotional material in an effort to recruit group business. Yet, satisfied meeting planners and delegates are the best and most economical advertising medium. If the hotel performs well, the meeting planner will likely return to the property. Delegates are well-traveled today and expect more from hotels. If your hotel has made a favorable impression, planners may recommend it to their peers, and delegates may stay with you on return visits—and recommend that their business associates and friends do the same.

To make that all-important favorable impression, it is necessary for the property's sales department and the convention services department to work as a team to ensure that the meeting planner's expectations are met. In the past, a property's convention service manager (CSM) generally stayed in the background until after the meeting or event was booked and their services were needed to execute meeting requirements. Today, however, the trend is to involve the hotel's CSM early in the sales process – usually starting with the site visit.

Having the CSM accompany the salesperson or sales manager during the site visit provides an opportunity for the CSM to establish rapport with the planner — and can greatly enhance sales efforts. The CSM has the knowledge and experience to answer specific questions, such as room capacities using various setups, and also offer suggestions to assist the planner to "see" his or her meeting at the property.

The CSM can be even more valuable if he or she has researched the group and the planner prior to meeting the planner on the site visit. The CSM should use the Internet to review the group's website and check its Facebook, Twitter, and LinkedIn pages for insights into the perception of the group and the activities in which the group is involved. Internet searches for the group and the planner will also yield news worthy articles; the CSM should be especially alert for "red flags," such as pending lawsuits or union issues that may affect the group's meeting.

Input from the CSM who will actually be servicing their meetings has become so important to meeting planners that many request the CSM's presence at their site visits. Julie Pingston, CMP, CTA, Senior Vice President & CEO of the Greater Lansing Convention & Visitors Bureau, says:

> The role of a CSM involves much more today than simply working with a meeting/event planner behind the scenes on banquet event orders and other tasks. CSMs, found at hotels, convention and conference centers, and convention and visitors bureaus, now strive to create a collaborative and consultative relationship.
> 
> A CSM has to be both engaging and innovative, as well as serve as a strong local on-site planner for their customers…Meeting and event

planners have indicated that the strength of their relationships with their CSMs is related to the success of their event. And, they will return to a facility or destination based on those relationships.[1]

Since nothing attracts another piece of group business more than a satisfied convention, it is crucial that all promises made in the selling process be fulfilled. An indelible impression will be made when the hotel provides service that is above and beyond the pre-convention promises.

---

**The Impact of Quality Convention Services on Rebooking**

A recent study conducted by the Event Service Professionals Association (ESPA) found that 71 percent (nearly three-quarters) of the meeting planners who responded based their rebooking decisions on the quality of their experiences with a property's convention services manager. Meeting planners also said the following about CSMs:

- 100 percent said that CSMs have a significant impact on the successful execution of events.
- 75 percent felt more comfortable and confident about the ability of a CSM who belonged to a professional organization.
- 88 percent indicated that the quality of a CSM's service greatly affected their perception of a hotel, convention center, or CVB.
- 81 percent said that continuing education was extremely important for CSMs; they felt that keeping up with industry trends, compliance, and best practices would enable CSMs to provide optimal service for their meetings.

Source: "Report: Convention Services Keep Groups Coming Back," *International Meetings Review*, October 24, 2014.

---

Presenting a "united front" – demonstrating that the sales and conventions services departments work together as a team – builds the meeting planner's confidence that the entire property is committed to providing superior service. In this chapter, we will discuss the relationship between salespersons and the convention services department, and we will show how the role of CSM has evolved and what attributes are important to be successful in this field. We will also take a look at the roles of convention services staff and learn the steps involved in booking and executing successful meetings.

## Service Is the Key

Sometimes, the service follow-through is regarded as an afterthought to the heavy emphasis placed on selling a convention or meeting. But failure in the essential service phase can be costly. A meeting planner evaluates the success of his or her convention on the extent to which the hotel's commitments were kept. Lack of communication, poorly trained or indifferent employees, failure to heed details, and rude responses to requests are all detriments that may result in lost future business.

How might the hotel better serve the convention group? Most important is a well-trained and courteous staff with a service attitude. The hotel industry is essentially a people business and it is important to communicate the property's willingness to assist the meeting planner during both the selling and servicing process (see box titled "Selling and Servicing Small Meetings"). Hotel staff members should be made aware of the importance of convention delegates and should be trained to understand that nothing short of top performance is expected.

## Chapter 10: The Service Function

**SELLING AND SERVICING SMALL MEETINGS**

*[Cartoon: A busy executive calls Marriott to plan a meeting for next week, and is transferred through a series of receptionists to various managers—Roone Block for guest rooms, Mr. Upsell the catering manager, Ms. Achtung the reservations manager, and Mr. Uptight the credit manager—before concluding, "Whew! — I never thought a small meeting was this complicated... there's got to be a better way!"]*

The cartoon above humorously depicts the importance of a single hotel contact person, particularly for small meetings, whose planners require easy accessibility to a source of assistance. After the Marriott Corporation conducted an extensive research study of its business, it found that the majority of its properties relied on small meetings to generate group business. The information gathered indicated that the majority of Marriott's group bookings consisted of simple catering events, involving room rental, refreshment breaks, continental breakfasts, and a single luncheon. The chain, which recognized that planners staging small meetings look for a single hotel contact, responded with the introduction of a new position, the Executive Meeting Manager. This person, who is responsible for booking and servicing small meetings and catering functions, is viewed as a one-stop shopping source to simplify planning for the small group client.

Other chains followed suit, either designating individuals to work one-on-one with meeting planners or developing programs designed to help planners of small meetings. Hyatt, for example, introduced the "Hyatt Meeting Connection," which is now The Hyatt Meetings Network. The chain's website (www.hyatt.com/hyatt/meetings/events/small-meetings.asp) for the planners of small meetings offers both search and quick response features (as well as a telephone number to a meetings expert) to make it easy to request a RFP. Once the RFP is received, the meeting planner is placed in direct contact with his or her own dedicated meeting contact.

Today, many hotels are using other technologies to communicate with meeting planners and to offer meeting planning tips. Several have developed apps that connect meeting planners directly to a salesperson or support staff, and communications with the planner are more likely to be in the form of e-mails or texts instead of letters and telephone calls.

Both sales and convention service staff can also use social media to connect with and build relationships with the planners of all sizes of meetings. Although the salesperson is often the first hotel staff member to make contact with meeting planners, he or she can "introduce" his connections to the convention services manager. This type of introduction usually appeals more to meeting planners than an invitation from someone they do not know. Once connected, both salespeople and convention services managers can build rapport by offering useful advice and sharing photos or videos of successful past events.

You can build goodwill in other ways—make arrangements with labor if exhibits are used, obtain any official permissions that are required by local government departments such as police or fire, and assist with transportation needs. Help convention delegates schedule their time and keep them informed about the facilities in the hotel. Book special entertainment, arrange tours to points of interest, and provide the highest-quality food and beverage service possible. In short, give convention delegates every reason for staying at your property—and returning in the future.

Regardless of how smoothly a program is planned, snags and slip-ups inevitably occur. If your hotel helps meeting planners solve these problems, future business is nearly always assured. It may be necessary to shuffle meeting rooms around, help find a last-minute substitute speaker, or prepare a special entrée for the wife of the chairman of the board. The attitude with which you accept these common occurences will, to a great extent, determine the location of next year's convention. The professionalism your staff demonstrates is the hotel's best promotion for future business from the convention organizer and it increases the likelihood of business referrals. If you conquer any crisis that threatens the flow of the meeting, the parting handshake may well be accompanied by the meeting planner's promise, "We'll see you next year."

## HISTORY OF CONVENTION SERVICES

**1960s** — *Beginning of the convention service position, but with limited authority.* Salespeople were now confronted with the problem of spending a considerable amount of their time servicing groups. Feeling the need to concentrate more time on the selling of the hotel and its facilities, many sales managers turned servicing over to either the sales secretary or the lowest-level salesperson.

**1970s** — *Role of convention service manager increased in importance.* As the number and complexity of the meetings held grew annually, so did the importance of the convention service manager. This increased recognition was advanced by the Society of Corporate Meeting Professionals, which opened its membership ranks to convention service managers.

**1980s** — *Gained industry respect.* Convention service managers formed their own association (seven hundred strong) called the Association for Convention Operations Management (ACOM) (the organization is now the Event Service Professionals Association — ESPA). Meeting planners came to rely on the dedication, knowledge, and hard work of the convention service department.

**1990s** — *Elevated to the hotel's executive committee.* Now most of the major hotel chains have a corporate-level position for convention services. Within the hotel, convention service managers generally report to marketing, occasionally to food and beverage or catering, and now increasingly directly to the general manager. In hotels that look to conventions for a major portion of their room nights, the director of convention services is part of the hotel's executive committee.

**2000s** — *Serve as meeting consultants.* The role of the convention service manager has expanded beyond delivering meetings service. Increasingly, meeting planners look for partners who can consult and present customized solutions to their problems. Most hotel chains have raised the bar, requiring their convention service managers to become certified with the same education and training as the customer.

**2010s** — Increased involvement during site inspections and sometimes during the request for proposal phase of the sales process. The focus on revenue management results in convention service managers working closely with the hotel's revenue manager as well as the property's general manager.

Chapter 10: The Service Function

# Who Services?

One of the frequently discussed issues in convention management is the extent to which the salesperson should be involved in the servicing process. The structure of the hotel staff is based in part on how this issue is resolved.

Some hotels say that a salesperson is just that, and that he or she shouldn't become involved in servicing the client. They claim that the service function is a specialty distinct from selling, and that there is a more efficient use of staff and a higher rebooking percentage when salespeople spend 100 percent of their time selling. Howard Feiertag, a veteran hotel salesperson, says:

> In my opinion, the person who books the business is not the best person to follow through on the details. Large hotels should pass the booking to a convention services manager. Small hotels should pass the food and beverage details to catering and the rooms details to a rooms division manager or front office manager. Although salespeople often do not like to let go of a piece of business, they should turn over the minutiae of the group to the operations staff, remove themselves from the details, and use their skills to book more business.[2]

Others hold that the convention salesperson should handle the sales and servicing completely. They suggest that the sales representative should follow up all hotel visits, write up the actual bookings, and coordinate the servicing of the group during its stay at the hotel. Their position is that the sales manager should sell, arrange, and work with the meeting from beginning to end. They feel that the salesperson who does not get involved in servicing may be concerned only with putting business on the books, thus perhaps making hasty promises that are impossible to keep.

Which approach should you practice? "The best approach is the one that works. No one procedure is best for all situations. However, if the size of the hotel justifies an in-house convention service manager, it is probably best that the sales and service functions be separated.

## The Convention Service Manager

Throughout the text, we have taken the position that the servicing responsibility is handled by the convention service manager. Such a practice assures the association, corporate, or nonprofit executive that whatever his or her requirements — reservations, banquet, meeting room setup—there is one individual with complete authority and responsibility for his or her meeting.

The title *convention service manager* has not been adopted by all hotels. Many use such other titles as event service manager, conference or convention service coordinator, convention manager, event coordinator, and, at many smaller properties, banquet or catering manager. (Chapter 14 offers a thorough discussion of the role of the banquet manager as practiced at most small properties.)

Regardless of the title, the position carries a lot of prestige and a hefty amount of responsibility (Figure 10.1 gives a sample job description that lists the numerous duties of a convention service manager). If any one person can make or break a conference, it is the convention service manager, often referred to as "the person who makes things happen." He or she is the meeting planner's contact person, and so should be readily available to handle

*Figure 10.1. SAMPLE JOB DESCRIPTION FOR CONVENTION SERVICE MANAGER.*

| | |
|---|---|
| | Job Title: Convention and Conference Service Manager<br>Reports to: Director of Convention and Conference Service<br>Department: Convention and Conference Service |
| **Summary of Position** | Services all convention and conference groups as assigned by the Director of Convention Service. Plans and coordinates all arrangements (i.e., golf bookings, audiovisual needs, etc.) related to assigned groups to ensure the success of the convention and to promote repeat business. |
| **Scope** | This position is responsible for identifying and communicating the needs of the customer to the hotel departments to ensure proper service throughout the hotel operation for assigned groups. |
| **Objectives/ Responsibilities** | A. Plans and executes conventions and conferences as the primary customer contact for assigned groups. *25% of time*<br><br>B. Coordinates and distributes all interdepartmental paperwork necessary for the successful implementation of assigned groups. *25% of time*<br><br>C. Oversees activities of assigned groups, and functions as the onsite contact for the Meeting Planner. *15% of time*<br><br>D. Assists with training of the Convention and Conference Coordinator as assigned by the Director of Convention and Conference Service. *15% of time*<br><br>E. Attends daily and/or weekly meetings as assigned by the Director as well as arranges and conducts Pre-Convention and Conference meetings for assigned convention groups. *15% of time*<br><br>F. Assists in preparation of forecasts and budgets. *3% of time*<br><br>G. Performs additional tasks as assigned by Director. *2% of time* |
| **Supervision Exercised** | Directly supervises: Assigned Clerical Staff<br>Indirectly supervises: Convention and Conference Coordinator<br>Floor Manager<br>Support Staff<br>Function Book Coordinator |
| **Supervision Received** | Responsible to the Director of Convention and Conference Service |
| **Responsibility/ Authority** | Employee Relations:<br>Responsible for communicating and following through with hotel management to ensure that the sales commitment is being fulfilled. Distribute written communications (resumes, event orders) detailing the needs of the customer and the sales commitment. Maintains effective relationship with Sales and Service Staff as well as all department heads.<br><br>Materials or Products:<br>Maintains up-to-date group files to ensure proper coordination of sales commitment as well as customer needs. Maintains trace system for these files.<br><br>Equipment:<br>Assists in properly using and maintaining an adequate inventory of meeting equipment to properly service all functions.<br><br>*continued* |

*Figure 10.1 continued*

|  |  |
|---|---|
|  | **Financial:**<br>Responsible for maximizing revenues associated with meetings for assigned group files as well as maximizing function space usage.<br><br>**Business Contacts:**<br>Maintains proper communications between groups, outside vendors, and hotel staff. Also responsible for establishing customer relationships that will encourage repeat business. |
| **Preferred Knowledge/ Qualifications** | **Equivalent Education Level:**<br>College degree (or equivalent convention and conference service experience) required.<br><br>**Experience:**<br>A minimum of two years in convention and conference coordination with exposure to office procedures; experience in function room setups and service ; strong interpersonal skills and organizational skills.<br><br>**Knowledge Required:**<br>Function space configuration, room setups, maximizing space, art of negotiating and selling. General knowledge of hotel management, operations, and facilities. |

all of the convening group's on-the-spot needs. Quite simply, he or she is the single most important communications link between the meeting planner and the hotel.

The convention service manager should not be satisfied with just selling rooms and food. He or she must be a problem solver and an excellent communicator. The convention service manager should request full and detailed information so the hotel can better serve the group. Likewise, the hotel should communicate accurate data to the client. Horst Schulze, former president of The Ritz-Carlton, says:

> Hoteliers must understand that a meeting planner has put his job on the line by selecting their hotel. The convention service manager (CSM) must build a quality product around that one customer, specifically and individually. The CSM must see himself as a true partner and loyal assistant to that planner. To supply a defect-free meeting, there must be communication between the planner and the hotelier. This communication helps the hotelier understand the planner's desired outcome for the meeting.[3]

The role of convention service manager has grown beyond service to meeting consultant at some hotels (see Figure 10.2). David Kassel, CMP, former senior conventions services manager, Walt Disney World Dolphin Hotel, states,

> I try to educate the planner on how to do events with a little more creativity. A lot of my expertise is anticipating needs — having the forethought to put myself in the planner's place. It also means that I find alternatives to save them dollars.[4]

Ideally, the convention service manager has the authority to get the job done and to get it done fast. The Loews Hotel chain, for example, has increased the stature of the chain's convention service managers, promoting them to the executive committees of their respective hotels (the executive committee is made up of senior-level hotel managers who report

**Figure 10.2. CONVENTION SERVICE MANAGERS AS EVENT PLANNERS.**

### MEETING YOUR NEEDS EVERY TIME

The next time you consider a meeting in the Phoenix area, give us a call and we will help you create an unforgettable event. With our two convenient locations, luxurious amenities, versatile meeting space, and first-class service, the Marriott is the perfect place for any event - business or social. Our professional staff will plan everything for you, down to the last detail and deliver impressive results. We offer up-to-date audiovisual technology and superb catering capabilities to complement our hallmark Marriott service.

IT'S THE MARRIOTT WAY.℠

**Marriott HOTELS & RESORTS**

The Buttes, a Marriott Resort
2000 Westcourt Way
Tempe, Arizona 85282
(602) 225-9000
marriott.com/phxtm

Phoenix Airport Marriott
1101 North 44th Street
Phoenix, Arizona 85008
(602) 273-7373
marriott.com/phxap

Call 1-800-MARRIOTT or visit marriott.com for more information or to make a reservation.

© 2007 Marriott International, Inc.

*Today's convention service managers do not just sell function space and food and beverage functions. Hotels have recognized the importance of assisting meeting planners with both large and small events, and most CSMs today take an active part in the planning and execution of events. This ad for Marriott Hotels & Resorts promotes the services offered to meeting planners by The Buttes, a Marriott Resort in Tempe, Arizona, including a highly trained hotel staff that will assist in planning every detail to ensure a successful event.*
**Source: Courtesy of Marriott International, Inc.**

directly to the general manager, and may include the director of food and beverage, the controller, the resident manager, the director of marketing, and the director of convention services). Jonathan M. Tisch, chairman of Loews Hotels, said the change came about because *he listened to meeting planners*. Meeting planners are able to rest much easier when

## Chapter 10: The Service Function

they have the assurance that their liaison has authority within the hotel as well as the responsibility to fulfill their needs.

A presenter at a meeting of the Hotel Sales & Marketing Association International (HSMAI) in Las Vegas suggested that the convention service department should report directly to the hotel's general manager, not to the director of sales.[5] He suggests that hotels should have an organizational structure that gives the convention service manager line control over the functions of the front desk, housekeeping, banquet, and food and beverage departments as related to conventions.

The working hours of the person in charge of convention service are often very long (see box titled "A Day in the Life of a Convention Service Manager"). Bill Tobin says of the

---

### A Day in the Life of a Convention Service Manager

Melissa LaBarbera, the former director of convention services at the Fairmont Chicago, became involved in each event after the sales department turned over meetings business to convention services. On a typical day, LaBarabera called planners to introduce herself; sent out pertinent information on such items as exhibits, production capabilities, and menus; scheduled pre-con and post-con meetings; and coordinated event details with other hotel departments. And, during an event, she was personally available to meeting planners and their attendees.

"I made sure I was involved from the day [attendees] arrived until the day they left," LaBarbera says. "Some hotels have 'floor' people who are on site at all times during the meeting. At the Fairmont, we – the CSMs – were on the floor, right along with the banqueting team. Ultimately, it was our job to make the planner look good."

To demonstrate how CSMs do just that, *Meetings & Conventions* magazine followed Patricia Sousa, the conference services manager at the 319-room Omni Berkshire Palace in New York City, on a Thursday in June. Sousa began her day at 9:00 a.m., when she entered her cubicle to catch up on daily reports, telephone calls, and e-mails, and then forwarded pertinent details to back-of-the house departments. Since there were already two financial meetings in-house, and a pharmaceutical client's event was scheduled to kick off that evening, Sousa's presence was required at the daily banquet-order meeting with the kitchen and catering staff, as well as at a weekly staff meeting to review upcoming events for the next two weeks.

By 10:00 a.m., the requirements for the upcoming pharmaceutical event had been changed a dozen times, resulting in numerous calls to various departments to make them aware of the changes. Since the group added a reception, Sousa personally met with the chef before the pre-con meeting at noon. At the close of the pre-con, Sousa gave her business card (on which she had written her personal cell number) to the planner, assuring her, "You may call me at any time, for anything."

Sousa's afternoon was spent reviewing materials for both the banquet order meeting and the staff meeting – and dealing with the unexpected problems that arose when one of the financial meetings ran overtime, requiring the banquet staff to flip the meeting room in a record 17 minutes to accommodate a plated lunch.

**Patricia Sousa**

At the 4:00 p.m. staff meeting, Sousa again faced – and met – challenges resulting from incoming groups' requests. On this particular day, the staff decided to hire an interpreter to meet the needs of a group from China, and they formulated a plan to provide extra power to high-level VIPs in another group.

At 5:15 p.m., Sousa's day was winding down, although she stayed at her post (catching up on paperwork) through the 6:00 p.m. pharmaceutical dinner. She would continue to monitor events at the hotel until approximately 8:30 p.m. Despite her long hours and the daily challenges, Sousa wouldn't change a thing. "This job is definitely not for everyone," says Sousa. "It's hard, and it is very fast-paced. But I really love what I do."

**Sources:** Lisa Grimaldi, "Miracle Workers: Profiles of Top CSMs and How They Make Meetings Shine," *Meetings & Conventions*; Cheryl-Anne Sturken, "A (Hectic) Day in the Life," *Meetings & Conventions*.

time he was convention service manager at Caesars Palace in Las Vegas, "I wanted to give the meeting planner the impression that I never went home." One hour before every function, he checked out the facilities with the group's coordinator. This is a commendable policy, but convention service managers typically work on three to five meetings simultaneously, each in different stages of completion. This work schedule underscores the need for convention service managers to possess the abilities to organize and multitask, but, no matter how skilled they may be, convention service managers often find they have little time for themselves. Cutting still further into time off are the pre-convention and post-convention meetings often scheduled for weekends.

But there are rewards for these long hours. In addition to the salary paid by the hotel, the convention service manager may receive compensation for long hours in the form of gifts and tips from the meeting planner. Association and corporate executives have been known to be extremely generous in saying thanks for a job well done. Further remuneration is sometimes received from the hotel. The Sheraton Waikiki, recognizing the importance of the convention service manager, has given a suite in the hotel to its CSM. Sheraton Hotels, like a growing number of chains, has also established advisory boards made up of meeting planners to help the chain respond to the needs and concerns of meeting planners. One of these concerns centers on the role of the convention service manager; in many cases, the advisory boards recommend giving convention service managers more authority to ensure that meeting details can be worked out through a single contact person. Brian Stevens, President of Sales & Marketing at Hilton Hotels, agrees:

> Today, more than ever, hotels need to make sure their customers work with the most experienced, most highly trained convention service managers possible — or there simply won't be any customers after a while.[6]

How does one become a convention service manager? Most have advanced through either the banquet or front office departments, where they were exposed to the problems frequently encountered in group business. Then some alert sponsor placed him or her over the department. Often the next step up the corporate rung is to convention sales. The salesperson who has had experience in group servicing knows what can be promised and what can be delivered, and thus is a most valued employee. However, many are not sure this move to sales is a promotion, and more and more managers are staying with convention services — or even becoming meeting planners themselves.

Another career move for some is promotion to resident manager. This is not surprising, since the convention service manager interacts with virtually all other hotel departments. In a recent speech, Joyce Inderbitzin, Vice President of Events at Hilton Hotels Corporation, estimated that 70 percent of Hilton's general managers were convention service managers at one time in their careers.

## Increased Recognition

The convention service manager's position has steadily been elevated in status in hotel organizations. The Society of Corporate Meeting Professionals invited convention service managers to join their ranks, and *Successful Meetings* instituted an annual Convention Service Manager of the Year award.

Convention service managers also have their own organization, the Event Service Professionals Association (ESPA). Membership includes convention service directors, managers, and coordinators from hotels, and event service managers from convention cen-

# Chapter 10: The Service Function

> **WORTH WATCHING**
>
> David Dvorak, former vice president of catering & convention services for Starwood Hotels & Resorts discusses meeting the challenges of today's meetings and important aspects of the chain's training for meeting & event managers at www.youtube.com/watch?v=3YdYcjLPQiY.

ters and convention bureaus. Hotel convention service managers can also join the Professional Convention Management Association (PCMA). This organization serves the convention industry with educational resources, networking, and an annual meeting that offers nearly 100 educational sessions to meeting planners.

Marketing gurus tell us that the best future customer is the one you've already got, and hotels are placing a heavy emphasis on the convention service manager's role in rebooking. Increasing the authority and responsibility of this department has been used by hotels to show commitment to the meetings business and convention service personnel.

A profile of ESPA's membership supports this contention. The average tenure of convention service managers is five years, with less than 10 percent of them going on into sales and marketing. Also, a number of convention service managers report directly to the general manager and are members of their hotel's executive committee, along with the directors of marketing, food and beverage, hotel operations, and the controller. A number of hotel chains have standardized the position of convention service manager and bring these managers together annually for networking and idea exchange. Hilton, Hyatt, Marriott, and Sheraton have established corporate directors of convention services.

Several chains have made major commitments to training their convention service managers and other convention support staff to better assist meeting planners (see box titled "Training Convention Services Personnel"). As part of its recently introduced "Network

---

**The Role of Convention Service Professionals**

Devon Sloan,
Event Management Specialist (Task Force)
Hilton Tucson El Conquistador

*"Convention service professionals have only one job, and that is to give the meeting professional the best meeting ever... The keys to producing a great meeting are communication and planning...The convention services personnel and meeting professional become a team, and communication between team members is critical...Pre-planning is so important to the success of the meeting. There will always be some little glitch when the meeting is on-site, and that is so much easier to deal with when everything else is running smoothly — because it has been planned...A convention services professional can expect to spend over 40 hours a week at the facility when there is a group in house... Depending on a group's evening activities, the convention service manager may be at the facility quite late, checking on a reception, dinner, or dance... But when the meeting professional and you sit down to conduct the post-convention evaluation and the former says it was the best one ever, that is tremendously rewarding...For those who enjoy working with new people daily, learning about new organizations, working hard, multi-tasking, delegating, administering, coordinating, juggling, creating, and working with details, this is the perfect job!"*

Chapter 10: The Service Function

## TRAINING CONVENTION SERVICES PERSONNEL

Many hotel chains have recognized the importance of the service function, and have introduced training programs for their convention service managers and other key convention personnel. This increased knowledge and meeting planning expertise helps build the confidence of meeting planners, and is an important selling point in today's highly competitive meetings market.

### OUR CONFERENCE DIRECTORS JUST MOVED UP IN THE WORLD. THANKS TO YOU.

" 'Listen to the customer'...that's something I've encouraged our people to do since I first became President and CEO of Loews Hotels. And once again that advice has resulted in a major change for the company. Specifically, at all of our properties, conference directors have now been given executive committee status. It's our way of recognizing and enhancing their critically important contribution – **something meeting planners have been suggesting right along.** These chain-wide promotions are just part of a broader new Conference Management Program at Loews. We hope you'll like the improvements. After all, they were inspired largely by you."

Jonathan M. Tisch
President and CEO, Loews Hotels

Loews Ventana Canyon Resort
Tucson, Arizona
★
Loews Santa Monica Beach Hotel
Los Angeles, California
★
Loews Coronado Bay Resort
San Diego, California
★
Loews Giorgio Hotel
Denver, Colorado
★
Loews Miami Beach Hotel
Miami, Florida
Opening Late 1997
★
Loews Annapolis Hotel
Annapolis, Maryland
★
The Regency Hotel
New York City
★
Loews New York Hotel
New York City
★
Loews Vanderbilt Plaza Hotel
Nashville, Tennessee
★
Loews L'enfant Plaza Hotel
Washington, D.C.
★
Loews Hotel Vogue
Montréal, Canada
★
Loews Le Concorde Hotel
Québec City, Canada
★
Loews Monte Carlo Hotel
Principality of Monaco

**LOEWS HOTELS**

National sales offices:
New York 212-545-2720
Los Angeles 310-576-6688
Chicago 312-540-3300
Washington, D.C. 202-452-7878

Plan," the Marriott chain has committed to staffing each of its convention properties with a minimum of two Certified Meeting Professionals (CMPs). Mary Beth Jones, former vice president of global sales and marketing for the Marriott chain, says:

> Our basic training for convention service managers comprises a two-to-four week, on-site program combined with courses that can be taken at a company "university" held 11 times a year across the globe. Our success centers around our ability to be consistent at our hotels. The four cornerstones that are key to all Marriott brands are: be the easiest company to do business with; be a consultant and partner in the client's success; deliver flawlessly on the details; and recognize and reward the most loyal customers.[7]

The CMP exam, given by the Convention Industry Council, also figures prominently in the Hyatt chain's "Learning Environment Specialist" (LES) program (passing the CMP exam is a pre-requisite for this advanced training). Developed in association with the Professional Convention Management Association (PCMA), this six-day program offers instruction to help enhance all phases of meeting planning. The Hilton Hotel chain developed its own program, Customer-Focused Convention Service Skills (CFCSS), to sharpen the skills of its convention service managers.

## Convention Service Staff

How the convention service department is staffed depends on the size of the hotel, the percentage of occupancy accounted for by convention groups, the size of the groups using the hotel, and the number and size of the property's meeting rooms. Figure 10.3 illustrates a sample organization chart of a convention service department.

*Figure 10.3 ORGANIZATIONAL STRUCTURE OF A CONVENTION SERVICE DEPARTMENT IN A LARGE HOTEL.*

```
                    Director of Convention Services
         ┌──────────────┬──────────────┬──────────────┐
    Director of    Convention        Floor         Function
     Exhibit        Service         Manager          Book
     Service       Managers                       Coordinator
                       │                │
                  Convention          Set-up
                 Coordinators      Crew/House-
                                     persons
```

> **starwood** Hotels and Resorts
>
> ## INTRODUCING THE CONFERENCE CONCIERGE
>
> As the convention industry has grown, the time commitment of the convention service manager has increased. Hotels that once realized 25 percent of their occupancy from meeting groups now look to capture 40-50 percent of their room nights from meetings, which would stretch even the most capable of convention service managers too thin to adequately service business.
>
> In response, Starwood Hotels (owner of the Sheraton and Westin brands, Four Points Hotels, the Luxury Collection, and the W hotels) is just one of the chains (Hyatt is another) that has introduced a new position: the *conference concierge*. The conference concierge's responsibilities begin when the group arrives. The concierge stays in constant communication with the planner, improving the level of attention and service that meeting planners receive. Typical tasks for the concierge might include getting copies made for the planner at the last minute or assisting with package shipment. With the addition of this position, planners now have two people on site to assist them, and the level of attention is greatly improved.
>
> The new position also frees up the convention service manager to spend more time with advance planning with groups whose meetings may be months in the future. And the position offers an opportunity for those wishing to break into convention services. David Dvorak, former vice president of catering and convention services for Starwood Hotels & Resorts Worldwide, Inc., says:
>
> "The new title creates a great entry-level position because the concierge sees room setups, how to deal with emergencies and meeting planners, and how to multi-task."

Some properties have expanded their convention service departments, creating new positions to better serve meeting planners (see box titled "Introducing the Conference Concierge"). In addition to the convention services manager, the following list provides the position titles and brief descriptions of the responsibilities of individuals who might work in the convention service department of a large convention-oriented property:

*Director of Convention Services* — oversees, trains, and assists the convention staff in all phases of managing meeting accounts. Assigns meeting accounts to convention service managers, keeping the workload evenly distributed among staff. Usually reports to the director of sales/marketing, but at large properties may report directly to the general manager.

*Convention Coordinator(s)* — entry-level position in the convention service department. Primary responsibilities are to service small meeting groups and to assist convention service managers.

*Floor Manager* — responsible for servicing and setup of all meeting room and food and beverage functions. Oversees housepersons to ensure instructions from the specification and function sheets are carried out. At some properties, particularly smaller hotels, this position may be given the title of *Banquet Set-Up Manager*.

*Set-Up Crew* (sometimes called *Housepersons*) — responsible for the physical setup of all meeting and banquet rooms.

*Director of Exhibit Service* — works closely with the meeting group's trade show manager when the hotel's exhibition facilities are utilized. This position is only present in hotels with substantial dedicated exhibit space.

*Function Book Coordinator* — the single person who inputs and retrieves entries from the function book reservation forms, responsible for ensuring the accuracy of the computerized function book. This individual works closely with the sales staff, catering, and the convention service manager(s).

*Convention Service Secretary(ies)* — performs secretarial duties, including typing of correspondence, specification sheets, and function sheets for the convention service department.

## Chapter 10: The Service Function

> ### 🖥️ INTERNET EXERCISE
>
> Log on to the home page of the Event Service Professionals Association (ESPA) at www.espaonline.org. Click on the "About ESPA" tab to learn about the history of this organization for convention service managers (CSMs).
>
> Navigate through the site to answer the following questions:
>
> 1. What categories of individuals and hospitality firms comprise ESPA membership?
>
> 2. What educational opportunities does ESPA offer to its members?
>
> 3. How would the organization be beneficial to students?

## Convention Service Managers at Convention and Visitors Bureaus

In addition to the convention personnel employed by hotels, CSMs can also be employed by convention and visitors bureaus. Unlike at hotels, however, CSMs employed by CVBs serve three separate clients – the external client (meeting manager), the internal client (bureau partners), and their employer (the city or CVB organization) – and they generally provide most of their services prior to the actual event. CVB CSMs are typically an integral part of the sales process, often taking part in the site inspections held before a host city is selected.

Eric Blanc, CMP, the director of sales, marketing, and convention services for the Tampa Convention Center, finds that all parties concerned benefit when salespeople and convention services staff work together, rather than as separate entities – especially in light of today's changing meetings environment. He says:

> It is imperative for professionals in both sales and service roles to collaborate and embrace each other's strengths to achieve success. From the convention center and destination marketing organization (DMO) perspective, there are many of us who recently took a hard look at our available resources and discovered that sales and services could have higher close rates and operate more efficiently and cost-effectively if they worked together rather than as separate entities.
>
> A destination team that clearly demonstrates collaboration between sales professionals and event service managers can be the differentiator if used properly during the sales process. For example, the service professional adds insight and creativity regarding specific factors such as food and beverage, flow, and space placement if brought along on a site visit. The sales team can utilize the service team as a key selling point and cultivate a long-term partnership based on performance. And, a team-based approach to follow-through can lead to not only successful meetings, but also repeat business and increased lead generation through referrals.[8]

During site inspections, CVB CSMs assess the group's needs and build a relationship with the planner. Because of their extensive knowledge of the area, CVB CSMs are able to assist meeting planners with finding the products and services needed for their meeting –

whether it will be held in a single hotel or city-wide, or at an alternative venue, such as a sports arena, college campus, or a fairground – while minimizing costs, as they are familiar with suppliers and discounts available. CVB CSMs also typically assist with such meeting details as housing, registration, tours, and spouse programs, and they also save time for meeting planners by acting as a contact between participating hotels and suppliers. The functions of CVB CSMs may also include such non-traditional services as assisting with special permits in the host city, obtaining sponsorship assistance, and offering creative suggestions for boosting meeting attendance.

## The Transition

A frequent debate in convention management is, "How and when should meeting planners be turned over to the individual within the hotel who will have charge of coordinating their conference?" Timing depends greatly on the meeting planner, the size and type of the meeting, and how far in advance the meeting has been booked. Four commonly used times for this transition include:

1. *During the site inspection* —The hotel salesperson is the key contact when booking the event, but some planners try to meet the convention service manager during the site inspection visit, saying there is a "reassurance factor" in making early contact with the person who will be handling the details of their meetings.
2. *Right before signing the contract* — Some meeting planners ask for an interview with convention services before signing the contract. This step helps ensure that promises made regarding space, set-ups, and meeting services can be met. One meeting planner has stated:

   > Before signing a contract, I want to meet the convention service manager and let him or her know who I'm bringing in and what my meeting is all about. The salesperson may wine and dine me, but the convention service manager makes it happen. That's the person I'm married to for three days.

3. *Immediately after the point of sale* — If the convention is large and complex, some planners start working with convention services as soon as the contract is signed.
4. *One year before the meeting* — Many planners feel no need to involve convention services before one year in advance to begin the formal planning process. This procedure will not work in the case of short-term bookings that will require immediate contact between the meeting planner and the convention service manager.

It is difficult to divorce the salesperson entirely from the service function. The salesperson who simply dismisses a client after the sale, assuming that the convention service manager will shoulder the burden, will probably not get a rebooking. One director of sales at a hotel and conference center uses a unique approach to ensure that both the salesperson and the convention service manager are known and trusted by the meeting planner:

> What we've introduced is a buddy system. Each sales associate is working with a conference service manager, and they actually work through

the sales process together. From day one, we introduce the conference services manager, who the sales associate knows and has been working with throughout the year.[9]

---

**Best Practices**

### Crowne Plaza Hotel and Resorts' "The Place to Meet" Program

In order to better meet the needs of meeting planners, Crowne Plaza Hotels and Resorts, a brand of the InterContinental Hotel Group (which also includes Holiday Inns), offers the "Place to Meet" program, which includes a two-hour response to a request for proposal, the services of a Crowne meetings director (CMD), and daily on-site meeting de-briefings.

Kevin Kowalski, Vice President, Crowne Plaza Brand, says the chain's advisory board told hotel management that "meeting planners want an experienced go-to person at the hotel; someone to partner with throughout their event." Therefore, the chain has taken steps to ensure that its convention service managers are a cut above the norm. Tina Lyle, manager of marketing operations for the chain, says:

"We want them (CMDs) to have the authority and empowerment to make something right, no matter what the service issue might be...When we started discussing what would enable a partnership between CMDs and buyers, we started looking at certifications, and we saw that the CMP would make our staff focus on the information meeting planners need, instead of just on what the hotel needs. It raises them to a level where they can speak to planners intelligently."

Crowne meetings directors (CMDs) must have at least eight years of meeting experience and must either hold or be working toward holding CMP credentials. To enable their staff to become CMPs, the chain launched a rigorous training program that includes a walk-through of the CMP application and an action plan for those who wish to take the CMP exam.

CMDs are also part of their properties' executive committees, meaning that they are included in weekly management meetings. This enables CMDs to learn about changes at the hotel; report in detail on incoming and departed group business; and work with other hotel departments, from housekeeping to engineering, to address a group's needs. At many properties, CMDs also report to the general manager rather than the director of sales or director of catering.

---

Repeatedly partnering the convention service manager with a specific salesperson creates strong bonds and efficient teamwork. If the sales staff is deployed by market segments, partnering benefits convention service managers by concentrating their work with similar types of groups. For example, working with a salesperson dedicated to medical groups allows the convention service manager to gain an in-depth understanding of how to service these types of meetings.

The transition from the salesperson to the convention service manager must be handled smoothly. Frequently the client has dealt exclusively with the salesperson for two or three years and has complete trust in the sales staff. The salesperson's exit can be traumatic if the planner has not been reassured of the service manager's competence.

> ### Using Social Media to Build Relationships Between CSMs and Meeting Planners
>
> It is far more likely that there will be a level of trust in the sales-to-service transition if a property's CSM has already built a relationship with the meeting planner. While the salesperson is most likely the first person from a property to make contact with planners, many CSMs today use social media to connect with planners and build a relationship with them before, during, and after their events.
>
> Since LinkedIn is the most popular social media site for planners, CSMs can benefit from joining and building a network of contacts. Rather than just doing a search and sending connection requests to planners, however, it is more effective to have a salesperson make an "introduction"; planners are more likely to be receptive to making a CSM a part of their network when they know the salesperson.
>
> Posts should always be informative and helpful (remember that social media is not about selling; it is about building relationships). CSMs can share their excitement about something new at the property, such as renovations to meeting rooms, a special seasonal menu, or a new theme for a banquet or party. They can also share about ideas they had to make a meeting more memorable – and show photographs or post links to videos of meetings and special events held at their property.
>
> Once a personal contact has been made with the planner, CSMs can invite him or her to post photos and videos of their event – and encourage attendees to do the same. CSMs should also ask for reviews – both on the social media sites of the planner and the attendees – and for recommendations on LinkedIn; many planners researching a property will look to these recommendations to make a final decision.
>
> In addition to having a personal network, CSMs can benefit from joining meeting-related groups, such as Event Planning & Event Management, MPI's Meeting & Event Discussion Group, and i-Meet, an online community for people who plan meetings and events. Properties can also set up its own group website to offer advice and blogs to make a meeting planner's life easier. If the hotel does so, CSMs should be sure to invite all their meeting planner contacts to join the group.
>
> CSMs can also make use of Facebook and Twitter to share news and information with meeting planners, although these sites are not as targeted as LinkedIn. CSMs can also share photographs on Instagram and use You Tube to showcase videos of meetings and events.

Ideally once the sale is made the salesperson steps aside and turns the meeting over to the service people. However, the client should not be abandoned by the salesperson. The salesperson should greet the planner, if possible, when the meeting comes to the hotel and reassure him or her that the meeting is in good hands. Further, the salesperson should keep in touch and reenter as the meeting closes to suggest a rebooking. It just makes good sense for a salesperson to maintain contact with a client who has bought the property as a meeting site, and could, of course, buy again in the future.

## An Overview of the Service Function

Thus far, we've talked about the importance of service, the role of the convention service manager, and his or her position in the hotel's organizational structure. In subsequent chapters, we will cover in detail every facet of this person's job and how he or she works with other departments within the hotel. To assist you in understanding the service process, an overview of the convention service manager's role follows. Additional information on each of these steps can be found in the Convention Service Checklist detailed in the Chapter Appendix.

*Step No. 1* — Once a group is booked, the convention service manager reviews all correspondence to find out what information has been documented and what information is still

## THE PERFECT CONVENTION SERVICE MANAGER

The Convention Industry Council advises meeting planners that the "perfect" convention service manager is one who: begins working with the planner as soon as the meeting is booked; knows his or her property and has the respect of people in other departments; has the authority to get things done; anticipates problems and has solutions at hand; offers creative suggestions for set-ups, programs, meals, and entertainment; considers himself or herself an extension of the planner's staff; is flexible and honest enough not to over-promise or to under-commit; balances the needs of the planner with the needs of his or her own property; and treats all meeting planners with equal respect.

Many CSMs think that this description is "too good to be true," especially in regard to working 24 hours a day, although the vast majority of CSMs put in long hours and have little free time. Therefore, it is not uncommon for hotel CSMs to become meeting planners (conversely, it is less likely that a meeting planner will join the hotel industry because of the long, demanding hours).

Hotel CSMs who become meeting planners bring a wealth of knowledge to their new positions. They know how hotels operate and they understand industry jargon. They are also familiar with the issues that are the most important in terms of meeting and event planning, and they know which issues can and cannot be negotiated in contracts.

*The convention service manager helps the meeting planner visualize how the meeting room layout will contribute to a successful event.*
**Source: Courtesy of InterContinental Hotel Group.**

required. Many times he or she will review **account files** from two or three years before the date of the convention. A **sales to service turnover data sheet** is now used by many hotels to quickly bring the CSM up to date on the group. This short form summarizes specifics negotiated by the salesperson, including guestroom block, preliminary meeting program, cut-off dates, and so on. With this information, the CSM begins to assemble the **working file** needed for servicing the group (refer to the Chapter Appendix, items 1-5).

*Step No. 2* — The booking is listed in the function book, and contact is made with the meeting planner through a **letter of introduction** (see Figure 10.4). Note that this letter specifies that the group will be dealing with the convention service manager while in the hotel, and it provides a timeline for crucial components of the event. Meeting planners have stressed the value of a written set of deadlines, saying that timelines give them a "handle" on

*Figure 10.4. SAMPLE LETTER OF INTRODUCTION AND TIMELINE SHEET.*

February 6, 20__

Ray Harper, President
Harper and Pritchard Construction
611 S. Bridge Street
Columbus, OH 48850

Dear Mr. Harper:

I would like to take this opportunity to introduce myself as your Convention Service Manager for your upcoming meeting which will take place at the Las Vegas Hilton during the dates of September 1-4, 20__. I will be responsible for all aspects of your meeting with the exception of food and beverage arrangements, which will be handled by Gus Moser in our Catering Department.

Below I have noted a few of the key items relating to your meeting. Please bring any discrepances to my attention as soon as possible so the appropriate changes may be made internally.

Room Block — 125 king rooms and 4 suites in the North Tower
Room Rate — $110 guest rooms, $150 suites
Method of Reservations — Rooming list
Billing — Master Account

Additionally, please find enclosed a time line for required information which will assist both of us in planning your upcoming convention. This schedule ensures that your program receives the attention and service that it deserves. Please review the schedule and advise me if any dates seem unattainable.

If you will be shipping any packages to the hotel in conjunction with your meeting, please ensure they are addressed to my attention in care of the Las Vegas Hilton Convention Service Department along with your organization's name and date of your function. However, due to storage requirements, we ask that these items be sent as close to the convention as possible.

Sincerely,

Cindy O'Keefe
Executive Director of Convention Se

cc: Sean Steward, Sales Manager
    Gus Moser, Catering Manager

**TIME LINE**

GROUP: Harper and Pritchard Construction
CONTACT: Ray Harper, President
MEETING DATES: September 1-4, 20__

Listed below are areas of concern with review dates that will assist us both to ensure a successful meeting.

| ITEM | DUE DATE |
| --- | --- |
| Preliminary meeting program | April 1 |
| Final meeting program | May 1 |
| Credit application finalized | July 1 |
| Cut-off date | August 1 |
| Meeting & audiovisual requirements | July 15 |
| Food & beverage menus finalized | July 15 |

Please make any changes as necessary, then sign and return the form to me. If these dates seem practical as listed above, I would appreciate your signing and returning this form to me. Thank you.

Ray Harper, President                    Cindy O'Keefe
Harper and Pritchard Construction        Executive Director of Convention Services

*The convention service manager and meeting planner should communicate often —and in writing — from the time the business is turned over to the convention service department. Today, the convention service manager and the meeting planner also exchange e-mail addresses early in the planning stage. Establishing a written timetable with the customer for pre-planning and communicating the group's requirements is essential to effectively service meeting groups. Most convention service managers tell us that their biggest problems in servicing groups stem from not getting enough information from their planners in a timely manner. A timeline such as the one in this figure alleviates that problem by setting dates when specific information is needed.*

their events, and help them to ensure that essential information is communicated between the planner and his or her contact at the hotel (whether it be the convention services manager or a designated back-up). At this point, the salesperson goes behind the scenes and the convention service manager begins to get answers to the three basics: *reservations, program and billing* (refer to the Chapter Appendix, items 6-10).

*Step No. 3* — **Tracing** — using follow-up letters, e-mails, text messages, telephone calls, faxes, and personal contact with the meeting executive — is initiated to build a relationship of trust and cooperation be-tween the two parties. Correspondence is made as clear as possible, and includes lots of detail. Technology has made tracing easier, more efficient, and faster. In the past, convention service managers relied on telephones and letters; today, e-mails, text messages, and faxes are used to speed up the tracing process (refer to the Chapter Appendix, items 11-27).

*Step No. 4* — Details of the program are formulated in a *personal interview* with the meeting planner at least six months before the event. Reservation requests are also mailed to the delegates at about this time in an effort to determine the number of guestrooms (see Chapter 11 for additional information and refer to the Chapter Appendix, items 28-42).

*Step No. 5* — A monthly preconvention meeting is held with all department heads to review upcoming groups (see Chapter 12). All convention *resumes* and *banquet event orders* are discussed in detail (refer to the Chapter Appendix, items 43-50).

*Step No. 6* — Two or three days before the conference opens, a pre-convention meeting is held with the front office manager (see Chapter 12), the supervisor in charge of room setup (see Chapter 13), the catering manager (see Chapter 14), and the meeting planner. The entire program is reviewed, the menus are reaffirmed, and the meeting setups are verified.

*Step No. 7* — During the event, the convention service manager is on hand as much as possible. He or she will be at each meeting location one hour ahead of time to view the setup, and check the audiovisual equipment (see Chapter 15), exhibit setup, and check security (see Chapters 16 and 17 and refer to the Chapter Appendix, items 51-62).

*Step No. 8* — A post-convention meeting is held at the end of the event (see Chapter 18). All charges to the master account are verified and initialed a second time by the client. The post-convention meeting is a review of the event by those persons in attendance at the pre-convention meeting. At this time, the salesperson steps in to sell the group on a repeat convention. When the service department does its job, a rebooking percentage of 70 percent is not uncommon (refer to the Chapter Appendix, items 63-70).

## Summary

Your attitude and professionalism in serving your guests will be what sets you and your property apart from the rest. And the foundation of your professionalism begins with knowledge. You must know what tangible products and services are required by meeting planners and how to deliver the successful meetings and functions that they demand.

In this chapter, we have presented an overview of the convention services structure and the importance of meeting with the planner to ensure that his or her requirements will be met. In the next chapter, we will discuss how to get the meeting or convention off to a good start by discussing the most efficient way to register guests. In subsequent chapters in this section, we will provide a foundation in other elements of service. Armed with this knowledge, you will have the confidence to embark on the most important aspect of your job: building the trust and rapport that results in satisfied customers and repeat business for your property.

## Endnotes

1. Julie Pingston, "The Role of the Convention Services Manager," *Michigan Meetings & Events*.
2. "Five Tips to Help the Sales Staff Perform at Their Best!" *The Rooms Chronicle*, Volume 8, Number 5, p. 6.
3. "Building Loyalty," *Convene*.
4. Robert Carey, "Leaders of the Pack," *Successful Meetings*.
5. Speech given at a Hospitality Sales and Marketing Association International (HAMAI) meeting in Las Vegas, Nevada.
6. Brian Stevens, "A New Commitment to Convention Service," *Convene*.
7. Terri Hardin, "Convention Services 101," *Meeting News*.
8. Eric Blanc, "Blurring the Lines Between Sales and Services," posted online at www.themeetingmagazines.com/cit/cvbs, September 1, 2013.
9. Connie Goldstein, "Productive Meetings," *Corporate Meetings & Incentives*. Additional References

## Study Questions

1. Should sales department personnel become involved with group servicing?
2. Where does the convention service manager fit into the hotel organizational structure?
3. What types of programs are available to train convention service managers and their staffs to better assist meeting planners?
4. Describe the titles and duties of the members of the convention services staff.
5. What is meant by the transition? At what four times can transitions take place?
6. What is tracing and how is it used to build a relationship with the meeting planner?
7. Briefly define the eight steps inherent to servicing a group's meeting.

## Key Terms

**account file**—A file prepared by the sales department that includes all correspondence, call reports, and information used in selling the group.

Additional information, such as the contract, the meeting agenda, room block data, and so on is added to the group's file if business is booked.

**letter of introduction**—Letter sent by the convention service manager to the meeting planner. Specifies whom the group will be dealing with while in the hotel.

**sales to service turnover data sheet**—Prepared by the salesperson, this sheet summarizes key information from the account file (room block, meeting program, cut-off dates, and so on) and is given to the convention service manager to assist in preparation of the working file.

**tracing**—Building a relationship with the client by using follow-up letters, e-mails, text messages, telephone calls, and personal contacts.

**working file**—A file set up by the convention service manager after a booking is definite. This file initially contains information from the account file. As the service manager works with the meeting planner, additional information, such as the group's resume and banquet event orders, is added. At the conclusion of the event, the working file is broken down and appropriate materials are re-filed in the group's account file for future reference.

# CHAPTER APPENDIX

## CONVENTION SERVICE CHECKLIST

Detailed checklists serve as planning guides and often prevent the overlooking of important items in staging a successful convention. Numerous checklists exist for helping the meeting planner avoid oversights, but few are available specifically for the convention service manager. This is the format used by Penta Hotels.

---

**Penta Hotels**
**CONVENTION SERVICE CHECKLIST**

NAME OF GROUP _____

DATES OF MEETING _____

MEETING PLANNER _____

MASTER ACCOUNT ADDRESS _____
_____

TELEPHONE NUMBER _____

SALES MANAGER _____

BANQUET MANAGER _____

| TWELVE (12) MONTHS AWAY FROM MEETING DUE DATE | Completion Date |
|---|---|

1. Sales manager to turn account file over to Convention Service with a copy of the signed contract, a copy of the approved booking notice, a copy of the approved room block, a copy of the credit form (if credit has not been determined, trace three days and follow-up), and a past history on pick-up for the last two (2) years. _____

2. Review account file. _____

3. Verify definite program, confirm diary space, meeting room rental, exhibit rental, set-up charges, and date all space hold to be released (if applicable). _____

4. Confirm room commitments with Front Office and Group Rooms Control for accuracy, based on past history; block VIP suites. Determine when room rate will be established, and trace if not already established. _____

5. Determine if all exhibit information is complete in contract and remind account of need for floor plans to be approved, exhibitor's contract to be approved, hold harmless clause signed, insurance certificate for $250,000.00. _____

6. Initial contact and letter of introduction — obtain names of other key meeting personnel. _____

   a) Request most recent convention history. _____

   b) Review credit procedures and billing address. _____

   c) Review reservation procedures, when mailing will go out, clarify need for approval of reservation form if they act as housing bureau. _____

# Chapter 10: The Service Function

6. d) Check need for hospitality suites, who will use them, their names and addresses, and previous suite number if annual. _____

   e) Ask about public relations opportunities, famous people, unusual events, and newsworthy issues. _____

   f) Inquire if account is tax exempt; ask for tax exempt form. _____

7. Discuss their needs and requirements for outside security per corporate policy. _____

8. Send Penta meeting planner fact book. _____

9. Send Penta convention kit. _____

10. Order reservation cards (if the salesperson has already done so, obtain a copy of this form). _____

**SIX (6) MONTHS AWAY FROM THE MEETING DUE DATE**

11. Contact public relations for coordination of publicity. Place director of Public Relations in contact with the meeting planner. (If this is applicable.) _____

12. Accentuate the need for the accounts to provide detailed instructions at an early date so that proper service may be administered. _____

13. Explain convention resume procedure. _____

14. Reconfirm staff and VIP housing requirements; double-check suites blocked. _____

15. Determine audiovisual needs. Discuss how extensive set-ups are. Sell in-house audiovisual company. _____

16. Discuss registration personnel and procedures. Penta needs to maintain integrity of our property. All signs must be professionally printed; no signs allowed on walls. No signs allowed in the main lobby, except by management approval. _____

17. Coordinate contact with banquet representative, give name, telephone number, have banquet representative call account. _____

18. Review account's needs in regard to office equipment, i.e., typewriters, telephones, need for decorations or decorators, florist. _____

19. Request name of drayage company. Review needs of union labor. This is a union house. _____

20. Inquire into anticipated companion programs, anticipated bus tours. Coordinate information regarding bus tour loadings and unloadings. _____

21. Request finalized meeting and exhibit floor plans for approval. _____

22. Review final meeting schedule and check diary. _____

**THREE (3) MONTHS AWAY FROM MEETING DUE DATE**

23. Reconfirm required suites and staff requirements with guest and Front Office. _____

24. Review billing arrangements, identify all master accounts and authorized signatures. _____

# Chapter 10: The Service Function

25. Remind client of cut-off date for rooms. _____

26. If rooms do not materialize, a rental may have to be implemented (if there is not a rental or sliding scale in the contract) by the salesperson. _____

27. Request official printed program. Compare published program to space requirements in regard to time, set-up times, coffee services, etc. _____

## SIX (6) WEEKS AWAY FROM MEETING DUE DATE

28. Process letter for VIPs. _____

29. Verify attendance at all functions, establish rental based on contractual agreement, and establish master account and billing instructions along with authorized signatures. _____

30. Secure deposit if required, due 30 days prior to arrival date, unless we have devised a payment schedule. _____

31. Review file on the departmental basis to alert key people of heavy or unusual requirements. _____

32. Review microphone requirements. _____

33. Review lighting requirements and any production set-up needs. _____

34. Review room block against pick-up and cut-off date with the convention service manager. _____

35. Review complimentary rooms. If pick-up is below what the client anticipated, causing a comp room assignment problem, confer with Sales Manager and Convention Service Manager to explore best means of satisfying customer. _____

36. Request complete set-up information. _____

37. Review room registration, check-in arrangements. _____

38. Review special housekeeping requirements, if applicable. _____

39. Obtain a copy of authorized signatures for the master account. _____

40. Review cash advance needs. _____

41. Review safe deposit needs. _____

42. Review shipping arrangements of materials. _____

## THREE (3) WEEKS AWAY FROM MEETING DUE DATE

43. Forward resume (specification sheet) and check with Catering on menu progress. _____

44. Distribute resume to hotel departments and include affiliated activities. _____

45. Establish date and time for a pre-convention meeting, process in-house memo. _____

46. Inquire if client wishes to guarantee rooms not picked up. _____

## TWO (2) WEEKS AWAY FROM MEETING DUE DATE

47. Order limousine if applicable. _____

## Chapter 10: The Service Function

48. Re-check program with diary for possible quick meeting room turn-over and enter proper times for all events. _____

49. Review complimentary room arrangements. _____

50. Request posting instructions. _____

### FORTY-EIGHT (48) HOURS AWAY FROM MEETING DUE DATE

51. Check hospitality and complimentary orders and VIP reservations. _____

52. Reconfirm pre-con meeting. _____

### DURING MEETING

53. Check setting of meeting rooms (a.m., afternoon, p.m.). _____

54. Public Space Mgr. or Asst. to complete checklist for each function room. _____

55. Assist with restaurant reservations for VIPs. _____

56. Review shipping arrangements for post-convention materials. _____

57. Review complimentary room arrangements. _____

58. Compare room pick-up to complimentary list, make necessary adjustments. _____

59. Set up post-convention meeting. _____

60. Verify booth and exhibit hall by walk-through with customer. _____

61. Determine exhibit rental charge if determined by booth. _____

62. Determine repeat booking potential and advise Sales Manager. _____

63. Review master account with account credit department at a predetermined meeting. This should be completed each day. _____

### IMMEDIATELY AFTER MEETING

64. Conduct post-convention meeting. _____

65. Call account and send thank you letter. _____

66. Complete report of convention and profit and loss statement and distribute. _____

67. Determine report on abnormal circumstances in the post-convention memo. _____

68. Post-convention report to include under "comments" section an objective evaluation of the hotel's performance. _____

69. Turn file over to Convention Service Manager for review. _____

### ONE (1) MONTH AFTER MEETING DUE DATE

70. Breakdown working file and return appropriate correspondence to account file. _____

# Chapter 10: The Service Function

## Industry Profile

*Kristine K Gagliardi, Former Corporate Director of Convention Services*

Hilton Hotels Corporation

*In over 20 years in the hospitality industry, Kristine has lent her expertise to both the Hilton and Marriott chains (in addition to serving on the corporate staff at Hilton, she was resident manager at the San Francisco Hilton). After moving to Marriott, Kristine was director of operations at the San Francisco Airport Marriott and hotel manager at the San Francisco Marriott before becoming the first woman general manager of that hotel. As corporate director of convention services at Hilton, she was responsible for the development and integration of convention service quality assurance programs throughout the chain. In addition to setting specific standards and guidelines for Hilton, Kristine also served as a liaison to meeting planners regarding the convention service function.*

## Effective Guestrooms Management

In the early development stages of Hilton's convention service standardization project, one of our fundamental goals was to create effective procedures which would *improve guestroom controls* for the group market segment…It was our intent to offer meeting groups an effective, accurate guestroom system during every stage of the meeting – pre-planning, on-site, and beyond — to post meeting information…All existing hotel-wide guestroom block procedures were examined.

An important part of our research was the initial booking process by sales. Was a group's historical data properly checked? Did this information correlate with the current booking? Was the pattern of arrival and departures in line with the group's meeting program? Did the proposed reservation method work to benefit the group and hotel? Did the group's cut-off date give the group and hotel enough time to react to casualty? Satisfied that our sales systems were sound, we then approached the next procedure category – reservations.

In order to monitor reservations closely, a convention service file activity checklist was developed to systematically track group pickup and other pertinent group arrangements. Using this checklist, the convention service managers could trace group block activity, and, if warranted, have subsequent discussion with the meeting planner regarding pick-up information. At each designated checklist time frame (six months prior to arrival, three months, one month, two weeks before cut-off date, etc.) a series of check-and-balance procedures were put into motion.

For example, three months prior to arrival, the reservation pick-up activity was checked and reviewed with the meeting planner. One month out, the group was contacted to discuss either adding or deleting rooms from the block. One week prior to the cut-off date, the group was contacted again to re-verify all room-related issues.

Equipped with valuable customer information regarding check-in/check-out expectations, the hotel could then prepare a strategy to ensure a smooth arrival. Arrival patterns, transportation methods, and peak check-in times were closely reviewed. Later, this information would be integrated with work schedules in order to properly staff the front desk and other lobby service areas. The pre-registration of rooms, suites, and VIP accommodations would also be accomplished in preparation for the group's arrival.

During the on-site and post-meeting stages, our CSMs observed and collected data that would be important to both the meeting planner and the hotel. This information was compiled into a "meeting report" that was sent directly to the meeting planner. This report covered all aspects of the meeting, including guestroom particulars, reservation method, sequence of hotel reservation pick-up, arrival/departure patterns, final pick-up date, casualty and no-show percentages, and so on. In today's competitive hotel sales environment, knowing group facts and being fully prepared to meet or exceed client expectations can make the difference in a group selecting your hotel over another.

**Learning Objectives:**

This portion of your text introduces you to the various systems used to make reservations for meeting and convention attendees. We will also take a look at how the room blocks for group meetings are managed, and see how the computer has changed the way in which group reservations are processed. When you have studied this chapter, you will:

- Know the methods commonly used to make reservations and the advantages and disadvantages of each.

- Be able to detail the factors that affect room assignments and identify factors that hotel staff take into consideration when managing room blocks.

- Be able to describe how the computer has changed reservations, registration and room assignments procedures and is being used to facilitate check-in and check-out and billing for convention groups.

**Outline**

Reservation Systems
- Hotel-Managed Reservations
- Rooming Lists
- Convention Center Housing Bureaus
- Third-party Housing Companies

Room Assignment
- Rate Structures
- Complimentary Arrangements
- Priorities
- Room Types
- The Group History
- Arrival/Departure Pattern
- Other Hotels

Managing Room Blocks
- No-Shows/Overbooking
- Attrition

Check-in/Check-out
- Check-in Procedure
- Check-out Procedure

Summary

# 11 Guestrooms

The letter of agreement has been signed and countersigned. The dates are firm. The room block is specified in the contract. At this point, many departments and organizations become involved as the service process branches out into different areas. One of these areas is the assignment of guestrooms, which plays an important part in the success of a convention. Cooperation between your reservations department and front desk and the convening organization's housing staff is essential to ensure that there are no unpleasant surprises for meeting attendees.

## Reservation Systems

Guestroom reservation information is typically sent to the group's membership three to six months before the event. While calling a toll-free number, faxing a reservation, or mailing a reservation form are options still used by some meeting attendees, most meeting planners today use one of the following methods (which we will discuss in detail in this chapter) to make their group reservations:

- **Hotel-managed reservations.** Hotels can either offer a reservations link on their own websites or provide a link on the group's website. Many hotels set up separate landing pages for groups, and the planner (using a password) can readily access group reservation information.
- **Rooming lists.** Usually used for corporate meetings, rooming lists provide the names and arrival and departure dates for all attendees (attendees at corporate meetings typically have similar arrival/departure dates). The planner provides this information to the hotel, which then downloads it into its reservation system.
- **Convention center housing bureaus.** A number of convention and visitors bureaus (CVBs) offer housing services to groups, and are especially beneficial if the meeting is spread out over several hotels, as CVBs usually have a strong working relationship with hotels in the city. In addition, planners often negotiate with the CVB to handle housing at no cost to the group.
- **Third-party housing companies.** Third-party firms are especially beneficial in cases in which the group's needs are complex. Because these firms are solely in the business of housing and/or registration, they typically offer the most streamlined reservations systems. In addition, third-party firms often become an extension of the group's staff – if a group uses the same company year after year, the third-party firm becomes familiar with the group's needs so the planner can leave housing and reservation details to the firm.

The use of the Internet is making it easier for meeting attendees and other guests to make their reservations. Marilyn Healey, past president of the Event Service Professionals Association (ESPA), says:

Housing programs have simplified the process for convention service professionals – gone are the days of running pick-up numbers for a conference or convention, transposing them to grids, and e-mailing them to clients on a weekly basis. These web-based applications greatly reduce the time CSMs spend on reservations and housing tasks, therefore providing them with the quality time necessary to exceed the expectations of their clients and their clients' attendees in the planning and execution of their events.[1]

Making reservations using such technology as hotel websites and housing bureau web-based applications is especially attractive to meeting attendees because of the convenience and speed of making the reservation and the capability for almost instant confirmation (or notification if there is a problem).

## Hotel-Managed Reservations

The easiest, most efficient way for hotels to manage group reservations is to receive them directly. Some meeting attendees opt to use the property's toll-free number to make their reservations; if that is the case, attendees should be notified beforehand that they must mention the meeting or convention when making reservations to ensure that their rooms will be credited to the group's block. Another alternative is for the hotel to offer a special toll-free number for the group's use (this is especially important if several groups will be meeting at the same time).

Other attendees may access a reservations form on the group's website and either fax or mail it to the hotel or meeting planner. While these methods appeal to attendees who worry about the security of online transactions, a study by *Convene* magazine showed that meeting planners are increasingly turning to the Internet to register their attendees.[2] Today, online reservations are the preferred choice of planners, as shown in the sidebar titled "What's Your Preferred Reservation Method?"

There are three primary ways for hotels to manage reservations online. The first is to set up an in-house reservations system (or be linked to the chain's reservation system). A planner who has reserved a **room block** at the property can advise attendees to go to the site to make their reservations and pay any specified deposits directly to the hotel. Reservations are tracked by the hotel, and the planner can view booking progress on a 24-hour basis through the use of a special password, as well as receive periodic reports on the group's booking status. This method is used primarily by small groups that need only one hotel for their housing and meeting needs.

The second method is for hotels to set up customized web pages for groups. Customized web pages are offered by many of the major chains, including the Hilton brands. At DoubleTree by Hilton, for example, the group's customized site offers 24/7 online booking at the rate contracted by the group as well as details about the event and surrounding attractions. The website is created after the group's room block is booked; the planner simply contacts the host hotel to provide pertinent content. Links to the customized site can be provided on the group's website or sent via e-mail or correspondence to attendees.

Some groups prefer to handle their reservations on their own sites, and many use a program, such as Cvent (www.cvent.com), to register attendees and process payments. Reservations information and payments are sent to the host hotel periodically to enable the hotel to monitor block pick-up.

Chapter 11: Guestrooms

> **WORTH WATCHING**
>
> Passkey offers a number of tutorials for using its Group Max software. Go to youtube.com and type in the following two titles:
>
> Group Max Attendee Website Experience
> Licensed Hotel Users: How to Setup The New Attendee Website
>
> When viewing these tutorials note how Passkay allows hotels to up-sell guestrooms and offers options for meeting attendees to extend their stays.

No matter which method is used, meeting planners have found that the best way to ensure that they fill their blocks is to *combine registration and reservations*; in other words, booking within the block is a condition of registration. This practice – or the offering of incentives, such as a discount on registration or free shuttle service during the meeting or convention — encourages attendees to reserve their rooms within the group's block, although there is a growing problem with *outside reservations*. The biggest "culprits" are millennials, who often use the Internet to find more appealing lodging, such as a nearby boutique hotel, and then use social media to invite their friends to book at the alternate hotel as well. While seasoned attendees are aware of the value of keeping the group's commitment at the host hotel to avoid attrition fees and the possible loss of negotiated concessions, that factor is lost on most millennials, who do not seem to be concerned about how their booking patterns impact the group.

In order to provide a seamless registration/reservations option for groups, most hotels are now using Passkey GroupMAX™ software, which offers an accessible centralized database to process housing reservations. This system also generates confirmations and acknowledgments for attendees, and provides alerts as well as periodic reports to enable meeting planners to better manage their room blocks. Hyatt was one of the first chains to use the system, which is now used by the majority of the major chains as well as CVB housing services and third-party housing firms. The box titled "Hyatt Uses Passkey to Market to Meeting Planners" provides an example of how the chain used its partnership with Passkey to attract meeting planners.

It is important that hotels offer secure online systems to protect both the personal data and financial information of meeting attendees. This is especially vital in light of rising incidents of cybercrime (see box titled "Pirates and Poachers"). Essential steps include installing anti-virus software, firewalls, and other deterrents to prevent hacking of reservations systems, and many hotels also offer a dedicated Wi-Fi network to protect sensitive data being communicated by today's mobile planners.

## Rooming Lists

Some planners, especially corporate and association planners with small to mid-sized blocks and incentive travel groups, prefer to handle their own reservations and provide a **rooming list** to the hotel (see Figure 11.1). When rooming lists are used, reservations are not made with the hotel, but with the housing staff at the planner's headquarters. The meeting planner prepares the rooming list from

**What's Your Preferred Reservation Method?**
PERCENTAGE OF RESPONDENTS

■ IN 2002   ■ IN 2017 projected by authors

| Method | 2002 | 2017 |
|---|---|---|
| Reservation cards, forms, or faxes | 31.5 | 10 |
| Telephone call-ins | 24.5 | 8 |
| 800 number | 19.8 | 7 |
| Internet (online) | 24.1 | 75 |

### Pirates and Poachers

The rise of online reservations has not escaped the notice of unscrupulous individuals and firms, called "poachers" and "pirates" in the industry, that wreak havoc on the group's room block commitment by engaging in illegal or unethical practices that include:

- **Selling fictitious reservations and credit card fraud.** Pirates accept deposits – or full payment for rooms to be used – but no reservations are made at the hotel. The charges processed on attendees' credit cards go straight to the pirates, who change "business" names or locations often to avoid prosecution.
- **Misrepresentations resulting in bookings outside the group's block.** Poachers attempt to entice attendees to book through them and bypass the group's block. Poachers may falsely say that the hotel's room block is full, or they may simply entice attendees with deals that turn out to be inferior to what was promised. In one case, poachers contacted attendees with a deal for one chain hotel, but the event was actually being hosted at another chain's property.
- **Trademark infringement.** Both pirates and poachers may use logos and other copyrighted data on correspondence in an attempt to be perceived as an official agent of the event.
- **Unauthorized access, use, and selling of data.** Lists and contact information on attendees and exhibitors are obtained from websites and databases or purchased from sources not authorized to sell this data.
- **Obtaining inventory through misrepresentation or omission.** Using deception, including failing to disclose the intent of the use of rooms to the hotel or its wholesalers, is a common practice of pirates and poachers. Once room inventory is obtained, it may be used in "bait and switch" schemes or sold to unsuspecting attendees for higher rates.

Unfortunately, it is relatively easy for poachers and pirates to obtain contact information for both exhibitors and attendees. Exhibitors are usually listed on the sponsoring group's website ahead of the event for benefit of customers and potential customers, and contact information for attendees can be obtained by hacking other websites, such as the group's reservations page. This information is then used to contact unwary victims, usually through telephone calls or e-mail offers.

Since many of these illegal firms require full payment at the time of "booking," there is no recourse for changes, transfers or cancellations. The unsuspecting attendees arrive at the destination to find they don't have a reservation – and may not be able to find another place to stay.

Other poachers may, indeed, book rooms, but these are generally outside the group's block. Like the larger, legitimate third-party firms, they charge hotels a ten percent fee for their bookings, but they also charge additional fees to attendees that have used their services.

In order to combat these practices, which can result in huge attrition fees for groups and monetary losses to attendees and exhibitors, the Convention Industry Council has prepared a white paper focusing on these predators and offering suggestions on how groups and hotels can minimize their chances of being victimized. You can view this white paper at www.conventionindustry.org/StandardsPractices/APEX.aspx (click on the Room Blocks tab to view this report and to access other articles and resources on the topic).

---

the reservations received and sends it to the hotel prior to the **cutoff date**. When the hotel receives the list, which is generally sent in its final form (partial lists are sometimes sent periodically), it is downloaded into its reservation system and the front office assigns rooms from the group's block to attendees, who are then pre-registered.

It is extremely important that the front office knows whether a group's reservations are coming individually or through a list. It is standard operating procedure that the trace file on any group for which a rooming list is expected is brought up in sufficient time to remind the customer that the list is expected.

There are both advantages and disadvantages to using rooming lists. First, it is difficult for the hotel to determine room pick-up if they have to wait until the cut-off date to receive information. On the planner's side, the rooming list must be continuously updated, and there is always room for error as another party, not the attendee, is handling the reservation.

Chapter 11: Guestrooms

---

### Hyatt Uses Passkey to Market to Meeting Planners

Hyatt Hotels & Resorts, which has offered the Passkey system to meeting planners for several years at more than 50 of its properties in the United States, Canada, and the Caribbean, has added Passkey's GroupLink[SM] enhancement tool to make meeting planners' work even easier – allowing them to track events up to the date of arrival and to manage city-wide events. The original Passkey system offered reservation capability, event and hotel information for attendees, and 24/7 access to more than 100 reports, including pick-up and booking reports to planners. The new GroupLink[SM] application provides meeting planners with even more cutting-edge solutions to efficiently manage their events, providing the ability to keep events open through the day of arrival and allowing for complete inventory management from one data source.

Irby Morvant, former director of sales and marketing at the Hyatt Regency New Orleans and now general manager of the Hyatt Regency Mission Bay Spa and Marina, says:

> Passkey elevates meeting planners to a new level of service and technology by giving them direct access to rooming lists and room pick-ups.

Offering Passkey has resulted in benefits to both the hotel chain and meeting planners. Arnetta Smith, an event manager for the American Petroleum Institute, says:

> I put the link (that Hyatt provides) into the e-mail marketing piece I send out, then attendees can click on it for Passkey, and make their hotel reservations at the same time that they do their conference registration. It's all in one e-mail document. I'm able to go into the Passkey system, quickly retrieve reports on room pick-up, see my numbers, and see who has registered.

In addition to Passkey, Hyatt also offers several other methods for making group reservations, including customized websites for specific meetings (hosted free of charge on hyatt.com), online reservations at hyatt.com, and toll-free numbers.

**Source: Hyatt.com.**

---

On the plus side, rooming lists can be conveniently downloaded into the hotel's reservation system at one time, eliminating the need for the hotel to make changes to individual reservations. Rooming lists are advantageous to planners whose attendees have a similar arrival/departure pattern (as in the case of corporate meetings, for example), and they have complete control over their group's reservations.

## Convention Center Housing Bureaus

When several hotels are used, the convention is commonly called **citywide** and the reservations may be handled by a convention center **housing bureau**. Many convention and visitors bureaus provide this service only when multiple hotels will be used. The housing services offered by the Anaheim/Orange County Visitors and Convention Bureau (AOCVCB), for example, are restricted to groups who will use two or more hotels at a minimum peak block of 500 rooms.

When a group contacts the CVB with their dates and room requirements, the CVB sends out a **bid sheet** to hotels to check the availability of requested types of rooms on the group's dates. Hotels return their bid sheet to the CVB, and include a stipulated cut-off date for reservations. The CVB then presents the bids to the sponsoring organization, which then chooses a host hotel and at least one overflow hotel.

*Figure 11.1. SAMPLE ROOMING LIST.*

Rooming lists are generally used for small corporate meetings for which the corporation will pay room charges and attendees will be responsible for their incidental charges. Some associations, however, also use them rather than having individual delegates contact the hotel for reservations directly. After the meeting planner obtains room information from delegates, he or she prepares a list to be sent to the hotel by an agreed-upon date. Information typically includes the names of attendees, the type of room desired (and how many will occupy a room), and arrival and departure dates.
**Source: Courtesy of The Hershey Lodge & Convention Center.**

About eight months before the convention, the CVB sets up a reservation system for the group. The group then prepares reservations forms that list each hotel and its rate for each type of room and sends them out to each attendee. In some cases, the reservation forms are returned to the CVB. The Seattle Housing Bureau (a division of Visit Seattle), for example, provides telephone numbers for reservations to be phoned in or faxed, a mailing address, and an online link to the group's website reservation system. Visit Seattle is one of many convention and visitors bureaus that use the Passkey software, which we described in the hotel-managed reservations system, to handle group reservations online.

Other CVB housing services also use Passkey to manage and monitor room blocks. The Austin (Texas) Convention and Visitors Bureau's Housing Bureau, for example, offers secure 24/7 access to online inventory and room block tools, and its services also include a customized event site for the group.

In other cases, reservation forms and deposit checks are returned to the sponsoring organization, which forwards the information and fees directly to the hotel. Many hotels prefer this method, as the fees can be quickly credited to the group's account.

Since city-wide conventions require more than one hotel, attendees must select their first and then subsequent choices. Rooms are

> **WORTH WATCHING**
>
> Do an Internet search for hedtalks.connectplusathiltonworldwide.com and click on the Driving Results tab. Scroll down to "Group Room Blocks" to view a video by Pam Henry, Hilton's deputy executive director of conference operations, on effective contracting and fulfillment of city-wide room blocks. In the following video, "Housing Services," Karen Malone, vice president of meeting services at housing service HIMMS, describes proven strategies for servicing attendees and exhibitors.

387

assigned on a first-come, first-served basis, and the CVB sends **reservation confirmations** to the registrants. The CVB also prepares a **reservation housing report** (illustrated in the box below) that is sent to both the hotel and the sponsoring organization to enable them to stay on top of group room block pick-up.

```
                       HOUSING REPORT
                     OCTOBER 19-21, 20__

                COMMITTED           ASSIGNED            BALANCE
HOTELS       ROOMS    SUITES      ROOMS    SUITES     ROOMS    SUITES
A            1400       70        1110       70        290
B             200                   86                 114
C            1000       11         386       11        614
D             300                   29                 271
E             400        3         167        3        233
VIP'S         200                                      200
   Totals--- 3500       84        1778       84
```

Copies of above sent to hotel sales officers, room reservation managers and association directors.

Should there be any discrepancies, please contact this office immediately.

*A form such as this one is used by the housing bureau to inform hotels of the meeting group's pickup on its room commitment. Reports are sent on a periodic basis to enable the individual hotels to adjust their reservations information.*

Although many CVB housing services have streamlined the reservations process by offering more online options, some planners cite problems with using these services, including understaffing (especially for large conventions) and busy phone lines. The inconsistency of housing services offered in different cities has resulted in associations that rotate their annual conventions geographically moving away from using CVB housing services and turning to third-party providers for their housing needs (see sidebar titled "What is Your Preferred Method for Handling Citywide Housing?"). Not only are third-party housing companies becoming more widely used by meeting planners, many CVBs have recognized the cost savings of using third-party companies and are now outsourcing housing to third-party vendors.

**What is your preferred method for handling citywide housing?**
For those who outsource, third parties are preferred to convention bureau housing services.
(PERCENTAGE OF RESPONDENTS)

- 8.9 Other
- 34.5 In-house (do it yourself)
- 32.5 Retain Third Party Housing Service
- 24.1 Convention Bureau Housing Service

*While a large number of associations handle citywide housing in-house, planners still rely on outside sources, such as convention bureau housing services and, increasingly, third-party providers.*
**Source:** *Convene's* Annual Meetings Market Report.

## Third-party Housing Companies

**Third-party housing providers**, private firms that typically use Internet-based technology to make housing arrangements for groups, are often used by large organizations that utilize several hotels for citywide conventions. The services offered by these third-party firms may vary widely; some offer housing services only, others may negotiate hotel contracts for the group and possibly generate rebates or discounts due to the large volume of business they produce, still others handle both housing and the registration process.

Third-party firms are the "preferred providers" for large conventions, especially those that are city-wide, but a growing number of planners for smaller meetings are also using them for housing services. There are several advantages to using a third-party firm:

- **Buying power.** Because they generate considerable business from a wide variety of clients, third-party firms can use their leverage to secure the lowest possible rates for a client.
- **Expertise and assistance.** Housing, especially for a large convention, is a complex process that requires a high level of expertise. In addition to handling all the housing details, which frees planners to concentrate on their programs, most third-party firms send a representative to the group's meeting to answer attendee questions and handle requests and any problems that might arise.
- **Data repository.** Third-party firms keep detailed records of their clients and can readily provide information on housing data from various hotels and post-convention data on the group's own meeting (the post-event audit will detail which attendees stayed at the contracted hotel but booked outside the group's block).
- **Sophisticated technology.** Most third-party firms use Passkey and other programs, such as Cvent (www.cvent.com), EventXL™ (Experient's software program), and RegOnline™ by Lanyon, which purchased Passkey, to manage room blocks and provide online access to rooms inventory to planners. Most third-party firms also monitor hotel rates weekly to ensure that the group rates are the lowest available. They may also create a dedicated group website that provides a registration feature and information on the meeting, the hotel(s), and the surrounding area.
- **Risk mitigation.** Because third-parties use technology to monitor room blocks, there is less chance of a group being charged attrition fees. If there is a possible "red flag" situation, the third-party firm can notify a planner immediately to enable him or her to contact attendees to ensure they are booking within the group's block.
- **Integrated approach.** Since most third-party firms handle both housing and registration functions, they provide "one-stop shopping" to attendees. This makes the process seamless and convenient, and builds a level of comfort for attendees. And, as we mentioned earlier in the chapter, using the same third-party firm over a period of time is also beneficial to the planner; the firm can be counted upon to understand the group's needs and almost becomes a part of the sponsoring organization's staff.

The downside to using a third-party firm is the cost. Third-party planners charge a fee that can run as high as ten percent of the room rate. A CVB will pay this fee when outsourcing its housing, but meeting planners must find a way to pay housing fees when they are not picked up by the CVB or hotel. It may be possible for the group to negotiate the rate with the third-party firm, especially if the group can be expected to generate a great deal of business over a long period of time. In other cases, the planner may negotiate fee payment as a concession from the hotel or add the cost – or a portion of it – to the registration fee.

There are three major third-party firms; they are (in alphabetical order) Conference Direct (conferencedirect.com), Experient (www.experient-inc.com), and HelmsBriscoe (www.helmsbriscoe.com). But there are numerous, smaller third-party housing firms, such as Orchid Event Solutions (www.orchideventsolutions.com), from which to choose, and the competition has resulted in innovation and better service.

## Room Assignment

The front desk carries off most convention and trade show room assignments without incident. Problems do occationally arise, however, and must be handled smoothly.

Prior to the meeting, the convention service manager should review and confirm with the customer:

- The rate structure by category of room
- Complimentary room assignments
- Guestroom priorities for VIPs and speakers
- The room block, including the types of rooms needed by the group
- The group's history in regard to guestroom pickup, no-shows, and cancellations
- The arrival and departure pattern for the group

### Rate Structures

Rates are extremely important to the planner. If the rates negotiated are beyond the budget of some attendees, they may book sleeping rooms elsewhere (outside the designated room block). This could significantly impact rental agreements for meeting rooms and could result in attrition fees.

Because most large-scale conventions are planned well in advance, most hotels do not commit themselves to any firm rates until one year prior to the reservation date. This policy is usually made clear during initial negotiations. It is also included in the final contract.

One of the preliminary decisions to be made in booking a convention is what rates to charge for delegates' rooms. Naturally the rates will vary between hotels and even within the hotel itself. Rates are determined according to a number of factors, including season (busy or slow), days of the week, size of the group, length of stay, type of room, number of persons in the room, and the known attendance and difficulty with the group's past conventions. Of course, the interpretation of these factors is up to the individual property. A resort hotel, for example, fills up with social guests on weekends, so it is not likely to offer dis-

---

**🖥️ INTERNET EXERCISE**

Visit the Hilton Hotels website at www3.hilton.com and click on the "Meetings & Events" tab. Scroll down to the "Meetings Simplified™" section.

1. What search criteria is available to meeting planners seeking group value dates?

2. Explain why the Guest List Manager and the Personalized Group Web Pages features are valuable to meeting planners who book with the Hilton chain.

3. What other tools are available on the site to assist meeting planners with their guestroom and meeting space requirements?

counted rates to a meeting group, while a downtown hotel that realizes the majority of its business during the middle of the week is more likely to offer discounted rates on the weekends.

Many hotels work within the limits of certain rate scales determined by management. The main ones are:

- **Rack rate.** All rates remain as posted, with no discounts or concessions. **Rack rates** are rarely used for conventions because convention groups are able to negotiate a group rate lower than rack rates.
- **Run-of-the-house-rate.** With a **run-of-the-house rate,** all similar rooms except suites are priced at the average between minimum and maximum rates, despite level or location. All guests pay the same rate. This is also called a *flat-rate arrangement.*
- **Split rate. Split rates** are offered to a group based on the room type. For example, regular guestrooms would be offered at a different rate than tower club rooms, ocean-view rooms priced differently than garden-view rooms, and so on.

It is important to remember that many conventions are planned years in advance, and that rates could vary a great deal over that time. This makes it essential to "peg" a rate of increase to determine the rates that the group will pay in the future.

In most cases, the hotel's rack rate is used to find the "peg rate." If, for example, the current rack rate is $150 per night and the group rate is $120 per night, the percentage below the "peg rate" is 20 percent. This percentage would be used to determine room rates at the time of the meeting (attendees would get 20 percent off the rack rate in effect at the time of the function). Other planners insist on more specific room rate guarantees; one planner, for example, specifies the following clause be included in the contract:

*The Hotel guarantees that room rates extended to the Symposium shall not exceed 85 percent of the rack rate and the present applicable rate shall not increase more than 5 percent per year. The final rate shall be established 12 months in advance of the Symposium.*

Small groups tend toward the use of flat rates, while large conventions find split rates more to their liking. Rack rates are seldom used for conventions unless the group is small or the hotel is running at high occupancy.

Discounts typically range up to 30 percent off the rack rate. Naturally, the hotel's objective is to ensure that it gets business, but at the highest possible rate. Questions often asked about the group to determine the amount of discount include:

- How much can they be expected to spend? Will they have cocktail parties? Banquets? Requests for meeting and exhibit space?
- What are the opportunities for future business with the group?
- Is the group willing to put down a firm financial hold on its room block?

Regardless of the rate decided upon, it is important to make the rate arrangements clear. If there is a range of rates, the reservation form should indicate the range and serve notice that rooms in the next higher category will be supplied if those at the requested rate are no longer available. Even if the contract calls for rack rates, it is best to indicate those on the reservation form.

Sometimes the association requests that the hotel charge the delegate more than the agreed-upon room rate and to refund the excess to the association. Hotels generally decline such requests for obvious ethical reasons, particularly if convention attendees are unaware of the arrangement.

## Chapter 11: Guestrooms

### Complimentary Arrangements

Most hotels offer concessions to get group business. It is common practice to extend one complimentary guestroom (**comp room**) for every 50 rooms used, or one suite for every 100 guestrooms.

A rooming list supplied by the meeting planner should specify who will occupy these rooms. To avoid heated arguments at the cashier's window, it is the planner's responsibility to spell out the extent of the complimentary arrangements to the guest and provide a copy to the hotel.

The meeting planner should tell his or her people, especially if complimentary rooms will be used by speakers and program members, what they must pay for themselves and what may be applied to the master account. It is easiest to use complimentary rooms for staff, but that is at the option of the meeting planner. It doesn't matter so long as everyone knows what is expected of him or her.

Some hotels provide a complimentary cocktail party or VIP welcome amenities upon arrival, complimentary travel to and from the airport, and free meeting space. There are no general guidelines for making concessions, but many hotels offer comp rooms and other concessions on the basis of guestroom pick-up. For example, if the group fails to pick up 80 percent of their contracted room block, it may only be allocated one comp room for every 100 rooms used instead of one for every 50 rooms used. There is no general guideline. A hotel must use sound judgment and integrity.

### Priorities

It is important that the convention planner supply a list of VIPs to the hotel. It is necessary to codify certain types of guests and the accomodations indicated for them. This is certainly important when you have accommodations in different buildings of the hotel. Association officials such as officers, board members, and staff usually get special treatment. Exhibitors, speakers, and entertainers may also require special attention.

It is important to block rooms so that oceanfront rooms and suites in resort hotels and the "best rooms available" in commercial properties are assigned to VIPs without question, regardless of the occupancy of the house. It is often the responsibility of the convention service manager to see that these reservations are in order. He or she should set up a procedure to check the day before arrival on what type of accommodations are blocked for VIPs and also on the day of arrival to make sure that these accommodations are delivered. In addition, the service manager might find out the VIPs' arrival times.

It is the policy of some hotels to have the sales office see that the VIPs get the proper attention. The feeling is that the salesperson's self-preservation is determined by his or her impression on the association's decision-makers, and the decision-makers are usually found on the priority list.

The VIP list should also be coded to include the possible supply of fruit, liquor, and/or flowers. The allocation of suites is also important, especially if the hotel has a limited number. Discuss this with the convention planner. Some associations have a rule that non-exhibitors cannot maintain hospitality suites.

Take care to hold a small number of rooms in a prime area of the hotel for late priority listings; they inevitably appear late in the game.

## Room Types

You must know the number and kinds of rooms to be held. Most agreements with convention planners call for a guarantee of a total *number* of rooms to be used. This may be fine at the negotiating table, but as the event approaches you need to know how many of these are singles, doubles, twins, or suites. Don't forget that there is much confusion about suite designation. Some hotels go so far as to indicate suites as having "one bedroom for two people" or "two bedrooms for four people." In addition, people confuse twins and doubles. This can be clarified by indicating "one bed for two people" or "two beds for two people." The box titled "Room Types" provides definitions that are common throughout the industry.

---

**Room Types**

- **Single room**—A room assigned to one person; may have one or more beds.
- **Double room**—A room assigned to two people; may have one or more beds.
- **Double-double room**—A room with two double beds (or sometimes queen beds); may be occupied by one or more people.
- **Triple room**—A room assigned to three people; may have two or more beds.
- **Twin room**—A room with two twin beds; may be occupied by one or more people.
- **Queen room**—A room with one queen-sized bed; may be occupied by one or more people.
- **King room**—A room with a king-sized bed; may be occupied by one or more people.
- **Quad**—A room assigned to four people; may have two or more beds.
- **Suite**—A room with a separate sitting area and one or more bedrooms.
- **Junior suite**—A single room with a bed and sitting area; sometimes the sleeping area is separate from the sitting area.
- **Studio**—A room with a studio couch that can be converted into a bed; may also have an additional bed.
- **Family room**—A double-double, triple, quad, or suite designed to accommodate a family; cribs and children's cots or roll-away beds are usually available.
- **Adjacent rooms**—Rooms close to each other; such as across the hall.
- **Adjoining rooms**—Rooms with a common wall but no connecting door.
- **Connecting rooms**—Rooms with a common door between them; guests can move between rooms without going through the hallway.

---

## The Group History

Since many conventions are booked far in advance, the number of rooms blocked out is an estimate, based on past conventions. Therefore, examining a group's *historical performance* can provide invaluable insights into what you can expect from the group in terms of room pick-up. You need to look at a group's history to determine if the group meets its commitments. Are there typically more attendees each year than anticipated? Are no-shows a problem? Is there an excessive amount of early departures?

In this era of revenue management, most hotels qualify a group before offering a proposal, as the group's impact on the hotel's bottom line is the main focus. Other hotels research the group's history after the contract has been signed. Whatever approach is used, there are several options available to review the group's historical performance and plan strategies to eliminate potential problems.

First, you can contact the sales managers of hotels where the group has met in the past. While they are ethically bound not to reveal financial information (such as rate paid, food and beverage revenue, attrition fees, and so on), sales managers who are familiar with the group can alert you to problems they have experienced. Sales managers can also advise

Chapter 11: Guestrooms

> **Best Practices** — **WESTIN** HOTELS & RESORTS
>
> ### Westin's Creative Approach to Tracking a Group's Historical Performance
>
> The Westin chain uses three interrelated procedures in an effort to assess the accuracy of a convention's commitment by observing its past performance. First, a standard letter of inquiry is sent, along with a questionnaire, to the last two hotels in which the group met. The letter states that the group has booked with a Westin property and asks the hotels to make a post-convention critique of the group. The critiques then are matched with the requirements that have been requested. If there is an indication that the group has exaggerated its needs, the hotel goes back to the customer to clarify the discrepancy.
>
> Westin's second procedure is to question a meeting planner who books a year or more in advance about his or her schedule of upcoming meetings. The Hotel reviews the file two weeks before the group's next meeting and two weeks after it.
>
> On the first date, the hotel wishes the meeting planner the best with the scheduled meeting and advises the planner of an evaluation questionnaire to be sent in four weeks. The planner usually is impressed with the hotel's meticulous approach to detail, and the hotel can be alerted to any change or trends that might alter the number of guestrooms or function space it is holding for the group.
>
> The third technique used by Westin might be called "pre-participation." When convention groups with complicated programs or unusual requirements are booked, the hotel salesperson and the convention service manager might request to be admitted as observers to the group's next meeting. By observing the meeting process and requirements, the convention service manager is better able to service the group at its forthcoming convention in his or her hotel. And, again, the client is reassured that he or she is in good hands.
>
> When the convention planner and the hotel executive have confidence in each other, they can work things out so that all delegates are housed and no one gets hurt by variations in expectations.
>
> Source: Courtesy of Le Westin Montreal.

you about the group's meeting planner; is the planner a seasoned professional who stays on top of the group's reservations and can be counted on to communicate with the hotel as needed, or is he or she an inexperienced planner who will require assistance in managing the group's room block? Most sales managers will freely share this information – especially since they know that they may need to call on your hotel for this type of information in the future.

Another option is to contact your local convention and visitors bureau. CVBs keep detailed records of groups they have housed in the city. These records include weekly room pick-up reports, which are also called **booking pace reports**, that show the inventory status of meeting planners' room blocks. These reports can be invaluable to hoteliers; if a group's history shows that the majority of the group does not book rooms until four weeks out, for example, the hotel need not be alarmed when the group's block is less than half full at six weeks out.

Since your letter of agreement with the group indicates the date by which the organization will either confirm or release rooms, the hotel and the group should re-examine room pick-up at regular intervals and readjust the number if necessary. The meeting planner must be alert for early signals that might affect attendance; perhaps the group will be celebrating a special occasion, such as its 50th anniversary, or feature a noted keynote speaker, which is likely to boost attendance. On the other hand, unforeseen circumstances, such as corporate downsizing, economic downturns, or a natural disaster, may result in fewer attendees. Careful, periodic monitoring of reservations patterns is necessary in order to adjust room blocks as needed to ensure there are no surprises at the onset of the event.

Another problem that may crop up is late reservations. Since reservations received after the cut-off date are usually accepted on a **space available basis** only, the group rate may no longer apply. If you have found that this has been a problem in the past, be sure to communicate your concerns to the meeting planner; this will provide an opportunity for him or her to take steps to ensure reservations are received on time. Communication between the hotel and the meeting planner is a key component in ensuring the success of meetings and building goodwill with groups.

## Arrival/Departure Pattern

In assigning rooms, you need an overall pattern that will indicate when people will arrive and depart. The convention planner may have some idea from previous years, but you will have to finalize detailed patterns when you get the reservations from the guests. Even for corporate meetings, where the meeting planner has greater control, attendees frequently arrive a day or two early because of transportation difficulties, personal travel plans, or the attraction of local tourist or recreational facilities.

For example, typical arrivals for a 400-room convention beginning on Monday and concluding on Thursday might look something like this:

| Day | Number of Rooms | Flow of Attendance |
| --- | --- | --- |
| Friday | 20 | meeting planner and staff |
| Saturday | 150 | early arrivals |
| Sunday | 360 | opening of convention |
| Monday | 400 | peak convention attendance |
| Tuesday | 400 | peak convention attendance |
| Wednesday | 350 | early departures |
| Thursday | 30 | post-convention meetings and extended days |

As you can see from this example, fewer rooms are required before the convention begins, and required rooms taper off as the convention winds down. In this case, Monday and Tuesday are the **peak nights** — the highest occupancy level. This type of arrival/departure pattern is typical for associations as well as other groups.

It is also wise to indicate the breakdown of the group's rooms into singles, doubles, twins, and suites. Arrival dates are easier to secure than check-out dates, but these too are important to you.

Be especially careful if you designate the availability of a *specific* suite. That extra-special VIP suite may be earmarked for the chairman of the board, who may very well decide to test your golf course and arrive a day or two before the meeting or stay in it several days after the event. Impress on your client that you must have advance notice of such plans to make sure the room is available and that there is no conflict with another group.

You will also need to determine the **major arrival/major departure** pattern of incoming convention guests. That is, the dates and times at which large numbers of attendees can be expected to check-in at the hotel and when large numbers will be checking out. The group's resume should provide this information, which is vital for planning staffing – you will need to have enough desk clerks and bellpersons available for a large influx of guests at particular times. The typical ratio is one bellperson and one front desk receptionist/cashier for every 75 guests arriving or departing. If a group is to arrive or depart en masse, however, one staff person for every 50 guests may be required.

Should the check-in for the group be early afternoon, the hotel may need to set up a hospitality area where attendees can wait until vacated rooms are readied by housekeeping. This is a problem for European hotels because most large planes arrive from the United States in the early morning but check-out time for departing guests is not until noon or so.

## Other Hotels

As we mentioned earlier in this chapter, sometimes a number of hotels are to be used for a large convention. In such instances, a competitor becomes a friend. It is nice to have a nearby hotel bail you out with a number of rooms when you may have overbooked. It is just as nice to receive guests from the other hotel when you have a number of rooms available — and to have the favors returned on other occasions. It pays to work together.

Similarly, you may be unable to supply a function room for the convention or for a local customer's banquet. Show the customer that you are interested in his welfare even when you are full by helping him to book the event at another hotel. The other hotel may appreciate the recommendation and reciprocate; your customer appreciates the help and the fact that you didn't turn your back on him or her when you didn't need the business. Always look to the future. The key to success in the hotel business is a good reputation for expertise and *caring*.

A variation may involve only the use of hotel facilities, such as golf courses or tennis courts. An inter-hotel billing arrangement also must be worked out in the case of multi-hotel involvements, which may bring local bus companies into the act.

## Managing Room Blocks

Hotels that cater to group meetings and conventions face potential difficulties when it comes to their rooms inventory. Meeting planners, naturally, want to ensure that there are enough rooms set aside for their attendees – and the number of rooms blocked can play a key role in negotiations for such perks as free meeting space and complimentary rooms. Hoteliers, of course, want to properly house the group, but the hotel's potential profitability can suffer if room blocks are overestimated or rooms otherwise go unfilled (not only do hotels lose money on unsold rooms, but revenue from such areas as food and beverage, recreational amenities, transportation, and other services may be far less than projected).

In this section, we will discuss some of the factors involved in managing room blocks. We will take a look at some of the most common potential problems that may arise when trying to manage room blocks and detail how hotels, meeting planners, and housing providers can work together to ensure that these problems can be avoided or minimized.

---

### INTERNET EXERCISE

Experient, a leading third-party meeting planner, has published an excellent resource titled "Guide to Room Block Management." Go to the Experient website (www.experient-inc.com) and click on "Knowledge Center." Then click on "Experient Publications" to view the 48-page booklet (you will have to register to access resources).

1. What types of historical information are needed to compile a meeting group's history?

2. How does combining housing and registration information in one mailing to meeting attendees aid groups in filling their room blocks?

3. What incentives are recommended for hotels to offer to assist in maximizing room pick-up?

---

## No-Shows/Overbooking

Attendees who fail to check into the hotel despite having a reservation are termed **no-shows**. No-shows may either be guests who fail to attend the convention, whether or not they cancel their reservations, or guests who attend the event but do not use the rooms booked in the group's block. In addition to no-shows, a hotel's profitability can be affected by guests who check out early. An **early departure** is a guest who leaves the hotel earlier than his or her scheduled departure date. Although this is less of a problem for city and airport hotels, which get a good amount of **walk-in** business, early departures can be devastating on resort hotels, which usually don't have the advantage of capturing transient business.

Early departures, like no-shows, can result in a significant loss of room revenue, as well as food and beverage, incidental, and recreational income. Scott Boone, former vice president of sales for InterContinental Hotels and Resorts, says:

> We've noticed an increase in early departures over the past three to four years, especially with convention attendees. Attendees usually book rooms months ahead for the whole conference, then adjust their schedules and neglect to notify the hotel...We just want guests to focus on their departure date so that we in turn will have inventory to offer.[4]

**Underdeparture.** Early outs are not the only challenge facing hoteliers in managing group room blocks. At the other end of the spectrum, problems may also arise if the guest decides to stay another day; this is called **underdeparture**. The hotel may have set aside a block of 250 rooms, and if 20 attendees decide to overstay, there may not be enough rooms available for other booked business (this can be especially critical if the group was booked at one rate but the hotel can get a higher rate for the rooms once they are vacated by the group).

Many hotels require a guest to initial the registration card indicating the day of departure; this institutes a contract between the hotel and the guest. The hotel meets its obligation by providing the room through that date. Once the date has passed, the guest may be considered a "trespasser." The hotel has two options: it can enter a new contract at a different rate (the hotel is not obligated to extend the convention rate); or, the hotel may evict the guest (the problem is that in the vast majority of states the hotel has to take the overstaying guest to court, which obviously is costly and time-consuming).

**Advance Deposits and Guarantees.** The increasing problem of no-shows and early departures has resulted in hotels taking additional measures to minimize losses. This is especially important to hotels that are unlikely to be able to fill unused rooms with other guests; a hotel in the city, for example, may have no trouble filling rooms with business travelers during the week, but experience slow weekends. A resort property (especially an isolated one), on the other hand, may be filled to capacity on weekends and holidays, but have few walk-ins during the week.

The Hospitality Sales & Marketing Association International (HSMA) strongly recommends the use of deposits as a solution to no-shows. Deposits are important to both a host hotel (a hotel that provides rooms for the entire meeting group or serves as the headquarters hotel for a large convention) and overflow hotels – properties that offer rooms to supplement the rooms available at the headquarters hotel. Overflow hotels commonly require a deposit that is sufficient to cover the cost of all nights booked. The reason for this policy is that the headquarters hotel may experience vacancies due to cancellations, no-shows, or early departures. Since delegates typically find rooms at the headquarters hotel more appealing, they may leave the overflow hotel to move to the headquarters hotel during the second or third day of the convention. This practice, of course, leaves the overflow hotel with unoccupied rooms to sell.

Host hotels usually ask for a smaller deposit. With an **advanced deposit reservation**, the hotel receives payment for at least the first night's lodging prior to the guest's arrival and is obligated to hold the room regardless of the guest's arrival time. If a guest holding an advance deposit reservation fails to check-in or cancel, the hotel may retain the deposit. A hotel that is going to take deposits must consider the necessary control and recordkeeping involved and the possibility of refunds.

Another solution offered is the use of guaranteed reservations. A **credit card guaranteed reservation** is a room being held, using the guest's credit card account number, for which payment is guaranteed; in the case of a no-show, billing takes place in the usual manner. But many hotels cite difficulties collecting such payments. The term is often misinterpreted; guests do not always understand that they are agreeing to guarantee payment regardless of whether or not the room is used.

Because the no-show problem is more significant at high-demand resorts than at city and airport properties, resorts have been the leaders in instituting stricter cancellation policies. In an effort to eliminate no-shows and control rooms inventory, some convention hotels have pushed their cancellation deadline to 72 hours before expected check-in. While the penalty for cancelling past the deadline is usually a single night's rate at most city and suburban hotels, it might be a two or three night's rate at some resorts; at some destinations, the penalty imposed may cover the cost of the room for the group's entire stay. Therefore, it is important that both the meeting planner and the meeting attendees understand your cancellation policy prior to booking their stay to avoid potential penalties.

**Overbooking.** In some cases, hotels that have experienced a great number of no-shows (and especially those that cannot rely on transient business to fill unused rooms) try to cover

> **SOME ASSOCIATION HOUSING POLICIES CONTRIBUTE TO HOTEL OVERBOOKING**
>
> In a perfect world, no hotel would ever overbook guestrooms. But hotels can't stop taking reservations when all their rooms "appear" to be sold. Because of "early departures" and "no-shows," hotels that do not confirm more than 100 percent of their rooms run the risk of going 10 percent to 15 percent unsold.
>
> The system is broken, and no one is fixing it. Consider the scenario for citywide conventions. Attendees return a form indicating which hotel(s) they prefer to be in. Registrants are asked to select their top three to six choices, in case the first choice is sold out.
>
> The housing organization attempts to assign the attendees to their desired hotel. If the No. 1 or No. 2 choice is available, there is a high probability the attendee will use the reservation. However, that likelihood decreases the further down the list you go. When all of an attendee's preferred hotels are sold out, most housing authorities will arbitrarily assign a hotel.
>
> This is where the real trouble begins.
>
> Hotels get notification of reservations from the housing organization without knowing if their hotel was a primary request or if it was an "assigned" reservation. (This information would be helpful because there is traditionally a larger "no-show" factor among attendees who are "assigned" rooms.) Many of these "assigned" attendees do not bother to call the hotel to cancel their reservations. Even advanced deposits made by credit card do not deter this practice because most travelers know that if they challenge a charge, most credit card companies will not pay the deposit to a canceled hotel.
>
> The net result: Hotels that don't overbook during a citywide convention have absolutely no hope of selling out their available rooms.
>
> Another reason for overbooking is when booking many years out, planners tend to be overly optimistic, resulting in hundreds (or even thousands) of excess room nights requested.
>
> If past history doesn't support the block, hotels are caught in a bind. If the group doesn't pick up, many rooms will go unsold. One strategy many hotels employ, whether they admit it or not, is to disregard the contractual block and instead protect a smaller block for the group. This enables the hotel to sell the remaining rooms to any interested buyers, be it other groups or individuals. Ideally, when the cut-off date arrives, the group will be under its contracted block by the same number of rooms that the hotel oversold.
>
> Unfortunately, this is not an ideal world. Walks result when a group picks up beyond its history...or when a hotel sells too deeply into its block. This creates the overbooked situation where some attendees have to be "walked" to a different hotel.
>
> The solution here is to establish realistic room blocks based on past performance. After each year's convention, future room blocks would be adjusted to reflect actual growth (or decline) in attendance. This would create a situation in which, at 12 months out, the room block would be within 3 percent to 4 percent of the previous year's pickup.
>
> This adjustment would give hotels a much tighter comfort level. And, instead of 10 percent to 15 percent, overbooking could drop to 5 percent or less.

projected losses by booking more rooms than they actually have available. This practice is known as **overbooking**.

If a hotel overbooks, a convention guest who arrives late may find that there are no rooms available. This constitutes a breach of contract by the hotel, which now owes damages to the latecomer. These guests are termed **walked customers**, as the hotel is responsible for finding other accommodations for them. This situation has led many meeting planners to specify that a *relocation, or walk, clause* be included in the group's contract. This clause provides for specific actions by the hotel in the event of overbooking, and may include such points as a complimentary room at a different hotel for each night that the attendee cannot be accommodated at the original hotel, a complimentary telephone call to allow the attendee to inform others of the change, complimentary transportation (or payment of the cost of transportation) to the new hotel, upgraded accommodations if the delegate returns to the original hotel, an in-room amenity upon the guest's return, and a letter of apology to the guest, in which the hotel accepts responsibility for the overbooking situation.

> **MORE ONLINE**
>
> Do an Internet search for "Room Blocks and Red Flags" How Hoteliers Think" to learn how hotels evaluate meetings business and allocate room blocks.

Hotels can minimize potential problems from overbooking by contacting properties previously used by the group to determine the group's no-show history. If a group typically fills its room block, the hotel will see less reason to overbook (the property may still oversell to a lesser degree to guard against any slippage). Conversely, it is a smart meeting planner who checks among his or her peers for a hotel's overbooking pattern. Wise planners also inform their members of the practice of hotels to hold reservations only until a certain hour, such as 5:00 p.m. They urge their members to arrive earlier than the hold deadline or to guarantee or pre-pay to make sure they get their rooms.

## Attrition

Many hotels protect themselves against no-shows, early outs, and underdepartures by inserting an **attrition clause** into their contracts. Since guestrooms are a perishable commodity, the hotel loses money if it is not able to resell rooms that meeting groups have booked but failed to fill. When hotels book blocks of rooms for groups, however, they normally allow for some **slippage**. While slippage amounts vary, many hotels expect groups to occupy or pay for 80 percent of the rooms blocked. Attrition fees, which are charged to the group, not the individual attendees, apply when the meeting group contracts for a specific number of rooms but the total amount of rooms used is below the original contracted block. Many meeting planners balk at such fees, and some fight the problem by reducing their room block. This practice, however, can cause a different set of problems; booking fewer rooms weakens a planner's negotiating position, perhaps adversely impacting meeting space or reducing the group's number of complimentary rooms.

Attrition has become such a large problem in such a short time that the Convention Industry Council launched Project Attrition, a nine-month study of the problem. The final report can be viewed online at www.conventionindustry.org.

While the CIC was developing guidelines that could be used industry-wide, many hotels and convention centers had already taken steps to help meeting planners minimize attrition. Hotels are not in the business of collecting fees; they want to fill rooms. Group guests spend more time in the hotel than other types of guests and therefore spend more money at the property, so it is important for hotels to find solutions to help a group to manage its block. Joel Pyser, former vice president of field sales for Marriott and now senior vice president of sales at Newmarket International, Inc., says:

> Attrition is the number one issue our customers talk about, and we want our customers to see us as providing them solutions.[5]

Rather than rely on attrition damages, which rarely make up a hotel's entire loss, many hotels are "partnering" with meeting planners — offering services and suggestions to help planners manage and promote their room blocks to avoid attrition fees. One such service is Hilton Hotels' Group Reservations Identification Program (GRIP) software, which interfaces with the chain's reservation system to provide a cross-reference of the group's reservations list in relationship to the rooms booked within its block. The GRIP system provides immediate, detailed summary reports of rooms booked outside the block, enabling the meeting planner to contact attendees that have made their reservations through other channels and encourage them to rebook their reservations correctly. If attendees do not wish to change their reservations, the GRIP system will ensure that their rooms are credited to the group, resulting in an accurate group history.

Several other properties have created event Web sites with registration and room reservations capabilities. These sites promote the value of staying at the headquarters hotel, including the proximity to events and opportunities for networking. And, to compete with possible lower Internet rates, some hotels, such as the Starwood chain, fix a price for guestrooms — no matter what the source of booking (including the Internet, travel agents, the hotel's own reservations system, and so on).

For hotels, it is all about time and space. The more time hotels have to react to reductions, the more likely they will be willing to work with the planner to minimize attrition fees. Some hotels now allow small meeting groups to adjust their room blocks 90 days out; blocks can be reduced by five or ten percent with no fees, providing that the group agrees to reduce meeting space a like percentage.

On the other hand, experienced meeting planners will keep hotels informed, and notify them as soon as possible if they feel they are going to meet or exceed their block. Hotels that can anticipate high occupancy levels will be able to cut down bookings from less profitable channels. Working together is the key in this age of revenue management.

**Booking Outside the Block.** When attendees bypass the group's housing service and book rooms at hotels other than those specified by the meeting planner, the hotel doesn't attribute those reservations to the group's block. This practice, called **booking outside the block**, is becoming more common, especially with easy access to hotel information on the Internet and the increasing use of third-party providers.

Many meeting planners cite room block headaches as their biggest professional challenge, and a majority report that the number of attendees booking outside the block has risen in recent years. Bill Drohan, CAE, president of Drohan Management Group, an association management company, attributes this trend to several factors:

> In many convention cities, limited-service hotels are popping up around convention centers, giving attendees lower-priced options. We have been losing a lot of business from our room blocks to these limited-service hotels.
>
> Online travel booking sites are also siphoning off the block as more attendees use the Internet to search for the lowest rates, often at the last minute. This was a huge concern during the recession, as these sites were offering significant discounts below the negotiated group rate. Now, the group rate is probably better, but the concern is that attendees have become accustomed to last-minute deals and are therefore waiting longer to register.
>
> And, hotel loyalty programs are a factor as well, as attendees choose chains where they can accumulate points. It all creates quite a pull on attendees.[6]

In some cases, especially when a large convention requires housing the delegates in a number of hotels, delegates may make multiple reservations because they fear they won't get a room at their first-choice hotel. Attendees frequently use the Internet to find travel "deals" (Hotels.com, Expedia, and Travelocity represent 75 percent of online sales).[7] It has become increasingly common to find that between 20-30 percent of a group's attendees book their rooms online, whether at the host hotel or at other properties in the convention city.[8]

Attendees who use the Internet may find cheaper rates at the host hotel and book rooms not designated in the group's contract. In other cases, convention guests book into a hotel in which they are members of a loyalty program. Whatever the reason, the group's block is adversely affected, impacting both the meeting planner, — who may lose free meeting space and other perks and possibly face attrition fees — and the hotel, which can lose financially when rooms go unused.

Hotels can help meeting planners fill their designated blocks by suggesting that planners "bundle" registration; that is, charge delegates one fee for the entire event (including registration, room, event attendance, and other services, such as transportation). Delegates who book outside the block would be required to pay a higher registration fee or be charged additional fees for specific events, such as an evening banquet. Planners can also discourage booking outside the block by including the reasons for booking within the group's block in promotional materials. Delegates tempted to book outside the block might be persuaded to change their minds when they realize that such benefits as free meeting space, complimentary receptions, audiovisual equipment, and other services are based on filling a guaranteed number of rooms.

**Room Audits.** As we have seen, attrition can be a problem for both hotels and meeting planners. Not only can failure to fill up its room block result in attrition fees for a meeting group, it also affects the group's leverage in future negotiations. If the group's history reflects a lack of room pick-up, it can lose a number of concessions, such as complimentary rooms, free or reduced rate meeting rooms, or perhaps complimentary beverage service between sessions.

Hotels, too, have a vested interest in assisting meeting planners to keep attendees in the contracted hotel and filling their room blocks. Rob Scypinski, VP of sales for Hilton Hotels Corp, says:

> Keeping people in the block obviously helps the association, because they won't run into attrition. It also helps the hotel, because even if we get a fraction of the room rate for attrition damages, we don't get them eating in our hotel, watching a movie, or using the high-speed Internet.[9]

One of the most effective ways to fight attrition is by using periodic room audits. We have already mentioned Hilton's GRIP software, which produces reports detailing which attendees are booked under the group's code and such other factors as which attendees are sharing rooms and which channels were used to book rooms. Starwood Hotels & Resorts uses a similar system, Starwood's Reservation Cross Check, in its properties in North America, and Experient offers DQ SureMatch, another automated room block auditing service, to its clients.

No matter which method is used, room audits should be conducted periodically to keep the registration and housing process on track. In order for both the meeting group and the hotel to reap the full benefits of room audits, the contract should include provisions that state how audits will be conducted and how these audits will affect concessions made to the group. This provides an incentive to the meeting planner to stay on top of his or her group's block pick-up and to look for any "red flags" that may affect concessions for the current meeting and leverage for future negotiations. The box titled "Industry-Wide Housing Practices" provides guidelines for maximizing the registration and housing process while minimizing problems with booking and attrition.

## Industry-Wide Housing Practices

The Convention Industry Council (CIC) has adopted best practices for event housing and registration as part of its APEX initiative. This initiative, which can be reviewed in its entirety at www.conventionindustry.org/StandardsPractices/APEX, deals with a number of issues in managing room blocks, including practices for collecting, reporting, and retrieving complete housing and registration data. Click on the Housing & Registration tab to see forms and templates that can be downloaded as either MS Word or PDF files. The Room Blocks tab offers information on how to manage room blocks and protect them from poaching.

Housing and registration accepted practices are organized into two parts – recommended forms for registration and housing, and accepted practices to be followed. The forms, which include templates for housing forms and rooming lists, include the complete and thorough information required by hotels in order to properly manage room blocks, can be customized to suit the character of the meeting (as with the other accepted practices adopted by the CIC, the housing and registration report can be adapted to any size meeting).

Best practices for blocking rooms, managing blocks, tracking, room audits, and information for post-event reports all make it easier for facilities to control room blocks, reduce rooms outside the blocks, and help clients to minimize attrition. These tools, while primarily a help to reservations departments, can certainly present opportunities for improved customer service by hotel sales and service professionals. These accepted practices were also developed to address housing-related terminology and the role of computerized technology in the industry's housing and registration process as well as room block management.

# Check-In/Check-Out

Once meeting attendees start arriving, it is important that the hotel be able to get them to their rooms quickly and efficiently – and that their first impression of the hotel is a favorable one. While the front desk has played a vital role in setting the tone of attendees' stays for many years, new advances in technology have greatly changed check-in/check-out procedures. In this section, we will discuss the role of the front desk, the popularity (and sophistication) of hotel check-in/check-out kiosks, and the use of mobile devices to check-in and access assigned guestrooms.

## Check-in Procedures

Today's computer technology has made it far easier for hotel front desk staff to register meeting attendees quickly. In most cases, **pre-registration** is used for groups; reservations are entered into the hotel's reservations system either individually (as attendees register) or as a group (in cases where a rooming list is prepared by the planner). Delegates are listed alphabetically within each meeting or convention group, and they are assigned rooms according to the type of accommodation requested and rate.

When an attendee arrives, the front desk staff pulls up his or her information in the computer and activates the room key. The front desk staff may also provide other materials, such as a map of the property, information about property services, and so on, but these should be prepared in advance to save on check-in time. The front desk staff must be courteous and helpful; in addition to being able to answer questions from each attendee,

## Chapter 11: Guestrooms

they can also enhance an attendee's stay by cross-selling (perhaps suggesting the hotel's restaurant for dinner or mentioning treatments offered by the property's spa).

Check-in time can be speeded along by determining the attendees' arrival patterns and staffing the front desk accordingly; delegates are not likely to form a favorable impression of the hotel if they have to wait in long lines. Some hotels offer special group check-in windows so attendees don't have to wait in line with leisure guests.

Other hotels offer separate counters away from the main desk to reduce traffic congestion for pre-registered guests. Hotels that service extensive group business may also have special lobbies for registration – or tables may be provided outside the group's meeting rooms. In these cases, room keys are typically placed into the attendee's convention or meeting packet.

In some cases, a **housing assistance desk** is set up near the registration area to enable the planner and members of the housing staff to greet and assist attendees (many hotels, in fact, request that the planner be present at check-in time to facilitate the process). Not only is this arrangement helpful to attendees who encounter reservation problems, but it also minimizes lobby confusion, long lines, and slow check-in procedures.

For even speedier service, many hotels offer kiosks that attendees can use to check-in and check-out. In some cases, the group will have a dedicated kiosk that displays a welcome message or other information, such as updates to the agenda. These kiosks, which have been promoted as "line-busting technology," allow guests with reservations to swipe their credit cards to receive their room keys and other information in less than 90 seconds.

Most major chains and some independent properties now offer these **self check-in, self check-out terminals**, which appeal to attendees who are familiar with kiosks in airports. Hyatt Hotels was a leader in this technology with its Touch and Go Instant Check-In Machine, while Hilton has installed kiosks that accept both credit cards and HHonors cards.

Tim Harvey, former senior vice president and chief information officer at Hilton, says:

> We found usage of these kiosks exceeded our early expectations. Some 10% to 12% of our guests [on average] used them, and, in some instances, usage was as high as 35%.[10]

*The Hilton Hotels Corp. is eliminating long lines at the front desk by offering free-standing automated check-in/check-out kiosks at its properties.*

That figure is much higher today, of course, and the kiosks themselves have evolved. In the past, room keys were dispensed when the guest entered information on a keypad. Today, it is becoming increasingly common for hotels to offer kiosks with 32-inch touch screens, and the kiosk may also offer the option to select additional services (a daily newspaper, laundry or valet, for example), make a reservation in the property's restaurant, or reserve a cabana at the pool. These features have eliminated many of the concerns about interaction with the front desk in terms of added revenue, and hotels have addressed the personal interaction issue by staffing hosts to assist attendees in using the machines and answering any questions they might have about the hotel. To provide even better service, additional kiosks are often located near elevators or meeting rooms to enable guests to get replacement key cards without having to walk back to the front desk.

## Best Practices

### Gaylord Hotels: Using Technology to Better Service Large Groups

Gaylord Hotels, which operates the 2,881-room Gaylord Opryland Resort & Convention Center in Nashville, Tennessee; the 1,406-room Gaylord Palms Resort & Convention Center in Kissimmee, Florida; and the 1,511-room Gaylord Opryland Texas Resort & Convention Center in Grapevine, Texas, is using technology to successfully host large groups and provide convention attendees with comprehensive information about their event online. Computers are used to manage group business, from centrally managing and distributing sales leads to automated check-in and check-out. Craig Ratterman, former director of strategic systems, says:

"Gaylord Hotels set up group-specific Web sites for attendees, and can accept rooming lists from any group that sends them in electronic format. They also use wireless terminals at check-in to give maximum flexibility, and give each attendee an individually customized map with directions to their room and to their conference's registration and location information...With the new Gaylord iConnect technology, convention goers can also see their group members' phone extensions and check their convention schedule. They can also view a welcome message and other e-mails from their group, check property maps to find their specific events, visit the layout of the exhibit hall and find out where the booths are – all online."

Other technology that is being used for more efficient service includes online check-in and specialized mobile apps. Radisson's "ExpressYourself[SM]" program, the first online guest check-in service, allows guests to reserve a room and then check-in at Radisson's website up to seven days prior to their stay. The guest then enters check-in information and makes specific requests, such as room location and preferred amenities. Upon arrival, the guest needs only to identify himself or herself at a designated Express Yourself area of the front desk to receive room keys and a hotel packet.

Bjorn Gullaksen, former executive vice president at Carlson Hospitality Worldwide, said of the program:

> Radisson is taking a bold step to transform what consumer research has consistently shown as the least-desirable experience in the hotel stay – standing in line for a slow check-in or slow check-out. We will never

# Chapter 11: Guestrooms

replace the human element of a friendly front desk person, but "Express Yourself" eliminates the paperwork that has traditionally been the main focus of the check-in process. By freeing staff from these procedural restraints, they can concentrate on welcoming the guest and getting them quickly to their room.[11]

Other properties, such as the Inn at St. Botolph in Boston, eliminate the need to stop at a reservations desk altogether. Guests who make reservations and enter their credit card information receive a confirmation e-mail that includes a room assignment and two key codes. The first code is entered into a keypad at the front door to allow entrance to the property, while the second is used to enter the guestroom.

The latest trend to streamline the check-in process is the use of mobile apps. This trend was fueled by millennials, who are technologically savvy and make extensive use of their smartphones or tablets to stay connected – and take care of business. A growing number of hotels are now offering mobile apps that allow guests to check-in on their mobile devices instead of having to wait in line or use a kiosk. Dolce, for example, was the first hotel to use MICRO's new Front Desk Mobile for OPERA 9 at its Aspen Meadows Resort. Guests were able to remotely check-in at the Aspen airport, where they were met by an agent who gave a pre-assigned room key to the guests, enabling them to go directly to their room when they reached the property. Other chains, including Hilton Worldwide, the InterContinental Hotels Group, and Marriott, also offer apps that allow a guest to check-in via their mobile devices. In most cases, guests are sent an e-mail with a barcode that can either be scanned on a smartphone or printed out to be scanned at a kiosk – or a special express line at the front desk — to receive room keys. Hilton's app also allows a guest to "see" his or her room before checking in, while Marriott's app alerts guests (via a text message to their phones) who have arrived early that their room is ready.

> **WORTH WATCHING**
> To view a short video on how kiosks are simplifying the registration process at Hotel La Tour, go to YouTube.com and search for hotel self-service kiosks; scroll down to "Hotel Kiosk" by Terry Chau.

The latest technology allows a guest to go directly to his or her room and unlock the door with their smartphones (guests using mobile apps are given a special code that they enter into the smartphone to access their rooms). The Starwood chain first offered the technology, SPG Keyless, for Starwood Preferred Guest members at select Aloft, W, and Element hotels; at the time of this writing, the app was compatible for iPhone 4 or newer models and Android phones running at 4.3 or more. Hilton also began offering keyless entry for its Hilton HHonors members at several of its domestic brands. Keyless entry is also being offered in Europe; the HTL Hotel chain, a new brand of boutique hotels, has replaced the traditional front desk/lobby with a lounge-type area where guests can check-in by smartphone and use a keyless entry system that emits a low-energy Bluetooth signal via smartphone to open room key locks.

> **WORTH WATCHING**
> View a video describing Starwood's SPG keyless mobile check-in app at www.youtube.com/watch?v=9MX7Mo4fDdY.

Since the technology is so new, several chains are taking a "wait and see" position and depending on mobile apps to fuel their business. Their concerns include the security of keyless systems – and the cost of replacing traditional magnetic stripe technology, especially since some guests do not use smartphones. In addition, only one phone can be linked

Chapter 11: Guestrooms

*The front desk is often the first contact for many convention delegates, and a friendly, efficient check-in sets the tone for a successful meeting.*
**Photo Courtesy of the Madinat Jumeriah Hotel in Dubai.**

to a room; if two or more people are staying in the room, traditional room keys would have to be issued.

## Check-out Procedures

While group check-out procedures may seem like a minor detail, problems when checking out can ruin the positive experience an attendee has had at the meeting. Hotels often estab-

407

Chapter 11: Guestrooms

lish a check-out time of noon or 1:00 p.m., but later check-outs may be offered if the event concludes with a luncheon – and if the final day's guest arrival patterns permit. If extending check-out times is not possible, attendees should be asked to check out before the established check-out time and arrangements should be made to store their baggage until departure time.

If attendees' charges are billed to the group's master account or if they have left a credit card for billing, there is generally no need for attendees to have to visit the front desk for check out. Some hotels offer dedicated check-out kiosks, which are usually smaller than regular check-in/check-out kiosks and are often located near the group's meeting rooms or on the floors occupied by the group's block. It is also common for guests to simply leave their keys in drop boxes near the lobby. And, in the case of hotels using a keyless entry system, no action on the part of the attendee is required; guestroom access codes will be inactivated by the hotel.

## Summary

A smooth reservations procedure sets the stage for a successful function. Fortunately, today's technology has streamlined the reservations process. Technology has made it easier than ever to process registrations over the Internet – credit card payments can be instantly processed, and confirmations can be immediately sent to both the attendee and the meeting planner. In addition, computer software has greatly facilitated the processing of registration and event information, especially when hotels make use of standardized forms and technology.

The downside of this technology is that attendees are more likely than ever to compare prices and book rooms over the Internet—often bypassing the group's designated block. This makes it necessary for planners to work with hotels to develop strategies to keep their group in their block to avoid lost concessions and possible attrition damages. This process is made easier by educating attendees about the importance of booking within the block—and sometimes offering incentives, such as registration discounts. Hotels can help planners to manage their blocks by providing periodic room audits to "flag" attendees who have bypassed the block and booked elsewhere in the hotel.

Both the hotel and the meeting planner should ensure that reservation information is communicated early and often to ensure that adjustments can be made. Proper room arrangements and efficient check-in and check-out procedures also add to a delegate's favorable impression of the property—and may result in future business from the meeting planner.

Getting the delegates into the hotel smoothly is just one segment of the servicing process, however. They are coming for a meeting or a function and their expectations are high. In the next chapter, we will see how the convention service manager communicates the numerous details required for the service staff to execute a successful meeting.

## Endnotes

1. Marilyn Healey, "Housing Technology: Ensure a Smoother Process for Your Client," HotelExecutive.com

2. Maxine Golding, "Convention Housing," *Convene*.
3. "The Broadmoor Simplifies Event Management with Passkey," www.hotel-online.com.
4. Linda Humphrey, "Early Check-Out Fees Gaining Momentum," *Business Travel News*.
5. *Meeting News*.
6. Dave Kovaleski, "36 Reasons to Think Inside the Block," MeetingsNet.
7. Mary Ann McNulty, "Pandora's Box," *PCMA Convene*.
8. Susan Hatch, "Online Booking Blues," *Corporate Meetings & Incentives*.
9. Jonathan Vatner, "Keeping Them in Line," *Meetings and Conventions*.
10. ehotelier.com.
11. Michael Billig, "Technology Snapshot," *HotelBusiness*.

## Study Questions

1. Describe in detail the types of reservations systems used to handle group bookings.
2. Trace the procedures used to service a citywide convention. Describe the forms used.
3. Distinguish between rack rates, run-of-the house-rates, spread rates, and split rates.
4. What three procedures are used by the Westin chain to assess the accuracy of a group's commitment?
5. What is the relationship between no-shows, underdepartures, and overbooking?
6. What factors are taken into consideration to ensure the smooth check-in and check-out of a convention group?
7. Assess the present-day application of the computer in servicing convention business and project technology's likely role in the future.

## Key Terms

**advance deposit reservation**—Payment to the hotel (prior to arrival) for the first night's lodging. The hotel is obligated to hold the room regardless of the guest's arrival time.

**attrition clause**—Contract wording that outlines potential damages or fees that a party may be required to pay in the event that it does not fulfill minimum commitments in the contract.

**bid sheet**—Form used by local convention bureaus to obtain room commitments and prices from local hotels. The list is later forwarded to the meeting planner or site selection committee.

**booking outside the block**—Meeting attendees book rooms at hotels other than those specified by the meeting planner or book rooms within the specified hotels but not as part of the convention group's block of rooms.

## Chapter 11: Guestrooms

**booking pace report**—A report listing the rate at which reservations are made.
**check-out time**—The time (set by the hotel) at which guests are expected to vacate their rooms.
**citywide**—A convention which, because of its size or special requirements, requires accommodations at several hotels for its delegates.
**comp rooms**—Complimentary rooms; rooms that the hotel offers to a group at no charge in ratio to the number of rooms occupied by the group. The standard is one comp room per fifty rooms occupied.
**credit card guaranteed reservation**—A reservation made by credit card that assures the guest that a room will be held until check-out time of the following day of arrival. The guest guarantees payment for the room, even if it is not used, unless the reservation is properly cancelled.
**cutoff date**—The deadline for holding the number of guestrooms booked by a group (the last day a meeting attendee can buy a guestroom from the room block reserved for the meeting). Generally, hotels specify a date (also called a **reservation review date**) 30 days before the first day of the meeting for the group to either guarantee, add to, or release the guestrooms booked for the convention. Reservation requests made after the cutoff date may be accepted on a space-available basis, but late bookers may not be entitled to the group room rate.
**early departure**—An attendee who checks out of the hotel earlier than scheduled. A fee may be charged by the hotel to make up for lost business. Also called an **understay** or an **early out**.
**housing assistance desk**—An area used to provide service to convention attendees who have concerns about their reservations.
**housing bureau**—Provided by a city's convention bureau, housing bureaus help place delegates into the city's hotels when large conventions are booked.
**major arrival/major departure**—The expected dates and times of arrivals and departures of large numbers of event attendees. Usually obtained from the group's resume, this information aids in staffing adequate front desk and bell staff.
**no-shows**—Customers who made reservations but do not show up at the hotel and did not cancel their reservation before the hotel's cancellation deadline.
**overbooking**—The hotel has committed more rooms that what are actually available for use (usually due to anticipated no-shows).
**peak night**—The night that the meeting has the highest demand for guestrooms. Guestroom numbers typically start out low (before the meeting), build to a peak (during the meeting), and then taper off (at the end of the meeting).
**pre-registration**—Often used for group business; with pre-registration, the hotel assigns the attendee a room that will be available upon the attendee's arrival.
**rack rate**—The standard rate established by a property for a particular category of room. May vary depending on the season.
**reservation confirmation**—Written agreement by a facility to accept a request for accommodations. To be binding, the agreement must state the intent of the parties – the particular date, the type of accommodations, and the number to be accommodated. Normally requires a credit card number.
**reservation housing report**—A report indicating the group's pickup of its room commitment. Sent by a housing bureau to both the hotel and the group.
**room block**—An agreed-upon number of rooms set aside for members of a group planning to stay at a hotel.
**rooming list**—A list of the names of attendees who will occupy the previously

reserved accommodations. Submitted by the meeting planner, it is also called a **housing list**.

**run-of-the-house rate**—An agreed-upon rate for all available rooms except suites. Generally priced at an average figure for group accommodations. Also called a **flat rate**.

**self check-in, check-out terminal**—A computerized kiosk system, usually located in the hotel lobby, that allows guests to review their registration information and receive their room keys at check-in. At check-out, they can review their folios and settle their accounts with the credit card used at check-in.

**slippage**—The number of guestrooms not used from the original room block. Also known as **wash**.

**space available basis**—Reservations that have no claim against the block of convention rooms because the request arrived after the official cut-off date.

**split rate**—The pricing of group guestrooms based on different room types, such as regular guestrooms versus tower rooms.

**sub-block**—A portion of the group's room block that is classified differently, such as VIP suites, exhibitors' rooms in various areas of the hotel, or rooms by type (double, double-double, and so on) or price range.

**third-party housing provider**—A private company that is contracted to manage the housing of convention delegates.

**underdeparture**—Occurs when a guest scheduled to leave decides to stay longer. Also called an **overstay**.

**walk-in**—A guest who does not have a reservation but requests accommodations at a hotel. Also called **transient business**.

**walked customers**—Guests holding confirmed reservations who are sent to another facility because of overbooking. If a hotel accepts a reservation but can't provide a room, the hotel has breached the contract and the injured guest is owed damages. The usual practice is for the guest to be compensated for the first night to stay at the second hotel (reimbursement for transportation between the two hotels is usually also included).

## Industry Profile

### Marilyn McIver, General Manager/Account Executive

**Southwest Conference Planners**

After working with the Marriott chain for three years, Marilyn was named convention service manager of the Maui Marriott. She later served on the opening team of the JW Marriott Desert Springs Resort & Spa, the chain's flagship property in Palm Desert, California, which offers 891 guestrooms, 85 suites, and 55,000 square feet of meeting space. In her current position at the largest destination management company in the southwest, Marilyn is involved in creating corporate meetings and incentive programs, including themed events, customized team-building challenges, tours/attractions, off-property events, transportation, and entertainment for a wide variety of clients, including most of the Fortune 500 companies.

## The Pre-Con: The Most Critical Meeting on the Program's Agenda

Ever feel that if you have to attend one more meeting, you just might lose your mind? Are you occasionally tempted to erase a meeting off your calendar or conveniently be unavailable? A word of caution…if the session you are *considering* missing is a pre-con meeting…don't!

Whether you are involved on the hotel's staff or are part of the association/corporate planning team, the pre-con meeting is possibly the most critical meeting on the program's agenda. This session is advisedly scheduled a couple of days prior to the opening of the convention, but *always* before any sizable number of attendees start arriving (it is also best to avoid meeting during traditionally busy times for hotel staff).

Hotels should always "educate" the planner as to what their format will be so planners won't be surprised. When I was a CSM, I always jotted down notes during the months of planning to assist in opening the pre-con…perhaps a bit of unusual association history or an amusing story from meetings past.

Executive support is of paramount importance for any event, so general manager attendance at pre-cons is a real plus. After introducing the planner and providing the opportunity for him or her to give a brief of the program, our staff introduced themselves and their departments' roles during the convention. Our GM was always the last to speak, and he or she would reaffirm the property's commitment to provide the group with the *best* meeting ever. My job was made easier by the fact that the GM meant that – and that the rest of the staff would follow the GM's lead.

It is not unusual for a department manager to bring a key hourly employee to the meeting. This exposure to the pre-con gives them a real sense of the importance of group business, and the word soon infiltrates associates' ranks. Technical directors and ground operators should also be included since they can provide important information regarding specialized aspects of the program.

Whether you elect to assume the role of a meeting planner or a CSM, always remember that you share one common objective: a successful program. Good meetings don't just happen…they are the result of the concerted efforts of a lot of people at many and varied levels. Communication is extremely critical to ensure good follow-through. Detailed function sheets, an accurate group resume with a timely distribution, and a well-run pre-con are all tools that we can use to make our common goal a reality.

**Learning Objectives:**

In this chapter, we will discuss the specifics of a pre-convention meeting and detail the forms used by the hotel to ensure that departments servicing the event execute it to the planner's specifications. When you have studied this chapter, you will:

- Know the purpose and importance of the pre-convention meeting and the function of a key personnel roster.

- Be able to describe the format and uses of the resume (specification sheet) and banquet event order (function sheet) in servicing conventions and group meetings.

- Recognize the importance of communication in the execution of an event and be able to describe how the computer is used to communicate meeting details.

**Outline**

Pre-convention Meeting
- Key Personnel Roster

Resume (Specification Sheet)

Banquet Event Order (Function Sheet)

The Importance of Communication

Communicating Details Electronically

The Importance of Follow-up

Summary

Chapter Appendix: Resume (Specification Sheet)

# 12 Preparing for the Event

After a letter of agreement has been signed by both parties and the reservation cards sent, the event must be planned in great detail. Some conventions are planned a number of years in advance; others, a year or two. Some member of the organization's staff will be the primary coordinator for the group. It may be the executive director for a small or medium-sized association or a convention coordinator for a large organization. It could also be a professional convention coordinator who is paid a fee by the association to run the event.

For the hotel, logistics are controlled by the convention service manager. As we discussed, the convention service manager is a most vital person on the hotel staff. He or she is the liaison person with the client and the control person within the hotel. It is not an exaggeration to consider the convention service manager as the key to the success or failure of an event. He or she is responsible for seeing that the event is properly planned and for taking quick, positive action should things go wrong during the event.

In many small hotels, the catering manager may serve as the convention service manager. It is not unusual in such a case for the catering manager also to be active in soliciting banquet business. If this is the case, communication with the sales department and use of the function book must be diligently controlled. This is doubly true when many promises are verbal, and not documented in correspondence or letters of agreement.

## Pre-convention Meeting

A **pre-convention meeting (pre-con)** is essential and goes a long way toward eliminating problems that may surface during a convention. Terry Matthews-Lombardo, CMP, an independent planner and well-known industry speaker, says of the pre-con:

> If run correctly, it has the power to make or break the success of so many aspects of the meeting. It's the final opportunity to discuss with all the key players how the details of each and every aspect of the program will play out in the next few days.[1]

A smart hotel sales executive will arrange for a pre-conference meeting to introduce the hotel's convention service personnel, the organization's people, and all outside contractors involved in serving the group. Hotels should make it a firm practice to bring the entire convention staff together for an unhurried pre-convention session with the meeting planner and contractors for goods and services. This get-together provides the opportunity for all parties to review the convention agenda item by item to ensure that everyone fully understands what is to take place and to finalize any last-minute details.

A pre-con meeting should be held a day or two before the arrival of the group's main delegation (many convention service personnel feel that the ideal time to hold a pre-con is two days prior to the group's meeting or event). The hotel's CSM should determine the best time to schedule the meeting; morning meetings are commonly held, but an afternoon pre-con may enable the hotel's staff from two different shifts to attend. At this time, the meeting planner and his or her staff meet with the convention service manager and all the hotel's department heads who are involved in the direct servicing of the group. The upcoming program is thoroughly reviewed.

Attendees at the meeting vary. For simple or one-day meetings, the pre-con may include only the meeting planner and the convention service manager. For a large convention with a number of banquets, meetings, and complex setups, the following individuals are likely to be in attendance:

- Meeting planner and his or her staff.
- Director of convention services and the convention service manager responsible for servicing the group.
- Salesperson who secured the group and perhaps the director of sales.
- Food and beverage manager, catering/banquet manager, and the chef.
- Hotel's general manager and perhaps the comptroller or credit manager.
- Director of exhibit service, floor manager, and a convention service secretary.
- Representatives from the following departments:

  | - front office | - reservations | - publicity/public relations |
  |---|---|---|
  | - security | - uniform services | - housekeeping |
  | - telephone | - recreational facilities | - concierge |
  | - room service | - audiovisual | |
  | - garage/valet | - spa director | |

- Outside vendors who will play a significant role, such as third-party housing companies, destination management companies, or audiovisual firms.
- For large programs, a representative of the Convention and Visitors Bureau may be invited.

Some astute hotel convention service managers suggest to the meeting planner that they invite a higher-up, such as the company president or association executive, to at least drop in at the introductions portion of the pre-con meeting. This helps the hotel's staff to recognize them as VIPs, gives the executives a clearer understanding of the complexities of managing meetings, and helps to strengthen the relationship between the hotel and the meeting group.

A small ceremony usually takes place at the end of the pre-convention meeting. The meeting planner and his or her key personnel may be given VIP pins, which serve two functions. First, they give distinction to the meeting planner and staff, recognizing that the hotel is aware of their positions and the importance of the meeting. Second, they help the hotel staff single out members who are in charge, should there be any last-minute changes or requests.

The "Best Practices" box titled "Westin's 'Operation Excell'" provides an excellent, step-by-step example of procedures that the chain formerly used to ensure optimum results from pre-con meetings. These procedures are not necessarily required for every convention, nor is it always necessary for all department heads to be present at a pre-con; the convention program will dictate which department heads should attend. Major conventions and smaller ones with complicated requirements, however, are preceded by a meeting similar to that described in the case study.

*Marriott's VIP pin for meeting planners.*

Regardless of who attends the pre-con, from that meeting on, it should be the service manager, not the salesperson, who deals with both the client and the hotel staff. If a hotel wants to succeed with convention business, it must develop good salespeople to bring in the right kind of business, and good convention service people, functioning in-house, to guide that business through to successful completion. In larger convention facilities, a convention service manager would have an assistant and possibly other specialists.

Chapter 12: Preparing for the Event

## Best Practices

## Westin's "Operation Excell"

It is important for meeting planners and a property to get off to a proper start. The following is a step-by-step overview of the "Operation Excell" checklist previously used by the Westin chain. This concept can be used by properties of all sizes to eliminate many of the unforeseen crises inherent to group meetings. An organized approach could well mean the difference between a successful convention and one that is plagued with unforeseen difficulties.

Source: Courtesy Westin New York at Times Square.

1. A pre-convention date and time is agreed upon by the hotel and the meeting planner. A reminder is sent to all departments involved, with a notation that all department heads are to be there ten minutes before the meeting begins. This is to give the convention service manager a chance to prepare the staff for any unusual characteristics or demands of the convention group. All the normal procedures used in setting up meeting rooms should be applied to the pre-con meeting. Taking care of details such as proper seating setup, the right-size meeting room, and comfortable chairs gives the client the impression that the hotel will service his or her meeting as well as it runs its own. Coffee, soft drinks and sweet rolls should be provided so there is an atmosphere of informality. To instill confidence that the hotel knows how to service meetings, the convention service manager should check the room an hour ahead of time for those little things — such as lighting, pads and pencils, and comfortable temperature — that make for a pleasant, attractive meeting setup.

2. An inventory of nameplates of all department heads should be maintained so that the client may relate in the meeting to the key people on the hotel's staff. VIP identification pins are presented to the meeting planner and his or her staff.

3. The meeting format gives department heads a chance to ask questions about matters that relate directly to their roles in servicing the group. The convention service manager then goes over the program event by event. A sample agenda might include:

- Review of the specification sheet and function sheets
- Review of the master account
- An updated room pick-up report

If there are areas of misunderstanding or changes are needed, the client has an opportunity to inject input. A secretary should be on hand to take note of these changes. These last-minute changes are typed up after the meeting and distributed to all involved.

4. A specification sheet (resume), which covers the entire convention program and is the hotel's in-house communication medium, should be distributed to every department in the hotel. Each department needs to be kept informed so it can forecast staffing needs. For example, if no luncheons or dinners are scheduled on a particular day, the people in charge of staffing the hotel's coffee shop and restaurants should be alerted to the possibility of extra volume. Likewise, if a late-evening activity is scheduled outside the hotel, security personnel should be informed to take extra precautions.

## Key Personnel Roster

Meeting planners often request a **key personnel roster** from the convention service manager so they have someone to contact should trouble arise (see Figure 12.1). This roster would list the names and telephone numbers of hotel department heads and other specialists (such as the in-house audiovisual contact). Many convention service managers, however, are hesitant to provide such a list, preferring to have all requests channeled through them. Perhaps the wisest course lies between these two positions.

If the convention service manager will *always* be on the scene and available to the meeting planner, it is possible for him or her to receive every request. But if this is not feasible, an assistant should be designated to act in such instances. If this is not practical, department heads should be trained to inform the convention service manager of all requests.

During a convention, a meeting planner will often refuse to wait until the manager can be located before taking action in what he or she deems a crisis. In any case, prompt action on the part of the hotel staff is crucial; communication between key personnel and the convention service manager is obviously essential.

Minita Wescott, past president of both the Chicago Trade Association Executives Forum and the American Trade Association Executives, suggested:

> One person on the hotel staff should be assigned to the convention for the duration of the meeting. This person should be readily available to handle all on-the-spot needs. It makes for a smoother meeting if the executive of the association can meet and get acquainted with all top members of the hotel staff with whom this executive and his staff will have to work.[2]

The Marriott chain responded to such meeting planners' requests for hotel contact people to act on last-minute needs and further expanded on it with the introduction of its Red Coat service (see Figure 12.2). A number of property convention staff personnel, easily identified by their red jackets, are both trained and empowered to handle last-minute details and crises. This program helps free up the property's convention service manager while still ensuring that immediate help is available to meeting planners who need it. The visibility and accessibility of these trained professionals helps to boost the confidence of even the least experienced meeting planner and demonstrates the chain's commitment to service.

A number of other chains and independent hotels also provide a dedicated liaison to meeting planners. Crowne Plaza Hotels & Resorts, for example, assigns a dedicated Meetings Director to each group. Delta Hotels and Resorts, Hyatt, and Wynn Resorts are among the hotels that employ meeting concierges. The duties of meeting concierges typically include pre- and daily inspection of meeting rooms to ensure that rooms are clean and properly set up and attending to the special needs of meeting planners, attendees, and VIP guests. Meeting concierges are highly visible during the event, and they can be instantly reached via apps (which we will discuss later in this chapter), e-mail, phone, or text message.

> **WORTH WATCHING**
>
> Gennice Carter, senior manager of meeting operations at AcademyHealth, shares her views on achieving event excellence by partnering with the hotel events management team at hedtalks.connectplusathiltonworldwide.com (click on the Driving Results tab and scroll down to the "Events Management" video).

# Chapter 12: Preparing for the Event

*Figure 12.1. HOTEL KEY PERSONNEL ROSTER.*

---

**HOTEL PERSONNEL**

**Hotel staff personnel contact for over-all service during the convention of** _____

| Period | Hours | Name | Title | Phone Extension |
|---|---|---|---|---|
| Early morning | ___a.m. to ___p.m. | _____ | _____ | _____ |
| Daytime | ___a.m. to ___p.m. | _____ | _____ | _____ |
| Evening | ___a.m. to ___p.m. | _____ | _____ | _____ |
| Saturdays | ___a.m. to ___p.m. | _____ | _____ | _____ |
| Sundays | ___a.m. to ___p.m. | _____ | _____ | _____ |
| Holidays | ___a.m. to ___p.m. | _____ | _____ | _____ |

**Hotel key staff by departments**
Check marks on the hotel staff list given below indicate the departmental key personnel with whom the organization will come in contact during the servicing of the convention.

| Check | Department | Name | Title | Phone Extension |
|---|---|---|---|---|
| ___ | _____ | _____ | _____ | _____ |
| ___ | _____ | _____ | _____ | _____ |
| ___ | _____ | _____ | _____ | _____ |
| ___ | _____ | _____ | _____ | _____ |

---

The meeting planner should have a principal contact on the hotel staff at all times during the day. In addition to key personnel rosters, some planners insist on being supplied with a mobile app for their own cellphone, two-way cellphones, or another direct communications device to ensure immediate contact with the hotel staff.

The key personnel roster is given to the meeting planner at the pre-con, at which time it is also customary for hotel and meeting staff to exchange business cards. Laura Himelson, senior conference services manager at the Montage Laguna Beach (California), provides a plastic sleeve to enable meeting planners to conveniently store business cards in one place.

**Sources:** Form reprinted with permission from the *Convention Liaison Manual*, published by the Convention Industry Council. Business cards and plastic sleeve courtesy of the Montage Laguna Beach; used with permission.

*Figure 12.2. MARRIOTT RED COAT SERVICE.*

Marriott's Red Coat service, which provides dedicated service staff for meetings and conventions, is promoted by individual properties within the chain, including the Oakland Marriott City Center.
**Source: Courtesy of Marriott Hotels. Used with permission.**

In the pressure cooker of an ongoing convention, meeting planners are most appreciative of reassurance that last-minute problems will be dealt with, and promptly. Gestures of such reassurance go a long way toward making a property a favorite of convention planners.

In summary, it is a good idea to furnish a roster of key hotel personnel to the client, along with the request that all action be taken through the convention service manager, *whenever possible*.

## Resume (Specification Sheet)

The convention service manager is responsible for writing a detailed schedule for each convention. The title for this schedule may vary. It may be known as the master prospectus, the bible, the summary, the specification sheet, or the resume. We will use the latter term, as it is most commonly used in the industry today.

Do not confuse the *resume* with the *banquet event order (function sheet)*, which is explained in the next section. The **resume** provides a comprehensive overview of the entire program in a chronological narrative, from pre-convention to post-convention, to the hotel staff. The banquet event order details only a single event.

All convention hotels use similarly constructed resumes when servicing groups that meet for more than one day. Resumes set forth activities day by day and hour by hour, covering meetings, meals, refreshment breaks, cocktails, reservation procedures, billing, exhibit instructions, special events, guest programs, recreational activities, and anything else that needs the hotel staff's attention. It is undoubtedly the single most important element of the convention servicing process, providing a tool for planning and communication between hotel departments.

The resume is prepared by the convention service manager in conjunction with the meeting planner. Much of the information is extracted from correspondence and discussion with the convention group and from **event specification guides (ESGs)** prepared by the meeting planner (see box titled "Industry-Wide Event Specification Guides"). For larger groups (such as associations that meet annually), the convention service manager may request a copy of the group's previous year's resume. The group's information is then put in the hotel's format and the resume is distributed to everyone involved with servicing the convention. This must be done far enough in advance to ensure that departments will have time to staff and prepare appropriately (in most cases, at least a week before the group arrives).

---

### Industry-Wide Event Specification Guides

Event Specification Guides (ESGs), prepared by meeting planners, differ from the resumes prepared for events by hotel personnel. To ensure that the details compiled by the meeting planner could be effectively incorporated into hotel resumes, APEX (the Accepted Practices Exchange), an initiation of the Convention Industry Council, developed a template that could be readily used for this important function.

The term Event Specifications Guide or ESG (acronym) should be the industry's official term for the document used by an event organizer to convey information clearly and accurately to appropriate venue(s) and/or suppliers regarding all requirements for an event. This is a four-part document which includes:

- Part I       The Narrative – general overview of the event.
- Part II      Function Schedule – timetable outlining all functions that compose the overall event.
- Part IIIa    Function Set-up Order – specifications for each function that is part of the overall event (each function of the event will have its own Function Set-up Order).
- Part IIIb    Function Set-up Order (Exhibitor Version) – specifications for each booth/stand that is part of an exhibition.

The 22-page template is essentially a staging guide. It can be accessed online at www.conventionindustry.org/StandardsPractices/APEX.aspx (click on Event Specifications to view a template that can be downloaded as a Microsoft Word or PDF file).

The new ESGs have been praised by planners and hotel personnel alike. Vicky Betzig, CMP, CTA, senior manager – client services at the Anaheim/Orange County Visitor & Convention Bureau, says:

> The amount of time a planner spends putting together event specifications is enormous. The template includes all of the specs most often required by hoteliers. I will be one of the first to use it.

ESGs are also extremely helpful to a CSM preparing the group's resume. The CSM can take required information from the ESG, prepare a resume and banquet event orders in the hotel's format, and return them to the planner for approval. Richard Green, former vice president of association sales and industry relations for Marriott International, states:

> Standardized events specifications will help planners to focus their requirements around the information that hotels and convention centers need to deliver a zero-defect meeting.

**Sources:** *The APEX Event Specifications Guide Template*; quotes from an APEX audio conference (Betzig and Green were among the speakers), published in *PCMA Convene*.

Chapter 12: Preparing for the Event

The length of the resume varies, of course, with the convention's size and number of days, and the amount of detailed planning required for each convention. We have seen some group resumes that were more than 40 pages long. Most, however, run eight to 12 pages for a three-day session. Simply put, a resume should be long enough to include all the details.

The importance of putting every detail in writing cannot be overstated. And the more detailed, the better. "Nobody told me" is heard too often in hotels. Putting everything in writing lessens the chance of this occuring.

Figure 12.3 illustrates an abbreviated resume written for a ficticious convention, the Architectural Draftsmen International. Note that the resume opens with a pre-convention setup and closes with a post-convention meeting. The resume begins with a general description of the group and a brief statement informing the hotel staff of the basic purpose and objectives of the meeting. A list of the individuals and departments that receive this information is listed on the left-hand side of the first page. To facilitate hotel staff recognition of key meeting personnel, such as the meeting planner and other VIPs, the Montage Laguna Beach in California also includes their photos within the resume. The first page also includes such information as complimentary accommodations, arrival and departure schedules, the reservation procedure, and billing to both master and individual accounts.

The next two pages provide an indication of the detail required in a resume. Every scheduled event is documented and thorough instructions provided regarding room setup and food and beverage arrangements. While reading through the sheet, keep in mind the importance of the meticulous recording required in the preparation of this form. As you can see, a large volume of information must be entered -- and often changed -- which is not only time-consuming, but may also result in costly errors.

## Banquet Event Order (Function Sheet)

When the program is finalized, each function should receive individual attention. Such attention to detail translates into service efficiency. This is done by means of a **banquet event order (BEO)**, such as the one illustrated in Figure 12.4. This banquet event order for a cocktail party shows the relationship between a resume and a banquet event order – the resume provides an overview of the event, while the banquet event order breaks the event down into minute details.

The banquet event order, like the resume, has been tagged with a variety of names: event form, worksheet, function sheet, and so on (we will use the term banquet event order, as that is the term most commonly used today). Banquet event orders can also vary from hotel to hotel in the amount of detail required. Individual banquet event orders, however, are generally prepared from the resume and are the working form for hourly employees (in Figure 12.4, for example, details are given regarding the staffing of a bartender, set-up crew, and cooks).

Ideally, the resume and any banquet event orders should be completed and two copies sent to the meeting planner two to three weeks in advance of the meeting and prior to distribution to the hotel staff. These materials should be accompanied by a letter asking the planner to review the copies, note any changes, and sign and return one copy to the hotel at least a week prior to the meeting (an example letter is shown in Figure 12.5).

Hotels require meeting planners to verify the ultra-specific details in each BEO with a signature. The BEO is a binding contract, so the meeting planner should carefully review each BEO prior to signing to ensure that the hotel has correctly translated his or her needs. Hotel staff members refer to BEOs – which may number 20 to 30 for a three-day convention — on a daily basis and deliver services based upon their content.

## Figure 12.3. SAMPLE GROUP RESUME.

* * * * * * * * * * * * * * * *
GROUP SPECIFICATION SHEET
* * * * * * * * * * * * * * * *

| | |
|---|---|
| SUBJECT: | Architectural Draftsmen International Attendees are the world's leading architects. The focus of the meeting is on customer service. The theme of the meeting is, "Building Better Relationships with Clients." |
| DATES: | February 16-20, 20__ |
| CONTACT: | Jay Bryan<br>Master Draftsman<br>206 Clark - Suite 307<br>Lakeview, Michigan 48850 |
| HOTEL SALESPERSON: | Larry Kingsbury, National Sales Manager |
| ARRIVAL/DEPARTURE PATTERN:<br>ROOM RES. MANAGER<br>ASSISTANT MANAGERS<br>FRONT DESK<br>HOTEL CASHIER | 300 rooms have been committed to this group. Most are arriving late Sunday, February 16 and departing Thursday, February 20, 20__. Arriving individually - Preregister |
| | RATES - European Plan<br>$95.00 Single or Double occupancy, plus 6% County room tax, net, non-commissionable. |
| | SUITE RATES - One Bedroom<br>$100.00 - Petite Suite<br>$120.00 - Deluxe Suite<br>$180.00 - Royal Suite |
| LOCATION: | DESERT VIEW, FOUNTAIN VIEW, POOLSIDE HEXAGON, CENTRAL TOWER |
| COMPLIMENTARY ACCOMMODATIONS: | A King Bedroom (North Tower) for Marney Vartanian, Associate Convention Manager<br>ARR: February 15, 20__<br>DEP: February 20, 20__ |
| | Additional complimentary units to be assigned based upon 1 complimentary unit for every 50 rooms actually occupied. (Names forthcoming) |
| HOSPITALITY REQUEST FOR: | Ms. Marney Vartanian<br>Dewars Scotch w/setups<br>ARR: February 15, 20__ |
| RESERVATION ACCEPTANCE PROCEDURE: | This group utilized our return reservation cards. |
| MASTER ACCOUNT: | All Group functions should be billed to the master account. Ms. Marney Vartanian will be the authorized signer. |
| INDIVIDUAL ACCOUNT: | Room, tax, and incidentals to be paid by individuals. |

Distribution list:
- General Manager
- Food/Bev. Dir.
- Front Office
- Showroom
- Exec. Chef
- Beverage Mgr. (2)
- Coffee Shop
- Room Service
- Group Billing
- Hotel Manager
- Asst. Hotel Mgrs. (2)
- Food Checker
- Reservations
- Publicity
- Security
- Housekeeping
- Head Houseman
- Head Banquet Waiter
- Sales (2)
- Food & Bev. Control
- Linen Control
- Doorman
- Benihana Manager
- Stage & Sound (2)
- Public Porters
- Steward
- Catering Director
- Group Services (4)
- Uniform Room
- Purchasing

(continued)

*This form for a fictitious convention is similar to those used by hotels to provide an overview of a group's event. At the left is a list of the people and departments that will receive this resume. In addition, the convention service manager usually sends the resume to the meeting planner well in advance of the pre-convention meeting to ensure that details are correct and that nothing has been overlooked. This saves time during the pre-convention meeting, as the major points have already been negotiated and accepted by both parties.*

*Figure 12.3. continued*

```
* * * * * * * * * * * *
    SCHEDULED FUNCTIONS
* * * * * * * * * * * *
```

Saturday, February 15, 20__

   3:00 P.M.                      ADI/HOTEL STAFF PRECONVENTION MEETING         Board Room

                               15 persons

   Attn: Set-up Crew             "U" shape

   Attn: Banquet Wtr.            Complimentary coffee, soft drinks, sweet rolls

Sunday, February 16, 20__

   6:00 - 8:00 P.M.               ARCHITECTURAL DRAFTSMEN INTERNATIONAL     Sec. F
                                COCKTAIL RECEPTION
                                Approximately 30 persons. All are convention officials
                                and board members

   Attn: Set-up Crew             Cabaret style

   Attn: Banquet Wtr.,
          Bar Manager                Call brand liquor to include: Beefeater, Johnny Walker Black,
                                Dewars, Smirnoff, Jack Daniels Black, Old Grand Dad, CC,
                                Bristol Cream Sherry @ $26.00 ++ and $30.00 ++. Two bottles
                                Chablis and Pinot Noir @ $7.00 per bottle ++. Beer @ $1.00 ++.

   Attn: Banquet Wtr.,
          Exec. Chef                 Following hors d'oeuvres: 5 orders Polynesian Pu-Pus @ $7.50++,
                                5 orders Selection #3 @ $6.75 ++, 10 orders Selection #4 @ $6.75 ++
                                10 orders hot seafood @ $8.00 ++, 10 orders cold seafood @ $8.50 ++,
                                and one shrimp bowl @ $100.00 ++. Hors d'oeuvre table to be
                                decorated with two gold candelabra and 6 silver chafing dishes, white tapers.
                                Cold hors d'oeuvres to be passed by waiters.

   Attn: Accounting               Bill to Texas Instruments - Exhibits Master Account.

Sunday, February 16, 20__

   3:00 - 6:00 P.M.               REGISTRATION                                      Foyer

   Attn: Set-up Crew             6' draped table rear of registration desk.
                                2 house phones. 1 directory board. Ice water
                                stand. Bb/c/e. (blackboard/chalk/eraser)

Monday, February 17, 20__

   9:00 A.M. - NOON            GENERAL BUSINESS SESSION                     Sec. F

                                500 Persons

   Attn: Set-up Crew             Theatre style with stage 12' x 40' x 24'
                                twenty feet out from kitchen wall. Projection platform
                                will be required against kitchen wall for rear screen projection.
                                Size to be determined. Head table for 8 on stage. American
                                Flag stage right. 1 35mm Carousel slide projector. 1 Lantern slide
                                projector. 1 electric pointer. 2 center aisle mikes. Central dimmer
                                to be located at projection platform. 1 projectionist.

   9:30 A.M. - NOON            EXHIBIT HALL SETUP                              Exhibit Hall

   Attn: Hall Supervisor          20 - 8' x 10' exhibit booth to be set up by
                                Scott Stubbs Service Company.

*(continued)*

*Figure 12.3. continued*

```
12:15 P.M.                    LUNCHEON                                          Sec. B
                              500 Persons

        Attn: Set-up Crew     Rounds of 10 with raised head tables on 32" dais
                              for 12 centered in south wall.

                              Lighted table podium mike center of head table.

        Attn: Banquet Wtr.    Tickets to be collected except at head table. Linen will probably
              Exec. Chef      be alternated on this function. This is to be advised.

        Attn: Banquet Wtr.    Serve our Group Luncheon Menu #7 with tomato juice
                              appetizer @ $6.10 ++.

        Attn: Accounting      Bill to ADI Master Account.

Thursday, February 20, 20

        3:00 - 5:00 P.M.      ADI/HOTEL STAFF POST-CONVENTION MEETING           Board Room
                              Same setup as on Saturday
```

Whether the function is a general session or a small committee meeting, document it. The basic seating layout, decorations, visual aids, and any other special services required should be detailed on the function sheet. Most hotels assign a specific number to each banquet event order for easy reference. Copies of each function sheet, as with the resume, should be distributed to hotel department heads at least a week prior to the event. There may be times when changes need to be made to banquet event orders. The most efficient way to communicate these changes is with a BEO addendum, commonly referred to as a banquet change order or banquet change sheet. These change orders contain the identification number and any other pertinent identifying information from the original banquet event order, and includes, very specifically, the changes to be made. In many cases, hotels use a color-coded system to immediately identify banquet event order status – the original BEO is printed on a white sheet, revisions can be printed on canary paper, and pink paper can be used for guarantees, for example. Other hotels reduce paper flow and instantly communicate changes via their computer systems.

It is essential that *each program segment* have its own banquet event order (function sheet) to ensure that all details will be handled. Document the head table, platform, basic seating layout, and all other arrangements. But also have a checklist for small but needed items, such as water glasses, pads and pencils, audiovisual equipment, sound systems, floral arrangements, and so on.

You may find that many well-organized association and corporate meeting planners make their own checklists of what is needed. As we mentioned earlier in this chapter, some meeting planners will even provide you with a complete **event specifications guide (ESG)**, also known as a **staging guide** or **specifications guidebook**, which is a concise document detailing how the meeting will proceed. ESGs include activities (by day, time, room, setup, and requirements), complimentary room assignments, signature authority, and other details authorized by the meeting planner. You can use these guides to prepare your own group resumes, incorporating the itemized requests contained in the ESGs. One convention service manager shared the following with us:

> Most people think that all the convention service manager does is handle the group while it's in-house, but 90 percent of our work is the extraction of details one to two years prior to arrival. My job is to direct, produce,

*Figure 12.4. BANQUET EVENT ORDER (FUNCTION SHEET).*

```
                    FUNCTION ORDER - FOOD AND BEVERAGE

EVENT DATE                              DAY                 ORDER
    February 16, 19-                        Sunday          NO.   126
ORGANIZATION                                                FILE
    Architectural Draftsman International                   NO.   N-614
POST AS
    Architectural Draftsman International Cocktail Reception
BILLING ADDRESS
    Bill to Master Account Texas Instruments, 120AK, Lakeview, MI 48851
CONTACT              ON SITE CONTACT           BUS PHONE NO      RES PHONE NO
 Deanne Pritchard     Robert Olson              363-1906
EXPECTED   GUARANTEED        SET UP             BOOKED BY        DATE TYPED
   30          30              33                Amber S.          2/1

TIME    SETUP REQUIREMENTS     LOCATION    TIME       MENU              LOCATION

6:00 PM - 8:00 PM  Cocktail   Sec. F       5 orders Polynesion Pu-Pus @ $22.50++,
-----------------------------------        5 orders selection #3 @ $20.25++,
Cabaret Style Set-Up                       10 orders selection #4 @ $20.25++,
Draped Cocktail Rounds with ashtrays,      10 orders hot seafood @ $25.50++,
no chairs                                  10 orders cold seafood @ $25.50++,
                                           1 shrimp bowl @ $300.00 ++

                                           Hors d'oeuvre table to be decorated
                                           with two gold candlabra and 6 silver
                                           chafing dishes.  White tapers.
                                           Cold hors d'oeuvres to be passed by
                                           waiters
                                           -----------------------------------
                                           Food     @ $ 20.25+T+T
                                           Seafood  @ $ 25.50+T+T
                                           Shrimp bowl @ $ 300.00 +T+T


            HOTEL TO ORDER
X Decorations
 3 Tropical Florals
 Charge to Master                                    REFRESHMENT BREAK
__ Entertainment

             AUDIO VISUAL




Time              Location
              SPECIAL NOTES
                                                BEVERAGE REQUIREMENTS
                                           RECEPTION
                                             Call Brand Liquor to include: Beefeater,
                                             Johnny Walker Black, Dewars, Smirnoff,
           SUMMARY OF CHARGES               Jack Daniels Black, Old Grand Dad, CC,
                                             Bristol Cream Sherry @ $78.00 ++, $84.00 ++
FOOD       See Menu                          and $90.00 ++.  Two bottles Chablis &
BEVERAGE   See Beverage Requirements        WINE SELECTION  Pinot Noir @ $21.00 ++ per
RENT                                         bottle.  Beer @ $3.00 ++.
LABOR
PARKING
DEPOSIT RECEIVED
METHOD OF PAYMENT
BALANCE DUE DATE                           TIME              LOCATION

   WE NEED YOUR ASSISTANCE IN MAKING YOUR BANQUET A SUCCESS. PLEASE CONFIRM YOUR ATTENDANCE AT LEAST 3
   BUSINESS DAYS IN ADVANCE. IF WE ARE NOT CONTACTED WITHIN THE SPECIFIED TIME, YOUR EXPECTED ATTENDANCE WILL
   SERVE AS YOUR GUARANTEE. THIS WILL BE CONSIDERED YOUR MINIMUM GUARANTEE. WE WILL ADD THE CUSTOMARY 17%
   SERVICE CHARGE AND SALES TAX. FOR GROUPS SERVED UNDER 25 THERE WILL BE A $50 LABOR CHARGE.
   I HAVE READ AND I UNDERSTAND THE REVERSE SIDE OF THIS DOCUMENT.
   IF IN AGREEMENT, PLEASE SIGN ONE COPY AND RETURN  X _____
```

*This form is used to detail each convention function listed on the specification sheet.*

and extract information from the meeting planner and in turn pass this information on to various department heads through specification and function sheets.

## Chapter 12: Preparing for the Event

*Figure 12.5. TRANSFER OF RESUME AND BANQUET EVENT ORDERS TO CLIENT.*

**MARRIOTT INTERNATIONAL, INC.**
Hawaii Area Sales Office

92-1001 Olani Street
Kapolei, Oahu, Hawaii 96707
Phone: 808/440-2356
Fax: 808/679-0293

February 28, 20xx

Ms Colleen Abee
The Meetings Group
Meeting Planner
1605 Iron Ridge Drive
Las Vegas, NV 89117

Dear Ms. Abee:

Enclosed for your review are two copies of your group resume and two copies of each Banquet Event Order. Please look them over carefully and note any changes. Please sign and return one copy of each BEO prior to your meeting.

Please notify our office of the exact number of guests attending each banquet function no later than 10 days prior to the event. As is our standard policy, the hotel will set and prepare for 5% over this guarantee. Once this number is received, you will be charged for the guarantee even if fewer attend of if you cancel over that time. Should your attendance go over that guarantee, you will be charged for the actual numbers served or for any higher subsequent guarantee that you submit to us.

Please feel free to contact me at any time should you have further questions or needs. I look forward to receiving your signed copies – and assisting you in staging a most successful event.

Warmest aloha,

Christopher Blunt
Director of National Accounts
Marriott International - Hawaiian Islands Hotels & Resort

*Hotels generally send copies of the group's resume to the meeting planner two to three weeks prior to the event for approval before distributing the resume and any accompanying banquet event orders to departments involved in servicing the event. This sample letter not only provides the meeting planner with these materials, but also requests attendance figures and reiterates the hotel's guarantee policy.*

A master schedule should be made. This will assist you in determining the number of pieces of anything needed anywhere at any particular time. You may have specified on a number of function sheets that a digital slide projector is needed, but the master schedule would indicate how many such projectors are needed at the same time.

Many hotel people feel that such details are truly the responsibility of the meeting planner. However, it is the hotel staff that will be called upon under crisis conditions to rectify any oversights. You could avoid those last-minute panics by being well organized; develop your own checklists and suggest that the meeting planner do the same.

If planners are inexperienced and fail to anticipate their needs correctly, they may say you gave them insufficient notice and you may end up as the victim. Given a choice between blaming you and accepting the blame themselves, they may find it all too easy to blame you.

Not only is it important to plan defensively, but your suggestions and organization also will establish your reputation. Clients will retain the memory that meetings at your hotel always run smoothly. That memory is the one you want to leave with clients.

## The Importance of Communication

Problems during meetings can be largely eliminated if a "pipeline" of communication has been established from the very beginning. It has been said that "the job of servicing meetings is 95 percent communication and 5 percent service." Securing detailed information and expectations from the meeting planner is one of the most important tasks of the convention service manager.

Letters, telephone calls, e-mails, text messages, and personal on-site visits are normally used to get initial information. Another excellent tool to initiate the communication process is to send a **resume questionnaire** (see the Chapter Appendix) to the meeting planner. This form consolidates a list of important questions and reduces the frequent telephone calls and exchanges of correspondence on individual items. Other ways to improve communication are for the convention service manager to provide the meeting planner with a formal and mutually agreed-upon timetable for communication of meeting details. Some convention service managers ask to be put on the meeting planner's mailing list, while others will send the meeting planners a sample specification sheet to inform the planner of the format used by the hotel.

It is important to remember that meeting planners have preferred methods of communications. Meeting planners today are multi-generational, so communications need to be tailored to their preferences. Some planners prefer e-mail, others would rather receive text messages, while still others prefer to be contacted by telephone or receive correspondence. Ed DiAntonio, director of catering and convention services at Walt Disney World Swan and Dolphin Resort, says:

> It's important to know how planners want to receive information. Many convention services managers are used to sending e-mails, but quite a few planners like phone calls. It's all about knowing your audience. We do everything electronically so we're not putting together 15 binders of information, which we feel is more environmentally friendly. We think it's the right thing to do.[3]

Once on-site, planners expect to have a CSM or other meetings staff available to communicate with them to ensure that meeting details are properly handled, and several chains have taken this concept further – offering a guarantee that the meeting will be successful. The Loews chain, for example, offers the Loews Service Guarantee, which provides planners with the direct telephone number of Jack Adler, the chain's president and chief operating officer (see Exhibit 12.6). The guarantee underscores the chain's commitment to the group and each hotel's accountability to deliver a successful meeting.

# Chapter 12: Preparing for the Event

*Figure 12.6. THE ULTIMATE COMMUNICATIONS PIPELINE.*

Although the Loews chain has a solid brand image for top-notch service due to its commitment to employee training, the chain took customer satisfaction to a new level with the introduction of the Loews Service Guarantee. If a meeting planner ever had a concern so great that it couldn't be handled by the general manager at the host hotel, the planner would be able to voice his or her concerns directly to Jack Adler, the chain's president and chief operating officer, on his direct telephone line. Adler, who is known as a hands-on COO, jumped at the chance to be on the front lines, but no one working for the chain expected that Adler's phone would ever ring.

**Source: Courtesy of Loews Hotels. Used with permission.**

Chapter 12: Preparing for the Event

# Communicating Details Electronically

Computer technology has altered the way resume and banquet event order information is created. Figure 12.7 illustrates a computer-generated banquet event order (function sheet). Automated sales systems can build a function sheet as information is gathered and input by the salesperson into the client's file. Also, a computerized system allows the creation of a number of forms that can be tailored to specific servicing needs. For example, you can

Figure 12.7. COMPUTERIZED BANQUET EVENT ORDER (FUNCTION SHEET).

**The Durham Resort**
44 Newmarket Road
Durham, New Hampshire 038244
(603) 868-1500

GROUP NAME: Automobile Travelers Association
POST AS: Annual Meeting
IN CHARGE: Mr. Harry McArthur          FUNCTION ORDER NO: 104

| DAY | DATE | TIME | FUNCTION | ROOM | PEOPLE | RENT |
|-----|------|------|----------|------|--------|------|
| Tue | 10/12 | 8:00 AM - 5:00 PM | Lunch Meeting | Cherry Room | 75 | $250 |

### BEVERAGES

Service: 17.5%   Tax: 9.5%
Bartender Fee: $65.00 each

### ARRANGEMENTS

In charge of service: Banquet Service

Chairs (18")
16mm Movie Projector
6' Round Dinner Table for Rounds of 10
Slide Projector with remote control
    capabilities
Rear Screen Projection (10' x 10')

### FOOD

*Stuffed Pork Chop from 8:00 AM to 5:00 PM*
*Room: Cherry Room   Attendance: 75*

Tender Pork Chop Filled with a Special
    Sausage Stuffing in a Mushroom Sauce
Whipped Potatoes
Vegetable du Jour
Tossed Garden Salad, Choice of Dressing
Assorted Rolls
Coffee, Tea & Decaf
*Charge: $18.00 Per Person*

Billing:   Master Account
Address:  1234 Albany Drive
          Atlanta, GA 01234
Phone:    (404) 555-2141

Client Signature:_____   Date:_____
Prepared By: Kathy McDonald_____   Date: June 14, 20_

The contents of the above meet with my approval. I consider our agreement definite and confirmed. Guarantees must be sumbitted 48 hours in advance of all functions (Monday functions, 72 hours). Prices are subject to 17.5% gratuity and 9.5% sales tax (where applicable).

*This function sheet, generated in an automated sales office, merges important account information and relative booking information on one display screen. This report retrieves the information from the hotel's meetings database.*

## Chapter 12: Preparing for the Event

create a form that contains just menu information for your chef, or a form containing just setup information for your service staff.

In order to standardize resume data and to minimize error, Newmarket® International developed its Daylight® "ultimate electronic resume" software. This electronically generated resume combines room block information, BEO information, and department information in one document (Figure 12.8 illustrates the initial page of a resume generated by the software).

Magnolia Hotels (www.magnoliahotels.com), a hotel management company, was one of the initial users of the ultimate electronic resume, and a representative of the chain states:

*Figure 12.8. NEWMARKET® INTERNATIONAL'S DAYLIGHT® ULTIMATE RESUME.*

**Stratford Portsmouth Hotel**
**Welcomes**
**LRB and Associates**

| Main Contact: | Jared Goldman | Arrival Date: | Sunday, July 13, 2008 |
|---|---|---|---|
| Address: | 100 Main Street | Departure Date: | Wednesday, July 16, 2008 |
| | Big Town, NY 10123 | Booking No: | AA234567 |
| Phone: | 212-555-4567 | Catering Mgr: | Susan O'Hara |
| Fax: | 212-555-2345 | Service Mgr: | Windy Hernandez |
| Email: | 212-555-5678 | Sales Mgr: | Jim Bento |

**Group Profile:** *Group is here to discuss next year's plans and goals. Spouses are attending and have separate functions. This meeting is the high point for the staff; they look forward to it every year.*

**Room Block:**

| Room Type | | Sunday July 13 | Monday July 14 | Tuesday July 15 | Wednesday July 16 |
|---|---|---|---|---|---|
| King | Agreed | 125 | 125 | 125 | 125 |
| | Pickup | 100 | 126 | 126 | 112 |
| | Rate | $250.00 | $250.00 | $250.00 | $250.00 |
| Double/Double | Agreed | 50 | 50 | 50 | 50 |
| | Pickup | 52 | 52 | 52 | 49 |
| | Rate | $350.00 | $350.00 | $350.00 | $350.00 |

**Total Rooms:**
Agreed:     700
Pickup:     669

**Billing:**                                                **Master Account Number:** A123456

| | Billing Method | Payment Method | Notes |
|---|---|---|---|
| Room & Tax | Combined | Direct Bill | Vendors as noted – pay their own Room & tax |
| Catering F & B | Master | Direct Bill | |
| On Own Dining | Individual | Credit Card | |
| On Own Beverage | Individual | Credit Card | |
| Incidentals | Combined | Direct Bill | Mr. and Mrs. Change have all incidentals posted |
| Transportation | Master | Direct Bill | |
| Golf | Combined | Direct Bill | Mr. and Mrs. Change have all incidentals posted |
| Spa | Combined | Direct Bill | Mr. and Mrs. Change have all incidentals posted |
| Tennis | Individual | Credit Card | |
| Internet | Combined | Direct Bill | Mr. and Mrs. Change have all incidentals posted |

**Program Details**
**Sunday, July 13, 2008**

| Times | Rooms | Event Type | Post As | EXP/GTD/SET | BEO # | Rental |
|---|---|---|---|---|---|---|
| 3:00 PM - 1:00 AM | Little Room 1 | Office | Office | 1/1/1 | 10 | $75.00 |
| SETUP | 2 - 6' Draped and Skirted Tables | | | | | |
| | 4 - Chairs | | | | | |
| | 1 - Large Trash Can | | | | | |
| | Clean Daily at prior to 8 am. | | | | | |
| SHIPPING | Please deliver all boxes marked for AASE to this room by 3:00 PM | | | | | |

| Times | Rooms | Event Type | Post As | EXP/GTD/SET | BEO # | Rental |
|---|---|---|---|---|---|---|
| 3:00 PM – 4:00 PM | ROOMS | DEPARTMENT | DEPARTMENT | 80/90/92 | | $0.00 |
| FRONT OFFICE | Guests will arrive by bus | | | | | |
| | Please have key packets ready for distribution | | | | | |
| GUEST SERVICES | 3 Buses to arrive | | | | | |
| | Have Bell Staff to assist with Luggage | | | | | |

Page 1 of 9

This is the first page of a nine-page electronic resume created by Newmarket® International's Daylight® software. The form combines all time-sensitive resume and BEO information for all departments in chronological order.
**Source:** Courtesy of Newmarket® International. Used with permission.

# Chapter 12: Preparing for the Event

*Post-convention meeting. When the event is over, convention service managers often meet with the meeting planner and key hotel personnel to review the convention. This is the opportunity to note what went well and to determine if there are areas for improvement.*
**Photo courtesy of InterContinental Hotel Group.**

As in many hotels, the catering staff at Magnolia was known to print out nine copies of a BEO. Now the team runs only one report. All the information and knowledge resides in one place, supporting seamless execution.

There are several other companies that offer software to manage functions. Cendyn/Arcaneo (www.cendynarcaneo.com), for example, offers computerized group resumes, BEOs, and post-convention surveys as well as other organizational tools in its get planning™ meetings program. Maestro PMS from NORTHWIND (www.maestropms.com) includes a number of programs to automate the entire event order process. To create a new event order, the hotel simply has to call up the client's file, block space on the meeting space grid, and enter food items or any audiovisual equipment requested.

Database management programs also allow meeting information stored in the computer to be isolated, manipulated, or sorted to answer specific requests. With just a few keystrokes, the meetings can be sorted by location, time, date, size, and so on. For example, you may wish to ask the computer to list all meetings scheduled in the convention area that require wireless microphones on Monday between 7:00 a.m. and 7:00 p.m., or which rooms require classroom setup this week. This information is available instantly on a computerized data management program and would not require searching through numerous typed re-

> **WORTH WATCHING**
>
> Jon Summersfield, co-founder and president of RoundTableHQ and executive vice president of sales at Cendyn/Arcaneo, presents a tutorial on cloud technology and the move to paperless meeting resumes at hedtalks.connectplusathiltonworldwide.com (click on the Driving Results tab and scroll down to the "Cloud-Based Event Planning" video).

sumes. Additionally, changes and deletions are made simply by calling up the meeting in question and revising the individual fields or deleting the record.

In addition, new technology processes driven by the Internet and e-commerce have altered the way in which specification and function sheet information is communicated. Increasingly, this information is transmitted electronically via a direct Internet link between the meeting planner and the hotel's convention service manager. Each will have all the details on his or her computer screen and will be able to make corrections online, eliminating the mailing of large amounts of paperwork.

Once approved by the meeting planner, the resume and banquet event orders are distributed electronically to departments within the hotel rather than having sheets (even computer-generated ones) copied and distributed. With the click of a mouse, the exacting details of the meeting will be distributed to all involved with servicing the group.

It is important to remember that most meeting planners today use their mobile devices for planning; it is no longer necessary for them to carry around heavy binders full of information or use staging guides to see specific aspects of their meetings. Paperless binders – tablet computers and mobile devices – have become the norm; the iPad, Kindle Fire, Android tablets, and more than 100 other tablet brands are available.

Mobile devices also play a vital role in keeping the meeting planner and the convention services staff in touch once the meeting is onsite. Several chains now offer **apps** designed specifically for this purpose. Marriott, for example, offers two apps – Red Coat Direct and JW Event Concierge. Both of these apps, which are available in 20 languages, are sent to the planner three days before the event begins. Should the planner have a request, such as additional coffee or the adjustment of a room's temperature, all he or she has to do is push a button on their mobile device to be connected to Red Coat staff (at selected Marriotts) or event concierges (at JW Marriott properties). You can learn more about these apps by searching for Meeting Services App – Marriott Hotel (or go to www.marriott.com/meeting-event-hotels/event-management-services.mi (scroll down to view brief videos of both apps).

Other hotels also provide similar apps. Starwood, for example, has developed the ProMeetings app, which it offers to its SPG and SPG Pro members; the app will be available globally in 2016. Hilton offers the getplanning by Hilton app, which allows the planner to connect with hotel staff, vendors, and partners. The app also provides access to meeting-related documents, floor plans, and menus. Omni offers two apps: OmniLink, which offers access to schedules, maps, videos, and downloads, and iMeetingPlanner, which was designed to allow planners to go paperless. Other meeting apps have also been developed by several software companies, including the firms we discussed earlier in this chapter.

## The Importance of Follow-up

Follow-up is an important part of showing your commitment to servicing a group's meeting. Follow-up, of course, should begin after initial contact with the client, as discussed in the communications section in this chapter. Checking details increases the likelihood that there will be fewer problems during the event.

During the meeting, frequent contact with the meeting planner and/or his or her staff is also important. Checking to ensure that all is going well reassures the meeting planner of your commitment to his or her group.

After an event, a **post-convention meeting** should be held. The same people who met for the pre-convention meeting should meet for an after-the-fact review of the convention. This meeting is an opportunity for both the planner and the hotel staff to assess the success of the event and to address any problems (and determine ways to solve them in the future).

## Summary

In this chapter, we have seen the necessity of working closely with the planner in the days leading up to a meeting or convention and the necessity of informing all hotel departments of their roles in the event. Pre-convention meetings, detailed resumes and banquet event orders, and communication with both the planner and hotel staff will ensure the success of a meeting and will leave a good impression of the property's commitment to service.

The group resume and the banquet event orders pull together hours of conversation and perhaps hundreds of e-mails and/or texts between the convention service manager and the meeting planner to capture all the details necessary to provide clear instructions to enable the hotel staff to execute the program successfully. The BEOs discussed in this chapter cover the requirements discussed by the planner and the property to set the tone for and properly execute the planner's event. These details include food and beverage requirements and room setups. In the next chapter, we will take a detailed look at the types of set-ups commonly used for meetings and other functions.

## Endnotes

1. Terry Matthews-Lombardo, "How Effective is Your Pre-con?" posted on planyourmeetings.com on October 8, 2014.
2. HSMAI Sales Manual.
3. Jennifer Juergens, "Working Together: Tips for Convention Services Managers Who Work with Independent Planners," posted on hospitality.event.com on February 22, 2012.

## Study Questions

1. What is the purpose of the pre-convention meeting? Who should attend?
2. What are the positions of the meeting planner and the convention service manager regarding a key personnel roster? What have some hotels done to compromise?
3. What key information is provided on a resume?
4. How does the the banquet event order differ from the resume?
5. How is the computer used to facilitate the communication of meeting details?
6. Why is follow-up so important? Describe three key times when hotel personnel commonly follow-up on a meeting.

# Chapter 12: Preparing for the Event

## Key Terms

**apps**—Software programs developed specifically for mobile devices. Apps may be developed by an outside provider or by the hotel itself to provide assistance with specific tasks, such as enabling meeting planners to communicate directly with the CSM or other designated hotel staff on their smartphones or other mobile devices.

**banquet event order (BEO)**—A form that provides a detailed breakdown of a single event. The banquet event order generally serves as a contract for the client and as a work order for the hotel's departments. Also called a **function sheet**.

**event specifications guide (ESG)**—A concise document, prepared and authorized by the meeting planner, detailing the specifics of a meeting or other event. ESGs include activities (by day, time, room, setup, and special requirements), complimentary room assignments, signature authority, and other important details. The ESG, which encompasses the full operation of the event, is shared with all key individuals. Also called a **staging guide** or a **specifications guidebook**.

**key personnel roster**—A list of hotel personnel who are available to the meeting planner to help service the event.

**post-convention meeting (post-con)**—A meeting held after the completion of a meeting or convention to evaluate the forecasting and planning that preceded the convention and the hotel's performance during the event.

**pre-convention meeting (pre-con)**—A meeting held before the convention or event to review the entire program to ensure that the planner and hotel understand each other's requirements and expectations. This meeting is attended by the planner and key hotel personnel who will be involved in servicing the event, to eliminate any misunderstandings and ensure a smooth event.

**resume**—A form providing a comprehensive overview of the entire convention program. Sent to the various hotel departments involved in the event, a resume provides specific instructions to the staff for servicing the event. Resumes include a summary of all group activities, billing instructions, key attendees, arrival and departure patterns, and other relevant information. Also called a **specification sheet**.

**resume questionnaire**—A form on which meeting planners answer questions relating to the upcoming event. Having detailed information readily available reduces the need for frequent contact with the meeting planner and assists hotels in preparing for both the pre-convention meeting and the event itself.

# CHAPTER APPENDIX

## RESUME (SPECIFICATION SHEET) QUESTIONNAIRE
Resume questionnaire to be completed by the meeting planner.
(By permission, Penta Hotels)

## Penta Hotel

### RESUME GUIDELINES

1. EVENT TO BE POSTED AS FOLLOWS:
   _____
   _____

2. OFFICIAL OFFICERS:

   NAME                          TITLE
   _____
   _____
   _____

3. AUTHORIZED SIGNATURES:

   NAME              SIGNATURES              TITLE
   _____
   _____

4. MASTER BILLING ADDRESS, TELEPHONE NUMBER AND TO WHOM'S ATTENTION IT SHOULD BE LISTED.
   (Upon approval of credit manager)
   _____
   _____
   _____

5. NEW YORK STATE TAX EXEMPT: ____YES ____NO

   (If your organization is tax exempt, please forward a copy of the certificate to the Convention Service Department.)

6. CONVENTION HEADQUARTERS HOTEL : _____

   OTHER HOTELS USED: _____
   _____

7. EXPECTED CONVENTION REGISTRATION: _____ADVANCE _____ON-SITE

8. WILL THERE BE A NECESSITY FOR HOTEL SAFETY BOXES FOR THE CONVENTION OFFICERS? ____YES ____NO
   (If yes): HOW MANY? ____ AND WHAT NAMES SHOULD THEY BE LISTED UNDER:
   _____
   _____
   _____

## Chapter 12: Preparing for the Event

-2-

9. MONEY EXCHANGE: Will there be a necessity for the officers to exchange large bills during the conference? _____ YES _____ NO
(If yes, in what denominations?)

    PENNIES _____    NICKELS _____    DIMES _____    QUARTERS _____

    $1 BILLS _____    $5 BILLS _____    $10 BILLS _____    $20 BILLS _____

10. RESERVATIONS: _____ HOTEL FORM _____ OWN FORM _____ HOUSING BUREAU
    _____ ROOMING LIST _____ PHONE IN

11. ARRIVALS: Will most of your arrivals be arriving by:

    _____ AUTOMOBILE _____ TRAIN _____ COMMERCIAL AIRLINE _____ CHARTERED BUS
    Note: For bus arrivals, please have the person(s) and/or organization contact our Reservation Manager directly.

12. HOSPITALITY SUITES: Please have the companies who will be sponsoring Hospitality Suites contact our Room Service Manager directly for their food and beverage needs. Also, our Reservation Manager and Credit Manager should be contacted to expedite their reservation and billing needs.

13. BUS DEPARTURES: Have you contracted for buses for tours, trips, etc. _____ YES _____ NO
    If yes, please advise us of your schedule in the program and setup instructions.

14. CELEBRITIES: Will any of your speakers attract media attention? _____ YES _____ NO
    If yes, please list their names and speaking date/time below:

    _____
    _____
    _____

15. SECURITY SPEECH: Do you require our Security Department to give a short speech on security tips on this city and the hotel?

    _____ YES _____ NO  If yes, it will be conducted at your first General Session.

16. OFFICERS, SPEAKERS AND VIP RESERVATIONS:

    NAME: _____    Double - 1 bed

    ADDRESS: _____    Twin - 2 single beds
    _____

    TELEPHONE #: _____

    ARRIVAL DATE: _____ ESTIMATED TIME: _____

    DEPARTURE DATE: _____ ESTIMATED TIME: _____

    ROOM TYPE: _____ SINGLE _____ DOUBLE _____ TWIN

               _____ 1 BEDROOM SUITE _____ 2 BEDROOM SUITE

    (Sharing with: _____)

    Arrival: _____ Departure _____

    BILLING INSTRUCTIONS: _____ Pays own room, tax and incidental charges

                                   _____ Room and tax to the Master Account

                                   _____ Room, tax and incidentals to the Master Account

    SPECIAL REQUIREMENTS: _____

-3-

17. REGISTRATION: (Speakers - Exhibitors - Registrants)

        DAY      DATE      TIME      LOCATIONS

_____

_____

18. ADMISSION: _____

19. EXHIBITS:              DAY/DATE        TIME        LOCATION(S)

    Drayage setup: _____

    Exhibitors Setup: _____

    Show Opens: _____

    Exhibitors Dismantle: _____

    Drayage Dismantle: _____

20. NUMBER OF EXHIBITORS: _____ TYPE OF BOOTHS: _____
    Forward the exhibitors contract to the Convention Service department.

21. HOTEL HOLD HARMLESS CLAUSE: Please sign and return.

22. CONTRACTORS: (Contact, address and telephone number)

    DRAYAGE CONTRACTOR           SECURITY CONTRACTOR

    _____           _____

    _____           _____

    _____           _____

    AUDIOVISUAL CONTRACTOR        TYPEWRITER CONTRACTOR

    _____           _____

    _____           _____

    _____           _____

    SIGN CONTRACTOR                COPY MACHINE/OFFICE EQUIP CONTRACTOR

    _____           _____

    _____           _____

    _____           _____

## Chapter 12: Preparing for the Event

-4-

    SOUND/LIGHTING CONTRACTOR                OTHER CONTRACTORS

    _____                _____

    _____                _____

    _____                _____

23. CONVENTION BUREAU PERSONNEL USED: _____ YES _____ NO

_____

_____

24. ROOM SERVICE/RESTAURANTS/BARS:    L=Light, M=Moderate, H=Heavy

| | BREAKFAST | LUNCH | DINNER | COCKTAILS |
|---|---|---|---|---|
| Room Service | _L _M _H | _L _M _H | _L _M _H | _L _M _H |
| Restaurants | _L _M _H | _L _M _H | _L _M _H | _L _M _H |
| Bars | _L _M _H | _L _M _H | _L _M _H | _L _M _H |

25. TELEPHONE INSTRUCTIONS:

    Will there be a need for outgoing calls? _____YES _____NO

    If yes: _____LOCAL     _____LONG DISTANCE     _____BOTH

    The special code word for all outgoing calls will be: _____

26. CHECKROOM FACILITIES:

    The hotel does have a Main Checkroom located in the lobby. Will you require a second checkroom? _____YES _____NO

    (If yes, our checkroom manager will contact you directly for charges incurred.)

27. PACKAGE ROOM:

    Will you be shipping boxes to the hotel Package Room? _____YES _____NO

    If yes, approximately how many? _____Basic Size _____Basic Weight

28. PROGRAM AND SET-UP INSTRUCTIONS:

    On the following page, please find an example of the format followed for the Convention Service resume. We suggest this format for simpler communications and easy understanding. For more detailed set-ups, we suggest attaching a diagram.

    This information will be included in the hotel's convention resume, which is distributed to all departments in the hotel.

# Chapter 12: Preparing for the Event

## Industry Profile

*David Scherbarth, CMP, Former Director of Banquets and Convention Service*

**Sheraton Bal Harbour Beach Resort**

*Before graduating with a degree in hotel/restaurant management, David Scherbarth already had experience in several areas of the hospitality field (convention houseman, bellman, desk clerk, night auditor, and banquet server). He decided on the convention service department as his career path, working first with Hyatt and then with Sheraton. During his career with Sheraton, David was chairman of the chain's Convention Service Committee, co-writing and introducing Sheraton's company-wide training program for convention and conference service managers.*

### How to Assign Function Rooms and Determine Meeting Room Set-Ups

Convention service managers are the meeting planner's primary contact. The impression made, the service provided, and the relationship that the CSM establishes with the planner are all critical to getting, and, even more important, keeping customers in this competitive market.

The convention service department is an extension of the sales department and must work closely with the sales manager to maximize function space while providing the group meeting with a comfortable environment to achieve the goals of the meeting. In order to block function space properly, the CSM must evaluate:

- **Day(s) of meeting.** If more than one day, try to keep the meeting in the same room. This minimizes labor and provides consistency to the group.

- **Beginning and ending times.** Accurate times can enable you to utilize the room more than once a day and as many as three or four times for different functions.

- **Set-up style and attendance.** The type of set-up and the number expected to attend has a direct impact on how much space is needed (a schoolroom set-up will use 30-35 percent more space than a theater-style set-up). You must know the various set-ups and the seating capacity of each for every function room in your facility.

- **Audiovisual and staging requirements.** These two items can dramatically alter the size of space needed. A complete understanding of the client's needs is necessary. A 24-hour hold may be necessary for extensive audiovisual and/or staging requirements.

- **Other items that need to be considered when assigning function space are:** noise conflicts with other meetings or banquets; traffic patterns of associated public space; lighting needs; ceiling heights; décor; electrical needs; and, competitive groups.

Because some meeting planners do not have a final agenda at the time they sign a contract with the hotel, the CSM has another important task – communicating with the meeting planner on a regular basis and refining the space as the group finalizes their agenda.

## Learning Objectives:

This portion of your text introduces you to the various types of function rooms and setups used for meetings and food functions. We will also discuss how to manage function room space to best serve groups while maintaining maximum profitability for the hotel. When you have studied this chapter, you will:

- Be able to identify factors that convention service managers consider before assigning function space to meeting planners.

- Be able to describe various meeting room setups and tell when each is commonly used.

- Understand how function rooms are broken down and be able to describe meeting rooms of the future.

- Know how to monitor function room usage and make the most of function space.

## Outline

Function Rooms
- Types of Function Rooms
- Function Room Size and Layout
- Meeting Room Plans
- Timetable for Setup and Breakdown

Managing Function Rooms
- Sales Restrictions on Function Space
- Function Room Charges
- Function and Meeting Room Revenue Management
- Release Dates
- Several Meetings Simultaneously
- Use of Meeting Rooms by Others
- Employee Procedure Manuals

Meeting Setups
- Function Room Furniture
- Basic Meeting Setups
- Setups with Tables

Breakdown of Function Rooms
Meeting Rooms of the Future
Monitoring Function Room Usage
Summary

# 13 Function Rooms and Meeting Setups

Any hotel can supply guestrooms. A convention hotel is one that has a sufficient number of function rooms and the trained staff needed to handle the many different kinds of meetings and conventions.

## Function Rooms

When the hotel sales representative originally solicited the convention, he or she presented the client with information about the hotel's meeting rooms. Most larger convention hotels have a number of suitable meeting rooms and often more than are needed for an event.

Often a convention planner will request that all the convention facilities be held for his or her event, at least until the program is roughed out and it is obvious what facilities are needed. This is rarely possible. Unless the convention is large and virtually sells out the house, the hotel's management cannot lock up a precious commodity like meeting rooms for any longer than absolutely necessary.

It is urgent, therefore, for you to get together with the meeting planner to place a hold on the rooms thought to be needed and to urge that planning be done to determine realistically the needs of the event. There is no pressure if you have no other meetings scheduled for those dates, but most sizable hotels handle a number of smaller meetings simultaneously.

### Types of Function Rooms

Before assigning rooms, the convention service manager must be aware of what the hotel has to offer. Some of the most common function rooms depicted in the hotel's convention brochure are exhibit halls, ballrooms for banquets and large meetings, conference rooms, and additional rooms or suites located near the main conference room to serve as **breakout rooms**. It has become increasingly common to use breakout rooms, including large rooms that can be subdivided with movable **air walls**, for training purposes and small group discussions. Unless meeting planners are advised otherwise, these are the rooms with which they will work as they lay out their schedules.

However, hoteliers should never assume that only traditional meeting space can be utilized by meeting planners (see Figure 13.1). Actually, all of the property's public space may be considered as function space, depending on the group and its needs. The unusual is often what makes a meeting experience memorable, so it is important to keep in mind such nontraditional options as hotel lobbies; hallways, foyers, or nooks near the meeting area; private, dedicated work spaces; rooftops; and outdoor settings, such as the property's pool area, lawns or gardens, parking lot, and property-front beaches.

We have already discussed how several chains are transforming their traditional lobbies into welcoming spaces for both socializing and working. Lobbies are becoming more open; they are being designed with eye-catching features, such as artwork, greenery, and water features, and comfortable furniture is arranged to accommodate social interaction – from meeting spaces for small groups to settings at which guests can enjoy coffee or a quick

## Chapter 13: Function Rooms and Meeting Setups

bite to eat while interacting with other meeting attendees (Westin, for example, offers a Grab & Go Café concept). Most lobbies offer Wi-Fi and Internet ports, and some also provide quiet areas where guests can work or connect online. To further appeal to meeting planners, some hotels have relocated their business centers closer to the lobby to make it easier for planners to quickly take care of any last-minute details.

*Hallways, foyers, and nooks* located near meeting rooms can be used both as **prefunction space** and for meetings of small groups. These areas are often used for morning and afternoon refreshment breaks and for cocktail receptions prior to an evening banquet, and they are increasingly being used for small group discussions and displays.

Some hotels also provide *private, dedicated work spaces* that are ideal for small meetings or breakout groups. Marriott's Workspring, for example, offers suites of five studios that accommodate from three to 75 attendees and feature common areas as well as work spaces. In addition to the studios, options also include Workspring Centers, break out spaces, individual pods, cafés, and outdoor spaces. The Westin brand offers Tangent, small meeting rooms that can be booked by the hour. The rooms are equipped with free Wi-Fi, video conferencing capabilities, and an Xbox 360 for DVDs or games.

This trend has largely been fueled by millennials, who prefer to work when and where they are comfortable. Today's mobile attendees prefer a comfortable, barrier-free environment over traditional meeting rooms with a center table or lectern and rows of chairs. More meetings today, therefore, can be termed an *unconference*, which is sometimes also called *participant-driven* or a *participatory event*. An unconference is held in a setting that encourages participant interaction, and these meetings typically feature a coffee-break type atmosphere that encourages interaction and creativity. Soft comfortable seating or lounge space with high tables and chairs is preferred, and, since attendees can stay connected through their mobile devices, the meeting may also include virtual elements (attendees can add their input from other locations within the hotel, such as their guestrooms, the lobby, or poolside).

*Rooftops* provide a dramatic setting for small meetings, cocktail receptions, meal functions, and socializing. The Yotel New York's Terrace (www.yotel.com/NewYork) is the largest outdoor hotel venue in New York City, but

---

**WORTH WATCHING**

Several chains have posted videos on how they are re-inventing their lobbies on YouTube:
- **Marriott International:** www.youtube.com/watch?v=fdzrEhtZLtM (or search for Reinventing the Hotel Lobby – Travel Brilliantly).
- **Hilton Hotels & Resorts:** www.youtube.com/watch?v=5XpnX50B4Ao (or search for Hilton Hotels & Resorts Presents the Ideal Lobby).
- **Holiday Inn Hotels & Resorts:** www.youtube.com/watch?v=9HNuvrEUUXg (or search for The Hub at Holiday Inn).
- **Starwood's Le Méridien Hub** – www.youtube.com/watch?v=ib9AMVbzsg8 (or search for Le Méridien Hub).

---

**WORTH WATCHING**

You can view videos on the dedicated work spaces provided by three hotel chains on YouTube:
- **Starwood** – GBTA Westin Tangent Meeting Rooms: www.youtube.com/watch?v=VE_N3qqCx5E (or search for GBTA Westin Tangent).
- **Marriott** – Workspace on Demand – Flexible Space to Work by Marriott: www.youtube.com/watch?v=lVHg2MSu1s8 (or search for Workspace on Demand – Flexible Space to Work by Marriott).
- **Radisson Blu** — Experience Meetings – Brain Box Breakout Rooms: www.youtube.com/watch?v=iPlEt7YW0DU (or search for Experience Meetings by Radisson Blu – Bookable at the Radisson Blu Hotel, Berlin; you can also search for Experience Meetings by Radisson Blu to view additional videos).

## Chapter 13: Function Rooms and Meeting Setups

**Figure 13.1. PROMOTING CREATIVE MEETING SPACE TO MEETING PLANNERS.**

"I need a partner who thinks outside the ballroom."

Annemarie O'Donoghue
Manager, Meetings & Sponsorships
American Gas Association

**Omni understands**

You want your meeting to be anything but ordinary. That's why Omni customizes each event based on your distinct needs. We offer unique venues. We deliver exceptional culinary options. And we recommend off-site activities that turn an ordinary event into an unforgettable experience.

Call today to learn how to earn multiple rewards with Omni.
800-788-6664 • omniunderstands.com

@OmniMeetings

OMNI HOTELS & RESORTS
a total departure

© 2012 Omni Hotels & Resorts

*Creative, memorable meetings are limited only by the imaginations of the meeting planner and the CSM. This ad promotes how Omni Hotels & Resorts customizes each event by offering unique venues and culinary options.*
**Source: Courtesy of Omni Hotels & Resorts.**

most rooftops, no matter what their size, can be converted into chic gathering places. Some hotels, especially those with multi-levels and/or towers, can design spaces to appeal to the specific needs of meeting planners.

There are, of course, some pitfalls inherent to this outdoor option. To compensate for the first -the weather- some rooftop venues are only open during certain times of the year (The Yotel New York's Terrace, for example, is typically open from the beginning of May until the end of September). Others feature acrylic walls to protect attendees from the winds, while overhead shelters range from canopies or other coverings to retracting ceilings or domes.

Another problem inherent to rooftop venues is quick and efficient food service. Some hotels, therefore, offer adjacent kitchens (demonstration kitchens tend to make the biggest impression) and indoor as well as outdoor dining. Others locate culinary facilities in a nearby area or on the floor below. And, of course, bars and snack options can be incorporated into the rooftop décor.

Other possible *outdoor settings* include poolside, lawns, gardens, and beachfront areas, and the property's parking lot can also be used for events ranging from welcoming receptions to large themed parties. It is a rare hotel that does not have a pool area large enough to hold a small group for informal meetings or small food and beverage functions. Resorts and conference centers often have expansive lawns or gardens that can be set with tables and chairs appropriate for a variety of meetings and other functions. These types of venues may also have private lake or oceanfront beaches that can be transformed into unique meeting space (see illustration below).

Of course, these options may be labor intensive as furniture, audiovisual equipment, and food and beverage items must be transported outside. Additionally, tents, cabanas, or booths may have to be set up, and the hotel and the meeting planner should always have a back-up plan in the event of inclement weather.

*Source: Courtesy of Marriott Fort Lauderdale Harbor Beach Resort & Spa.*

## Function Room Size and Layout

Many factors come into play when discussing meeting room size. First and foremost, of course, is the number expected to attend. Then you must consider the room setup desired and the number and type of audiovisual equipment needed. Additional space may be required for clothes racks, props, or tables to distribute literature. And you must allow more space if refreshment breaks are scheduled.

The basic layout indicates the style of seating. It is wasteful of labor to set each room to utmost capacity, but you obviously must provide enough seating. This is the time to examine the kind of sessions that will go on just before and just after this specific program to make sure the setup is the same or enough time is allotted to make the change. Hotels are

## Chapter 13: Function Rooms and Meeting Setups

frequently able to schedule similar meetings back to back and thus keep manpower and equipment change-over time to a minimum.

The meeting planner will also have to confer with you about the style and size of the head table. Pads, pencils, folders, and printed material may all be placed on chairs and tables. And water glasses and pitchers may be put at a number of tables, or stations, if tables are not used. Each session has its own requirements; some, for example, call for name signs. Attention to details is the key to service.

## Meeting Room Plans

It is important to include meeting room plans on resources used by meeting planners, including the hotel's convention brochure, websites, and directory advertising. For years, convention brochures gave general — often approximate — dimensions of meeting rooms, and meeting planners were often dismayed to arrive to a hotel and find that there was not enough room to stage their functions. To eliminate this problem, the Professional Convention Management Association (PCMA) developed a program to help both properties and meeting planners by actually measuring the dimensions and capacities of meeting rooms. After the rooms are measured with sophisticated laser-powered equipment, computer software is used to accurately map out the room and determine room setup capacities. The detailed computer printouts generated are given to the property to be used in presentations. Properties that have had their space certified are provided with gummed seals that can be affixed to current promotional materials, and are given permission to use the PCMA seal in advertising to assure planners that they are getting the space promised.

In addition to the dimensions of rooms, meeting planners need to know the capacity of each under a variety of setups. Figure 13.2 illustrates a **capacity chart**, a diagram that shows the capacity of a room when various setups are used. While planners are made aware of the kinds of rooms available to them during a sales presentation, the convention service

**Figure 13.2. MEETING ROOM CAPACITIES AND DIMENSIONS.**

INTERCONTINENTAL · TORONTO CENTRE

| Name of Room | Banquet | Theatre | Classroom | Reception | Conference | U-Shape | Hollow Square | Dimensions | Area sq. ft. | Height |
|---|---|---|---|---|---|---|---|---|---|---|
| Ballroom 'A' | 200 | 275 | 135 | 275 | — | 50 | 65 | 60x39 | 2340 | 9' 11" |
| Ballroom 'B' | 270 | 400 | 198 | 400 | — | 65 | 80 | 60x57 | 3420 | 9' 11" |
| A&B Combined | 510 | 700 | 342 | 700 | — | — | — | 60x96 | 5760 | 9' 11" |
| Simcoe | 20 | 20 | 16 | 20 | 20 | — | — | 21x17 | 357 | 9' 6" |
| Ontario | 150 | 200 | 84 | 200 | — | 42 | 52 | 53x38 | 2014 | 9' 6" |
| Niagara | 70 | 100 | 45 | 100 | 28 | 32 | 38 | 29x38 | 1102 | 9' 6" |
| Ontario & Niagara Combined | 240 | 280 | 120 | 320 | — | — | — | 82x38 | 3116 | 9' 6" |

Dimensions are approximate and in feet

*Most hotels, conference centers, and city convention facilities offer charts such as this one to meeting planners. This is a particularly good example, as it includes seating capacities for a variety of seating arrangements as well as detailed information on room dimensions, square footage, and ceiling heights. These statistics, coupled with the computerized scaled drawings now available, help meeting planners to assess the ability of properties to meet their requirements for various types of meetings and functions.*

**Source: Courtesy of InterContinental - Toronto Centre.**

manager should also be available to help planners decide which function would work best in each room. We will discuss the setups commonly used and how capacity is affected by various setups later in this chapter.

Convention service managers should also be aware of the impact of the **Americans with Disabilities Act (ADA)** in regard to their property's function space. While there are still a number of "gray areas" in terms of responsibilities of the property, certain physical requirements must be met by properties offering convention space. These include (but are not limited to) adequate handicapped parking, easy accessibility (ramps, wide doorways, etc.), adapted restroom facilities, and assistive devices for the hearing and visually impaired. It is important to note that after the U.S. ADA was passed, other countries, including Australia, the United Kingdom, and Canada passed similar laws.

Not only must hotels be **barrier-free** (free of obstacles that prevent disabled persons from moving freely to all public areas), but meeting planners may also have special requirements for accommodating their attendees with disabilities. Wider aisles and increased space for seating arrangements may be needed to allow wheelchair access or a signer may be required for hearing-impaired attendees. In some cases, it is not difficult for a property to make the necessary adjustments; in others, it will be up to the property and the meeting planner to determine who is responsible for providing the additional services needed.

**Scaled Drawings.** Most properties prepare **floor plans** - scaled drawings of each room (see Figure 13.3). These should indicate doors, windows, pillars, elevators, electrical outlets, and any obstructions that might affect the setup of the meeting. Meeting planners will probably ask for scaled drawings of each room, so you should have accurately scaled drawings of each function room for your own use and for distribution to customers.

These drawings should be accurate enough to be used to designate meeting or exhibit layouts. If you indicate capacity on the drawings, keep in mind that different setups accommodate widely differing numbers of people.

In addition, meeting planners also like to visualize the overall daily flow of their attendees as they participate in convention activities. Figure 13.4 shows an overall schematic of a facility. While this plan does not provide the detail inherent to scaled drawings of the meeting rooms itself, it may prove helpful to the planner in planning his or her program.

Not only are scaled drawings of function rooms and overall schematics important to meeting planners as they plan their events, they are also used to ensure a safe event. For large events, detailed scaled drawings of the function are required by local fire marshals. These scaled drawings, unlike the scaled drawings provided to the meeting planner by the hotel, must include both the room's schematics and the proposed room setup. In most cases, this finalized scaled drawing is the responsibility of the meeting planner and should be a part of a hotel's contractual terms with the meeting planner. For example, the Westgate Las Vegas Resort & Casino advises:

*"Your Company or Association is responsible for scaled diagrams for events with attendance of 300 guests or more. These must be approved by the Clark County Fire Marshal. The Westgate Las Vegas Resort & Casino cannot guarantee these diagrams will be approved if submitted less than 30 days prior to your function. The Westgate Las Vegas Resort & Casino can assist in providing a scaled diagram of your event."*

**Using Computer Technology to Assist Meeting Planners.** Many properties are taking advantage of today's computer technology to assist meeting planners in determining optimum room setups. Using **computer-assisted design (CAD)** programs is far quicker than manually drawing floorplans (often to find that the space does not accommodate the function), and offers the advantage of flexibility (features of a room — pillars, curved spaces, etc. can be considered when determining the best layouts — and a number of room setups

## Chapter 13: Function Rooms and Meeting Setups

*Figure 13.3.* DETAILED MEETING ROOM PLANS.

448

Chapter 13: Function Rooms and Meeting Setups

*Figure 13.4. AN OVERALL FACILITY SCHEMATIC AS A SALES TOOL.*

Using a plan as illustrated here, a salesperson can help the meeting planner visualize the attendees' flow from guestrooms to function rooms.
**Source: Courtesy of Camelback Inn, Scottsdale, Arizona.**

can be compared). Additionally, they can show a number of options that the meeting planner (and the convention services staff) may not have previously considered, they enable meeting planners to see at a glance how various setups will work in terms of traffic flow as well as capacity, and they can be stored to enable them to be used for future functions.

Many hotel chains such as Marriott (which utilizes its own software to offer computerized room drawings to meeting planners), are finding this technology to be an invaluable tool for the varied needs of meeting planners. This technology is expected to be increasingly

449

used by both properties and meeting planners themselves, and should be considered as part of your property's program to assist meeting planners with staging a successful function.

A number of software programs that "draw" room setups have been developed. MeetingMatrix (www.newmarketinc.com/product/interactive-floor-plans-and-diagrams), can be used by planners online or they can download a copy and work offline. Delphi Diagrams is offered to planners by over 1,000 hotels and venues already in Delphi's system. Social Tables (www.socialtables.com) provides room diagrams seamlessly over computers, tablets, and mobile devices. Vivien, an innovative virtual event designer by CAST Software (cast-soft.com/vivien/overview), provides three-dimensional renderings of room setups, enabling meeting planners to view table seating patterns or the stage from different angles; this enables planners to "see" the room exactly as attendees would (see box titled "Using Computer Technology to Assist Meeting Planners"). Jim Barr, former catering & convention services manager at the Sheraton Chicago Hotel and Towers, states:

> MeetingMatrix diagrams are complete and easy to modify and read, and that helps us both with sales and operations. From a sales perspective, clients are more confident about their buying decision when we use MeetingMatrix to show how their function will work in our space. On the operations side, using the diagrams during final event preparations keeps questions, miscommunications, and re-sets to a minimum.[1]

Another innovation is the use of special apps to measure meeting space (see sidebar titled "Apps for Measuring Meeting Rooms"). Most meeting planners today carry their smartphones and/or tablets on site visits, and these apps provide a simple, convenient way for them to measure meeting space and create floor plans.

## Timetable for Setup and Breakdown

Most hotel brochures do an adequate job of presenting the basic contours of each meeting room, and many are designed to show how a room is used in a variety of ways. Few, however, tell the convention organizer how much time is required for room setup and breakdown. But there is a great need to communicate that information.

It is very important to know exactly how long it takes a crew to set up each room under the many seating arrangements. Many a meeting program has failed because those planning it did not take into account the time it takes to set up and break down, and the program was de-

### Apps for Measuring Meeting Rooms

**Point and Measure.** This app from Tap TapSoft turns an iPhone into a measuring tape. An iPhone camera is pointed at an object to be measured, and, based on the height of the camera lens and the iPhone tilt angle, Point & Measure will calculate its height and distance using the phone's sensors. An overview and demonstration video is available at www.tapsoft.com/our-apps/pointmeasure.

**MagicPlan.** The Sensopia MagicPlan app measures rooms and draws floor plans via photographs taken on a mobile device's camera. The app creates a 360-degree image and floor plan of a meeting room, and "furniture" of varying types can be inserted into the diagram with the touch of a finger. Floor plans are available in pdf, jpg, and dfx formats, and interactive floorplans can also be published on the web. A video of the app in a home setting can be seen at www.sensopia.com/english/index./html.

**RoomScan and RoomScan Pro.** These apps create instant floor plans of a space when an iPhone is tapped against each wall. The app calculates dimensions and square footage, and meeting planners can e-mail the floor plans directly from the property. You can view a demo at locometric.com.

Chapter 13: Function Rooms and Meeting Setups

## Using Computer Technology to Assist Meeting Planners

MeetingMatrix is one software program used to enable meeting planners to see which setups will work best for their functions. After entering such basic information as room dimensions, number of attendees, and special requirements (size or shape of tables, space needed for exhibits, etc.), the program "draws" one or more possible room configurations, enabling the meeting planner to see which one will be best — and providing the convention services department with a list of function room furniture and equipment needed for the setup chosen.

### Sample Banquet Setup

FUNCTION SPECIFICATION:   Meeting name: Sample meeting   Facility name: Sample facility

| Function name: | Banquet | Setup items used: | QTY | ITEM | |
|---|---|---|---|---|---|
| Room name: | Ballroom | | 209 | 18" x 18" | Chairs |
| Number of people: | 209 | | 8 | 6' x 30" | Rectangular tables |
| Setup: | Banquet — | | 3 | 8' x 30" | Rectangular tables |
| | 10 per 5 foot diameter table | | 20 | 5' dia | Round tables |
| Distance between rows: | 75 inches | | 2 | 5' dia | Quarter-round tables |
| Center aisle width: | 5.0 feet | | 9 | 6' x 30" | Crescent tables |
| Side aisle width: | 5.0 feet | | 25 | 3' x 3' | Dance floor squares |
| Cross aisle width: | 5.0 feet | | | | |

signed much too tightly to permit good service. The planner would have developed the program more realistically if he or she had some idea of the time needed to perform these services.

Too often, the hotel bears the stigma of failing to perform well, give good service, or show much expertise, so the hotel staff should make the meeting planner aware of its **func-**

tion room turnover time – the amount of time needed to tear down and reset a function room. Most meeting planners would gladly loosen up their timetables if they knew what was involved to assure that their shows ran smoothly and on time.

Convention service managers should have charts made up indicating turnover time requirements. These charts should list the time it takes to set up each room for maximum capacity under each seating arrangement. They should give the time it takes to break them down, plus union regulations regarding workday, hours, overtime charges, and any unusual characteristics that may affect costs and time. Specify the number of people needed. Time may be saved by using a larger crew but this will cost more; at times a meeting planner might choose such an option.

## Managing Function Rooms

Your hotel function space is a precious asset, and your goal as a convention service manager is to maximize its utilization. Empty rooms, whether guestrooms or function rooms, are a perishable product.

The convention service manager is the person most qualified to assign rooms for specific events. This should be done in communication with the meeting planner. The service manager knows the hotel's facilities; the planner knows the event's characteristics.

In assigning a room, its size, its capacity under a specific layout, the type of event, and the presentation style should all be considered. The room size should "match" the expected attendance. Too much space or too many empty seats can create the wrong psychological setting. These fundamental requirements probably were hashed out during the sales presentations, but other factors must be considered, too.

Consider the room's location within the hotel in regard to traffic in corridors, elevators, escalators, parking arrangements, and coat check rooms. All program segments must be definitely allocated to specific locations about sixty days before the event, at the latest. This is especially important if a group wishes to reserve their space on a 24-hour basis. According to Maria Dempsey, regional director of sales, western region, Pan Pacific Hotels, this can pose a problem for the hotel:

> The request for access to public meeting space on a 24-hour basis means no other groups may use those rooms, even if the room is not occupied overnight.[2]

A number of groups, however, wish to reserve their rooms for the duration of their meeting, especially if functions involve exhibits or extensive staging or if there is the possibility that a meeting will not end on schedule. David Kilman, CMP, past president of MPI, offers this perspective:

> There is a tug-of-war between planners and suppliers regarding 24-hour space holds. It all comes down to the total value of the meeting. If a planner expects, or demands, the luxury of a round-the-clock hold on space, there must be an appropriate financial return to the supplier...Once the economic impact of a meeting is resolved, it should be easy to determine if a 24-hour hold is a reasonable request.[3]

When considering a **24-hour hold**, therefore, it is vital to analyze the economic impact of the meeting, including the value of the meeting itself and subsequent business from the group, and the time of year. If, for example, the group wishes to book during the Christmas holidays when you can expect to generate a large volume of lucrative catering business, it may not be a sound business decision to reserve function rooms on a 24-hour basis (see Sales Restrictions section in this chapter). If you decide to reserve the rooms around the clock, a clause should be included in the group's contract guaranteeing the 24-hour hold and any restrictions put upon it by the hotel.

You should get a list from the client of all the people on his or her staff who are authorized to move an event to a different location, should the need arise. Just before the event, and especially during it, it is absolutely essential to know the channels of authority within the convention staff. Time may be too short and the need for action too great to let you double-check any instructions. Cancellations of sessions, changes in timetables and the like may be made at the last minute.

Such a list should be in writing, of course. And the degree of authority should be specified. What can these staff members order? Changes in layout or location can be costly in terms of time and labor.

The list you get from the convention organizer should be similar to the list of your department heads that you give to the organizer. The key people of both the hotel and convention group staffs should attend the preconvention meetings. Let them get acquainted before the pressure begins. Discuss possible changes. This is the time to indicate what the hotel staff will need in the way of time and labor to bring about such program alterations.

Because association conventions must cope with optional attendance at both the convention and individual programs, it is often necessary to move workshops and meetings from one room to another to accommodate smaller or larger groups. Airing such possibilities in advance allows your staff and the client's staff to understand such conditions and to react more quickly and constructively in crisis situations.

## Sales Restrictions on Function Space

Both the hotel sales staff and the catering department are involved in selling function space. The sales department is responsible for selling space that is used by convention groups requiring sleeping rooms. The catering department is responsible for selling function space to local groups. Since hotels are primarily interested in filling sleeping accommodations because of their high profit margin, the hotel sales department should have preference in booking the available function space.

Therefore, most hotels have local catering sales restrictions. For example, during its peak convention season, a hotel may limit local catering to a short booking cycle. That is, the catering department may only sell function space to local groups after the hotel is assured that the needs of groups needing sleeping rooms have been met. Once the hotel sales staff sells their group room allotment on a given day, any function space still available may be sold by catering.

In some cases, special **day packages** are created for groups that do not require overnight accommodations. Day packages typically include a single price per attendee for the entire day. This price is inclusive of all food and beverage, instead of having meals and breaks priced separately, so these packages can be an economical option for local groups or other groups that do not require sleeping rooms.

The further out a commitment is made by convention groups, the greater the opportunity for catering to sell the unused space. This period of time is frequently referred to as the **open sale period**. Holidays are often designated as open sales periods, as group guestroom business is traditionally slow around Christmas, Thanksgiving, and the Fourth of

## Chapter 13: Function Rooms and Meeting Setups

July. Any hotel business booked by catering during those times is not likely to displace conventions needing meeting space.

## Function Room Charges

How do you determine what to charge for meeting space? Brochures list rates for guestrooms but rarely for meeting rooms. The latter situation is most flexible; it depends on the meeting group, the time, and the space required. If a group uses enough guestrooms, there is often no charge for meeting rooms.

As mentioned in Chapter 9, the guestroom-to-meeting-space ratio is an important variable when negotiating. Meetings that require an excess of meeting rooms relative to their guestroom block may warrant a charge for meeting space.

Properties with unique function space may be able to charge more for their room rental. Function space characteristics that might command a premium include:

> **WORTH WATCHING**
> View a short video titled "Negotiation Leverage – Guestroom-to-Meeting-Room Ratio" at www.youtube.com/watch?v=K3I1C0B9CnM (or go to YouTube and type the video's title in the search box).

- Large ballrooms that are free of pillars or other obstructions
- High ceilings with retractable chandeliers
- Tiered theater-style auditoriums
- Advanced audiovisual-equipped rooms
- Meeting rooms that are convenient to guestrooms

It is important that the meeting planner understands your property's policy regarding function room charges. Many hotels include a clause similar to the one below to eliminate potential misunderstandings:

> *Meeting and function space is assigned based on the type of setup and the number of people in attendance. Should advance setup and late teardown or an abnormal amount of meeting space be required, a charge may be incurred. Specified meeting rooms cannot be guaranteed and are subject to change. If the final attendance figures are less than the original estimate, an adjustment to the meeting and function space will become necessary. Any changes requested in your agenda after receipt of this contract are based upon space availability at the time of your request. Any cancellation of food and beverage functions after acceptance of this agreement will result in the organization being charged the full dollar value of that function based on either the actual menu price or an average menu price. Should the hotel be able to resell a function of similar value in the originally scheduled room, there will be no charge assessed.*

There may well be circumstances in which the hotel management prefers to charge for a function room. A hotel that hosts a catering event where no guestroom nights are used, for example, may specify a *minimum sales amount* on the room. Typically, the more meeting space reserved, the higher the minimum sales amount required by the property. If a meeting group cuts back on food and beverage, the hotel will likely increase charges for meeting space.

In the case of food functions, the cost per person often covers the use of the room. That is, the hotel could require that a group not using sleeping rooms spend a specific amount, such as $20,000, to secure a large ballroom for their event. Jil Larson, director of revenue management at Omni Hotels, makes a strong argument that hotels should consider *group catering revenue per room night*, rather than the traditional guestroom-to-meeting-space ratio. She states:

> A guestrooms-to- meeting-space ratio advises how much function space a group should receive based on how many room nights are provided. That's great, but a group taking a lot of guestrooms is automatically rewarded with a lot of function space, which is only warranted if they're actually paying for that space. I prefer to allocate space based on how much catering revenue, including room rental, is being collected per room night booked. In my opinion, a small group with a lot of catering revenue can take as much or more space than a large group paying very little for the function space.[4]

You should consider having a listed price for each room; after all, it looks great when you waive the fee. When you do charge for a function room, a list of charges should be available. Function room rental rates should be determined for each meeting room by time of day. Some properties will list specific rates for morning, afternoon, evening, full-day, and 24-hour weekday hold, and weekend rates.

You might outline a sliding scale arrangement, tying the meeting room fees to the number of guestrooms used for the convention (see Figure 13.5). For example, if the group picks up 200 room nights or more, the $1,000 fee for the ballroom could be waived; if 100-199 room nights are used, the cost would be $500; and if the group uses fewer than 100 room nights, the cost would be $750 to $1,000 depending on the number of room nights.

There is a trend today to charge for space. A hotel that handles a number of small meetings would be wise to consider a fee, particularly if the group plans to meet in one room, hold a food function in another, and conduct breakout meetings in another three to five rooms.

In such situations, room charges should be stipulated if the guestroom commitment is not enough to cover the labor costs of setting up, servicing, cleaning, and tearing down. After all, a hotel is in business to make a profit. Astute convention service managers often advise planners to schedule meetings and meal functions in rooms that can keep the same setup. A hotel can turn a **quick set** when all that is necessary is cleaning off table tops and setting up a lectern.

You might also want to charge for meeting rooms when companies participating in a trade show take the opportunity to hold dealer or sales meetings. The people attending may already be registered for the trade show, and the requirements of the trade show would place great strain on the allocation of meeting rooms. Of course, if the food functions of such additional meetings mount up, it may justify not charging for the use of the room. But a room charge may be justified if the food function is only a refreshment break. In the final analysis, there is no hard and fast rule on charging for meeting space. A hotel needs to look at the food, the rooms, and all other profit areas to determine its rate structure.

*Figure 13.5. GUIDE TO FUNCTION SPACE CHARGES.*

---

### SHERATON FUNCTION SPACE CHARGES

The Sheraton Waikiki charges for function space under the following circumstances:

1. All exhibits.
2. All function rooms that are held on a 24-hour block.
3. All function space for groups that have meetings only and are holding no sleeping rooms at the Sheraton Waikiki Hotel.
4. All function space when unusual or costly setups are required.
5. All function space when the sleeping rooms decrease proportionately from the original commitment.

### FUNCTION SPACE VS. SLEEPING ROOM CONSUMPTION (PROPORTIONATE SLIDING SCALE)

| Percent of Decrease From Original Block | Amount of Meeting Room Charges |
|---|---|
| Up to 40% decrease | No charge. |
| 41%-60% decrease | 50% charge for meeting rooms as listed on "meeting room charge sheet." |
| 61%-80% decrease | 75% charge for meeting rooms as listed on "meeting room charge sheet." |
| 81%-100% decrease | 100% charge for meeting rooms as listed on "meeting room charge sheet." |

In addition to the above "sliding scale," the hotel will also take into consideration your definite food and beverage events when determining your meeting room charges.

---

The Sheraton Waikiki provides meeting planners with detailed space pricing policy. Note the charges increase if sleeping rooms slip from the original room block commitment. In determining meeting room charges, many hotels consider "slippage" — when guestroom pickup decreases significantly, the charge for the group's function space increases. Meeting room rental at this 1,900-room property totals over $250,000 annually.
**Source: Courtesy of the Sheraton Waikiki.**

## Function and Meeting Room Revenue Management

Increasingly, hotels are applying traditional guestroom yield management methods to meeting and function rooms. Yield management sets prices based on the forecasted demand for function space. Rental rates are increased or decreased from the established rates depending on the time and date of the meeting and on the total revenue the event brings to the property. Several Hiltons, for example, have begun to determine intricate yield management formulas for pricing their function space. Steve Armitage, former senior vice president of sales at Hilton Hotels Corporation, states:

> The meeting buyer can expect to see meeting room yield management become more widespread as technology advances.[5]

The use of yield management techniques can be beneficial to both hotels and meeting planners. Setting prices according to predicted demand levels not only helps hotels to manage their revenues but also provides the opportunity for price-sensitive customers who are willing to purchase at off-peak times to do so at favorable rates. It is necessary, however, to identify and communicate high and low demand periods and to be able to justify the different rates available to different clients at different times of the year. And any fee increases should be made incrementally, to avoid alienating corporate buyers.

If the meeting contract includes an option for meeting planners to reduce their room blocks prior to the meeting date, a corresponding clause should be in place that allows the hotel to reduce the meeting room space allocation if the reduction in room block is exercised. Sometimes, groups will drop room nights per their agreement but cling to their original meeting space allocation; this presents a problem to the hotel in both guestrooms lost as well as the inability to book another group due to a lack of available meeting space.

When establishing your yield management strategy, you will want to consider a number of factors, including the performance of each of your function rooms (a large ballroom, for example, may actually yield a lower occupancy rate than a smaller meeting room that is used several times a day), physical "rate fences" (such as amenities offered, location, and so on, that can justify a higher charge), and non-physical "rate fences," such as customer characteristics (a property can justify lower rates to a potential customer likely to use other hotel facilities, such as sleeping rooms, restaurants, and so on).

Once these factors have been determined, you will want to develop a strategy that can be easily implemented. One simple approach is to color-code demand periods on a calendar or table. High-demand periods, for example, can be coded in red for instant recognition as a "hot" period, moderately high-demand periods can be coded in yellow to signify "warm" periods, and low-demand periods can be coded in blue. Each of the demand levels (colors) should have a different set of prices associated with it, and those prices should be communicated to all staff members involved in selling meeting space or catering functions. It is also important to communicate when qualified discounts can be offered to meeting planners or groups (usually in low-demand periods).[6]

## Release Dates

When a convention buys out the house, a request to **hold all function space** seems reasonable. Such requests are typical from large groups that are booking two to three years out. But a request to "hold all function space" is difficult for a hotel, especially in periods of high demand. Groups requesting an all-space block on your function space should be closely monitored, and all space-blocks should be negotiated with reasonable **release date** increments, such as one year, nine months, or six months, to allow your property to sell the space with some lead time should the large group not materialize as anticipated.

Release dates should be set in every letter of agreement. At some early date when a rough program is available, the room assignments can be tentatively made. At this point, *some* function rooms can be released if there seems to be more than enough. The convention in the house should have a priority for meeting rooms, but you may get other calls. Here again, it is obvious why there is a need to have just one function book, under one person's control.

At a somewhat later date, when a detailed program is worked out, try to get unneeded rooms released. Planners often to try to hold onto every room indefinitely, to have a reserve for some occasion that may come up. But this practice can inhibit your other sales efforts.

Many properties specify their release date policies in meeting contracts. The following clause spells out one property's policy:

> *In order to ensure that adequate space is available for your meeting, please provide the Convention Service Department with a tentative function schedule six months prior to your meeting/convention, or as soon as possible. A final program is required no later than 90 days prior to the*

> *start of your convention. Space not assigned at 90 days will be released to the hotel for scheduling of other functions, as required.*

## Several Meetings Simultaneously

Most meetings are small. More than 75 percent of all corporate meetings have fewer than 100 in attendance. To do much business in meetings, you must be able to house more than one simultaneously. Naturally, this is not the case when you virtually sell out the house, but most often the function book fills up with a number of more modest events.

Handling several smaller meetings calls for careful planning. You cannot negotiate with all groups at the same time, so you must take care not to commit all your public space to one group, leaving you with no facilities for other groups. Most hotels want the option of moving groups around to maximize usage, especially when groups are not using guestrooms, and often include a function room assignment clause in their contracts. A typical clause might read:

> *The function room assignments listed in this contract are tentative. Final function and meeting rooms will be assigned by the Hotel three months prior to the meeting dates. The Hotel reserves the right to reassign function rooms to accommodate both Group and all other groups or parties using the Hotel's facilities during Group's meeting.*

Avoid naming specific meeting rooms in the contract. Most convention service managers can point to times when new business was lost because they were unable to re-assign function space due to the sales team guaranteeing specific meeting rooms in the contract. Jil Larson of Omni Hotels states:

> There are groups that will absolutely insist upon reserving specific meeting rooms, but it is costly to the hotel and therefore should be charged if offered. Several hotels I've worked with will only agree to guarantee specific meeting rooms with rack room rental or a set fee ($500, for example). Once there is a price to pay for guaranteed named rooms, clients occasionally find ways to be flexible on this issue.[7]

Some meeting planners who feel that they have negotiated for a specific room or rooms that will meet the objective(s) of their function object to such a clause and try to negotiate it out of the contract. A hotel can address the concerns of the meeting planner by pointing out the reasonable time frame (most groups do not publish a program with specific room names more than three months before the function) and assuring him or her that the hotel will meet specific requirements if another room is substituted. The hotel should then follow through on its promises, ensuring that basic requirements (such as square footage and other needs, such as hard walls to minimize noise) are met.

Traffic patterns must be carefully planned to avoid confusion and congestion. Give thought, too, to the proximity of different kinds of groups. Don't forget to find out what will be going on in the room next door. Holding a training session next door to a college reunion is asking for trouble; a rock band next door to a speech could be disastrous. And even a seemingly ordinary meeting can become quite noisy merely by adding a sound film.

You may find it extremely profitable to go after smaller meetings. To begin with, there are more of them. And smaller meeting organizers are generally not as demanding of price and concessions, often can offer much repeat business, and tax your staff less in serving them. It is tempting to hit that home run by bagging a full-house convention. But a steady stream of good base hits in the form of modest-size meetings often wins the ball game by providing what every hotel wants — profitable business.

## Use of Meeting Rooms by Others

Some organizations ask, or demand, that all requests by other groups for meeting facilities in the hotel at the time of their event be cleared with them. They are trying to control the entire environment of their event and they don't want rival organizations meeting at the same time under the same roof. Apprehensions of industrial security cannot be dismissed lightly.

The hotel must be careful about this. Imagine an IBM research seminar in the house at the same time as Toshiba or Honeywell meetings! When a competitive organization appears on the scene, the usually easygoing meeting planner gets quite uptight. And you may find yourself needing strict security systems for a relatively easy, small seminar.

And should you be concerned about only the exact date of the meeting, or must you worry, too, about the days immediately before and after the event?

Small properties that can handle only one average-size group at a time can use such situations to sell themselves. In the off season the small resort can claim that walk-in business from competitive personnel is highly unlikely. The meeting organizer is assured of receiving all your facility and attention, and need not worry about traffic pattern and unwanted guests.

The convention organizer may want to veto a meeting held in the hotel during his or her dates. Many companies hold dealer meetings at trade shows. Most association executives have no objections, and many feel that it adds importance to their event. But many worry that the timing of such meetings may pull delegates away from the main sessions or events.

It is safe to say that you can expect meeting planners to be interested in who and what is scheduled in the hotel during *their* time.

## Employee Procedure Manuals

Convention service managers, as we have said, are the in-house coordinators of the convention. They work with virtually every department in the hotel. Their authority in dealing with these departments is to a great extent determined by their character and the respect they have earned from those with whom they work. In many hotels, convention service managers do not have direct line authority over rooms or food and beverage departments. This often necessitates that they use tact and discretion in getting the job done.

However, they do have line authority within their own department and must function as managers there. Serving under them are three to ten housepersons who set up the function rooms. Each of these people should be trained in the various types of meeting setups. This is best accomplished with the use of an **employee procedure manual** (see Figure 13.6).

A procedure manual is not a job description. A procedure manual tells the employee how to do the job, whereas the job description is prepared primarily for management and states the job's responsibility and authority. Ideally, the procedure manual should include illustrations or drawings. For example, setup illustrations similar to those used in this chap-

## Chapter 13: Function Rooms and Meeting Setups

*Figure 13.6. EMPLOYEE PROCEDURE MANUAL*

### SetUp Support Services for Functions

| STEPS: | HOW-TO'S: | TIPS: |
|---|---|---|
| To complete all steps, you will need tables, a banquet event order (BEO), change orders (if any), tablecloths, table skirts, standard amenities, trash cans, an easel, a message corkboard, and tacks or stick pins. | | |
| 1. Set up registration Tables. | Check the banquet event order (BEO) for the number and type of tables to set up.<br><br>Place tables in the lobby or near the entrance to the function room as stated in the BEO. | |
| 2. Cover, skirt, and flounce registration tables according to the BEO. | Place Tablecloths on Function Room Tables and Skirt and Flounce Function Room Tables. | |
| 3. Place amenities on registration tables. | Place the following items on registration tables:<br>- Pens or pencils<br>- Message pads<br>- Pitcher with water and water glasses<br><br>Arrange other items supplied by guests as indicated on the BEO. | Guests may have items sent ahead for the function. |
| 4. Place a trash can near the tables. | | |
| 5. Set up a message board. | Put a message corkboard on an easel near the registration table to hold messages for guests who are at the function.<br><br>Provide tacks or stick pins. | The message board prevents the interruption of meetings. Participants can check the message board during breaks. |

*Employee procedure manuals, such as this one, provide specific instructions for setting up the various components of a meeting or convention (this example provides instructions for setting up a registration area). Having detailed guidelines ensures that all aspects of the job are handled consistently.*
**Source: Adapted from Hospitality Skills Training Series, Banquet Setup Employee Guide, American Hotel & Lodging Educational Institute.**

ter should be included. The manual also should include a step-by-step outline of the houseperson's job.

The procedure manual will have the same importance for employees in the convention service department as the master recipe card does for a cook. Successful restaurants are successful largely because of consistency; the same should be true for convention servicing. A procedure manual will help ensure that setups will not be done in a slightly different way each day.

It is often difficult for employees to recall each procedure in a setup and all the required supplies. The manual eliminates the exclusion of certain setups, as well as serving as a valuable training tool for new employees. Manuals might also include rules and regulations that apply to the setup houseperson.

Efforts should be made to personalize the manual. It should be published in a small booklet form that can easily fit into a shirt pocket for quick reference.

No such manual is permanent. On the contrary, new tables, chairs, and operating techniques will necessitate updating. Hopefully, the employees themselves may suggest ways to perform certain aspects of the job better.

# Meeting Setups

**WORTH WATCHING**

Dr. Paul Radde of The Thrival Institute (www.thrival.com) has written a comprehensive guide, *Seating Matters: State of the Art Seating Arrangements*, that is not only helpful to meeting planners, but is also an excellent resource for CSMs. CSMs can use the concepts presented in this guide to enhance their consultative approach in assisting meeting planners to manage the logistics of their meetings. You can view a video of Dr. Radde's "Key Tips for Event Seating" at www.youtube.com/watch?v=C-pTRz5pwXM (or go to YouTube and search for Paul O. Radde's Key Tips for Event Seating).

The physical arrangement of chairs and tables plays an important role in meetings, and hotels are becoming more innovative in their use of meeting room furniture. Convention planners know that the atmosphere of a meeting can be enhanced or destroyed by the size of the room and the manner in which it is arranged. Thus it is essential that you have an orderly presentation for each of your facility's meeting rooms, giving its dimensions and its capacities under a variety of layout designs.

## Function Room Furniture

Hotel function rooms get heavy use. Often a number of functions are scheduled on one day for a single room, with only an hour or two between events. These events are usually quite different, and housepersons must work quickly to set up a variety of functions — business meetings, lectures, training sessions, fashion shows, banquets, and others. The only flexibility the room can provide is through the use of air walls or folding division doors. The major change must be provided by the equipment and setup within the room.

*Function room furniture* is the term coined for equipment used in meeting and banquet rooms. Jacob Felsenstein, the author of a book on function room furniture, has suggested four general features to look for in function room furniture:

- *Strength and durability.* Watch for the weakest link, such as mechanical folding devices which are easily broken, or strong components which may depend on a weak hinge or spring. Safety of guests is a foremost consideration. There are simple and effective folding devices that minimize the possibility of failure. Keep in mind, frequency of use means frequency of cleaning. Parts in contact with the floor must be made to withstand and facilitate frequent scrubbing, waxings, and vacuuming.

- *Ease of handling.* All folding or knock-down equipment should be simple to set up. Equipment that is light in weight may not be the most durable. There are a wide variety of carriers, such as dollies and trucks, which are designed to aid in handling.
- *Ease of storage.* Equipment should be able to be stacked so that one piece does not mar the next, and in a manner that prevents vulnerable parts from protruding. In choosing dollies or trucks, check to see that they are designed to handle the particular piece of equipment in your particular setting.
- *Flexibility.* It may be advisable to buy function room furniture that serves two or more purposes in order to avoid extra handling or storage. For example, a Knockdown Cabaret Table allows for different sized tops to be used interchangeably with one column and base, enabling it to fill many different needs; one Dual-Height Folding Platform serves two different levels, many different purposes, can save up to 50 percent on initial outlay, and an additional 50 percent on handling costs and storage space.[8]

**Chairs and Tables.** Meeting room chairs and tables vary a great deal, but there are certain types and sizes that are used most frequently. Your capacity figures should be based on such equipment, and will vary when you use equipment other than the standard. Most variations are used in small meeting setups, such as board room facsimiles; many such meetings use posh swivel chairs. Conference centers frequently boast **ergonomic** chairs, which are bigger than a regular chair, upholstered in leather, come with a cushion seat and swivel, and are said to be comfortable for 18 hours at a stretch (see box titled "Crowne Paza ® Rolls Out Ergonomic Chairs").

Most chairs used for meetings are 18 inches wide by 18 inches deep by 17 inches high. *Stacking armchairs* (not the type mentioned in the previous paragraph) are slightly larger, such as 20 inches by 20 inches by 17 inches. Most folding chairs are smaller and not as comfortable, and are generally used for last-minute overflow accommodations. Planners want their attendees comfortable so they can concentrate on the program.

Kevin Shanley, corporate director of sales for Kalahari Resorts, says:

> **WORTH WATCHING**
>
> Watch a short video on the difference between typical meeting room chairs and the ergonomic chairs used at The Woodland Resort and Conference Center at www.youtube.com/watch?v=dMLxuQJY0SA (or go to YouTube and search for Woodland Resort and Conference Center ergonomic chairs).

> You don't want people thinking about how uncomfortable they are or how much they want to get up and stretch [instead of paying attention to the presentation].[9]

Hotels today are responding by offering much more comfortable seating options, including sofas, club chairs, and higher chairs; even bean bag chairs may be used at smaller, more informal meetings. A number of these options can be viewed in the Inspiration Gallery on the Marriott chain's Meetings Imagined website (www.meetingsimagined.com/inspiration/); add the following after the slash to see these photographs: vip- seating; casual-

## CROWNE PLAZA ROLLS OUT ERGONOMIC CHAIRS

Just as the Westin chain revolutionized the guestroom with its Heavenly Bed, the Crowne Plaza® Hotels & Resorts brought comfort to the meeting room with ergonomic seating. After a survey commissioned by the chain revealed that over 60 percent of the respondents felt that a more comfortable chair would help them focus during meetings, the chain refitted meeting rooms in its properties in the United States and Canada with Herman Miller Caper® chairs. The chairs, which offer greater comfort with their ergonomic backs, flexible mesh net seat, and casters for mobility, are just the chain's first step in meeting the demand for more comfortable seating. Crowne Plaza® is also outfitting larger rooms with flex-back banquet-style chairs that feature contoured seats and flexible backs.

**Source: Courtesy of Crowne Plaza Hotels & Resorts.**

lecture-seating; modern-club-chairs; and nontraditional-presentation, which shows a mix of soft seating.

Rigid chairs are recommended for food functions. They are more comfortable than folding chairs, which are smaller and lower. Folding chairs should only be used for emergency backup or for outdoor events.

*These tables, which feature a plastic-coated top, are stylish enough to not require a tablecloth, and they are easy to clean. The drop down on the front of each table is called a modesty panel.*
**Source: Courtesy of Chicago Conrad Hilton Hotel.**

Most hotels inventory several types of tables: rectangular; square; serpentine; round; half rounds; quarter rounds; and, cocktail rounds. One new innovation being used for meetings is the touch screen conference table, which comes in a variety of sizes and styles, and many hotels now also stock schoolroom and banquet tables that feature a plastic-coated surface that does not require a tablecloth (see illustration); these tables are stylish, save on laundry costs, and send a message to the planner that the hotel is environmentally conscious. There are downsides to these types of tables, however – they are expensive, and some planners feel that they lack the warmth and color of tablecloths.

The standard height for tables is 30 inches; the standard depth, either 30 or 18 inches. When people are to be seated opposite each other, the 30-inch table is required. When people sit on only one side of the table, as we shall discuss in *schoolroom* setups, the 18-inch depth is sufficient and saves much space. The 30-inch-deep rectangular table, however, is used most frequently for head tables, even when people are seated on only one side. This deeper table is also used as display tables, exhibit stands, and for other purposes. It is most versatile and comes in lengths of four, six, and eight feet so that a variety of total lengths may be achieved easily.

Round tables (which are also referred to simply as **rounds**) are used for many food functions and also for some kinds of meeting sessions. They most often are five, five-and-one-half, or six feet in diameter. Comfortable seating calls for a five-foot round table for six to eight people; a five-and-one-half foot table for eight to ten guests; and a six-foot table for ten to 12. A **cocktail round** (also called a cabaret or highboy table) of about three feet in diameter is used for **reception style** setups. In this type of setup, the tables, which vary in height from 30 to 50 inches, are placed throughout the room to allow for the mixing and mingling of guests. There is usually limited or no seating — if seats are provided, they are usually set against the perimeter of the room. Some planners request that the hotel mix the room with five-foot rounds that include six seats for those who do not wish to stand and mingle during the reception.

An almost infinite number of variations can be created by using half-rounds and quarter-rounds. The more imaginative curved **serpentine** tables (also termed **crescent** tables) are commonly used for buffets. You are restricted only by your imagination in developing unique buffet arrangements.

*Square tables* may also be found in some setups. The four-foot square table is the size most commonly used.

Tablecloths, mitered on the corners, are used on tables because most banquet and meeting room tables are damaged and unsightly from continual breakdown and storage. When ordering tablecloths, you will have to specify the exact measurements needed (see box titled "Tablecloth Sizes for Round Tables"). Tablecloths for round tables should be approximately 18 inches wider than the table diameter to allow for a nine-inch drape over the sides (a 90-inch round tablecloth should be used for a 72-inch diameter table, for example). Since the standard table measures 30 inches from the floor and the average chair seat is 17 inches from the floor, the nine-inch drape will not touch the chair seats or interfere with the guests' comfort. Floor-length tablecloths are sometimes used at formal functions, however.

| TABLECLOTH SIZES FOR ROUND TABLES ||| 
|---|---|---|
| Table Size (Round Diameter) | Standard: Banquet-Length Tablecloth | Formal: Floor-Length Tablecloth |
| 72" | 90" | 132" |
| 66" | 84" | 126" |
| 60" | 78" | 120" |
| 36" (cocktail) | 54" | 96" |

**Head tables**, as well as display and buffet tables, stages, and platforms, require special drapery. Traditionally, T-pins and tacks have been used to attach floor-length linens for such setups, but **velcro** is now being used by many hotels.

*Snap-drape skirting* is also available. Plastic clips are fitted along the top edge of platforms and tables, and grippers sewn into the upper pleat of the skirting are snapped into place quickly. Snap-drape skirting is made of permanent-crease polyester and fiberglass, making it easy to clean and wrinkle-free.

**Platforms and Staging.** Folding platforms are used in many ways; they elevate head tables for banquets and speakers. They come in different sizes, with different names: platform, riser, stage, **dais**, podium, or rostrum. You must construct them to size. Check local safety regulations carefully. The usual heights are six, eight, 12, 16, and 24 inches, plus a 32-inch high *riser*. Lengths may be four, six, or eight feet, or any combination of these. Widths vary from four to six feet. If you maintain adequate stocks, a variety of combinations can be created. If the platforms are old and unsightly, put pleated skirting around the bottom and perhaps carpeting on top.

Staging height is determined by the room length. In general, divide the room length by 50 to determine the stage height. For example, a room that is 100 feet in length would require a 24-inch (two-foot high) stage or platform. A room that is 75 feet in length divided by 50 equals 1.5 feet or 18 inches needed for stage height.

**Cocktail Rounds**
Courtesy of Shelby Williams Industries, Inc.

**Serpentine (Crescent) Table**
Courtesy of Shelby Williams Industries, Inc.

**Sample Platform Staging**
Courtesy of Sisco Companies.

**Lecterns. Lecterns** are reading desks used to hold the speaker's papers and come in two basic types. The smaller *table lecterns* are placed on tables, while full-size *floor lecterns* are set on the floor. Both sizes should feature built-in light fixtures to enable the speaker to manipulate lighting and audiovisual equipment directly, and enough connecting wire to reach wall outlets.

Many a room becomes difficult to set up because the wall outlets are on the same circuits as the overhead lights and are controlled by a common switch. Make sure the lectern's light unit is connected to a wall outlet that will not be cut off with the overhead lights. Cables, like those for microphones or light units must be taped — tripping the guest speaker is not a recommended way to start a session.

House lights are often dimmed for effect or for greater visibility of audiovisual presentations. Check each setup carefully; smart meeting planners will double-check such items themselves.

Lecterns (and head tables) should be easily accessible. They often must be approached in a relatively darkened room, so the access path must have some illumination. They should not be located near an entrance or other high-traffic area to ensure that speakers and their audiences are not distracted by people moving about. If a video or PowerPoint presentation is planned, the room should be set up so that any doors are off to the side so latecomers will not have to walk in front of the projector.

You should have a good inventory of table lecterns, floor models, and some lecterns with contained sound systems. It is helpful if the lectern has a flat area that securely holds at least a water glass. This area should be large enough so that writing implements, such as a pen, pencil, chalk, or an electric pointer, can be stored.

Permanent stages allow you to develop more sophisticated lecterns with full audiovisual controls. Such units don't lend themselves to the temporary setups of most meeting rooms, but they are received most enthusiastically by program members. Consider these units whenever a permanent installation is possible. A must item that is most versatile for temporary setups is a portable lectern with a built-in sound system that plugs into an ordinary outlet.

Most hotels have their names or logos painted on the lectern faces. Because speakers are commonly televised or photographed, the hotel name can result in much publicity through local and national news media. It is often necessary to show some goodwill gestures to the TV people so they will compose the scene large enough to include the hotel logo.

## Basic Meeting Setups

A number of basic seating arrangements have evolved. Be sure that your customer is using the terminology correctly. Layout or schematic sheets will help in this area, and the Quick Calculation guide in this chapter will enable you and the meeting planner to ensure that there is enough space for each type of meeting.

**Auditorium or Theater Style.** One of the most common seating arrangements, termed the **auditorium/theater style**, calls for chairs to be set up in rows facing the speaker, stage, or head table. Good for lecture sessions with limited note taking (see Figure 13.7), it is used in both large and small meetings.

To set auditorium style, place two chairs first to position the aisle. The chairs should never be abutted; a minimum of two inches, called the *space*, must be left between chairs side by side. The *distance* is the dimension from a chair to the one in front of it. Minimum distance is 36 inches from chair center to center. When chairs have been positioned to indicate the aisles, the bulk of the chairs can be placed. One-square-foot carpet patterns is the

*Figure 13.7. VARIATIONS OF THE AUDITORIUM STYLE SEATING ARRANGEMENT.*

Straight

Senate

Semi-circular

V-shape or Chevron

Many planners prefer the V-shape or semi-circular rather than the straight setup because more chairs can be placed in the same amount of space and attendees will have a more direct line of sight to the speaker. Aisles are generally four to six feet wide, and, when possible, should align with exit doors. Aisles are required across the front and rear of the room as well as along the sides. When attendance is large, requiring several rows of chairs, cross aisles should be placed for every 15 rows.

Source: Reprinted with permission from *Function Room Set-Up Manual* by Gerhard M. Peter; published by the Hospitality Sales & Marketing Association International.

most popular with hotel people because it helps to align setups. If there is no carpeting, the lines in hardwood floors might guide you.

Aisle sizes and numbers are regulated by local fire departments. If you have any doubts, get the specifications from the fire department. Most regulations call for aisles to be six feet wide if 400 or more people are involved; aisles of four or five feet are sufficient for smaller groups. Double aisles are preferred if the meeting format calls for questions from

## Seating Principles

1. *Avoid center aisles whenever possible.* The center area should be used for seating meeting attendees because it offers the best viewing.

2. *V-shaped and semicircular seating is preferred over straight-line seating.* Angled seating improves sight lines and brings attendees at the outside ends of the rows closer to the speaker.

3. *The speaker should be positioned on the long side of rectangular meeting rooms.* While not as space efficient, placing the presenter on one of the long sides of the room allows the audience to be closer to the speaker.

4. *Plan for quick sets.* A "quick set" refers to how quickly the function space can be set up and rearranged. For example, a general session set at crescent rounds can be more quickly converted into banquet-style seating than a general session set in theatre style.

**Source:** Schoolroom V-shape setup photograph courtesy of Fairmont Hotel Vancouver. From the Fairmont Hotels' Image Gallery.

---

the floor or anything that will result in back-and-forth movement of people or passing of objects such as microphones.

The first row of chairs should be about six feet from the front edge of the head table or platform. The most popular auditorium style uses a center aisle, but many experienced planners avoid a middle aisle because the presenter is facing an empty space. Many planners prefer to divide the seating area into three sections with two aisles of four feet. In larger halls, fire departments may require aisles across the front and back of the room and an additional horizontal aisle halfway down. It pays to check and to keep a record of local fire regulations.

Keep in mind the number of chairs in a row. It is extremely uncomfortable for an attendee to have to make his or her way across fifteen people to find a seat in the middle of the row. Many planners opt for a "mini row" of no more than seven seats. There are variations, but they require more room. One is *auditorium style, semi-circular, center aisle.* You need at least 12 feet from the head table or platform to the front row of chairs. Set the outside chair where you want it. Use a piece of string tied loosely between the two ends of the curved row. Line up the rest of the rows measured from the first one.

*Auditorium, V-shape* (sometimes referred to as a **chevron setup**) sets up similarly; the side sections form an angle to the center aisle. This is an ideal setup if space isn't an issue; by offsetting each row, attendees are not sitting directly behind one another.

Space and distance vary from the norm when armchairs with writing arms are used. Because of the bigger dimensions of these chairs, use three-inch spacing and a 40-inch distance from chair center to center.

When on a dais, regardless of the floor arrangement, make sure that the head tables are draped down to the floor. Place water and glasses at the lectern and on the head table. Use one water carafe for every two people seated on the stage.

New trends in seating arrangements include mixed and tiered seating. *Mixed seating* may include a combination of sofas, chairs, stools, and cubes to enhance a casual atmosphere and draw attendees into the conversation. *Tiered seating*, which is most often used for small meetings, also includes seating of varying heights, with stools placed farthest away from the speaker. Sometimes tall "breakout tables" are placed along the sides and back of the room for attendees who do not wish to sit for the presentation.

## Setups with Tables

A great many meetings and most food functions require tables as well as chairs. Room sets require different types of configurations in order to facilitate communication at meetings. In this section, we will take a look at some of the most commonly used table setups and their variations.

**Schoolroom Style**. One of the most popular setups among both large and small groups is the **schoolroom/classroom style** (see Figure 13.8.). This is the best setup for meetings in which most of the talking will be done by a presenter and attendees will take notes, refer to information in binders, or work on computer equipment such as laptops. It is also the most comfortable design for very long sessions. This setup, however, is not the preferred setup for encouraging conversation among attendees, although it can be used for small group interaction – participants at every other table can turn to face those behind them. In the most common arrangement, people sit on just one side of the table. In such cases, use the 18-inch-deep rectangular tables and, most of the time, allow for a center aisle. Allow about 24 inches of space for each person. However, if attendees will be using binders or laptop computers, allow 2.5-3 feet per person. While this means that a six-foot table will seat only two people, it is better than seating three people uncomfortably (both physically and psychologically).

Schoolroom tables are either six or eight feet in length. Six-foot tables can seat two or three persons per table; eight foot tables seat three or four. For groups requiring space to spread out, the smaller number should be set for each table.

The 30-inch-deep tables are usually too wasteful to use in schoolroom setups because people are seated on only one side. But there are instances when you do have to use them, especially if a great deal of paperwork is to be done. In such cases, allow 60 inches from center of table to center of table. The length of each row depends on the room size and attendance.

The tables should be draped. Place pads and pencils at each setting, plus water pitchers for every 16 persons. You can put a glass at each setting or provide a tray with ten or 12 glasses for every 16 persons. A variation is *schoolroom, perpendicular style*. In this arrangement, the rows of tables are perpendicular to the speaker's table. The 30-inch-deep tables are used because people will be seated on both sides. It is necessary to allow additional room for each person because the seats must be turned somewhat to face the speaker. Allow 30 inches of table space per person instead of 24 for the wide table and 60 inches from center of table to center of table. Tables should be six feet from the head table, with six-foot aisles on both sides of the room and a four-foot horizontal aisle in the center.

Schoolroom setups may also be *V-shape*, off a center aisle. Angled seating improves sight lines and gives attendees a sense of being closer together. Angling the rows to form a herringbone or chevron pattern brings attendees at the outside ends of the rows closer to the speaker. Schoolrom styles may also be set up using round tables. The **crescent-round** setup uses either 60-, 66-, or 72-inch diameter rounds. Seating is used on only one side, so all attendees can face the speaker. This setup works well when the same room will be used for meals and an educational session, and for general sessions in which attendees break into small discussion groups in the same room.

Chapter 13: Function Rooms and Meeting Setups

*Figure 13.8.* THE SCHOOLROOM STYLE ARRANGEMENT AND VARIATIONS.

Straight

Perpendicular

Crescent-round

V-shape

The V-shape schoolroom allows the best sight-lines between attendees and the speaker. If attendees are expected to use laptops, 30-inch-wide tables are preferred rather than the standard 18-inch-wide tables. The crescent-round setup is often used when a planner wishes to follow a meal function with a presentation and desires to keep participants in the same room. Once the meal is finished and tables are cleared, attendees are seated on one side of the round, facing the speaker.

**Source: Reprinted with permission from *Function Room Set-Up Manual.***

Many groups schedule a break if a meeting is longer than two hours. The break should be programmed so that your staff can take the opportunity to **refresh the meeting room**. When the meeting breaks, housepersons should refill ice water pitchers, replace dirty glasses with clean ones, replace soiled or wet linen, straighten all chairs, and pick up all obvious trash on the tables and floor. Such procedures help project a positive image of the hotel.

**U-Shape.** Some smaller meetings require a more face-to-face arrangement, making the **U-shape setup** popular (see Figure 13.9.). This setup is often used for board of directors meetings, committee meetings, and breakout sessions with audiovisual presentations, as all attendees can see the presentation when it is placed at the open end of the U (for optimal learning, group size should be limited to 20-24 people). The U-shape can also be used for banquets, with seating on all sides of the U.

Use 30-inch rectangular tables if people will be seated on both sides. Eighteen-inch-deep tables can be used if only the outsides will be used, but most planners prefer 30-inch-deep tables. The usual per-person allowance is 24 inches, but training and technical groups may need more space (2.5-3 feet per person) if attendees will be using training materials or computer equipment.

Drape the front part of the U all the way to the floor. When the tables are draped, make sure that the crease is straight; it should run continuously along the center of the table.

*Figure 13.9. THE U-SHAPE SEATING ARRANGEMENT.*

Source: Reprinted with permission from *Function Room Set-Up Manual.*

**Horseshoe.** The **horseshoe setup** is just like the U-shape except the head table is connected to both legs with serpentine sections to soften the corners (see Figure 13.10.). The U-shape and horseshoe arrangements are good for board meetings and idea exchange and lend themselves well to audiovisual presentations. The horseshoe and U-shape setups are ideal for training meetings in which the speaker needs access to the participants. These setups allow all participants to see and hear each other, but the size of the group is limited to approximately 24 persons.

**Hollow Square and Hollow Circular.** The **hollow square setup** and the **hollow circular setup** are preferred by meeting planners who want to do away with the head table concept (see Figure 13.11.). This setup, which makes efficient use of space in a room, works best for small groups (up to 30 people) for which there is a facilitator leading the discussion, or for decision-making or problem-solving sessions, as there are good sight lines and the setup is conducive to eye contact between participants. There is also no sense of preferential seating, so there is a sense of equality among participants. This type of setup, however, does not work well for sessions requiring audiovisuals.

## Chapter 13: Function Rooms and Meeting Setups

**Figure 13.10. THE HORSESHOE ARRANGEMENT.**

Source: Reprinted with permission from *Function Room Set-Up Manual.*

Exhibit 13.11 also shows two variations to the traditional hollow square and hollow circular setups. The *octagonal arrangement* is made up of eight tables whose upper left corners are in close proximity to the upper right corners of the next table. The *angled hollow square* setup includes four sets of double tables that face each other on the upper and lower portions and the left and right center sides; a single table is angled between each of the sets of double tables. In both of these arrangements, seating is along the outside edges only.

These setups are formed like the U-shape (using 30-inch-wide tables) except that the open end is filled in. Naturally, chairs are placed only on the outside. The hollow square and the hollow circular are popular for small meetings. Both arrangements should be skirted on the inside and are usually constructed to accommodate up to 30 persons.

**Variations.** The **E-shape setup style** is a variation of the U-shape (see Figure 13.12.). You need about four feet between the backs of the chairs to facilitate traffic. The *T-shape setup* has a head table 30 inches deep. A single leg extends from the center of the head table for as long as is needed. The leg is often set with double tables to make a 60-inch solid rectangular unit.

**Board of Directors.** The **board of directors/conference setup** is a popular arrangement for small meetings. It calls for a single column of double tables making a draped table of 60 inches by as long as necessary (see Figure 13.13.). Allow 24 inches of table space per person. The board of directors arrangement is so popular with meeting planners that many convention hotels have permanent setups with fine wooden tables and deluxe executive-type chairs. Suites equipped with such permanent fixtures are versatile small meeting rooms.

The *board of directors oval setup* is simply the board setup with a 60-inch half-round table at each end of the long table. Chairs may be set at the curved end.

Two relatively new and innovative setups include pod seating and eyebrow pattern seating. **Pod seating** features two long rectangular tables facing each other with three chairs on each side and one at

---

### Quick Calculations

**Theater Style.** Allow 12 square feet per person for groups of less than 60 people; 11 square feet per person for groups of 60-300 (the most common size for a breakout session); and, ten square feet per person for groups of more than 300 people.

**Schoolroom Style.** Allow 22 square feet per person for groups of less than 60 people; 20 square feet per person for groups of 60-300 (the most common size breakout session); and, 17 square feet per person for groups of more than 300 people.

**U-Shape and Horseshoe.** Allow 35 square feet per person.

**Hollow Square and Conference.** Allow 30 square feet per person.

Chapter 13: Function Rooms and Meeting Setups

*Figure 13.11. THE HOLLOW SQUARE, HOLLOW CIRCULAR, OCTAGONAL, AND ANGLED HOLLOW SQUARE ARRANGEMENTS.*

Hollow Square

Hollow Circular

Octagonal

Angled Hollow Square

*These setups are used for groups that do not want a head table concept.*
**Source: Reprinted with permission from** *Function Room Set-Up Manual.*

*Figure 13.12. THE E-SHAPE AND T-SHAPE ARRANGEMENTS.*

*The T-shape arrangement shown here uses a row of two tables for the base of the "T"; the T-shape is also commonly seen with a row of single tables forming the base.*
**Source: Reprinted with permission from** *Function Room Set-Up Manual.*

473

Chapter 13: Function Rooms and Meeting Setups

*Figure 13.13 THE BOARD OF DIRECTORS SETUP.*

*Popular seating arrangement for small meetings shown with its oval variation.*
**Source: Reprinted with permission from *Function Room Set-Up Manual.***

the far end of the tables (the ends closest to the speaker should remain open). This setup is best used for small group discussion and to facilitate presenter interaction with small groups. **Eyebrow pattern seating** consists of two rows of five chairs each that face each other in a crescent shape. This type of seating is ideal for sensitive conversations, debates, in-depth presentations, or viewing a video or film presentation while remaining close enough to engage with other attendees. Diagrams of these seating arrangements are shown in Figure 13.14.

*Figure 13.14. POD AND EYEBROW PATTERN SEATING*

*These two innovative meeting setups are primarily used for small group interaction. Pod seating allows facilitators to walk into the open end of each pod to converse with participants, while the eyebrow pattern gives an intimate feel to the meeting. Both setups provide unobstructed views of screens or lecterns.*

**Round Tables.** *Round tables* (see Figure 13.15.) can be used when meetings break up into smaller discussion groups without leaving the room. Round tables are also used most often for food functions.

Use the design in the carpet or lines in the floor to align the tables in neat rows. Allow at least 54 inches between round tables for chair and service space for banquet setups (see diagram).

Waiters need 36 inches between chairs and walls. Place chairs near the tables and position after the waiters have set the tables. The front edge of the chair should just touch the tablecloth. Afterward, stack the chairs immediately to facilitate cleanup and breakdown.

**Banquet Spacing**

*Figure 13.15. ROUND TABLE ARRANGEMENTS.*

| Diameter | Seats |
|---|---|
| 72-inch diameter | 10 to 12 persons |
| 66-inch diameter | 8 to 10 persons |
| 60-inch diameter | 6 to 8 persons |

*Rounds can be used for food functions and for meetings that break up into smaller discussion groups. Seventy-two-inch rounds seat ten to 12 people. Sixty-inch rounds seat six to eight persons. There are also 66-inch rounds, that seat eight to ten. For greatest comfort, the lesser number of seats is preferred.*
**Source:** Reprinted with permission from *Function Room Set-Up Manual.*

## Breakdown of Function Rooms

After a meeting or party is completed, housepersons should break down the room and clean it. The reason for this is obvious. Business could be lost, or a poor impression given, if a prospective customer saw an untidy meeting room while walking through the convention area.

Chairs and tables need to be stacked. Function chairs probably receive more damage than any other furnishings in a hotel. Housepersons who display more speed than caution in setup and dismantling should be instructed to avoid such carelessness.

If the meeting room isn't scheduled for immediate use, tables and chairs may need to be stored. Storage is a common headache to convention servicing. Hotels unfortunately often do not allot adequate and accessible storage space for function room equipment. Space that is too small or is too difficult to maneuver in shortens the life of the equipment. Furniture that is "forced" into storage is often damaged.

Some properties keep formal control over the location and storage of their equipment. In large convention hotels where the volume justifies it, a requisition system is used for issuing equipment and supplies. An inventory is taken periodically and all articles are locked up when not in use.

## Meeting Rooms of the Future

As we entered the 21st century, dramatic changes were already taking place in how meeting rooms were designed and equipped. Hyatt Hotels, for example, replaced drywall construction with open-structured ceilings in their ballrooms, providing greater versatility as well as faster setup time. In its meeting rooms, the chain installed infrared lighting controls, giving the speaker the ability to make instant adjustments to the lighting system. Distracting noises were eliminated by adding light and sound vestibules between public areas and the actual meeting space, and by creating double walls between the subdivisions of the ballroom to eliminate noises from adjacent meetings. The chain also installed permanent state-of-the-art communications systems featuring fiber-optic cable, Category 5 data cable, and ample telephone wiring.[10]

> **WORTH WATCHING**
>
> Go to www.youtube.com and search for "meeting rooms of the future" to view several videos showing the latest in technology, including ICE (Interactive Collaborative Environment), which allows the use of multiple devices from multiple locations.

Most properties today provide wireless, high-speed Internet access in their meeting rooms – and throughout the hotel (including lobbies, guestrooms, business centers, and even food and beverage areas). While Internet service has been offered for some time, the wireless technology has made accessing such information as exhibit directories, seminar schedules, and other data easier than ever before, and both meeting planners and attendees have come to expect the technology to make their meetings more productive.

Today, it is not uncommon for meeting rooms to have multiple screens for Internet-based presentations and attendee participation. Another innovation is the touchscreen conference table, which allows attendees to view information displayed on the table's top and interact with the presenter and each other.

Another development for meeting rooms of the future is the use of plasma screens. These one- to three-inch-thick, self-contained units will not only change the way in which presentations are made, but will also change the shape of meeting rooms. As plasma screens become the dominant feature in meeting rooms, lighting requirements will change -- and the sizes of the rooms themselves will have to be adjusted to accommodate the new wide screens. Acording to Martin Dempsey, director of the media and business center at the

Scottsdale Conference Center in Arizona, "Ambient light is not an issue with the plasma screen."[11] There is no need to dim lights to see the image.

Other changes cited by architects in the field include changes in table shapes, room decor, and simplifying controls used for presentations. Tomorrow's tables, although they will have the look of heavy wooden tables, will be hollow, light, and easily moved. Rooms will be white or light-colored to provide for better contrast when video cameras are used, while rooms in which plasma screens are dominant can be painted in lively hues. While high technology will continue to play a major part in presentations, it is expected that control panels will become less visible (concealed yet readily accessible). To see a virtual tour of some of these innovations, visit the site of Next Gen Boardrooms (www.ngboardroom.com/features.html).

In terms of room décor, both the wellness movement and environmentally conscious groups have impacted how meeting rooms are designed. More meeting spaces feature natural materials, such as stone or wood, as well as recycled materials, and natural sources of light and energy, including skylights and solar panels, are being increasingly incorporated. Meetings are also being designed to be aesthetically pleasing to attendees with elements that appeal to their senses (see box titled "A Sensory Approach to Meeting Rooms of the Future" to learn about pioneering efforts in this area).

## A SENSORY APPROACH TO MEETING ROOMS OF THE FUTURE

When Omni Hotels set about to craft the perfect meeting room, it wanted to go beyond the three essential elements — proper room temperature, the ability to hear well, and the ability to clearly see the presentation — and create an atmosphere that would provide the type of environment that would ensure that the goals of a meeting were met. To do so, the chain started with a year of research, which included creating a Sensory Advisory Board, staffed by representatives from several high-profile companies (including the Elizabeth Arden Red Door Spa, the Julliard School, and Whole Foods Market). The panel focused on the five human senses to determine which colors, lighting, sounds, scents, and even tastes best contributed to the optimum experience for meeting attendees.

The result was the chain's Sensational Meetings program, which offers customized settings for three meeting approaches: Energetic Meetings, Challenging Meetings, and Recognition Meetings. For **Energetic Meetings**, brainstorming, planning, and training is enhanced by the use of vibrant, high-energy colors and stimulating flavors for meals and break fare. **Challenging Meetings** settings provide a relaxed environment to mitigate stressful points of discussion through the use of subdued lighting and soothing music (and breaks featuring green tea). **Recognition Meetings**, which focus on honoring past success and building on them for the future, are highlighted by upbeat music, vibrant floral designs, decadent champagne truffles, and stimulating scents.

Loew's Hotels has also picked up on the trend, offering the Color Break option that allows meeting planners to theme their meeting rooms — and even food choices — by color. The program is currently available in three color themes: **blue** (representing peace, spirituality, and youth), which stimulates thought and communication; **yellow**, which represents wisdom and happiness — and sharpens memory and concentration skills; and, **green** which represents nature and well-being, to encourages ideas.

The elements of each theme color include wall coloring, color-inspired floral centerpieces, and onscreen color flashes. The color schemes also translate well to meals and break snacks. A yellow theme, for example, would feature a mix of sweet, healthy, and salty foods — personal dishes of pineapple, yellow M&Ms, and potato chips — in individual dishes.

Both the hotels and meeting planners are seeing positive results with the new programs. According to Ellen Burke Van Slyke, former corporate creative director of food and beverage at Loew's Hotels, "The value of color as a stimulant is undeniable. All elements of a meeting room must be in place to create the right mindset."

# Chapter 13: Function Rooms and Meeting Setups

## PUTTING IT ALL TOGETHER

In this exercise, *you* will be using the information that you have learned in this chapter to demonstrate how a property's meeting space can be utilized to its maximum potential. You have been named convention service manager of a hotel with fairly limited meeting space (see diagram below). It is your job to fill this space as effectively as possible, so you have booked a number of functions. On Thursday of next week, your property will be hosting:

1. A morning (9:00 a.m.-noon) training seminar for 50 distributors of a multi-level marketing company. The distributors will need to check in and will receive packets of information before entering the training room. A refreshment break will be taken at 10:30 a.m.
2. An afternoon (1:00 p.m.) press conference for a local official announcing her candidacy for Congress. Attendance is projected to include approximately 20 news reporters, three television crews, and the candidate's key staff of nine people. In addition, the candidate has requested the provision of additional seating in the event the public wishes to attend. She has also requested the availability of floor microphones for a question and answer session.
3. A two-hour afternoon (2:00 p.m. - 4:00 p.m.) meeting of twelve directors of the board of the community's hospital.
4. A local charity's evening fund-raising dinner. A cocktail reception will be held from 6:00 p.m.- 6:30 p.m., with dinner following at 7:00 p.m. Dancing will follow from 8:30 p.m. until midnight. Expected attendance is 300 people. Special requirements include a head table for 20 VIPs and the availability of an area for ticket collection and the viewing of prizes that will be raffled throughout the evening.

The following morning, another training session will be held from 9:00 a.m.-noon, and you will want the room set up before the staff goes on overtime at 1:00 p.m.

1. Which room(s) would be most suitable for each meeting? What factors did you take into consideration in making your decision?
2. What style of seating would you choose for each meeting? Draw up a sample floorplan for each function.
3. Develop sample function sheets that detail the special needs for each function and how these requirements will be met.

Environmentally-friendly practices also include "going green" by eliminating the need for copious amounts of paper. Individual computer terminals are provided for attendees who do not bring laptops or tablets, and laser pointers are often used in place of disposable markers. Many properties have also established recycling programs for paper and other consumables, such as ink and toner cartridges, and have demonstrated their commitment to the environment by offering water only when requested and providing locally produced food and beverage options.

Whatever trends finally emerge as dominant, it is important that hotels keep abreast of the latest innovations but make decisions concerning design and function with the actual needs of the meeting planners they are serving in mind. If a hotel caters primarily to SMERF segments, for example, a large investment in plasma screens and other high-tech gadgets would be a waste of money. Corporate groups, however, would demand the latest in technology.

The InterContinental Toronto Centre is regarded as the most technologically advanced hotel in Canada. The property's two Next Generation Boardrooms, named Conquest and Visionary, offer drop-down LCD projector screens, 60-inch plasma SMART boards, high-end sound equipment, and video web conferencing. Attendees sit in sleek, ergonomic black leather chairs around contemporary oval conference tables that feature recessed "Plug & Surf" high-speed dataports and electrical outlets for each participant.
**Source: Photo courtesy of InterContinental Hotel Group.**

## Monitoring Function Room Usage

It is important to understand the dollar value of function room space. One chain calculated that meeting space cost $.08 per square foot per day when it was not being utilized. In other words, a 10,000-square-foot ballroom costs $800 per day just sitting vacant. To get a handle on function space utilization, it is useful to track and monitor the following:

- Function room occupancy by meal period
- Types of functions
- Use of guestrooms by function groups
- Popularity of individual banquet menu items
- Sales revenue per square foot of function space
- Average banquet check by type of function
- Pattern of unused times and days
- Average number of persons by type of function

Reporting function room statistics can be revealing. While the hotel's function rooms may seem very busy, during certain times of the year only one function per day is often booked in each of the meeting rooms. The data gathered will help you to develop an effective strategy for yield management, which was discussed earlier in this chapter.

## Summary

In this chapter we have taken a look at the various types of function rooms and the setups that are commonly used when servicing convention groups. We have discussed the importance of assigning function rooms for maximum efficiency and revenue, and detailed the factors that should be considered when assigning function room space. We have also seen that the use of function rooms must be monitored to ensure maximum profitablilty for your hotel. In the next chapter, we will take a look at how some of the function room setups we have discussed are used when servicing one part of the convention business: food functions.

## Endnotes

1. Jim Barr, Catering/Convention Service Manager, Sheraton Chicago Hotel and Towers, MeetingMatrix advertising brochure.
2. M. Jill Wien, "Holiday Holds," *The Meeting Manager*.
3. Ibid.
4. Jil Larson, "A Checklist for Function Space Management," Revenue for Hotels blog, posted March 20, 2011.
5. Chris Davis, *Business Travel News*.
6. Information in this section adapted from Sheryl L. Kimes and Kelly A. McGuire, "Function-space Revenue Management: A Case Study from Singapore," *Cornell Hotel and Restaurant Administration Quarterly*.
7. Jil Larson, "A Checklist for Function Space Management," www.hospitalitynet.org, posted on March 4, 2015.
8. *Guide to Function-Room Furniture*, Jacob Felsenstein; King Arthur Incorporated, Pennsauken, NJ.
9. Elaine Yetzer Simon, "Comfort, ease of use help determine seating selection," *Hotel & Motel Management*, April 7, 2003, p. 30.
10. Doug Fox, "Hyatt's Improvements Upgrade Presentations," *Convene*.
11. Justin Henderson, "21st Century Box," *Successful Meetings*, January 2000, p. 20.

# Chapter 13: Function Rooms and Meeting Setups

## Study Questions

1. What is a function room? List the basic types of function rooms.
2. What is mean by the statement: "All public space may be function areas depending on the group and its needs." What other hotel areas can be used to host functions?
3. What factors must be considered in charging a group for meeting space? For assigning meeting rooms?
4. List the basic styles of meeting room setups and tell when each is used. What styles are commonly used for food functions?
5. What is "function room furniture"? What features should you look for when selecting function room furniture?
6. How will meeting rooms of the future differ from today's meeting space?
7. What methods are used to monitor function room space?

## Key Terms

**air walls**—Moveable barriers that usually slide on tracks in the ceiling to divide one large room into multiple smaller spaces. Not necessarily soundproof.

**Americans with Disabilities Act**—U.S. legislation that requires public buildings (offices, hotels, restaurants, etc.) to make adjustments to meet minimum standards to make their facilities accessible to individuals with physical disabilities.

**angled hollow square**—A variation of a hollow square setup, with seating on one side of four sets of double tables angled by placing a single table between each set.

**auditorium/theater style**—Chairs set up in rows facing the head table, stage or speaker. Number of aisles may vary. Some variations are V-setup and semicircular.

**barrier-free**—Absence of obstacles preventing handicapped persons from moving freely to all public areas within a building.

**board of directors/conference setup**—One wide table or series of tables set up in a rectangular shape with chairs on both sides and at the end. Some hotels have permanent board setups featuring expensive furniture and executive chairs. Oval setup is also used.

**breakout rooms**—Smaller meeting rooms used when larger sessions divide into smaller groups for discussions and group work. Usually planners request that these rooms be located near the main meeting facilities. Multiple breakouts can take place simultaneously at some meetings; attendees may rotate through the breakouts to hear different presentations.

**capacity chart**—A diagram that details the specifics of a meeting room, including the name of the space, the dimensions of the room, and the room's capacity in various room setups, including classroom, rounds, boardroom, and so on.

**chevron setup**—Seating arrangement in which chairs are arranged in rows slanted in a V shape facing the head table or speaker (rows are separated by a

Chapter 13: Function Rooms and Meeting Setups

center aisle). Also called a **herringbone set-up** and a **V-shape set-up**.
**cocktail round**—Small round table, available in 18-, 24-, 30- or 36-inch diameters, used for cocktail-type parties. Also called **cabaret table**. For sit-down service, use 30-inch height; use bar height for stand-up service.
**computer-assisted design (CAD)**—A computer program that allows meeting planners to graphically implement meeting room designs and layouts.
**crescent-round**—Seating arrangement in which 60-, 66-, or 72-inch diameter rounds have seats on two-thirds to three-quarters of the table and no seats with their backs to the speaker. It is often used for banquet-to-meeting or meeting-to-banquet quick setups. Also called **half-moon seating**.
**dais**—Raised platform on which the head table is placed or where people stand while speaking to an audience or performing.
**day package**—A special package created for groups that will be utilizing the hotel only during daylight hours. A day package is often the most economical option for meetings that do not require overnight accommodations, as they typically include a single price per attendee for the entire day — the price is inclusive of all food and beverage, rather than having meals and breaks broken down.
**E-shape setup style**—Tables set in the shape of an E with chairs on the outside of the closed ends and on both sides of each leg.
**employee procedure manual**—Instructions for employees to do specific jobs. Often includes illustrations or drawings. Helps ensure consistent setups.
**ergonomic**—Furnishings, especially tables and chairs, specifically designed to provide maximum comfort and alertness in a conference environment.
**eyebrow pattern seating**—Contains two rows of five chairs each that face each other in a crescent shape. It is an ideal formation for sensitive conversations, debates, in-depth conversations, or viewing a video presentation or film, as attendees can engage with each other without having to move around.
**floor plan**—A scaled diagram of the size and arrangement of a room, including both permanent and temporary objects and fixtures.
**function room turnover time**—The amount of time needed to tear down and reset a function room.
**function rooms**—Rooms specifically designed to house meetings or social gatherings.
**head table**—A table, often elevated on a dais or stage, used to seat VIPs, speakers, and other dignitaries.
**hold all function space**—Blanket hold on all available space in a facility without specific meeting or function rooms named.
**hollow circular setup**—Same as horseshoe setup except both ends are closed; chairs placed on the outside.
**hollow square setup**—Tables set in a square with a hollow middle; chairs placed only on the outside.
**horseshoe setup**—Similar to U-shape style; set in the shape of a horseshoe. Chairs can be placed around both the inside and outside.
**lectern**—A reading desk used to hold the speaker's papers. Either rests on the floor (full size) or on a table.
**octagonal setup**—A hollow setup using eight tables whose upper left corners are in close proximity to the upper right corners of the next table. Seating is on the outside only.
**open sale period**—Period of time during which catering is free to sell function space due to projected slow convention business (catered events would not be

## Chapter 13: Function Rooms and Meeting Setups

likely to displace convention groups needing meeting space).

**pod seating**—A seating setup with two long rectangular tables facing each other and three chairs on each side and one at one end (the open end should face the presenter). Best used for small group discussion as well as presenter interaction with small groups.

**pre-function space**—Area adjacent to the main event room; used to assemble attendees prior to a function. Often used for receptions prior to a meal or for refreshment breaks during an event.

**quick set**—Function room setup that saves turnover time, limits the function rooms required, and eliminates additional charges for changing room setups. Examples include the use of round tables for lunch and dinner functions in the same room and the use of a classroom-style setup for both morning and afternoon sessions.

**reception style**—A room setup designed to encourage the flow of traffic to enable participants to mix and mingle. Usually consists of high-top tables placed throughout the room, and limited or no seating is provided (if chairs are used, they are usually placed along the perimeter of the room).

**recognition meetings**—Meetings held for the purpose of honoring past successes and building on them for the future. Typically festive events, featuring awards presentations, guest speakers, and possibly entertainment to motivate attendees.

**refresh the meeting room**—Clean a room after or between meetings (refilling water pitchers, changing glassware, and other general housekeeping).

**release date**—Date when the hotel or conference facility will require the meeting planner to designate final space needs and release any unneeded space back to the facility.

**rounds**—Circular banquet tables, usually 60 inches (152 centimeters) in diameter (also available in 66-inch and 72-inch — 168- and 183-centimeter — sizes). The 60-inch diameter table provides place settings for up to eight people; the 72-inch size for up to ten people.

**schoolroom/classroom style**—Tables six feet by 18 inches are lined up in rows on each side of a good-sized center aisle. All tables and chairs face the head table. Variations are the V-shape and perpendicular style. Classroom is usually set at two or three people per six-foot table or three people per eight-foot table. Tables are usually draped with a tablecloth.

**serpentine**—Curved, S-shaped tables that make a snake form when placed together.

**24-hour hold**—A hold on a meeting room that gives the group sole, continuous access to the room 24 hours a day. Typically requested when the group wants to keep the existing setup for the duration of the meeting (such as having an audiovisual or production setup that can't be torn down each day).

**U-shape setup**—Tables set up in the shape of the block letter U; usually used for small meetings. Chairs are placed on the outside of the closed end and on both sides of each leg.

**velcro**—Brand-name special tape with loops and fabric that is used to adhere table drapery.

## Industry Profile

## Gene Meoni, General Manager - Hospitality

**The Darden School Foundation**

After his graduation from Johnson and Wales with a degree in Food Service Management and Culinary Arts, Meoni began working at the Waldorf Astoria in New York City. Over his more than two-decade career, he has served as director of food and beverage for the Grand Traverse Resort Village in Michigan, the Hershey Lodge in Pennsylvania, the Stein Eriksen Lodge in Park City, Utah, and the Homestead Hotsprings in West Virginia. He is currently employed by the Darden School Foundation, which supports the Darden School of Business at the University of Virginia; the school and the university operate the Inn at Darden.

## Planning Food Functions

The catering/convention services department is the most profitable division of any hotel food and beverage operation – provided the proper planning, controls, service, and creativity are utilized for each event, be it a refreshment break for twenty or a five-course gala dinner for a thousand guests.

The most exciting aspect of catering for me is the development of menus for a property. Banquet menus should be varied in selection and price range to meet the needs of your market segments. Menus should include regional specialties, property specialties, and upgraded menus that were executed for past events. Your ability to customize menus for each group, which is a trend in today's marketplace, will enhance the success of your operation.

When developing customized menus, a skilled catering/convention services manager will take a team approach. The kitchen and service staff must be involved in creating the menu to offer assistance regarding product quality and availability, product cost, staffing, room size limitations, equipment, production limitations, and service limitations. Remember, when you promise products and services to a group, you must deliver, which makes the menu development phase paramount to your success.

When planning meetings, conventions, or catered events, you must utilize the controls planned to guarantee service to your guests and the profitability of your operation. Function sheets (BEOs) for food and beverage products and services must be detailed and specific, as they will become your contract with the meeting/event planner. Your _guarantee policy_, charges for set up, meeting room rental, additional staffing, and any other information to be communicated to the client must be contained in the BEOs. If attendance is under guarantee, the catering/convention services manager must hold the planner to the guarantee. Catering is very profitable, and the guarantee policy is a control to guarantee that profit. At the time of the event, food and beverage product has been purchased and front and back of the house staff have reported, so if lower revenue is received due to a group being under guarantee, your profit will certainly be affected.

When setting up for a convention, meeting, or catered event, organization and pre-planning are necessary for a successful execution. The catering/convention services manager must obtain complete information regarding all events and communicate this information to the operational staff. When dealing with experienced planners, the CSM's role will be to answer questions, offer suggestions, and discuss information provided; inexperienced meeting planners will require assistance on a larger scale – they will depend on the CSM and the creativity of his or her team to develop a memorable event.

**Learning Objectives:**

This portion of your text introduces you to the various types of food and beverage functions typically held at a convention hotel. When you have studied this chapter, you will:

- Know the different types of banquet food service and understand both the service and control issues related to banquet food functions.

- Be able to describe several types of beverage service and explain how beverage service is billed.

- Be able to describe service and control issues related to beverage functions.

- Be able to describe post-function activities for food and beverage functions and understand in-house coordination at both large and small properties.

**Outline**

Food Service
- Types of Food Functions
- Themed and Special Events
- Off-premises Catering
- Changing Tastes
- Types of Service
- Chef's Tastings
- Pricing Food Functions
- Attendance
- Attrition
- Function Rooms
- Control Procedures
- Staffing
- Uniserve or Duoserve

Beverage Service
- Types of Setups
- Hospitality Suites
- Brands
- Pricing Methods
- Beverage Control

Post-Function Actions

In-house Coordination: Large vs. Small Properties
- Role of the Catering Manager
- Servicing and Selling
- Communication and Cooperation

Summary

# 14 Food and Beverage Service

Food and beverage functions have always played an important part in meeting and convention programs, but the "traditional" food and beverage options of past years, such as the choice between one chicken and one beef entree at a banquet or simply providing an urn of coffee and hot water for tea for meeting delegates, have been replaced with new choices that add variety and excitement to meetings and conventions (see box titled "Latest Food and Beverage Trends").

These changes have resulted from the public becoming more knowledgeable about food and beverages and meal presentation, thanks in part to such food personalities as Emeril Lagasse and Rachel Ray.

Professor Robert "Bob" Briggs of the Culinary Institute of America in Hyde Park, New York, says:

> People are reading culinary magazines, watching the Food Network, taking cooking classes, traveling, and becoming much more food savvy in recent years.[1]

The result is that attendees have higher expectations regarding the food and beverages served at their meetings or conventions, they are more willing to experiment with new foods, and they expect attractive presentations. Hotels are responding to their demands with creative menus, including incorporating local specialties into meals and staging themed functions, and offering alternate food and beverage options.

The Hyatt chain, for example, has led the way in several service trends. George Vizer, former vice president of food and beverage for the Global Hyatt Corp., says:

> We are trying to create a restaurant-quality dining experience in a banquet setting. Having a banquet doesn't have to mean that you have servers in a banquet setting with large service trays, distributing food in an institutional manner. Instead, servers come to the table and introduce themselves to the guests. They recite the menu. They announce what wine they're pouring. So that there's interaction with the guests, just as you find in a restaurant setting.[2]

This concept is part of the chain's Personal Preference Menus for banquets (see box titled "Hyatt's Personal Preference Banquet Menus"). The concept allows planners of groups from 20-2,000 to select one appetizer, a salad, and a dessert, and to choose three entrees from a selection of six. Banquet attendees are served the pre-selected appetizer and salad, but then opt for one of the three entree choices (a vegetarian entree is also available).

Both meeting planners and hoteliers are well aware that food and beverage functions can make or break the meeting. A well-run, interesting program takes a backseat to the quality and attractiveness of the food and drink provided during the meeting. Even if attendees have enjoyed a guest speaker or an interesting workshop, the element that will stand out most is the food; if it was unsatisfactory or unappealing, that, unfortunately, will be remembered – and discussed – long after the meeting is over. Attendee satisfaction, on the other hand, means more attendees at an organization's next function – and repeat and word-of-mouth business for a hotel that makes food and beverage functions memorable. In this

## LATEST FOOD AND BEVERAGE TRENDS

Years ago, foods and setups available for meetings were generally unimaginative and predictable. Banquet attendees, for example, were all usually served the same dish (or possibly a choice of chicken or beef), buffet tables were typically square and skirted, while banquets were set at round, skirted tables, and refreshment breaks usually consisted of sugary pastries and the choice of coffee or tea.

Today's food and presentation methods are a far cry from that standard fare. As attendees have become more health-conscious and food savvy, the old "stand-bys" have become a thing of the past. New food and beverage trends, which we will be discussing in greater detail in this chapter, include:

**Presentation** — The skirted buffet or banquet table is fast becoming a relic, and yesterday's round banquet tables are being replaced with clean, exciting looks. At the Four Seasons Hotel Philadelphia, for example, elegant, unskirted tables are put together in a variety of ways, while Hyatt Hotels & Resorts opts for an assortment of benches, ladders, and stainless steel tables to add atmosphere to the function.

Even the presentation of the food has changed. At buffets, chafing dishes are rapidly being replaced by woks, paella pans, cast-iron skillets, heated bricks, and marble slabs, while other foods are presented on risers or as part of an elegant display or edible centerpiece. Today's banquets now rival fine-restaurant dining, with attendees being offered a menu of entrées from which to choose, and other options, such as mini-meals and tasting stations, are replacing traditional sit-down dinners. The Harbor Castle Westin in Toronto promotes tasting stations as an opportunity for attendees to mingle as well as try a variety of bite-sized foods.

**Food and Beverage Options** — Today's meeting attendees are both food savvy and health-conscious, and hotels have responded by offering **organic foods**, low-fat foods, low-carb choices, sugar-free options, and foods prepared with no trans-fats or corn syrup. And not only is fresh food preferred, attendees want smaller portions of healthy foods — and a wide choice — making such options as tapas, dim sum, and mini-desserts popular. Also popular are "trendy" foods, such as sushi, "spa cuisine," and "bad foods with good ingredients" (blueberry muffins, zucchini bread, carrot cake, pumpkin pie, and banana nut bread instead of sugary doughnuts and Danish).

Dolce Hotels and Resorts emphasizes nourishment with such break offerings as fresh fruit and vegetable juices, vitamin water, fruit, yogurt and granola bowls, small salads, and interactive juice bar stations, while the Hilton Suites Phoenix offers interactive F&B stations featuring made-to-order juice beverages blended for each guest, stations for custom-made salads, and "Fire and Ice" bars with cold stations (chefs preparing sashimi) and hot stations (chefs cooking up spicy Cajun-style fare).

**Other Innovations** — Other innovations in the F&B industry include online banquet menus and the "customization" of banquet events. Rarely do today's meeting planners order strictly off a pre-printed menu; they prefer to work with a hotel or convention bureau's catering staff to create "signature events" using local regional fare.

### WORTH WATCHING

View a video of Dino Michael, director of global restaurant development for Hilton Worldwide, describing the difference between food trends and fads and highlighting how technology may be applied to food and beverage events at hedtalks.connectplusathiltonworldwide.com/#s-HgPV-cZo6kA (or search for Hilton Elevated Discussions, click on the "Creating Experiences" tab, and scroll down to the "Food and Beverage Trends" video). In the video following this one, he discusses "Sustainable Food & Beverage."

chapter, we will discuss the various types of food functions typically staged for meetings and conventions, and detail how creativity and communication play important roles in successful functions ranging from simple refreshment breaks to elaborate, themed events.

## Food Service

Banquets, parties, and other business or social functions involving food and beverage can produce additional, often high, revenues for your hotel. Bill Carlin, former managing editor of *Nation's Restaurant News*, states:

> Banquets are the most profitable area of hotel food and beverage operations.[3]

Successful banquets can contribute greatly to overall profitability, because the profit margin on sales for banquets often runs 35-40 percent, as opposed to 10-15 percent for hotel restaurants. There are several reasons for this difference:

- In convention-oriented hotels, banquet sales volume often exceeds restaurant volume by as much as two to one.
- Banquets allow flexibility in pricing. A New York steak dinner priced at $60 on the restaurant menu may bring $85 on the banquet menu. The justification for this difference is the cost of setting up and tearing down the banquet area and also the short time allowed for serving a large number of people in one seating.
- Food costs are lower for banquets due to volume preparation and no large inventory is required, since ordering can be done as needed and all attendees normally receive identical meals.
- Beverage profits are high because beverage costs are easily controlled and revenues are greater because of pricing flexibility.
- Labor costs are significantly lower because banquet servers and bartenders are often part-time employees used on an as-needed basis. The cost of restaurant employees, in contrast, is largely fixed, because a regular staff must be maintained - even during slow periods.
- Employee productivity is high, since staffing levels can be set for a predetermined, guaranteed attendance.

It is therefore very important that the hotel build a relationship with the planner as early as possible. Astute CMS or catering directors should get the meeting planner and the facility's chef together no later than the site inspection. The chef can detail favorites of other groups, explain what seasonal items are likely to be available, and work with the planner to develop cost-cutting menus. The latter can involve using the same ingredients in creative ways, using cheaper cuts of meat in more elaborate dishes, and creating customized menus for the group.

While this process often saves money for the planner, that doesn't mean that hotel profits will suffer. These early planning stages provide excellent opportunities for hotel staff – the CSM, catering manager, and chef – to upsell. A planner who can save money in one area, such as on wine for an event, may opt to choose to spend those additional dollars on an upgraded dessert or creative refreshment break.

Some planners are not bound by tight budget restraints. A catering department can increase revenue by providing innovative opportunities for planners to experience what the hotel has to offer. If a planner is more concerned about having a memorable welcoming reception, for example, the catering department can set up a sample of what it has to offer in that area (food, setting, and atmosphere). Other areas to consider are adding additional staffing for more personalized attention to attendees, offering more elaborate presentations instead of a simple buffet, and upgrading beverage service (creating a "make your own Mojito" bar, for example).

## Types of Food Functions

Meetings may call for breakfasts; luncheons; dinners; dinners with entertainment and/or dancing; refreshment breaks; bars; receptions; buffets; and continuous hospitality setups in suites, meeting rooms, or exhibit halls. Gene Meoni, who contributed his expertise to the opening of this chapter, says that banquet menus should be varied in selection and price range to meet your market segments. Menus should include regional specialties, property specialties, and upgraded menus that have been executed during past events.

Meoni states:

> As our guests become more informed regarding nutrition and the negative impact on health caused by some foods, clients are more interested in healthier foods. Meeting planners are arranging healthy breakfasts by use of continental breakfasts containing the traditional breakfast pastries along with healthier muffins, fruits, yogurt, and granola. Full breakfast buffets are also utilized with enhancements that will give guests a choice of traditional or healthy items. Creative refreshment breaks emphasize stretching, yoga, juices, nonalcoholic specialty drinks, and health bars.
>
> Lunches are lighter, and most dinner menus offer both a fish or vegetarian selection as an alternative to the beef entrée. Some studies prove that there is a greater alertness and retention in seminars when lighter, more nutritious meals and/or breaks are offered to guests.

In designing your group menus, your presentation is just as important as the choices you offer. Begin by collecting sample menus from other properties to glean ideas you may

---

### 🖥️ INTERNET EXERCISE

Log on to the websites of the hotels listed below and review their banquet menus:

- Westin La Paloma Resort —
  lapalomaresortandspa.westinemenus.com
- The Palms Hotel & Spa —
  www.thepalmshotel.com/meetings/catering-menus
- Fairmont Hotel Vancouver —
  www.fairmont.com/hotel-vancouver/meetings-weddings/banquet-menus

1. How well do each of the menus reflect the menu guidelines presented in the chapter?

2. Which hotel's menus do you feel are most appealing to meeting planners? Why?

3. What service charges does each hotel impose?

Chapter 14: Food and Beverage Service

> ## HYATT'S PERSONAL PREFERENCE BANQUET MENUS
>
> In response to the increased emphasis on updating meetings cuisine, the Hyatt chain introduced its Personal Preference Menus for banquets, which allows attendees to choose their own dinner entrees, just as they would in a fine-dining restaurant.
>
> Troy Wood, former director of catering and convention services at the Hyatt Regency Tamaya Resort & Spa in Santa Ana Pueblo, New Mexico, stated:
>
>> Often our client is planning grand closing dinners or special occasions as a part of the booking, and that's when Personal Preference Menus are a perfect fit. When we discuss Personal Preference Menus with our clients, the first response is, "Wow, can you do that?"
>
> The concept works as follows:
>
> - The meeting planner selects one appetizer and one salad that will be served to each attendee.
> - The meeting planner chooses three entrees from a selection of six. At their table, attendees may pick from these three entrees or choose a vegetarian option.
> - A dessert sampler is also included.
>
> Helen S. Pollard, CMP, director of conventions & meetings planning for the American Association of Nurse Anesthetists, is enthusiastic about the program:
>
>> At our big lunches or galas, you always have people who won't touch the food — people who are allergic to seafood, or won't touch meat, or just will eat chicken. Our population is so varied, something like the Personal Preference Menus is appealing.
>
> Not only do Personal Preference Menus for banquets offer unique selections that appeal to food savvy attendees, the experience itself rivals that of a fine-dining restaurant. Eye-catching four-color menus are presented to each guest, and, once waiters explain the concept to attendees, the appetizer course is served. Bread is served between the appetizer and salad, giving the kitchen staff enough time to prepare the entrées. The final course, a trio of three elegantly presented desserts, caps off the "fine dining" experience.

want to incorporate into your own design. Be sure to use detailed descriptions and colorful illustrations, when possible. If your budget is limited and you can't afford expensive graphics, you can still get your point across with mouth-watering word images (words such as "melt in your mouth," "piping hot," "savory," "flaky," and so on create a word picture – and a desire to purchase).

Be sure that your menu conveys your image – and generates sales – by following basic design elements, such as an attractive cover, an appealing design format, and an easy-to-read layout. Menus should always be printed on a good, quality paper stock. Dark ink on ivory or cream paper stock gives a more "cultured" look. Pages should not look cluttered – always allow plenty of white space between items and columns. Don't forget contact information – always include your property's logo, name, address, telephone numbers, and e-mail addresses. An original copy (not a photocopy) should always be presented to meeting planners (the only exception to this rule is sending menu information to a meeting planner via fax, e-mail, or text message).

Two other types of food functions held in conjunction with beverage service are **refreshment breaks**, which are increasingly being called **energy breaks**, and cocktail **receptions**. Refreshment breaks, which take place between meeting sessions, are generally offered for 30 minutes at mid-morning and mid-afternoon. Ideally, breaks should be set up in a room adjacent to the meeting room. If this is not possible, beverages and/or food items can be setup in the hallway or lobby outside the meeting room (you will want to ensure that any setup required will not disturb the meeting program) or brought to the meeting room itself. Serving carts or portable tables can be used outside the meeting room, or the items can be carted outside the meeting room and wheeled in when the person in charge of the group gives a signal for the food service staff to enter (see box titled "Refreshment Break Guidelines").

Refreshment breaks generally include such beverages as coffee, tea, soft drinks, and bottled water, and usually feature various light food items. A break between morning sessions, for example, may include muffins, low-fat yogurt, and fruit in addition to beverages. Serving heavy, sugar-laden foods may lead to attendee sluggishness, especially between afternoon sessions. Receptions are usually stand-up social functions that bring attendees together to socialize, and they may be held at various times during a meeting program. Sometimes, there are welcoming receptions for attendees; other receptions precede a meal function (this ensures that all guests are in the same place before a sit-down dinner), or receptions may be held to enable attendees to socialize with outside participants, such as vendors, outside sales representatives, and so on.

---

### Refreshment Break Guidelines

1. Prices for breaks may be quoted per person or on a consumption basis.
2. Space stations so bottlenecks are kept to a minimum.
3. Open stations farthest from the main entrance first to draw people into the room.
4. Separate coffee and soda stations.
5. Identify each hot beverage with a sign.
6. Lay out stations for quick service: coffee cups, followed by regular coffee, decaf, tea bags, and hot water. Accessories, cream, sugar, sweetener, and spoons should be available on a separate table a short distance from the beverage station.
7. Set one beverage station per 75 to 100 attendees.
8. Staff one server per 100 people for refreshment breaks; one server per 50 people at receptions and buffets.
9. Figure 20 six-ounce cups of coffee in a gallon.
10. "Marry" (combine) coffee stations toward the end of the break.

#### REFRESHMENT BREAK ESTIMATES FOR 200 PEOPLE

| | A.M. | | P.M. |
|---|---|---|---|
| Coffee | 65% x 200 = 130 cups = 6.5 gals | Coffee | 35% x 200 = 70 cups = 3.5 gals |
| Decaf | 30% x 200 = 60 cups = 3 gals | Decaf | 20% x 200 = 40 cups = 2 gals |
| Tea | 10% x 200 = 20 cups = 1 gal | Tea | 10% x 200 = 20 cups = 1 gal |
| Soda/Water | 25% x 200 = 50 drinks = 50 sodas | Soda/Water | 70% x 200 = 140 drinks = 140 sodas |

## Chapter 14: Food and Beverage Service

At most receptions, beverages, usually including alcoholic beverages, and light foods, often **hors d'oeuvres** (hot or cold finger foods) and **canapés** (hot or cold appetizers with a bread or cracker base), are served. Foods may be presented on small buffet tables or passed by servers.

When presenting foods in a buffet style, keep in mind that easy access to food results in greater consumption. Figure 14.1 details how different types of buffet setups affect the amount of food that would be required for a reception. If a planner has a limited budget or simply wants to ensure that the food he or she has ordered lasts through the event, you should suggest the round buffet or 180-degree buffet arrangements.

*Figure 14.1. SAMPLE RECEPTION BUFFET SETUPS.*

**Round Buffet**
If you're using this buffet for hors d'oeuvres, it has no beginning and no end for lines to form naturally, so it actually helps limit consumption. This type of buffet setup, used as more of an elaborate display with height (i.e., fruit, cheeses, or vegetables), is an attractive and elegant addition to a reception.

**180° Buffet**
Buffets with only 180° access are useful in limiting or minimizing consumption. If a budget is limited or insufficient for comfortable/unlimited hors d'oeuvres, then this type of buffet setup can help the food last for a longer period due to reduced access.

Food access = 7-8 pieces per person with plates and 5 pieces per person without plates (napkins only).

**360° Buffet**
This buffet provides convenient and fairly easy access to food, thereby increasing consumption.

Food access = 8-10 pieces per person with plates and 6-8 pieces per person without plates (napkins only).

The physical layout of a reception buffet controls access to food, therefore limiting or expanding the amount of time that food lasts. This chart details how much food can be expected to be consumed per person using the three most common reception buffet setups, enabling you to assist a meeting planner in deciding which setup to use and how much food to order for the event.
**Source: From the *Experient Guide to the Food and Beverage Experience*, sponsored by Hilton Hospitality, Inc., and published by Hammock Publishing. Used with permission.**

The cocktail reception with hors d'oeuvres should create a festive atmosphere, so many receptions include music, dancing, and entertainment. There should also be plenty of room to allow attendees to socialize (as a rule of thumb, allow seven to ten square feet per attendee and provide seating for 25 percent of attendees). Not only do these activities put attendees in a good frame of mind, they also serve as distractions that will cut down on reception food consumption (this not only ensures that attendees will have room for dinner if the reception precedes a meal, but also helps the meeting planner's budget).

To assist meeting planners in ordering food for receptions, the following guidelines have been developed:

| | |
|---|---|
| Dry snacks | 1 ounce per person |
| Anchor foods (cheese, vegetables, fruits) | enough for 1/3 of attendees |
| Action stations (carving station, pasta station) | enough for 1/2 to 2/3 of attendees |
| Passed hors d'oeuvres | 1 of each for all attendees |
| Dessert and coffee | enough for 1/3 to 1/2 of attendees |

Source: From the *Experient Guide to the Food and Beverage Experience*, sponsored by Hilton Hospitality, Inc., and published by Hammock Publishing. Used with permission.

Keep in mind that many guests at receptions enjoy sampling every item. Therefore, encourage meeting planners to order at least one piece of every item for each attendee. For a reception for 500, for example, it is wiser to order 500 pieces of three types of hors d'oeuvres rather than 250 pieces of six different types. If the planner wants more variety, the menu can be supplemented with less expensive items, such as cheese and crackers, chips and dip, and vegetable and fruit trays.

Two basic methods are used in charging for hors d'oeuvres and **finger food**: by the person per hour, and by the bowl or tray. Figure 14.2 shows these two methods.

Each function should be dealt with separately to make sure of details. A banquet event order should be filled out for each event, listing all the information needed for smooth execution.

*Figure 14.2. PRICING CATERED ITEMS.*

### Canapés and Hors D'Oeuvres

**No.1: $12.50 per person**

**Hot**
Grilled Cocktail Franks, Mustard Sauce
Swedish Savory Meatballs
Knishes
Chinese Egg Rolls
Butterfly Shrimp, Cocktail Sauce

**Cold Canapes**
Savory Cheese Spread, Pimento
Cornets of Imported Genoa Salami
Smoked Nova Scotia Salmon
Deviled Eggs with Anchovies

**No. 2:**

**Cold Canapes**
Large Tray...$98.50
(Serves approximately 25 persons)
Medium Tray...$78.00
(Serves approximately 15 persons)

Selection: A variety of Assorted Cold Canapes, including Stuffed Eggs Moscovite

*This hors d'oeuvres menu shows two methods of pricing: by the person per hour and by the tray or bowl. While the eating habits of groups may vary, the industry standard for a two-hour reception is eight pieces per person for the first hour and four per person during the second hour.*

## Themed and Special Events

Every meeting planner tries to do something different at each event. Most conventions have a high percentage of people who repeatedly attend, so planners often want to "add a new twist" to the program, from adding flair to the cocktail party to staging a themed banquet.

Experienced meeting planners disguise the same old cocktail party by introducing a different theme each year. **Themed events**, both large and small, are very popular and are remembered by the attendees. In addition, themed events do much to enhance the reputation of the hotel. One event service manager states:

> Theme parties are frequently used, and as a catering/convention services manager, you should be prepared to offer assistance to planners in the form of services and ideas. The catering/convention services manager should have resources available for the planner, including florists, prop companies, theme companies, and entertainment agencies. You should become acquainted with services and pricing from each outside vendor to ensure successful pre-planning with the meeting/event manager. As part of your annual budget, you should designate a dollar amount to be utilized to purchase your own inventory of props. Be sure to keep up on the latest themes and increase/upgrade your inventory annually. The purchase price will be returned in rental income passed along to your clients.

**WORTH WATCHING**

View a video of on-site and specialty events at Starwood Hotels and Resorts at www.youtube.com/watch?v=qFtPnPuJq88 (or go to www.youtube.com and search for on-site specialty events at starwood hotels & resorts).

The focal point of any such function is the menu, and hotels that offer several different types of themed menus are a step ahead of the competition. There are many themes that can be effectively executed, even if the meeting planner has a limited budget. An "Old Mexico" theme, for example, can offer taco bars, a chili bar, an interactive fajita bar, and chips with salsa and guacamole. Not only are most of these menu items inexpensive, but it also takes time for guests to assemble a taco, which greatly cuts down on the amount of food consumed. Other low-cost themes include a State Fair or Fourth of July theme (featuring traditional, low-cost foods such as hot dogs, hamburgers, and so on) and a Western theme (beef stew served from a "chuck wagon," or typical barbecued foods).

If you are in a locale that offers unique cuisine, consider featuring a locally grown themed menu. In Calgary, for example, themed "local" menus might include Alberta beef, caribou, lamb, salmon, halibut, or goat cheese. Amy Johnson, former director of catering and convention services at the Hyatt Regency Calgary, says:

> One of our biggest sellers right now for banquets is venison.[4]

At a recent event, Johnson served Alberta venison and wild mushroom soup in an acorn squash, veal wrapped in an Alberta potato, and a Canadian cheese platter. These menu items were an excellent way to introduce delegates to the "flavor" of the destination.

The menu should be served in creative ways that will enhance the theme. **Action stations** featuring costumed chefs, for example, are more memorable than having a guest simply choose from pre-prepared dishes on a buffet table. A chef wearing colorful garb as he or she makes fajitas at an Old Mexico event, or dressed as a cowboy while preparing cooked-to-order steaks for a Western-themed party, are just two examples. Costumes for servers can also add to the atmosphere, as can creative decorations and entertainment. Incorporate the theme into your table and serving ware; use clay dishes and colorfully decorated serving platters and bowls for a Mexican theme, tin plates and cups at a barbecue, and so on. The theme should also be reflected in table and wall decorations and lighting (paper lanterns for an Oriental theme, or torches for a Hawaiian luau, for example).

## Chapter 14: Food and Beverage Service

Many decorations and other enhancements, such as bubble machines, fog machines, and other "effects," are inexpensive and can be easily stored for future functions. Themed props may also be obtained at low or even no-cost from such sources as vendors (most beverage vendors can supply "game themed" props, such as Super Bowl decorations or NASCAR posters), travel agencies, and airlines (good sources for travel posters). If you have requests for unusually themed events, it can be cost-effective to work with outside sources and rent props needed for special functions.

When you have developed functions that work well, these can easily be promoted to other groups. Some properties and chains, such as Fairmont Hotels & Resorts, offer brochures promoting their popular themed events. Brochure pages detail the setting and decorations for the event, the food and beverages that will be served, entertainment provided as part of the function, and "extras," such as a fireworks show to end the evening. Themes range from a Mexican party (complete with a performance of the Mexican Folkloric ballet) to a Bohemia Party to a Las Vegas Night.

*Action stations featuring chefs serving or carving food are more memorable than having a guest simply choose from a buffet table.*
**Source: Photograph courtesy of Loews Hotels and Resorts.**

This type of promotional material (as well as photographs taken during past events) is a great help in selling other business. If you have successfully staged themed events, clients will likely respond to your suggestions. This is especially true if you can offer not only the expertise but also the other elements needed to stage such an event. While planners usually love themed events, many have budget constraints or need help with stimulating their thinking. When you help meeting planners stage events that guests remember long after the meeting or convention, everyone benefits. The guests have a memorable experience and meeting planners have the confidence to book more, bigger, and better events with the hotel, which can look forward to both future repeat business and word-of-mouth bookings resulting from satisfied planners and guests.

In addition to themed events, meeting planners may also want to include other **special events** in their programs. These functions, which are primarily social in nature and are generally celebratory, can range from receptions for attendees, VIPs, and speakers to elegant, black-tie **gala dinners** that include gour-

> **MORE ONLINE**
>
> Marriott's Meetings Imagined is another program designed to help meeting planners and hotel CSMs to collaborate on creative events. Search for Marriott's Meetings Imagined or go to www.meetingsimagined.com to view the Inspiration Gallery that shows hundreds of ideas for setups and food and drink options. Meeting planners are encouraged to share photographs from their own successful functions on the site.

met food, music, dancing, other entertainment, and awards presentations.

No matter what type of event is planned, the property's food and beverage department will play a major role in making it a success. That means offering special foods and beverages, perhaps serving the food more elegantly (served by waiters in tuxedos, for example), and creating a setting that gives the event the "flavor" desired by the meeting planner.

A property's food and beverage department is critical for the execution of special events. While some hotels have an in-house special events manager and can provide a vast inventory of linens, serving ware, and so on, many hotels work closely with destination management companies (DMCs) or special event companies that are hired by the meeting planner. These companies may be better able to work with specific vendors or arrange for off-site locations, such as private homes, clubs, and golf courses for the function.

## Off-premises Catering

In addition to servicing functions in-house (known as **on-premises catering**), a great many hotels and restaurants are turning to **off-premises catering**, — preparing food and/or beverages for events away from the hotel,— to boost food and beverage revenues. While some events are held on the grounds of a property or restaurant, these are still serviced directly by the hotel's on-premises kitchen(s). With off-premises catering, food must be either partially

### Best Practices

*Fairmont*
THE QUEEN ELIZABETH
MONTRÉAL

### Off-Premises Catering:
### Fairmont The Queen Elizabeth, Montreal, Quebec, Canada

The 1,039-room Fairmont The Queen Elizabeth in Montreal generates $1.6 to $1.9 million annually with its off-site catering department, which brings in almost 18 percent of the hotel's total food and beverage revenues. The service, which began when the hotel began catering meals to one nearby office building in 1976, now handles some 300 events a year, which translates into 130,000 to 140,000 covers.

Formerly under the direction of longtime director of outside catering, Armando Arruda, the department prepares a variety of cuisine, including Canadian, continental, and French dishes. Most of the food for the off-site events, which range from continental breakfasts to high-end gala dinners, is prepared in the hotel's kitchen, which is manned by 80 chefs. For some events, the food is finished in off-site kitchens. Although outside help, including wait staff, is sometimes hired for large events, the hotel maintains quality control by employing its own chefs.

*Head Chef Pignard*

In addition to providing food for corporate events, the Fairmont also caters a number of off-premises functions, such as fund-raising or award dinners, for hospitals, art organizations, and other groups.

Other Fairmont hotels, such as the Fairmont Pallister in Calgary, Alberta, and the Fairmont San Jose in California, also offer off-premises catering at venues that range from large barbecues at Calgary's rodeo grounds to intimate dinners on private jets.

or fully prepared in the hotel's kitchen and then transported to the site of the function or fully prepared at the event site.

Off-premises events can be held at a local attraction (in Dallas, some events are held at the Southfork Ranch, where the *Dallas* TV show was filmed, for example), or at other venues, such as a fund-raising dinner at a museum, an opening reception at an art gallery, or at outdoor locations. The location of the event will be an important factor in determining both the menu and the method of food preparation.

Before a hotel or restaurant gets into the off-premises catering business, it is important to determine the feasibility of such an operation. Off-premises catering can be an expensive proposition. Mobile kitchen equipment and other equipment, such as portable furniture and decorations, may have to be purchased. Since off-premises catering may be seasonal in some locales, storage would have to be arranged for equipment not being used on a regular basis.

Some hotels opt to partner with local venues or work with destination management companies to get the maximum value from off-premises catering. In some cities, hotels can partner with unique local venues, such as art museums, historic theaters, or public gardens, or a reception facility (such a facility usually stocks its own furniture and props; all the hotel or restaurant would have to do is provide the food and/or beverages). Destination management companies can help with such off-site arrangements as equipment, decorations, entertainment, and other services.

Revenue potential can also be maximized by preparing menus that are both cost-effective and easily prepared and transportable. A barbecue menu can easily be executed at local parks or other facilities, for example, or a property may opt for catering only one or two types of events, such as receptions or buffet breakfasts, off-site.

Yet another creative option is to use *food trucks* to provide unique offerings both off-site and on-site. When the JW Marriott Los Angeles hosts L.A. LIVE events, for example, it creates an authentic experience by bringing in food trucks with such diverse offerings as Mexican food, Korean BBQ, burgers and sliders, and even vegetarian and vegan dishes. While these trucks were parked outside at the Marriott (and can be used at remote locations as long as electrical outlets are available), other hotels have brought them inside as part of a themed event.

The benefits to using food trucks are that they are unique and offer a wide variety of foods. In addition, guests can interact with the chef at each truck and place custom orders. Food truck operators benefit by having a steady flow of customers over a specific time, rather than having to rely on the hit-or-miss foot traffic inherent to busy streets.

Hotels can make revenue from this option in several ways: some simply charge for space and electricity; others receive a portion of the profits made during the event; or, a combination of the two may be contracted. The hotel also benefits by not having to staff its own chefs and servers, and clean-up is minimal since each truck is responsible for its area.

## Changing Tastes

Banquet menus should reflect meeting attendees' desire for a more healthful diet. People are increasingly conscious that the food they eat and the way it is prepared has an impact on their overall health. Hotels have responded by offering lighter, low-cholesterol items and providing alternative menus for attendees with dietary or religious restrictions. These menus may offer vegetarian, gluten-free, and lactose-intolerant substitutes, and offer choices that reflect the latest dietary trends (see box titled "The 'Greening' of Banquets").

Ruth Butler, CMP, CMM, manager, meeting & event operations at Experient, says:

## Chapter 14: Food and Beverage Service

### The "Greening" of Banquets

Healthy, natural food is becoming more important to both meeting planners and attendees, and many hotels are responding to this trend by offering organic foods, including locally-grown produce that is free from pesticides and chemical fertilizers; and beef, chicken, and other meats that have not been injected with anabolic steroids, antibiotics, and growth hormones.

The Fairmont Hotels & Resorts chain was the first hotel company to commit to using sustainable, locally sourced and organically grown products as part of everyday food service operations whenever possible. Serge Simard, former vice president of food and beverage for Fairmont and now general manager of the Fairmont the Queen Elizabeth and regional vice president, Eastern Canada, says:

> Our guests are very savvy, experienced diners, and they also are becoming more conscious of how their consumer choices affect the planet. We want our guests to know that when they dine at Fairmont, not only can they count on the very best, freshest ingredients and a true experience of the destination through their culinary choices, there will always be a range of sustainable options for them to consider.

Other hotels and chains offering organic choices include the InterContinental Chicago, which promotes "Green Menus" that are anchored by local vendors who supply products that are organic and cruelty-free in addition to being locally grown. The chain reports that their green menus now account for approximately 50 percent of their event business, and other properties, including the Walt Disney World Swan and Dolphin Resort, have also introduced organic banquet menus.

Buying local produce isn't always an option for some properties, especially those in arid climates. Some hotels, such as The Boulders Resort & Spa in Carefree, Arizona, have responded by creating their own gardens. The 5,280-square-foot garden at The Boulders not only supplies the property's restaurants and spa café, but has also become a refreshing event space for small groups. Some hotels have to resort to having organic produce shipped in, and some of their choices may be limited — it may be impossible to serve range-free chicken to a large group, for example.

Keeping costs reasonable is another concern. Organic produce, for example, may be ten to 50 percent higher (although the average is 25 percent) than traditionally farmed fruits and vegetables, and the cost of free-range chicken and grass-feed beef may be prohibitive. The key is to offer as many organic, locally-grown products as possible to appeal to health- and environmentally-conscious meeting planners and attendees.

*Rooftop herb garden.*
**Source: Photograph courtesy of Fairmont Royal York Hotel, Toronto, Ontario, Canada.**

The low-carb craze has really hit. All the meeting and event managers in our office are dealing with it.[5]

The Sheraton chain has responded to the low-carb trend by introducing Lo-Carb Lifestyle, the most extensive line of low-carb food offerings in the hotel industry. Also, four senior chefs from Hilton Hotels Corporation attended an extensive three-day nutrition course at Johnson and Wales University. Upon their return, they created a roster of recipes geared toward low-carb dieters and people with diabetes.[6] New York-based Loews Hotels responded to the trend with its "No Carb-tails" drink menu, which includes such libations as diet-friendly daiquiris and vodka-infused green tea,[7] while Marriott has a program called Fit for You, and Renaissance offers Eat, Drink, and Balance.

**MORE ONLINE**

- Go to westinwellbeing.starwood promos.com/eat-well to learn about the chain's partnerships with Super Chefs™ and The Juicery to offer healthy alternatives for food and beverage functions.
- You can view information about Fairmont's Lifestyle Cuisine Plus Menus at www.fairmont.com/promo tions/lifestyle-cuisine-plus/. A video is also available at www.youtube.com/watch?v=cpMTsVyRBr0.

The biggest change in eating habits has occurred at breakfast. Meagan Kiessling, conference manager for Alcoholism & Substance Abuse Providers of New York State in Albany, New York, says:

> Low-carb and protein are definitely playing a larger role in menu planning, particularly with breakfast. There is almost no point to adding a continental breakfast for your group without at least two low-carb options.[8]

Eggs, potatoes, bacon, and sausage have given way to a variety of lighter, health-conscious offerings such as whole grain muffins and rolls, low calorie yogurt, fresh fruits, and low-fat dairy products. Hot oatmeal, cooked wheat cereal, and shredded wheat are very popular alternatives to traditional breakfast fare. Lunches and dinners have also become less formal. Diet-conscious attendees appreciate extensive salad bars featuring fresh vegetables and low-calorie dressings. Poultry, fish, veal, and lean pork entrees, grilled rather than fried, are popular with fitness-conscious attendees. Heavy meals promote sleepiness, so many meeting planners desire to offer attendees moderate portions and food groups that are high in protein (see box titled "Catering Menus Feature 'Brain Food'").

Today, new technology is being used to assist planners in making their decisions — and to improve the quality and variety of food and beverages offered to meeting and function guests. Sheraton's "Sheraton Cuisine," the umbrella name for the chain's hotel kitchen software, provides colored pictures of the 365 dishes offered in its "Cuisine of the Americas" menu, along with the recipes and a breakdown of the nutritional content of each entrée. Scott Geraghty, former director of culinary services for the Sheraton New York Hotel Complex, is enthusiastic about this program and its next phase, which calculates nutritional content after substitutions have been made. He states:

> A catering manager will be able to sit down with a meeting planner, call up a color picture of what a plated dish would look like, and make substitutions like: "What would this dish look like with carrots instead of zucchini?"[9]

Refreshment breaks no longer require doughnuts, Danish, and other sugary bakery items. Health-conscious participants know that simple sugars provide few nutrients and play havoc with the waistline. Fruit juices; flavored mineral waters; yogurt; muffins; fresh

## Catering Menus Feature "Brain Food"

Today's "brain food" movement is based on the concept that diet plays a pivotal role in a person's alertness and intellectual performance. These two factors are of utmost importance to meeting planners, who want their attendees to get the most out of their programs, but this trend is also being embraced by other diners who want to remain at their best throughout the day.

One of the leading proponents of the "brain food" concept was celebrity chef Jamie Oliver, who worked with Europe's Scandic Hotels to eliminate serving foods that are heavy and carb- and sugar-laden at meetings; they have been replaced with soups and slow-release energy foods, such as complex carbs and lean meats. Major U.S. hotel chains are also rethinking traditional meeting foods. The Hyatt chain, for example, uses fewer sugars and white flours and more whole grains, fiber, and protein to keep meeting attendees sharp. Marriott International is focusing on more complex carbohydrates, whole grains, fruits, vegetables, and anti-oxidants in its meal and refreshment break offerings. Omni Hotels & Resorts introduced menu items designed for "energetic meetings," "challenge meetings," and "recognition" meetings into its Sensational Meetings program.

At Loews Coronado Bay Resort near San Diego, California, former executive chef Mark Leighton Ching developed a Brain Food luncheon menu that offers a balance of foods that provide a "slow burn" throughout the afternoon. Chef Ching says, "You want a balance between carbs and protein and enough of the right fats to satisfy the appetite. Metabolic satisfaction comes from fats, ideally healthy fats, and if there's a balance, energy is released slowly and consistently."

His menu starts with organic heirloom bean soup and features such dishes as smoked salmon flatbread, chicken almandine, rosemary-orange flank steak, roasted cauliflower and Brussels sprouts, and steamed broccoli; desserts include vanilla panna cotta with blackberry jam, dark chocolate banana bread pudding, and mini fruit cocktail martinis. The menu eliminates "sugar highs" and crashes – and their inherent aftereffects of decreased cognitive ability and focus.

Other foods that are known for their brain-boosting benefits include such breakfast choices as oatmeal with walnuts and honey, yogurt with fresh fruit, whole-wheat waffles or pancakes, bran or oat muffins, and vegetable omelets on whole-wheat English muffins. Satisfying – and balanced – lunch choices include light salads, vegetarian whole-grain wraps, roasted chicken, salmon, and brown rice dishes, such as Chef Ching's brown rice lettuce cups with dried blueberries, dried cherries, bleu cheese crumbles, and red cabbage with an acai-banyuls vinaigrette.

### WORTH WATCHING

Go to www.meetings-conventions.com/Hot-Ideas/Food-and-Beverage/VIDEO—Help-Yourself or search for Video: Help Yourself: Meetings and Conventions to see a video of healthy foods offered by the International Association of Exhibitions and Events at their annual Expo! Expo! convention in Los Angeles. The energy-boosting spread featured bowls of nuts, wasabi peas, and dried fruits that the attendees could scoop into individual, disposable bowls as well as fresh fruit that could be eaten as a fruit salad or taken to a nearby station to be made into smoothies.

## INTERNET EXERCISE

Experient, one of the leading independent meeting planning firms, provides a wealth of information for both meeting planners and meeting suppliers, including hotels, convention and visitors bureaus, and conference centers. Log on to the home page of Experient (www.experient-inc.com), and then go to "Knowledge Center." Click on "Experient Publications" and then "Guide to the Food & Beverage Experience" to download the guide (registration is required). Read through the guide to answer the following questions:

1. Explain the difference between break packages and consumption breaks.
2. Discuss planning guidelines for food and liquor for receptions.
3. Explain the benefits of a banquet ticket exchange.

fruits such as pineapple, melon, and strawberries; plus decaffeinated coffee and hot tea are popular items. One conference service manager tells us that today's meeting breaks also feature such healthy options as fresh vegetables, nuts, power bars, and other foods "that can help to keep the brain power going during the day." Because of this growing health-conscious trend, many hotels now market **energy breaks** instead of refreshment breaks.

## Types of Service

An important planning decision is the type of service to be used at food functions. The kind of banquet service selected influences pricing, staffing, and the overall effect of the function.

**American/plated service** is the most common form of banquet service. The food is assembled in the kitchen and waiters deliver plates to the tables. Cold food may be plated ahead of time and stored in refrigerators. Hot food is plated just prior to delivery and is sometimes served from a number of stations set up in the kitchen. Guests are served food from the left and beverages from the right. All items are picked up from the right at the end of the course. Plate service requires the least skill on the part of the service personnel.

With **Russian service**, all food is fully prepared in the kitchen and courses are served to the guests directly from soup tureens, platters, or an escoffier dish by waiters working in teams. While Russian service, also called *platter service*, requires more space between tables to enable waiters to move freely, as well as a larger, skilled labor force, it is an efficient way to control portions, as waiters place a pre-determined amount of food in the bowls or on the plates of guests.

**French service**, also called *cart or tableside service,* is generally used only for small groups, but also requires sufficient space between tables for waiters to move about freely. More experienced waiters are required for this type of service, as much of the food is prepared tableside on a gueridon (rolling cart).

**Pre-set service** is frequently used for luncheons where fast service is needed. The first course of soup, salad, or appetizer is set on the table prior to the guests' arrival; occasionally the dessert may also be pre-set. While pre-set service works well when the schedule is tight, pre-set food is rarely as attractive as food delivered in courses during the meal.

**English/family-style service** is similar to Russian service, as food is brought to the table on a platter or tray. In most cases, the food is presented to the host, who either cuts the main course himself or herself or chooses to have it done by the server away from the table. Vegetables and other accompaniments are placed in bowls or other serving dishes on the table, allowing the guests to serve themselves.

**Buffet service** is a presentation of several food items from which the attendee makes a selection. Buffet service is efficient because a large number of people can be served in a short period of time with a small serving staff. Since buffets can be more expensive to serve than plated meals, because there is no portion control and surplus food must be ordered to ensure adequate amounts of offerings, hotels may suggest several alternatives to the "traditional" unlimited buffet. These choices can include *attended buffets*, at which guests are served by chefs or attendants (this not only offers better portion control, but is also more elegant), *combination buffets*, in which inexpensive items, such as salads, are presented buffet style and expensive items, such as meats, are served by an attendant for portion control, and *plated buffets*, at which a selection of pre-plated foods is set on the buffet table.

**Butler service** is sometimes used at receptions or upscale dinners. At receptions, servers circulate with trays, from which guests help themselves. At formal dinners, food is presented on silver trays, and serving utensils are offered to allow guests to help themselves from the tray.

Another trend in food functions is **à la carte catering**, which offers more options to both planners and diners. Under the à la carte system, catering departments develop menus offering two or three items from which guests can choose, or unique combinations of entrées to suit more palates (a *combination* of meat and seafood or creative vegetarian entrées, for example).

Just as Hyatt introduced its Personal Preference Menus for banquets, mentioned earlier in this chapter, the Marriott chain has made extensive use of à la carte catering, even offering seated guests a menu to give more of a sense of fine dining. The Peabody Orlando,

*Butler-style service, such as this example of hors d'oeuvres being passed on silver trays by waiters wearing white gloves, conveys an upscale atmosphere.*
**Source: Photograph courtesy of Jumeriah Hotels and Resorts.**

which has offered a choice between beef and chicken for some time, has extended its à la carte service to include duo and trio entrée choices in its regionally-oriented banquet dishes (such as jerk chicken and Caribbean-style pork). Karl Edlbauer, corporate executive chef of the hotel, explains:

> The clientele is looking for more upscale menus that are daring, but with a classical presentation.[10]

## Chef's Tastings

In order to enable planners to sample banquet dishes so they'll know in advance how the food will look and taste, many hotels offer a "tasting dinner," also called a **chef's tasting**. A chef's tasting is especially important to meeting planners who are staging larger, unusual events or one that is extremely important, such as a board dinner.

Chef Gordon Marr, food and beverage director at the Washington (D.C.) Hilton Hotel, recommends that the tasting meal be an exact replica of the banquet meal and that it should approximate meal service. Figure 14.3 shows a sample tasting given by the Grand Hyatt New York.

Chef's tastings can take place at two crucial times during the meeting planning process. Some planners opt for a tasting shortly after they have selected the menu. This gives them the opportunity to talk with the chef to let him or her know what they hope to achieve with the banquet. Chefs can then come up with other inventive ideas to enhance the experi-

*Figure 14.3. CHEF'S TASTINGS.*

*The elements of a tasting firsthand at the Grand Hyatt New York by* Convene *staff members Jamie Roberts and Michelle Russell. They were joined by Grand Hyatt staff James Dale, senior director of catering; Chef Arbeeny; Jerry Perez, executive sous chef; Ricardo Morales, banquet captain; and Chris Reed, sous chef. Terry Dale, formerly of NYC & Co., sits next to PCMA's Peter Shure.*
**Source: Reprinted with permission of** Convene, **the magazine of the Professional Convention Management Association, www.pcma.org ©2005. Photo courtesy of Grand Hyatt, New York.**

ence for attendees. Planners may also schedule tastings one or two weeks before the function to enable them to experience seasonal foods that may be on the menu.

Hotels do not charge for chef's tastings, but properties sometimes limit the number of attendees. To be fair to the venue, attendees should be directly involved in the function. Therefore, attendees would include the meeting planner and such executives as the executive director of an association or the program chairman of a group event. Some hotels also allow one or two guests to attend, but it is more cost-effective if these guests will have direct input into the meeting (a board member who will be attending a function, an actual attendee, and so on).

## Pricing Food Functions

Many convention planners prefer to complete all negotiations in detail before signing the letter of agreement. Some even want to go so far as to select menus and agree on prices. A planner would prefer this because it makes budget projections so much easier. But with conventions planned years in advance, it is not possible for a hotel to make exact quotations.

Most hotels will gladly say what they charge for menus currently in use, feeling that this is a sufficient guide for meeting planners. There is obvious danger in pricing a menu so far in advance. Most meeting planners with any experience at all realize that any such agreements may have to be modified because of rising costs. If you examine the currency values of the past fifty years, you see constant inflation. When the spiral goes up sharply, everyone recognizes the inflation, but in reality there has been a steady curve upwards over the years.

You must be very careful when you have to make price guarantees for dates several years ahead. Most hotels have adopted a policy of quoting room rates not more than one year in advance and firm menu prices not more than six months before the event. Some hotels even quote a more restricted policy. For example, an Orlando-area Marriott's contract reads:

> *Menu prices cannot be confirmed more than 60 days prior to the function due to the daily fluctuation of market prices. The organization grants the hotel the right to make reasonable substitutions on the menu to meet increased market prices or commodity shortages.*

You cannot avoid such a policy unless you have no need to be competitive and can build in a fat reserve in your quotations. But few of us have such prerogatives. To be competitive, you figure prices closely and cannot absorb inflationary additions to cost.

You will find some exceptions, but most meeting planners understand such limitations and are concerned about unduly squeezing a hotel. After all, each event is a custom production and the planners are concerned with the quality of what they will receive. If they *are* obliged to set an early price on tickets, they understand that a flexible attitude on the menu can enable them to carry out the meal function while allowing the hotel a fair profit. Some astute meeting planners attach a copy of the hotel's current menu to the contract and specify that prices cannot be raised "more than X percent per year" over current prices.

All agreements on menus, prices, and terms must be made in writing and signed by both parties. This eliminates misunderstandings.

## Attendance

The planner initially will estimate attendance at a food function. This is vital, as it indicates the scope of the event. The figure is only for preliminary preparations, and must be reviewed.

The convention planner owes it to the facility to keep it informed of the closest possible estimates of attendance at each food event. The planner may not know for sure, but a time will be set by which a firm guarantee must be given in order to prepare for the event.

Properties doing banquet business face the problem of determining a fair and workable **guarantee** policy. A typical guarantee clause might read:

> *In order to best serve your guests, a final confirmation of attendance or "guarantee" is required by NOON, three (3) business days prior to your meal event. The guarantee is not subject to reduction after the 72-hour deadline. If no guarantee is received, the hotel will charge for the expected number of guests indicated on the Banquet Event Order (BEO) or the original contract, whichever amount is greater. The hotel will set 5% over the guarantee for all food functions with less than 500 attendees and 3% for all groups exceeding 500 guests. Guests arriving over and above the guaranteed number may be served an alternate menu.*

The convention service manager can assist the planner in determining banquet attendance figures by suggesting that there be a **ticket exchange** and reserved seating for the *final* banquet, which is usually the most cost- and labor-intensive function. A ticket exchange is a control procedure that requires attendees to exchange a coupon from their registration packet for an actual event ticket and a reserved seating arrangement for the final gala banquet. The attendee typically turns in the ticket shortly after registering. Using this method, the planner can set a reservation deadline that falls during the meeting but still within the hotel's deadline for a head count.

No one policy is applicable to all hotels or all situations. However, the Hospitality Sales & Marketing Association International surveyed a number of hotels and found that most adhere strictly to their guarantee policies. Those surveyed stressed the importance of explaining the guarantee and working with the planner to set a realistic attendance figure.

Most hotels require a guarantee either 48 or 72 hours before a food function. The meeting planner then agrees to pay for the guaranteed number of people whether or not that many appear. If 200 people are guaranteed for luncheon at a per-head charge and only 185 show up, the organization will pay for all 200. It is a touchy situation, but the obligation is clear-cut.

What happens when more show up? The experienced planner will ask that places be set for more than the guaranteed number; an **overset safety margin** of three to five percent is common. It is to the advantage of both the hotel and the convening group to avoid last minute scrambling with chairs, tables, and place settings.

Often the guarantee is included in the function sheet and is signed by both the hotel and a convention representative. Any agreement between the hotel and client is binding. If the guarantee calls for 200 and the hotel agrees to set for 5 percent over, the hotel sets tables and chairs for 210. If 210 show up, all is in readiness and the bill indicates 210. If 230 show up, the hotel is allowed to substitute 20 meals of a quickly prepared item.

Another guarantee method suggested by meeting planners, but seldom used, is to guarantee only labor. If only 185 of the guaranteed 200 showed up, the association would pay for only the cost of one waiter and not the extra fifteen meals prepared. Obviously, a hotel should never consent to this unless the extra meals can be used somewhere else.

## Chapter 14: Food and Beverage Service

The organization must designate, in writing, who is authorized to make changes in attendance estimates, menus, and prices. A guarantee sheet (see Figure 14.4) summarizing the functions and the guarantees for each day is printed daily and distributed to appropriate staff.

*Figure 14.4. GUARANTEE SHEET.*

### The Durham Resort
### Guarantee Sheet
### For February 8, 20_

| Time | BEO # | Room | Func. | GTD | Set | Sources | Post As |
|---|---|---|---|---|---|---|---|
| 4:00A-4:00A | 121 | Madison | EXHB | 25 | 28 | DJ/AO/JH/CH | Kopykat Sales |
| 7:00A-9:00A | 378 | Monroe | BMTG | 150 | 165 | AO/AO/JH/JH | Auto Travelers Assn |
| 7:00A-9:00A | 127 | Grant | BMTG | 100 | 110 | DJ/DJ/AO/AO | Auto Travelers Assn |
| 7:00-11:00A | 382 | Ballroom J | RECP | 200 | 220 | KZ/KZ/JH/JH | Kopykat Sales |
| 7:30A-8:00A | 352 | Ballroom J | CONT | 50 | 55 | AO/AO/JH/JH | Kopykat Sales |
| 8:00A-4:00P | 482 | Ballroom A | EXHB | 20 | 22 | ML/ML/MW/MW | Auto Travelers Assn |
| 8:00A-6:00P | 482 | Ballroom A | EXHB | 20 | 22 | DJ/DJ/AO/AO | Auto Travelers Assn |
| 8:00A-6:00P | 371 | Webster | EXHB | 20 | 22 | AO/AO/JH/JH | Auto Travelers Assn |
| 8:00A-12:00P | 487 | Coolidge | REG | 20 | 22 | AO/AO/JH/JH | Auto Travelers Assn |
| 8:00A-5:00P | 877 | Washington | GS | 80 | 88 | DJ/DJ/AO/AO | Kopykat Sales |
| 10:30A-4:30P | 472 | Jackson | MTG | 75 | 85 | JH/JH/DJ/DJ | Kopykat Sales |

*This computer printout lists all food functions on a particular day. Copies of the form are generally distributed to the executive chef, banquet chef, executive steward, food and beverage controller, function book coordinator, banquet manager, and convention service manager.*

## Attrition

Hotels must be certain that the food and beverage revenue generated by a group can support the amount of space required for the event. Increasingly, hotels are using clauses that deal with attrition and/or cancellations to protect themselves. Attrition is the difference between the actual number of food and beverage covers consumed and the number agreed to in the contract between the meeting planner and the hotel. When hotels book a piece of business, they often base the room rate quoted to the group on a **food and beverage minimum**; that is, the amount of food and beverage and the meeting room rental anticipated. Typically, hotels look at the type and size of functions planned for the convention, put a dollar value on each one, add up the numbers, and then allow about 20 percent of that number for attrition (slippage). The resulting number is the minimum amount the group is expected to spend on food and beverage and meeting room rental. If the group fails to spend this amount because of poor attendance or the need to cancel banquets, the attrition clause in the contract allows the hotel to collect damages for lost profits.

A typical clause might read:

> **WORTH WATCHING**
>
> Rick Tedrick, chief financial officer of the NRA Foundation, explains how gathering and sharing years of F&B and ancillary spending data results in better contract negotiations for both meeting planners and hotels (especially for city-wide conventions), at hedtalks.connectplusathiltonhworldwide.com/#-d0k-vaHNAZA (or search for Hilton Elevated Discussions, click on the "Driving Results" tab, and scroll down to the "F&B Ancillary Spend Negotiation" video).

*The Hotel is relying on, and the Group agrees to provide, a guaranteed minimum of 80 percent of the total anticipated food and beverage revenue ($_____). If Group's total actual food and beverage revenue slips below this amount, Group agrees to pay as liquidated damages (agreed not to constitute a penalty) the lost profit on the food and beverage revenue; 30 percent of the difference between the agreed minimum and the actual total food and beverage revenue. Group also agrees that, with respect to guaranteed functions, Group will pay the greater of (1) actual attendance or (2) the guaranteed attendance, with the revenue from such payments counting toward the satisfaction of Group's minimum total food and beverage revenue commitment.*

## Function Rooms

The type of function room to be used for a food event depends on the nature of the session, its location in relation to other functions and the hotel traffic flow, and the kind of seating arrangement desired. Pay attention, too, to the decor, lighting, and other decoration requested. And, thought must be given to heating and cooling controls.

All these factors must be considered when the convention service manager sits down with his or her counterpart in the convention organization to select a room for the function. Priorities may dictate that the most suitable room go to another event, but any room used for a food function must be able to provide satisfactory results.

A reminder is in order here to note the time it takes to set up the food function room and clean it up afterward. It is important to know whether the cleanup noises will disturb the meeting session going on next door. It may not be possible to avoid such proximity, but it shouldn't come about because no one thought about it. The clash of silver and china can be most distracting at a serious meeting and can reflect on the hotel's image.

On one occasion, the Salvation Army had a meeting scheduled next door to a luncheon for the governor of Hawaii. As the governor was presenting his opening remarks, the Salvation Army opened its meeting in the traditional way with a song to the resounding beat of the bass drum. Needless to say, the hotel's convention service manager gave greater consideration to a group's program after this incident.

## Control Procedures

Most food functions are charged on a per-head basis. Every hotel should devise a **head count** procedure to determine the actual number of **covers** (meals) served. Guesswork has no place in banquet billing. The charges should be agreed to in writing, and the menu selection should be indicated.

Many meeting planners prefer to use coupons or tickets. The meeting delegates at registration are issued a coupon book with tear-out tickets for each function. There is need for caution if this system is suggested. Here are the two most common methods of ticket collection:

*At the door* — A table should be set up with a representative from the association and one from the hotel there to collect tickets.

*At the banquet table* — In this case, the waiter collects the tickets. This can be a touchy area if delegates do not have their tickets. A common delegate response is, "I left my ticket in my room." This is a difficult situation to police; if the hotel is paid for only the tickets collected, the waiter is forced to refuse service. Hotel personnel should be instructed what to do if a conferee shows up without the proper ticket.

Counting the dishes expected to be used in advance is another method of determining the number of covers served. The chef or convention service manager then counts the number of dishes that were not used and subtracts this from the first figure. Perhaps the best system is to simply count the people seated. The convention service manager and the meeting planner should both take counts. This should be done immediately after the entree has been served.

Some food functions, such as refreshment breaks and hospitality centers, obviously cannot be charged in this way. Spell out clearly the formula used. You may charge for coffee by the cup or by the gallon, fruit juice by the gallon, Danish pastry by the piece or by the tray, and so on.

Some canny sales managers will give away hors d'oeuvres or favors. In such cases, it enables them to close the deal at higher rates for rooms or meals. Psychologically, the practice may make for a better presentation; economically it may represent less than the price advantage. In addition, the higher rate will bring in a further dividend should more people attend. The buffet and hors d'oeuvres are fixed costs on your part, while the higher rate for additional guests adds to your profit.

Small food functions are often tagged with additional charges. If the function is not large enough to cover labor and setup costs, hotels frequently add on to the bill. Figure 14.5 provides an example of banquet labor and miscellaneous charges.

## Staffing

Hotels generally provide more waiters per guest as the price per cover increases. The minimum wait service for standard plated dinners is one waiter per 20 guests (at rounds of ten, one waiter per two tables; at rounds of eight, two waiters per five tables). French and Russian service generally require one server for every ten guests. For buffet meals, the standard is one wait staff to 40 persons for breakfast and one wait staff for 30 persons at lunch and dinner. The minimum bus staff is one for every three waiters. If the menu calls for wine service poured by wait staff, the minimum is one waiter per 16 guests.

Pre-meal briefings should be conducted before all large banquets by the **banquet captains** (one banquet captain should be staffed for every ten to 12 servers). Menus, special service requirements, station assignments, and other pertinent items should be reviewed.

*Figure 14.5. MISCELLANEOUS FUNCTION CHARGES.*

### Banquet Labor and Miscellaneous Charges

A. Waiter Labor Charge...........$50.00
   All functions with less than 20 guests

B. Overtime Charge, Waiter...$18.00/hr
   Breakfast over 2 hours
   Lunch over 3 hours
   Dinner over 4 hours

C. Service Charge $20.00/extra table
   For setting less than 10 covers per table

D. Carver (Chef).............. $60.00/hour
   After 2 hours

E. Housepersons............$18.00/hour
   4 hours minimum

F. Early Setup of Banquet
   Rooms........$18.00/hour per waiter
   Prior to meal functions

G. Porter....................$120.00/8 hours
   If no food functions and meeting room complimentary

Hotels frequently add on to the bill if the food function is not large enough to cover labor and setup costs. In addition to the charges listed above, it is common for properties to apply a flat service charge to food and beverage functions under a certain size (typically 25 people or less). In some cases, labor and charges are waived entirely or based on the total dollar amount spent on the function. Any specifics negotiated should be clearly spelled out in the contract.

The setting up and service of the head table should be assigned to the captains. Special attention is paid to silverware, glasses, and proper arrangement of place settings.

Finally, the times for serving must be carefully controlled. The salad course typically takes about 20 to 30 minutes, the entrée about 30 to 50 minutes (from serving to the removal of plates), and desserts can usually be handled in 20 to 30 minutes. Normally, complete service takes about 1½-hours for a lunch and about two hours for a dinner event. Keep in mind, however, that a more elaborate function will take additional time, so staff accordingly.

It is necessary to adhere closely to scheduled meal times, so extension of cocktail parties should be kept to a minimum. Meal functions should also run on schedule. Not only are some attendees reluctant to attend a catered event that will run over two hours, but an overly long event may also give the impression that there is something wrong with the catering department.

## Uniserve or Duoserve

The food and beverage service is generally handled in one of two ways by hotels. In a **uniserve** system, the meeting planner makes all arrangements for both function space and food and beverage through one service contact, the convention service manager. In this system the banquet/catering department reports to convention services.

With a **duoserve** system, the food and beverage responsibilities are separated from the scheduling of function space. In this case, meeting planners must work with the banquet/catering department for their food and beverage requests and with the convention services department for their function room needs. When the duoserve approach is used, the banquet/catering personnel generally report to the food and beverage director. As we indicated earlier, most meeting planners want to deal with only one contact person at a hotel. The assistant director of convention services at the former Sheraton Tucson El Conquistador (now the Hilton Tucson El Conquistador Golf & Tennis Resort) makes a strong case for

## Should Hotel Catering and Convention Services Departments Be Combined?

by Nora May, Assistant Director Convention Services at the former Sheraton Tucson El Conquistador (now the Hilton Tucson El Conquistador Golf & Tennis Resort)

"UNISERVE" — the word used by the Sheraton Tucson El Conquistador to define a manager who specializes in catering AND convention services.

When it was announced that our hotel would be switching to the Uniserve concept, there was a definite concern that arose in my mind on how a person could "do it all!" After all, in my experience as assistant catering director, catering alone took all of my time, including my personal family time, and now they want to add to my responsibilities? It seemed almost impossible.

Several years have passed since the Uniserve concept was put into action, and there is no doubt in my mind that this is THE BEST way to run the business. The positive aspects of this concept outweigh the negative aspects. As a matter of fact, I can't think of a negative aspect. These are the positives:

1. **Efficiency!** The meeting planner benefits from working with just one person. It simplifies the job. Plus it saves on communication time for the meeting planner and the Uniserve convention service manager. When working the split method, oftentimes I would get little notes on my desk from convention services that said something like, "Spoke with ABC Company on the phone. They want to add a continental breakfast to the meeting on Monday." It is incredible how much time it takes to find out exactly what this message means. Which meeting? There are three breakouts and a board meeting scheduled. How many people? First you go to the convention services person to obtain more details, and usually you have to call the client to confirm. Uniserve eliminates this type of time waste.
2. **Control!** As a sole person handling all of the group's conference requirements, one has a grasp of the whole picture. The Uniserve CSM is responsible for every detail of the conference.
3. **Rewarding!** Opportunities and challenges continuously arise prior to a group's conference and during the conference. There is no getting around the problem-solving issues that tend to keep our blood flowing in the hospitality industry. That is what makes our jobs so interesting, exciting, and sometimes exhausting. In Uniserve, when the group departs and the guests are grinning from ear-to-ear, sending compliments in every direction, and the meeting planner re-books for the following year on the condition that YOU are assigned to work their file... rewarding? You bet!
4. **Free Time!** It's the best part of Uniserve! Prior to Uniserve, I literally spent 90% of my time at work. Family life barely existed. And although this type of job can be addicting, everyone has a right to a personal life. Uniserve permits a personal life. I say this with caution, as this is dependent on a number of things:

A. Adequate staffing is necessary in the Uniserve department. The Sheraton El Conquistador convention services department consisted of four Uniserve people who handle the convention groups, one local catering manager, and a one-stop-shop manager who blocks, contracts, and caters to groups of 20 sleeping rooms and under. Of course, staffing varies from hotel to hotel and is dependent on the type of market the hotel pulls.
B. The convention files must be assigned strategically between managers to allow adequate days for paperwork between groups and allowing for *days off*.
C. The banquet manager, banquet captains, and conference floor manager *must* be trained to handle problem-solving situations effectively and with confidence. The same captain should handle as many of the group's meal functions as possible so that the meeting planner can feel comfortable with familiar faces.
D. A daily meeting with the hotel staff to include the chef, banquet manager, conference floor manager, and Uniserve CSMs is a MUST! The purpose of the daily meeting is to cover all functions in the hotel for the upcoming three days.

I cannot claim that the Uniserve system will work for all hotels. However, I believe there are many hotels that could use this system and it would relieve many of those catering and convention service managers who are "burned out."

# Chapter 14: Food and Beverage Service

the uniserve system (see box titled "Should Hotel Catering and Convention Services Departments Be Combined?").

## Beverage Service

More discontent has been voiced over beverage service and charges than over most factors of a convention. Of all the price policies at a convention, the liquor arrangement brings the loudest and most frequent outcry.

Unfortunately, meeting planners or the hosts at hospitality suites usually specify their favorite brands of liquor, and they are familiar with package store prices. Many planners and hosts resent what they consider to be unfair markups on name-brand liquor by the hotel. Some hotels have taken to charging the same prices as local liquor stores, but most have a much higher rate — two, three, or even four times the cost. This is a management decision. The additional revenue gained by marking up must be weighed against the frequent ill will engendered.

### Types of Setups

A number of beverage arrangements are used in catering to private parties. We will discuss the four most common procedures specified by meeting planners:

The **host bar**, also called an *open bar* or *sponsored bar*, is used most frequently by corporate meeting planners. At a host bar, guests drink freely of the beverages offered and the host pays the bill at the end of the function (average consumption at a hosted bar is two to three drinks per person for a one-hour open bar). This type of bar is stocked to prepare for all types of drinks and is staffed by a bartender. A purchase amount is almost always guaranteed. If, for example, at least $300 worth of beverage is not consumed, the host will pay for what was consumed, plus an additional amount to cover labor. Figure 14.6 shows typical labor costs for beverage service.

*Figure 14.6. TYPICAL LABOR COSTS FOR BEVERAGE SERVICE.*

**Beverage Labor and Miscellaneous Charges**

A. Bartender Charge —
   If less than $300 sales, labor charge
   ...............................................$200.00

B. Bar Supplies — If group supplies liquor
   Cocktail Napkins
   Stir Sticks ......................$2.00/person
   Assorted Bar Fruit
   Mix - Sodas ....................$7.50/quart
   Bloody Mary Mix, Orange Juice,
   and Sweet and Sour........$16.00/quart
   Blenders.........................$20.00/each

C. Extra Bartender Charge $40.00/hour
   4-hour minimum

D. Extra Barback Charge $160.00/8 hrs
   8-hour minimum

*In addition to the charges listed above, it is common for properties to apply a flat service charge to functions under a certain size (typically 25 people or less). In some cases, labor and charges are waived entirely or based on the total dollar amount spent on the function. Sometimes, bartender fees are waived altogether (many meeting planners insist that they not pay bartender fees for the staffing of large hosted bars). Any specifics negotiated should be clearly spelled out in the contract.*

The **cash bar**, also called a *C.O.D. bar* or *no-host bar*, is the second most common arrangement. At a cash bar, each person pays for his or her own drinks. A minimum guarantee is also specified by the hotel in this case. Beverage consumption at a cash bar is usually lower than when the bar is hosted; during a one-hour cash bar, the consumption is about 1½ to two drinks per person.

**Coupon sales** are used at many private parties. Delegates buy tickets or coupons ahead of time and give them to the bartender when the drinks are served. The coupons may be sold by the hotel management or the host organization. Coupon sales eliminate the use of cash and the need for a cashier at the function.

The late Stanley H. Stearman, longtime executive director of the National Society of Accountants, said of the use of coupons for beverage functions:

> We give everyone two drink tickets along with their banquet ticket. They are actually perforated stubs which are turned in to the bartender in return for drinks. Not only does this method limit consumption to two drinks per person, but it gives me control over my liquor costs. I pay a certain amount for each stub that has been turned in. The only disadvantage to me is that I have to pay full price even if someone redeems his stub for a soft drink.[11]

The South Coast Plaza in Costa Mesa, California, uses still a different method in servicing private parties. The **captain's bar** is a self-service or make-your-own-drink bar that has been stocked with full bottles of liquor and mixes needed to make all the basic bar drinks. This bar is always hosted. The meeting planner and the convention service manager inventory the bar before and after the party, and the group is charged for how much is consumed. There is no guarantee on this type of setup because there is no bartender labor cost.

## Hospitality Suites

**Hospitality suites** are beverage or food and beverage functions held by the sponsoring organization or by other groups (such as exhibitors at an organization's trade show). They are usually held in a suite on a sleeping room floor, which means that hospitality suites are typically sold by the catering department but serviced by room service. Larger functions, such as those offering entertainment, are held in public function rooms (in this case, they would be both sold and serviced by the catering department).

While hospitality suites have traditionally been evening hospitality functions, there has been a trend for hosting breakfast or luncheon events as well. These hospitality suites are **auxiliary business**, commonly referred to as in-conjunction-with (ICW) business, for hotels. This means that even if the ICW business is not necessarily booked directly by the meeting sponsor, it should be considered part of the group's meeting history, as it increases the value of the meeting to the hotel.

Some meeting planners and exhibitors wish to avoid what they consider to be excessive prices charged by the hotel by bringing in liquor purchased outside the hotel. They then order mixers, ice, and glasses from room service. Hotels have varying policies regarding such action. Some hotels have a **corkage** charge to cover the use of liquor that is purchased elsewhere.

Katie Kannapell, the banquet manager of Cipiriani 42nd Street in New York City, tells of a recent corporate event in which the champagne provided by the sponsor was $20 pricier than Cipriani's in-house stock due to the corkage charge. She says:

Corkage is complicated. People often think corkage is cheaper, but you [the meeting planner] have to ask what is included and then compare it to what the venue serves. Very often you are not saving anything.[12]

Union regulations often dictate the circumstances under which a bartender must be employed. Tell your client in advance about such regulations. Explain the hours involved, overtime charges, and other pertinent details. Spell out the circumstances under which no such help is required. Include information about gratuities and taxes.

## Brands

Most hotels offer a varied selection of liquor brands to the meeting planner. Brands are commonly offered in three categories: house (well) brands, call brands, and premium brands. **House brands** are the least-expensive liquors and wines, and will be used for the function unless the meeting planner requests otherwise. Actual brands of liquor offered may vary from venue to venue, so be sure to inform meeting planners of the brands your hotel uses to avoid any confusion.

**Call brands** are brands specifically asked for by name, such as when a meeting planner requests Jim Beam Bourbon or Beefeater's Gin. These brands are generally priced in the mid-range and must be requested as replacements for house brands.

**Premium brands** are quality, expensive liquors, such as Crown Royal, Chivas Regal, or Tanqueray Gin. When a planner selects a top-of-the-line drink menu, a guest at the function will not have to settle for the one brand offered on the standard drink menu. He or she will likely be able to choose from two or three brands of quality liquor.

Be sure that the meeting planner understands these categories, his or her options (using house wines but call brands, for example), and associated charges so that he or she can make an informed decision. This will help to avoid complaints over liquor charges.

## Pricing Methods

Meeting planners often ask for advice on how much liquor will be needed. The consumption of liquor varies, of course, with the makeup of the attendees. A chart such as the one shown in Figure 14.7 should prove helpful to you and your customers in making such decisions.

Liquor charges can be figured *by the person, by the bottle,* or *by the individual drink.* Whichever is used, make sure that someone on the convention staff has been designated to tally up after the affair with a designated member of the hotel staff. This will help avoid misunderstandings after the event and avoid last-minute searching for someone of authority on the convention management staff to corroborate the tally.

**By the Person.** When liquor is priced **by the person**, a flat rate is charged for each person present during a specified period of time. This type of pricing is also referred to as the *per person/unlimited consumption plan.* Sometimes a flat rate is charged for a cocktail party of a specified time period and additional time is charged on an hourly basis. At other times, the rate is given only as an hourly charge. If food is to be served, what kind and how much must be discussed and listed in the agreement.

## Chapter 14: Food and Beverage Service

*Figure 14.7. GUIDE TO HELP ESTIMATE THE AMOUNT OF LIQUOR NEEDED FOR A BEVERAGE FUNCTION.*

### Reception Drink Estimator

Based on an all-male attendance and easy access to bars. With 50% female attendance, average is 2 1/2 to 3 per hour, with 100% female attendance, average is 2 to 2 1/2 per hour.

| Number of Guests | 1/2 hr | 3/4 hr | One hr | 1 1/4 hrs | 1 1/2 hrs | 1 3/4 hrs | Two hrs |
|---|---|---|---|---|---|---|---|
| 25-55 | 2 | 3 | 3 3/4 | 4 | 4 1/4 | 4 1/2 | 4 3/4 |
| 60-104 | 2 | 3 | 3 3/4 | 4 | 4 | 4 1/2 | 4 3/4 |
| 105-225 | 1 3/4 | 2 1/2 | 3 | 3 1/2 | 4 | 4 | 4 1/2 |
| 230-300 | 1 1/2 | 2 | 2 1/2 | 2 3/4 | 3 | 3 1/4 | 3 1/2 |
| 315 & up | 1 1/2 | 2 | 2 1/2 | 2 3/4 | 3 | 3 1/4 | 3 1/2 |

### Drink Estimator

| Bottle size | Drink size | Number of drinks |
|---|---|---|
| **Liquor** | | |
| 4/5 quart | 1 oz. | 25 |
| 4/5 quart | 1 1/4 oz. | 20 |
| 4/5 quart | 1 1/2 oz. | 17 |
| Quart | 1 oz. | 31 |
| Quart | 1 1/4 oz. | 25 |
| Quart | 1 1/2 oz. | 21 |
| **Wine** | | |
| 750 ml | 5 oz. | 5 |
| Liter | 5 oz. | 6.7 |
| Magnum | 5 oz. | 10.2 |

*While guides such as the one above can be helpful in determining how much liquor will be needed for an event, several other variables should also be considered. Alcohol consumption is usually less if the event is on the evening of a major arrival day, the event is before 5:00 p.m. or after 8:00 p.m., hors d'oeuvres are served, or if there are other activities available in the function area. Consumption typically increases if the event is on the final night of the meeting, is held between 6:00-7:30 p.m., only dry (salted) snacks are served, or if the event is held during a major sporting event and a large video screen is in use.*
**Source: Reprinted with permission from *The Schenley Guide to Professional Hosting*. Published by Schenley Affiliated Brands Corp.**

From the meeting planner's perspective, this flat rate per person can be the simplest, but not necessarily the cheapest, pricing method. Unless the group has a lot of drinkers, this is usually an expensive plan.

You will need a way to determine the number in attendance. Collecting tickets or invitations at the door is one way to do this.

Extension of the time period and the admission of people who do not have tickets require approval by an authorized person. The head count and the time period should be acknowledged immediately after the event by having the authorized person initial the tally.

**By the Bottle.** The convention organizer may prefer to pay **by the bottle** consumed. Liquor by the bottle can be cost-effective for large groups. If you are charging $9 per drink and serving one-ounce drinks from a fifth, the meeting group pays $225 for the bottle (25 drinks per fifth). A by-the-bottle charge would reduce this cost to $100 to $120 per bottle.

The by-the-bottle system is very popular for hospitality suites, both with and without bartenders. This system calls for charges on all bottles opened regardless of how much of the contents is consumed. Some hotels permit the host to keep the opened bottles; others do not. Some hotels agree to store opened bottles of liquor from one reception and use them for the group's next reception. Obviously, the bartender must be made aware of the arrangement, and it must be made part of the work order for the beverage event.

Sometimes the charges for the bartender are part of the per-bottle price. If so, this should be indicated in the work order or agreement; if not, list the rates and hours.

Make sure that the liquor supply given is stored securely. Good hotel people assist their guests in arranging storage. It is imperative that both the hotel and the convention organization have people designated to tally and record the number of bottles used and returned for credit. Meeting planners will want to ensure that they have a good inventory system in place to ensure proper billing. This means taking an inventory of the bars both before and after a function (this should always be done in the company of a hotel banquet person, who verifies the planner's totals). The inventory should not only include bottles of liquor, but also mixers, soft drinks, and bottled water (as well as any other items for which the group is being charged). Soft drinks are usually charged at about $4 each, so it is becoming more prevalent for these items to be inventoried.

When buying liquor by the bottle, meeting planners often request that banquet bars be closed in staggered order, moving the partials from one to the other (this is termed *marrying* the bars). Their instructions also frequently call for the bartenders to pour measured drinks, as bartenders could pad the bill by overpouring.

Food may be served, but is charged separately. And, under certain conditions, there may be a room charge. Much depends on the anticipated volume and the basic agreement under which the event takes place.

**By the Drink.** Charges can also be made **by the drink**, based on the number of individual drinks served. This type of function always includes the mandatory use of bartender service (no less than one bartender for every 75 guests is the rule of thumb). There should be an agreement on the size of the drink to be poured, and the bartenders so instructed. Meeting planners often specify that portion control measuring pourers (called Posi-Pours) be used.

This arrangement is used by many meeting planners, especially those planning for small groups. Most meeting planners feel the most economical bar for receptions of under 100 persons is by the drink; for over 100 persons, by the bottle.

The guests may pay for drinks in cash or prepaid coupons, or the host may pay for it all. Food charges are a separate item, and there may be a room charge. Give the meeting planner advance notice of gratuities, taxes, and a schedule of bartenders' work regulations.

## Beverage Control

Rigid procedures for issuing liquor and the use of it should be maintained. The banquet department is generally responsible for issuing the liquor. Since it is impossible to judge how much or what kind of liquor will be preferred, it is customary to stock 25 percent over what the group is estimated to consume. This policy eliminates shortages, but it must be controlled.

The excess must be returned to the storeroom at the end of the function. Special banquet requisition forms are used for private parties, showing all the bottles issued, consumed, and returned. Immediately after each function, all bottles — full, empty and partially used — should be accounted for.

The Renaissance Hotel uses the requisition form shown in Figure 14.8. The banquet manager uses this form for each function, showing the number of bottles originally issued, any additional issues, and all returns. Each bottle issued is marked with a distinctive means of identification. At the end of the party, the banquet manager totals the requisition by determining the amount of each item consumed and its price, and then making the appropriate extensions. The total is transferred to the banquet guest check, which is verified and signed by the meeting planner. A percentage of the check total is usually added to the bill as a gratuity for the staff.

**Automated Bars.** Several hotels are making use of automated bar systems. A long-standing complaint of meeting planners is the tendency of bartenders to over-pour in host bar setups (pouring drinks without the use of shot glasses or other measuring devices is called **free pour**). They feel the staff members are encouraged to pour on the heavy side because their tips are figured as a percentage of sales. Another problem area is the counting and storing of open bottles. Both of these problems are eliminated with automated bar setups.

Automated bars operate much like soft drink bars, with individual push buttons for each liquor item — vodka, gin, bourbon, scotch, rye, etc. Quart bottles are placed upside down in the wells and dispensed by a vacuum system. Each bottle has its own dispensing unit and meter. The size of the drink is determined by the meeting planner, and the dispensing unit is set accordingly (this method of dispensing exact amounts of liquor per drink is known as **electronic pour**). The meters are checked and recorded before and after the party, with the difference being the amount consumed.

The control feature offered by the metered bars is what makes them attractive to both the meeting planner and the hotel. They provide a consistent drink and eliminate overpouring, but they are not without their limitations. The machine dispenses only the alcohol; mixed and blended drinks still must be prepared by a bartender. And only eight bottles can be filled on most units, limiting the choice of drinks. Some observers also say that metered bars are impersonal, lending a mechanical atmosphere to cocktail parties.

The Peabody Memphis uses a RFID tracker system to monitor its bar and banquet operations. RFID, which is short for "radio frequency identification," is a technology similar in theory to bar code identification. RFID-enabled liquor pour spouts provide a clear picture of how each drink is prepared, identifying over-pouring, missing drinks, and unaccounted pours — all of which translate into reduced liquor costs.

**Liquor Liability.** Can a hotel be held liable to an innocent third party for wrongful acts of an intoxicated attendee? The answer depends on the individual state, but due to alcohol related automobile accidents, many states have passed **dram shop laws** imposing liability on the dispenser of alcohol sold illegally, terming a sale is illegal if to a minor, intoxicated person, or known alcoholic. Management must take reasonable care in serving alcoholic beverages at functions. Managers should be trained to be alert to potential problems with intoxicated patrons and how to deal with unruly meeting attendees. A typical contract clause might read:

> *If alcoholic beverages are to be served on the Hotel premises (or elsewhere under the Hotel's alcoholic beverage license) the Hotel will require that beverages be dispensed only by Hotel servers and bartenders. The Hotel's license requires the Hotel to (1) request identification (Photo ID) of any person of questionable age and refuse service if the person is either under age or proper identification cannot be produced, and (2) refuse alcoholic beverage service to any person who, in the Hotel's judgment, appears intoxicated.*

Chapter 14: Food and Beverage Service

*Figure 14.8. BAR REQUISITION FORM.*

**RENAISSANCE HOTEL**
**BANQUET WINE/LIQUOR REQUISITION**
NO. 001399

DATE: 8-25-
DAY OF WEEK: MONDAY
TIME: 6:00 PM
FUNCTION: RECEPTION
ROOM: Foyer / Renaissance Ballroom
ORGANIZATION NAME: SINGER
BANQUET CHECK #: 06272
BANQUET EVENT ORDER #: 02135
TENDERS IN CHARGE: Bill / Cheryle
CLIENT'S ACCOUNT #: 12948
NUMBER OF GUESTS: 275

MANNER OF SALE: ☒ BY DRINK ☐ BY BOTTLE ☐ BY HOUR
TYPE OF BEVERAGE: ☐ PREMIUM ☒ HOUSE ☐ SPECIAL LIST
TYPE OF SALE: ☒ HOSTED ☐ CASH BAR

| CODE | DESCRIPTION | ISSUED QUANT | SIZE | RETD BOTT | USED BOTT | NO DRINKS | DRINK PRICE | TOTAL | LIQUOR | WINE | MISC | % POT |
|---|---|---|---|---|---|---|---|---|---|---|---|---|
| | HOUSE BOURBON | 3 | | 1.7 | 1.3 | 43 | 3.00 | $129. | 8.30 | | | 6.5% |
| | HOUSE SCOTCH | 3 | | 1.9 | 1.1 | | | | | | | |
| | HOUSE GIN | 4 | | 2.4 | 1.6 | | | | | | | |
| | HOUSE VODKA | 4 | | 1.1 | 2.9 | | | | | | | |
| | HOUSE BRANDY | 2 | | 1.8 | .2 | | | | | | | |
| | HOUSE RUM | 2 | | 1.6 | .4 | | | | | | | |
| | HOUSE TEQUILA | 2 | | 1.3 | .7 | | | | | | | |
| | HOUSE WHISKEY | 2 | | 1.8 | .2 | | | | | | | |
| | HOUSE WHITE WINE | 18 | | 2 | 16 | | | | | | | |
| | HOUSE RED WINE | 6 | | 3 | 3 | | | | | | | |
| | MILLER LITE BEER | 24 | | 5 | 19 | | | | | | | |
| | HEINEKEN BEER | | | | | | | | | | | |
| | PREMIUM BOURBON | | | | | | | | | | | |
| | PREMIUM SCOTCH | | | | | | | | | | | |
| | PREMIUM GIN | | | | | | | | | | | |
| | PREMIUM VODKA | | | | | | | | | | | |
| | PREMIUM BRANDY | | | | | | | | | | | |
| | PREMIUM WHISKEY | | | | | | | | | | | |
| | PREMIUM TEQUILA | | | | | | | | | | | |
| | PREMIUM RUM | | | | | | | | | | | |

**TOTALS**

ISSUED BY _____ RETURNED BY _____ APPROVED BY _____
RECEIVED BY _____ RECEIVED BY _____

WHITE - FOOD AND BEVERAGE CONTROL   CANARY - BANQUET MAITRE D'   GOLDEN ROD - BEVERAGE MGR.

*This form details the number of bottles issued, consumed, and returned. The form also specifies the pricing method to be used (by drink, by bottle, by hour), the type of brand (premium, house, special list), and the type of setup (hosted, cash bar).*

Some provisions are stricter, prohibiting attendees from bringing alcoholic beverages into the hotel from outside:

> *Alcoholic beverages may not be brought into the hotel from outside sources. The sales, service, and consumption of alcoholic beverages are regulated by the State Alcoholic Beverage Commission. The Hotel, as a licensee, is subject to the regulations promulgated by the Commission, violations of which may jeopardize the Hotel's license. Consequently, it is the Hotel's policy that alcoholic beverages may not be brought into the hotel from outside sources.*

**Staffing and Logistics.** A typical rule of thumb is to staff one bartender per 75 to 100 people. You will also need to staff one bar back for every three bartenders (bar backs are responsible for replenishing stocks of liquor, ice, glassware, and garnishes used during the function). When food is served at receptions, staff one server per 50 people, and one waiter per 100 people for receptions without food service.

Bar locations will vary according to the room's dimensions and the placement of other provisions such as staging, dance floors, and buffet tables. Generally, one bar station is required for every 75-100 guests. Avoid grouping bars too close together. With large receptions requiring several beverage stations, open those bars farthest from the entrance first in order to bring people into the room. This helps to spread the crowds. The chart below summarizes staffing requirements for receptions based on attendance:

### Reception Service Estimator

| Number of Guests | Number of bartenders | Number of waiters with food | Number of waiters without food |
|---|---|---|---|
| 25-100 | 1 | 2 | 1 |
| 105-205 | 2 | 3 | 2 |
| 215-325 | 3 | 3 | 2 |
| 350-475 | 4 | 4 | 3 |

**Beverage Labor Charges.** In addition to charges for the liquor and other drinks served at beverage functions, hotels also assess labor and miscellaneous fees for events. Generally, clients must hire a minimum number of bartenders for a minimum number of hours (typically for shifts of four hours). Some bartender fees, for example, are based on a sliding scale, such as $200 for the first hour, $150 for the second hour, and $100 for each hour thereafter. If bartenders are hired for a four-hour shift and the function extends beyond four hours, additional overtime charges may be assessed. In addition to bartenders, beverage functions require bar backs. Some hotels include the salaries for these employees in the bartender charge, except in cases where additional bar backs are required.

Some beverage functions may also require cashiers. Many hotels do not allow clients to schedule cash bars unless at least one cashier is employed. Having a cashier eliminates the need for the bartender to handle cash, which slows down beverage production and service and can create security problems. Cashiers can be eliminated if the client sells drink tickets that guests can redeem for beverages.

Planners may also wish to employ cocktail servers, although servers can cost almost as much as bartenders. Therefore, most meeting planners eliminate the need for servers by having two or three portable bars set up in the room and having guests give their orders directly to the bartenders. If the client wishes to have cocktail servers, however, they can be used to best advantage by circulating the room with trays of poured wine or champagne. This eliminates the need for wine drinkers to slow down the flow at bar stations.

Other charges incurred at beverage functions are the costs for supplies and mixers, which are not considered part of a liquor order. It is important that all charges, whether they be for labor or supplies, be clearly spelled out in the contract in order to avoid any misunderstandings.

## Post-Function Actions

Prompt action must be taken at the end of each food function to eliminate possible billing difficulties and to bring each function segment to a satisfactory close. It is recommended that the planner and the CSM (or hotel manager) meet daily to discuss both the things the hotel did well as well as any areas for improvement at each function. In some cases, this meeting can be held immediately after the function; if the function is held in the evening, the meeting should be held no later than the next day so details are fresh in the planner's mind. Setting a specific time is the best approach, and these meetings should be scheduled well in advance of the group's arrival to enable the hotel ample time to clear its schedule for the daily de-briefings.

If billing is based on attendance, the captain in charge should tally the number of persons served or the number of tickets collected and have the authorized convention person sign an acknowledgment of the total. Make sure the person signing is designated in writing as a person who is authorized to sign.

If beverages were served, tally the unopened bottles of liquor and/or soft drinks and have the amount acknowledged by signature. Bottles to be returned for credit must be signed for.

Most convention groups use a master billing account for the food functions. If the terms are cash, the money or check should be presented when the tally is certified as correct. If cash is collected by the organization, the hotel should provide a safe place for it or accept it in payment and give a suitable receipt. Place a summary of the food functions in the file folder for the analysis of the convention.

## In-house Coodination: Large vs. Small Properties

We have referred to the convention service manager as the person who coordinates the convention. This person, however, does not do it all; many departments are involved. The competence of the department heads determines the extent to which the convention service manager becomes involved. If the reservations, front-desk, and catering managers are on top of their jobs, the convention service manager's headaches are minimized. If not, the convention service manager must spend more time overseeing the operation.

### Role of the Catering Manager

The in-house coordination at *small properties* is generally not handled the same way as at larger properties; the major difference is the role played by the *catering manager.* At larger properties, catering managers are only in charge of food and beverage; seldom do they become involved in sales and seldom are they required to account for more than the food and beverage service. But at small properties, their areas of responsibility branch out.

A property with insufficient sales volume to justify carrying a convention coordinator must nevertheless give one person that responsibility. Usually, it is the banquet or catering manager who wears two hats: head of his or her department and head of group business.

What distinguishes a large property from a small one? There is no definition, but hotels with fewer than 250 guestrooms might well handle servicing differently than larger ones.

Figure 14.9 gives a catering manager's job description adapted from the operating manual of Doubletree Hotels, whose hotels range from 140 to 300 guestrooms and are typical of such properties whose catering managers double as convention service managers.

> **WORTH WATCHING**
>
> - Do an Internet search for "Every Role a Starring Role – Disney Catering" (or go to www.youtube.com/watch?v=9ibJzhtFfTw) to see a video on the duties of Chris Anderson, the catering/convention services manager at the Disneyland Resort in California.
> - Search for Ghada Alamdar Hilton Worldwide (or go to www.youtube.com/watch?v=_RHjVVQy5rU) to view a career profile of banquet manager Ghada Alamdar.

## Servicing and Selling

The division between servicing and selling is less pronounced at small hotels than at large ones. As we discussed in Chapter 10, there is wide variation among hotels in the extent to which the sales department participates in servicing.

At small hotels, servicing and sales, particularly of food and beverage functions, are more likely to be handled by the same person. Part of the catering manager's job might be to actively solicit and schedule group banquet business. Often, the catering manager is given charge of the function book. This is fine as long as the lines of authority, responsibility, and communication are clearly understood.

Problems arise when the left hand does not know what the right hand is doing; for example, when the sales department books a convention that conflicts with the catering department's efforts. The problem is likely to be acute when the two departments are located in different areas of the hotel. In this case, the sales department must rely on the phone or memos to communicate with the catering department. There may even be inter-departmental rivalry for function space, with each trying to show greater sales and profit.

## Communication and Cooperation

Servicing requires clear communication channels at small properties. When the property has a convention service manager, there is generally good cooperation, with one independent person coordinating the efforts of other departments. But when the catering manager serves as the coordinator, there seems to be more autonomy of departments. The catering manager may be unfamiliar with the problems in the front of the house; reservation and front office departments lack understanding of the handling of food and beverage.

*Figure 14.9. JOB DESCRIPTION OF A CATERING MANAGER.*

### Catering Manager's Job Description

1. **Basic Function**
   To service all phases of group meeting/banquet functions; coordinate these activities on a daily basis; assist clients in program planning and menu selection; solicit local group catering business.

2. **General Responsibility**
   To maintain the services and reputation of Doubletree and act as management representative to group clients.

3. **Specific Responsibilities**

   a. To maintain function book. Coordinate the booking of all meeting space with the Sales Department.
   b. To solicit local food and beverage functions.
   c. To coordinate with all group meeting/banquet planners their specific group requirements with the services and facilities offered.
   d. To confirm all details relative to group functions with meeting/banquet planners.
   e. To distribute to the necessary inter-hotel departments detailed information relative to group activities.
   f. To supervise and coordinate all phases of catering, hiring, and training programs.
   g. To supervise and coordinate daily operation of meeting/banquet setups and service.
   h. To assist in menu planning, preparation, and pricing.
   i. To assist in referrals to the Sales Department and in booking group activities.
   j. To set up and maintain catering files.
   k. To be responsive to group requests/needs while in the hotel.
   l. To work toward achieving Annual Plan figures relating to the Catering Department (revenues, labor percentages, average checks, covers, etc.).
   m. To handle all scheduling and coverage for the servicing of catering functions.

4. **Organizational Relationship and Authority**
   Is directly responsible and accountable to the Food and Beverage Manager. Responsible for coordination with kitchen, catering service personnel and accounting.

*As seen by these duties detailed by Doubletree Hotels, the catering manager often serves as the convention service manager at small properties.*
**Source: Courtesy of Doubletree Hotels.**

Such a situation is not necessarily detrimental, as long as each department does its job and there is good inter-departmental communication. The difficulty may arise when the association executive questions the hotel's handling of his or her membership's registration. If the catering manager is the planner's contact in the hotel, the planner may find little relief for the problem. Perhaps the catering manager is too busy with the upcoming dinner or has not been schooled in the procedure for registering guests. Or perhaps — and this is a more common problem — the catering manager doesn't have the authority to go to the rooms department to straighten out the situation. The meeting planner's nightmare is a contact without the muscle to get the job done.

The autonomy of departments also leads to the lack of resumes (specification sheets), which are the backbone of control and communication in servicing. Substituting for the resumes (specification sheets) are memos from the sales department to the rooms department and individual function sheets prepared by the catering manager for all meeting room and food and beverage setups. Memos and function sheets are fine ways of communicating, but a comprehensive schedule of the overall convention program is still needed.

# Chapter 14: Food and Beverage Service

## PUTTING IT ALL TOGETHER

Your property has been approached by the corporate office of a large multi-level marketing company that wishes to hold a convention for approximately 600 distributors and spouses. While funds are unlimited, the meeting planner is totally inexperienced and will need your help to plan a successful function.

At this time, plans are sketchy. The meeting planner does want to incorporate the company's "Pot of Gold" promotion into an Awards Banquet and stage a luau to celebrate the vacations won by the company's top five distributors. The meeting planner is open to your suggestions regarding creative menus for these two functions, but wants to serve traditional American fare for the buffets and other meal functions.

The convention will run from Wednesday afternoon through Sunday afternoon. Events currently being considered are:

| Day | Time | Event |
|---|---|---|
| Wednesday | (Afternoon) | **Registration** |
| | (Evening) | Registration and **Hospitality Suite** |
| | | Dinner on own |
| Thursday | (Morning) | **Three seminars** (Approx. 100 people each room) |
| | | **Refreshment Break** |
| | (Afternoon) | **Three seminars** (Approx.100 people each room) |
| | | **Refreshment Break** |
| | (Evening) | **Buffet Dinner** (Approx. 500 attendees) |
| Friday | (Morning) | Same as Thursday |
| | (Afternoon) | **Buffet lunch** (Approx. 500 attendees) |
| | (Afternoon) | Same as Thursday |
| | (Evening) | **Directors Dinner** (24 in attendance) |
| | | Other attendees: optional dinner show (on own) |
| Saturday | (Morning) | **President's Breakfast** (approx. 300 attendees) |
| | | **General Session** (600 attendees) |
| | | Lunch on own |
| | (Afternoon) | **Continuation of General Session** |
| | (Evening) | **Awards Banquet**, **Entertainment** (music and dancing) |
| | | (600 attendees) |
| Sunday | (Morning) | Breakfast on own |
| | (Afternoon) | **Farewell Luau** (Approx. 350 attendees) |

Using what you have learned in Chapters 12, 13 and 14, develop a presentation that you will use in your pre-convention planning session with the meeting planner. Cover the following areas:

1. A proposal detailing what food and beverages could be offered at the food functions (hospitality suite, refreshment breaks, buffet lunch and dinner, the directors dinner, president's breakfast, the awards banquet and luau). Include how the client could be charged for each function.
2. An outline of what your property can offer in the way of decorations, staffing, and meeting requirements (musicians, additional entertainment, staging, lighting, etc.) for the awards banquet and the luau. Provide room set-up plans detailing suggested seating, food service, and entertainment area options.
3. A sample room set-up for the seminars and the general session. Include the style of seating, a list of available audiovisual equipment, and staffing (set-up, registration personnel, etc.) that your property can provide.

*Beverage stations should be set up toward the rear of the function room to draw people into the room. The most popular beverage pricing plans are by the person, by the bottle, and by the drink.*
**Source: Photograph courtesy of Dolce Hotels and Resorts.**

## Summary

Food and beverage functions are an integral part of most meetings. Both association and corporate meeting planners rate the quality of food and beverage service as "very important" in their selection of meeting facilities. Food and beverage functions are second only to guestrooms in generating revenue at most convention hotels.

So, while hotel sales and service people are generally primarily concerned with filling guestrooms, it is imperative that convention sales and service managers also be knowledgeable in the food and beverage area.

In addition to food and beverage functions, the success of a meeting is often judged by its impact on attendees. In today's world of high technology, it is a rare delegate who leaves a meeting whose highlight was a simple flip chart presentation. In the next chapter, we will take a look at how hotels are using today's sophisticated audiovisual equipment to enhance both large and small meetings and generate repeat sales for the property.

## Endnotes

1. Carol Bialkowski, "Emerging Trends: A Conversation with Top Hyatt F&B Executives," *Unconventional Cuisine*, Hyatt Hotels Corporation.
2. Ibid.
3. *Meetings & Conventions*.
4. Carol Bialkowski, "Infusing Your Meeting With Local Flavor," *Unconventional Cuisine*, Hyatt Hotels Corporation.

# Chapter 14: Food and Beverage Service

5. Carol Bialkowski, "What's on the Menu?: Staying Ahead of Attendees' Food Issues," *pcma convene*.
6. Ibid.
7. Bruce Myint, "Hotels Scramble to Cut Carbs," *Meetings & Conventions*.
8. Ruth Hill, "Association Meetings," *Meetings West*.
9. Jeanne O'Brien, "Sheraton Reveals New Food & Beverage Program," *Meeting News*.
10. Toni Giovanetti, "A La Carte Catering Emerges as the Favored Choice of Meeting Planners," *Hotel Business*.
11. Bob Skalnik, "Liquor Control," *Association and Society Manager*, ©Barrington Publications.
12. Cheryl-Anne Sturken, "Bar Codes: Understanding How Liquor Tabs Are Tallied," *Meetings & Conventions*.

## Study Questions

1. Explain why the profit margin for banquets is considerably higher than that of hotel restaurants.
2. Name several types of food and beverage functions commonly requested by meeting planners. Why is it necessary to have a separate function sheet for each?
3. What trends have affected the types of food served at functions? How have hotels responded to these trends?
4. What types of service are used for food functions? What factors determine the most effective type of service for a function?
5. Discuss the procedures used in establishing a guarantee for food functions. In what ways is attendance monitored to ensure the guarantee has been met?
6. What three different pricing methods are used to bill for liquor? How is control maintained for billing purposes?
7. Discuss the staffing and logistics common to beverage functions.
8. How does control of the food and beverage function differ between large and small properties? Distinguish between the role of catering manager and convention service manager.

## Key Terms

**à la carte catering**—Catered events at which guests may choose from a number of different menu items.

**action station**—At action stations, chefs prepare foods to order and serve them to guests. Popular items for action stations include omelets, crepes, pasta, grilled meat or shrimp, carved meats, sushi, Caesar salad, and flaming desserts. These chef-attended food stations provide an interactive dining experience for attendees and allow them to customize their orders. Also called **performance stations** or **exhibition cooking**.

**American/plated service**—Food is arranged on plates in the kitchen and brought to the guests.
**auxiliary business**—Affiliate and sub-group business that is brought to the hotel because of the meeting or event. Also called **in-conjunction-with (ICW)** business.
**banquet captain**—Person in charge of banquet service at food functions; supervisor of the servers. For small functions, the banquet captain also serves as maitre d'; for larger functions, he or she may be responsible for a specific area of the dining room.
**buffet service**—A presentation of several food items from which the guests choose and serve themselves. Variations include **attended buffets**, at which chefs serve attendees, and **plated buffets**, at which a selection of pre-plated foods is set on a table from which attendees choose. Buffets are typically chosen for less formal events.
**butler service**—At receptions, servers offer a variety of hors d'oeuvres on platters to guests. At dinners, food is presented by butlers on silver trays.
**by the bottle**—A charge for liquor based on full bottles served.
**by the drink**—A charge for liquor based on the number of drinks served.
**by the person**—A fixed price for liquor per attendee. This charge may cover all consumption of food and beverage (this is sometimes referred to as the **per person/unlimited consumption plan**). In some cases, beverages are charged per the person and food is ordered separately by the piece.
**call brand**—Brand name liquor, distinguished from "house brand," selected by customer according to personal preference. Usually of higher quality than house brands.
**canapé**—Hot or cold appetizer with a bread or cracker base.
**captain's bar**—Self-service bar at which guests make their own drinks. This type of bar is always hosted.
**cash bar**—Guests pay for their own drinks. Also called a **no-host bar** or **C.O.D. bar**.
**chef's tasting**—The opportunity to sample a menu in advance of the event, usually in the company of the chef.
**corkage**—Charge that is placed on beer, wine, and liquor purchased elsewhere and brought into the facility.
**coupon sales**—Attendees at a function purchase tickets for drinks from the hotel or from the host organization.
**covers**—The number of meals served at a meal function.
**dram shop laws**—Laws covering the liability of people serving alcoholic beverages. Under dram shop laws, a party injured by an intoxicated person can sue the establishment that contributed to that person's intoxication.
**duoserve**—A meeting service system in which food and beverage responsibilities are handled by catering while other aspects of servicing the group are handled by the convention service manager. Because responsibilities are separated, meeting planners have two hotel contacts.
**electronic pour**—System of dispensing pre-determined exact amounts of liquor or non-alcoholic beverages per drink.
**energy break**—Refreshment break at which nutritious food and beverages are served. These breaks also may include some form of exercise.
**English/family style service**—Food is brought to the table and guests serve themselves. In some cases, the host cuts the meat and passes the tray to guests; the host may also have the meat cut by a server away from the table

before it is placed before guests.

**finger food**—Food, typically served at a reception, that does not require the use of a knife, fork, or spoon.

**food & beverage minimum**—The minimum catering revenue required for a meeting or event. Fees or other penalties are imposed if the minimum is not met.

**free pour**—Alcoholic drinks poured without the use of shot glasses or other measuring devices.

**French service**—Food service in which items are prepared tableside from a cart or gueridon. This type of service is best suited to small groups.

**gala dinner**—An evening event at which a multi-course, seated dinner is accompanied by entertainment, such as dancing, speeches, or the presentation of awards. Standard dress is black-tie.

**guarantee**—The minimum number of meals to be paid for by the client, even if some are not consumed. Usually, the hotel requires the planner to set this number no less than 48 hours prior to the event.

**head count**—The actual number of people attending a food function.

**hors d'oeuvres**—Small appetizers; hot and/or cold finger foods served at a reception. Heavy hors d'oeuvres are served with the intention of providing more of a meal (in the form of small appetizers) to guests; typically eight to ten pieces per person are served.

**hospitality suite**—Guestroom or suite used for receptions and entertainment. Usually stocked with beverages and light food. Often used by exhibitors at trade shows to entertain and sell delegates on their firms' products.

**host bar**—Beverage plan for banquets or other functions in which the guests do not pay for drinks; the host is charged either by the drink or by the bottle. Also called an **open bar** or a **sponsored bar**.

**house brand**—Brand of wine or distilled spirits selected by a hotel or restaurant as their standard when no specific brand is specified. Also called a **well brand**.

**off-premises catering**—The transportation of food, either fully prepared or in various stages of preparation, from a hotel's kitchen to a site away from the hotel.

**on-premises catering**—Servicing food and/or beverage functions in meeting rooms, function rooms, and sleeping rooms within the hotel. Some on-premises events may extend to the hotel or restaurant grounds, but food and/or beverage is still served within the confines of the establishment.

**organic foods**—Food products that are free of pesticides, commercial fertilizers, or other chemicals.

**overset safety margin**—Number of covers set over the guarantee. Billed to the client only if actually consumed.

**premium brand**—High-quality, high-priced hard liquor (spirits). The best and most expensive brands.

**pre-set service**—Placement of some foods on banquet tables prior to the seating of the guests.

**reception**—Stand-up social function, sometimes preceding a meal, at which beverages and light foods are served. Foods may be presented on small buffet tables or passed by servers.

**refreshment break**—Short breaks between meeting sessions. Usually offering beverages and/or light food items, some are planned around a theme. See also **energy break**.

**Russian service**—Food is fully prepared in the kitchen and all courses are served on platters (or from tureens) to guests at their tables. A plate is placed in front of each diner and a server places food from the tray or platter on each plate.

**special events**—Unique activities or functions staged one time, usually for the purpose of entertaining event attendees. See also **themed event**.

**themed event**—A function with a creative theme to make it more memorable. Themed events utilize elements that appeal to all five senses, incorporating sights (decorations and costumes), sounds, tastes (special food and beverages), touch, and smells to create a unique experience for attendees.

**ticket exchange**—Banquet control procedure whereby guests exchange an event coupon from their registration packet for an actual event ticket and seat assignment. This procedure increases control and tends to reduce the number of "no shows" to provide more accurate guarantees.

**uniserve**—A meeting service system in which the meeting planner makes arrangements for both function space and food and beverage events through one service contact, the convention service manager.

## Industry Profile

## Shawna Suckow, CMP, Founder

**SPiN and The HIVE Network**

*Award-winning speaker, author, and customer expert Shawna Suckow has been planning meetings and events for over 20 years. In 2008, she founded SPiN (the Senior Planners Industry Network), which is now the world's largest association comprised strictly of senior-level planners. In 2014, Shawna founded a sister organization, The HIVE Network, a community just for salespeople, which offers a new CCSE (Customer-Certified Sales Expert) designation. The goal of the organization is to bridge the communications gap between planners and hotel salespeople to make the buying process easier for everyone.* Successful Meetings *magazine has recognized her as one of the "25 Most Influential People in the Meetings Industry" for four consecutive years, and Shawna has also been honored by being included in Meetings Trendsetters by* Meetings Focus *magazine, as one of the Favorite Speakers by* Meetings & Conventions *magazine, and as part of Favorite 8 Speakers by* MeetingsNet .com.

## The Planner's Perspective

Planners and suppliers come from two different planets; planners are from Saturn (hard to reach and protected), while suppliers are from Venus (all about love – "love me, love my property"). One of my passions is bridging this gap in understanding between salespeople and meeting planners.

Our industry continues to evolve and technology continues to transform everything. There is a lot of frustration out there among hotel salespeople just trying to do their job — while meeting planners are better than ever at ignoring them. In the meeting and event industry, planners don't buy the same way we did before. The way hotels have sold to us in the past just won't work anymore.

First, cold calls are one of our primary pet peeves. We are time-pressed, budget-crunched, and frazzled. We don't have time to talk to suppliers we don't know. Ninety-five percent of cold-calling is ineffective now – it doesn't work.

So how do you break through the protected fortress? The key to the kingdom is the social networking site, LinkedIn. This is the one way we planners are letting you into our world right now. LinkedIn can help hotel salespeople make that personal connection. But don't try to connect with planners you don't know.

Secondly, dispel any reason for distrust. If I know you, I trust you. Relationships matter. Meeting planners, like everyone else, are bombarded with marketing that all sounds the same. Everyone says they are the best. Planners hate surprises.

Be yourself, not your company. Be a real person, a peer rather than a salesperson. On your LinkedIn profile, don't list your accomplishments like it's a resume; make it more personal. Talk about your philosophy, your involvement in your market segment, or why you like your job.

We've launched a new project for hotel salespeople called the HIVE Network (www.hivenetwork.org). It is all about cross-pollination between meeting planners and hotel salespeople. Meeting industry education is typically focused on planners. Our education will help hotels stop spinning their wheels, stop being ignored, and get access to planners in ways that really work.

My advice to those entering the industry is, "What are you waiting for?" Take the risk or you will never know what could have been.

## Learning Objectives:

This portion of your text introduces you to the wide variety of audiovisual equipment available to meeting planners today. We will also discuss the best options for meeting AV needs and provide guidelines for charging for audiovisual equipment and service. When you have studied this chapter, you will:

- Be able to describe the common types of audiovisual equipment and tell when each type is commonly used.

- Be able to detail the advantages and disadvantages of owning expensive audiovisual equipment versus contracting with outside sources for audiovisual needs.

- Understand how the increased use of high-tech presentations and mobile devices has led to the need for hotels to evaluate their bandwidths to enable them to adequately provide high-speed Internet and Wi-Fi capabilities.

## Outline

Types of Audiovisual Equipment
- Sound Systems
- Lighting
- Screens
- Projectors
- Projector Stands
- Multimedia Presentations
- Simultaneous Interpretations
- Virtual Conferencing
- Other Presentation Devices

Bandwidth and High-Speed Internet Access

Outside or Inside?
- Audiovisual Specialists
- In-House Equipment

Charging for Audiovisual Equipment

Union Regulations

Summary

# 15 Audiovisual Requirements

In the past, most meeting needs were fairly simple. Meeting planners typically requested a few microphones, a slide projector and screen, paper flip charts, and an occasional movie projector. Over the past two decades, however, technological developments in communications have resulted in **audiovisual** equipment and techniques that have greatly enhanced the meetings market. And today's tech-savvy meeting planners want to take full advantage of these advanced capabilities.

It is a rare meeting today that doesn't incorporate an audiovisual (AV) presentation in its program. And more tech-savvy requests are becoming common as new technology is released. To remain competitive, it is necessary for hotels today to offer smart boards (interactive white boards on which information can be easily manipulated, saved, and downloaded by attendees), smart touch lecterns, and wide-screen, high-resolution plasma monitors.

Advertising a meeting facility's "state-of-the-art" equipment is meaningless if the hotel's convention services staff or the meeting planner do not know how to use the new equipment. The key to a successful and positive meeting experience is ensuring the meeting coordinator and guest speakers understand that your high-tech AV equipment is easy to use – and that assistance is available for technical support.

The more seasoned users of AV systems require little help from the hotel staff. They know precisely what equipment they need and what they require the hotel to be able to provide. They sometimes bring their own equipment or contact an AV company for support.

The meeting planner who is less knowledgeable about AV systems will need support. Someone on the hotel staff should at least be familiar with, if not expert at, AV systems to provide needed service or help the planner to find it locally. It is not realistic to expect everyone on the convention sales and service staff to be expert in every facet of AV systems, but all, especially the convention service manager (CSM), should keep abreast of new developments and be conversant in the terminology and requirements of today's AV technology. Planners will have a greater comfort level with a professional CSM who is consistently working to keep up to speed with the latest technology.

Lee Sterbens, regional general manager of GES Global Experience Specialists, says:

> CSMs should be able to assist meeting planners with the selection of appropriate space and proper audiovisual equipment. Having a basic understanding of what equipment is required to achieve the desired goal will allow you to better serve your meetings groups and yourself.

Hotels that do a large volume of meetings and conventions business generally have at least one person – or a staff of AV professionals — available for technical support. Fairmont Hotels & Resorts, for example, has partnered with PSAV Presentation Services to provide a "technology concierge." The chain's Event Technology Concierge Service offers a single point of contact to support planners' AV needs. Designated personnel typically attend client meetings, suggest event technology solutions, and respond to client concerns and problems while the group is in-house. At the end of the group's program, the technology concierge will go over AV charges and answer any questions, and he or she will also build relationships with planners by sending post-event correspondence.

# Types of Audiovisual Equipment

The audiovisual equipment used for today's meetings can range from a simple flip chart to a sophisticated computer-generated multi-media presentation. In this section, we will take a look at the various types of AV equipment commonly used by meeting planners and see how each can be used to help stage a successful meeting.

## Sound Systems

A sound system is the kind of AV system that most hotels own. A supply of microphones, microphone stands, amplifiers, and speakers is typically the first purchased by a hotel staff.

Top-quality sound **amplifier** systems are a must. Most meeting rooms in hotels and convention centers have built-in public address (PA) systems. There are times, however, when meeting planners want to use an external PA system, which involves providing speakers, an amplifier, a mixer, and one or more microphones. External PA systems are typically used for general sessions, awards banquets, or special events that involve elaborate audiovisual presentations or audio tracks that are in stereo or rich in sound. Depending on the size of the group and its need for quality sound, it would be easy for a group to spend several thousand dollars a day on an external PA system. When using a built-in PA system, on the other hand, the planner only needs to pay for the mic and perhaps a mixer.

> **MORE ONLINE**
>
> To learn more about the audiovisual equipment we will be discussing in this chapter, go to the website of Conference Room Systems (www.conferencesystems.com). Click on the Guides link to view descriptions and tutorials for various categories of AV equipment. There is also a Resources tab that includes additional information.

With either system, speakers should be distributed so that there are no "dead spots" in sound throughout the meeting room. When sound systems are used with projection equipment, they should be located in the same area as the screen. Studies have shown that people tend to comprehend better when the sound and the visuals come from the same direction.

You need a variety of microphones, stands, and long extension cables to handle meeting situations. It may be necessary to supply a mic for every panelist at the head table or for every speaker at lecterns, and/or to have several microphones on the floor for questions from the audience. Ideally, the moderator and each speaker on a panel should have a microphone; if this is too costly, only then should microphones be limited to one for every two or three panelists (who should be reminded beforehand to speak into the nearest microphone).

Generally, if there are less than 60 people in the room, a microphone isn't needed unless the presenter is soft-spoken or the ceiling height is 15 feet or more. A mic is definitely required if the session is being taped, however.

Microphones are recommended for larger groups (greater than 60-75 people). While some speakers feel they can project sufficiently for a group of 100, it may be difficult for the audience in the back of the room to hear because of background noises, such as throat clearing, coughing, or paper shuffling.

When audience participation is part of the program, audience microphones will be required, as will a mixer to enable the volume on the different mics to be controlled. Mixers will be discussed later in this section.

If you join any but a brand-new facility, take inventory and have a list ready of what is available for use, in good working order. Call in a consultant on sound systems and find

## Chapter 15: Audiovisual Requirements

out what constitutes a suitable basic inventory of AV equipment. Discuss this with experienced convention coordinators too.

Any basic inventory should include a variety of microphones. A **lavaliere microphone** is popular with speakers because it hooks around the neck with a ribbon or cord, leaving the hands free. This type of mic, which is also called a *lapel*, *neck*, or *pendant microphone*, has a variety of optional positions. For best results, however, the head of the mic should be as close to the speaker's mouth as possible – men should be encouraged to place their mics on their neckties or coat lapels, and women should wear their mics high on their blouses or on the upper part of a jacket lapel.

It is important that all microphones used with public address systems (lectern, table, and floor mikes) be unidirectional. A **unidirectional microphone** picks up sound from only one direction (the speaker) and background noise (sounds coming from the sides and back of the microphone) is rejected. Windscreens (porous covers) also reduce the possibility of distracting sounds, such as blowing or popping.

A **standing microphone** is attached to a free-standing floor stand that is adjustable for height and angle. The stand has a sleeve or collar into which the mic can easily be placed. This type of mic, which is omni-directional (which means it picks up sounds from all directions), is typically used for questions or comments from the audience (in which case it is usually positioned in one of the aisles) or it can be used by a speaker or entertainer from the floor or stage.

A **roving microphone**, which is used to reach different parts of the audience, can also be equipped with a floor stand. Some models require a long cable to reach audience members, but some meeting planners prefer a **cordless/wireless microphone** when roving mics are required. Cordless/wireless mikes come in two types: UHF (ultra high frequency) and VHF (very high frequency). UHF is usually preferred, but both types work well and offer freedom of movement. Wireless mics offer the convenience of being able to move around the room without worrying about a cord (although you will want to make sure that these mics have fresh batteries), but they are more expensive than microphones with cords and, in some cases, an audio mixer is required to control the sound if the cordless mic doesn't feature a volume adjustment.

A **table microphone** has a short stand that rests on a table, desk, or lectern (the microphones, therefore, are sometimes called **lectern/podium mics**). The mics are usually attached to a gooseneck mic holder, enabling more than one speaker to use a mike in close proximity to his or her position on the stage.

Mics should be tested in each room to make sure the signal doesn't come through neighboring amplifiers. Cordless microphones should only be used in situations where freedom of movement is important, as they can cause problems. Signal interference is possible from a number of sources: metal structures in the room, wire mesh in the walls, and even suspended ceiling framework can cause disruptions or distortion in the sound. Even the more expensive models can face such problems as weak signals and poor quality sound as batteries wear down. If wireless microphones are used, then, it is wise to have a back-up system (such as a wired lavaliere microphone) immediately available.

All cables should be taped to the floor or carpet to avoid tripping accidents in a darkened room. Avoid at all costs cables that run across the dais. Run such connectors along the front of the stage, hiding them in the draped skirting.

Have an AV attendant available during conventions. It helps to have this person on hand for the larger events and available for troubleshooting at smaller events, such as workshops.

All systems should be set up and *tested* before the meeting. Find out if the meeting group plans to have someone in charge of volume control and distribution of microphones. The amplification system is crucial to the success of the meeting, and is an important part of the testing process. In cases where multiple microphones will be used, or when proceedings will be recorded, a sound technician will be needed to run an **audio mixer board**; the mixer board (sound board) raises and lowers the volume from each input source, and should be located in the audience to enable the technician to hear exactly what the audience is hearing. In general, one mixer is required for two to four microphones, and two mixers should be used for five to eight mics.

If your hotel uses Muzak or similar background music or a paging system, make sure you can control or eliminate such distractions in each meeting room. This is essential. Many times larger rooms are subdivided by temporary walls, and the controls are in only one room segment. The meeting planner may not know which subdivision of the room has the controls. Orient the convening organization's staff to control locations.

## Lighting

Lighting requirements should be handled by a specialist. If the hotel has a permanent stage, a professional service company should equip it for versatile lighting. But most often, platforms are temporary and lights must be furnished on stands. If platforms are always placed in the same position in certain rooms, a permanent lighting booth may be constructed and equipped. Even smaller rooms need skillful light placement to improve visibility of screened presentations.

While the technical details should be left to a lighting professional, the convention service manager should have a working knowledge of the basic types and uses of lighting equipment.

Lighting requirements for small rooms are simple; for large rooms and audioriums they are more complex. Union regulations recognize this (see the Union Regulations section in this chapter). Attendants are required for spotlight use when large rooms use stage lighting, and so on. Attendants are usually not required for simple setups in small rooms. Don't forget to tell the client about union regulations and rates.

Some of the basic types of lighting include profile spots, follow spots, floodlights, and special effects lighting. **Profile spots** are also known as *ellipsoidal spots* or *lekos*, and are ceiling mounted with a range from 500 to 1,000 watts. Employing an LED lamp, profile spots are used to light lecterns, signs, and the area of the stage nearest the audience to project background light patterns (colored filters may be used for this effect). Profile spots can also project **gobo patterns**, pre-cut designs that fit over the projected light to form light shapes, such as a company logo.

It is important to note that LED lights have replaced the standard halogen bulbs used in the past. These energy-efficient units (which use four to six times less electricity than halogen bulbs), can display nearly any color (except brown), allowing more creativity for altering the mood or energy of the room. Another benefit is that LED lights are cool to the touch, unlike halogen bulbs, which can cause burns when touched. Because of the cost-effectiveness and safety of LEDs, they are also used to light public areas throughout the hotel.

**Follow-spots** are cannon-shaped, movable lighting devices that are usually located to the rear of the auditorium. They are used to highlight and follow the speaker or performer, and require the services of a technician to ensure this added visibility is maintained. These lights are extremely brilliant, and may also be used with colored filters for a variety of effects.

**Floodlights** are usually used to light objects rather than people, and are often used to light backdrops (known as cycloramas) that serve as neutral backgrounds for the speakers.

Floodlights are used to project a diffused, even light, and feature frames that can accommodate color filters for different effects.

LED par can lights are the most commonly used floodlight. This type of floodlight can be used for a variety of lighting options, from filling large areas with light to creating mood and atmosphere by lighting only the front of the stage or providing "mood" lighting as a backdrop. In addition, gels can be inserted to provide color, creating a dramatic effect.

Another effective and convenient option for enhancing the ambience of a room are **uplights**. Uplights use LED par cans that shine from the ground upward. They are easy to set up and control and use very little power.

*Special effects lighting* is used both for illumination and to "create the mood." Ballroom globes, strobe lights, ultraviolet lighting, and laser lighting can be used to create a number of effects that enhance special functions — and can serve as visual centerpieces.

A commonly used lighting technique is the **stage wash** – filling the stage with even light and color. A number of different types of lights can be used to achieve this effect. Lighting trees (stands that can be used to raise mounted lighting equipment) are used to ensure that all areas of the stage are illuminated uniformly.

Computer-controlled lighting instruments, which are commonly called **intelligent lighting**, are capable of performing a wide variety of functions with the touch of a button. Although intelligent lighting equipment is significantly more costly than traditional lighting, its flexibility makes it a popular option with hotels that frequently host theme parties and large-scale productions that require complex lighting effects.

Dimmer switches on house lights are a must for meeting rooms. Delegates need partial illumination to take notes, while still being able to see the projection on the screen clearly. A control board is used to balance lighting to achieve the desired effect. Depending on the complexity of the board, it may require lighting personnel or a lighting technician.

## Screens

Projection screens are often purchased by hotels. Larger ones must be tailor-made for the larger rooms, especially those hampered by a low ceiling. The chart in Figure 15.1 offers a guide to screen size selection under a variety of conditions and can help you decide where to place the projection stands when setting up.

There are several formulas used for determining seating capacity and screen placement. The two most commonly used are the *five feet rule* and the *two by eight rule*.

The five feet rule states that the minimum distance from the bottom of the screen to the floor is five feet, while the average height of a seated person is four feet, six inches. Therefore, to view the screen clearly, the bottom of the screen must be a minimum of five feet off the floor.

The two by eight rule states that no one should be seated closer to the screen than two times the screen's height or farther from the screen than eight times the screen's height. For example, if the meeting room's ceiling height is 15 feet, the maximum height for the projection screen is 10 feet, and if a 7½-foot-high by 10-foot-wide screen is used, the farthest seat from the screen should be no more than 60 feet and the closest seat no closer than 15 feet. Screen sizes are always listed height first, so a 7' x 10' screen is 7 feet high and 10 feet wide.

Several other guidelines also apply to ensure maximum visibility. First, the distance from the projector to the screen should be at least 1.5 times the width of the screen. Second, the projection platform must elevate the projector to at least the bottom of the screen. Third, the projection platform should be placed at a 90-degree angle to the screen.

*Figure 15.1. GUIDE TO SCREEN SIZE SELECTION AND SEATING DISTANCE FROM SCREEN.*

**Choosing a screen size** that takes full advantage of the specific type of projector and room size is as important as choosing the proper screen surface. Today's shorter projection lenses and larger rooms permit bigger, more lifelike projecting than ever.

Audience Capacity

Farthest Seat — Eight times the screen height. First consideration when picking ideal screen for any room. (Assuming choice of lenses.)
Closest Seat — Two times the screen height
Audience capacity — Ten square feet per person after aisle space is deducted. (Assumes ideal seating arrangement.)

| Screen Size H W | Farthest Seat from Screen | Closest Seat to Screen | Audience Capacity | Square Feet Seating Space |
|---|---|---|---|---|
| 6' x 8' | 48' | 12' | 150 | 1,500 |
| 7½' x 10' | 60' | 15' | 200 | 2,000 |
| 9' x 12' | 72' | 18' | 300 | 3,000 |
| 10½' x 14' | 84' | 21' | 500 | 5,000 |
| 12' x 16' | 96' | 24' | 750 | 7,500 |
| 15' x 20' | 120' | 30' | 1,500 | 15,000 |

There are three options for placement of a screen: the center of the stage, to one side of center stage, or in a corner. In deciding where to place the screen, it is important to determine which is more important in the presentation – the speaker or the information on the screen. If the speaker is conducting training, for example, the screen should be centered and the speaker should stand or sit off to the side. If the presenter is a motivational speaker or other special guest, he or she should be the focal point and the screen should be placed off to the side. Placing the screen in a corner is usually only done as a space-saving measure when rear-screen projection is used.

You will also want to have a seating arrangement that offers an optimum relationship of the audience to the screen. The most desirable angle is between 45 and 90 degrees, although an angle of 22-45 degrees is acceptable, especially if the on-screen presentation is secondary to the speaker. Angles of less than 22 degrees are undesirable, as these angles would make it difficult to read the projected material (see box titled "Angle of Screen in Relationship to Attendees" on page 357).

When placing screens, you will also want to be sure that you do not block fire exits and that lighted exit signs or other lighting do not shine through the rear of the screen. The darker the area above the screen, the brighter the projected image will be. And, since most people are right-handed, place the screen to the speaker's right to enable the presenter to refer to projected material with his or her right hand.

There are many types of screens available. Figure 15.2 compares the advantages and disadvantages of the three most common screen types:

- Fastfold screens
- Wall and ceiling screens
- Tripod screens

## Chapter 15: Audiovisual Requirements

*Figure 15.2. ADVANTAGES/DISADVANTAGES OF TYPES OF SCREENS.*

| SCREEN TYPE | ADVANTAGES | DISADVANTAGES | AUDIENCE SIZE |
|---|---|---|---|
| Fastfold | Excellent appearance<br>Available in large sizes<br>Good for rear projection<br>Dress kits available to improve appearance | More expensive<br>No anti-keystoning device available<br>More labor intensive | 6'x8' - up to 150 people<br>7.5'x10' - up to 200 people<br>9'x12' - up to 300 people<br>10.5'x14' - up to 500 people<br>12'x16' - up to 750 people<br>15'x20' - up to 1500 people |
| Wall/Ceiling Screens | Usually complimentary<br>Can be large in size | Screen can't be moved<br>Meeting room must be set around screen | Audience size will vary depending on size of screen |
| Tripod | Less expensive<br>Anti-keystoning device available in sizes less than 8 ft.<br>Fast installation | Largest size is 8-ft.<br>Less attractive<br>Full dress kit not available<br>Cannot be used for rear-projection | 60"x60" - up to 25 people<br>70"x70" - up to 50 people<br>84"x84" - up to 100 people<br>96"x96" - up to 150 people |

Tripod Screen | Standard Fastfold Screen System | Wall and Ceiling Mounted Electric Screen

*Different types of screens have inherent advantages and disadvantages that should be taken into consideration when determining the best screen(s) to be used for presentations. This chart provides an "at-a-glance" comparison for easy reference.*
**Source: Courtesy of Da-Lite Screen Company, Inc. Used with permission.**

The most popular of the larger screens is the **fastfold**, available in sizes up to 30 feet high. The screen comes with adjustable legs to vary the height of placement off the floor (or it may be hung from the ceiling). They last a long time when taken care of and the smaller fastfolds represent a relatively minor investment. Local AV dealers may have a hard time supplying the huge screens, but no trouble supplying any number of small units.

You can give your fastfold screens a "movie theater" look by purchasing full dress kits made especially for these screens. Dress kits are curtains designed to be placed at the top and around the sides of the screen. The curtains add weight to the top of the screen, but additional support brackets will eliminate any potential problems. While using dress kits

**Angle of Screen in Relationship to Attendees**

```
          SCREEN
0° ━━━━━━━━━━━━━━━━━━━━━━ 0°
    Undesirable        Undesirable
 22°
      Acceptable      Acceptable
    45°  Recommended  Recommended
              90°
```

increases costs somewhat, meeting planners appreciate the "finished" look that dress kits provide for general or plenary sessions or other types of meetings for which a professional-looking backdrop is important.

*Wall* or *ceiling screens* come in a variety of sizes and are designed to be hung from hooks or lines, or mounted on the wall or ceiling. They are inexpensive, and the metal tube casings make for easy storage. They are activated like the old-fashioned window shades.

**Tripod screens**, which come in a metal tube like the wall or ceiling screen, are mounted permanently on folding tripod stands so that they can be placed anywhere. Light, portable, versatile, and inexpensive, they are extremely useful in smaller meetings. Tripod screens should be tilted forward or back at the top to avoid **keystoning**, an effect in which an image appears noticeably wider at the top than at the bottom and appears unfocused. And, for a more professional image, the bottom of the screen should be skirted.

There is a variety of screen fabric in use today. A favorite is **glass-beaded** (white), which offers great brilliance. As their name implies, these screens have surfaces covered with tiny glass beads that reflect a bright image back toward the audience. A disadvantage of this type of screen is that they have a narrow viewing angle. Smooth white **matte-surface screens** offer consistent brilliance from a wider angle, which is important in small rooms where some seats may be at a sharp angle to the screen, and are the most commonly used types of screens. Silver metallic and **lenticular screen** surfaces combine the best features of both types, offering maximum brilliance and wide-angle light consistency. They are somewhat more costly than the others. Any local AV dealer can assist you in selecting the proper screens for your facility.

## Projectors

Slide projectors were once the mainstay of the meetings industry, but today they have been almost completely replaced by high-tech computer projection systems. In cases in which slide projectors are still used, the most popular option is the 35mm, 80-slide **carousel projector**. A remote control device is often used in conjunction with these projectors. Both wired remotes and cordless remotes are available, with the wireless device giving the speaker additional mobility.

An **overhead projector** is occasionally used for instructional purposes. The projector is positioned near the speaker and projects behind him or her onto a screen. Overhead projectors handle any brands of transparencies up to nine by nine inches. Such units are relatively inexpensive and rarely break.

## Chapter 15: Audiovisual Requirements

The **LCD projector** has largely replaced traditional overhead transparencies and the 35mm slide projector, and it is the instrument of choice for PowerPoint slides and Web presentations. The special attachment is attached to a personal computer, projecting whatever is on the computer monitor to the projection screen. Not only does this device make the image large enough for easy audience viewing, but it can also store and select data at the operator's command.

A more recent innovation, and one that is preferred by many meeting planners, is the **computer data projector**. These stand-alone projectors are equipped with their own built-in light source into which the computer plugs directly.

Computer programs, such as Microsoft PowerPoint, are commonly used with this type of projector. These programs allow color, animation, and graphics to be projected from computers onto a screen.

An even higher-end projector used in large function rooms where a large screen is required is the **DLP projector (digital light projection)**. DLPs are lighter (three to seven pounds is common), more portable, brighter (with extremely high light output of up to 15,000 lumens), and have a better image quality. While more expensive, they provide better resolution at greater distances.

A visual presentation that is widely used is **rearview projection**. The term "rearview" is somewhat of a misnomer, because the audience still views the picture from the front (see Figure 15.2). The projector, however, is set up behind the screen. By using a curtain or similar room divider, hotels can cut off one part of a room from the other. The audience sits on one side of the partition, the projector on the other. A **translucent rear-projection screen** is framed by the curtain, and the projection equipment is hidden on the darkened rear side.

The primary advantage of this technique is that all projection equipment is hidden from the audience, eliminating the need for an aisle. Additionally, the projection area can be blacked out, allowing for higher **ambient light** in the audience area without washing out the image. The disadvantage is that the room cannot be fully used for seating (rearview projection reduces the available square footage for seating by up to one-third). Another disadvantage is that rear projection requires an almost completely dark projection area behind the screen, requiring complete draping of the screen -- sides, bottom, and top. In addition, if space behind the screen is limited, a more expensive wide-angle lens may be required. On the positive side, however, rearview projection allows the speaker more freedom of movement, and the presentation can appear more dramatic because the image seems to appear out of nowhere.

It is wise for the convention service manager to check out the room setup and the audiovisual equipment supplied before the meeting starts. He or she should check:

- The *screen*, to see if it is above the audience's heads so that all will be able to see clearly from where they sit
- The *projector*, to see that it is secure on the stand and that an extra lamp is available
- The *speaker*, to see that he or she is near the screen
- The *electrical cords,* to be sure they are out of the aisles and hidden

With the use of DVD for meeting presentations, many properties are finding it imperative to provide playback equipment and support.

*Figure 15.2. COMPARISON OF COMMON PROJECTION SYSTEMS.*

*There are both advantages and disadvantages to the two common projection systems detailed in this figure. Frontview projection systems do not take up a lot of space. Disadvantages include possible interference (as when attendees walk across the projected beam of light) and the danger of speakers or attendees tripping over cords or other equipment. With rearview projection systems, there is no need to dim lights, allowing attendees to take notes. The primary disadvantage of these systems is their size; not only do they take up a lot of space (typically 15 to 30 feet behind the screen), but the area behind the screen must also be completely dark, reducing the square footage available for seating. Another disadvantage is that special projector lenses are required, which also adds to the expense.*

Video projectors and DVD projectors are essential for viewing videotapes or DVDs in all but small groups. A self-contained video projector has a curved six-foot screen that can easily be seen by audiences of up to 100 people.

While several of these units can be used for larger groups, it is usually more effective to use a detached video or DVD projector and a fastfold projector screen in larger rooms. This equipment offers a quality image 12 feet wide, and can be used for both front or rear projection.

For arenas and other larger areas, light-valve video projectors must be used. This type of projector projects up to 400 feet and creates an image roughly 40 feet wide. It may not be feasible to purchase this type of projector. It is more practical to rent a light-valve video projector when the need arises.

On the other end of the meetings spectrum, television sets can be used to service small meetings. Television screens fall into two categories: monitors and receivers.

Chapter 15: Audiovisual Requirements

A **monitor** has no tuner, and interprets signals directly from a videotape player, DVD player, or video camera. Monitors are more costly than television receivers, but are often requested by meeting planners due to the crisper image they produce. The next level of video monitors is high-definition television (HDTV) and plasma screens. These monitors are only one- to three-inches thick and up to 110 inches in size. Although these monitors are costly, they are being increasingly used by meeting planners.

**Receivers** are used to interpret and reproduce television signals, but cannot play videotapes or DVDs without an appropriate player. While television receivers have built-in audio systems, these are usually of a mediocre quality; it is advisable to patch sound into the property's sound system rather than rely on the units' audio systems.

Signals from videotapes can be split to feed a number of monitors and television receivers, and the number of units needed will depend on the size of the audience. A general rule of thumb is 25 viewers per 25-inch set and 50 viewers per 25- to 52-inch set.

The brightness of a projector is measured in **lumens**; the higher the lumen rating, the brighter the projector. LCD projectors come in a wide variety of lumens. Hotels commonly use 2500 to 5000 lumen projectors, which are small, light-weight, and easy to handle in smaller meeting spaces. Larger spaces, such as convention halls, might require projectors with lumen levels of 12000 or more (projectors of up to 10000 and 20000 lumens are now available).

*Figure 15.4. SEATING ARRANGEMENTS WHEN USING PROJECTORS.*

*When using a projector, the room should be arranged so that the audience's view of the screen is not blocked by the speaker and the projector. The seating arrangement on the left is best for viewing.*
**Source: Courtesy of the 3M Company.**

540

Chapter 15: Audiovisual Requirements

The **aspect ratio** is the ratio between the width and height of an image. There are two aspect ratios available on projectors; 4:3 is the standard format, and 16:9 is the widescreen format. The industry is rapidly moving to the 16:9 widescreen aspect ratio, as the majority of presentations use a laptop, which are programmed with a widescreen format and delivered to a digital projector (see sidebar).

Although most meeting planners are well versed in the layout of meeting rooms, occasionally the convention service manager will be called upon to advise on the placement of audiovisual equipment. Few things can destroy the effectiveness of a meeting more than the improper positioning of projectors and screens. No one wants to look down the back of someone's neck while the speaker explains the visuals.

Obscured views can be prevented with a simple understanding of AV layout. Figure 15.4 illustrates the proper positioning of a projector so that the speaker does not block

*Figure 15.5. PROJECTOR ARRANGEMENT IN U-SHAPED SETUP.*

*This diagram illustrates the best position for a projector in a U-shape table arrangement.*

541

the audience's view. Figure 15.5 shows the best positioning of a projector in a U-shaped setup. Review these illustrations thoroughly. Good visibility is foremost in communicating with visual techniques.

## Projector Stands

Projectors have to be placed on something. It may be a table or desk, but it is more versatile and convenient to have special projection tables or stands. These come in folding and rigid types. Some have casters for easy movement; with these stands, projectors may be placed anywhere in a room.

There are two basic types of projector stands: the **Safelock stand** and the rolling cart. The Safelock is ideal for large projectors, and has four telescoping legs that adjust to heights up to 56 inches. Rolling carts come in several fixed heights, with the 32-inch and the 54-inch the most commonly used. The 32-inch rolling cart is ideal for overhead projectors, while the 54-inch cart is usually used for television monitors. When using rolling carts, regardless of height, **skirting** (pleated or ruffled draping) should be used to wrap the lower portion of the cart. (Skirting, which gives a professional, finished look, should also be used at the bottom of projection screens.)

## Multimedia Presentations

Multimedia presentation uses several types of audio and visual equipment to create total sight/sound environments. **Multimedia** can range from the very simple to highly sophisticated systems. Convention service managers should have a working knowledge of the basic types of equipment commonly requested by meeting planners.

Even simple shows have more than one source of graphics or video, so a **switcher** or router is used to take inputs from different sources (a computer or video device, for example) and then send the individual signals to the screen. High-end switcher systems have an enormous capacity, and they have the ability to generate real-time special effects, picture-in-picture windows, and green screen effects. This type of system requires a dedicated and specially trained technician.

Programmers are the ultimate in multimedia equipment. The computerized control can be used to synchronize sound tracks and multiple projectors on multiple screens (and can even turn the lights off in the room) for a stunning audiovisual performance. And, as video continues to become a popular alternative to slides, multimedia is becoming even more exciting as a motivational and communications tool.

## Simultaneous Interpretations

As meetings become more international in scope, many properties have found it necessary to provide **simultaneous interpretation** facilities. This involves having a speaker's words translated into the language(s) of the meeting participants, and requires specialized equipment and personnel.

In most cases, the speaker addresses the group and interpreters in soundproof booths relay what the speaker has said to the attendees via wireless headsets. The number of booths and headsets needed will depend on the number of languages required for the meeting.

Today's technology has enhanced this process. Loop antennas can be used within certain areas to enable attendees to hear their language within that area. Infrared signals are also used to beam a language to attendees. Another development is multiple channel selection, which enables attendees to channel back and forth between different languages.

While simultaneous interpretation can be costly, both in terms of equipment (sound booths, headsets, and antennas or infrared radiators) and personnel (interpreters and technicians), more meeting planners will require this service in today's increasingly international business world, and the properties that offer this capability can capture a share of this growing — and lucrative — market.

## Virtual Conferencing

In an increasing number of cases, meeting planners have found that it is virtually impossible — or too costly — to bring everyone who should be involved in a meeting together in person. Conflicting schedules and the high cost of travel are the prime factors for the use of **virtual conferencing**. The most recent Meetings Market Report conducted by *Meetings & Conventions* found that approximately 25 percent of corporate meeting planners use virtual conferencing.

Virtual conferencing can be broadly defined as the electronic linking of more than two people at different sites, and falls into four basic categories: audio, audiographic, video, and web conferencing.

**Audio conferencing,** the most basic form, is generally used when budget is a major consideration. Audio conferencing simply utilizes telephone lines and speaker phones to connect several parties. A speaker can give a presentation to meeting "attendees" at several locations via speaker phones or special microphones and amplifier systems tied directly to telephone lines of the participating properties or alternate remote sites.

**Audiographic conferencing** is generally used for planning sessions, project reviews, and briefings because it combines both audio interaction and visual capabilities. Specially designed conference rooms offer the ability to "show" documents, slides, and objects via television monitors at the remote sites.

**Video satellite conferencing** provides full-motion, "face-to-face" networking, and is the most expensive and sophisticated form of virtual conferencing. Remote sites are "linked" through the use of satellite technology; many properties now offer this type of conferencing network.

Video conferencing involves considerable expense. First, it is necessary to provide full video production, which involves multiple video cameras, technicians, and special effects equipment. Second, it is necessary to provide a playback system at each location. This equipment includes multiple video monitors or video projectors. Third, uplink/downlink and satellite facilities are required. Special equipment (telephone lines, cables, or a microwave system) sends the signal from the origination point to a satellite dish ("uplink" or "earth station") which beams the image to the satellite (22,000 miles or more above the earth). The signal is received by a transponder (an access point on the satellite), the frequency is changed, and the signal is beamed down to satellite dishes ("downlink") at each remote location before it travels, again via telephone lines, cables, or microwave system, to the remote receivers.

While this process requires a large initial investment, many properties have found it worthwhile to purchase or lease uplink systems or find other ways to offer video-conferencing services. Sheraton Hotels & Resorts, for example, went into partnership with VueCom, which provides videoconferencing services transmitted over high-speed, fiber-optic lines. The system, which is easily adapted to various meeting sizes, is installed at approximately 140 properties.

Other chains, including Marriott, Westin, and Hyatt, currently offer videoconferencing or are in the process of reintroducing this service. Their investments in this technology may pay future dividends, as adverse circumstances — a fuel crisis, worsening economic trends, or other negative shifts in the business world — make video conferencing a viable alternative to costly meeting travel and accommodations.

Another alternative to face-to-face meetings is **web conferencing**. Web conferencing refers to conducting meetings, events, and seminars over the Internet. Web-based presentations utilize an Internet connection rather than satellites. The sponsoring organizations have the advantage of saving time and travel expenses as "attendees" can participate without leaving their offices, plus the Internet is less costly than satellite uplink/downlink services.

There are a number of different ways that speakers can connect to the Internet. The easiest, least expensive, but slowest connection is through a telephone line. Many planners find this access too slow and prefer the high-speed connections possible with ISDN (Integrated Services Digital Network), T1, T3, or T5 lines (T1 lines operate at a higher capacity than an ISDN line and can be "split" to accommodate several users at once; T3 and T5 lines are even faster, allowing more tasks to be performed simultaneously at the higher speed). Since these lines ensure that Web information will appear very quickly on computer and projection screens, many hotels, conference facilities, and convention centers are installing these types of lines throughout their meeting rooms.

Today, content can be directly accessed by mobile devices via a direct Internet connection or by Wi-Fi. Content is made available at a specific web address, and attendees click on the link to download the content into their mobile devices. A great deal of content for mobile devices is available only for Apple products; however, more presentations are being developed to be viewed on Android devices. Some applications, such as Periscope, offer both IOS and Android links and can also be seen on a PC; the comment feature is only available on mobile devices, as is a replay feature, although plans have been announced to offer replay on PCs.

## Other Presentation Devices

Not all presentation is done by projectors, of course. Many speakers use whiteboards. Dry-erase markers are used, and many whiteboards are marked like graph paper, making it easy for a speaker to write or draw in a straight line.

Whiteboards are also available in electronic, interactive versions. Interactive whiteboards are an excellent way to provide information in interesting formats; graphs, charts, sales numbers, and other significant data can be displayed – and modified, as these whiteboards

> **WORTH WATCHING**
>
> Watch a demonstration of Epson's BrightLink Pro Interactive Whiteboard at www.youtube.com/watch?v=FZyhjU2mLgI (or go to www.youtube.com, search for Epson WhiteLink Pro Interactive Whiteboard – See it in Action).

## Advantages and Disadvantages of Popular AV Equipment

| Advantages | Disadvantages |
|---|---|
| **Slide Projectors**<br>1. Can be operated with wireless remote control device.<br>2. Can be connected with audio-sync tape.<br>3. Excellent color reproduction on slides. | 1. Limited motion capabilities compared to video.<br>2. Fan noise can be distracting. |
| **Flip Charts**<br>1. Very inexpensive.<br>2. Take up very little seating space.<br>3. Ideal for "brainstorming" and training meetings. | 1. Limited to small audiences (50 persons or less). |
| **Computer-Based Projectors**<br>1. Most are compatible with laptop computers.<br>2. PowerPoint and electronic graphics make for powerful presentations.<br>3. Possible to provide Internet connection. | 1. Technology changes about every 18 months, so equipment can become obsolete. |
| **Overhead Projectors**<br>1. Can be used in a lighted room.<br>2. Simple to operate, and transparencies can be produced quickly on a copy machine. | 1. Noise from built-in fans can be a distraction.<br>2. Limited color reproduction. |
| **Video Projectors**<br>1. Instant playback capabilities.<br>2. Full motion and color capabilities.<br>3. Simple to operate.<br>4. Video display of computer-generated information is possible. | 1. Various formats of playback equipment are incompatible.<br>2. Difficult to project to large audiences. |

are connected to computers and essentially become a live computer desktop. The material being displayed can also be printed out and distributed to group members.

One whiteboard model, Panasonic's Panofax, reproduces everything written on it or taped to it. When desired, a photocopy of everything on the board can be made with the push of a button. This eliminates extensive note-taking, which often distracts attendees from what the speaker is saying.

The SoftBoard, shown in Figure 15.6, is another example of this technology. SoftBoards are connected to a computer and store everything written on them into the computer using two infrared lasers mounted at the upper corners of the boards. Information is generated through the use of bar-coded dry erase markers, allowing the lasers to track their position and color. Information is captured stroke by stroke and can be "played back" at various speeds or stored on disks, e-mailed, or cut and pasted into other files.

*Paper easel pads* or **flip charts** are commonly used with broad soft-point pens or markers. Flip charts are portable, using handy tripod easels. There are special cabinets to house them. If you have rooms used extensively for training classrooms, you may find it convenient to mount such flip charts.

Flip charts are generally 27x34 inches in size, and should be limited to use in small meeting rooms. When ordering flip charts, the convention services department needs to specify "flip chart easel with pad"; this will differentiate from the order for "tripod easels," which support signs but not the heavy flip chart pads. Some properties charge extra for pads and markers and supply the easels only; others include all materials needed for the presentation (easel, pad, and specified colors of markers) in the basic charge.

## Chapter 15: Audiovisual Requirements

*Figure 15.6. HIGH-TECH COMPUTER APPLICATIONS FOR PRESENTATIONS.*

*The SoftBoard shown above connects to a computer, that stores information written on the board with bar-coded dry erase markers. The device's playback mode works like a VCR, or DVD, and information generated can also be stored on a disk, e-mailed, or cut and pasted into other files.*

*Pointers* have become more sophisticated since the days of long wooden ones. Many speakers use metal pointers that telescope down to ball-point pen size. There are also electric hand-held **laser pointers** that can project an arrowhead onto the screen from 100 feet away, allowing a greater freedom of movement for the speaker.

Another device, used for presentations, communication, and training is the personal computer. Most meeting planners realize that computers can easily become damaged in transit, and look for properties that can supply personal computers for workshops and training sessions (as well as for on-site convention registration).

Because the cost of stocking computers can be prohibitive, many properties make arrangements with a local computer rental center when a number of computers are requested by a meeting group.

Since most attendees today travel with their mobile devices, hotels must also supply Wi-Fi to accomodate cell phones, smartphones, and other mobile devices. We will discuss this additional component of Internet service in the next section.

Hotels are not expected to supply the gear for sophisticated AV presentations such as multi-screen extravaganzas. These are usually handled by specialists. Local AV dealers or service organizations can handle such needs if you get requests for such sources.

It is usually enough for hotels to be able to supply on short notice such basics as projectors, screens, whiteboards, and easel pads. Beyond this, advance notice should be given and a specialist dealer called in. A meeting planner should supply a list of all AV needs in advance.

To sum up, a hotel should have a good working relationship with a local audiovisual dealer/service organization. If such a company is not available, the hotel may decide to

## INTERNET EXERCISE

Visit the websites for Freeman Audio Visual Solutions (www.freemanco.com/freemanco/ourservices/audioVisual.jsp) and PSAV Presentation Services (www.psav.com). Both of these companies provide extensive audiovisual services to hotels and resorts. Navigate through these sites and answer the following questions:

1. Which of these sites offers a Resource Library?
2. Which offers a bandwidth calculator?
3. What additional information have you learned about audiovisual equipment?

stock a department of its own. In either case, a hotel may choose to stock a minimum number of basic items and train staff people to maintain and operate them.

## Bandwidth and High-Speed Internet Access

Since meeting planners today are incorporating more Internet-based elements, such as computer-generated presentations and video streaming, into their meetings, offering high-speed Internet access (HSIA) is essential for hotels to stay competitive. In the past, meeting rooms were wired with Internet connections, and Internet was also available in guestrooms (sometimes for a fee). But wired Internet connections are not enough for today's planners and their attendees.

Tech-savvy meeting planners increasingly expect a Wireless Local Area Network (WLAN) to be available in meeting rooms to accommodate the use of wireless devices for presentations and attendee interaction. Many meeting attendees also see a wired Internet connection as cumbersome; they expect to be able to use their mobile devices in meeting rooms and throughout the hotel (guestrooms, public spaces, at the pool, and so on). Hotels have responded by offering increased wireless capabilities – and by installing charging stations for guests' multiple mobile devices.

There are two types of wireless technology that are typically used for meetings: the IEEE 802 series (also known as wireless fidelity, or Wi-Fi), which has a transmission range of 100 feet or more, and Bluetooth, which has a shorter transmission range of about 30 feet (Bluetooth-enabled devices are not only used for social networks; they can also be used in meeting rooms for such applications as sending questions to the presenter).

In today's high-tech meetings environment, it is important that the hotel provide enough **bandwidth** to ensure both connectivity and quality presentations. The APEX Bandwidth and Connectivity Workshop of the Con-

### WORTH WATCHING

- The Profession Convention Management Association (PCMA) offers an excellent video, titled "The Intersection Part 4: Bandwidth," on Internet connectivity and bandwidth. Use a search engine and type in the title to access the video.
- Todd Marinko, vice president of strategic accounts at PSAV, explains the fundamentals of Internet delivery and the importance of creating customized solutions for Wi-Fi needs at hedtalks.connectplusathilton worldwide.com (click on the Driving Results tab and scroll down to the "Customizing Wi-Fi Solutions" video).
- Hilton Elevated Discussions also features another video on Wi-Fi from Vivian Eickhoff, group event marketing manager at Microsoft, at hedtalks.connectplusathilton worldwide.com (click on the "Creating Experiences" tab and scroll down to the "Wi-Fi" video).

547

## Chapter 15: Audiovisual Requirements

vention Industry Council (CIC) defines bandwidth as the amount of data that can be transmitted (uploaded) or received (downloaded) per second; it defines Wi-Fi as the technology that distributes the bandwidth to wireless devices.

Different devices – cell phones, smartphones, tablets, laptops, audio response systems, and so on – require a different amount of bandwidth to operate properly, so the hotel's bandwidth determines how many devices can be used concurrently inside meeting rooms, public areas, and guestrooms without interference or crashes. Bandwidth also determines whether streaming video presentations will be transmitted over the Internet fast enough to project crisply and clearly on the screen; a less-than-optimal bandwidth can limit the type, size, and quality of presentations that speakers or instructors will be able to upload or download.

It is important, then, that planners estimate their bandwidth needs (web access, streaming, peer-to-peer communications, and so on) and plan in advance to ensure that enough Internet access and Wi-Fi will be available during their events. An audiovisual professional or a member of the convention services staff should be able to assist in this area, but there are also several apps that can help, including Speedtest (www.speedtest.net/mobile), a free app that measures the wireless signal in a venue, and TechSpec, an app for Androids that can be downloaded from the Google app store (this tool is frequently used for site inspections, as it provides complete technical information – from the number of electrical outlets in a room to the strength of the Wi-Fi signal). There are also several bandwidth estimators available on the Internet; PSAV, for example, has created the APEX Bandwidth Estimator for the CIC as a courtesy to the industry.

It is also important to determine where Wi-Fi access points (AP) are located. Knowing exactly where access is available will enable a meeting planner to determine seating arrangements and staging. If Wi-Fi is strongest in the front of a room, for example, that area would be used for presentations, while the back of the room could be set up for socializing, which does not require extra wireless service.

> **MORE ONLINE**
>
> The Convention Industry Council (CIC) offers the following educational resources on bandwidth:
> - A white paper titled "Getting Up to Speed on Event Bandwidth"
> - An APEX bandwidth terminology download
> - An article titled "Strike up the Bandwidth"
> - A bandwidth estimator tool.
>
> To view these resources, go to www.conventionindustry.org, click on Standards and Practices, and scroll down to the Internet Access link. The site also features links to outside sources for additional information.
>
> Several other organizations and firms, such as the International Association of Conference Centers, also offer bandwidth calculators. You can find additional information on these services with an Internet search.

Free Wi-Fi is available in most hotel lobbies – and planners expect free high-speed Internet in guestrooms — but bandwidth above and beyond these services is likely to result in additional costs to the meeting group. Hotels charge for upgrades in bandwidth and connectivity, so meetings that require multiple mobile devices (or have a large number of attendees that can be expected to use mobile devices) are likely to incur fees and pay a premium for extra connectivity.

Many meeting planners, who are used to receiving free Wi-Fi at coffee shops, libraries, and the airport, balk at these fees. But reconfiguring a meeting room for Wi-Fi requirements or supplying wireless connections to thousands of attendees at once is far more costly than providing service to clientele at a small establishment.

Providing a wireless infrastructure – and keeping up with the latest technologies – costs money, and hotels typically assess charges in several ways to recoup their investment:

- A set fee based on bandwidth used.
- A charge based on both bandwidth and the number of locations where connectivity is needed.
- Fees based on concurrent connections (the number of users connected at one time; fees are imposed based on peak use).
- Fees based on unique connections (connecting all devices to a network via access codes; the planner is charged an agreed-upon amount for each connection).
- A daily fee charged to individual attendees.

It is sometimes challenging for planners to budget these costs, especially since they can vary in price from hotel and hotel – and sometimes at the same hotel, where it will cost more to provide service in a large exhibit hall, for example. To avoid potential problems and ill will, hotels should clearly spell out their Internet policies and charges in their contracts. This gives planners several options: they can try to negotiate costs; they can plan their programs around wireless limitations (deciding how many bandwidth access points are required and how they should be distributed); or they can choose a more affordable venue.

## Outside or Inside?

Since audiovisual equipment plays such a vital part in today's meetings business, properties are faced with the dilemma of how to make AV equipment available. Is it feasible to maintain a large in-house inventory, and, if so, what should be stocked? Or, would it be more cost-effective to have an outside AV firm provide the requested equipment? Or, as yet a third alternative, should the most commonly used items be stocked in-house and outside AV firms be called upon to supply any special equipment requested by the meeting planner? In this section, we will take a look at the advantages and disadvantages of supplying AV equipment from outside sources or in-house (see box titled "Outside or Inside?") and look at what factors figure into a property's decision on meeting AV requirements.

### Audiovisual Specialists

Many hotel managers prefer to use a local AV service organization rather than cope with this area in-house. Outside rental firms are used when:

- The hotel lacks adequate storage space
- Equipment is used so infrequently that investment in a piece cannot be justified
- The call for certain equipment, such as thin, high resolution, wide screen monitors, is so heavy that it is not feasible for a hotel to inventory so many pieces

There are four main categories of outside audiovisual suppliers:

- Exclusive
- Recommended
- Non-exclusive
- In-house

An **exclusive contractor** is an AV firm that has been contracted by the hotel to provide all audiovisual equipment and services at the property; this firm has the sole right to

## Outside or Inside?

Hotels are faced with the decision of either owning AV equipment and leasing it to the meeting group or entrusting the AV needs of a group to an outside firm. The final decision will vary depending on individual property needs, and the following factors should be taken into consideration when making that decision.

### Advantages of Using an AV Company Outside the Hotel

1. Audiovisual equipment is expensive. In the event of theft or lost items, the outside firm, rather than the hotel, would incur the loss.
2. Many audiovisual pieces are used so infrequently that the cost of maintaining an inventory would be prohibitive.
3. The cost of maintaining and repairing equipment is expensive and may not justify the hiring of a staff specialist to service audiovisual items.
4. With advances in audiovisual equipment, some items may become obsolete, which would require additional expenditure by the hotel.

### Advantages of Owning AV Equipment and Leasing It to the Meeting Group

1. There may be a lack of suppliers in the area, or it may be difficult to rent a particular piece.
2. The property can purchase pieces that best meet its needs rather than have to rely on an outside contractor whose equipment may not be adequate.
3. The property has greater control over the quality of equipment if it owns it. Rental equipment may have been misused and may not function properly.
4. The property directly benefits from renting its own equipment to meeting groups, rather than turning the profits over to an outside firm.

provide AV services within that particular hotel or convention center. Some hotels impose fees to block outside AV suppliers, and they may include clauses in their contracts regarding penalties for not using their exclusive contractor. A typical clause might read:

> The hotel has an exclusive contract with American Audio Visual for audiovisual services. A $100 fee per room, per day, will be assessed for technical services and additional set-up requirements for audio visual equipment supplied by a source other than Hilton Milwaukee or American Audio Visual. Audio visual equipment contracted outside the hotel must be removed immediately following the conclusion of the event. The hotel and American Audio Visual assume no responsibility for services contracted outside the hotel.

Other clauses might specify that the hotel's exclusive contractor will be required to manage and oversee any outside AV company. These restrictions do not sit well with meeting planners, as many may already have a supplier of choice, so many meeting planners try to negotiate around them before signing their contracts. Smart planners also insist on a full disclosure of all potential charges, and some include a "buyer's freedom to choose" clause in their own contracts.

A *recommended contractor* is an AV firm that has the hotel's "stamp of approval". The hotel may have used the firm or firms in the past and been satisfied with the equipment and level of service provided. Unlike with an exclusive contractor, however, planners are under no obligation to choose a recommended contractor; they will not be assessed any penalties for going with the AV provider of their choice.

*Non-exclusive contractors* can be any AV firms that are appropriately qualified and insured, but the firm must adhere to the hotel's rules and regulations. Sometimes, meeting planners will "shop" local vendors to determine the best price for equipment and services. The planners of large conventions may contract with a specific AV company that will provide services wherever the organization meets. The fees that this type of company charges to the planner are usually a small price to pay for proven, consistent service for large events.

On rare occasions, meeting planners may wish to bring in their own audiovisual equipment, particularly lightweight LCD projectors. To accommodate these planners, many hotels now offer "bring your own projector" packages that include screen setup assistance, a powered projection cart, and all special signal and power cables. This often results insignificant savings to the meeting planner who is holding training sessions.

An **in-house contractor** is an AV firm that is retained by the facility to provide on-site equipment and services as needed. These firms set up an office and store equipment at the hotel. In some cases, these AV firms are provided with rent-free space, but they are required to pay a commission to the hotel when they are contracted for AV equipment (commissions vary, but 30 percent is common).

Figure 15.7 shows an example of an AV rate schedule for The Yarrow Hotel & Conference Center in Park City, Utah, for equipment provided by its in-house contractor, Wasatch Audio Visual. AV firms such as these know the facility and what will and what won't work in each meeting room. Last-minute needs can be quickly met from the on-site storage of AV equipment.

In addition, in-house contractors provide convenient, consolidated billing for the planner. In some cases, planners are not required to use the services of an in-house contractor, but they may be charged a surcharge or facility fee for using outside contractors that provide the same service.

When an outside firm is used, many convention service managers prefer to order the equipment themselves rather than have the corporation or association do it. There are three reasons for this. First, they are assured that the equipment will arrive in plenty of time to set it up. Second, they can determine how large to set the stage, since the screen is often placed on a raised platform. A third reason is that AV companies often pay a commission to hotels that book them instead of the competition.

An outside company offers the hotel's client a specialist with a full staff and inventory of equipment. An expert staff can be relied upon to maintain the equipment and to handle any on-the-scene malfunctions. Many hotel managers have said that they would install an inventory of such equipment only when the volume of such rental would enable them to hire at least one full-time specialist to manage a small department. That person would assist in planning, setup, operation, and service.

This is sound thinking when the hotel is in an area with good service companies. But in remote resort areas, the nearest AV dealer may be some distance away. If that is the case, last-minute malfunctions or additional needs can constitute a severe problem. A convention services manager in Lake Tahoe, Nevada, for example, gave this explanation for opting to stock equipment in-house:

> We are in a very isolated area, so each time I need to order a single piece of equipment due to a group change, the service charge is outrageous. The AV company's office is in Reno, 35 miles away, and the weather can be a factor on equipment delivery nine months out of the year.[1]

## Chapter 15: Audiovisual Requirements

*Figure 15.7. SAMPLE AUDIOVISUAL EQUIPMENT RATES.*

### AUDIO VISUAL

**PROJECTORS**
- Overhead Projector .......... $30.00
- 35mm Slide Projector ....... $30.00
- 35mm 50% Brighter ........ $75.00

**SCREENS**
- 6' Tripod Screen .............. $30.00
- 8' Tripod Screen .............. $40.00
- 12' Cradle Screen ............ $65.00

**MICROPHONES**
- Handheld Podium Mic. ... $15.00
- Wireless Lavalier ............. $60.00
- Wireless Handheld .......... $60.00

**SPEAKER PHONES**
- Speaker Phone
  (6 people) ...................... $30.00
- Polycom System
  (20 people) .................... $75.00
- Gentner System
  (large groups) .............. $250.00

**TAPE RECORDERS**
- Portable Cassette ............. $15.00
- Stereo Cassette ................ $40.00
- CD Player ....................... $40.00

**VIDEO CAMERAS**
- Camcorder ..................... $100.00
- Digital Video Camera .... $550.00

**VIDEO MONITORS & TV's**
- 25" Monitor .................... $80.00
- 31" Monitor .................. $150.00
- 51" Monitor .................. $275.00

**VIDEO PLAYERS/RECORDERS**
- 1/2" VHS ........................ $50.00
- Beta SP ......................... $400.00

**DATA & VIDEO PROJECTION**
- LCD for Computer ....... $350.00
- LCD for Video ............. $400.00
- LCD 2000 Lumens ....... $550.00

**PRESENTATION AIDS**
- Easel Only ...................... $10.00
- Flipchart (pad & easel) ..... $25.00
- Whiteboard .................... $20.00
- Corkboard ...................... $15.00

**CARTS & STANDS**
- Projection Carts .............. $15.00
- TV/VCR Cart .................. $20.00
- Safe Lock Stand
  (adjustable) ................... $10.00

Additional Information:
Please call (435) 655-9898
Fax (435) 655-9899

**WASATCH AUDIO VISUAL BUSINESS CENTER**

Equipment is supplied and serviced by our on-site audio visual specialists, Wasatch A/V Business Center.

An experienced event consultant will preview your needs and arrange for hardware and technical support. This could range from the latest in giant screen projection from video or computer sources to an overhead projector and screen or a simple flipchart with colored markers.

*Prices subject to change. Equipment subject to availability. This is a partial list only.*

The Yarrow Hotel contracts with Wasatch Audio Visual to supply AV equipment to meeting planners. As ann in-house contractor, the company maintains an office within the hotel.
**Source: Courtesy of Yarrow Hotel, Park City, Utah.**

## In-House Equipment

If an arrangement with a local AV service company cannot be made, a hotel may decide to stock at least the basic AV requirements. Rick Stanfield, CHA, former vice president of administration at Opryland Hospitality, cautions:

> It is essential to track usage before investing in equipment. Do you have enough demand? Who will coordinate the AV service? These are important questions to answer. Go through a year's worth of records to see how often certain equipment is rented and calculate how many rentals will be necessary to break even. Look carefully, plot it on a graph, because it's hard to get payback if your equipment is sitting on a shelf.[2]

The question might well be asked, "If a hotel is going to have its own equipment, what types and how much of each must be stocked?" Naturally, the type and quantity vary from hotel to hotel. No one list or rate schedule can be applied to every hotel; a hotel must consider the needs of its clients in offering the proper assortment of AV equipment.

Some hotels are reluctant to bring in local companies on a one-time rental basis for fear that the service may not be up to their own staff's standards. But if you call on a local company frequently, you have the muscle to demand *excellent service*, rather than the business-as-usual kind. After all, AV malfunctions generally happen on the weekend or at night. If you can achieve a good working relationship with an alert and eager AV company, your problems are solved. If not, you had better set up some sort of department of your own.

Equipment used at a convention, then, can come from any of three sources — the *convening organization*, the *hotel*, or an *outside AV specialist* hired by either the convention organization or the hotel. And equipment may come from any combination of the three.

The first need is to coordinate service. Another is to identify hotel equipment permanently to facilitate sorting equipment afterwards. Use decals or permanent stencil imprints in paint. Many properties with in-house audiovisual departments are utilizing *bar coding* to both inventory equipment and to facilitate billing. Each type of equipment is labeled with its own bar code that can be scanned to generate reports as to where and how much it is used, and charges can be instantly calculated and posted to the client's account.

Your own equipment will fare better from security and maintenance standpoints if responsibility for it is assigned to specific individuals. These people should receive special training in the care and operation of such equipment. Everyone in convention sales and service should be at home with the kind of equipment needed for most meetings. The dealer from whom the merchandise is purchased should agree to train your personnel; it requires merely some demonstration, not a lengthy course. Technical representatives of AV equipment manufacturers can be reached through the dealer to provide advice and training assistance.

## Charging for Audiovisual Equipment

No single rule can be established for how much a hotel should charge for AV equipment. Competition and the availability of outside firms, the number of guestrooms occupied, the extent of food and beverage functions, and the amount invested in equipment are some of the variables that must be considered in establishing a policy.

In some cases, the client deals directly with the AV supplier if an outside supplier is used. In other cases, you may contract with the outside service and pass the charges along to the client. Whether you use outside services or provide in-house equipment, you should supply a list of your prices to the client. A form detailing the specific equipment to be used and the cost for each piece is commonly used to provide an at-a-glance overview of AV charges (see box titled "Sample AV Equipment List/Price Sheet").

Remember when figuring your prices to include any additional charges, such as delivery costs, set-up charges, labor requirements (technician, sound mixer, etc.), and other miscellaneous fees (the cost of bringing extra electricity to a room, for example). These costs may be figured into the price of the equipment, in which case you may wish to add a notation to that effect on your form. Or, additional costs may be listed separately on your form.

In any case, it is bad business to surprise the meeting planner with hidden costs; he or she must often work within an AV budget and should know exactly what will be charged for the entire meeting beforehand. A recent survey by *PCMA Convene* magazine found that AV

# Chapter 15: Audiovisual Requirements

## Sample AV Equipment List/Price Sheet

A listing such as this one can be used to give the meeting planner an at-a-glance look at exactly what audiovisual equipment will be used for a meeting or function and its overall costs. This list can also be helpful to the property's convention service department, as it provides an overview of the equipment that will be in use on specific days.

**Source:** Bill Masheter, "AV Bids," *Association Meetings*. Used with permission.

### AV Flowsheet

Meeting: **American Association of Widget Waxers**
Property: **Hotel Unique**
City: **Heartland**
Room: **All**
Session:

| EQUIPMENT | BASE COST | Day/Date Thu 14 QTY | Day/Date Fri 15 QTY | Day/Date Sat 16 QTY | Day/Date Sun 17 QTY | Day/Date Mon 18 QTY | Day/Date Tues 19 QTY | Day/Date Wed 20 QTY | TOTAL |
|---|---|---|---|---|---|---|---|---|---|
| Tripod screen 70" x 70" | $18.00 | 5 | 5 $90.00 | 8 $144.00 | 6 $108.00 | 6 $108.00 | 7 $126.00 | | $576.00 |
| Tripod screen 84" x 84" | $24.00 | | 1 $24.00 | 1 $24.00 | 1 $24.00 | 1 $24.00 | 2 $48.00 | 1 $24.00 | $168.00 |
| Tripod screen 96" x 96" | $30.00 | | | | | | | 2 $60.00 | $60.00 |
| CPE fastfold screen 10' x 10' front | $55.00 | | 2 $110.00 | 1 $55.00 | 1 $55.00 | 1 $55.00 | 2 $110.00 | | $385.00 |
| CPE fastfold screen 12' x 12' front | $85.00 | | 1 $85.00 | 2 $170.00 | 2 $170.00 | 2 $170.00 | 2 $170.00 | 1 $85.00 | $850.00 |
| 2 x 2–35mm slide projector Kodak EKIII | $27.50 | | 4 $110.00 | 7 $192.50 | 6 $165.00 | 5 $137.50 | 8 $220.00 | | $825.00 |
| 2 x 2–35mm slide projector Kodak EKIII Britelite projector | $48.00 | | 4 $192.00 | 3 $144.00 | 2 $96.00 | 3 $144.00 | 2 $96.00 | 4 $192.00 | $864.00 |
| 2 x 2–35mm slide projector 500w xenon | $200.00 | | | 1 $200.00 | 2 $400.00 | 1 $200.00 | 2 $400.00 | | $1200.00 |
| 2 x 2 long lens | $15.00 | | 7 $105.00 | 7 $105.00 | 7 $105.00 | 7 $105.00 | 8 $120.00 | 4 $60.00 | $600.00 |
| Safelock stand | $10.00 | | 5 $50.00 | 9 $90.00 | 7 $70.00 | 6 $60.00 | 8 $80.00 | 1 $10.00 | $360.00 |
| Overhead projector | $27.50 | | 5 $137.50 | 10 $275.00 | 6 $165.00 | 5 $137.50 | 8 $220.00 | | $935.00 |
| 32" cart w/drape | $15.00 | | 5 $75.00 | 10 $150.00 | 4 $60.00 | 8 $120.00 | 11 $165.00 | 3 $45.00 | $615.00 |
| 16mm projector | $35.00 | | 1 $35.00 | | | | 1 $35.00 | | $70.00 |

554

expenditures typically account for 13 percent of the budget for respondents' largest meetings.[3] Therefore, hotels must do their best to work within these budgets; sometimes an alternative piece of equipment may be suggested, or a discount may be given if the group's meeting spend warrants it.

A logbook should be used to control the rental of audiovisual equipment. The log should contain the date ordered, the item, the delivery date, the guest billed, and the banquet check number. If an outside agency is billing the hotel, each invoice should be approved by the convention service manager and recorded in the logbook before sending it to accounting.

## Union Regulations

One of the biggest complaints of meeting planners is the influence that unions have on the operation of audiovisual equipment. When AV equipment is ordered from outside firms, technicians are often part of the package. Projectionists, sound recording engineers, spotlight operators, and other specialists with expertise in complicated equipment are required. The problem arises when the services of a projectionist really aren't needed, but the union contract calls for such a person whenever the equipment is used. According to one convention manager:

> One of the biggest complaints by convention groups coming to our city is the requirement to pay the high union scale for some person to sit idly by and run a machine that anyone can operate. In some cities the meeting planner or his people can't even plug the equipment in, but must wait for a union projectionist.

While this may seem a little farfetched, the situation is actually becoming more common. And it is unlikely that union restrictions will be eased. Hotels should inform meeting planners of such rigid union regulations; a violation can lead to a work stoppage and a crisis in the convention.

## Summary

Convention programs are becoming more sophisticated and often involve the services of both the hotel and a number of outside suppliers to carry them out. Today's hotels must have — or be able to obtain — the latest in presentation devices in addition to the simple presentation aids used in the past. Today's meeting and convention attendees expect a professional presentation and come to the meeting with high expectations. In the next chapter, we will take a look at servicing meeting attendees. We will see how admission systems are set up and detail the wide variety of support services that are being used to make the convention or meeting a memorable event for all concerned.

## Endnotes

1. *Hotel Convention Sales, Services, and Operations*, Pat Golden-Romero, Elsevier.

2. Vicki Meade, "Picture This," *Lodging*.
3. Michelle Russell, "You Can't Skimp on AV," *PCMA Convene*.

## Study Questions

1. In what cases would a hotel prefer an outside AV specialist rather than coping with in-house service? What have some hotels done to offer on-site service without the expense of purchasing AV equipment?
2. Discuss the types of sound systems, lighting, lecterns, and projection screens usually offered by hotels.
3. What types of projectors are commonly used in meeting presentations? When is each type typically used?
4. How has technology changed the presentation of information? What high-tech AV equipment is commonly used today?
5. What is bandwidth and how does a planner determine how much bandwidth is needed?
6. How do union regulations affect meeting presentations?
7. What factors are considered when hotels determine charges for AV equipment?

## Key Terms

**ambient light**—Level of illumination from natural lighting sources already existing in an environment.

**amplifier**—A device that enables sound signals to be intensified.

**aspect ratio**—The ratio of image width to image height.

**audio conferencing**—A conference between two or more sites using only voice transmissions.

**audiographic conferencing**—Conference that combines visual capabilities with voice transmissions.

**audiovisual (AV)**—Equipment used for visuals and sound during a presentation. May include screens, projectors, and microphones. AV equipment needs are listed in the event's Banquet Event Order (BEO).

**bandwidth**—The transmission capacity of an electronic communication device and the speed of data transfer. More bandwidth allows more people to be doing more things online at once.

**carousel projector**—Most popular 2" by 2" (35mm) slide projector. Projects images from slides in mounts measuring 2 by 2 inches, presorted in round trays.

**cordless/wireless microphone**—Small, portable microphone that operates without any direct electrical connection. Often used when taking questions or comments from the audience.

**DLP projector (digital light projection)**—High-end projector with extremely high light (up to 15,000 lumens) and scan output. Most commonly used for very large screen and room applications.

**easel**—Portable three-legged stand with a rack that is used to hold signs, boards,

## Chapter 15: Audiovisual Requirements

posters, charts, cork boards, magnetic boards, or other objects.

**exclusive contractor**—The audiovisual provider selected by the hotel to exclusively provide audiovisual equipment and services.

**fastfold screen**—A large screen with a frame. The legs of this screen are attached at the sides to allow the screen to be folded down into a small case for storage (some fastfold screens are also suspended above the viewing area). Most popular of the large viewing screens. Available in sizes up to 30 feet high.

**flip charts**—Large pads on a tripod stand. Used by speakers for illustrations and drawings.

**floodlights**—Lights designed to provide general illumination.

**follow-spots**—Movable lights used to highlight the speaker or performance.

**glass-beaded screen**—Screen on which the surface is covered with tiny glass beads that reflect a bright image back at the audience but have a narrow viewing angle.

**gobo patterns**–Possibly derived from "go between," gobos are metal plates perforated with a pattern of holes to produce a projected image or outline, such as a corporate logo, when placed in front of a light (more sophisticated gobos rotate to create moving patterns). Gobos can also be made of glass that contains colored patterns.

**in-house contractor**—Contractor retained by a facility to provide on-site services as needed. In some cases, planners are not required to use their services, but may be charged a surcharge or facility fee for using outside contractors to provide the same service.

**intelligent lighting**–Lighting instruments that can be computer-controlled to move light around the room and project color and patterns on screens, scenery, walls, or the floor.

**keystoning**—Distortion of a projected image; the image is wider on the top and narrower on the bottom. Tilting the top of the screen can correct the problem, and many data projectors allow the operator to tilt the lens to correct keystoning.

**laser pointers**—Compact instruments consisting of a visible light laser. Used for pointing out features on a projected visual display.

**lavaliere microphone**—A microphone that hangs around the neck, leaving the hands free. Also called a **lapel, neck, or pendant microphone**.

**LCD projector**—A device that projects the image on a computer monitor onto a screen. The self-contained unit, which contains a **liquid crystal display** panel, light source, and lens, works with both PC and Mac computers and DVD, VCR and digital HDTV signals.

**lectern/podium mic**—A type of microphone used by speakers who present from a lectern or podium. The mic is usually attached to a gooseneck mic holder mounted to the lectern or podium.

**LED lights**—Short for Light Emitting Diode, these lights give off light and little-or-no heat and are more environmentally friendly than standard lights.

**lenticular screen**—Screen with a silver-colored finish that has brighter reflective characteristics than a matte screen and a wider viewing angle than a beaded screen.

**lumen(s)**—A measure of the total amount of visible light emitted. A measure of brightness used when referring to video projectors. Brighter projectors are required for larger screens or in rooms with natural light.

**matte-surface screen**—Screen having a flat or matte white finish that does not reflect as effectively as a glass-bead screen but can be viewed from virtually all front angles.

## Chapter 15: Audiovisual Requirements

**mixer board**—Regulates the sound from multiple microphones. Also called a **sound board**.

**monitor**—Device used to view a video or computer image.

**multimedia**—Refers to the use of two or more audiovisual devices for a presentation.

**overhead projector**—Projects a transparency onto a screen. Speakers can write on transparencies as they are projected.

**profile spots**—Adjustable spotlights used to light lecterns, signs, and areas that need a tightly focused pool of light.

**rearview projection**—Movie, slide, or computer image projected from a projector positioned behind the screen onto the back of a screen placed between the viewer and the projector. Also called **back projection**.

**receivers**—Devices that convert electric currents or waves into visible or audible signals. Similar to a monitor, but with poorer picture quality.

**roving microphone**—Hand microphone, with or without a cord, that can be moved easily through an audience to take questions.

**Safelock stand**—Audiovisual equipment stand with four adjustable telescoping legs.

**skirting**—Pleated or ruffled draping used on audiovisual stands and stagings. Also used to drape buffet, reception, and head tables for food and beverage functions.

**simultaneous interpretation**—The interpretation of the presentation into another language while the speech is in progress.

**stage wash**—Lighting that provides an even, overall illumination to the stage area.

**standing microphone**—Microphone attached to a metal stand placed on the floor. Can be adjusted for angle and height. Also called a **floor microphone**.

**switchers**—Audiovisual switchers allow the connection of multiple components to a projector or monitor and the easy switching between inputs.

**table microphone**—Microphone attached to a small stand placed on a table, desk, or lectern.

**translucent rear-projection screen**—Plastic screen with a special gray coating that allows images to be projected from behind the screen and viewed by the audience in front.

**tripod screen**—Portable projection screen with three folding legs and a pull-up surface supported by a rod on the back. Usually not larger than 10-12 feet.

**unidirectional microphone**—A microphone that picks up sound from only one direction. Used for speeches, it is different from omni-directional devices, that pick up sound from all directions.

**uplights**—LED lights that shine upward from the ground.

**video satellite conferencing**—Two-way, full motion, full-color, interactive electronic form of communication. Various transmission technologies can be used to link groups of people at two or more locations for face-to-face meetings, seminars, or conferences.

**virtual conferencing**—Any meeting at which people at two or more distant locations are linked using video, audio, and data for two-way communication via satellite communications or the Internet. Parties see and hear each other via TV screens or computer monitors and audio speakers.

**web conferencing**—Multiple participants take part in an online, real-time meeting via web-based video.

# Chapter 15: Audiovisual Requirements

## Industry Profile

## Reggie Aggarwal, Founder and CEO

### Cvent

A former attorney, and founder and chairman emeritus of the Indian CEO Tech Council (now "TiE-DC"), Reggie founded Cvent, a cloud-based software company focused on event management, in September 1999. Under his entrepreneurship, Cvent grew from a two-person start-up to a 1,700-person company with branch offices around the globe. Reggie's many honors include being named CEO of the Year by the Washington Business Journal, Entrepreneur of the Year by Ernst and Young, and a rising star by Forbes magazine.

## Lessons from a Successful Entrepreneur

Cvent's growth has been largely fueled by an entrepreneurial attitude and start-up mentality. However, it wasn't easy. Our company went through many ups and downs before we got to where we are today – a company with 145,000 clients. During the difficult years, we had to rebuild the company by concentrating on the basics:

1. Hire great people. Your employees are the DNA of your company.
2. Make the best product.
3. Service your customers.

In starting our company, I saw how difficult event planning was and decided there must be a way to automate all the details required of the meeting planner and a way to make it easier for hotels to market and sell to meeting groups. The real reason businesspeople attend conferences is to make connections in person and to expand their networks. Business gets done when people meet, and our goal was to bring that experience into the 21$^{st}$ century.

Cvent's original product was its online event management offering. In the years since, the company has vastly expanded its offerings. Our focus is on helping organizations get more ROI from their meetings and events; making events more engaging and beneficial for attendees; and, assisting hotels, venues, and meeting suppliers to connect with meeting planners. Our products include online meeting event registration and marketing, online surveys for post-event reporting, event management, social meeting tools, and a comprehensive supplier network for submitting requests for proposals.

The meetings industry is huge – half a trillion dollars a year is spent on meetings and events worldwide. Twenty-five percent of a typical company's spend goes to meetings and trade shows. It is a huge part of an organization's budget, but few recognized how important it was because it was seldom centralized in one department. You have marketing, human resources, training, travel. It makes a massive impact to the most important parts of an organization, which are its employees, its customers, and its prospects. The meetings market is poised for growth, and our focus is on showing hotels and meeting planners how technology can contribute to meetings and events.

As our company has grown, we have continued to focus on customer's needs; how we can save them time and money and how we can help them get better results. We look for pain points in the planner and hotel experience, and then we find the aspirin.

### WORTH WATCHING

Watch a short video of Reggie Aggarwal explaining "how Cvent rebuilt itself into a billion-dollar meetings and events titan" at www.youtube.com/watch?v=b0kK6YL8GIw (you can also find this video and a number of related videos by going to www.youtube.com and typing Reggie Aggarwal in the search box).

**Learning Objectives:**

This portion of your text introduces you to a number of the details inherent to a successful meeting or convention. We will discuss convention admission systems and security, additional services provided by the hotel to enhance events and ways to build attendance by offering special programs for the adult guests and/or children of attendees or delegates. When you have studied this chapter, you will:

- Be able to explain the registration process for conventions, describe the types of admission systems used for meetings, and summarize security issues at conventions.

- Be able to describe special services offered by hospitality properties, including programs for guests and the children of meeting attendees.

- Be able to explain the importance of checklists for planning conventions and meetings.

**Outline**

Convention Registration

Convention Security
- Controlled Admission
- Ticket Arrangements
- Uncontrolled Admission
- Exhibit Security

Other Services
- Signs and Notices
  - Hotel Rules
  - Sign Responsibility
  - Price Schedule
  - Locations
- Convention Headquarters Room
- Convention Hospitality Suites
- Guest Packages
- Telephones
- Printing and Duplication
- Decorations
- Entertainment
- Preferred Suppliers/Exclusives

Guest/Companion Programs
- Building Guest/Companion Attendance
- Activities for the Attendees' Guests
- Activities for Children

Summary

# 16 Admission Systems and Other Services

Once the planner has made arrangements with the hotel for his or her event, the next step is to get the word out to the organization's membership and provide a way for them to register for the convention. While registration is a function of the convening organization (it is not the same as room reservations, which are handled by the hotel), it is up to the property to ensure that everything runs smoothly on-site and to assist the planner with other aspects of the event, including security and activities for attendees and their guests. If problems arise, attendees may unfairly blame the hotel, so it is important to take whatever steps are necessary to ensure that convention guests have a positive impression of the hotel. In this chapter, we will take a step-by-step look at the registration process and detail ways that hotels can help with registration and other aspects of the organization's program, both before and during the event.

## Convention Registration

The first step in the **convention registration** process is getting the word out to potential **attendees**, who may be called delegates at some conventions. This may be done by mail, e-mail, fax, via the organization's newsletter, or over the Internet (many organizations today set up a link to their convention information and registration on their home pages or create a dedicated convention website, such as the one illustrated in Figure 16.1). No matter which method is used, the planner should include complete program details, including dates and times of the event and specific functions, housing options (some are handled by the organization; others require that reservations be made directly through the hotel or an outside party designated to handle room reservations), and other services available, such as details on transportation, free shuttles, guest and children's programs, and so on.

Registration information is of special importance, so the **registration form** should clearly spell out fees, cut-off dates, and methods of payment accepted. Some registration fees are all-inclusive (the registration fee covers both the program and housing), while others include only the convention program or portions of it. If the registration fee is not all-inclusive, it is important to detail any extra charges, such as special events, tours, spouse and children's programs, and so on. Some organizations keep the registration fee as low as possible by offering attendees the option of choosing which functions they wish to attend (a budget-conscious attendee, for example, may opt for a less-expensive luncheon rather than the more expensive closing banquet, or forego smaller functions in favor of the banquet).

Most planners prefer **advance registration** over **on-site registration**. When attendees are given the opportunity to register in advance of the event, attendance is usually better, there are less on-site traffic problems, planners are able to create customized convention packets containing badges and tickets to selected functions ahead of time, and, last but not least, advance registration generates cash flow before the event. In order to encourage advance registration, some organizations offer a discount to attendees and/or promote the advantage of having a guaranteed place at functions that may be sold out by the time of the event.

Typically, a majority of attendees pre-register by mail, fax, and the Internet (the number of **registrants** opting for **online registration** is growing year by year), while a small

Chapter 16: Admission Systems and Other Services

*Figure 16.1. ONLINE CONVENTION INFORMATION AND REGISTRATION.*

This website, created by the National Association of Broadcasters to promote their annual convention in Las Vegas, is one of many examples of how organizations create an online presence to provide information to potential attendees — and to allow them to register securely online for the event. Online information can also be offered on the convening organization's main site as well as on a separate site, such as the one that the NAB created, or the host hotel may offer a dedicated web space for the convenience of the planner and his or her organization.
Source: Courtesy of the National Association of Broadcasters.

percentage register on-site (this can vary, of course, depending on the organization). No matter which method is used for advance registration, it is important to follow up immediately with a confirmation that includes specific details, including the fee paid (and any balance due) and functions, courses, or activities selected; this eliminates the possibility of errors when the delegate arrives on-site. In addition to a confirmation, some organizations send out a registration packet that contains program information for registrants.

563

Sending pre-convention information is an excellent way to market products and services. The organization, for example, may offer CDs of the meeting program or provide details on baby-sitting and other services. Hotels can also take advantage of this opportunity to reach future guests early by providing brochures or other printed advertising, or a link to the hotel's website can be sent to attendees with the pre-convention information.

Once attendance is confirmed, the planner can begin to put together a **convention packet/kit** to be distributed to each attendee on site. Items provided by the convening organization in convention packets typically include:

- An introductory letter stating the purposes and aims of the meeting
- A list of scheduled events
- Information about speakers and entertainers
- Coupons or tickets to all pre-paid functions
- A badge or name tag

Hotels often provide meeting planners with information to be included in convention packets. Items commonly included are:

- Hotel facilities available to guests
- Times of operation for hotel restaurants and hospitality suites
- Details on check-in and check-out procedures and the handling of hotel bills
- Special favors, such as notepads and pens imprinted with the hotel's logo

Convention packets can be distributed in several ways. If rooms have been pre-assigned, packets can be left in guestrooms. Or, a pre-registered guest may pick up his or her packet upon registering at the front desk. Most planners prefer to hand out packets at the group's **registration area**, even though the first two methods help to eliminate traffic congestion (in most cases, the group has a separate area for pre-registered guests). Handing out packets gives event staff the opportunity to welcome attendees, answer questions, and immediately attend to any problems.

Several hotels and chains have eliminated the need to distribute packets by developing *event apps* to assist meeting planners in managing their events and communicating with attendees. The Omni chain, for example, offers OmniLink, which provides customized information to attendees' smartphones or tablets. The app, which is free of charge to both the planner and attendees, is customized by the planner, except for the Facilities section, which includes property information and maps downloaded by the hotel. Customizable sections include Agenda (a complete listing of meeting information, places, and times), Speakers (speaker profiles, photos, and session listings), Attendees (photos, bios, and direct e-mail contact), and Link and Download sections.

> **WORTH WATCHING**
> Watch a two-minute video detailing the features of the OmniLink app at www.omnihotels.com/meetings/omni-link.

Since most meeting planners and attendees today travel with their mobile devices, event apps are expected to continue to grow in popularity (see sidebar titled "The Future of Mobile Event Apps"). These apps, which are available from outside vendors as well as hotels, are increasingly being used by meeting planners and attendees. Grupio (www.grupio.com), for example, offers several apps that are compatible with iPhone, iPad, Android, and mobile web devices. These include Grupio Express, Grupio Custom, and Grupio Multi-Event (which can be modified for use at future meetings).

## Chapter 16: Admission Systems and Other Services

> ### The Future of Mobile Event Apps
>
> A recent study by The Event Marketing Institute (EMI) and Cvent found that the use of mobile event apps continues to grow:
>
> - By 2016, 88 percent of planners expect their attendees to consider mobile event apps as crucial to their event experience, and 86 percent of planners will have an app at their event.
>
> - By 2016, 94 percent of attendees are expected to use mobile event apps, up from 85 percent in 2015.
>
> - Mobile app spending levels will be maintained or increased by 94 percent of the industry.
>
> **Source:** Matt Alderton, "Event Apps on Upward Trajectory, Study Finds," posted on www.incentivemag.com on April 15, 2015.

The location of the registration area is important, and may vary depending on the size of a group. An area may be set aside off the lobby or in front of the meeting rooms for a small group; a larger group will require a separate room (many convention hotels have separate lobbies near their meeting rooms) or, in the case of large conventions, may even be placed in a tent in the facility's parking lot. No matter which type of location is required, the registration area is usually broken down into three stations: a *packet pick-up area*, where pre-registered attendees sign in and receive their packets; an *area for on-site registration*, where delegates register and payment exchanges hands; and an *information or tour desk*, where delegates may register for special tours and other optional services.

Robert Paluzzi of Caesars Palace in Las Vegas, speaking to a class of ours, defined the convention registration area as the "headquarters place for the meeting." Since it will be visited by all the attendees at one time or another, careful attention must be given to the traffic flow and other aspects of the registration process. It is a wise convention service manager who works with the planner to ensure smooth traffic flow. In the case of smaller conventions, a straight line queue can be used to register attendees. With larger conventions, however, a **serpentine queue** is often used to minimize space needed for lines (to see examples of both types of lines, see sidebar titled "Registration System with Queue"). Serpentine queues offer the advantage of being positioned to direct people to various stations, and portions of the barricades can be removed as traffic lessens. This type of line also provides an opportunity for face-to-face communications between attendees.

It is important to remember that no one likes to stand in line. Therefore, offering diversions can make the time pass more quickly. Some registration areas are set up near video screens that provide information on the convention and the property, including directions to meeting rooms, information about property amenities and services, and information about area attractions. An electronic **message board** may also be set up in the registration area to provide up-to-date program information (nearly every convention registration area includes a "traditional" message board that enables attendees to post notes to each other, but an electronic board makes it easier for convention staff to provide last-minute updates).

The second station in the registration area, which is for on-site registration, is generally handled exclusively by the meeting planner. The hotel, however, can make a positive impression and ensure that things run smoothly by having an adequate supply of back-up computers and printers (and other supplies) available for use in an emergency. The hotel may also offer assistance to the meeting planner regarding staffing needs.

Since convention registration has gone "high-tech," it is important that registration staff be fully trained to understand the computer programs used in the registration process (one such program is Experient's EventXL™). They should also be trained in payment procedures and be able to answer any questions that may arise (or know whom to contact if the problem is beyond their expertise). For these reasons, registration is sometimes handled by the convening organization's staff; in other cases, outside help is contracted through the city's convention and visitors bureau. In some cities, convention bureaus have temporary help, which they offer at no charge or for a nominal fee. Temporary workers can be contracted through outside staffing agencies (these temporary workers are usually referred to as **temps**). If the convening organization wishes to use temps, the hotel or convention and visitors bureau should be able to provide a list of reputable staffing agencies.

The third stop in the registration process is the tour and special service desk. Here, attendees can find information on city tours and trips to local attractions as well as area maps; in many cases, there is an area for brochures and special discounts offered by local businesses and entertainment venues. This desk may also provide informational materials, such as exhibit setup instructions.

## Convention Security

Another important area of concern to meeting planners is staging a worry-free event. Meeting planners want to ensure that their attendees and exhibitors don't have to worry about their personal safety or their property. Hotels have responded to this requirement for greater security by installing electronic door locks, providing well-lighted parking and public areas, and offering high-tech alarm and surveillance systems in their public areas and exhibit halls.

In the wake of the terrorism threat following the attacks of September 11, 2001, hotels are also taking other measures to ensure the safety of their guests and their facilities. This begins with having all employees wear hotel-issued photo identification badges and putting plans in place to ensure heightened security at both front-of-the-house and back-of-the-house areas.

Some hotels require checks of car trunks and baggage during heightened security alerts, while other properties, such as the Wynn Las Vegas, have beefed up security by putting specially trained dogs on patrol (see box titled "Security Goes to the Dogs").

Depending on the risk level, spot checks of delegates and their luggage may be made at the front desk and in the registration area; if the risk level is elevated, inspection may be mandated for all delegates and their belongings.

There should also be plans in place for back-of-the-house areas, such as entry points for exhibitors and loading docks. In some cases, exhibitors may be required to be accompanied from the loading docks to the exhibit area; if the security risk level is high, exhibitors may be barred from the loading docks.

## Chapter 16: Admission Systems and Other Services

### Security Goes to the Dogs

Security officers are a common sight in the hotels and casinos of Las Vegas, but eight "officers" stand out — the two Labrador retrievers and six German shepherds that patrol the Wynn Las Vegas. Wearing harnesses that say "Security" and displaying official hotel employee identification badges, the dogs, who have such Vegas-themed names as "Ace," "Blackjack," "Casino," "Jackpot," and "Keno," patrol all areas of the property — the two main entrances, the public promenade, the luggage distribution center, and back-of-the-house facilities. Former Wynn Las Vegas Vice President of Security Jerry Keller, a former two-term Metropolitan Police Department Sheriff, said of his canine "officers":

> The dogs are a deterrent. We want them visible for both our employees and guests. Visibility is a key element. The dogs are part of the overall security measures we've developed.

The dogs, who were specially trained in explosives detection techniques in Europe, accompany a select group of eight officers who have more than 35 years of combined canine-handling experience. If a suspicious scent is detected while on patrol, the dogs give a subtle reaction to their handlers, and a security team and the Las Vegas Metropolitan Police are notified to deal with the situation.

Although the dogs, like those in other canine units, go through extensive training with their handlers to build bonds, the Wynn security dogs do not go home with their handlers, as is typical in canine units. Instead, the dogs are housed in a $500,000 climate-control kennel complete with a bathing area and two large outdoor exercise pens.

Source: Howard Stutz, "Two Labrador Retrievers and Six German Shepherds Key Components of Wynn Las Vegas Security Operations," *Las Vegas Review-Journal*. Photograph courtesy of Wynn Las Vegas.

To assist hotels in planning for safety and security at their convention centers and exhibit halls, the International Association of Venue Managers (IAVM at www.iavm.org) offers several resources, including a "Post 9/11 Safety Security Planning" video and an annual Safety and Security Report.[1] This information can help with assessing security risks and taking the necessary steps to ensure a safe event.

The meeting planner can also contribute to a hassle-free meeting by controlling access to the group's functions. This is especially important in light of two unscrupulous practices that are plaguing the trade show industry today: suitcasing and outboarding. **Suitcasing** refers to the practice of individuals who are not official exhibitors but promote their own competing products on the exhibit floor. They often leave promotional materials at the booths of official, paid exhibitors; or, they may engage directly with attendees and hand out materials or their business cards. While it is sometimes difficult to identify them (some may even have registered as an attendee), convention organizers should stay on the alert for any questionable activities.

**Outboarding**, which also affects the business of paid exhibitors, refers to organizing a similar show or exhibit at the same time – and often in close proximity – to the official show. Sometimes, promotions may even be held in a suite at the same hotel to lure attendees away from the exhibition for which they have registered.

Both of these practices, of course, hurt both the sponsoring organization and the exhibitors who have paid to participate. If exhibitors do not do well, they may decline to exhibit at the organization's next show. This, of course, hurts the sponsoring organization, which depends on revenues from booth rentals. Therefore, organizations are increasingly

Chapter 16: Admission Systems and Other Services

developing and posting policies to curtail these activities, and several organizations, including the International Association of Exhibitions and Events (IAEE), have developed sample policies that show organizers can customize for their events. The IAEE's policy – as well as a four-page ad that planners can download for display at their events — can be viewed at www.iaee.com/resources/tools/suitcasing_toolkit.

There are a number of measures that meeting planners can use to help to control admission and protect the integrity of their events. The following sections will provide insight into methods commonly used to control access to events.

## Controlled Admission

Most conventions insist upon registering all attendees, even when there are no charges for admission. At the very least, good mailing lists are derived from the data collected at the registration desk.

Admission often is limited to people with particular jobs or professions. People are screened at a central registration desk, fees are collected, and some sort of credential, usually a **badge**, is presented (Figure 16.2 shows two different types of badges). The registrant's name and affiliation are typed, printed, or written on the badge. Since adhesives, pins, and even clips can damage garments, several companies have developed alternative ways for attaching badges. Badgetec (badgetec-usa.com), for example, offers badges (printed on thick cardstock or polyester) that slip into a Contour Clip that folds over fabric, eliminating the damage caused by metal teeth or adhesives. Imprint Plus (www.imprintplus.com), which uses recycled materials and vegetable-based inks, developed the recyclable Pocket Fastener, a plastic holder that enables wearers to slip their badges into their pockets.

*Figure 16.2. Sample Convention Badges.*

*Badges for attendees and exhibitors at conventions can range from an adhesive name tag (not pictured); to a badge placed into a plastic holder and worn around the neck; to today's sophisticated, interactive badges, such as the nTAG by nTAG Interactive. This badge not only displays the name of each meeting and convention attendee, but can also communicate with other badges to facilitate the tracking of attendees and provide networking opportunities.*
**Sources:** Name badge courtesy of *Corporate Meetings & Incentives*; nTAG photograph courtesy of nTAG Interactive.

Plastic-encased badges can also be hung on a **lanyard** that can be worn around the neck is a popular choice (if using this type of badge, names and other pertinent information should be visible on both sides in case the badge flips over). To avoid tangled lanyard cords, some planners include this type of badge in the attendees' individual registration packets. Another planner tells us that he places lanyard badges on jewelry stanchions purchased for this purpose; this practice not only eliminates tangled cords, but also makes the registration area look more organized and professional.

A more sophisticated type of badge is a plastic or aluminum badge embossed with the registrant's name and address, similar to a charge card. Exhibitors are supplied with "lead retrieval" devices that scan the badges of the attendees. At the end of the show, the exhibitor returns the machine to the lead retrieval company and receives a printout of all the attendees who visited the booth. (Exhibitors use trade shows to develop new trade contacts, and follow-up of these new contacts may result in additional business. That's the system that feeds the exhibits, which certainly support the entire convention.)

More sophisticated systems include bar coded badges, which can be used not only for on-site registration to identify guests, but also for billing purposes. Some registrants, for example, are coded to authorize the rental of audiovisual equipment or meals and special services. The bar codes will permit instant access to these charges, making cost-accounting far more accurate and up-to-date.

Another type of sophisticated badge that is used by meeting organizers *is the* **radio frequency identification tag** (RFID). Each RFID SmartBadge has a small (often one-quarter inch or smaller) chip — which is part computer chip, part transmitter — that is encoded with a unique identification number. The identification number, which corresponds to information in individual attendees' registration files, can be accessed by other badges via infrared sensors over a wireless network with a central server. One such badge, the nTAG by nTAG Interactive, allows badges to exchange data and find mutual areas of interest to facilitate networking.

RFID devices, which can also be accessed by special readers located at such strategic points as the registration desk, outside meeting and banquet rooms, and at exhibitors' displays, have proven invaluable in a number of areas besides networking. Meeting planners can use the ID codes to analyze registration information, track attendance at various events (the technology is often used to track attendance at educational sessions to verify completion of Continuing Education Units — CEUs), and even to help attendees find colleagues and friends at large sessions or banquets. Exhibitors can use ID codes to determine traffic flow to their booths and to qualify prospects and then follow up with them.

Two other sophisticated technologies that are growing in popularity are near field communications (NFC) and beacon technology. **Near field communications (NFC)** is a short-range wireless connectivity that enables attendees to use their smartphones to buy tickets, make payments, exchange networking information, track CEU credits, and even open guestroom doors. With the NFC technology, an attendee's smartphone becomes his or her "ticket" – the phone is simply tapped on an entrance turnstile or reader to gain admittance. Networking information is exchanged by either tapping two phones together or tapping the phone against a badge containing an NFC chip.

**Beacon technology** uses *Bluetooth Low Energy (BLE)* radio transmitters to share information between Apple and later model Android mobile devices (Apple's version of the technol-

> **WORTH WATCHING**
>
> To view more information on NFC and beacon technology, go to www.youtube.com and search for near field communication and then beacon technology. There are several excellent videos on each topic, ranging from an introduction to each to specific examples on how these technologies are being used.

ogy is called the iBeacon). Beacons are commonly used for location information and navigation, tracking attendee entrance into a meeting room or an exhibit hall, and for networking. The advantages of this technology are that the cost is low (usually about ten dollars per unit), the units require minimal maintenance (a battery usually lasts a year or more), and beacons aid in loss prevention (an alert is sent to the venue when equipment is moved by an unauthorized person). A disadvantage is that each radio transmitter's range is limited to 150-feet (this area is called a *geo-fence*). This can be overcome with the use of several transmitters, and beacon technology is increasing being used in exhibit halls.

The convention service manager should be able to supply the names of local companies that stock different kinds of badges. However, it is generally not the hotel's responsibility to supply badges. This is the job of the convening organization. No matter what type of badge is used, the meeting planner should prepare a written plan regarding admittance to an event. The hotel's security team, registration staff, and other personnel associated with the event should familiarize themselves with the plan, which usually covers such areas as:

- Criteria for attendance (ticket, invitation, presentation of a photo I.D., and so on).
- Levels and categories of registration, such as general admission, VIP status, exhibitors, sponsors, and so on. As we have mentioned, if registration is tiered, there should be some unique feature, such as a color-coded badge, to enable each level to be immediately recognized.
- Any exceptions to the standard registration process and details on how these situations should be handled.

Badges are often color-coded to sort out the different categories of registrants. In some cases, all but exhibitors are barred from the exhibit hall area except during certain show hours, and the color-coding helps the security guards police this policy. Color-coding also helps the exhibitors recognize prospective customers.

## Ticket Arrangements

Tickets provide a simple way of presenting evidence on which to base charges. If the agreement is to charge thirty dollars for each person served at a luncheon, each of those lunch tickets represents thirty dollars in cash. The tickets must be counted immediately after the affair, and the number verified by an authorized person from the convention staff.

Systems for collecting tickets are simple enough, but nothing should be left for the staff to improvise. Suggest one system.

If the admission is to be by ticket, a small table or two, with chairs, is set up to handle the transactions. The table is especially needed if tickets may be purchased at the door and not merely presented. Sometimes tickets or badges are to be claimed at such a table. If you expect a crowd, you'll need several table stations. It is easier to bring up the subject and discuss it in advance than to scramble for tables and chairs at the last minute.

The tables and chairs may be placed just outside or just inside the door of the function room. Space is a consideration in deciding where to put the tables.

Waiters can collect tickets at a sit-down meal, while a hotel employee can collect tickets at the door for a buffet. It is worth repeating that a person on the convention staff should be at the door, too, to troubleshoot and to identify and greet VIPs. The tables also serve as a focal point for those who have questions, for notices to be placed, and for material to be picked up.

Tickets are often sold in advance by convention organizers. Associations make money from such functions in many ways. The price they charge might be more than they pay the hotel. In addition, not every ticket is used and no refunds are made. This most usually happens when the convention sells a package of tickets for all the meals of the event at a flat fee.

Lots of ruffled feathers can be avoided if the hotel staff meets with the convention staff to decide what to do when delegates lose or forget their tickets. Don't expect a security guard or a waiter to improvise in such cases. If a convention executive is authorized to approve admission at each function, make some provision for recording that number. The simplest way to handle the problem of lost or forgotten tickets is for the convention executive to have extra tickets to supply when he or she sees fit to do so.

Sometimes, the count must be verified and the bill submitted to someone other than the convention organization. Many companies sponsor food functions as a way of helping an organization and to promote their image within that industry. The procedures are all the same except that you deal with another person. Arrangements should be made to ascertain who should be billed — the convention organization or the sponsor. And an authorized person should be designated to verify counts. Payment arrangements should be spelled out.

## Uncontrolled Admission

There are times when the doors are open to all who care to enter. However, this is relatively rare. But it is common to permit all who have badges to enter, allowing a free flow of people into and out of the meeting and function areas. This is where color-coding helps a great deal. When admission requires only a badge, and the badge is readily available, a security guard or other hotel person, such as a captain, stationed at the door may be all that is needed.

In such uncontrolled arrangements, it is most common for all liquor and food to be paid for with cash or coupons.

## Exhibit Security

Conventions accompanied by exhibitions pose a number of potential problems that can be both embarrassing and costly to a hotel. Communication is needed between the convention service manager and the person responsible for security. Coordination and cooperation are necessary to provide the protection required.

When exhibitors are involved, the hotel's security force may have to be supplemented with outside help. The extra cost should be figured into the selling price and absorbed by the organizing group. There are a number of national **security contractors** that might be called in. However, many hotels maintain an on-call list of reliable off-duty police and fire officers. They have been trained in basic security procedures and are an excellent source of help.

All security personnel, whether part-time or full-time, experienced or inexperienced, should go through a training session and orientation of the hotel's facilities. A job description such as that shown in Figure 16.3 might be given to each guard. It outlines the guard's duties and responsibilities as an employee of the hotel.

Security in the modern hotel is becoming a more complex problem. There are four critical periods involved in security: move-in; open show hours; closed show hours; and move-out. Each is different.

Move-in and move-out periods are the most critical times because of the many transitory, poorly identified persons who have access to exhibits and displays. People have been

## Chapter 16: Admission Systems and Other Services

*Figure 16.3. A TYPICAL JOB DESCRIPTION FOR HOTEL SECURITY GUARDS.*

> **Hotel Security Personnel Job Duties and Responsibilities**
>
> 1. *Help take care of an antagonist calmly.* Security must know how to take care of troublemakers through the use of logic or force without attracting too much attention from the guests.
> 2. *Watch for fire.* Security must know what to do about extinguishing small fires when fire trucks are still in transit.
> 3. *Report accidents.* A report must be presented to the hotel office for insurance purposes.
> 4. *Know how to take care of bomb threats.* Security must learn how to warn guests of bomb threats without making them panic.
> 5. *Emergency evacuation plan.* Security must know the hotel's exits so that they can direct people in the event of an emergency.
> 6. *Crowd control.* Security guards must know how to handle crowds during a mass panic.
> 7. *Policing loading areas.* Loading areas must be checked for stolen hotel property or stolen exhibits.
>
> And in addition to these duties, a security officer must have a law enforcement background and be familiar with local and state laws.

known to take anything from calculators to operating tables. Security personnel must be wary of anyone who looks suspicious. For example, it is strange to see someone wearing an overcoat when it is quite hot outside. The security guard should make tactful inquiries of such people immediately. Security guards must be alert and observant to spot the unusual.

Tight security is essential at the loading docks and truck entries during move-in. Any materials or displays that go in and out of the door should have a pass-check from show management. Security personnel often encourage exhibitors during move-in to put their display goods in a "safe room," if one is available. If it is not available, they are encouraged to put their displays under their booths, away from the view of passing persons. This will help to eliminate theft.

It is advisable to have a roving officer rather than one who merely stands at the door; this more often is a psychological deterrent to would-be thieves.

During the show or exhibit, much of the responsibility for guarding the booths falls on the exhibitors themselves rather than the security guards; this is especially true of large conventions, where it is just not feasible to have a security guard at each exhibit. Exhibitors who decide to leave their booths for any period of time should have replacements so the booths are never left unattended.

Burns Security Institute once surveyed exhibitors and show personnel around the nation about exhibit hall security problems. The 200 exhibitors who responded to that survey felt that one of the primary problems in exhibit areas was internal pilferage, with both exhibit hall and exhibit workers taking advantage of managements' trust by stealing items.

Likely times for employees to steal is during dismantling. Security needs are crucial at this time because so much is going on in the hall. The employee knows the hotel, its hiding places, and the exits that are unguarded. Because of this, employee thefts are often successful.

Exhibits are also very vulnerable to theft during the evening when exhibitors are gone. Exhibitors often leave in a hurry to join the merriment without putting expensive exhibits in the security rooms, if they are available.

Electronic surveillance is an important part of hotel security systems. Burglar alarms and closed-circuit television are used, but not to the extent that people might believe. Certainly there is going to be better control with such equipment, but there will be a greater expense, which the organizing group will have to bear. Thus many conventions will decide not to use such surveillance because of their tight budgets. If, however, the exhibition is a large one with highly valued items, this electronic equipment will be used.

## Other Services

There are a number of other services that may have to be arranged by the convening organization or that will require your input and assistance to execute. Press facilities may have to be designated (most **press rooms** include a place for the press to do interviews, as well as telephones and computer access to enable reporters and photographers to submit coverage). Sources for computer and printer rentals and other needed equipment must also be found. Local modeling agencies, public stenographers, and similar services may have to be called in. Most of these services do not require special handling, just advance notice and some thought.

The responsibility for ensuring that all these elements come together to create a successful event rests on the hotel's convention service manager. Mary Healey, convention service manager at the Hyatt Long Beach, explains:

> **MORE ONLINE**
>
> The hotel's convention service manager provides a copy of facility guidelines and procedures to the meeting planner prior to preparing the group's resume. These guidelines cover such areas as catering, billing, security, banners and signs, décor, preferred vendors, shipping, insurance, and so on. In many cases, the hotel requires a signed acknowledgement of these guidelines.
> You can view the guidelines and policies for the Hyatt Regency Denver at Colorado Convention Center by searching for Facility Guideline, Hyatt Regency Denver. The guidelines for JW Marriott Indianapolis can be viewed by searching for JW Marriott Catering and Convention Guidelines.

Today's CSM has evolved into a proactive, creative champion for ideas and suggestions, event themes, entertainment and culinary options, and an impresario of myriad vendors and off-site specialty venues. The CSM's role continues to grow through our responsibilities as a one-stop, can-do resource.[2]

### Signs and Notices

Proper signage can add a great deal of visual impact to a convention or meeting as well as provide needed information. Only the simplest meeting can make do without *signs* and *notices.* They are most obvious when absent. The convention organization has a great stake in making sure that all goes smoothly, and signs are a great help within the convention area. Many convention planners are inexperienced, so the hotel must stand ready to advise and supply. Unless you want to scramble at the last moment, you should remind the client of the need for such signs and notices, and expedite the creation of them.

### Hotel Rules

Most hotels have restrictions on the types of signs allowed and their placement. Some, for example, do not permit signs in their lobbies or where they will obscure other hotel signage, such as the name of a meeting room; other policies restrict the use of tape and tacks, which can damage walls. Safety, too, is a major concern – signs should not obstruct walkways or access points, and hanging signs must conform to the maximum weight allowed at rigging points.

Many hotels provide sign holders in crucial areas of the convention area, such as near the doors of meeting rooms. These permanent frames are usually designed to hold standard-sized card stock for signs. Bulletin boards and other movable signboards are handled easily on short notice. Those reliable tripod easels make great sign holders and are most versatile.

A printed form outlining the hotel rules on signs should be submitted to the convention organizers to be included in their convention manuals. This practice eliminates any misunderstandings; a meeting planner is spared the frustration of bringing in a sign that will not be allowed. The sidebar titled "Hotel Sign Policies" is an example of the typical sign policy regarding signs and their placement.

Hotel rules regarding distribution of notices also should be outlined clearly. Companies at trade conventions frequently request to distribute printed material at strategic points within the hotel or even to place them at the door of each delegate's room. Daily convention newspapers, newsletters, and advertising material are distributed in this manner.

The hotel should inform the organization if it is willing and able to undertake such distribution and if it charges for the service. The convention organizer should be directed to inform the participants about the recommended procedure to follow for such service.

It is important to learn if the convening organization has any policy about signs and distribution of newspapers, magazines, newsletters, advertising materials, or any other printed matter. The policy should be aided by the hotel staff's compliance, and all such requests should be referred to the convention staff. Hotel personnel should either handle or supervise the hanging of posters or signs.

## Sign Responsibility

It is the convening organization's responsibility to create signs. The convention service manager should be alert and advise when he or she notices that they are not being planned. A discussion of signs is helpful. The inexperienced meeting planner will appreciate it; the old pro won't mind the reminder.

### Hotel Sign Policies

- All signs must be professionally printed or painted. Handwritten signs are not permitted.
- All signs must be displayed from easels.
- Placement of signs is restricted to meeting room area.
- No signs allowed in main lobby or guestroom corridors. The hotel has an electronic event board in the lobby for daily meeting room and registration information, as well as electronic signs outside of each function room.
- No pins, tacks, or adhesives of any sort are permitted on any hotel wall or door.
- No tape or glue permitted on painted walls. We realize that visual aids have to be displayed occasionally on the vinyl walls of our meeting rooms, but please check with your convention service manager on the type of tape to use on vinyl walls.
- The hotel's staff will be happy to assist in hanging any banners or large signs. Please check with your convention service manager for any restrictions.
- Please be advised that you will be held liable for damages if the above mentioned policies are not adhered to.

The program indicates the need for signs. If the organization supplies them, the hotel is freed from the responsibility. We would suggest documenting that decision with a memo or letter. Most often, however, it is easier for the organization to have the signs made through the hotel to save the bother of transporting them.

Regardless of who accepts the responsibility of supplying signs, invariably a few more are needed at the last minute. Some arrangement must be made for such service. If the hotel cannot do the job in-house, a local supplier must be on call. In view of the fact that setup usually is on weekends and evenings, it is a wise convention hotel that sets up some sort of sign-making capability in-house.

## Price Schedule

Establish a price schedule for all sign work, whether the hotel has an in-house shop or uses an outside sign company. A work order should be made out for each sign; its location, if predetermined, should be noted. No verbal orders should be taken. State whether the hotel will bill the organization or the group will deal directly with a local sign company.

## Locations

The purpose of signs is to give information, direct pedestrian traffic and activity, and assure a smoothly flowing meeting. Thus signs are needed in logical locations. Trace the progress of attendees step by step to determine what signs are needed and where.

To facilitate this process, which is especially important for large conventions, a convention service manager should provide a facility floor plan to meeting planners. This will enable the hotel and the meeting planner to develop a *way-finding plan*, which will not only show the convention attendees how to get around the hotel, but will also help the meeting planner to determine exactly where signs will be placed, what each sign should convey, and the size of the sign, among other details. A way-finding plan is especially useful if the convention service manager indicates the most common sign locations within the hotel and suggests sign sizes and recommended materials (in today's eco-friendly environment, natural materials are often suggested or requested). It is important to note that all signs should serve a distinctive purpose – a giant at-a-glance agenda sign, for example, may be obsolete before the meeting starts, so the wise convention service manager should suggest alternate choices, such as a video display board, to convey information.

Large banners may be placed outside the hotel entrance or over the marquee. Or, **reader boards** listing the day's events, times, and locations can either be printed or displayed on video screens. The goals are to prevent delegates from milling around and to direct traffic.

Notices on the bulletin board in the lobby, in elevators, and at crucial places in the corridors will help facilitate movement of people. The hotel staff also must be informed about events so it can answer questions intelligently. Such informed staff people should include the assistant manager, the bell captains, the door attendants, and front desk personnel.

**Aisle signs** are often used in exhibit halls to help attendees locate a specific booth. Aisle signs are usually hung above each aisle to enable them to be readily seen, but some exhibitions also feature signs attached to either a permanent or temporary fixture at the beginning and ending of each aisle that connects to a main aisle.

At some properties, the creation and placement of signs and notices may come under union contract. In this case, the client should be notified about any union jurisdiction to avoid difficulties.

Today's technology is also being used to convey convention information. Many hotels have an in-house television channel that is programmed to display meeting information (in most cases, there is no charge for scheduling information, and the convention organizer or vendors have the option to purchase time for additional messages or advertisements approved by the hotel). When guests awaken, they merely turn on the TV to access the schedule of events for the day. This method of communication is especially useful when last-minute changes have been made in the convention program.

An increasing number of properties are using **digital signs** to convey information outside meeting rooms and in high-traffic areas. While the initial cost of installing digital signs is higher due to installation or rental of the flat panel screens, programming costs, and electrical work needed for the units, the use of digital signs is appealing to meeting planners as there are reduced costs (there is no need to change out placards daily, saving on labor and material) and less environmental impact. Janus Displays (www.janusdisplays.com), offers motion video, live RSS feeds, and flash animations to enable hotels to promote both convention events and advertise hotel amenities. Other applications of the software include way- finding displays and floor plans, and the broadcast of emergency warnings.

At the Hyatt Regency Chicago, way-finding LCD displays and digital signage are used throughout the hotel to provide information and guide convention attendees to meeting rooms and hotel facilities. The project initially started with about 50 monitors and four way-finding kiosks, but has grown to almost 60 LCD screens and 200 projector displays.

**Sample Way-finding Digital Displays**

Two examples of how digital signs are used to assist convention attendees in finding their way around the convention facility. The hotel has advertised its amenities at the lower portion of the display on the right.

## Convention Headquarters Room

The administration of a large convention often requires a staff of five to ten people, so the association needs a room to work out of as an office. Hotels recognize this need and usually provide such a room free as part of the package. Ideally, this room should be adjacent to the meeting rooms and equipped with tables, computers and printers, duplicating machines and perhaps a stenographer. Naturally, the hotel will charge for any such equipment supplied.

The Sonesta Hotel chain has gone a step further. A secretary is assigned to large groups free of charge to work in the headquarters room. The secretary's functions might include typing, handling messages, and arranging show tickets, among others.

## Convention Hospitality Suites

Planning something for the evening hours is sometimes a real problem for meeting sponsors. One solution a convention manager might suggest to a client is a company **hospitality suite**. This calls for coffee, a bartender, card table, television — in general, a lounging atmosphere where the members may congregate informally. The advantage to the hotel is that the delegates stay in the hotel and spend their money there rather than being out on the town.

Another service provided by the hotel is what might be called "controlled hospitality suites." There is a tremendous demand for hospitality suites when a large convention and exhibition move into a hotel. Exhibitors rush for these rooms as places to entertain and transact sales. But the association executive also needs these suites for board and convention officials. When the demand for hospitality suites is greater than the number available, *the hotel's first obligation is to the meeting planner.*

Meeting planners are specific about the assigning of suites. Ground rules often state that:

- Exhibitors are not to have their hospitality suites open while meetings are scheduled.
- Non-exhibitors will not be allowed to have hospitality suites.

## Guest Packages

Convention exhibitors and convention delegates frequently bring samples and promotional material that they would like to distribute at the meeting. Procedures for accepting these guest packages must be determined and communicated to the employees involved. If adequate storage space is available, packages are generally stored free. But it should not be a hotel's practice to store large packages, or any packages for an extended period of time.

To avoid any misunderstandings, the hotel's policy can be stated in a clause, such as the following, in the organization's contract:

> *Storage of Exhibit Materials*
> *The Hotel cannot accept and store shipments of exhibit materials in advance of a show. Due to County fire department regulations, crates, boxes, and other items to be used for the storage of exhibit materials cannot be stored on the Hotel premises during a show. It will be necessary for you to make arrangements with your exhibitor service to receive and store exhibits for delivery to the Hotel on the move-in date. These arrangements must also include the removal of empty crates, their storage during the show, and their subsequent return to the Hotel on the move-out date. Should any property not be removed by the designated*

*move-out date, the Hotel management may store, or cause to be stored, any such property and your organization or the exhibitor will be charged a reasonable fee for all expenses incurred.*

A package log book should be maintained, showing the date of receipt, where a package is stored, and both the addressee and addresser.

Exhibitors occasionally misdirect packages to the hotel. Such packages should be referred to the decorator's warehouse for later delivery. If exhibitors ask the hotel at the end of the convention to wrap and send out packages, the service should be provided at a charge.

## Telephones

Telephone service should be discussed with the convention staff before the event; it may be necessary to bring in telephone company representatives. Many conventions want provisions made for incoming calls to meeting rooms and exhibit areas. Outgoing telephone service from meeting rooms can be abused if it is not controlled. If outgoing service is requested, it must be planned. You should discuss who is to pay and when. Figure 16.4 details the fees of the former Ritz-Carlton Lake Las Vegas for telephones and other communications.

## Printing and Duplication

Most printing is done by the organization before the event, but last-minute work is often needed. You should be able to supply the names of cooperative printers nearby who have proved their reliability. Some hotels have in-house print shops.

You should inform the convention staff of what types of duplication you can handle, what the lead time is, the costs, and the kinds of material you can handle. Have a fee schedule printed and presented beforehand or on display. You may have an in-house shop with offset printing capability, or one of the more sophisticated models of office copiers. All of these can handle notices and the like. The convening organization is not the only one to seek such services. Many of the exhibitors look for last-minute printing to fill needs of their exhibits and/or the sales meetings that are frequently held in conjunction with the convention.

Hotels that handle a large number of meetings and conventions often have business centers to meet printing and duplicating needs and other secretarial or business services. The box titled "Executive Business Center Services" details some of the services (and their costs) offered to meeting planners at the Ritz-Carlton Lake Las Vegas.

## Decorations

From time to time, you will get calls for special draperies, flowers and plants, and special flags and banners. Exhibit decorators usually handle such items; they have the expertise and the trained personnel to take care of these requests.

Hospitality suites may need floral decorations. You should have an arrangement with a florist to facilitate service and billing. Make clear to your clients whether they are to pay you or deal directly with the florist. Unless you have an arrangement with a florist for exclusive business, you really shouldn't care if the florist and your clients make their own

*Figure 16.4. SAMPLE TELEPHONE AND COMMUNICATION CHARGES.*

---

**THE RITZ-CARLTON®**
LAKE LAS VEGAS

## Event Technology
CONNECTIVITY
PRICING GUIDE:

## Meeting Space Connectivity:

- **House Phone: <u>No Charge</u> for first house phone.**
  ($25.00 per phone/per day for each additional phone.)

- **D.I.D. Phone Line: $50.00 per day + calls**
  (All calls billed through PBX.)

- **Conference Phone: $125.00**

- **Speaker Phone: $75.00**

- **T1 Connection: $700.00 Per room or location**
  **Up to 5 terminals per location.** (One time connection charge.)

## Client Communications:

- **Client Walkie Talkies: $35.00 Per day.**
  (Each includes spare battery and charger.)

- **Nextel Communicators: $125.00 Per Week.**
  **Phone capabilities $1.00 per minute**
  (Includes incoming/outgoing and Long Distance.)

---

*Most hotels prepare a detailed listing of charges for telephones and other communications equipment available for meetings and conventions. This form details the fees that the Ritz-Carlton Lake Las Vegas charges for telephones, high-speed Internet connections, and other communication devices.*
**Source: Courtesy of the Ritz-Carlton Lake Las Vegas. Used with permission.**

arrangements. Often, clients are happy to be steered to firms in the house or recommended by the hotel so that they can feel sure of prompt service, especially when they are not obliged to use that particular vendor.

## Entertainment

There are union regulations and tax liabilities to be considered when live entertainment is used. This varies from area to area and should be part of the general information included in the letter of agreement and discussed at the pre-event meetings.

## Executive Business Center Services

### Facsimile
| | |
|---|---|
| Local Fax: | $1.00/page |
| Domestic Fax: | |
|     First Page | $4.00 |
|     Additional Pages | $2.50/page |
| International Fax: | |
|     First Page | $10.00 |
|     Additional Pages | $3.00/page |

### Computer
*Workstation:*
| | |
|---|---|
|     Word Processing | $25.00/hour |
|     Printing | $0.25/page |

*Includes Complimentary Internet*

*Clerical:*
| | |
|---|---|
|     Typing | $10.00/page |
|     Statistical Typing | $15.00/page |

### Rental Equipment
| | |
|---|---|
| Fax Machine | $400/3-7 days |
| Copier | $400/3-7 days |
| Printer | $190/2 days |
| Color Printer | $440/2 days |

*Additional equipment available upon request*

### Comb Binding
| | |
|---|---|
| Small Comb | $4.50/each |
| Medium Comb | $5.00/each |
| Large Comb | $6.00/each |

### Office Supplies
| | |
|---|---|
| Legal Copy Paper | $12.00/ream |
| Formatted Diskette | $1.00/each |
| Legal Note Pad | $2.00/each |
| Name Badges | $2.00/badge |
| (plastic sleeve, clip, printing) | |

*Additional supplies available upon request*

## Photocopying

**Black & White Copies:**

Letter Size
| | |
|---|---|
| 1-200 | $0.25/page |
| 200-500 | $0.20/page |
| 500-1000 | $0.15/page |
| 1000+ | $0.10/page |

Legal Size
| | |
|---|---|
| 1-200 | $0.30/page |
| 200-500 | $0.25/page |
| 500-1000 | $0.20/page |
| 1000+ | $0.15/page |

Ledger Size
| | |
|---|---|
| 1-200 | $0.50/page |
| 200-500 | $0.45/page |
| 500+ | $0.40/page |

*Double sided copies, add $0.10/page*

**Color Copies:**

Letter Size
| | |
|---|---|
| 1-100 | $2.50/page |
| 100-200 | $2.00/page |
| 200-300 | $1.50/page |
| 300+ | $1.00 page |

Legal Size
| | |
|---|---|
| 1-100 | $3.00/page |
| 100-200 | $2.50/page |
| 200-300 | $2.00/page |
| 300+ | $1.50/page |

*Double sided copies, add $0.50/page*
*Colored and Three-hole Paper, add $0.10/page*

### Transparencies
| | |
|---|---|
| Black & White | $2.50/page |
| Color | $5.00/page |

*Taxes not included in copy and facsimile prices*

The Ritz-Carlton, Lake Las Vegas
1610 Lake Las Vegas Parkway
Henderson, NV 89011
Phone: (702) 567-4700
Fax: (702) 567-4777

---

Live entertainment will also affect your table and chair setups. Bands may call for raised platforms. Entertainers have different requirements, too. The entire stage area should be discussed to make sure you have enough space and can meet all specifications.

Hotels are often called upon to supply dressing rooms for entertainers. A problem is that entertainers prefer to rehearse on the scene, which may not be possible because the room may be in use for other convention events. This should be taken into consideration when the program is arranged and rooms selected. It may not be possible to honor such requests.

## Preferred Suppliers/Exclusives

Because meetings and conventions have gotten so sophisticated and complex, it is not always possible for the planner to make the necessary arrangements for each of the services described in this section. In this case, the help of an outside party is often sought. Convention decorators, drayage companies, florists, printers and duplicators, photographers, **ground operators,** and audiovisual specialists are a few of the outside organizations that can be used.

Yet another outside source is the **special event planner.** The services of special event planners vary a great deal; some catering and production companies, for example, advertise "event planning services" to give the impression that they provide complete planning services, when, in fact, they do not. A true special event planner brings together a combination of the best vendors (florists, caterers, entertainers, staging companies, and so on) to meet a client's needs and budget. In an effort to identify qualified special event planners, the International Special Events Society (www.ises.com) offers a certification program. Meeting planners who hire a planner with the CSEP designation are ensured of getting a highly trained professional who can, indeed, provide all needed services.[2]

Today, many meeting planners turn to **destination management companies** to manage such details of their meetings as transportation, group tours, and elaborate functions. The advantages to using a DMC are that they are experts on their particular area and that they have built relationships with local vendors who can provide reliable services, often at a discounted rate due to the volume of business that DMCs generate. As with special event planners, however, the expertise and services offered by DMCs can vary. The sidebar titled "A Sampling of Specialized DMC Services" provides a list of services most commonly offered.

DMCs can range from one-person shops to franchise operations to large companies, and they may handle diverse business; some, for example, handle specific groups, such as corporate or incentive groups, others may service only associations, while the larger DMCs typically handle a mix of all three categories of clients. Location can also play a part in the focus of a DMC; for example, The Meeting Manager Company, which has offices in Southern California, specializes in association programs in San Diego and incentive business in Palm Springs.

---

**A Sampling of Specialized DMC Services**
(Including but not limited to)

- Creative proposals for on- or off-site themed special events—including decor, conception, audiovisual, sound and lighting professionals, entertainment, centerpieces, and more.
- Entertainment procurement—DJs, musicians, impersonators, comedians, games
- Customized off-site tours—historic, industry related, spouse, or fun
- Off-site venue and entertainment logistics and suggestions
- Airport transfers—sedans to coaches—including VIP Meet and Greet
- Shuttle services—hotel to venue
- Company picnics: catering, entertainment, and permits
- On-site registration and hospitality services
- Teambuilding design: ropes Courses, scavengers hunts
- VIP amenities—themed gift baskets and promotional items

Source: Vivian K. Elba and Renee T. Mulvey, "The Destination Management Company: A Hotel's Partner in Sales," *HSMAI Marketing Review.*

## Chapter 16: Admission Systems and Other Services

> ### 🖥 INTERNET EXERCISE
>
> ### Destination Management Companies Join Forces to Form a Global Presence
>
> The DMC Network, an Orlando, Florida-based company representing more than 50 North American destinations, formed an alliance with Ovation Global DMC, a Dublin, Ireland-based consortium of European and Middle Eastern DMCs. Log on to the companies' websites, listed below, to answer the following questions.
>
> - dmcnetwork.com
> - ovationdmc.com
>
> 1. What are the key points in the mission statements of each group?
> 2. What standards must be met for consideration in the DMC Network?
> 3. Briefly describe the Ovation Strategic Partner Programme.
> 4. What advantages has teaming up provided to each company?

Costs and methods of payment for DMC services will also vary. Some DMCs bill by the hour, while others have a set commission. When a commission is charged, most DMCs charge 15 to 20 percent above their costs, which may actually be a bargain, as DMCs can often negotiate lower rates with vendors.

In addition to planners, hotels that have their own convention services departments can benefit from joining forces with local DMCs. Partnering with a DMC that can handle outside details allows the property's staff to concentrate on meeting needs and food functions. Rather than tie up staff to research special requests, a DMC that is familiar with what is available in the area can provide an immediate solution to a meeting planner.

> **ⓔ WORTH WATCHING**
>
> To view an overview of destination management companies, go to www.youtube.com/watch?v=sS3481PPK-k (or go to www.youtube.com and search for What Exactly is a DMC).

DMCs that regularly work for hotels are familiar with the specific needs of planners and the importance of providing reliable service to them. And a hotel's willingness to leave important details to a trusted outside firm demonstrates that the property is committed to ensuring the best experience possible. Payment for the use of DMC services can be billed separately, or, as is often the case, added to the master billing.

The increasing use and success of outside DMC services has prompted some hotels and chains to establish their own DMCs (see Marriott "Best Practices" box). Nashville's Gaylord Opryland Resort & Convention Center and the Pointe Hilton Resorts, for example, own and operate their own DMC services outright rather than deal with outside suppliers. At the Boulders Resort & Spa in Arizona, the Destination Service Department and the Catering/Conference Services department work together to provide complete in-house destination management services, including off-property theme events, recreational activities, tours and sightseeing, transportation services, and room amenities and gifts in addition to meetings support and team-building programs. By providing in-house, "one-stop shopping" to meeting planners, the hotel generates additional revenue that would otherwise have gone to an outside vendor.

**Receptive agents**, who perform such services for delegates as guided tours and local transportation, are also extremely important to the success of a convention, as are local talent and modeling agencies, speakers bureaus, and temporary personnel services. Most

> ## BEST PRACTICES
>
> ### Marriott
>
> ### The San Francisco Marriott: In-House Destination Management
>
> Marriott has led the way in offering in-house destination management services. Destinations by Marriott, a new division of Marriott Lodging, has been established at several properties. Resort properties were the first to offer in-house event planning, but now a growing number of city hotels are adding it as well.
>
> The trend toward more elaborate meetings and conventions has been on a collision course with company downsizing, forcing more meeting planners to rely on outside help for planning the myriad details associated with group functions. More and more, planners have been turning for help at the scene of their functions—destination management companies (DMCs) that can arrange for everything from ground transportation to decorations to elaborate theme parties.
>
> Many properties, who see this type of service as a logical extension of the sales effort, are getting into the act as well; either offering hotel office space to outside DMCs or setting up their own in-house DMCs. This enables the hotel to offer everything required by the meeting planner—from planning through execution of the function—with the added benefits of consolidating deposits and posting all charges to the group's master account.
>
> Barbara Morris, former director of Destinations by Marriott at the San Francisco Marriott, says her hotel's in-house destination management program is "awesome." She says:
>
>> Customers are so pleased to have the ability to work with one supplier. They like the Marriott name and the service level behind it...It's wonderful for the meeting planner who comes to us. They have a master account with everything on it. And they generally get a better deal if everything is done in-house.
>
> Naturally, the entry of hotels into this area has sparked some resentment from private DMCs. They claim that the DMC staff at the hotel may not have the experience—or contacts—of established DMCs. But the entry of hotels into this arena can only make things better for meeting planners—there will be increased competition for business, resulting in even more creative options—and better service.
>
> Meeting planners are not required to use the services of an in-house DMC; a property's service bids for the business just as outside services do. Many meeting planners, however, appreciate this "one-stop shopping" option, making it likely that the number of in-house DMCs will continue to grow—and offer more and better service to stay competitive.
>
> Source: Ruth A. Hill, "The Entertainers: Hotels Assume the Role of Destination Managers," *Lodging*.

hotels maintain a list of *preferred suppliers* who can provide specific services to meeting planners. In many cases, the hotel receives a commission for recommending these suppliers.

Many times, hotels allow their preferred suppliers to maintain an **on-site office**. In this case, the supplier has a greater chance of getting most of the convention business, and pays the hotel rent and a percentage of sales. While some meeting planners appreciate the convenience of such on-site service, many are expressing concern over the growing number of properties that insist that the convening organizations use the property's preferred supplier (see box titled "Preferred Suppliers: What Meeting Planners Have to Say").

Sometimes, hotels and convention centers not only have a list of preferred suppliers or their own DMCs, but also have **exclusives** with some vendors. This means that only a specified vendor is allowed to provide a service or product (catered food and beverage, Internet/telecommunications equipment, decorating and/or floral service, security, cleaning services, and so on) within the facility. When a hotel has an exclusive, meeting planners do not have a choice of suppliers – and cannot bring in products or services from off-property sources.

## Chapter 16: Admission Systems and Other Services

> **Preferred Suppliers: What Meeting Planners Have To Say**
>
> "The value of a preferred supplier list depends on where my meeting is located. In my home area — Greater Chicago — I have my own resources and preferred suppliers. I have had experience with most suppliers or know someone else who has used the vendors and service providers.
>    "Away from my home base, I'd welcome a preferred supplier list to tell me who does a good job in the area, but I still would do my own calling to compare prices. I wouldn't be bound to using that list, but I would appreciate that the hotel offered it."
> *Roseanne M. Hoban, former senior account executive, Association Management Systems, and now owner of Association Dynamics.*
>
> "I like to find my own suppliers and negotiate with them directly. I think you get a better price. If you go through the hotel to book your photographer, for example, there's going to be an added cost. The hotel is going to make some money. But it takes a lot of time to find suppliers on your own. The advantages of using a hotel's preferred suppliers are that they are familiar with the property's quirks and are likely to do a good job because their position with the hotel is at stake. And even if a planner is working with an in-house supplier, he or she can still negotiate with them directly and pay them directly."
> *Pat Fagan, conference service manager, Sun Life Assurance Company of Canada.*
>
> "The issue of preferred suppliers is a hot one right now. More and more hotels are doing it, and I have even heard of hotels that are telling meeting planners that there will be a 15-percent surcharge if they do not use a preferred supplier. That's because the hotels are getting a commission from suppliers they recommend.
>    "I don't like it. I want to be able to choose the decorating firm, the florist, and the audiovisual company I use for my meetings. Now, if I am in a city where I have no contacts, a list of preferred suppliers might be helpful. But I don't want to be bound by it.
>    "Hotels that tell planners which suppliers they should use — or penalize them with a surcharge — should realize that the practice is going to cut into their business...for example, our association has a decorator we've used for the past seven or eight years. He knows our show and travels with us on site visits to cities we'll be using. While I am negotiating with the hotel, he meets with local decorators to explain exactly what we need and to find someone to contract for the job. I want his advice, not that of the hotel.
>    "Other groups have two- or three-year contracts with audiovisual people who will go to their meeting sites and run locally rented equipment to make sure the show goes the way it's supposed to. Now, if the hotel insists the planner employ a preferred supplier, the association is still bound to a contract with its own audiovisual firm and duplicate services could get very expensive."
> *Janet Balletto, former national meetings coordinator, American Mathematical Society.*

Exclusives, which benefit hotels by generating more revenue, are becoming more common, but they are not popular with all meeting planners. Hotels can "sell" these exclusives to meeting planners by promising a better service level (hotels must select vendors that deliver, of course, and can point out vendors' familiarity with the facility and locale and his or her accessibility). Sometimes, hotels can also demonstrate that their exclusive vendors can offer services or products (such as audiovisual equipment, for example) cheaper than the organization can purchase or rent them and have them delivered to the function.

Meeting planners are more likely to accept the idea of exclusive suppliers if they understand the rationale behind using them. John Houghton, executive vice president of the Metro Toronto Convention Centre, says:

> When you talk about the benefits of using an exclusive supplier, you need to keep in mind the service they provide. Electrical services are exclusive because we don't want just any company having access to critical systems like electrical. You want someone who is intimately familiar with our infrastructure and knows what can and cannot be done. We never want the lights to go out during an event due to someone who "thinks it

should have worked without any problems," but didn't understand the electrical load of everything else that is going on in the building.

Our exclusive suppliers maintain offices within our facility and are linked into our communication systems. They have a warehouse full of gear on-site to be able to deal with last-minute requests or last-minute changes. These are also "event savvy" people who are used to *working with the idiosyncrasies of the business and people who have immovable deadlines.*[3]

In some cases, hotels may compromise to secure the group's business; they may allow the convening organization to bring in its own decorator if it agrees to use the property's photographer, for example. Meeting planners should always be advised beforehand of existing exclusives, and all arrangements made—whether agreeing to the sole use of exclusive vendors or otherwise— should be clearly understood during the negotiating process and spelled out in the group's contract to avoid any misunderstandings.

## Guest/Companion Programs

Many hotels have neglected a potentially profitable market in not promoting guest attendance at conventions. The average convention delegate spends approximately $250 per day in the hotel. If the delegate brought a guest, the expenditures for both might well exceed $350 per day. It is a general conclusion that members stay longer and spend more money when a spouse or guest is along; both result in more money for the hotel.

This additional revenue, which is known as **auxiliary business**, typically comes from money spent in the property's restaurants, lounges, and gift shops and for the use of its recreational facilities; it also includes extra revenue for guestrooms and other services rendered to exhibitors at conventions and trade shows. The hotel can also generate extra income by offering **ancillary services or activities**, such as baby-sitting services or local tours and other programs to complement the meeting. This is added revenue for the hotel and doesn't require the selling of another guestroom. For a 500-delegate convention, this could mean an *additional* $50,000 a day in sales—no small sum for any hotel.

More often than not, attendance at today's conventions includes the spouse or a guest. According to the most recent *Meetings & Conventions* Meetings Market Report, over 11 million spouses or guests attend conventions and association meetings each year. And for some groups the annual convention has become a family affair. Business meetings, too, can be a source of additional revenue as meeting attendees often combine business and leisure, perhaps arriving with their spouses or family to enjoy vacation time together a few days before or staying a few days after the meeting (this practice has led to the coining of the term *bleisure*). Convention service people should make provisions for entertaining these additional guests.

The first step, after recognizing the significance of attendance by spouses, is to sell the idea of a **guest/companion program** to the meeting planner, who after all must increase the convention budget if these programs are part of the plan. Point out that the presence of spouses and guests may be healthy for the meeting. The attendees are less likely to come to the morning session bleary-eyed after a late night on the town if their spouses or guests are accompanying them. Sessions will probably be more businesslike and delegates more alert, attentive, and receptive. In addition, ticket sales for food and social functions will increase markedly, with positive effects on the meeting planner's anticipated revenue.

*Cooking classes are popular activities for guests/companions at conventions.*
**Source: Photograph courtesy of The Ritz Hotel, Paris, France.**

Suggest to meeting planners that they often determine the attendance figure. If delegates anticipate they'll have a good time, they encourage their mates or guests to attend the convention. Spouse and guest attendance at conventions fosters a close-knit family feeling, which improves the company's image. If a poll were taken, it would probably show that the most successful meetings were those attended by both the husband and wife. This is a strong factor in corporate decisions to invite the spouse or a guest to attend.

Discussing options to cover the costs of these activities may also increase their appeal. In some cases, the organization subsidizes all or part of the costs of additional activities, but attendees may pay themselves, which does not add to the meeting planner's budget. Activities, such as tours, may be added as options to the group's program and included in the convention fees, or the attendee may purchase tickets for a tour directly from the tour operator. A third — and often attractive — option is to arrange for sponsorships for outside programs. A local attraction, such as an outlet mall or theme park, for example, may cover part of the costs, offer discounts, or provide transportation to and from the hotel because the attraction can expect to generate additional revenue from the participants.

## Building Guest/Companion Attendance

Once a meeting planner is convinced of the value of inviting guests, much can be done by hotels to promote their attendance. Working in conjunction with the meeting group, the convention service manager should suggest ways to create interest and thus increase attendance. The following methods might be used:

## Chapter 16: Admission Systems and Other Services

- Supply the meeting planner with the hotel's brochures and internal marketing pieces and suggest that he or she include them with group mailings. Or, provide a special link to activities that can be promoted on the group's website or in correspondence to attendees. Include such items as menus, pictures of the hotel, and highlights of the city.
- In addition, you might secure a complete and up-to-date membership mailing list from the meeting planner and send personalized letters, e-mails, or texts describing the planned activities. Also tell potential guests about the climate and offer suggestions on appropriate attire.
- Suggest that the convening group designate a chairperson for a guest/companion program. Offer to work with this person in arranging shows, sight-seeing, and other interesting programs.
- Advertise in the popular trade journals of the conferring group. Your ad should extol the virtues of having the delegates' guests come along.

## Activities for the Attendees' Guests

Hotels have recently taken positive steps to increase spouse and guest attendance; a few properties have even created guest/companion service departments with directors to meet the needs of these attendees. Working alongside the convention service manager, the program's director helps convention committees plan and coordinate interesting programs.

Most hotels cannot afford to staff a special director for spouses and guests, but every hotel dealing in group business should at least prepare a directory of possible activities for these attendees. This directory should be freely distributed to meeting planners. Figure 16.5 provides examples of unique guest programs created by several properties.

**WORTH WATCHING**

The Wild Dunes Resort in Charleston, South Carolina, partnered with the Lee Brothers Culinary Experience to create a unique, local experience for convention attendees. You can view a video of the brothers in action at www.youtube.com/watch?v=EJygVKEVnSk (or go to www.youtube.com and search for Lee Brothers Culinary Experience).

**Shopping Trips.** A very popular event that promotes goodwill is the shopping trip. Proper planning is very important. Normally, chartered buses take care of the transportation. A store guide should be scheduled to greet the attendees and, if possible, the group should be shown behind the scenes.

Timing is important. Often the attendees will break into smaller groups to go through different stores, so a rendezvous time should be clearly communicated. Be sure that the attendees are back at the hotel in time to get ready for the evening's festivities.

**Sightseeing and City Tours.** Sightseeing and city tours are also popular. A competent guide is paramount. The convention service manager should have a list of sightseeing and tour agencies contacted in advance.

All cities have points of interest: colleges, historic spots, gardens, and so on. One of the best-received tours is the home and garden type. Local residents open their homes for conventioneers' guests, often in an effort to raise money for charity. Generally five homes for viewing is ample. As in the case of shopping trips, timing is important. Discourage the use of cars; go by bus to keep the group together.

587

## Chapter 16: Admission Systems and Other Services

> **Developing Attendance With Guest/Companion Programs**
>
> Janet H. Wright, CEM
> President, The Wright Organization, Inc.
>
> *"One of the most challenging aspects of meeting and exposition management is developing memorable recreational and social programs for both attendees and spouses and guests. In order to do so, you must know what the local area has to offer, and, equally important, know your audience...In some recreational areas, such as Orlando, Anaheim, etc., it is foolish to plan tours that compete with existing recreation. In those cases, we try to negotiate discounted tickets, line passes, etc. Yet in many locales where there is an abundance of activities we have found our more successful activities are those which we have created with the help of a convention service manager or a destination management company...Since we know our audience, the broad strokes of an idea are normally generated by us, with the convention service manager supplying the details and implementation. For example, one of our corporate meetings featured a 'Beach Olympics.' Since it was obvious we would lose attendees to the beach in the afternoon anyway, we made the beach part of the corporate program...The event consisted of surfing, volleyball, sand castle building, hula dancing contests, and, during rest periods, participants heard a brief — and usually humorous, always instructive — message from the sponsor...With the tightening of tax laws, it is imperative that these supplementary activities fall within IRS guidelines as education rather than recreation to be considered tax-deductible...."*

**Guest Lecturers.** Many guest/companion programs present speeches by professional people, such as doctors, lawyers, chefs, company executives, and psychiatrists; questions and answers follow. Perhaps there are local speakers you might suggest to the organization. The range of these lectures is great, from flower arranging and dancing lessons to how to prepare a will.

**Other Activities.** Certainly the list of possibilities is nearly inexhaustible. Other suggestions gleaned from our readings and discussions with convention service managers include theaters and concerts, special business meetings for spouses and guests only, and finale parties. Local cultural activities, such as visits to museums, galleries and historical districts; "behind-the-scenes" tours of the property and nearby attractions; and tours of local businesses (such as wineries, chocolate factories and manufacturers of popular products) are also well received. Or, you may wish to offer self-improvement courses, such as cooking classes and classes on time management, stress reduction, dress for success, family life, parenting, child development, and so on, based on the interests of members of the group and their guests.

Since many convention attendees today are health conscious, fitness courses are popular. If your hotel has limited spa facilities, you can partner with a local spa to offer on-site or off-site classes in yoga, Pilates, or Zumba. Other possibilities include golf and tennis tournaments and active team-building exercises, such as rope courses and Olympic-style games.

When planning guest activities, it is important to know your audience and gear your program to their specific interests and tastes. For example, the Hudson Valley Resort and Spa in Kerhonkson, New York, has developed a "menu" of ideas to customize activities to match the interests and personalities of the meeting group. Planners can choose from indoor and/or outdoor activities. A sampling of offers includes paintball battles, rock climbing excursions, and wine or antiquing tours. If possible, find out what was done in previous years (you won't want to duplicate last year's program) and gauge which activities were most favorably received.

You will also want to schedule activities carefully. Keep in mind that many spouses and guests consider conventions as vacations and like to sleep in; suggest that guest/com-

*Figure 16.5. CREATIVE GUEST PROGRAMS.*

When creating memorable guest programs, it is important to take both the location of the property and the guests' preferences into consideration. The properties in the examples below have each put a "twist" on typical guest program activities by offering an experience unique to their locales.

**Las Ventanas al Paraiso, Los Cabos, Mexico.** The 71-suite Rosewood Resort offers tequila lessons taught by "trained tequileros." Groups learn about the history, classification and distillation of tequila — and get practical advice on how to drink it. Guests can earn a "Tequila Aficionado" certificate after tasting three different kinds of the liquor and passing a quiz.

**Ojai Valley Inn & Spa, Ojai, California.** Located in California's wine country, the 312-room property on an 800-acre ranch offers several "Short Courses in Living Better." Local artisans conduct group workshops in drawing, painting to music, and making sarongs using the batik dyeing technique. Other courses include horsemanship, aromatherapy, and golf etiquette.

**Sheraton Wild Horse Pass Resort & Spa, Chandler, Arizona.** The 500-room resort serves as a cultural liaison to guests, working with groups to incorporate Pima and Maricopa tribe culture into meetings and activities. Pottery, basket weaving, and other artistic workshops are available, and tribal elders are available to speak at functions. Team-building activities include building bicycles for children who live on the nearby reservations.

**The Equinox Resort & Spa, Manchester Village, Vermont.** The 183-room property offers such unique programs as falconry sessions, as well as an archery school and the opportunity to drive its fleet of Land Rovers and Hummers over 80 acres of off-road vehicle trails.

**Mohonk Mountain House, New Paltz, New York.** The 261-room property in New York's Catskill Mountains has developed wacky group activities that include game shows, remote-control car races, tricycle polo, and "human foosball." Other activities include gnome hunts, a "musical chairs" painting workshop, during which participants contribute to a group canvas, and cardboard boat regattas.

Hotels often offer guest/companion programs to boost attendance at conventions and meetings. The properties featured above have developed creative programs that provide unique activities and appeal to a wide range of interests.
**Source:** Tom Isler, "Property Rites: Inspiring On-Site Activities for Groups," *Meetings & Conventions.* Photographs courtesy of The Equinox Resort & Spa.

## Chapter 16: Admission Systems and Other Services

panion programs be scheduled in the afternoons. Spouses and guests may also dislike being rushed from one activity to the next; ample free time should be allotted.

## Activities for Children

Over the past several years, a growing number of attendees have been combining the annual convention with their family vacation. Smart meeting planners are aware that working parents want to spend more time with their children, so many organizations are inviting the entire family to conventions as a way to boost attendance (see Figure 16.6). Hotels also benefit from family attendance, but some properties have found it a challenge to balance family-friendly services with the needs of business travelers, who may also be an important market segment for the property. Anne Hamilton, vice president of global travel at the Walt Disney Company says:

*Figure 16.6. GUEST AND CHILDREN'S PROGRAMS.*

### Arranging Guest Programs

Percent of Corporate Planners: 46% / 54%
Percent of Association Planners: 22% / 78%

■ Yes ■ No

### Arranging Children's Programs

Percent of Corporate Planners: 64% / 36%
Percent of Association Planners: 92% / 8%

■ Yes ■ No

*The most recent "Meetings Market Report" conducted by* Meetings & Conventions *magazine shows the extent to which corporation and association planners accommodate guests and children at meetings.*

We identified that we would have two types of guests before the actual construction of our resorts, so because of the layout, there's no reason for, say, a leisure guest to walk through the convention center. We pre-block the groups' sleeping rooms in an area where they're together. Groups normally like that anyway, and it limits the concerns of being disturbed by, or disturbing, other guests.[4]

*The Kids-Club at Brenners Park – Hotel & Spa in Baden-Baden, Germany, offers a number of indoor and outdoor activities for children from three to 12 years of age. Activities include sports, games, baking and cooking classes, crafts, behind-the-scenes tours of the hotel, and a "Splash Hour" at the hotel's pool as well as field trips. The Kids-Club also offers a library stocked with children's books and access to DVDs, a PlayStation3, and Nintendo Wii.*
**Courtesy of the Brenners Park – Hotel & Spa.**

Another challenge for hotels and meeting planners wishing to build attendance is having to plan activities and supervision for children of various ages. Some hotels have established in-house programs for junior attendees. The Hyatt chain, for example, offers Camp Hyatt, a program that offers structured recreation and learning activities for several age groups. The Walt Disney World Swan offers Camp Swan, with activities (featuring Disney characters) available until midnight. The box titled "A Rundown of Kid-Friendly Programs at the Major Hotel Chains" lists programs and activities for children and teens that are offered by major hotel chains.

Other properties may offer licensed child-care facilities on site or, at the very least, provide a list of registered baby-sitters for the youngest children. Some hotels contract with an outside service, such as Kids Quest, which provides hourly child-care and entertainment at the property. Or the hotel or sponsoring organization can look to such companies as KiddieCorp and KidsAlong to create programs that are customized for the children of at-

## Chapter 16: Admission Systems and Other Services

### A rundown of kid-friendly programs at the major hotel chains

| Hotel chain | Program | Ages | Notable features |
| --- | --- | --- | --- |
| Doubletree | kidsCAREpak | 3-12 | Gift bags for children during the summer |
| Holiday Inn | KidSuites | All ages | Special guest rooms to give kids their own "fun" space |
| Hyatt | Camp Hyatt | 3-12 | Activities that incorporate local culture |
| Four Seasons | Kids for All Seasons | 5-12 (may vary) | Children's bathrobes; supervised activities |
| Hilton | Hilton Vacation Station | 2-12 | Free toy rental; supervised activities at some resorts |
| Le Méridien | Penguin Club | 4-12 | Supervised activities available at offshore properties |
| Loews | Loews Loves Kids | 10 and under | Family concierge trained to cater to children's needs |
| Omni | Omni Kids | 13 and under | Pre-trip planning at www.omnikidsrule.com |
| Ritz-Carlton | Ritz Kids | 4-13 | Healthful kids' menu; etiquette classes for ages 8-12 |
| Sonesta | Just Us Kids | 5-12 | Free activities and excursions |
| Westin | Westin Kids Club | 12 and under | "Heavenly" cribs; free beverages and teddy bears |
| Wyndham | Wyndham Family Retreat | All ages | Program for families to cook and play games together |

tendees. One of KiddieCorp's clients is the Rancho Bernardo Inn near San Diego, where the children of attendees enjoy "Camp RBI" during the summer and on various holidays.

There is a wide variety of choices available, from on-site supervised recreational activities to field trips to local attractions. The wise meeting planner will schedule children's activities to entertain young guests while their parents are tied up in meetings as well as activities for the entire family to enjoy together after the meetings (one organization, for example, stages a variety show for the entire family, while others may arrange for discounted family passes to nearby attractions).

No matter which avenue is chosen, there are a number of factors to consider when hosting family-oriented groups. First and foremost is liability. The hotel must protect itself (and its guests) in regard to the safety of facilities used and the personnel supervising children. All child-care facilities should carry a minimum of $1 million in liability coverage, and most require that parents sign a waiver when dropping off children; this should also be done for any in-house programs, and especially for any field trips off-site. Background checks should be performed on all personnel having direct contact with children, and the hotel should ensure that there is a small ratio of children to staffers to ensure adequate supervision (the accepted **adult-staff-to-child ratio** is one adult for every three infants, one adult for every four toddlers, and one adult for every six children up to eight years of age).

When the details have been worked out, it should be up to the meeting planner to communicate to the attendees exactly what will be offered—and who is responsible for paying for various activities and programs. This will eliminate any misunderstanding by participants, ensure a happier time for all involved, and establish the hotel as a family-friendly property that will likely be considered for future group activities and family vacations.

## Summary

Hotel personnel are often involved in a number of activities to ensure that convention programs run smoothly. When servicing a large convention, the convention service department may be involved in everything from suggesting effective admissions systems to providing security to delegates and exhibits to arranging for in-house or outsourced decorations, entertainment, and printing services. To be effective, your property must be willing to "go the extra mile" in assisting the meeting planner with these details -- as well as helping to build attendance through guest/companion and/or children's programs.

Building your skills in these areas will enable you to handle any type of meeting -- including the largest of conventions and trade shows. In the next chapter, we will take a closer look at the trade show, which provides a true test of a hotel's ability to organize and execute minute details.

## Endnotes

1. Julie Pingston, "How CSMs Can Help Drive Higher ROI for Hotel Executives Looking to Grow Their Event/Marketing Business," *Hotel Business Review*, September 22, 2014.
2. Barbara Scofidio, "Up Front: Special Events Intelligence," *Corporate Meetings & Incentives*.
3. "Leave Your Vendors Behind: Exclusive and Preferred Providers," *Meeting Budget*.
4. Susie Amer, "The Family Business," *Successful Meetings*.

## Study Questions

1. What is the difference between hotel registration and convention registration? What three methods are used to distribute delegates' convention packets?
2. There are four critical periods for convention exhibit security. Identify them and detail the methods for control of each.
3. Why is it important for hotels to work with or to be able to recommend reliable outside suppliers? How do these arrangements benefit the hotel? the meeting planner? the outside supplier?
4. Discuss the importance of guest/companion attendance at conventions. List possible programs for encouraging adult attendance.
5. Many conventions are planned at vacation resorts or other "family-friendly" locations so delegates can bring their children along. What activities are typically planned to entertain children while their parent(s) are occupied with convention business?

## Key Terms

**adult staff-to-child ratio**—The ratio of adults to children required during a child-care/youth program. Accepted ratios are 3:1 for infants, 4:1 for toddlers, and 6:1 for children up to eight years old.

## Chapter 16: Admission Systems and Other Services

**advance registration**—Attendees register for an event before it takes place, either by mail, fax, phone, or over the Internet. Also called **pre-registration**.

**aisle sign**—Typically used in exhibit halls, these directional signs are typically hung over each aisle to enable attendees to find specific booths. May also be placed on temporary or permanent fixtures at the beginning and ending of each aisle off main aisles.

**ancillary services or activities**—All event-related support services, including stewards, technicians, interpreters, and tour guides. Many activities, such as local tours, are arranged or promoted by the meeting manager to complement the meeting, and these non-essential meeting components may result in extra revenue to the hotel if facility services are used (see auxiliary business).

**attendees**—People present at the convention; may be determined in terms of registered members of the convening organization or may also include spouses, children, guests, and vendors.

**auxiliary business**—Business that is brought into the facility because of or in conjunction with an event.

**badge**—Identification card with registrant's name and affiliation printed on it for control and security reasons. Usually given out during convention registration, a badge can be an adhesive, pin, clip-on, or necklace style, or a digital interactive badge.

**beacon technology**—Low-cost radio transmitters that use low-energy Bluetooth connections to transmit messages or prompts to a smartphone or tablet. Commonly used to track attendance at a meeting room or exhibit hall and as navigation and networking tools.

**convention packet/kit**—A comprehensive collection of conference documentation and/or event materials presented in a bag, binder, envelope or folder. Materials can include a program book, tickets, maps and so on, and hotels often provide information about the property for inclusion in the packet. Sometimes called a **registration packet**.

**convention registration**—Process during which attendees pay convention registration fees and receive packets outlining the convention program.

**destination management companies (DMCs)**—Professional management companies that specialize in the creation and delivery of events, activities, tours, staffing, and transportation, utilizing their local knowledge, expertise, and resources.

**digital signs**—Signage that features electronic displays rather than printed copy.

**exclusives**—Agreements that limit who may provide specific products or services. A florist or a photographer, for example, may have an **exclusive contract** in a particular facility, meaning that no other contractor is allowed to provide the same services or products in that facility.

**ground operators**—Company or person in a city that handles local transportation and/or other local travel needs.

**guest/companion program**—Entertainment or activities, such as sightseeing, shopping, and lectures, planned for guests and companions of those attending conventions.

**hospitality suite**—Suite or room for the convenience, comfort, and socialization of attendees and/or guests. Drinks and snacks are usually available.

**lanyard**—A cord or string worn around the neck, as in corded badges.

**message board**—Board, also sometimes called a *bulletin board*, on which convention attendees can review messages left by others and leave their own messages if they desire. May also be electronic or online **message centers** for

attendees.
**near field communications (NFC)**—A short-range wireless connectivity that enables attendees to use their smartphones to buy tickets and gain admittance to an event by simply tapping them on an entrance turnstile or reader. Also used for networking by tapping two smartphones together or tapping the phone against a badge containing an NFC chip.
**online registration**—Attendees register for an event on the sponsoring organization's website.
**on-site office**—A convening organization's temporary headquarters, which is set up at the site to handle business during the event.
**on-site registration**—Attendees register at the site of the event, usually on the day the event starts (or sometimes the day before or while the event is in progress).
**outboarding**—The practice of holding a competing show or exhibition at the same time as (and usually in close proximity to) the sponsored show to avoid paying exhibit fees and siphon attendees away from the primary exhibition.
**press room**—A separate area in which members of the press may obtain exhibitor kits, conduct interviews, and file their stories by telephone, fax, or the Internet.
**radio frequency identification tags (RFID)**——Interactive badges that share information between a receiver and a small transponder.
**reader board**—A listing, either printed or electronic, of the day's events, times, and locations for attendees.
**receptive agents**—Tour operators or travel agents who specialize in services for incoming visitors.
**registrant**—Individual who has submitted a registration form and attends an event; also called an **attendee** or a **delegate**.
**registration area**—Designated area where event registration takes place.
**registration form**—A form, either printed or online, that is filled in by an attendee to sign up for the event and specific functions during the program. May also include housing options.
**security contractors**—Companies hired by exhibit or event management to keep the entire event floor and individual exhibits safe during the function. Guards, closed circuit TV, and other methods may be used.
**serpentine queue**—Unlike a straight-line queue, a serpentine queue makes use of barriers, such as ropes, to either save space or direct attendees to different service stations. As the crowd thins, barriers may be removed, resulting in a straight line queue.
**special event planner**—A person or company that manages all the details and logistics of a project, including conventions, trade shows, ceremonies, and other functions. An event planner must deal with such areas as budgets, selecting and reserving event venues, acquiring necessary permits, planning food functions, and selecting speakers and entertainment to ensure that the event will meet the sponsoring organization's goal and provide a memorable experience for attendees.
**suitcasing**—The practice of promoting competing products or services to attendees by an unauthorized person. The offender may often leave his or her own promotional materials at another exhibitor's booth or directly engage with attendees, providing promotional materials or a business card to them.
**temps**—Temporary workers hired for convention registration and other duties, such as clerical support, traffic control and security.

## Industry Profile

*Sam Lippman,
Founder and CEO*

**Lippman Connects**

Sam Lippman started his career in 1977 as an account executive for United Exposition Service Company. During the next three years, he worked with carpenters, decorators, riggers, and teamsters, staging the largest trade shows in Chicago, Detroit, and New York City. Prior to forming his own company, he was the director of operations for the Consumer Electronics Show. Sam also shares his expertise as a lecturer at George Washington University.

## Exhibitions Require a Team Effort

Producing trade shows is an exciting, demanding, complex challenge that requires teamwork and communications. Show managers, contractors, facilities, labor, and exhibitors must all work together, under incredible time restraints, to create these live marketing events.

Show managers must pull together a diverse team of professionals to ensure the successful production of their shows. The selection of the exposition service contractor; official contractors, such as registration, security, and transportation; and, the consultants and free-lancers that support the effort on-site must be made carefully so that all chosen will excel as a team. This team must work together, through an intricate series of opportunities and challenges, to create a show that benefits everyone: the exhibitors; the attendees; and the host community.

The most important member of this trade show team is the exposition service contractor. The exposition service contractor's account executive is the show manager's "eyes and ears" on the exhibit floor, allowing the show managers to focus on their many other responsibilities. From the unloading of the first truck to the dismantling of the last exhibit, a happy exhibitor is the goal of both the show manager and the exposition service contractor. Exhibitors that have a successful show will increase their budgets for the next show, for more exhibit space and for more complex displays, which means more revenues for both show management and their exposition service contractor.

The most important tool the exposition service contractor provides to show management is the exhibit hall's to-scale floor plan. As soon as the preliminary floor plan is complete, the show manager and exposition service contractor should meet with their facility's convention service manager to confirm their move-in and move-out schedule. Find out exactly what type of show is being followed and what other business will be in the facility at the same time.

The trade show industry is completely interdependent. Associations depend on the income generated by trade shows to keep their membership fees low and still offer many benefits and services to their members. Show managers depend on their trade show team for the success of their trade show. Trade show contractors depend on healthy trade shows for their livelihood. Facility managers depend on accurate floor plans to deliver their services to the correct booths. Exhibitors depend on qualified labor to set up and dismantle their displays. Because of this interdependency, successful trade shows have a commitment to communications. Trade show managers communicate early and constantly with their exposition contractors, facilities, labor, and exhibitors. This constant, interactive communication among all members of the trade show team helps to create shows that provide a cost-efficient marketing and education forum for exhibitors and attendees.

**Learning Objectives:**

This portion of your text introduces one of the most lucrative — and most detailed — segments of the meetings and conventions industry: the exhibit and trade shows market. Trade shows require extensive planning in a number of areas, which we will cover in this chapter. When you have studied this chapter, you will:

- Be able to describe the scope of exhibitions and trade shows and identify the types of exhibits commonly used.
- Be able to identify and discuss the elements of exhibit planning, including the duties and responsibilities of key exhibition and trade show personnel.
- Be able to explain exhibit billing procedures and discuss the shipping and receiving concerns of exhibitors and the properties that host them.

**Outline**

The Scope of Exhibits and Trade Shows
- Types of Exhibits

Exhibit Planning
- Key Trade Show and Exhibit Personnel
  - The Trade Show Manager
  - Exhibition Service Contractors/Decorators
  - Exhibitors
- Scaled Drawings
- Layouts
- Photo File
- Timetable
- Show Hours and Room Assignments
- Labor Regulations
- Insurance

Exhibit Billing Procedures
- Hotel's Rental Charge
- Exhibition Service Contractor's Fee

Convention Shipping and Receiving
- Exhibit Shipping
- Recommended Address Terminology
- Shipping Methods
- Incoming Shipping Costs

Summary

# 17 Exhibits and Trade Shows

The exhibit is a very important part of the convention business. It is a key element in most trade conventions, with over 80 percent including an **exhibition** in their annual meeting, and is a very important part of technical, scientific, and professional conferences as well. Associations see exhibits both as a way to attract attendance and as a very essential revenue producer. Additionally, trade shows are viewed by organizers as educational opportunities for attendees — an extra component of the event's educational program, supplementing seminars and workshops.

Exhibitors, in turn, consider exhibitions as unique opportunities to market their products. There is no other way they could reach so many buyers so quickly, and face to face. Most of the attendees present at the shows are decision-makers, so much effort is put into exhibits as marketing tools.

## The Scope of Exhibits and Trade Shows

Exhibits and trade shows are a lucrative and fast-growing segment of today's convention and meetings market. Exhibits and trade shows are growing at an annual rate of over four percent, so, as you can see, an increasing number of companies are taking advantage of this excellent marketing opportunity. Many trade shows are becoming major international events.

> **WORTH WATCHING**
>
> The International Association of Exhibitions and Events (IAEE) offers a video on the scope of trade shows on YouTube. Go to www.youtube.com, type "Education About the Meetings Industry" in the search box, and click on the "by IAEEHeadquarters" video (or go to www.youtube.com/watch?v=w2j1n3w2H8Y).

We explained in Chapter 4, "Selling the Association Market," that the association makes a profit from exhibits by charging exhibitors for booth space. Exhibits also offer the association a cash flow, which helps finance the convention planning. The exhibitor's reservation for booth space is usually accompanied by a check for half the cost of the space. The rest is sent in later, but still in advance of the convention.

The association's only costs at this stage have been for promotion of the event and payroll, a year-round burden. This advance money from exhibitors amounts to a great deal, and it literally finances the convention. The only additional revenue of any consequence comes from admission and registration fees. It, too, is solicited in advance for the same reason.

The importance of the trade show is reflected in the development of hotels with considerable convention space. These hotels have had great success in going after conventions with exhibits.

It is a rare convention organizer who does not prefer to house the entire convention under one roof. When this is not possible, separate exhibit centers are often used in conjunction with neighboring hotels. The largest exhibitions use huge convention centers such as McCormick Place in Chicago, which has 2.6 million square feet, and the Las Vegas Convention Center, which boasts over 3.2 million square feet of space.

Convention hotels with built-in exhibit areas are successful even in a city with a giant convention center. In Las Vegas, for example, the attraction of a one-house event brings lots of business to individual properties, even with the convention center available. While the very largest conventions would use the convention center and several hotels near it, a somewhat smaller event might be held at the MGM Grand Hotel (5,700 rooms and suites and over 600,000 square feet of exhibit space), Wynn Las Vegas and its sister property, Encore (4.750 combined rooms and 260,000 square feet of exhibit space), or Mandalay Bay (3,754 rooms and suites and an exhibit area of nearly 1.7 million square feet). All of these hotels, as well as other hotels in the city, have the necessary supporting rooms that can accommodate conventions with exhibits.

Las Vegas enjoys as much event business as it does because of its excellent convention facilities and tourist attractions. Other cities are attracting more convention business by offering the latest technology. The Boston Convention and Exhibition Center, for example, is using **beacon technology** to guide attendees to individual booths. Its ActivLocator system consists of 270 Bluetooth beacons which can measure an attendee's location to within six feet, and the app does not require Internet connectivity. Although the system cost $250,000 to install, it is a money-maker for the facility, which can charge hosts to use the system and upload maps of convention layouts.

However, trade show business is not limited to large properties only. Smaller hotels around the country use in-house exhibit areas as an asset in selling convention business and as a lucrative source of revenue. Research by the Center for Exhibition Industry Research (CEIR) reveals that approximately one-third of the conventions involving trade shows have fewer than 50 exhibits per convention. A common rule of thumb is that twice the amount of space is needed for each square foot of booth space. For example, 50 eight-by-ten-foot booths need 4,000 square feet of space for the actual booths, plus an additional 4,000 square feet of space for aisles, entrance and exit areas, and registration desks (see box titled "Formula for Determining Exhibit Space Needs).[1]

---

### Formula for Determining Exhibit Space Needs

Factors that need to be considered when determining the space needed for an exhibition include:

- The number and size of regular and nonstandard booths (island booths, peninsula booths, and so on).

- Space needed for additional features, including special feature exhibits, display areas, lounge areas, concessions, and so on.

- Placement of the show's registration area and management office — additional space will be needed if these are located inside the exhibit hall.

Square footage needed for an exhibit is determined by doubling the net square footage required for the booths and adding any space required for ancillary needs. The basic formula is to multiply the number of booths x booth length x booth width x two. This formula also works in reverse. If you have 12,000 square feet of exhibit space available and want to determine how many 8'x10' booths would fit in the space, for example, you would divide 12,000 by two, then by eight (length of booths), then by 10 (width of booths) — or simply divide the square footage once by 160. Using this formula, you would see that 75 booths would fit into the 12,000-square-foot space.

## Types of Exhibits

Exhibits are used to showcase or demonstrate products or services at trade shows. There are three basic types of exhibits: a **table top exhibit**, that is often used when there are few exhibitors or space is limited; an **area exhibit**, in which the exhibitor is assigned a specific floor space for displaying large, tall equipment, or two-tier displays or **multi-level exhibits**; and a **booth exhibit**, which is usually constructed with either **pipe and drape** or **hardwall**.

> **MORE ONLINE**
>
> For a comprehensive glossary of terms and language used in the trade show and exhibitions industry, go to www.equinox-design.com/exhibition_glossary.html (or search for Exhibition Glossary – Equinox Design Ltd.).

The most common arrangement is the booth plan. Exhibit booths are ten feet wide by eight feet deep or ten feet wide by ten feet deep and limited in height to eight feet or 12 feet along the back wall with four-foot high side dividers. There are four basic types of booths: (1) **standard booths** (also known as in-line booths) are placed back-to-back with adjacent booths on the sides and have maximum heights of eight feet; (2) **perimeter booths** are located on outside walls and maximum heights of 12 feet are allowed; (3) **peninsula booths** consist of four or more spaces and are bordered on three sides with aisles; and (4) **island booths** are bordered on all four sides by aisles and include four or more spaces (see box titled "The Four Basic Booth Types.")

In some cases, organizers may utilize either the same type or different types of booths to create a **pavilion** – a grouping of booths that feature a similar product or consist of exhibitors from the same country; *international pavilions* are typically used to test the viability of a specific trade show or marketplace. Exhibitors can save money with pavilions, as the participants can share resources. Attendees benefit by being able to compare and shop similar products or services without having to wander around the exhibit hall.

## Exhibit Planning

Normally the trade show is held in conjunction with the trade association's annual meeting, but other groups or corporations may also sponsor a trade show as a profit-making venture. The association or corporation may manage the trade show from in-house, using its own personnel, or may hire an outside show manager to plan, organize, market, and operate the show.

Trade show managers who work directly for a particular association or corporation are represented by the International Association of Exhibitions and Events (IAEE), formerly the International Association for Event Management (IAEM), a professional association of approximately 7,000 trade show managers. The Society of Independent Show Organizers (SISO) also provides information on the value and role of exhibitions, and offers practical tips and how-to information on exhibition management.

> **MORE ONLINE**
>
> Log on to www.siso.org to learn about the Society of Independent Show Organizers (SISO). Scroll down to the bottom of the home page to view seven videos of industry professionals discussing the benefits of SISO, the role of technology in trade shows, how globalization is changing the industry, and the future of the trade show industry. You can also view a video about the International Meeting Exchange – America by clicking on the SISO-TV tab on the home page and then clicking on IMEX America

**Source: Courtesy of the Convention Industry Council.**

As mentioned in Chapter 10, some hotels with substantial dedicated exhibit space may staff a director of exhibit service. This person functions as the principal liaison between the hotel's convention service manager and the meeting group's show manager. There is a wide range of professionalism in show management. Local committees generally have little background in exposition management, while association and corporate meeting planners responsible for annual shows have developed considerable expertise in conducting a show. Hotels committed to the trade show market are well advised to employ a knowledgeable director of exhibit service with a good understanding of exhibit and trade show jargon to assist committees and meeting planners in producing a successful event.

## Key Trade Show and Exhibit Personnel

**Trade shows** provide a forum at which companies can exhibit their products and services to convention attendees. They are, essentially, a "live" marketing event, with about 60 percent of today's trade shows held in conjunction with an association convention and 40 percent sponsored by independent corporations.

Both associations and independent corporations have also taken advantage of today's technology to offer **virtual trade shows** — exhibits, displays, and programs are made accessible to remote "attendees" through Internet and data feeds. No matter how an exhibit is managed, if your property plays host to such an event, you will be working with a number of different people, including:

- Trade show managers,
- Exhibition service contractors/decorators
- Exhibitors

**Trade Show Manager.** The **trade show manager** (also called the show producer, exhibition manager, or show organizer) produces and manages the exhibition. He or she is responsible for developing a list of potential exhibitors, marketing the show to both exhibitors and attendees, contracting with an exhibition service contractor, and overseeing all logistical planning.[2] The trade show managers you work with will be employed in one of two ways:

- *As an in-house staff member* assigned to organize, market, and manage the show for the association (the National Restaurant Association operates in this manner). Or, the trade show manager may be an outside individual or firm contracting with the association to oversee the trade show aspect of the convention.
- *As a private entrepreneur or corporate entity*, organizing an independent trade show for profit. A recent trend is for associations to either sell their trade show and use the invested funds to benefit the association, or partner with a multi-management trade show firm and get a percentage of the profits. Examples of such trade shows include the sale of the American Booksellers Association's trade show to Reed Exhibition Companies and the sale of the National Sporting Goods show to Miller Freeman, Inc.

The show manager's first priority is to sell floor space to exhibitors. To attract exhibitors, the trade show manager prepares an **exhibitor prospectus** that includes the location and dates of the show, a profile of prospective and past attendees, floor rental prices, and other pertinent information to assist potential exhibitors in making a decision as to whether to participate (see box titled "The Exhibitor Prospectus"). High attendance figures from past shows are particularly important in recruiting exhibitors.

**Exhibition Service Contractors/Decorators.** It is customary for the hotel to furnish the basic exhibit area, perhaps with a floor covering, but perhaps with nothing. The trade show manager usually selects an exhibition service company to work as an "official" **exhibition service contractor** (decorator, and general service contractor) for the event. While the trade show manager will contract with an exhibition service firm, this does not generally preclude exhibitors from using an outside contractor for the installation and dismantling of their booths. Some companies have contractual agreements with firms that travel around the country setting up the corporation's exhibits. These firms, called **exhibitor appointed contractors**, participate in several shows throughout the year (see box titled "Changes in the Role of an Exhibition Services Contractor"). Show management and the "official" service contractor require a letter of intent to use an outside contractor.

The contract with the show manager generally calls for general decorating of the ex-

**WORTH WATCHING**

To view videos on the role of exposition service contractors:
• Search for Shepard Exposition Services – Servicing the Exhibitor or go to www.youtube.com/watch?v=qGBQu_bmNkE.
• Search for Freeman Exhibitor Experience at www.youtube.com/watch?v=cuYSdC71WRg.

## The Exhibitor Prospectus

The exhibitor prospectus is the most important marketing piece that will be produced for the event, as it will help to influence an exhibitor's decision to participate. The exhibitor prospectus should include:

- A cover letter, on official letterhead from the show's sponsor (which should prominently feature contact information), inviting the exhibitor to the show. It is particularly effective if the invitation comes from an industry leader who has had past experience with the show.
- The show's unique rationale (and, if applicable, brief highlights of the show's educational content).
- The show's important statistics and successes (exhibitor and attendee testimonials should be included).
- The features of the show and benefits for exhibitors (photographs of crowded aisles are a good selling point).
- A listing of attendee categories and demographics (location, buying power, influence).
- A listing of other exhibiting companies.
- A listing of the products and services that will be displayed at the show.
- The exhibit floor plan.
- General information (hours, days, booth furnishings).
- Pricing, payment schedule, and deposit information.
- The exhibitor contract with rules and regulations.

hibit hall (includes entrance signage, aisle carpeting, and basic construction of pipe and drape booths), the design of the **exhibition floor plan**, and the on-site coordination for the show. The floor plan is a scaled, schematic drawing of the exhibit area, including dimensions, design, shape, entrances, aisles, numbered exhibit booths, lounges, concession areas, restrooms, and electrical/plumbing accessibility. Sam Lippman, who is quoted in the Industry Profile at the start of this chapter, states:

> An accurate floor plan, laid out to identify structural obstacles, such as columns, freight doors, and low ceilings, will save time, money, and aggravation for the show manager, the contractor, and their exhibitors from the beginning of the sales cycle to the last day of move-out. The experienced exposition service contractor will design a floor plan that maximizes the exhibit hall's booth layout, get the floor plan approved by the fire marshal, and offer creative layout options to the show manager.[3]

It is the exhibition service contractor's job to organize, coordinate, and execute all the services required to set up the exhibit area. The old-time decorator was basically a window trimmer, carpenter, and sign painter whose function was to construct eight-by-ten foot booths. Decorators' work today is much more encompassing. They are in charge of labor, plumbing, electrical work, signs, cleaning, telephones, florists, booth hostesses, audiovisual information, and drayage (shipping and warehouse storage of exhibits).

In fact, exhibition service contractors are key persons in the convention process. They work with meeting planners from the pre-show planning until the exhibit hall is cleaned and all the exhibitors' equipment is returned to the home offices. They prepare floor plans for approval by local fire marshals. They contract with a number of suppliers, such as audiovisual dealers and florists, removing this task from the meeting planners. They provide **floor managers** to supervise and control the setup and dismantling of exhibit booths.

Chapter 17: Exhibits and Trade Shows

---

## Changes in the Role of an Exhibition Services Contractor

Don Freeman is chairman of Freeman, which has grown into a family of full-service contractor services that includes AVW-TELAV Audio Visual Solutions, Party Time Rentals, and Stage Rigging. Many of his clients are shows that move around the country, and Freeman has seen a dramatic shift in how his firm meets the needs of these exhibitors:

> Since I started in the 1960s, the biggest change I've seen is the increasing sophistication of shows. It used to be a trade show was either hard-wall booths or pipe and drape. We were essentially a furniture rental company, and we didn't even do a lot of materials handling. Then we progressed to a full-service contractor and now things are moving even beyond that. We do so much more than take orders for signs and carpet. We consult with clients about how they want to convey their brand's image.

Today, exhibitors want more than themed show graphics and signage — they are focusing more on reflecting their show brands, and Freeman says:

> We have to better understand the objectives of the organizations we're working for and the objectives they have for each event. Then we've got to find ways to support those objectives and bring value to the table.

To do so, Freeman, which had focused primarily on the service his company provided for show organizers, stepped up efforts to better meet the needs of exhibitors. The company constantly looks for ways to improve the exhibitor experience, including redesigning its Exhibitor Service Centers to be easier to use and more consistent from show to show. One thing, however, remains the same — the company's commitment to customer service. Freeman says:

> Now every one of our 3,000 employees receives customer service training, even if they don't deal with outside clients...There's no secret to creating great customer service. It's just something you've got to build into your culture in everything you do and remind people of it often.

**Source:** "5-minute interview: Don Freeman, Chairman of Freeman," *Expo.*

---

Equally important, they consult with hotel convention sales and service staffs in an effort to bring about understanding and acceptance of each other's procedures and responsibilities (see box titled "Do's and Don'ts of Exhibit Planning"). This mutual understanding is best facilitated through a pre-event meeting or a series of meetings between the decorator and the convention service manager.

The exhibition service company's contract with the exhibitors is initiated through the **exhibitor service kit** (see Figure 17.1). This kit or manual provides information, pricing, and order forms for booth items including floor coverings, signage, janitorial services, electrical services, furniture rental, shipping of mate-

**WORTH WATCHING**

To see a video showing the range of services offered to exhibitors and show managers by the Oregon Convention Center, go to www.youtube.com and type "Exhibiting at the OCC" in the search box (or go to www.youtube.com/watch?v=acTulqdDbuI).

*Figure 17.1. SAMPLE EXHIBITOR'S SERVICE KIT.*

*A typical exhibitor's service kit includes a number of forms, such as the ones above, that provide information and enable the planner to order specific products and services for various aspects of the function. The forms above can be accessed online to allow planners to quickly and easily enter required information and forward it to the convention facility. While it was previously necessary to either mail or fax requests to hotels or other convention facilities, many venues now make their forms available online to facilitate the ordering process.*
**Courtesy of Sands Expo, Las Vegas, Nevada.**

rials, and so on (see box titled "The Exhibitor Service Kit"). The service contractor of today frequently uses the power of technology to carry on business with exhibitors. Using the Internet, the exhibition service contractor can display the floor plan, allowing exhibitors to determine space availability. Additional linking allows the exhibitor to browse the exhibitor's service kit and complete forms for drayage, carpet, phone lines, and other needs on-line.

Often, the exhibition service contractor will subcontract special services, such as floral, catering, and audiovisual, to specialty contractors. But, regardless, the exhibitor normally contracts directly with the exhibition service contractor for all services.

## Do's and Don'ts of Exhibit Planning

Exhibition service contractors do find fault with hotels sometimes. Global Experience Specialists, a leading decorator with offices nationwide, has outlined the following hotel problem areas from actual convention situations:

**1. Poor Planning for Exhibit Layout**
How many times has an exhibitor walked into his assigned booth space to find a beautiful gigantic and low-hanging chandelier right smack in the middle of the booth — or a column or similar obstruction? Reason? The convention sales personnel just pulled out a basic stock floor plan and submitted it to the client — without consulting the exhibition service contractor— and nowhere did the plan indicate the column or chandelier.

**2. Plumbing**
Neither the plumbing contractor nor the exhibitors will ever be the same after this session — 140 booths in 30,000 sq. ft. of exhibit space...and two water and drain outlets from which to supply all the plumbing lines and connections required by the exhibitors.

**3. Electrical**
This was an electronics show; power load was so great that existing equipment in the hotel was inadequate to provide half the required current. Additional lines had to be brought in by the utility company at the time of the show move-in. An electronics show obviously involves a heavy power load, and the hotel could have saved everybody a lot of headaches if this had been taken into consideration while booking the show — balancing requirements against electrical facilities available — and increasing the power in advance.

**4. Labor**
How many times have we set up a one hundred or two hundred booth show, all custom constructed displays, and found we would be allowed six hours for dismantle, pack-up and move out from the area? This unreasonable rush causes breakage and damage to property, misdirected shipments, and worst of all, an unhappy client who will not do business with you again.

**5. Heavy Equipment**
Heavy equipment shows do not belong on ballroom floors, nor should this heavyweight material have to be moved over marble or plush carpet. Further, the live load limit of a floor is not equal to the static load limit. One of the machines exhibited in a ballroom weighed 12,800 pounds, in a single unit 12' long and 8' wide. Not only that, but there was another part meant to be attached to the machine, weighing an additional 6,000 pounds all by itself, which was to be hoisted and attached to the top of the machine, to complete the unit, to a total height of 20'. We regret to say the hotel took a dim view of the whole operation, and refused to allow use of the hoisting rig necessary to raise the 6,000 pound attachment, so the show went on without it. A perfect show for a concrete floor, but never a ballroom.

**6. Control of Dock**
Here, we meet the drayage contractor's most serious problem. The most important single function of the drayage contractor is to get the exhibit freight in and out on schedule, a schedule not determined by him, for his convenience, but predetermined by the meeting group and the hotel. No hotel has unlimited facilities for receiving, storing and handling tons of exhibit freight. Most have limited dock space. Some much tighter than others, but none so extensive that they can accommodate miscellaneous common carriers, display house vans and independent exhibitors' vehicles, out of control of the official drayage contractor. The official drayage contractor assumes the responsibility for prompt, orderly move-in and move-out of all freight for the show, and the only way he or she can fulfill this obligation is by being allowed absolute control of the loading dock, and with all freight movement going through his or her hands.

*As we said, a meeting of the convention service manager and the decorator before showtime is a must. Most of the difficulties outlined above could be resolved through communication and joint cooperation.*

## The Exhibitor Service Kit

The exhibitor service kit, which is sent to exhibitors who have contracted for and been assigned booth space, should be sent to exhibitors or posted on the Internet at least 90 days prior to move-in and should include such information as:

- List of official service contractors
- Checklist of forms and deadlines for their return
- Days/dates and hours for move-in and move-out
- Pertinent rules and regulations (fire/safety regulations, labor union rules, and so on)
- Rates and pricing and order forms for such items as:

    | | |
    |---|---|
    | booth furniture, carpeting and signage | labor and equipment |
    | utilities | telephone/internet connections |
    | booth security | booth cleaning |
    | audiovisual equipment | computer rental |
    | catering | photographers |
    | floral needs | greeters, demonstrators, models and other personnel |
    | exhibitor insurance | lead retrieval |

- Contractor's payment policies, liability, labor, and material-handling authorizations
- Information and order forms for promotional opportunities (list rentals, invitations, sponsorships)
- Exhibitor registration, housing information, and other pertinent forms

The exhibition service manager oversees the move-in, set-up, and teardown of the trade show and is present throughout the event to service any last-minute needs of either of its two main clients — the exhibitors or the trade show manager.

Because of the tremendous coordination required in staging an annual show, many associations and independent trade show sponsors seek multi-year contracts with an exhibition service company. A good working relationship between the sponsoring organization and the exhibition service contractor is of obvious importance and should receive the very highest priority by all parties.

**Exhibitors.** The **exhibitor,** who can be an individual or a firm, sees the trade show as an opportunity to demonstrate products or services to prime decision-makers and is therefore diligent in selecting and participating in what he or she considers to be the most important events.

Exhibitors are first contacted by the trade show manager through the prospectus. After deciding to participate, they rent floor space from the trade show manager. The exhibitors are then introduced to the exhibition service contractor via the exhibitors service kit and buy (or rent) other services and materials, such as booth signage and decorating from the exhibition service contractor.

Many participating companies appoint an **exhibit manager** to coordinate the exhibit. Large companies that participate in several shows throughout the year may assign a corporate exhibit manager to coordinate their company's exhibit. Smaller companies give sales managers or sales staff managers the additional part-time responsibility of organizing the exhibit and selling at trade shows.

While many properties do not deal directly with exhibitors, it can be very beneficial for properties to work with an **exhibitor advisory committee**, which consists of representatives of an event's exhibiting companies. Committee members update properties and show management on industry trends and issues, and they act as a liaison between show management and exhibitors in regard to show rules and procedures.

Exhibitors can have an enormous impact on the property. They require guestrooms, patronize food and beverage outlets, and often host hospitality suites. It is a wise convention service manager who works with a show organizer to ensure that the organization's overall plan includes analyzing how exhibitors will affect the overall strategy for the function. In some cases, for example, a limited amount of guestrooms may be available at the host property, and an overabundance of exhibitors may result in convention attendees being forced to find lodging elsewhere. The convention service manager may suggest that exhibitor registration be limited to ensure that enough guestrooms are available for convention delegates. Or, the convention service manager may work with the trade show manager to find alternate accommodations for exhibitors.

In cities that host a number of conventions, such as New York, Chicago, Orlando, and Las Vegas, hotels have addressed this problem by building larger convention facilities so they can both provide accommodations for large groups and hold all exhibits in-house. These **hotel shows**—exhibitions held entirely within the hotel rather than at a convention facility—have become increasingly common as a result of both meeting space expansion and the downsizing of some exhibits that previously required extensive floor space.

Hotel shows offer a number of advantages. Meeting planners like the idea that their attendees are somewhat of a "captive" audience in the hotel. They also like hotel shows for the financial advantages they can offer. While convention centers rely on exhibition hall and meeting room charges and other fees, the planner can often get free function space by booking blocks of rooms and other business, such as food and beverage functions. Hotels, of course, benefit from the extra business, but careful thought should be given regarding how many rooms are set aside for hotel shows - and when. Booking shows during peak times, for example, can result in the loss of large blocks of rooms that could have been sold at higher rates. Conversely, booking exhibits during valley or shoulder times can greatly contribute to the hotel's bottom line.

## Scaled Drawings

We have discussed the need for the hotel to have scaled drawings of its meeting rooms. Obviously, the same need exists for the exhibit area (see Figure 17.2). Large, accurate draw-

---

### 🖳 INTERNET EXERCISE

The exhibit and trade show industry was quick to embrace the Internet because of the high costs of producing and sending the many forms necessary to stage a trade show. Many groups now make their forms available online, rather than faxing or mailing documentation.

Using a search engine, search for "exhibitor service kit" or "exhibitor service manual" (or, alternately, "exhibitor service handbook") and then search for "exhibitor prospectus." You will find examples of these forms posted by meeting groups and exhibition service contractors.

Using the criteria presented in this chapter for each type of form, evaluate the quality and thoroughness of two of each of these online forms and answer the following questions:

1. Was the exhibitor prospectus from an association or corporate meeting group? Who posted the prospectus — the meeting group or the exhibition service contractor?
2. Is a floor plan included in the exhibitor service kit? Does the exhibitor contract with the exhibition contractor or the meeting group?
3. Explain the difference between the "Exhibitor Prospectus" and the "Exhibitor Service Manual."

ings to scale should note the presence of columns, doors, windows, obstructions of any kind, the **floor load** capacity, and ceiling heights. The latter two factors are essential, because some displays rise high in the air and some merchandise is heavy.

Supply the drawings to association clients in sizes that make good work sheets. It is important to keep drawings to scale. Many office copiers reduce the image to save paper or to increase sharpness. Some do it slightly; some, a great deal. But reduction destroys the key to the scale. If the scale is given as one-quarter inch equaling one foot, a *reduced* drawing carries such a notice, but a rule laid across the drawing would give a false reading. Imagine setup day with a layout that was planned on the basis of such a false print!

If you have your scaled drawings printed, perhaps in a fair quantity by the offset printing process in a convention booklet, be sure to inform your printer of the need to maintain the strict scale. Usually, printers reproduce your copy exactly as it is presented, but it doesn't hurt to make sure. Sometimes, a slight reduction in overall size helps the job get done on a specific-size sheet of paper, and it usually does not affect the overall quality of a job. But not in your case. If the printer knows the importance of maintaining your scale, you might eliminate costly and aggravating problems later on.

As with other trade show functions, it is common today for scaled drawings to be computerized and made available over the Internet or optimized for the mobile devices commonly used by industry professionals. Computerized drawings are not only easy to update, but today's software provides the capabilities of "arranging" the various components of the hall or booth into the scaled drawing to find the best configurations.

*Figure 17.2. SCALED DRAWINGS.*

This scaled drawing for the Boca Raton Hotel and Club provides information on ceiling heights, sizes of door openings, and floor load limits. Note that although a scale is provided, it is approximate.
**Source: Courtesy of the Boca Raton Hotel and Club, Boca Raton, Florida.**

Chapter 17: Exhibits and Trade Shows

## Layouts

You should also offer a convention planner a variety of layout schemes for a specific hall (see Figure 17.3). An exhibit in a hall seemingly too large for it looks awful — it carries the stigma of failure on the part of the convening group to attract enough exhibitors. A different

Geneva, Switzerland, is the site of ITU Telecom World, an international telecommunications trade show held every four years. Coordinated by the International Telecommunications Union (ITU), a subcommittee of the United Nations, this high-tech exposition features exhibitors from 36 countries. It is attended by over 150,000 visitors — including ministers of communications from 77 countries and hundreds of CEOs and executives from multinational corporations.

To attract the attention of these buyers, over $900 million is spent on elaborate displays created by the foremost designers in the world. Company products are presented using today's high technology, and exhibits often feature **multi-level exhibits**, accessed by elevators and escalators. Upper-level meeting rooms and hospitality lounges are available for face-to-face discussions.

### WORTH WATCHING

To view three short videos on the global growth of meetings and expositions, search for "Video: How Destinations Use Conventions to Gain Edge in Growth" or go to www.interntionalmeetingsreview.com/meetings-events/video-how-destinations-use-conventions-to-gain-edge-in-growth.

layout might provide wider aisles, or conference or rest areas; or perhaps the exhibitors could be spaced out to make for a better looking, more efficient exhibit. Screens (run-off drapes) or temporary walls could be used to block off unoccupied areas. The appearance of the exhibit is important to the hotel as well as to the convention planner. It is in your interest to make the exhibit look great.

The schematics should be presented to the convention executive early enough to help him or her prepare convention solicitation brochures. After all, the executive sells specific areas designated by numbers, not general space. It is difficult to change the layout after positions have been assigned. Exhibition service contractors might be helpful in supplying these exhibit layouts for your hall.

Chapter 17: Exhibits and Trade Shows

*Figure 17.3. BOOTH LAYOUTS.*

Booth Size: 8' x 10'
Aisle Width: 7' 6"
Number of Booths: 235

Booth Size: 8' x 10'
Aisle Width: 8'
Number of Booths: 313

*These graphics from the Bally Grand Hotel's convention brochure show two examples of booth layouts for the same room. Note that the layouts shown are based on both 8'x10' booths and 10'x10' booths. Aisle widths are also noted.*
**Source: Courtesy of the Bally Grand Hotel, Las Vegas.**

## Chapter 17: Exhibits and Trade Shows

The service conractor will know the local fire regulations in regard to aisle width, room capacity, access to exits, and anything peculiar to that locality. In many places, the local fire inspector must approve exhibit layout and setup. It is so much easier to conform to local fire regulations from the very onset of the planning of the exhibit. It avoids those headache-provoking late changes and explanations that can plague a planner.

*Carlson Hotels Worldwide used a unique booth configuration for its Annual Business Conference Customers First Partner Trade Show at the Bellagio in Las Vegas. Instead of the traditional 10'x10' booth, each booth is pie-shaped and set within a pod (each pod of booths showcases exhibitors selling similar products). The back of each booth is 10' wide — large enough for a standard portable display — and each space contains 58 square feet. The distance from the outer edge of the seating area in the center of each pod to each exhibition table is approximately 12.5 feet. The unique floor plan is a major tool for selling exhibit space. Freeman, the exhibition service contractor for Carlson Hotels Worldwide, prepared this floor plan (drawn to scale) on a template of Bellagio's Grand Ballroom.*
**Source: Courtesy of Carlson Hotels Worldwide and Freeman.**

## Photo File

It is also helpful to maintain a file of photographs of conventions held previously in your establishment. The convention executive can check out aisle width, exhibit heights, and overall appearance from the photos. All too often, printed material shows only open rooms. Besides guiding the planner for his or her layout, photos of conventions carry the endorsement of past patronage by convention organizations.

Guide the photographer by listing the characteristics you want shown clearly in the photographs. Build a file of floor setups with and without people in the scene.

## Timetable

When planning for the exhibit, it is necessary to block out the time that each exhibit area will be in use. This includes the time needed to bring in the exhibit material, remove it from the crates, set it up, remove the packing cases, and clean up before the exhibit opens (this process is known as **move-in**).

After the event, the exhibition contractor must plan the logistics of bringing in the packing cases, delivering them to the individual booth areas, dismantling the booths, arranging for shipping or storage of the units, and cleaning up in time for the next exhibit to move in (this is commonly referred to as **move-out**).

A day or two is needed for **installation and dismantle** at most exhibitions. Labor charges are important in this process. The most common complaint of exhibitors is the need to use high-priced labor at overtime rates.

In an effort to negotiate the improvements they feel are needed, exhibitors have joined together to form their own trade associations. Exhibitors in the health care industry are represented by the Healthcare Convention and Exhibitors Association (HECA at www.hcea.org). The International Association of Exhibitions and Events (IAEE at www.iaee.com) is another professional association of exhibit managers. Companies and individuals who design and produce the exhibits are represented by the Exhibit Designers & Producers Association (EPDA at www.edpa.com). These groups have their own annual trade shows at which the newest ideas and designs in exhibit building are presented.

## Show Hours and Room Assignments

Two other common complaints of exhibitors are the hours the exhibit hall is scheduled to be open and the method in which guestrooms are assigned. Actually, both of these are determined by the meeting group, not the hotel, but it is important for the convention service manager at least to be aware that there are complaints.

Exhibitors feel that delegates should have free time from meetings during the day to browse through the exhibit area. Many are annoyed at the long days of sitting in their booths with little delegate traffic flow. They maintain that they are too tired after sitting all day and that there is too little time left to make their important business appointments, which is why they came to the convention.

How does this all relate to the convention service manager? Bill Tobin of Caesars Palace said: "If I notice there is a particularly busy meeting and function schedule, I will tactfully encourage the meeting planner to give exhibitors more exposure."

One solution to this problem is the *hosted-buyer programs* that we previously discussed. Hosted-buyer shows provide an opportunity for exhibitors to meet one-on-one with pre-qualified buyers on an appointment basis. This ensures that exhibitors have a steady flow of attendees who have need of their products or services.

Another option is to provide *product theaters* and *learning lounges* on the exhibit floor. Product theaters, which are typically set up by exhibitors, provide an opportunity for education as well as for selling. Learning lounges use a similar concept; speakers from the educational sessions can continue their presentations on the exhibit floor. Other ways to keep attendees on the floor are scheduling educational sessions at different times than the exhibition, limiting the number of concurrent sessions, using pavilions for easier navigation of the exhibit floor, and adding snack bars or restaurants as well as comfortable seating.

The assigning of guestrooms is another source of exhibitor discontent. One of the services provided to the planners by the hotel is "controlled hospitality suites," which means the meeting group gets first choice on all of the hotel rooms and suites it needs. After all, it is the group's meeting. Exhibitors would like to see less of this policy, however, because it leaves many of them in hotels other than the headquarters hotel. And when forced to stay in a different hotel than the delegates, the exhibitors naturally find it more difficult to transact, and close, important evening sales.

So what can the hotel do? One solution is for the hotel to rent its smaller meeting rooms to exhibitors for evening hours. This arrangement would help delegates, exhibitors, and hotels.

## Labor Regulations

The quality of the labor hired can make or break an exhibition. Sam Lippman, former director of operations for the Consumer Electronics Show (CES), explains:

> The show's manager, exposition service contractor, and facility could not exist without qualified labor. A trained workforce has been instrumental in the rapid growth that trade shows have experienced these last fifteen years. Therefore, it is crucial that any and all union jurisdictions be understood by the entire show management staff and constantly be communicated to the other contractors and their exhibitors. Many show managers run successful pre-show meetings in the exhibit facility three to five months before their show. At this meeting, exhibitors can meet the leaders of local unions and physically inspect the exact location of the booths on the exhibit floor.[4]

The trend of trade shows beginning on Sunday has made it difficult to avoid night and weekend labor charges. This overtime, added to what many exhibitors consider already exorbitant labor rates, has caused some to reconsider their commitment to exhibitions. Whenever possible, a hotel should allow exhibitors to set up early to avoid such charges.

Some cities, such as Chicago, New York, and San Francisco, are referred to as "union cities," as there are formal working arrangements between the city, labor unions, and primary convention facilities. While surrounding hotels are not always bound by such agreements, some are **union houses** — properties that have agreed to abide by negotiated labor agreements. Typically, these labor agreements cover *teamsters*, who are licensed to handle and unload freight and oversee drayage; *decorators, riggers, and show installers*, who install booths and carpeting and decorate the finished booths and exhibition area; *electricians*, who handle all electrical needs; *stage hands*, who facilitate the installation of stages, lighting, and audiovisual equipment; and *food and beverage workers* (this category sometimes includes janitorial functions as well).

While it is understandable that some functions, such as the installation of complicated electrical connections and lighting, are best left in the hands of an expert, labor regulations in some cities prohibit exhibitors from even plugging in a projector or pounding a nail. The labor contractor does all the work, even the simple jobs that the exhibitor could easily do. Ed Johnson, past president of the Exhibit & Event Marketers Association (www.e2ma.org), says of this situation:

> Every show contract specifies an official contractor and spells out certain functions the official contractor will perform exclusively. Usually these services are limited to plumbing, electrical work, and drayage, but some contracts include carpenters, model agencies, and photographers. We believe the exhibitor should be able to select his own florist, photographer, and models rather than have to be forced to use someone who may not suit his needs. (Often these subcontracted services lead to a kickback situation.) We want to make it clear, however, that if we use someone besides the official contractor, he will be a bonafide contractor located in the show or convention city. Associations are afraid the exhibitor wants to bring in non-union help, and that just isn't true.[5]

Labor regulations vary a great deal throughout the country. In San Francisco, for example, stage hands and riggers often perform similar functions; in Chicago, teamsters can carry power strips to the floor, but only electricians can plug them into sockets. Convention service managers should not close their eyes to the varying restrictions and trust to luck. Remind the association to alert its exhibitors to the labor regulations that apply to your hall. The convention service manager must also keep abreast of labor developments and advise the show organizer and exhibitors of any potential problems, such as impending labor disputes. The membership of some organizations will honor union picket lines, so it is important to have a contingency plan. One option is the purchase of strike insurance, which should include coverage for such losses as shipping and transportation costs and the reimbursement of sponsorship fees as well as covering the refund of fees paid by the show organizer and exhibitors.

You must live with the labor contracts in your city. Most experienced convention executives are aware of the labor situations in their localities and have learned to live with them, but be wary of the inexperienced client.

## Insurance

Accidents do happen, and claims do come up, so insurance coverage is absolutely essential. It should be provided by the convening organization, and smart exhibitors will carry their own as well.

The convention organization should be encouraged to contact its own insurance agents to provide full coverage for liability, fire, theft, and breakage. In turn, if notified early, the convention staff should pass along such advice to exhibitors.

Too often the subject is not discussed until the need for coverage is at hand. Then someone says that he thought the hotel was covered. This is another area in which the hotel must be wary of inexperienced convention personnel.

For the protection of the hotel, each exhibitor should be presented with a contract containing a **hold harmless clause** such as the one shown in Figure 17.4. A hold harmless clause releases the hotel from liability should there be an injury, loss, or breakage. These clauses also spell out exhibitor liability; if exhibitors damage hotel property, they should be held liable for repair charges.

*Figure 17.4. INSURANCE AND HOLD HARMLESS CLAUSE.*

**THE WESTIN BAYSHORE**
Vancouver

**EXHIBIT INSURANCE**
The Group acknowledges that the Hotel and its owners do not maintain insurance covering property brought onto the Hotel premises by exhibitors and that it is the sole responsibility of the exhibitor to obtain insurance covering such losses. The Group shall give written notice of such to any exhibitors that it permits to use the function or Exhibit Space to be furnished by the Hotel.

**EXHIBITS AND EXHIBITION INDEMNITY AND HOLD HARMLESS AGREEMENT**
The Group assumes the entire responsibility and liability for losses, damages and claims arising out of injury or damages to displays, equipment and other property brought upon the Hotel premises, and shall indemnify, defend and hold harmless the Hotel, its owners, affiliated companies, agents, servants and employees from any and all such losses, damages and claims. Should the Group allow exhibitors to use the function space to be furnished by the Hotel, then the Group shall cause all such exhibitors bringing displays, equipment, and other property upon the Hotel premises to execute an Indemnity and Hold Harmless agreement in the form of this paragraph and thereby indemnify and hold harmless both the Group and the Hotel, its owners, affiliated companies, agents, servants and employees.

Exhibit insurance clearly spells out the responsibilities of both the hotel and exhibitors in the case of loss or damage. In the example above, exhibitors are required to carry their own insurance, and they assume the responsibility for loss or damages to their property as well as damages incurred by the hotel.
**Source:** Used with permission of the Westin Bayshore, Vancouver, B.C.

## Exhibit Billing Procedures

What does the hotel charge for? There is no reason why a hotel cannot set its own policy regarding any aspect of the exhibit, providing, of course, that the client agrees to it (see Figure 17.5).

*Figure 17.5. EXHIBIT AND DECORATOR'S CHARGES.*

## Exhibit and Decorator's Charges

There are *two charges* that you should be aware of for your budget purposes:
    A)   *Hotel Exhibit Charge*        B)   *Decorator Charge*

### A. Hotel Exhibit Charge

Sheraton-Waikiki exhibit charge is on a *Sliding Scale Per Room basis*. *Sliding Scale* is based on a *Per Booth Basis Per Room Per Day*, as follows (When we use the terminology "Booth", we are speaking of an 8' x 10' area):

*Sliding Scale*

| Number of Booths in a Room Respectively | Per Room Respectively Kauai/Maui/Molokai/Lanai |
|---|---|
| 35 - 44 | $30.00 per 8' x 10' booth per day. |
| 26 - 34 | $35.00 per 8' x 10' booth per day. |
| 18 - 25 | $40.00 per 8' x 10' booth per day. |
| 10 - 17 | $60.00 per 8' x 10' booth per day. |
| 05 - 09 | $180.00 per 8' x 10' booth per day. |

All Foyer booths $30.00 per 8' x 10' booth per day. Entrance and exit days are full price on Fridays and Saturdays. One-half (1/2) price on Sunday through Thursday.

    *Exhibit Pavilion:*    $2000.00 each day, plus 4.16% tax Daily charges include set-up days and exit days.

*All above subject to 4.16% sales tax.*

There are two *money-saving opportunities* contained in the above:
a)   By careful planning of your entrance and exit dates and time, you can save money.
b)   By containing your exhibits to the capacities that the respective rooms will hold offers money savings.

| | | | |
|---|---|---|---|
| Kauai Room | (44) 8' x 10' exhibits | Maui Room | (44) 8' x 10' exhibits |
| Molokai Room | (44) 8' x 10' exhibits | Lanai Room | (37) 8' x 10' exhibits |
| 2nd Floor Foyer | (28) 8' x 10' exhibits | | |

### B. Decorator Charge

The decorator, when selected, also has a booth charge which includes rod and drape, electrical outlets and other specific equipment as negotiated between the decorator and the association.

The hotel agreement with the decorator is as follows:

a)   The decorator will provide all chairs and tables negotiated with the association. The hotel cannot provide the tables and chairs for exhibits.
b)   The respective booth electrical specifications, including spotlights, are negotiated between the decorator and the association. The hotel is not involved.
c)   Storage equipment responsibility rests with the decorator. Equipment is stored in the decorator's warehouse prior to and after each convention.
d)   Drayage — The decorator is responsible for the following:
    1. Receipt of exhibits from the mainland.
    2. Storing of goods.
    3. Transfer to hotel.
    4. Transfer to second floor exhibit area.
    5. Removal of exhibits back to warehouse.
    6. Shipping to mainland.

Source: Courtesy of the Sheraton Waikiki.

Common trade practice calls for the hotel to make a basic charge for the room. This charge may be (1) a flat fee, or (2) based on the number of booths sold.

This latter method of pricing is popular with meeting planners because it protects them from a poor showing by exhibitors. Of course, it means that the hotel is locked into the convention's success, or lack of it, in selling exhibit space. And the hotel's role in such sales efforts is necessarily a passive one.

## Hotel's Rental Charge

Hotels historically have been paid for guestrooms and food and beverage, but only recently have they capitalized on the sale of exhibit space. Exhibitions more and more frequently are held concurrently with conventions, and hotels with adequate exhibit areas are in the best position to book these groups. Some hotels have not only been able to show profits from the rental of their exhibit areas, but they have also taken on the role of decorator, providing booths, furniture, drapery, etc., for which there is an additional rental fee. This is not the rule, however; most meeting groups use independent decorating firms.

There are two common types of exhibit arrangements for shows held within a hotel — the exhibit held concurrently with a convention (typically defined as *business-to-business*, or B2B), and the exhibit held as part of a trade show (*business-to-consumer*, or B2C). The first is sometimes termed a private trade show, with preregistration required and attendance restricted to individuals within the association. The latter, often called a **consumer show** or *gate show*, is targeted directly to consumers and open to the public, although attendees are usually charged an entrance fee at most shows. These categories require different considerations in determining rental charges.

*The exhibit held concurrently with a convention* is the more common type of arrangement, and rental charges vary to a greater extent. As we mentioned, it is a common hotel practice to make a basic charge for the exhibit area. Associations, which make a sizable profit reselling the space to exhibitors, are willing to pay a reasonable fee. While there are no hard numbers and fees vary from city to city, time of year, and demand, it is common for the facility to charge the association or trade show company from $2.00 to $8.00 per square foot. The association or trade show company then resells the space for considerably more – in the $15-$30 per square foot range or even more.

Hotels frequently establish a figure from which they are willing to negotiate. Each group must be analyzed individually. Various factors must be considered in arriving at an agreed rate, just as in determining the charges for meeting rooms. Here are some of the considerations:

- What is the extent of the group's guestroom commitment? Its meeting room commitment?
- How much can the members be expected to spend for food and beverage?
- Is there the possibility of repeat business with this group?
- Are there any unusual problems in catering to this group (e.g., a large electronics show)?
- How great is the demand from other groups for these particular days?
- How much of an exhibit area will the group need?

*The exhibit held as part of a trade show* is often open to the public, as in the cases of boat, gem, and antique shows. In other cases, such as the Snowsports Industry of America, the exhibit is restricted to dealers. Trade show organizers are primarily in the business for a profit and fully intend to make their profit from subleasing the hotel exhibit space. In this case, the markup for exhibit space is considerable.

Hotels can generally command a bigger rental charge for trade show exhibitions than those used in conjunction with conventions. Meeting rooms are seldom used by trade shows, and there is no assurance that attendees will stay in the hotel guestrooms. In the case of an antiques show, booked into the Las Vegas Hilton, most of the antiques dealers were not financially able to pay the Hilton's high room rates, so they stayed in nearby budget motels.

Another consideration justifying a higher rental charge is the likelihood of damage to the hotel due to the increased traffic flow. Such business, however, might well provide the hotel with increased food and beverage revenue in its restaurants and lounges.

## Exhibition Service Contractor's Fee

The exhibition service contractor usually receives a flat fee of $200 to $300 for setting up each booth, using pipe frame dividers and drapery for separation on the back and sides (see Figure 17.6.). The service contractor charges the exhibitor extra for such furnishings as tables, chairs, and wastepaper baskets. Sometimes, the exhibition service contractor will offer a **booth package** to exhibitors. In this case, the exhibitor pays a single price for the booth and such additions as a table, chair, carpet, electrical outlets, and so on instead of having to pay for the added items separately.

The fees the hotel charges for the exhibit room usually include the overall lighting (but not that for individual exhibits), heating and air conditioning, and cleaning services. The individual exhibitor orders from the decorator and pays directly for extra lighting, booth decorations, the furnishings described above, electrical connections, water and gas connections, telephone service and installation, extra signs, graphics, floral decoration, and photography.

# Convention Shipping and Receiving

The convention service manager can avoid many frayed tempers and difficulties by advising the convention organization about shipping procedures. Such advice should be given early enough for the convention executive to include it in mailings to exhibitors. This is accomplished by working backwards from the meeting date to create a schedule to ensure that materials are ready for shipment and arrive when they are needed on site. Specific instructions should also be provided for the routing and storage of exhibit materials (see Figure 17.7). In some cases, small packages (such as attendee handouts) may be addressed directly to a hotel contact person; in most cases, however, exhibit materials are handled by outside companies. It is important, then, to provide detailed information on the procedures and costs for handling exhibition materials.

## Exhibit Shipping

Many hotels do not have adequate storage space to receive and store exhibit material prior to the event. A **drayage company** thus plays an essential role in the flow of exhibit material. **Drayage** refers to material handling, and is the work and cost of transferring an exhibitor's materials to and from the booth.

## Chapter 17: Exhibits and Trade Shows

*Figure 17.6. EXHIBITION SERVICE CONTRACTOR'S FEES*

**FREEMAN**      **INVOICE**

HOWARD JOHNSON/TRAVELODGE/KNIGHTS INN
BALLYS CASINO & RESORT - LAS VEGAS, NV

BOOTH #: 522
BILL TO: AAA
EXHIBITOR: AAA

INVOICE #: 124444-54
INVOICE DATE:
BRANCH #: 111
PO #:

| DESCRIPTION | MEN | HOURS | QTY | UOM | RATE | EXT | TAX |
|---|---|---|---|---|---|---|---|
| 6'L X 42"H DRAPED COUNTER | | | 1 | EA | 123.60 | 123.60 | |
| 8'L X 42"H DRAPED COUNTER | | | 1 | EA | 138.40 | 138.40 | |
| CASEY PADDED STOOL | | | 4 | EA | 65.75 | 263.00 | |
| 9' X 10' CARPET | | | 1 | EA | 113.00 | 113.00 | |
| CARPET PADDING - (SQFT) | | | 90 | SQFT | .50 | 45.00 | |
| **BOOTH FURNISHINGS TOTAL** | | | | | | **$683.00** | |
| WAREHOUSE-CRATED-OT ONE WAY | | | 2 | CWT | 65.40 | 130.80 | |
| Received DT: 05/20/05 02:23 pm   Target DT: | | | | | | | |
| Shipper: AAA   Receiver #: 1000087 | | | | | | | |
| Carrier: FREEMAN DECORATING COMPANY   Pc Cnt: 4 Pro #: 67884-71 | | | | | | | |
| WAREHOUSE-CRATED-OT ONE WAY | | | 2 | CWT | 65.40 | 130.80 | |
| Received DT: 05/16/05 02:46 pm   Target DT: | | | | | | | |
| Shipper: AAA   Receiver #: 1000015 | | | | | | | |
| Carrier: AIRBORNE EXPRESS   Pc Cnt: 5 Pro #: W38589624371 | | | | | | | |
| SHOWSITE-CRATED-OT ONE WAY | | | 1 | CWT | 62.20 | 62.20 | |
| Received DT: 05/24/05 10:00 am   Target DT: | | | | | | | |
| Shipper: AAA   Receiver #: 2000025 | | | | | | | |
| Carrier: DHL WORLDWIDE EXPRESS   Pc Cnt: 2 Pro #: 38589689073 | | | | | | | |
| **MATERIAL HANDLING CHARGES** | | | | | | **$323.80** | |

*Most exhibitor service contractors charge a flat fee for setting up simple booths and charge additional fees for additional items, including furnishings and booth decorations. This excerpt from an exhibitor service contractor's invoice details the charges for booth furnishings and carpet and padding, as well as shipping costs for the listed items.*
**Source: Freeman.**

The drayage company receives all the exhibit material. It has adequate storage facilities in another part of town, probably where real estate is less expensive and zoning allows large warehousing operations. It also has adequate trucking equipment to move the material from its storage area to the convention site within a day or two of setup time. It is the aim of every exhibition hall manager to reduce to an absolute minimum the time the hall is not used for an active exhibit. When setup day comes, the manager wants the material moved in quickly.

Exhibit handling and storage are paid for by the exhibitors. When the exhibitor doesn't understand that the drayage company is to store all material, cases start coming to the hotel. But if the drayage company is selected early enough, such shipments are rerouted to the drayage company facility, and the drayage company can have the convention organizer include its facility as the proper shipping address for the exhibit crates. The exhibitor

*Figure 17.7. HOTEL SHIPPING GUIDELINE*

---

**THE BOULDERS**
RESORT AND GOLDEN DOOR SPA

**Incoming Shipping Guidelines**

Please make sure that the following information is on the outside of the packages when shipping materials for your event

- Address the packages to the individual (with your company) who will be receiving them once on property (i.e. Joe Smith, guest with _____ group).
- Send To:

  The Boulders Resort
  34505 N. Scottsdale Road, Suite K1
  Scottsdale, Arizona 85262

- The name of the Catering/Conference Service Manager
- Number of Pieces (i.e. 1 of 10, etc.)
- Conference Name and Dates

Send your packages to arrive approximately 3 days before your function begins. Packages cannot arrive any earlier than 5 days prior to the conference due to limited storage facilities. Any shipments that do arrive earlier will be charged a storage fee of $5.00 per box per day. Crates and/or large boxes will be charged $25.00 per box per day.

Incoming packages will be charged the following handling charges:

| Boxes | Charge |
|---|---|
| 1 – 5 boxes | $15.00 |
| 6 – 10 boxes | $25.00 |
| 11 – 20 boxes | $50.00 |
| 21 – 30 boxes | $70.00 |
| 31 – 50 boxes | $100.00 |
| 51 – 99 boxes | $150.00 |
| 100+ boxes | $200.00 |
| Crates/Pallets | $125.00 each |

All shipments must be prepaid. The Boulders Resort cannot be responsible for collecting shipments.

Please Note:
The preferred carriers for The Boulders Resort are UPS and Federal Express. They arrive once daily, usually between 10am and 2pm, regardless of the package service used. Both couriers will deliver on Saturday, but only when specifically requested.

34505 North Scottsdale Rd. Suite K1 Scottsdale, Arizona 85262 Phone 480-488-6720 Fax 480-488-7462

---

*In order to ensure prompt delivery of materials needed for exhibitions and trade shows, hotels prepare guidelines for organizers and exhibitors and mail the required information out well in advance of the show date to avoid any problems with the receipt of materials. In some cases, materials are handled by drayage companies or shipped to an outside facility; in this example, The Boulders Resort and Golden Door Spa in Scottsdale, Arizona, provides guidelines for materials to be sent directly to the property. Note that arrival date and storage information/fees are provided, and the property also lists its preferred carriers.*
**Source: Courtesy of The Boulders Resort and Golden Door Spa.**

then ships directly to the drayage company, which accepts the material, stores it, and starts to deliver all the crates to the convention site on setup day. When the time comes to break down, the entire process works in reverse.

## Chapter 17: Exhibits and Trade Shows

*Pictured are exhibits using only a portion of the more than 218,000 square feet of the exhibit space available at the John B. Hynes Veterans Memorial Convention Center in Boston, Massachusetts.*
**Source: Courtesy of the Massachusetts Convention Center Authority.**

Frequently, the decorator will handle all the drayage. He or she will send the exhibitor labels for any freight that will be sent to the convention. The labels are pre-stamped with the name of the convention to ensure that the service company gets the freight to the right show. The service company sometimes gives exhibitors thirty days of free storage prior to the convention; this is to make sure all freight arrives in time.

Drayage material will be delivered to the booths prior to the show. After the convention, the service company delivers the freight to a common carrier or other means of transportation, such as airplane or padded van.

It is important that the decorator know the truck line and invoice number of the shipment in order to trace freight if it is not received in time. Re-forwarding instructions are also required by the service company.

## Recommended Address Terminology

Proper address terminology facilitates handling and delivery of crates and parcels. If a drayage company is used, have all shipments addressed and consigned directly to its facility.

The *event* the shipment is intended for and the *dates* of the event should be marked clearly. This is essential, even if in-house storage is provided. It is also important for small parcels sent through the mail, so there can be a logical grouping and storage within your hotel package room.

A convention service manager often will prefer to have the association address its material marked to his or her attention. Lost or misplaced crates create havoc; the first inquiries made by exhibitors are often in regard to their crates and parcels.

It is important to set up a procedure on handling material addressed to the hotel. Even if the exhibitors' manual instructed that shipments were to be sent directly to the drayage company, you'll always get some sent to the hotel. How you handle such shipments depends on how much room you have at the hotel and how much time is left before the event.

Lost shipments are always a problem. It is difficult for convention service managers to help when cases are lost en route, but they should do what they can to calm concerned and aggravated exhibitors. They, of course, should help exhibitors trace their shipments and expedite installation at the earliest moment after arrival.

## Shipping Methods

You help your client and you help yourself if you indicate a preferred shipping method. There are several options:

- Air freight/parcel delivery (overnight or two-day service) gets packages to the facility quickly and facilitates tracking, but this option is expensive and there are often weight/size limitations for packages.

- Common carriers are trucking companies that combine shipments (from several clients) that are going to the same destination. This is an economical way to ship, but delivery dates are not always guaranteed and tracking can be difficult.

- Trucks can be hired exclusively from van lines or trucking companies — or exhibitors, especially those who participate in numerous shows, may own or rent their own delivery vehicles.

- Using an exhibit contractor as a shipping agent.

From your vantage point, a preferred carrier or trucking company may mean smooth delivery of many shipments. The client is assured of delivery with little trouble.

Local companies don't all offer the same degree of service. Some truckers may have a larger installation in your city, or more trucks, or perhaps just a better, more concerned traffic manager. One desirable characteristic is delivery on weekends. Whatever the reason, recommended firms with consistently good performances ease the bottlenecks that appear on setup day. Good local trucking arrangements help a great deal.

Even using the best trucking company available does not always eliminate problems. To reduce risk, some planners opt to insure their materials. This decision is made based on the value of their items, how critical the materials are to the meeting, and the risk of their loss or damage due to the shipping method. If, for example, a package of speaker handouts is lost in transit, insurance would cover the cost of replacement printing and copying.

On the hotel's part, you will also want to ensure that there are no scheduling conflicts at your **loading docks**, the area where goods are received. This is especially important if you are using your loading docks for more than one function - or if exhibitors are bringing in goods or merchandise (such as a fleet of cars, for example) that may tie up the docks for some time. The hotel's convention service manager should be aware of the number and type of deliveries expected and the amount of time required to unload incoming trucks to avoid conflicts with additional deliveries or the receipt of incoming shipments.

## Chapter 17: Exhibits and Trade Shows

### Incoming Shipping Costs

Some arrangements must be made to handle shipments that come in with postage or freight charges due. Drivers are not empowered to leave shipments when money is due. Without a clear arrangement, a truck might remain at the loading platform, keeping others from unloading and generally causing havoc.

Exhibitors should be advised to prepay all shipping charges, but inevitably a number of cases and cartons arrive with some money due. A procedure should be set up to pay such charges and arrange for reimbursement. This responsibility clearly belongs to the convention organization, but the hotel should make sure that some sort of system is set up. When it isn't, the hotel is generally blamed as being unable to handle incoming shipments without trouble.

Outgoing shipments should be handled properly, too. One reason so many shipments come in with charges due is the ease of shipping that way, eliminating the need to weigh and evaluate shipping costs on the scene. If exhibitors prefer to ship that way from your hotel, keep in mind that those shipments may not be going back home. Many go to other events. Similarly, the exhibit cases you receive may be coming from another event freight-collect.

Working with good shipping companies can ease your outgoing shipment problem. Alert them to the breakdown schedule of the show, and they can arrange for the trucks and drivers to be there. Those companies that work well with you to clear the cases out of your hotel are very likely the companies you'll be recommending for incoming shipments. Good local service companies are a comfort to a convention service manager, and they should be cultivated carefully.

Inform the convention staff of the time needed to set up the exhibit and to break it down. Reminding exhibitors about overtime charges works well. Some exhibitors rush to get ready for the exhibit but have to be prodded to get out quickly.

## Summary

Trade shows can be a lucrative business for hotels that are willing to make the effort to organize for them. This involves developing a capable sales and service staff that understands the needs of both the trade show organizer and the exhibitor. While a hotel's role in the trade show may vary, it is important that its staff be able to assist meeting groups or trade show companies as needed. This may involve contracting exhibition service contractors or other outside services (such as florists, security staff, personnel to set up and dismantle booths, and drayage companies), or directly assisting with specific requirements. No matter what the hotel's involvement, the property has a stake in the success of a trade show. Trade shows bring in guestroom and food and beverage business, and satisfied exhibitors and trade show organizers often result in repeat business -- not only for future trade shows but also for other meetings and leisure stays.

**MORE ONLINE**

To explore trends in the industry, view the International Association of Exhibitors and Events white paper titled "Future Trends Impacting the Exhibitions and Events Industry" at www.iaee.com/articles/detail/IAEE-White-Paper-Examines-Future-Trends-in-the-Exhibitions-and-Events-Industry (click on link below bulleted points to download this 12-page resource). In addition, MeetingsNet offers a slide show titled "14 Trends Shaping the Exhibition and Event Industry" at meetingsnet.com/trade-shows/14-trends-shaping-the-exhibition-and-event-industry.

The trade show industry is expected to grow both nationally and globally; industry professionals expect to see a greater international presence at events, and U.S. firms are expected to increase their involvement in trade shows overseas, especially in emerging markets such as China and India. Technology will also play a role in how trade show exhibitors connect with prospective buyers and enhance the buying experience. It is expected that hybrid events, combining a live presence and virtual elements, will continue to grow, so hotels that wish to capture a share of this market must keep up with the latest developments and be able to provide technological tools to both exhibitors and attendees.

## Endnotes

1. Total number of booths = 50 booths
   Size of each booth (8'x10') = 80 square feet
   Total number of booths multiplied by the size of booths
   80 square feet x 50 booths = 4,000 net square feet
   Net square feet multiplied by 2 = 8,000 gross square feet
2. To view the most recent salary surveys for both association and independent show managers, go to www.expoweb.com.
3. From correspondence with Sam Lippman. Used with permission.
4. Ibid.
5. Jane Chase, "Exhibitors Have Their Say," *Association & Society Manager*, ©Barrington Publications.

## Study Questions

1. Why are trade shows important to both meeting planners and hotels?
2. What are the three types of exhibits used at trade shows? Describe the four basic booth configurations.
3. Who are the key personnel responsible for executing trade shows? What is the role of each?
4. Explain the difference between the exhibitor's service kit and the exhibit prospectus.
5. List the types of information and some of the forms provided in the exhibitor's service kit.
6. Identify the two types of clients served by exhibition service contractors and detail the services provided to each.
7. Discuss how such factors as labor regulations and insurance coverage affect exhibitors.

## Key Terms

**area exhibit**—Exhibitors are assigned specific floor space for displaying

## Chapter 17: Exhibits and Trade Shows

equipment and other displays.

**beacon technology**—Low-cost radio transmitters that use low-energy Bluetooth connections to transmit messages or prompts to a smartphone or tablet. Commonly used to track attendance at a meeting room or exhibit hall and as navigation and networking tools.

**booth exhibit**—A standard unit of exhibit space (usually 10 ft. by 10 ft.) occupied by an exhibitor. Usually constructed of pipe and draping.

**booth package**—An exhibitor receives a variety of services for a single price. Carpet, a six-foot draped table, a 500-watt outlet, and 500 pounds of drayage may be included in the price of each booth, for example.

**consumer show**—Show open to the general public. Also called a **gate show** or **public show**, these shows may include travel destination shows, recreation shows, home and garden shows, and so on. These shows are not generally connected to any convention or meeting and usually charge an entrance fee.

**drayage**—Delivery of exhibit materials from the dock to the assigned exhibit space, removal of emptied crates, return of the crates to be repacked at the end of the event, and delivery of the crated exhibit materials back to the dock.

**drayage company**—Company that handles drayage for a show and returns exhibit materials to the exhibitor.

**exhibition**—An event at which products and services are displayed. In addition to stimulating sales and enhancing public relations efforts, exhibitions provide face-to-face contact with prospective buyers and the opportunity to build business-to-business (B2B) relationships.

**exhibit manager**—Person in charge of individual exhibit booth/stand.

**exhibition floor plan**—To-scale floor plan showing spacing of booths, aisles, and design of the exhibition. Prepared by the exhibition service contractor for the show manager and approved by the fire marshal.

**exhibition service contractor**—Independent firm or individual responsible for setting up and dismantling an exhibit, including supplying booth and display equipment, rental furnishings, floor coverings, labor, drayage, and signage. Sometimes referred to as a **general service contractor** or a **decorator**. Usually contracted by the planner's organization. If the sole agent, said to be the **exclusive contractor**.

**exhibitor**—Person or firm that displays products or services at the show. Also refers to the staff of a booth or display.

**exhibitor advisory committee**—Representatives from an event's exhibiting companies who act as advisers to show managers regarding rules and procedures; also advise managers of industry trends and issues.

**exhibitor appointed contractor (EAC)**—Any person or firm other than the designated "official" contractor providing a service to an exhibitor. Can refer to an install and dismantle company (I&D house), florist, or any other type of contractor. Rather than working in one city, exhibitor appointed contractors often travel throughout the country to set up and dismantle the booths for companies that exhibit at a number of shows throughout the year.

**exhibitor prospectus**—Promotional materials that promote the benefits of exhibiting in a show, sent to current and prospective exhibitors to encourage their participation. Information includes a floor plan of the exhibition, cost of exhibition space, special requirements, and an application for participation. Today, this information is commonly posted on the sponsoring organization's website.

**exhibitor service kit**—Contains information about the services needed by the exhibitor for a successful convention. Usually developed by the exhibition service contractor. Contains general event information, labor/service order forms, and rules and regulations pertinent to an exhibitor's participation in an exhibition. Also called an **exhibitor's manual**.

**floor load**—Weight per square foot/meter that the exhibit can safely accommodate.

**floor manager**—Person retained by event management to supervise the installation, operation, and dismantling of the exhibit area.

**hardwall**—A type of exhibit construction in which the walls are made of a solid material, such as plywood, plastic, or similar materials, rather than the fabric used in pipe and drape.

**hold harmless clause**—A type of indemnity clause that requires one party to fully protect the other from a claim (this would include the payment of costs for attorney fees). States that neither party will hold the other responsible for any damages to or theft of materials or equipment.

**hotel shows**—Exhibitions held in hotels as opposed to a city's convention center.

**installation and dismantle**—The set up and tear down of exhibits. Also, the firm that does this work.

**island booth**—Booth or display with aisles on all four sides.

**loading dock**—The area on premises where goods are received. Loading docks are usually raised areas that facilitate the unloading and loading of trucks.

**move-in**—Date or dates set for the installation of exhibits.

**move-out**—Date or dates designated for the dismantling of exhibits.

**multi-level exhibit**—An exhibit with two or more levels or stories. Often used by large companies to expand their exhibit space without taking up more floor space.

**pavilion**—A grouping of booth spaces on the exhibit floor that share a common factor, such as companies showcasing the same type of product or a grouping of companies from a specific region or country. Exhibitors share resources to save money; attendees benefit from a more efficient way to compare and shop.

**peninsula booth**—A booth or exhibit with aisles on three sides.

**perimeter booth**—A booth or exhibit located on an outside wall. **Also called a perimeter wall booth**.

**pipe and drape**—Lightweight aluminum tubing draped with fabric to create separate exhibit booths.

**standard booth**—A basic 8'x10' or 10'x10' booth configured in rows of adjacent and back-to-back booths of the same size. Also called an in-line booth.

**table top exhibit**—Used where space is limited or where there is a limited number of exhibitors.

**trade show**—An exhibition of products and services held for members of a common or related industry. Not open to the general public.

**trade show manager**—Individual who plans, organizes, and operates the trade show. Responsible for renting the site and soliciting exhibitors. May work directly for the association or corporation or as an independent. Also called the **show organizer** or **show producer**.

**union house**—Facility at which workers are governed and regulated by an organized union.

**virtual trade show**—Exhibition of products or services that can be viewed over the Internet.

### Industry Profile

## Sherry Taylor Cummins, CMP, CMM, Past President

**Meeting Professionals International, Michigan Chapter, Lansing, Michigan**

*Sherry Taylor Cummins, director of HR and communications for a private company in southeast Michigan, has a BA degree in Human Resources and is a Certified Meeting Professional with a Certification in Meeting Management. She is a blog writer for Cvent, an event management software company, serves on the RISE award committee for Meeting Professionals International, and is a past president of the Michigan Chapter of MPI. Sherry, who resides in the Detroit metro area, has published two books and has contributed to several newspapers, magazines, and books.*

## Conducting a Successful Post-Conference

The post-conference meeting is a valuable tool often overlooked. Hotels dedicate extensive resources and energy into landing the group sale, detailing events with the planner, preparing a comprehensive resume, and interfacing with the hotel team to ensure execution. Once a meeting is successfully executed, guests are out the door, and the invoice is presented, all details seem complete, and before a collective sigh is released, the next meeting is already in motion. Working with a convention or conference services manager (CSM), a planner can expect to receive a pre-conference, or "pre-con," meeting with all members of the hotel team that will touch their event. But how often is a post-con (post-conference review of every aspect of the meeting) delivered?

To make a commitment to conduct a comprehensive event review with the planner can bring valuable group business to your hotel and cement a relationship between you and the planner. The adept sales manager understands that the proverbial "bird in the hand," the current planner, is much easier business to acquire than new business. Using the post-con as a tool, you show that you care about the planner's business and that you care about being the best that you can be. Below are principles for creating and using a valuable post-con – one that is hospitality marketing in action!

### How Do You Acquire Feedback?

Acquire data by providing a post-event survey for evaluation immediately after a meeting or event to all department heads. Response results improve when the survey is easy to complete and has a short deadline for return. Making the survey easy to complete provides better data, data that is more relevant and timely. Provide a survey to the planner as well, covering every aspect of each meeting or event that was part of the planner's overall event. Once results are received, follow up with any questions you have regarding comments or survey answers so that you fully understand the information shared. Even better, invite the planner back if possible or touch base by telephone so that all comments are best understood.

### What's in a Post-Con Report?

What is included in the post-con report depends on who will be reading the report. You will provide a comprehensive report for your files and historic information. The financials, room revenue, room blocks, room actuals, food and beverage, number of guests, rooms used, room set-up, a detailed timeline, including staff names, roles, responsibilities, hours worked, etc., will be included.

A clear and compellingly written and delivered post-conference report with the right components will tie up the loose ends of your events and is an effective learning tool for both the hotel and the planner. The planner will appreciate that you cared enough to find out what did not go so well and that you have a plan to improve the issues. You can then celebrate with the planner those things that went well and affirm that you will continue them as best practices. By wrapping up the meeting on this positive note, you have come full circle. Using the post-conference meeting as a tool, you will build strong and lasting partnerships with planners and expect to see group business grow stronger as well.

## Learning Objectives:

This portion of your text introduces you to how meetings and conventions are billed and the need for post-convention or meeting follow up to assess the performance of both the group and your property. When you have studied this chapter you will:

- Be able to detail the factors that must be considered when establishing billing procedures for group meetings.

- Be able to explain the procedures that hospitality properties most commonly use for group billings.

- Know the typical procedures for conducting a post-convention review.

## Outline

Convention Billing
- The Master Account
- Time of Payment
- Guest Credit
- Gratuities and Service Charges
  - Gratuities for Hourly Personnel
  - Service Charges
  - Blanket Service Charges
  - Special Gratuities
- Surcharges and Resort Fees
- HSMAI's Suggested Payment Schedule

Post-Convention Review
- Comparison with Projections
- Function Attendance
- Special Services
- Individual Comments
- Post-Convention Reporting
- Final Appraisal

Summary

# 18 Convention Billing and Post-convention Review

After a booking has "gone definite," the convention service manager begins to collect information from the meeting planner about various aspects of the convention so that he or she can prepare the meeting **resume**. (As we explained in Chapter 12, the resume, or specification sheet, is the major internal means of communication for hotel personnel involved with the convention.) There are three basic areas that every convention service manager looks at as he or she puts together the resume: reservations, program, and billing.

Open and honest communication is paramount in all three of these areas. We have already discussed the reservations and program segments. In this chapter, we will address questions about function *billings*.

## Convention Billing

Convention billing is much too important to be handled haphazardly. Ranking near the top of the list of meeting planners' pet peeves are surprise billing charges. Open communications can help tremendously to have the event end on a happy note. When it is clear who pays for what, everything seems to go more smoothly.

As with most aspects of convention planning, the time to avoid billing problems is at the beginning and not at the end. Billing policy is usually established months before the group gets into the hotel, not at the end of the convention, and should address:

- What areas does the master account cover?
- How are the delegates' charges to be handled?
- Will there be more than one master account?
- Who is authorized to sign?
- What about tips and gratuities?
- How should early arrivals and late departures be handled?
- Should the hotel or the group be billed by outside service companies such as florists and audiovisual suppliers?
- What are the charges for the various types of guestrooms? Meeting rooms? Exhibit area?
- What are the arrangements for food and beverage?
- How are transportation charges to be handled? How are special events, such as golf tournaments and tours, to be priced?
- What are the arrangements for audiovisual, electrical, and phone charges?
- Will there be a charge for security and other labor provided by the hotel?
- How does the meeting planner want the bill broken down?
- Are deposits required?
- Who will prepare and collect chits? Tickets? Banquet checks?

All of these aspects need to be prearranged, and each detail should be clearly spelled out. **Billing instructions** for each function should be clearly outlined in the resume, as shown in Figure 18.1. The accounting department, as well as the other service departments in the hotel, wants explicit instructions on the billing procedure. You definitely want to avoid the problems that arise at the check-out desk when the specification sheet doesn't deal in detail with billing arrangements.

*Figure 18.1. CORPORATION AND ASSOCIATION BILLING EXAMPLES.*

---

### Example I — Arizona Biltmore Hotel, Phoenix

_____Corporation

**Controller:** Corporation will guarantee all personal checks up to $250 for all members.
Reserve suites 67-66-63-62-61-59-58 from 4/28. Charge 5 to Master Account — other 2 to be complimentary.

**Billing:** MASTER ACCOUNT to cover American plan room rate, tax and service charge of all guests.
Master Account also to cover: receptions, surcharges, recreational activities on tournament day, breakfast trail ride, cowboy hats, bandanas, refreshment breaks, entertainment, hostesses, etc.
PREPARE INCIDENTAL FOLIO for each guest. Post all incidental charges to their respective accounts. To be paid prior to departure. (LIST IN ACCOUNTING OFFICE OF ENTIRE ACCOUNTS TO BE TRANSFERRED TO M/A).

**Night Auditor:** NOTE: Extend $4.50 inclusive credit per person for those taking shopping tour on 4/4 or leaving prior to luncheon on 4/5. MUST NOTIFY CASHIER 24 HOURS IN ADVANCE IN ORDER TO RECEIVE THIS CREDIT. THIS CREDIT GOES TO MASTER ACCOUNT — NOT INCIDENTAL ACCOUNT.

---

### Example II — Caesars Palace, Las Vegas

_____Association

**Master Account I:** All group functions should be added to the master account. Mr. _____ and Ms. _____ will be the authorized signers.
NOTE: Please post a charge in the total amount of $250 to this group's master account. This charge is for the purchase of 250 Caesars Palace medallions at a cost of $1.00 per medallion.

**Master Account II:** A second master account is to be set up. To this master, charge the entire accounts of all _____ Association Directors and Staff.
Mr. John M. _____ will be the authorized signer.

**Individual Account:** Rooms, tax, and incidentals to be paid by the individuals.

---

*Billing instructions from actual resumes for a corporate meeting and an association convention.*
**Source: Courtesy of the Arizona Biltmore Hotel and Caesars Palace.**

## The Master Account

The biggest problem when working with convention billing is usually unclear communication. Therefore, an understanding of billing procedures begins with terminology.

A *folio* is a collection of charges incurred by an individual or an organization. There are three types of folios to which charges are posted:

- **Master Account Folio** — charges are paid entirely by the sponsoring organization.
- **Individual Guest Folio** — charges are paid entirely by the individual guest.
- **Split Folio** — charges are paid partially by the sponsoring organization and partially by the individual guest. Most meetings in hotels are accounted for as split folios.

A **master account** is generally set up to facilitate billing to the convention organization. The hotel executive and the convention executive should discuss the charges that should be billed to this account. All other charges are billed to the guests on their individual accounts.

Increasingly, meeting planners are looking for hotels that are willing to divide the overall bill into sub-master accounts to enable planners to quickly and accurately review actual charges against their budgets. For example, many groups will specifiy a separate master account for group food and beverage functions, another for audiovisual, and still another for miscellaneous items such as telephone and business center use. Sometimes a participating company will sponsor a program event, such as a luncheon or cocktail party, and a separate master account is set up for this affair.

Deirdre Bourke, CMP, former account executive at Experient and Conferon, advises meeting planners to:

- Provide clear instructions to the hotel about specific charges that should be posted to the master account, such as room and tax, food and beverage, audiovisual, electrical, telecommunications, and business center.
- Advise the hotel in advance if separate master accounts are required. Establishing multiple master accounts is a simple way for meeting planners to segregate bills in advance so they don't have to be sorted out after the event.
- Confirm with the hotel that all charges posted to the master account must have backup, including invoices, signed checks, and banquet event orders (BEOs).[1]

It is imperative that the convention organization put down in writing all people authorized to charge to the master account, and they sometimes provide samples of **authorized signatures**. Signers are usually the convention staff personnel. If *all* their charges are to be allowed on the master account, say so. The understanding is that these people are also authorized to sign charges. If this area of authority is to be limited in any way, those limitations should be spelled out.

Failure by the meeting planner to detail the extent of what will be charged to the master account can lead to difficulties. The hotel doesn't care who pays what or how, so long as it is made clear who is to pay. It is the convention staff's responsibility to inform attendees and speakers as to what hotel services are included on the master account, and therefore will be paid by the convening organization.

Ask the convention staff to inform you, as well as the guests, who will pay for rooms, food, beverage, telephone, valet charges, and other incidentals. It helps to inform the guest when he or she checks in that the room charges will be paid for by the association, but many

Chapter 18: Convention Billing and Post-convention Review

> **Establishing Convention Billing Procedures**
> Karen Hudson,
> Director of Sales/Independent Contractor
> Relais & Chateaux/Western Region properties
>
> *"When I was sales manager at the Four Seasons Hotel in Newport Beach (now the Island Hotel Newport Beach), our hotel convention billing procedures were set up prior to the meeting. Once a contract is signed and the group requests direct billing of charges, a credit application is forwarded to the client...If the credit manager approves the credit application, a master account is established for the group. In the event credit is not approved, a deposit is then required either immediately or at some point prior to group arrival...When a master account is established in the computer system, any and all charges that the company or association is responsible for are posted to that account. These charges are processed through the front desk, which posts these charges daily. Once the group checks out, charges are collected by the credit department and compiled into one bill...If the group uses outside vendors such as entertainment or special flowers or plants, it is the responsibility of the conference service manager to post the supplier or vendor charges to the group's master account...."*

hotels feel that this is the convention staff's task. Unfortunately, it is surprising how infrequently the convention staff follows through to tell its guests the extent to which they are responsible for charges. Bringing the matter to the attention of convention executives will at least alert them to potential embarrassing problems and maybe move them to set policy.

Such arrangements apply to corporate meetings as well those of associations, since corporate meetings may be attended by people other than company employees. The arrangements should be spelled out completely. This applies to corporate personnel, too. Some companies pay *all* charges through the master account, while some pay only room and food charges, with the rest paid through individual expense accounts. All variations will be encountered.

The hotel should have no policy of its own, but should merely follow the *clear* instructions of the company meeting planner. These instructions should be in writing. Generally speaking, if you get the meeting planner to spell it out to you in writing, the corporate personnel stand a much better chance of receiving detailed instructional memos telling them how to check out.

In some cases, group deposits are required. The need for group deposits is based upon such factors as credit worthiness and group history. The Financial & Insurance Conference Planners organization has prepared a guide providing possible solutions to problems usually associated with master account billing to be used by meeting planners and hoteliers alike. Two forms from this guide are illustrated in this chapter. Figure 18.2 illustrates a **master account billing authorization form**, which provides a comprehensive set of instructions on:

- How hotel charges are to be posted (master account or individual guest's room folio).
- The limit of financial responsibility the meeting group will accept.
- The names and specimen signatures of those who are authorized to sign for any master account expenses (only those with an authorized signature are permitted to sign for group charges).

# Chapter 18: Convention Billing and Post-convention Review

*Figure 18.2. MASTER ACCOUNT BILLING AUTHORIZATION FORM.*

MASTER ACCOUNT BILLING AUTHORIZATION

Convention Name _____
Dates _____
Food Plan _____

NOTE: Please post charges as indicated below. Master Account charges noted here apply only on meeting dates. See separate letter for exceptions and additional Master Account information.

| ROOM & FOOD PLAN | MA | IND | HOTEL SERVICES | MA | IND | SPORTS | MA | IND |
|---|---|---|---|---|---|---|---|---|
| Room & Tax | | | Telephone • Local | | | Golf Greens Fees | | |
| MAP (FAP)* Guest | | | • Long Distance | | | Golf Lessons | | |
| MAP(FAP)* Spouse | | | Parking | | | Golf Driving Range | | |
| Other | | | Valet & Laundry | | | Golf • Caddie Fee | | |
| | | | Bellmen | | | Golf • Cart Rental | | |
| FOOD & BEVERAGE | | | Maids | | | Tennis • Court Fees | | |
| | | | Pool/Beach Attendants | | | Tennis • Lessons | | |
| Restaurant • Food | | | TV Movies | | | Tennis • Racquet Rentals | | |
| Restaurant • Bar | | | Beauty Salon | | | Sports Merchandise | | |
| Room Service • Food | | | Barber Shop | | | Spa/Health Club | | |
| Room Service • Bar | | | Merchandise Shops | | | Stables | | |
| Bar Charges | | | Other | | | Other | | |
| Cover Charge | | | | | | | | |
| Other | | | MISCELLANEOUS | | | TOURNAMENTS | | |
| BANQUET CHARGES | | | Airport Transfers | | | Refreshments | | |
| | | | Other | | | Club/Racquet Rental | | |
| | | | | | | Golf/Tennis Balls | | |
| | | | | | | Greens Fees | | |
| | | | | | | Cart Rental | | |
| | | | | | | Caddie Fees | | |
| | | | | | | Court Fees | | |
| | | | | | | Other | | |

*Including tax & Service Charge, if any.

The _____ Company
  (Sponsor Organization)

1. (Is/Is not) responsible for payment of delinquent charges to individual accounts.
2. (Will/Will not) guarantee payment of its attendees' hotel bill whether paid by check or charge card.
3. (Will/Will not) guarantee personal checks cashed by its attendees up to $_____.
4. Some persons (list attached) will have entire room and incidental accounts posted to Master. These persons should be preregistered and will not check themselves out. Their room bills will be reviewed and signed by the sponsor organization's planner.
5. Authorizes these signatures (Type) _____ _____ _____
   for its MA charges (Sign) _____ _____ _____
The hotel should consider these billing instructions definite and authorized by _____
                                                            (Planner/ Date/Telephone Number)

*The meeting planner uses this form to provide the hotel with a comprehensive set of instructions on how specific charges are to be billed.*
**Source: Courtesy of the Financial & Insurance Conference Planners.**

Figure 18.3 illustrates a **rates and charges bulletin**, which communicates to the convention attendees the specific rates for rooms, meals, **incidental charges,** and billing procedures, as agreed to by the convening group and the hotel. Typically this bulletin is sent to the convention attendees about one month prior to the convention date. Use of this communication bulletin reduces disputes and speeds guest check-out.

*Figure 18.3. SAMPLE RATES AND CHARGES BULLETIN.*

## SPECIMEN RATES AND CHARGES BULLETIN

To: Convention Attendees

The following rates and charges, which have been agreed to by ABC Company and the XYZ Hotel, will be in effect during your stay at the XYZ Hotel. The rates listed in this bulletin represent the maximum you should be charged for the listed services during the length of your stay at this convention.

DAILY ROOM RATE: Modified American Plan (2 meals)

| | |
|---|---|
| $ 140.00 Per Person, per day plus<br> 11.00 Per Person,<br>    daily service charge* plus<br> 4.53 Daily state tax (3%) | $ 230.00 Per Person, per day plus<br> 11.00 Per Person,<br>    daily service charge* plus<br> 7.23 Daily state tax (3%) |
| $ 155.53 Daily Total | $ 248.23 Daily Total |

These Rates: Include lodging, breakfast & dinner daily, and gratuities for maids and MAP dining room personnel.

Don't include bellman, doorman or limo driver gratuities, parlor charges or incidental charges.

MAP CREDITS

Tavern Room — A credit of $8.00 per person will apply and the balance would be charged at a la carte prices.

Golf Club — Dinner in Golf Club carries a surcharge depending on items selected.

Main Dining Room — A few items are a la carte, depending on items selected.

All Extra Meals — (A la carte) charges will be billed to your individual hotel account.

Room Service — A room service charge of $2.00 per person ($2.50 in cottages) will apply to all room service orders.

NOTE: MAP includes dinner on check-in day, and breakfast on check-out day. Should you dine in a group, be certain that all room numbers are listed or only that person who signs will get the total charges for the group.

TRANSPORTATION

Airport to Hotel — $6.50 per person
$3.25 per person (small children)

*Applicable if the hotel imposes a Service Charge

*One month prior to the convention, a listing of specific rates and charges is sent to the convention attendee by the meeting planner. This type of communication clearly spells out exactly what is covered by the convening group and what charges the individual attendee will be responsible for, greatly reducing the chances of any misunderstandings at the time of the meeting or convention.*
**Source: Courtesy of the Financial & Insurance Conference Planners.**

## Time of Payment

Methods and time of payment vary a great deal, depending on the policy of the hotel, the credit and reputation of the convening organization, past history, the frequency of group business, and other factors.

Master accounts can add up to a considerable amount of money, and it is hard to blame hotel managers if they try to get as much of it as possible up front. This is not only because of concern about being paid, but also because of a desire to accelerate the time of payment and to ease the hotel's cash flow.

The usual practice in the trade is a payment when the contract is signed, a pre-convention payment at an agreed upon date, on-the-scene payments, and a final payment. The final payment can be broken into two parts — one at the end of the event, and a final settlement later. In most cases, payment is due in full approximately 30 days after the event. To ensure prompt payment, some hotels offer discounts to groups that pay their master account charges in full within ten days after departure. In other cases, hotels offer discounts to groups who pay with certain credit cards. The American Express® program, for example, offers discounts and other amenities at several hotel chains and properties when the card is used for payment.

Hotels have been known to be flexible about payments, depending on what they know about the client. Political organizations certainly should not be allowed to run up large bills, because the payment may be uncertain or delayed. But a prestigious local corporation that has dealt with you many times may cause your controller little concern about the bill.

Many meeting planners insist on talking with someone from the hotel's accounting department before the convention begins. The standard policy for the Hyatt Hotel chain is to take the meeting planner to the accounting office at the first mutually convenient time to go over billing procedures. The understanding agreed upon earlier is reinforced and problems are solved before the service is performed.

Convention organizers frequently complain that hotels cannot present the final accounting at the end of the event, while the convention staff is still on the premises and memories are fresh. If complete billing is not ready, organizers can still review the charges and initial their approval. Some charges lag, but at least the bulk of the account can be settled. The Hilton chain requires that if bills are not available at the post-convention billing, they be sent out within five days after the meeting (and, to further facilitate the billing process for the planner, bill formats are consistent at all properties within the chain).

A good practice, endorsed by many convention service managers, is to arrange for the meeting planner to meet with the property controller daily to go over the previous day's charges on the master account. Some hotel chains, such as the Crowne Plaza Hotels & Resorts, offer a *daily meeting debriefing* to allow meeting planners to review an itemized accounting of that day's expenditures (Figure 18.4 shows how the chain promotes this service).

Michele Geller, corporate sales manager at the Crowne Plaza Dallas, says that daily debriefings lift a huge burden off the planner. She explains:

> This really helps when you get back to the office a week after the program and have to dig through reams of paperwork when the next meeting is already looming.[2]

Daily meeting debriefings allow meeting planners to track and manage the function budget on a frequent basis, and any discrepancies and questions can be addressed during these meetings. The daily reviews eliminate surprises for the meeting planner and, since

Chapter 18: Convention Billing and Post-convention Review

*Figure 18.4. DAILY MEETING DEBRIEFINGS.*

## Daily Meeting Debrief

**Daily Meeting Debrief** – With a limited budget and lots of attendees, it's common for even a well-planned budget to run over. Now, at the end of every day of your meeting, you'll get a Daily Meeting Debrief. This itemized accounting of your bill will be presented by your Crowne Meetings Director so that you may discuss, in detail, all of that day's expenditures. This will provide the perfect opportunity for you to track and manage your budget before it becomes a problem. During the Daily Meeting Debrief, you'll also be able to raise any issues, special requests or needs for the following day so your meeting will continue to run smoothly and as you planned.

The Daily Meeting Debrief: another way we set the standard.

FOR MORE INFORMATION ON HOLDING A SUCCESSFUL MEETING WITH
CROWNE PLAZA HOTELS, CONTACT US AT 1-800-MEETING,
VISIT MEETINGS.CROWNEPLAZA.COM OR CALL A HOTEL DIRECTLY.

**CROWNE PLAZA**
HOTELS & RESORTS

The Crowne Plaza Hotels & Resorts has developed a "Meeting Success" program to assist meeting planners to plan and host successful meetings and events within their budgets. Part of this service is the Daily Meeting Debrief, which provides planners with an itemized accounting of each day's expenditures to enable them to track and manage the function budget.
**Source: Courtesy of Crowne Plaza Hotels & Resorts.**

issues are clarified before the group leaves the hotel, they facilitate the correct posting of master account charges (ideally, the master account can be presented before the event organizers leave the hotel). All banquet checks, audiovisual charges, and other service invoices should be reviewed and signed daily by the meeting planner. Days or weeks after the event, it is extremely difficult to dispute details such as the number of dinners served at a banquet or soft drinks consumed during a break.

The hotel doesn't want the entire account held up while a relatively minor matter is adjudicated, of course. One suggestion is to set this amount aside pending further investiga-

637

## Chapter 18: Convention Billing and Post-convention Review

tion and/or discussion while the rest of the bill is settled. Some meeting planners ask that a certain amount be held back after the event to handle any adjustments. The amount of money held back and the time allowed should be part of the letter of agreement or other correspondence. Otherwise, the entire bill might be held up and perhaps used unfairly for leverage.

At some conventions, a considerable amount of cash is generated through registration and ticket sales. Some arrangements should be made to count this money and keep it safe. If such cash is applied against the master account, receipts should be issued for all payments. If agreed-upon payments have been made on schedule, organizations may request checks from the hotel in return for such cash. Clear such arrangements with the hotel controller.

The use of computers for accounting functions has greatly enhanced the billing process. Hyatt, for example, offers Group Bill, which allows planners to see all charges in real time during the event. The interactive PDF document features linked budget items that include overviews as well as individual charges for rooms and refreshment breaks. The streamlined system replaces the cumbersome old-style bill, which often ran to 300 pages. Steve Enselein, vice president of catering and convention services for the Global Hyatt Corporation, says:

> If you've ever planned a meeting you know it used to take a week to reconcile the bill. We are giving [planners] time back – this is a huge timesaver.[3]

Westin is also using technology to better serve meeting planners. David Moore, CMP, meetings and events manager at the Westin Charlotte, explains:

> We have two digital client programs that we are just introducing, eBill and ePortfolio. Clients enter a password-protected portal where they can access daily billing, meeting notes, files, and communications.[4]

But in addition to more efficient billing (some charges can be added instantaneously if the property uses point-of-sale terminals), computers increase the speed with which hotels can analyze convention groups for future billing. One hotel sales executive sees technology helping both the hotel and the meeting planner:

> Among the things that are different these days is that you can see the arrival/departure pattern of a group. You can see what food and beverage sales are per occupied room because they play a role in what's charged for meeting and sleeping rooms. Now the planner can get a report that will show the exact value of his or her group to the hotel. We still need to offer good meeting space, but now a lot of the competition is going to revolve around who can make the planner's job easier. And technology is helping us to accomplish that.[5]

With computer systems, the bill can be broken down for each function and quickly tallied to provide the total charge within an hour of the last meeting. Confusion and long hours of labor to put together the bill are minimized, and the bill can be reviewed and finalized while details are still fresh in the minds of the hotel staff and the meeting planner.

## Guest Credit

Another matter to be discussed by the hotel staff and the meeting planner is **guest credit**. With national credit cards, it is simply a matter of saying which cards the hotel will accept. If the hotel limits the cards it will take, this information should be given in time for inclusion in the convention brochure so guests will be forewarned. But most national and international cards are accepted in most hotels, so this seldom constitutes much of a problem.

The extension of credit directly to the guest is more of a risk. The convention executive should be told if this is contrary to hotel policy. Then the recommended procedure by which a guest could establish credit with the hotel might be outlined.

The hotel should also state its policy about cashing checks for guests. Maximum amounts should be made clear. Cashing checks for people with no established credit is a courtesy, not an obligation. Many associations, and certainly corporations, guarantee the checks cashed for members or employees. A maximum limit, if any, should be indicated.

## Gratuities and Service Charges

Gratuities and service charges are a generally accepted part of convention costs. These items are always covered in all sales proposals and later in the contract (letter of agreement), yet few areas of convention management seem to cause as much controversy. While the common industry practice is to use the terms tips, gratuities, and service charges interchangeably, the CIC glossary makes clear distinctions between the terms. **Gratuities** are monetary gifts given *voluntarily* in appreciation of excellent service by specific individuals. A **service charge**, generally a set percentage of the total bill, is a *mandatory* fee added to the group's bill (the fee is then distributed among service personnel).

Meeting planners are often confused about how much to tip, who should be tipped, and when the tip should be given. One hotelier states:

> The end of tipping is a long way off in America. I feel the planner should settle the gratuities subject in advance. If he or she feels uncomfortable with the amount specified, he or she should go to another hotel. Likewise, if he or she feels there is dissatisfaction with the amount of the gratuities, he or she should think twice about returning to that hotel. Most of the problems with gratuities are the result of not discussing the matter with the hotel convention staff — in the beginning, when everything else is being settled. Nobody should ever feel strange about asking the hotel for advice on this matter.[6]

When hotels are approached for advice on tipping, they should be prepared to explain the types of gratuities typically given and the usual amounts given to specific personnel. Although tipping procedures and amounts may vary by location and type of facility, gratuities and service charges can be categorized into four distinct groups:

- Gratuities (tips) for hotel hourly personnel, such as bellpersons, food servers, housekeepers, and door attendants (see sidebar titled "Typical Gratuities (Tips) for Hourly Personnel").
- Service charges for group functions and banquets. These are automatic and mandatory, and are generally figured as a percentage of the bill and added to the check.

## Typical Gratuities (Tips) for Hourly Personnel

| | |
|---|---|
| Shuttle Drivers | $1-$2 per person |
| Valet | $1-$2 when car is returned |
| Bell person | $1-$2 per bag |
| Concierge | $3-$10 per assist, depending on difficulty of request |
| Housekeeper | $2 per day, paid on a daily basis |
| Room Service | Most hotels add a gratuity charge of 15%-25% |
| Bartender | $30-$50 per event |
| Sommelier | 15%-20% of wine expenditure |
| Housemen/set-up crew | $5-$7 per person, per day, per function |
| Shipping & Receiving | $2-$3 per box delivered; $50 if an inordinate amount of boxes delivered; $20-$30 for handling boxes to/from cars |
| Miscellaneous | $15-$20 to anyone providing special service/exceptional customer services |

Source: Christy Lamagna, "Gratuity Guidelines," *MeetingsNet.com*.

- Blanket service charges. These charges are added to the room charge and delegates are not encumbered with further tipping.
- Special gratuities given to management personnel, such as the convention service manager, banquet manager, and head houseperson.

## Gratuities for Hourly Personnel

Our first classification, tips for hourly service personnel, primarily covers the following:

| | |
|---|---|
| Door Attendants | Restaurant Servers |
| Bell Staff | Cocktail Servers and Bartenders |
| Concierge | Wine Stewards |
| Valet Parking Attendants | Room Service Staff (unless tip is included |
| Housekeeping Staff | in room charge) |

Other hourly service personnel may include shuttle drivers, recreational personnel (golf and tennis pros, pool attendants), childcare workers, and so on. Hourly service personnel may be tipped by individual delegates or by the event staff, depending on meeting arrangements. If a meeting organizer is handling tips, he or she should take into consideration such factors as the size of the group, the complexity of an event, and the destination, since expected gratuity amounts can vary from location to location — and from venue to venue.

Generally, gratuities for hourly service personnel are given when the service is rendered — a valet parking attendant is tipped when he or she returns a car, housekeepers appreciate a daily tip, and banquet staff should be tipped at the end of the meal. But, especially if gratuities are handed out by the convening organization, tips can be given to department managers to be distributed at the end of the event — or even after the post-con meeting takes place.

In those cases where a meeting organizer handles gratuities, a hotel convention service manager may be asked to issue **paid-out slips** to employees. These in-house forms authorize the hotel to charge the group's master account for the tips, eliminating the need for the planner to handle large amounts of cash. Employees present their slips to the facility's cashier or payroll or accounting department to receive their cash. Amounts needed can be gauged from past events or by calculating three to five percent of the event's spending and integrating gratuity money into the event budget. Whether tips are handled through paid-out slips or distributed through department management, it is totally acceptable for the planner to ask for proof that the money was distributed — and to whom.

## Service Charges

Our second classification, service charges, seems to present the most problems. The flat service charge rate is 15 to 22 percent or more in most cities, and many meeting planners justifiably decry being assessed a 15-plus-percent service charge regardless of the service. In many cases, however, the hotel is following the terms of a union contract, and this should be explained in the initial negotiations to avoid misunderstandings.

It is important to note that in some states the amount will be subject to sales tax if it is listed as a service charge rather than a gratuity. If a planner hosts a lunch for 100 people at $25 per person, for example, and a service charge of 18 percent ($450) was added, the resulting total of $2,950 would be subject to the state's sales tax—not just the original cost of $2,500.

To combat this problem, some hotels eliminate the term *service charge* and replace it with *gratuity*. A gratuity can legally be added to the bill after the state sales tax has been levied on the cost of meals only. This results in major savings for meeting planners, and most of them prefer to be charged in this way.

No matter which approach is used, it is important that your hotel clearly spell out its policy to eliminate unpleasant surprises for the meeting planner. If mandatory service charges on food and beverage functions or sleeping rooms can legally be replaced with agreed-upon gratuities not subject to state taxes, this arrangement should be spelled out in the convention contract.

> **WORTH WATCHING**
>
> To watch a video of Shawna Suckow, the founder of the Senior Planners Industry Network (SPiN) and The Hive Network for sales professionals, discussing the importance of meeting gratuities, search for Video: Build Tipping Into Your Budget (or go to www.meetings-conventions.com/Savvy/Budget/VIDEO — Build-Tipping-Into-Your-Budget).

When there is a flat percentage on food and beverage setups, the hotel normally distributes the service charge among the service personnel. While the bulk of any mandated service charge will go to the workers servicing the function, it is not uncommon for a portion to be distributed to other hotel staff members. The Royal Palms, an upscale resort in Phoenix, Arizona, for example, charges a 22-percent service charge on food and beverage service. This money is distributed beyond the service staff — both the catering director and the convention service manager receive a portion of the service charge, although no portion is given to the hotel's executives, sales-staff, or owners.[7]

Many planners will ask the convention service manager for a breakdown of who shares in the distribution. There is a greater willingness to pay a mandatory service charge if the planner knows it will go to employees and not be used as an additional source of revenue by the property. In fact, a recent survey conducted by *Meeting News* showed that knowing how the service charge was distributed was "Very Important" to over half of the planners interviewed and "Somewhat Important" to over another third (see box titled "Show Me The Money").

Meeting planners should be advised, however, that it is not uncommon for a portion of a service charge to be used by management to offset labor costs. The director of convention services at a well-known San Francisco hotel says:

The union contract specifies the apportionment of the 19 percent gratuity. No part goes to convention service staff, banquet managers, or room setup; but just 75 percent is equally distributed among the waiters -- the people who worked the function. The other 25 percent is allocated to a category called "salaries recovered," reducing labor costs on the profit and loss statement.[8]

## Show Me The Money

How important is it to you what a supplier does with mandatory gratuities and service charges (i.e., pocket all or some of it versus giving all or some to service workers)?

- Not at all important 0.7%
- Not too important 9.2%
- Somewhat important 35.5%
- Very important 54.6%

Source: MeetingNews survey of 296 meetings buyers

*A recent survey by MeetingNews showed that knowing how mandatory gratuities and service charges were distributed was considered important to 90.1 percent of the 296 meeting planners surveyed.*
**Source: Rayna Katz, "Planners Nix No-Choice Tips," *MeetingNews*.**

## Blanket Service Charges

**Blanket service charges**, our third classification, are becoming more common. Planners and delegates often favor this form of tipping; it means they tip only once -- when they register -- and are not faced with it again. Some resorts have used this method for years, and now commercial convention hotels are trying the system, which is called the **American plan** — a single charge for rooms, meals, and gratuities (the more common **European plan** prices rooms, meals, and tips separately).

If a blanket tipping policy is to be used, this must be communicated to the delegates to avoid double tipping. Often the meeting planner will point out the policy in the registration packet. Notices declaring "Your gratuities are completely covered in the room charge; do not tip hotel personnel" are common. Similarly, the hotel must communicate this procedure to its employees and discourage them from accepting tips. Again, the resume is the medium whereby the tipping policy is communicated internally.

To help clarify blanket tipping charges, we have outlined below the policies of two well-known resorts:

- The Greenbrier
  White Sulphur Springs, West Virginia

  *In lieu of gratuities for housekeeping and Modified American Plan food service personnel, a service charge of $12.00 per person is added daily to guests' accounts. Bellmen, doormen, and others who render personal services are not included in the service charge.*

- Boca Raton Hotel and Club
  Boca Raton, Florida

*For the convenience of the convention group, the hotel adds $14.00 per day per person to cover the following hotel personnel:*

- *Front door and parking attendants*
- *Handling of luggage on arrival and departure*
- *Chamber maids*
- *Dining room personnel for meals served under the meal plan*

*For a la carte food and beverages an automatic service charge of 15 percent is added to the check. Other personnel are tipped at the convention group's discretion.*

Even if gratuities for hourly employees are included in service charges, there may be occasions when either the meeting planner or the event's attendees wish to recognize exceptional service with an additional gratuity. A meeting planner may give a tip to a banquet captain whose expert handling of a function has made the event especially memorable, for example. Or, a delegate may wish to show appreciation to a staff member who has provided an additional or unexpected service.

## Special Gratuities

The final type of gratuity is that used in rewarding special personnel. Meeting planners may ask the hotel about the accepted practice and internal policies for giving such tips. Hotels that do recommend tipping for special services will offer a suggested minimum scale. Figure 18.5 details the way in which special service personnel are typically rewarded.

*Figure 18.5. TYPICAL SPECIAL GRATUITIES (TIPS) GIVEN TO MANAGEMENT PERSONNEL.*

| | |
|---|---|
| Sales Manager | Gift valued at less than $125 |
| Convention Service Manager | $100-$500 per entire program |
| Food & Beverage Manager | $100-$150 per entire program |
| Head Chef | $50-$75 per function |
| Banquet Chefs | $30-$50 if carving stations are used |
| Banquet Captains | $10-$20 per function |
| Front Desk Supervisor | $30-$75 if there are many special requests |
| Reservations Manager | $40-$75 per entire program |
| Head Houseperson | $50-$100 per entire program |
| Audiovisual Manager | $50-$75 per entire program |
| Other Managers (Security, Bell desk, and so on) | $40-$60, depending on involvement with entire program |

## Surcharges and Resort Fees

While surcharges and resort fees may seem similar to blanket service charges, they are far more encompassing. **Surcharges**, which have been implemented to bring additional revenue to hotels, are often added to guestroom bills for energy usage and Internet access, telephone calls and faxes, mini-bar restocking, and baggage handling. Meeting charges may include such surcharges as fees for electricity for audiovisual equipment and lighting, fees to cover the cost of banquet staff, and even charges for using credit cards to pay the master account.

Like service charges, surcharges are mandatory, and many meeting planners and delegates feel that they are paying for services they don't need. One SMERF meeting planner says of surcharges and resort fees:

> The whole concept of surcharges goes against our grain. The so-called daily resort fee is another way hotels try to squeeze extra dollars from their customers. For $10 a day, for example, they will cover a number of things "for your convenience!" Well, all my luggage is on wheels and I don't need the bellman to carry my luggage. I'm smart enough to open the hotel room door, and even smart enough to turn on the light. Free telephone access for local calls doesn't help, because I don't know anybody local to call. For long distance, I've long since learned that it's a lot cheaper and easier to use my cell phone. So paying $10 a day for a newspaper I don't normally read is simply not for my convenience. That's why, if I sign a contract, I make sure that the rate specified is "all-inclusive" except for taxes, an element beyond the control of the hotel.[9]

**WORTH WATCHING**

Caesars Entertainment, whose ten Las Vegas properties include Bally's, Caesars Palace, the Cromwell, the Flamingo, Harrah's, the Linq, Paris Las Vegas, Planet Hollywood, and the Rio, as well as the Nobu Hotel at Caesars Palace, uses a no-fee policy as an important strategy to attract meeting planners. Watch a short video promoting Harrah's no resort fee policy at www.youtube.com (type Harrah's "No Resort Fees" in the search box) or go to www.youtube.com/watch?v=d8C6-WGfXUI.

It should be noted that a surcharge does not always include fees for other services and facilities that planners and attendees may use. Some hotels charge daily fees for valet and self-parking, the use of its fitness center, spa access, tennis court access and racquet rental, sports equipment storage, and Internet access, if that is not included in the surcharge. The difference between these fees and the surcharge is that they are only paid if meeting attendees make use of them, and planners should make attendees aware of these additional charges — especially if guestrooms and gratuities are covered by an all-inclusive plan.

The **resort fee**, which is similar to blanket service charges and surcharges, was originally added by resorts, especially those in out-of-the-way locations, to help raise revenue as they did not enjoy the benefits of walk-in traffic. These fees, which are now common in most resorts, are automatically added by resorts for services ranging from in-room amenities to local telephone services to resort facilities such as business centers, fitness centers, and tennis courts. The Boulders Resort in Arizona, for example, lists a number of amenities that are included in its resort fee:

> *A Resort Service Charge currently of $29.00 per Casita per day and $33.00 per Villa per day will apply to all guestrooms utilized. This fee includes daily newspaper, nightly turndown service, valet parking, all cash gratuities for bellstaff, housekeepers, on-property drivers, pool attendants, concierge, and all other service personnel (**excluding food and beverage gratuities**). This nightly service charge also includes a daily membership to the Golden Door Spa. This membership allows access to the locker room and all the amenities, full use of the weight room and cardio room, access to the sauna, steam room and O'Furo, Golden Door Spa pool area, Niwa, Labyrinth and Access to the Golden Door Spa Café (**excludes treatments and classes**).*

Other resorts may include such amenities as in-room coffee and movies, shuttle service, mini-bar restocking fees, charges for in-room safes, baggage holding fees, business center charges, access to sports facilities, Internet access, newspapers, and valet parking.

It is understandable that meeting planners balk at resort fees – especially if they are "hidden" and come as a surprise at the end of the event. Hotels, however, continue to impose them, as fees have an incremental profitability of over 80 percent for hotels (representing nearly all pure profit). It is estimated that the amount of resort fees and surcharges collected by hotels in 2018 will top three billion dollars.

The problem arises when the hotel does not disclose these fees, which should be clearly posted on the hotel's website and explained in hotel contracts. Meeting planners are becoming more vocal about being "nickeled and dimed" at every turn – especially if they were not aware of these fees or if some of the amenities included in resort fees (which average $15-$25 a day) are not used by attendees. Planners are increasingly insisting on a full disclosure of all resort fees and surcharges prior to signing a contract, and hotels that do so are more likely to capture meetings business (see Figure 18.6).

Most meeting planners attempt to negotiate these fees, and over 50 percent of them are successful in either eliminating or reducing them. If that is not possible, they may ask that resort fees be rolled over into the overall room rate.

Another tactic to combat the fees, which are becoming more prevalent – and more costly – is for planners to insist on contract clauses that protect them from unexpected (undisclosed) fees. John Foster, CHME, an attorney with the Atlanta law firm of Foster, Jensen & Gully LLC, which specializes in the legal aspects of meetings and conventions, trade shows, and events, adds the following clause to all his contracts:

> *1) No additional charges not specified in this contract, or any addendum, will be incurred by XYZ Group for work performed or for service items provided by HOTEL unless HOTEL has first obtained prior written permission from XYZ Group to have the work completed or the service or item provided.*
>
> *2) Neither XYZ group nor attendees will be responsible for additional surcharges, gratuities, or service fees not included in this contract without XYZ Group's or an attendee's written consent, respectively.*[10]

Hotels are responding to the concerns of meeting planners in several ways. Marriott, for example, rarely charges resort fees, and it bundles telephone and Internet charges to save money for their customers. While Hilton continues to use add-on fees, including resort fees, these charges are now optional for meeting planners — and a full disclosure is always made before the customer is charged; a group cannot be charged an additional fee unless it "opts in."

In conclusion, the handling of gratuities and service charges, as with all elements of convention management, should be carefully reviewed and understood by both the meeting planner and the convention service manager. Even though tipping is a touchy area, no difficulties should arise if guidelines are clearly established at the outset.

**Figure 18.6. OMNI HOTELS PROMOTES ITS NO HIDDEN FEES POLICY.**

In this ad, Omni Hotels & Resorts promotes its commitment to a full disclosure of charges to meeting planners, promising there will be no extra costs or hidden fees.
Source: Courtesy of Omni Hotels & Resorts.

## HSMAI's Suggested Payment Schedule

The Hospitality Sales & Marketing Association International offers a list of standardized procedures that help reduce problems in convention accounting. Here are the guidelines:

- Establish a formal procedure for the hotel and the meeting planner to review periodically the room block arrangements before the meeting. The recommended schedule: up to one year before the meeting; six months before; then every month; and, with one month to go, weekly. The use of rooming lists is encouraged.
- Meeting room usage and charges should be thoroughly reviewed before the meeting.
- The hotel should clearly specify what credit cards are accepted and the maximum that can be charged.
- A master statement of all functions should be organized daily.
- Night auditors and cashiers should be instructed about the details of posting convention charges.
- It is desirable to have corporate meeting planners guarantee all attendees' bills.
- The hotel should inform the company of any delinquent accounts after thirty days.
- A representative from accounting, the head cashier, and perhaps the accounts receivable department head should also attend the pre-convention meeting.
- The resume and individual function forms are to be supplied to the meeting planner before the convention; charges to be clearly specified in advance.
- At the conclusion of each function, a copy of the master statement and supporting vouchers should be furnished to the meeting planner for his or her signature.
- It is recommended that the master account be submitted in full no more than five days after the event. Prepayment of a portion of the master account is encouraged.

The emphasis of this checklist is *communication*. Every aspect of billing must be clearly and concisely communicated to the accounting department and the meeting planner.

## Post-convention Review

It is wise to review a job when it is completed. Much can be learned. Such a review should be done with an eye toward constructive improvement. The purpose of a review is to evaluate performance during the event and the forecasting and planning that preceded the convention. The goal is to improve technique so that the next event will go even smoother.

According to one convention service manager:

> A good, thorough pre-convention meeting can lead to a very short and satisfying post-convention wrap-up.

We recommend two review sessions. The first, an intra-staff meeting, should involve the hotel staff only. The second, termed a **post-convention meeting (post-con)** should be attended by both the hotel staff and the meeting planning staff.

The hotel meeting should include the hotel sales manager, convention service manager, and all departments involved in servicing the group. The purposes of this meeting are to review the meeting's rough spots, to discuss how the event could have been expedited, and to recognize any efforts that went well as examples for the future. Often in such a meeting an internal report, called a **performance report**, is prepared. Kirby Smith, vice president of sales and marketing for Marriott International, Inc., says his company takes post-meeting performance reports seriously:

> **Post-convention Reporting**
>
> Mike Gamble
> Former Sr. Vice President, Sales and Marketing
> Philadelphia Convention & Visitors Bureau
>
> *"Post-convention reporting has become one of the overlooked, underrated, and irritating duties that convention professionals face every day. Cities and hotels are still faced with inaccurate reporting of history and typically do not have the adequate information available to make a good business decision on whether or not to book a group or convention. With the fast pace of the hospitality industry, it is easy to move on to the next meeting or convention and forget about the one that has just finished....A thorough post-convention report will give a much better picture of the overall value of the meeting that most times is not conveyed. During the qualifying and pre-sales activities, the hotels and convention bureaus often ask for an extraordinary amount of information about the group's history, buying habits, and ancillary spending...The irony is that typically hotels and cities are unable to provide the same amount of information back to the planner once the meeting is completed...."*

We use one form that's designed to hold people accountable in every facet of a hotel's operation, channeling to them with our bonus system. The form is broken down into the sales process -- pre-event, event, and post-event phases -- and addresses transitions from sales to service.[11]

The second meeting should involve both the meeting planner and his or her staff and the hotel staff. If the convention is city-wide, the convention bureau, exposition service contractor, destination management company, and audiovisual supplier may be invited. This meeting is also held to go over the many things that happened at the convention while they are fresh in everyone's mind. A good time to hold this meeting is when the master account gets its final review and approval. Everyone is in the hotel and relaxed after the great effort.

Don't duck discussions about the rough spots. Talk them out and try to agree on how they can be handled in the future. Both teams learn much from these inter-staff meetings.

This is also a time to begin the pitch for more business. Many hotel staff people are reluctant to start selling at this time, but if all went well, it may very well be the best time to make the pitch. If not for the next convention itself, for other types of meetings. Corporations hold meetings all the time, and you should make your bid for more of their business.

Every aspect of the meeting should be reviewed and discussed candidly. Association executives should feel free to express their views on the staff's service and performance. Meeting planners appreciate having the opportunity to share their comments. If they sense the hotel is honestly concerned about improvement, they will more readily book future business.

## Comparison with Projections

Compare what happened with what was expected to happen. Prepare a **pick-up report**, comparing the number of guestrooms originally blocked out with the number actually used.

# Chapter 18: Convention Billing and Post-convention Review

Review the flow into and out of the hotel. Were there early check-outs or late departures? Did you have adequate help on hand to receive the guests? Were no-shows a problem? Did you overbook? If so, how did you handle it? Compare attendance with that of other years.

Early departures wreak havoc with hotel income. Yet they generally reflect at least as much on the convention programing as on the hotel attractions. If early departures were greater than in previous years, the program could be at fault; but the hotel still might give some thought to what it can do to make its facilities or area more inviting.

If this convention continually has a problem with early departures, the executive should make some effort to get members to estimate their stays more accurately and honestly. Most convention executives realize that healthy hotels are their concern, too.

Late departures create a different problem when they interfere with other group commitments that are beginning. There is enough evidence of intentional overbooking by hotels that late departures add fuel to the fire. Late departures are a problem, of course, only when the house is overfilled. Otherwise, it's a pleasant bonus.

The entire projection of arrival and departure patterns should be reviewed. The mix of rooms used—single, doubles, twins, and suites—should be compared with what was blocked out in order to polish the technique for the next time. Compare the pattern with the work schedule of your front desk people and other personnel needed for heavy arrival traffic.

## Function Attendance

Both the hotel staff and the convention executive are most interested in how actual attendance at special functions compared with expectations. Guarantees at food functions don't tell the whole story. If actual attendance fell below the guarantee, the convention executive still has to pay for the full number guaranteed or try to persuade the hotel to accept payment for only those served. On the other hand, if more than an extra five percent showed up, the hotel is hard-pressed to seat and serve the additional guests. The convention organization is chagrined not to serve its members; the hotel is undeservedly shown in a bad light.

Review function room allocations. It is difficult to conduct a meeting in a room only 30-percent filled. A smaller room would have helped, if one were available. If not, dividers and screens could have been used. Perhaps the larger room could have been used for something else.

## Special Services

Feedback on the hotel's services also is of interest. Each convention is different, but the hotel can learn from each one about room service, the restaurants, the play at the athletic facilities, the elevator service, and so on. Keep an eye on these services because hotel reputations depend on them. It is an interesting phenomenon that the people who shape the image of hotels are the ones who get the least pay. The telephone operator and the front desk people probably have more contact with hotel guests than anyone else on the staff. If they have been congenial throughout the convention, the customer probably will carry away a good image of the hotel.

## Individual Comments

A very different picture may emerge if you take the trouble to invite comments from your own staff, too. Staff members have a different vantage point than the convention service manager. Ask the bell staff, housekeepers, and front desk people how they think the convention went.

Stand near the cashier at check-out time to hear candid comments from guests. Some hotels make post-event mailings to guests. The benefits are twofold: the hotel projects a sincere desire to render good service, and it is often able to detect unspotted problem areas.

The Grand Sierra Resort, for example, uses a service evaluation questionnaire (see Figure 18.7) to quiz the respondent on all service aspects of the meeting. An analysis of the results has proven to be very advantageous when it comes to booking repeat business.

Hyatt Hotels recently employed third-party telemarketing assistance to receive feedback from planners about service delivery. Fred Shea, former vice president of sales operations, says:

> Nobody can tell you what to do better than your customers. Hyatt commissioned the Gallup polling organization to survey meeting planners by telephone. With results of the canvassing, the company is making changes in its culture that are tied to service accountability.[12]

Whatever your approach, some effort should be made to determine the staff's and guests' feelings about how the event went and how the hotel fared.

## Post-convention Reporting

**Post-convention reports** have become one of the most discussed topics in today's meetings market, as accurate and thorough reports are important to both planners and hoteliers. Meeting planners know that information is power, and when it comes to negotiating, a thorough meetings history provides leverage in ensuring better rates. Catherine Roper, former vice president and strategic development program coordinator for the Health Industry Distributors Association, says:

> As a planner, I need help from the hotel in knowing the value of my business. This is so I have a history to bring to negotiations. For instance, my people are in the gift shops, the restaurants, playing golf and tennis, and using the spa. I want to know the total picture of my meeting's value.[13]

Another meeting planner says:

Writing a clear and compelling post-convention report is as important as the flawless execution of the event itself. A post-convention report is a summary of our meeting experiences that creates history, and showcases our talents and professionalism. Post-convention reports assist us in manag-

**MORE ONLINE**

To view an infograph prepared by DMAI's EmpowerMINT on the importance of post-convention reports, search for 4 Tips to Ensure Your Meeting History is Accurate and Complete (or go to blog.empowermint.com/infographics/meeting-history-accuracy).

## Chapter 18: Convention Billing and Post-convention Review

*Figure 18.7. SERVICE EVALUATION QUESTIONNAIRE.*

**GRAND SIERRA**
RESORT AND CASINO · RENO

Name:
Group:
Dates:

M & C Manager:
Catering Manager:

### Performance Survey

PLEASE RATE YOUR SATISFACTION WITH OUR PERFORMANCE:

**MEETINGS & CONVENTIONS — 1: NOT SATISFIED - 5: EXTREMELY SATISFIED**

| # | Question | | | | | | |
|---|---|---|---|---|---|---|---|
| 1. | The review and confirmation of your meeting arrangements? | N/A | 1 | 2 | 3 | 4 | 5 |
| 2. | Requests were responded to in a timely manner? | N/A | 1 | 2 | 3 | 4 | 5 |
| 3. | The Service Manager Team's visibility and accessibility during your meeting? | N/A | 1 | 2 | 3 | 4 | 5 |
| 4. | The meeting rooms were set-up on time and according to your specifications? | N/A | 1 | 2 | 3 | 4 | 5 |

**CATERING & BANQUETS**

| # | Question | | | | | | |
|---|---|---|---|---|---|---|---|
| 1. | The review & confirmation of your Banquet Event Orders (BEO's)? | N/A | 1 | 2 | 3 | 4 | 5 |
| 2. | Requests were responded to in a timely manner? | N/A | 1 | 2 | 3 | 4 | 5 |
| 3. | The Catering Team's visibility and accessibility during your meeting? | N/A | 1 | 2 | 3 | 4 | 5 |
| 4. | The banquet rooms were setup on time and according to your specifications? | N/A | 1 | 2 | 3 | 4 | 5 |
| 5. | The quality of banquet food & beverage selections? | N/A | 1 | 2 | 3 | 4 | 5 |
| 6. | The banquet service level during meals? | N/A | 1 | 2 | 3 | 4 | 5 |

**AUDIO VISUAL PRODUCTIONS PLUS!**

| # | Question | | | | | | |
|---|---|---|---|---|---|---|---|
| 1. | The AV equipment set-up according to your specifications? | N/A | 1 | 2 | 3 | 4 | 5 |
| 2. | The AV equipment working properly? | N/A | 1 | 2 | 3 | 4 | 5 |

**PRIORITY NETWORKS HIGH SPEED INTERNET SERVICE**

| | | | | | | | |
|---|---|---|---|---|---|---|---|
| 1. | Quality of service & equipment provided by Priority Networks? | N/A | 1 | 2 | 3 | 4 | 5 |

**OVERALL EXPERIENCE AND SUGGESTIONS**

What did we do well?

Where can we improve?

Were there members of our staff that went above and beyond your expectations?

Prepared by:

NAME: _____
Please print

DATE: _____

Forms such as this one, used by the Grand Sierra in Reno, Nevada, ask meeting planners to give their rating of the hotel's performance during a meeting or convention. Used with permission.

ing and controlling event management systems, and they summarize information and facts (not emotions), persuade change, and move others into action.[14]

Hotels, likewise, recognize that post-convention reports allow them to more accurately evaluate and qualify business. The Hilton chain, for example, offers a guaranteed Post-Event Report (PER) that will be delivered electronically within 14 days after the end of the event (see Figure 18.8). Convention bureaus need accurate histories when trying to es-

# Chapter 18: Convention Billing and Post-convention Review

*Figure 18.8.* **HILTON'S POST-EVENT REPORT COMMITMENT.**

## PROPRIETARY BEDS *AND* PROPRIETARY PLANNING TOOLS. SO YOU'LL STILL RESPECT US IN THE MORNING.

While others have been trying to lure you with their proprietary new bed systems alone, we've been developing proprietary new planning tools and working on building lasting relationships. Because as your partner, we know that powerful tools and world-class support are what you really need to help you take charge of your meeting or convention experience. Call 1-800-321-3232, or visit us at hiltondirect.com.

- *RAPID!* (Reservations Automated Processing Input and Delivery): Web-based application that automates the creation of reservations from meeting professional rooming lists.
- *G.R.I.P.* (Group Reservations Identification Program): Manage room blocks proactively with automated cross-reference of group registration lists against hotel reservations.
- *POG* (Private Online Group Page): Attendee direct reservations through a customized group home page linked to organization's registration site.
- *PER* (Post-Event Report): Comprehensive analysis delivered electronically, within 14 days after meeting concludes.
- *Master Account Processing*: Accurate, easy to understand and delivered 5 days after your event!

*Get our exclusive tools and services at these great Hilton® destinations:*
Hilton Anaheim · Hilton Atlanta · Hilton Austin · Hilton Chicago · Hilton Hawaiian Village® · Hilton Waikoloa Village®
Hilton Houston · Hilton New York · Hilton New Orleans · Hilton San Francisco · Hilton Washington, DC

©2005 Hilton Hospitality, Inc.

**Hilton**

One of the most important tools that the Hilton chain offers to meeting planners is the Post-Event Report (PER), which is guaranteed to be delivered electronically within 14 days after the end of an event. The chain also promises to provide the group's master account billing five days after the event's conclusion.
**Source: Courtesy of Hilton Hospitality, Inc.**

tablish room blocks for city-wide conventions, and hotels need them to determine their level of participation.

Accurate post-convention reports also lead to better service. For example, the convention service manager can staff to handle peak arrivals based on past experience.

To ensure they receive post-convention reports, some planners are stipulating in the contract that they won't pay until they get an accurate report. Planners are also asking hotels

## Industry-Wide Post-Event Report

Since compiling accurate meeting histories is essential in evaluating business, standardized information is becoming increasingly necessary. To ensure that complete, standardized data could be collected for analysis, APEX (the Accepted Practices Exchange), an initiation of the Convention Industry Council, developed a template that could be readily used for this important function.

After extensive research, the History/Post-Event Reports Panel of APEX spent a year compiling a History/Post-Event Report (PER), that meets an established set of guidelines, including:

- The necessity of a Post Event Report (PER) citing details and activities of an event—its history
- A face-to-face meeting between the primary event organizer and each venue or facility involved in an event (which should occur immediately following the end of the event,) to focus on completion of the PER
- Once the PER is complete, the organizer should file report copies with each venue or facility used for the event (i.e. CVB, hotel, conference center, etc.)
- The most recent PER for an event should accompany any request for proposals sent to solicit proposals for future occurrences of same
- The APEX PER should be completed for events of all sizes, especially those of 25 peak room nights or more

Approved as an "Accepted Practice" by the CIC, the 14-page template, which is available on line at www.conventionindustry.org/APEX/StandardPractices (click on Post-Event Reporting link to download the template as either an MS word file or a PDF file). The template includes instructions for use; forms for entering information on group event(s), contacts, hotel rooms, room blocks, food and beverage, function space, exhibit space, and future event dates; a section on report distribution; and tracking and Post-Event Report FAQs.

The report has proven invaluable to both hotels and meeting planners. Dave Scypinski, senior vice president at ConferenceDirect, says:

> All the information we want to report on is contained in the APEX post-event report. If this is to become our industry standard, we said let's get a jump on it for internal purposes.

One meeting planner who praises the PER is Barbara Zamora-Appel, former program director for the Association of Hispanic Advertising Agencies. She says:

> It is very thorough; there is no room for error. The PER can be customized for small or large groups; I use it for both my larger meetings, and even for board meetings. Suppliers and planners can communicate much more effectively.

**Sources: The APEX Post-Event Report Template, Convention Industry Council; Christie Hicks and Christine Shimisaki, CMP, "APEX in Action: Bridging the Gap,"** *PCMA Convene.*

## Chapter 18: Convention Billing and Post-convention Review

*When the event concludes, the hotel's convention service manager and the meeting planner should schedule a time for convention analysis and review. An on-site review of the master account should be done prior to the group's departure, while the meeting is still fresh in the minds of both parties.*
**Source: Photo courtesy of InterContinental Hotel Group.**

to provide post-convention information on **auxiliary business** -- affiliates and subgroups as well as exhibitors. Planners recognize that the auxiliary revenue to hotels from associations with exhibits can be huge. Not only do exhibitors utilize guestrooms, but many also hold events ranging from meals to hospitality suites to meetings.

Responding to the need for post-convention reports, most major hotel chains now have a company-wide standardized system for post-convention reporting. Hyatt, Hilton, and Marriott automatically provide post-convention reports for all groups using 100 rooms or more on peak nights.

Many in the meetings industry would like to see an industry-wide, single database of post-convention information. One possibility proposed by industry groups is to have post-convention information submitted by hotels to their convention bureaus. The EmpowerMINT program developed by the Destination Marketing Association International (DMAI) offers a way for important historical data to be maintained and shared with planners. The information is collected by host Destination Management Organizations (DMOs) and convention and visitors bureaus, and can be accessed by planners who have used these entities to book their meetings and events. If a planner has not used a DMO or CVB, he or she should request histories from hotels or other venues the group has used in the past.

It is important to note that databases and other exchanges of information regarding a group's history should never include dollar amounts. It is a violation of antitrust law to exchange pricing information, such as room rates or banquet charges. Exchanging the number of rooms blocked, rooms picked up, number and size of food functions, and describing room service and restaurant volume as light, moderate, or heavy is an acceptable practice.

Since it is so important to get accurate meeting statistics, there has been a growing consensus within the industry that standardized forms would facilitate the process. In response, the Convention Industry Council (CIC), which has been active in trying to standardize many areas of the hospitality industry, developed a post-event report template. The box titled "Industry-Wide Post-Event Report" on page 653 further explains the Post-Event Report (PER) and its importance to meeting planners and hotels alike.

## Final Appraisal

Before breaking down the working file and returning appropriate correspondence to the account file, ask if you could do a better job if the clock could be turned back to give you another chance. That question should be considered with complete frankness in the cold light of post-convention experience. If the answer discloses areas of difficulty, you should take steps to eliminate such problems in the future. The problems could deal with personnel or facilities. Solving them could help the sales manager set priorities on the kind of business you want and can handle. If the answers please you, don't forget to send a thank-you letter to the meeting planner, and to put that name in your follow-up file for some time in the very near future.

## Summary

You can see, selling to and servicing the conventions and meetings market requires careful planning and attention to details. The convention billing process and post-convention follow-up are important factors in building a group's goodwill and generating future business. A property must clearly spell out billing procedures and make it easy and convenient for the meeting planner to keep abreast of meeting charges. After the convention or meeting, follow-up is necessary to determine areas of strengths and weaknesses and to build a group history that can be used in the future to negotiate additional events.

## Endnotes

1. Deirdre Bourke, "Bill Review Made Easy," Experient special to PCMA.
2. Nikki Gloudeman, "Mastering Your Master Bill," *smartmeetings.com*.
3. Les Jakobson, "Hyatt Modernizes Group Billing," *Successful Meetings*.
4. Julie Pingston, "How CSMs Can Help Drive Higher ROI for Hotel Executives Looking to Grow Their Event/Meeting Business," *Hotel Business Review*.
5. Don Nichols, "High-Tech Comes to Hotels," *Association Meetings*.
6. Roger Sonnabend, "The Hotelier Looks at the Business of Meetings," *3M Business Press*.
7. *Meeting News*.
8. Julie Barker, "The Ultimate Guide to Tipping and Gratuities," *Successful Meetings*.
9. "A Good Contract," *TRNews*.
10. Nicole Brudos Ferrara, "Stop Those Surcharges!" *Meetingsnet.com*.
11. Ruth Hill, "Planner's Lament," *Lodging*.
12. Ibid.
13. Ruth Hill, "Confronting the Bull in Today's Market," *HSMAI Marketing Review*.
14. Michele Wierzgae, "Writing a Post-Con Report," *Meetings South*.

# Chapter 18: Convention Billing and Post-convention Review

## Study Questions

1. Discuss the statement: "As with most aspects of convention planning, the time to avoid billing problems is in the beginning and not at the end." What procedures are recommended for avoiding billing problems?
2. What are the three different folios that can be used for a meeting or convention? Who pays the charges for each?
3. What factors should be considered when determining a time of payment for a meeting group? When are charges typically billed?
4. List the four groupings for service gratuities and distinguish between blanket service charges and special tipping.
5. Outline the HSMAI's suggested payment schedule.
6. Why is a post-convention review important? Who should attend post-convention review meetings?
7. What should be included in the post-convention report? What are the benefits of post-convention reports? Design a sample report that would help your hotel to gauge the success of a convention.

## Key Terms

**American plan**—Charge includes room, food and beverage, and gratuities. Includes three meals per day.

**authorized signature**—Signature of person(s) with the authority to charge to a group master account.

**auxiliary business**—Affiliates and subgroups, such as exhibitors, who contribute to the overall value of the meeting. Often, this type of business that is brought to a facility because of an event, is called **in conjunction with** business.

**billing instructions**—Notice as to how charges for an event should be handled and to whom invoices should be addressed.

**blanket service charges**—Service charges added into the room charge so that attendees do not have to tip during their stay. Primarily used with the American Plan (AP) system.

**European plan**—Guestrooms, food and beverage, and tips are priced separately.

**gratuity**—A voluntary payment added to a bill to signify good service. Also called a **tip**.

**guest credit**—Credit extended to a guest based on information collected by the hotel's credit department. This is a courtesy of the hotel, not an obligation.

**incidental charges**—Expenses (telephone, room service, and so on), other than guestroom charges and taxes that are billed to a guest's folio.

**individual guest folio**—An account on which all individual guest charges not covered by the group's master account will be posted for payment by the individual guest.

**master account**—The group's primary record of transactions to be paid for by the event's sponsoring organization. Charges may include guestrooms, taxes, food and beverage, audiovisual equipment, decorations, incidentals, and so on.

Since delegates may be responsible for some charges at some events, all items to be charged to this account should be agreed-upon in advance. Also called a **master account folio** or a **master bill**.

**master account billing authorization form**—A form that provides instructions on the types of folios to be established, limits of the group's financial responsibility, and the names and signatures of personnel authorized to sign for group charges.

**paid-out slips**—In-house forms that allow cash withdrawals to be charged to the event's master account for employee tips. Using paid-out slips eliminates the need for the event organizer to have to carry large amounts of cash for tips distribution.

**performance report**—An internal report used by hotels to evaluate a convention. The hotel can use this research to determine how the convention facilities matched the client's needs.

**pick-up report**—A post-meeting document detailing the number of hotel rooms used each day of an event. This report includes the total number of guestrooms originally blocked for each night and how many were actually used.

**post-convention meeting (post-con)**—A meeting at the primary facility at which an event occurred just after the event has ended. Attendees at this meeting usually include the primary event organizer, representatives of the host organization, department heads of the facility, other facility staff as required, and event contractors. Its purpose is to evaluate the implementation of the event and to complete the post-convention report. A final review of the master account with a representative from the hotel's accounts payable department is usually part of the post-con meeting.

**post-convention report**—A report of the details and activities of an event. A collection of post-convention reports over time provides a complete history for an event. Also called a **post-event report**.

**rates and charges bulletin**—Communicates specific rates for rooms, meals, gratuities, and billing procedures agreed upon by the various parties involved.

**resort fees**—Charges automatically added by a hotel for services ranging from in-room amenities to local telephone services to resort facilities, such as business centers, fitness centers, and tennis courts.

**resume**—A form that provides a comprehensive overview of an entire event, from pre-convention to post-convention, for the hotel staff. Resume sheets detail activities from day to day (and hour by hour), and cover complete details of functions, reservations procedures, billing, recreational activities, and anything else that may require the attention of the hotel's staff. Also called a **specification sheet**.

**service charge**—An automatic and mandatory amount added to standard food and beverage charges or other hotel services.

**split folio**—Charges are paid partially by the sponsoring organization and partially by the guest. Communication is needed to ensure that all parties involved understand who is responsible for specific charges.

**surcharge**—A mandatory charge added to the guestroom charge for such items as energy, Internet access, and telephone usage, and to meeting rooms for products and services from electricity to additional charges for service personnel.

# Index

## A

A la carte catering, 524
Account file, 99
Account mapping, 188
Account penetration, 188
Action plans, 61
Action stations, 494, 524
Activities for children, 590
Addendums, 340
Advance deposit reservation, 398
Advertising, 270
   agencies, 301
   brochures, 288
   collateral materials, 288
   cooperative and strategic partnerships, 299
   direct mail, 294
   e-mail, 286
   exchange trade, 299
   fax transmissions, 288
   print, 271
   social media, 284
   strategies, 296
   trade magazines, 271
   web site, 279
AIDA, 275
Airport Hotels, 17
Alcoholic beverages, 511
All-Suite hotels, 17
Ambient light, 538
American pricing plan, 642
American/plated service, 501
Americans with Disabilities, 341, 481
Amplifier, 531
Ancillary services/activities, 585
Annual conventions, 125
Apex
   glossary, 10
   contracts, 327
   housing, 403
   post-event report, 653
   specification guide, 420
Application for direct billing, 332
Apps, 280, 434, 565
Arbitration clause, 339
Area exhibits, 600
Arrival/departure pattern, 323
Aspect Ratio, 541
Assigning account management, 94
Association bid, 142
Association Management Companies Institute, 140
Association management companies, 3, 27, 120, 140
Association meetings,
   attendance, 137
   characteristics, 130
   decision-makers, 138
   financial impact, 120
   how they earn money, 121
   kind of meetings, 134
   prospecting, 118
   site selection criteria, 123
   sources for finding, 143
Attrition clause
   food and beverage, 338
   guestrooms, 336
   meeting rooms, 338
Attrition liability calculator, 337
Attrition, 400
Audio conferencing, 543
Audiographic conferencing, 543
Audiovisual
   sound systems, 531
   specialists, 549
   advantages and disadvantages, 545
   charging for, 553
   flow charts, 554
   in-house contractors, 551
   pricing, 553
   projectors, 537
   screen size and seating, 534-537
   source of supply, 549-550
   types of equipment, 552
   union regulations, 555
Audit clause, 338, 347
Auditorium/theater style, 466-469
Authorized signatures, 632
Automated bars, 516
Auxiliary business, 512, 654

## B

Bandwidth, 13, 547
Banner ad, 283
Banquet /catering department, 81
Banquet captain, 508
Banquet department, 81
Banquet event order, 421
Banquet manager, 508
Banquet profitability, 488
Banquet round tables, 464
Banquet
   control procedures, 508
   menus, 489
   staffing, 508
   changing tastes, 497
   greening of, 498
   role of catering manager, 519
   small properties, 519
   types of service, 501
Bar requisition form, 517
Barrier–free meeting space, 447
Beacon technology, 23, 569, 594, 599

# Index

Bed taxes, 259
Beverage service labor charges, 511
Beverage service, 511-519
   automated bars, 516
   control, 515
   hospitality suites, 512
   liquor liability, 516
   pricing, 513
   staffing and logistics, 518
   types of setups, 511
Bid sheet, 386
Billing instructions, 630, 631
Blanket service charges, 642
Block, 336, 347
Blog, 286
Board and committee meetings, 129
Board of director setup, 472, 474
Board of directors, 142
Body copy in advertising, 271
Booking outside the block, 401
Booking pace report, 394
Booth exhibits, 600
Boutique hotels, 17, 158
Breakout rooms, 442, 481
Breakout session, 125
Broadcast fax, 288
Brochures, 288
Budgeting, 63
Buffet service, 502
Business center, 156
Business mix, 49
Butler service, 502
By the bottle beverage pricing, 514
By the drink beverage pricing, 515
By the person beverage pricing, 513

## C

Call brand, 513
Call report, 247
Canapes, 493
Cancellation clause, 333
Canine security, 567
Capacity chart for function space, 446
Captains bar, 512
Carousel projector, 556
Cash bar, 511
Catering manager job description, 521
Catering, off-premise, 496, 497
Catering, on-premise, 496
Catering, role of catering manager, 519
Certifications, 9
Certified Meeting Professional, 9
Characteristics of association meetings, 130-138
   convention duration, 137
   cycle and pattern, 130
   geographic restrictions, 132
   lead time, kind of site, 133, 134
   price, 138
   voluntary attendance, 137
Characteristics of corporate meetings, 165
   duration, 173
   exhibits, 173
   geographical patterns, 169
   kinds of sites, 170
   multiple-booking potential, 174
   one meeting, one check, 174
   small meetings, 165
   time cycle, 167
Check-in/Check-out procedure, 403, 408
Chef's tastings, 503
Chevron setup, 468
Citywide convention, 386
Citywide housing, 386
Class and family reunions, 199
Close-ended questions, 240
Closing and follow-up, 244
Cocktail receptions, 492

Cocktail round tables, 464
Collateral materials, 288
College fraternal groups, 205
Comparison of association and corporate meetings, 153
Competition analysis, 51
Competition rate analysis, 51
Competitive analysis need fulfillment by market segment, 52
Competitive set, 51
Complete meeting package, 33
Complimentary guestrooms, 392
Complimentary rooms, 325
Computer data projector, 538
Computer-assisted design, 447
Concurrent session, 125
Conference centers, 172
Conference concierge, 365
Consistency in advertising, 298
Construction/renovation clause, 341
Consultative selling, 233
Consumer Price Index, 322
Consumer research, 59
Consumer show, 34
Content Marketing, 278
Continuous refreshment break, 13
Contract negotiations, 310
Contract standardization, 341
Contract/letter of agreement, 316
Control books, 100-103
Convention and visitor bureaus, 185
Convention badge, 568
Convention billing, 630-647
   gratuities and service charges, 639
   guest credit, 639

659

# Index

HSMAI's payment schedule, 646
time of payment, 636
Convention brochures, 288
  electronic, 290
  printed, 289
Convention center housing bureaus, 286
Convention Industry Council, 330
Convention lead form, 259, 260
Convention packet, 564
Convention registration, 562
  advance registration, 562
  online registration, 562
  on-site registration, 562
  registration form, 563
  registration packet, 564
Convention sales manager, 84
Convention security, 566
  controlled admission, 568
  uncontrolled admission, 571
Convention service manager, 356
  communication role, 81
  CVB, 366
  day in the life, 360
  job description, 357
  letter of introduction, 371
  recognition, 361
  tracing, 372
  transition from sales, 367
Convention service staff, 364
Convention service,
  best practices, 368
  communication role, 81
  history, 355
  organization chart, 364
  overview, 369
  selling and servicing small meetings, 354
  who services, 356
Conventions
  economic impact, 5-8
  professional certifications, 9

who holds, 12-15
Cooperative advertising, 299
Cordless/wireless microphone, 556
Corkage, 512
Corporate meeting decision-makers
  advertising/sales promotion manager, 177
  company president, 176
  full-time planner, 176
  marketing and sales, 177
  meeting specialist/third-party planners, 179
  passenger traffic, 178
  procurement (purchasing) managers, 178
  training director, 179
Corporate meetings, 12, 152
  account penetration, 186
  characteristics, 165
  corporate positions, 175
  decision-makers, 175-182
  financial impact, 152
  kinds of meetings, 159-165
  number of meetings and attendance, 160
  requirements, 154
  selection criteria, 156
  shrinking lead times, 168
  sources for finding 182
  trade shows, 173
  when held, 167
Corporate retreats, 164
Corporate social responsibility, 32
Coupon sales, 512
Credit application, 390
Credit card guaranteed reservation, 398
Crescent-round setup, 470
Customer's lifetime value, 315
Customer-oriented, 38
Cutoff date, 321, 385

## D

Daily meeting debriefings, 636
Dais, 482
Damage clause, 334
Database marketing, 109
Day packages, 453
Dealer meetings, 188
Decision-maker/association meetings, 138
Decision-maker/corporate meetings, 175
Delphi, 100
Delta hotels meeting maestros, 86
Destination management companies, 23, 27, 581
Destination Marketing Association International, 145
Destination marketing, 259
Developing action plans, 61
Difference between sales and marketing, 38, 39
Digital light projector, 538
Digital signs, 576
Direct mail, 294
Direct mail novelties, 295
Director of marketing, 40
Director of revenue management, 82
Director of sales and marketing, 83
Director of sales, 83, 84
Directories and databases, 141
Dispute resolution, 339
Destination Marketing Association International, 259
Double booking, 102
Dram shop laws, 516
Drayage, 619-621
Duoserve, 509, 510

## E

Early departure fee, 323

660

# Index

Early departure, 397
Economic impact, 5, 8
Educational meetings, 200
Electronic brochures, 290
Electronic pour, 516
Elements of a print ad, 272
Elements of filing systems, 100
E-mail advertising, 286
Employee procedure manuals, 459-460
Energy break, 491
English/family-style service, 502
Enviromental responsibility, 30
Ergonomic, 482
E-shape setup, 473
Establishing objectives, 60
European pricing plan, 642
Evaluating the sales effort, 98
Event specification guide, 420
Exchange trade advertising, 299
Exclusives, 557
Executive director, 139
Exhibit billing procedures, 616-619
Exhibit manager, 607
Exhibit security, 571
Exhibit shipping methods, 623
Exhibit shipping, 619
Exhibit shows, 253
Exhibiting at trade shows, 255
Exhibition floor plan, 603
Exhibition service contractor, 602, 604
Exhibition service contractor's fee, 619
Exhibitor appointed contractors, 602
Exhibitor prospectus, 602
Exhibitor service kit, 604, 606
Exhibitors, 607
Exhibits, booth layouts, 611, 612

Exhibits, 598-615
  billing procedures, 616
  held as part of a trade show, 618
  held concurrently with convention, 618
  insurance, 615
  key personnel, 601
  labor regulations, 614
  photo file, 613
  planning, 600
  rental charges, 618
  scaled drawings, 608
  shipping and receiving, 619-624
  show hours/room assignments, 613
  types, 600
Experient, 180

## F

Familiarization tours, 261-264
Fastfold screen, 535-536
Fax response for reservations, 283
Fax transmissions, 288
Fax-on-demand, 288
Feeder cities, 50
Financial Insurance Conference Planners, 217
Flip charts, 545
Floodlights, 533
Floor load, 609
Flow chart for guestroom pickup, 323
Follow-spot lighting, 533
Food function guarantees, 505
Food service, 488-511
  attrition, 506
  changing tastes, 497
  control procedures, 508
  guarantees, 505
  post-function actions, 519
  pricing, 504
  role of catering manager, 519

staffing, 508
themed and special events, 493
trends, 488
types, 489
Formula for determining exhibit space needs, 599
Fraternal meetings, 204-208
Free pour, 526
French service, 501
Frequency in advertising, 298
Front view projection, 539
Full American plan, 19
Full-time meeting planner, 176
Function book, 100, 104
Function book reservation sheet, 104
Function room turnover time, 451
Function room
  release dates, 457
  square feet for setups, 472
  assigning, 452
  breakdown, 475
  certified meeting space, 446
  charging for, 454
  computer-assisted design, 447
  for banquets, 464, 475
  furniture, 461
  managing, 452-453
  meeting room plans, 446
  monitoring usage, 479
  of the future, 476
  sales restrictions, 453
  seating principles, 468
  size and layout, 445
  timetable for setup, 450
  types, 442

## G

Gala dinners, 495
Gate show, 626
General managers involvement in sales 75, 78

661

# Index

General session, 125
Geographic origin study, 50
Getting prospect involvement, 240
Global referral associations, 92
Globalization, 2
Government agencies, 209-212
Gratuities/tips, 330, 639
Green meetings, 30
Group ceiling, 324
Group history, 393
Group room allotment, 102
Guarantee (food service), 505
Guest credit, 639
Guest history analysis, 50
Guest mix, 57
Guest packages, 577
Guest registration cards, 50
Guest/companion programs, 585
Guestroom attrition, 336
Guestroom control book, 102, 105
Guestroom management, 380
Guestroom rate structures, 390
Guestroom types, 366, 367
Guestroom to meeting space ratio, 324

## H

Handling inquires, 248
Handling objections, 242
Head tables, 464
Headline in advertising, 271
HelmsBriscoe, 181
Hilton hotels, e-events, 166
HIVE Network, 5
Hold all function space, 428
Hold harmless clause, 457
Hollow square setup, 473
Home run accounts, 97
Hors d' oeuvres, 492
Horseshoe setup, 471, 472

Hospitality suites, 512
Host bar, 511
Hosted-buyer trade show, 256
Hotel directories, 276
Hotel exhibit shows, 608
Hotel internet reservations, 383
House brand, 513
Housing assistance desk, 404
Housing policies, 399
Hyatt hotels, personal preference menus, 490
Hybrid meetings, 23, 130

## I

ICAA, 5
Importance of marketing, 39
Incentive meetings, 163
   individual travel, 213
   site selection criteria, 214, 215
   trends, 215
Incentive travel houses, 28, 216
Incidental charges, 634
Indemnification clause, 340
Independent hotel representative, 89-91
   how to choose, 91
   internet exercise, 90
Individual guest folio, 632
In-house destination management companies, 583
Inquiry questionnaire, 317
In-room technology, 22
Installation and dismantle of exhibits, 613
Insurance, 340
Insurance/financial service meetings, 217-219
Integrated marketing, 298
Intelligent lighting, 534
International Association of Conference Centers, 19
Internet advertising, 278

Internet, 20-24

## J - K

Job description, 84
Job description, catering manager, 52
Key account management, 95-97
Key personnel roster, 447
Keystoning, 557
Kinds of association meetings, 124
   annual conventions, 125
   board and committee, 129
   conferences, 129
   seminars and workshops, 129
   state and regional, 125
Kinds of company meetings, 159

## L

Labor unions, 212
Laser pointers, 546
Lavaliere microphone, 532
Layout of sales offices, 79
Lead time, 133
Lecterns, 466, 557
LED lights, 553
Letter of agreement/contract, 316
Lighting, 533-534
LinkIn, 528
Liquid crystal display 512, 517
Liquidated damages, 334
Liquor liability, 516
Loading docks, 623
Logo in advertising, 275
Lumens, 540

## M

Magazine advertising rates, 276

# Index

Mailing list, 294
Major arrival/ major departure pattern, 396
Major close, 244
Management meetings, 162
Managing room blocks, 396
Market segment plan, 69-73
Marketing budget form, 64
Marketing budget, 60, 62
Marketing defined, 38
Marketing mix, 39
Marketing objectives, 60
Marketing plan
   conducting marketing research, 42
   sales committee, 41
   steps, 41, 42
   time period covered, 41
Marketplace analysis, 54-55
Marriott hotels, red coat service, 359
Master account billing authorization form, 634
Master account folio, 632
Master account, 331
Master card, 100, 101
Media chart, 297
Medical meetings, 220-224
Meeting activity in Canada, 5
Meeting activity in the United States, 7-9
Meeting magazines, 275
Meeting management companies, 27
Meeting planner profile, 16
Meeting rooms of the future, 476
Meeting setups, 466
Meeting-related web sites, 282
Meetings
   technology, 20
   trends, 19
   types of customers, 15
   types of facilities used, 16-19
   types of, 11
   who holds, 12-14
Methods of filing, 98
MICE, 6

Microphones, 532
Military and other reunions, 196
Milennials, 25
MINT, 143
Mitigated damages, 334
Mixer board, 533
Monitor, 540
Multi-booking potential, 174
Multimedia presentation, 542
Multiple-meeting contracts, 342

# N

National and regional sales meetings, 160
National sales office, 88-90
Near field communication, 23, 569, 595
Need fulfillment by market segment, 52
Negotiations, 26, 310
   customer's lifetime value, 315
   factors to consider, 315
New product introduction/ dealer meetings, 161
Newsletters, 293
Nonprofit meetings, 14, 193
Nonprofit organization, 14, 193
No-shows, 397

# O

Occupancy chart, 57
Off-premise catering, 496
On-premise catering, 496
Open sale period, 453
Open-ended questions, 240
Opening the sales call, 239
Option date, 106
Organization chart, 78
Organizing for convention sales, 76

Outboarding, 567
Outsourcing, 26
Overbooking, 397
Overbooking/relocation clause, 341
Overhead projectors, 537
Overset safety margin, 505

# P

Paid-out slips, 640
Passenger traffic manager, 178
Passkey, 384
Peak period, 313, 395
Per-diem, 209
Performance report, 647
Permission marketing, 287
Personal sales calls, 233-245
   closing and follow-up, 244
   getting prospect involvement, 240
   handling objections, 242
   opening the sales call, 239
   pre-call planning, 234
   presenting the property, 241
Pick-up report, 648
Pick-up, 336
Platforms and staging, 465
Plus, plus, 327
Positioning of an ad, 275
Positioning the property, 36, 56-60
Post-convention meeting, 434, 628
Post-convention review, 647-655
   comparison with projections, 648
   final appraisal, 655
   function attendance, 649
   reporting, 24, 650
   service evaluation questionnaire, 651
Poster sessions, 222
Preamble to contract, 320

# Index

Pre-call planning, 234
Pre-con meeting agenda, 412
Pre-convention meeting, 414
Predictable attendance, 171
Preferred suppliers, 551
Pre-function space, 443
Premium brand, 513
Pre-registration, 403
Presentation book, 239
Presenting your property, 241
Pre-set service, 501
Press kit, 305
Press releases, 305
Press room, 576
Print advertising, 271
    hotel directories, 276
    positioning ads, 275
    trade magazines, 271
Printed brochures, 289
Procurement manager, 178
Professional congress organizer, 22
Professional/technical meetings, 162
Profile of association meeting planner, 142
Profile of corporate meeting planners, 176
Profile spot lighting, 558
Projector stands, 542
Property analysis, 42, 43
    business status and trends summaries, 47-49
    strengths and weaknesses analysis, 44
Property fact book, 235, 236
Proposal letter, 319
Public relations, 303
Publicity, 303
Putting the marketing plan into action, 65

## R

Rack rate, 391
Rate analysis, 51
Rates and charges bulletin, 635
Reach in advertising, 298
Reader boards, 575
Reader file, 98
Rearview projection, 538
Receivers, 540
Reception drink estimator, 514
Reception style setup, 464
Receptive agents, 582
Reduced-rate rooms, 322
Refresh the meeting room, 483
Refreshment break guidelines, 491
Refreshment break, 328, 491
Regional sales office, 88-89
Relationship marketing, 86, 87
Release date, 324
Release dates on function rooms, 457
Religious Conference Management Association, 201
Religious meetings, 201-204
Request for proposal, 21, 319
Reservation confirmation form, 386
Reservation housing report, 386
Reservation systems, 382-390
    convention center housing bureaus, 382
    hotel internet site, 382
    postal reply/fax response, 383
    rooming lists, 384
    third-party housing companies, 388
    toll-free telephone numbers, 383
Reservations, 382
Resorts, 18
Resort fees, 644
Resume questionnaire, 427, 435-438
Resume, 419
Retreat, 164
Revenue centers, 41
Revenue management, 112, 113
    director, 82
    meetings, 93
Review/monitoring the marketing plan, 64
Rolling Green Resort case study, 43
Room assignment, 390
Room audits, 402
Room taxes, 259
Rooming list, 382, 384
Roving microphone, 532
Run-of-the-house rate, 391
Russian service, 501

## S

Safelock audiovisual stand, 542
Sales blitz selling, 252-255
Sales blitz survey sheet, 254
Sales calls, 233
    appointment calls, 238
    cold calls, 237, 528
    presentation book, 239
    six steps, 234
    telephone sales calls, 245-251
    third-party endorsement letters, 239
    turning features to benefits, 242
Sales forms, 106
    cancellation form, 106
    definite booking form, 106
    lost business report, 106
    tentative booking form 106
Sales letters, 295, 296
Sales manager turnover, 87
Sales managers, 83
Sales meetings, 93, 160
Sales office automation, 106
    advantages, 107

# Index

personalization, 112
virtual office, 110
yield and revenue management, 112-115
Sales office interfaces with other departments, 79
Sales office, 77
control books, 100-104
large properties, 77
organization chart, 78
positions, 83-93
small properties, 77
Sales records, 98
control books, 100
filing systems 99-100
sales forms, 106
Sales staff turnover, 87
Sales staff, 83
assigning account management, 94
clerical support, 88
director of advertising and public relations, 86
evaluating the sales effort, 96-98
independent hotel representative, 90-92
key account management, 95-96
managing the sales effort, 92-98
regional sales office, 88-90
sales meetings, 93
standard operating procedures, 92-93
supplemental, 88-92
Sales structures, Marriott's sales force one, 76, 89
Sales to service turnover data sheet, 370
Scaled drawing, meeting space, 447, 448, 608
Schoolroom/classroom style, 469, 470
Screening prospects, 246
Screens, projection, 534
Search engine optimization, 279
Second-tier cities, 34, 135
Segment profitability, 56

Selecting an advertising agency, 302
Selecting target markets, 56-60
Self check-in/check-out terminals, 404
Selling to the meeting planner, 253
personal sales calls, 233
sales blitz selling, 252
selling with CVBs, 257
site inspections/fam tours, 261
telephone sales, 245
trade show selling, 253
Seminars and workshops, 128
Serpentine queue, 565
Serpentine tables, 464
Service charge, 330, 641
Service fraternal groups, 208
Setting appointments by telephone, 246
Shoulder period, 314
Signs and notices, 573-576
digital signs, 576
hotel rules, 573
price schedule and locations, 575
sign responsibility, 575
Simultaneous interpretations, 542
Site inspection selling, 261-262
Site inspection tour, 262
Site inspections, 139
Skirting, 542
Slide projectors, 537
Slippage, 336, 400
SMERF, 14, 192, 194
average expenditure, 192
class and family reunions, 199
educational meetings, 200
fraternal meetings, 204
military and other re-unions, 195
monthly meeting pattern, 195
religious meetings, 201

social, 195
market at a glance, 194
Social groups, 195
Social media, 21, 53, 284
Social responsibility, 126
Sound systems. 531
Sources for finding association business, 143-148
Sources for finding reunion business, 197
Sources for reaching the fraternal market, 206
Sources of association's income, 121
Space available basis, 395
SPiN, 528
Special events, 527
Specialty items, 294
Split contract, 336
Split folio, 632
Split rate, 391
Stage wash, 558
Staging guide, 424
Standard operating procedures, 92
State and regional conventions, 126
Stockholder/public meetings, 163
Strategic meetings management, 25, 152
Strategic partnerships, 299, 300
Supplemental sales staff, 88
Surcharges, 643
Switcher, 542

# T

Table top exhibits, 600
Target markets, 58
Team-building activities, 30
Technical societies, 14
Telemarketing, 251
Telephone sales techniques, 245-251
follow-up, 246
handling inquires, 248
screening prospects, 246

**665**

# Index

setting appointments, 246
telemarketing, 251
Telepresence, 23
Termination clause, 333
Themed events, 493-495
Third- party endorsement letters, 341
Third -party housing companies, 382, 388
Third-party meeting planners, 15, 179
Ticket exchange, 505
Tickler file, 100
computerized, 103
Timing in advertising, 298
Tour and travel sales manager, 85
Trace file, 100
Trade associations, 178
Trade directories and publications, 183
Trade magazines, 271
Trade show manager, 602
Trade show selling, 253-257
Trade show, 627
Training meetings, 162
Translucent rear-projection screen, 538
Travel agents, 28
Trial close, 244
Tripod screen, 535
Types of exhibit booths, 600
Types of exhibits, 600
Types of group customers, 15-16
Types of meeting facilities, 16
Types of meetings, 11

## U - V

Underdeparture, 397
Unidirectional microphone, 532
Union houses, 627
Union regulations, 331
Uniserve, 509, 510
U-shape setup, 471
Valley period, 313

Video satellite conferencing, 543
Video streaming, 23
Videotape/DVD projectors, 539
Virtual conferencing, 543
Virtual sales office, 110
Virtual site inspections, 261
Virtual site tours, 261
Virtual trade shows, 601
Voluntary attendance, 137

## W - X

Walkable cities, 135
Walked customers, 399
Walk-in, 397
Wall/ceiling screen, 535
Warranty of authority clause, 339
Wayfinding signs, 576
Web conferencing, 544
Westin hotels, 376, 389
Where association delegates spend money, 7
Whiteboards, 544
Who holds meetings, 12
Working file, 107, 342
Writing sales letters, 296

## Y - Z

Yield management, 112
Zero based budget, 63

# Index